Public Works Inspectors' Manual

Third Edition

SILAS B. BIRCH, JR.

Published by —
BNI Books, Division of Building News, Inc.
Los Angeles, California 90034

Distributed by —
McGraw-Hill Book Company
New York, St. Louis, San Francisco, Auckland, Bogotá, Hamburg, London, Madrid, Mexico, Milan, Montreal, New Delhi, Panama, Paris, São Paulo, Singapore, Sydney, Tokyo, Toronto

Library of Congress Cataloging-in-Publication Data

Birch, Silas B.
  Public works inspectors' manual.

  Includes index.
  1. Public works — Inspection — Handbooks, Manuals, etc.
I. Jaffe, Sam.   II. Title.
TA153.B57   1988   624'.038'7   87-22816
ISBN 0-07-005298-0 (McGraw-Hill)

1 2 3 4 5 6 7 8 9   8 9 2 1 0 9 8 7

ISBN 0-07-005298-0

The editors for this book were Sam Jaffe and Silas B. Birch, Jr.,
the designer was Ramón López and the production supervisor
was Richard Berlanga. It was set in Century by BNI Books.
Printed by Griffin Printing Co. and bound by Stauffer Edition
Binding Co., Inc.

Foreword

The *Public Works Inspector's Manual* is a complete operational and technical guidebook for professionals charged with the responsibility of inspecting all types of public works construction for city, county, state and federal agencies. It is unique as the most comprehensive and authentic text of its kind ever written and published. The contents should prove to be of considerable value, not only to inspection personnel but also to contractors, engineers, architects and to students considering public works inspection as a career.

The first edition of this manual was written in 1957 for use by personnel of the Bureau of Contract Administration Department of Public Works, City of Los Angeles, and published in that year. This agency is one of the largest administrators of public works construction in the world and widely acknowledged for its expertise in modern materials and methods of construction. The publishers recognized the non-availability of such a work to serve the needs of countless other governmental agencies. To this end, the manual was edited and recast with references to departments and bureaus of the City of Los Angeles eliminated in order that the text might have general application by any other governmental agency which might adopt it for its own use.

The second edition was updated and revised in 1978 by the key management personnel of the Bureau of Contract Administration. This third edition has been revised and edited by the original author, Mr. Birch, to reflect the changing technology of the construction industry to the present state of the art.

The original author was Silas B. Birch, Jr., former Director of the Bureau of Contract Administration.

References to particular departments and bureaus and to job titles of various personnel of the public works agency which is the model for this manual are those in use by the City of Los Angeles, which is the model for the entire text.

If other public works agencies adopt this manual for their own use, and if their terminology for various departments, bureaus and personnel are different from the text of this manual, they can simply devise and declare a list of synonyms which will made all references herein workable for their local agency's counterparts.

Smaller agencies will probably have many of the functions and job responsibilities which are called out in this book combined into a lesser number of operating entities — but, by the process of co-relating these combined functions with those of the larger agencies, smaller agencies should not be inhibited from making use of the procedures and forms set forth in this manual.

Many of the specimen forms reproduced as plates in the appendix section are actual copies or variations of forms now is use by the City of Los Angeles. These reproductions can easily be adopted by other agencies by a simple title change or slight modification.

Because of the magnitude and complexities of projects in a large city and the inter-relationship between many different departments and bureaus, some procedures might appear to be cumbersome and complicated. With a little imagination, these procedures can be simplified and streamlined for use as models in smaller agencies.

Otherwise, the text material is of universal application in modern engineering construction and contains most of the background and technical information essential to the effective performance of the Construction Inspector.

The procedures set forth in this manual are designed to be compatible with the provisions of the well-known document, *Standard Specifications for Public Works Construction*. This manual, however, is intended as a corollary book of reference and would not take precedence over provisions of *Standard Specifications* or other contract documents in the event of conflict. The Inspector is emphatically reminded to read the contract documents.

The *Standard Specifications for Public Works Construction*, now in its seventh edition, is just what its name implies . . . a uniform standard for all public works construction to be followed by governmental agencies in a given jurisdiction who officially adopt these standards.

The first edition of the *Standard Specifications*, published in 1967, was researched and written by a 400-man task force representing the Joint Cooperative Committee of the Southern California Chapter, American Public Works Association, and Southern California Districts, Associated General Contractors of California. It is updated and republished every three years. As of this date, over 200 cities, counties and other agencies in the United States, follow the *Standard Specifications* with its state of origin, California, being the major user.

The *Work Area Traffic Control Handbook ("WATCH")* is referenced in this manual. The 1985 (sixth edition) of this handbook is approved and endorsed by the Institute of Transportation Engineers (Southern California Section), American Public Works Association (Southern California Chapter) and City Traffic Engineers Association.

The publisher of this manual and the other public works documents described above is the firm of Building News, Inc., experts in the field of code book publishing for governmental agencies. The publisher is prepared to offer standard or customized versions of all forms depicted to all agencies interested in their adoption and use. All interested parties should contact the publisher at its headquarters, 3055 Overland Ave., Los Angeles, California 90034, (213) 202-7775.

Editor's Note

The procedures and methods set forth in this Manual are widely used in the engineering construction industry, but can vary considerably with different jurisdictions, dependent upon the engineering and construction concepts prevailing in the area. This does not mean that any particular concept is necessarily better than another, but that the historical experience with a particular construction method or material has been found to produce an acceptable end product with which the jurisdiction can feel comfortable.

Wide variations in weather and the availability of suitable native materials for aggregates are just two important reasons for the Engineer to adapt methods and materials to local conditions.

One purpose of this Manual is to provide a source of reference and background material to inspection personnel so as to expand their field of knowledge in the engineering construction industry, thereby assisting them to build confidence in themselves through a better understanding of their work.

It is requested that any error or omission noted be brought to the attention of the editor, as well as any new method, material or equipment that may evolve subsequent to the publication of this edition. It will greatly assist in updating future editions.

About the Author

Silas B. "Si" Birch, Jr. is eminently qualified to serve as the compiler, editor and author of such an important document as the *Public Works Inspectors' Manual*.

A graduate of West Virginia University, the author is a civil engineer who has spent his adult life in heavy engineering construction as a military constructor, contractor, public works official, consultant, teacher, lecturer and author.

He served in the U.S. Army Corps of Engineers from 1940 to 1946, including a year in Alaska, and rose to the rank of lieutenant colonel. He is now a colonel in the Corps of Engineers (Reserve).

After the War he entered the employ of the City of Los Angeles, Department of Public Works, as a construction inspector, where he rose rapidly to the top position in his bureau as Inspector of Public Works. It was during this tenure that he served as a key author and guiding light to the 400-man task force which compiled, wrote and continues to update and publish the triennial *Standard Specifications for Public Works Construction*, upon which this Inspectors' Manual is based.

He retired from public service in 1975 and with his wife, Lee, settled in the spectacularly scenic Arizona community of Sedona, where he built a home and became an active leader in civic affairs, in addition to serving as a consultant to the State of Arizona on local road building projects.

He has received recognition by colleagues in his profession as the recipient of two outstanding citations: the "SIR" award of the Associated General Contractors of California; and the Henry S. Swearingen Memorial Award of the American Public Works Association.

TABLE OF CONTENTS
PART 1 — GENERAL INFORMATION

PART 2 – CONSTRUCTION MATERIALS AND MATERIALS CONTROL PROCEDURES

Table of Contents

PART 3 — CONSTRUCTION METHODS AND INSPECTION PROCEDURES

PART 4 — PREVIEW, FINAL INSPECTION AND ACCEPTANCE

PART 1

GENERAL INFORMATION

1-1 INTRODUCTION TO PUBLIC WORKS CONSTRUCTION INSPECTION

1-1.1 General. Information in this part of the Manual is designed as an introduction to public works construction inspection and the technical information is contained in Parts 2 and 3. Included are general policies and procedures of a good public works construction inspection and contract administration agency as well as information to orient the Construction Inspector to his duties and responsibilities.

Agency Inspectors must work constantly to achieve a high standard of excellence in the administration and quality control inspection of public works improvement contracts. The accomplishment and stature of the Agency must inevitably stem from the individual commitment and performance of each employee and each individual has a responsibility to perform in such a manner that personal goals and the Agency goals are not in conflict.

The Agency organization must deal effectively with a relatively difficult control and communication problem. Inspectors are widely dispersed to the various project sites and spend the entire workday there. Isolated from immediate supervisory resources and control much of the time, the Inspector must make literally hundreds of individual judgments affecting the quality of construction. Under these circumstances management must see to it that the Inspector maintains the feeling of being a part of and responsible to the organization and that he has its support. Communication is vital under these conditions and the Inspector and the Agency Management must utilize all available resources and opportunities to discuss and resolve problems as they arise.

The Inspector must have the perspective of knowing the role or function and purposes of other organization elements and groups of the Agency and the relationship they have to his own immediate area of participation and responsibility. With such understanding the Inspector can utilize their support in the process of accomplishing the work of the Agency.

Each Inspector must be motivated to increase personal knowledge and skills and to be informed regarding the latest construction materials and techniques.

Ideally, the Construction Inspector at the jobsite is a leader who gains the confidence and respect of the people he is dealing with by demonstrating his knowledge and ability. He does not depend solely on the rights and powers vested in him by the Agency because he knows that such an exclusive and arbitrary approach is not likely to produce the result he and the Agency are seeking.

He has to have a thorough knowledge of the project or phase of work to which he is assigned.

He must know sound construction methods and the latest techniques for their implementation.

He has to be experienced in all standard inspection and testing procedures and coordinate his work with the contractor or his representative so that the combined effort will produce the specified quantity and quality required by the specifications.

He must be timely, but not hasty to condemn. However, once he is aware of work that endangers the quality, he is to be firm in his insistence on corrective action. He must keep in mind that an order to "tear it out" is sometimes necessary, but realizes such action often is of questionable benefit to the public, which very often pays the cost in delay, inconvenience and eventually in money represented by rising construction costs on future work.

1-1.2 Legal Aspects of Construction Inspection. State and local laws require detailed and continuous inspection of all work paid for with public funds or which is performed in a public way. These laws are the result of many years of experience in the field of contractor-public relationship and gradually developed as a safeguard against the natural tendency of individuals or groups to divert portions of the benefits to themselves.

In basic intention, the Construction Inspector is the representative of the Agency at the site of the work who is empowered to enforce the provisions of the contract or permit. He is authorized to reject materials and workmanship not in conformity with the contract or permit requirements.

1-1.3 Characteristics and Training of the Inspector. The Inspector must be mature, confident, patient, meticulous in carrying out his duties, and a person of integrity who also possesses good judgment. He should have had practical experience in engineering construction and possess an understanding of the principles involved, as well as having a thorough knowledge of the policies, procedures and specifications applicable to his work.

To be successful, the Inspector must have a character and personality of such strength as to merit the respect of those with whom he works. He must be firm but fair in his decisions and follow through to insure that he obtains compliance with his instructions. He should be understanding of the contractor's problems and willing to cooperate at all times to secure acceptable work at the least cost without compromise of the plans and specifications. He should command respect of his associates through his knowledge of the work, impartial decisions, exercise of good judgment, his personal dress and conduct, and exemplary performance.

The Inspector must be alert and observant. He must maintain a spotless service record and conduct himself in such a manner that it will reflect credit upon the Agency. A proper sense of proportion will enable him to give greater attention to the more important matters.

Perhaps an Inspector can be best defined by stating the things he is NOT. The author of the following is no longer known, but the message it conveys is as applicable as ever:

He is NOT a designer, although by using plans and specifications, he must know what the designer is trying to do. He is quite often consulted by the designer and rightly so.

He is NOT a surveyor, yet he must often suggest that the surveyor approach the problem from a particular angle. In this way, he often solves the problem of proper surveying.

He is NOT a superintendent, yet he must be of that same caliber and know construction and all its problems. He must have all the foresight of a good superintendent in that he must be aware of and appreciative of good job planning. Conversely, he should be on the alert against those inescapable results of bad planning.

He is NOT a policeman, yet he must gain compliance with the law.

He is NOT a lawyer, yet he must know and enforce codes and ordinances.

He is NOT a carpenter, cement finisher, or mechanic; yet he must know when such craftsmen are qualified.

He is NOT an accountant, yet he must use detailed methods of accounting and bookkeeping in his record work.

Summarizing, the public works inspector is a designer without a drafting room; a surveyor without a transit; a superintendent without a crew or equipment. He is a policeman without a club or a warrant; a lawyer without a briefcase; a craftsman without tools or a union card; and an accountant without a machine.

The following extracts from an editorial from the February, 1957, issue of *Western Construction*, by Jim Ballard, Editorial Director, is appropriate and informative:

TOUGHEST JOB IN CONSTRUCTION

The toughest job in construction is that of "Inspector." It is the vital link between design and its fulfillment in the field. The inspector is too often underrated in the engineering organization and looked upon as a necessary evil by contracting forces. However, the function is essential in the contract system; inspectors and their problems deserve more understanding and upgrading from both sides.

It is grossly unfair to consider the inspector a detective trying to find intentional deviations from plans and written specifications. Any contractor with the attitude that the inspector is placed on the job to hunt for dishonesty does not deserve to be in contracting.

If all inspectors possessed ideal qualifications, if they had experience coming from years in engineering and contracting, if they had wisdom adequate for a supreme court judge, if they were masters in the art of human relations, there would be little reason for the usual misunderstandings. However, there are factors that rule against complete harmony.

It is a stubborn fact that an inspector has authority to point out deviations from specifications, but does not have corresponding authority to approve changes, however minor. This leads the contractor, or his harassed general superintendent, to complain that the inspector can always say "No," but is never able to say "Yes." This is not a fair or logical complaint. The function of the inspector begins and ends with seeing that field operations produce results called for in the plans.

Occasionally an inspector appears to take delight in using his authority in situations that exhibit pure cussedness. To illustrate: Several years ago during an editorial trip over a job with the construction engineer we found the pouring of the invert in a by-pass tunnel temporarily shut down and the foreman fuming over the action of the inspector. The work stoppage resulted from the inspector finding boot tracks made by a finisher on the concrete surface and stopping the pour until they were removed. This was concrete to be covered by rock ballast for the railroad and at the end of construction the tunnel was to be permanently plugged. Such action of the inspector would appear to be lacking in reasonable judgment although it must have been in accord with the letter of the specifications. However, there is always the other side to such an incident. Possibly this inspector had been pushed around by the contractor's supervisory staff until he was waiting in desperation for some opportunity to retaliate and assert his authority.

Working under strict orders and guided by the legal phases of the specifications, the inspector fills a most difficult position as he watches over the results of each day's work.

If he has the qualities of firmness with patience, and judgment with a desire to be correct but practical, he will fulfill his function on the construction team. And if the contractor advises his staff to appreciate the function of the inspector, even as they use their own methods for accomplishing the results he must secure, then the other half of the team is in harmony. This combination will result in securing the completion of the contract with minimum friction, maximum speed, and complete effectiveness.

(Reprinted by permission from Western Construction, 1957.)

One of the most enlightening and complete treatises on the subject of construction inspection was given by Vaughn Marker, Managing Engineer for the Pacific Coast Division of the Asphalt Institute. By his permission it is reprinted here from the Proceedings of the California Street and Highway conference, published by the Institute of Transportation and Traffic Engineering, University of California:

AIDING THE YOUNG OR INEXPERIENCED INSPECTOR

There has been such an expansion in the field of highway construction in recent years that the experience level of inspector personnel has been considerably lowered. Experienced field engineers and inspectors have been elevated to supervisory positions, while new and younger men have been hired to perform inspection. These new inspectors, in general, have been sincere and have performed diligently. There has, however, been a noticeable deterioration in the quality of inspection, primarily because of the relative inexperience of these new men. This is reflected by more frequent complaints by contractors that "those inspectors don't know their business . . . " or " . . . we would sure like to have a good, tough inspector who knew what he was talking about . . ." Engineering administrators and supervisors have noticed more and more work being accepted by inspectors that is of borderline or even substandard quality.

In all fairness, it must be said that the tempo of construction has greatly increased, making inspection more difficult. In addition, contractors have been finding it more difficult to hire experienced crews, resulting in the need for greater effort to maintain the quality of workmanship. This, of course, requires more experience and ability on the part of the inspector.

It has been written that inspection is the toughest job in construction, is the vital link between design and fulfillment, and is essential in the contract system. Even though the vast majority of highway construction is performed under contract, wherein one party agrees to perform certain work to a given standard in return for an agreed remuneration by the other party, it has been necessary for one party to check on the other to see that the contractual agreements are met. This has been the traditional function of the inspector. His duty is to see that the field operations produce the results called for by the plans and specifications. In this capacity, he has the responsibility to point out deviations from the specifications but not the authority to approve minor changes, even for improvement.

It is generally agreed that the inspector nearly always looks upon his work seriously and tries to do the best job possible. It is an extremely rare occurrence when the inspector is not interested in seeing the work performed correctly. He sometimes loses sight of the over-all picture because of his concentrated interest, but on the other hand, his duties usually do not include an appreciation of the over-all picture. He will usually do a good job within the limits of his knowledge and ability.

The engineering administrator and, often, the engineering supervisor look upon the job of inspection as routine. They are usually aware of its importance but prone to accept the quality of inspection that exists. Quite frequently, they feel they are unable to do otherwise because of the press of their many duties. They instruct the inspector to inspect a specfic item of work and then accept his results. In some cases, if the inspector has never been exposed to the particular item of work, the supervisor will give him a short verbal lesson on what to do or turn him over to an "old timer" with one or two jobs under his belt. Supervisory personnel generally bewail the need for inspector training but produce innumerable excuses why such a program cannot be instituted in their particular organzation.

The contractor and his supervisory personnel have two distinct viewpoints concerning the inspector and his work. James I. Ballard, editor of *Western Construction* magazine, has written: "The inspector is . . . looked upon as a necessary evil by contracting forces." They either wish they didn't have to put up with him at all or try to inveigle him into superintending the work. In the first instance, they may be able to slight some of the specification requirements, in the interests of job economy, while in the second instance, the inspector is prone to accept whatever work has been done, since he directed a portion of it.

At the opposite extreme is the new inspector who, for the first time in his life, is thrust into a position of authority. Occasionally the individual is greatly over-impressed with his own importance and position and begins to throw his weight around unnecessarily. In doing so, the new inspector probably thinks he is behaving in the correct manner. The trouble with this approach, however, is that there are probably several things concerning the work which he doesn't know, thus making him ludicrous. And, his demeanor is such that the people he is dealing with get the impression of supreme arrogance. This man frequently makes the mistake of so behaving that he assumes superintendence of the work, putting him in the untenable position of judging the quality of results reached by means that he dictated. It is this type of inspector who draws the most fire from the contractor.

Requirements for a Good Inspector

The inspector invariably works under the strict requirements of contract plans and specifications in addition to the further instructions of his supervisor. He must deal with a myriad of minor and major problems and details. In doing this, the ideal inspector must have desire, sagacity, firmness, good judgment, knowledge and courtesy. His relations with the contractor's crew must be friendly and firm without familiarity, and must be conducted with the skill of a diplomat. How can we help this poor, much-maligned inspector? In order to help, we should first decide what the fundamental requirements for a good inspector are.

Knowledge. First, it is of paramount importance that the inspector have a knowledge of the work he is inspecting. This knowledge should include information concerning the materials, as well as considerable acquaintance with the equipment and procedures. There is a school of thought that the less the inspector knows about a specific item, the better and more objectively he can enforce the letter of the specifications. I believe this is fallacious. The more knowledge the inspector has, the better prepared he will be to discharge his duties.

Common Sense. The second commodity that is invaluable to a good inspector is an abundance of common sense. While it cannot be substituted for knowledge and specifications, it is the means of applying one to the other, and of interpreting the specifications to properly enforce their intent. It may grow on knowledge but it cannot be learned out of a book.

Observation. The inspector must perform his function by observation of what is going on about him. Thus, another basic requirement is the ability to see what he looks at. "Seeing" in this context includes observation with the eyes as well as considered thought about the image observed. It is amazing how an inspector can observe an incorrect condition and not realize it as such. This situation is aggravated by lack of knowledge or common sense and, most seriously, by mental laziness. Too many inspectors just don't bother to think about what they are looking at.

Physical Tools. Besides the personal requirements of the inspector, there are tools he must use to perform his function. These include the general run of measuring devices as well as necessary testing equipment. Perhaps the most important tools are a notebook and pencil.

The importance of job records listed in the inspector's notebook cannot be over-emphasized. It may be that the information recorded will never be needed and never be reviewed, but, if it is ever needed, it will be needed badly. The notebook should contain every bit of information possible concerning the work being inspected. Such related information as weather conditions, the time and place any incident occurred, breakdown of equipment, length of work stoppages, number of men and type of equipment affected by work stoppage, any unusual incident or condition, even a change in color of a material should be recorded. If the item seems unusually important, it should be recorded and analyzed in sufficient detail to make it fully understandable at some later date. The notebook information will become a reference for future performance of the work, a certain reference in the event of legal action or litigation by any interested party, and, possibly most important, it may contain a clue for a future investigator, in the event the job fails. There is nothing too trivial to be included in the inspector's notebook, and the very act of recording will help him to learn and remember.

Courtesy. A major part of the inspector's job is to inform the contractor when unsatisfactory conditions exist or when the specifications are not being met. This is accepted and expected by the contractor, yet is the source of most of the poor relations that can develop on the job between the contractor and the inspector. Since valid criticism or objections by the inspector are expected by the contractor, it cannot be this factor that strains relations; it must be, not what is said, so much as the way it is said that is important. Of course, an aggravating manner of speech is not limited to inspectors. But when poor relations develop between the inspector and the contractor, the work suffers as well as everyone connected with it. A little common courtesy will go a long way.

Improving the Inspector

In light of the requirements for a good inspector and the situations that develop on the job, what can be done to improve inspectors? It can be seen that many of the things that might need improvement depend entirely on the individual. While some assistance may be possible with such things as the employment of common sense, the ability to observe, and the development of personality, the main effort in these things must come from the inspector himself. The main area of assistance is in increasing knowledge through education, better specifications, and training in the use of the tools of inspection.

Better Plans and Specifications

Specifications are the means of communication between the designer and the constructor in achieving the completed structure. The inspector, as well as the contractor, is stuck with the specifications. Both the inspector and the contractor must thoroughly understand the specifications, and they are legally and morally bound by them. Specifications play an important part in the inspector's behavior. These are the rules by which he must referee the game of construction. Their clarity and simplicity play a big part in his performance. In the matter of plans and specifications, the designer can do much to reduce the burden on the inspector. Simple, concise wording of specifications makes their intent clear and minimizes the amount of interpretation needed. The same can be said of the plans. The designer should have in mind some of the problems of construction when the plans are drawn so that they can readily be transposed into the desired structure. These two things alone can greatly simplify the inspector's work, providing instructions do not become so sparse that the inspector must make design decisions in the field that should have been settled long before. It is interesting to note that good plans and specifications will frequently reduce the bid price because the contractor knows better what he must do and, therefore, how he can do it more efficiently.

Aid in Acquiring Knowledge

The primary assistance that can be given the inspector is by increasing his knowledge. This education must be a continuous thing because new people are constantly entering the field and because new developments are constantly appearing. In many items of inspection, the individual will have contact with the item only infrequently and needs a periodic refreshing of his knowledge. There has never been a formal training program for inspectors, to my knowledge, and those who started twenty or thirty years ago learned through experience. Unfortunately, some of the things learned by these "old timers" may have been learned wrong in the first place and these incorrect procedures have been perpetuated through their influence. In other words, even the "old timers" may be able to learn something.

There are several ways for inspectors to increase their knowledge, some of which can be taken advantage of concurrently. For technical education concerning materials, theory, etc., there are courses offered by various colleges. These courses give the inspector a better background of information regarding the materials and theories he is dealing with and allow him to perform his function more intelligently. Formal schooling alone, however, is not enough and must be used in conjunction with other methods of education.

Probably the best place for inspectors to increase their knowledge is on the job. Here the very things they are trying to learn are happening. It is the ideal place to learn. However, it is of great importance to have a qualified individual available to give explanations of things to be learned. Only in this manner can the new or inexperienced inspector learn and, at the same time, avoid the pitfalls of inexperience. It is true he can probably learn without a tutor, but it will take much longer and he will be making the very mistakes it is desirable to avoid. Furthermore, with explanations of why certain things occur or why it is best to use a certain method, the lesson is retained better and the reasoning can be adapted and applied in future instances.

This on-the-job training can be set up in many ways, from a completely informal, hit-or-miss method to a carefully planned and integrated program. Unfortunately, if anything prevails, it is the former. Planned and integrated programs are practically non-existent. The administrator or supervisor often says such programs are impossible in his organization for many reasons. I wonder where this administrator thinks the trained inspector is going to come from or what organization can afford to plan some training on the job? It is my belief that if training and education are desired for inspectors by any engineering supervisor, then that supervisor must instigate it. His efforts will be almost useless, however, unless he is honestly interested and wants to provide planned training on an intelligent, sustained basis. The only weakness may be that the supervisor has no one capable or qualified (including himself) to train the inexperienced man. But nothing will be accomplished if nothing is attempted.

The literature is another very important source of knowledge. For many years, technical papers have been presented on a wide variety of subjects dealing with highway engineering or construction. In addition, most construction trade magazines make a continuing practice of printing articles concerning proper methods. Articles such as these can be invaluable to the inspector as well as the contractor's crew as a reference source for any particular item or work. Supplementing these sources are many of the manufacturers of materials and equipment who publish literature dealing with their particular line. Trade associations increase the availability of technical literature. All these sources should be drawn upon for information in any training program. Since it is difficult for the individual to determine what to read and where to find it, a real contribution would be the development of a list of suggested reading for inspectors, to be published yearly.

Training aids such as movies, film strips and models have been produced by many of the larger contracting organizations. These can be put to good use in any training program. For example, the California Division of Highways has produced several film strips dealing with different types of construction and aimed at informing the inspector. Many trade associations have also produced movies dealing with their product that can be of great help to the new inspector. Most of these organizations are willing to make training aids available, on request, to any agency desiring them.

Handling the Inspector

One of the intangibles in increasing the knowledge of the inspector is his desire for self-improvement. Plans and training are of little value if the object of their attention is disinterested. If desire is lacking in the inexperienced inspector, he should either be shifted to some other line of endeavor or an attempt should be made to instill the desire.

The inspector is a very important person in our system of contracting for construction work. At the same time, mainly because of tradition and economy, the inspector-designate is usually the newest, youngest and most inexperienced engineer on the job. He is thrust into a position of considerable authority, frequently with little preparation. He can be helped if his supervisor makes clear the inspector's position as well as giving him some technical instruction. The psychology of personnel management dictates that the supervisor encourage and support the subordinate. This is doubly true in the case of the inspector. In order to build up his confidence, as well as his technical knowledge and personality, he must be equitably supported by his supervisor. If it becomes necessary to overrule one of his decisions, the reasons should be explained in such a way as not to humiliate him. The inexperienced inspector should be tactfully and fairly handled by the supervisor in order to develop fully his potential.

Cooperation by the Contractor

The people who are most in contact with the inspector are contractor personnel. They do much to influence and mold the inspector, especially the new one. It is also true that most contractors' supervisory personnel will do their best to **please** the inspector even though this involves a slight change in operation. Unfortunately, there are few contractors who try to **help** the inspector. Yet, it would seem that some assistance by the contractor might be in order since he is one of the parties most interested in the inspector's work. Still more unfortunate, there are some contractors and their representatives who actually seem to harass the inspector. Their philosophy seems to be that the most advantageous position for them is to get the inspector on the defensive and keep him there. Assistance by the contractor and his representatives might take the form of explaining the reasons for doing certain items of work in a particular way. This assistance, of course, becomes valuable only if the one giving it knows what he is talking about.

Possibly the greatest assistance that could be rendered by the contractor would be a deliberate effort to appreciate the function and the problems of the inspector. At the same time, the inspector will assist himself, as well as the contractor, if he will try to understand the problems of the contractor. The inspector is primarily interested in quality, while the contractor is primarily interested in quantity. Under no condition should the contractor expect, nor the inspector permit, a reduction in quality in the interests of quantity, although within specified limits of quality all efforts for maximum quantity should be encouraged. Right here, in fact, is the crux of the understanding that is needed by both parties.

Summary

In summary, some of the things that are needed to assist the inexperienced inspector are:

(1) Desire for self-improvement on the part of the inspector.

(2) Planned training programs on a sustained basis to increase knowledge. The supervisor must interest himself in the program to make it successful.

(3) The taking into account by designers and specification writers of the construction problems connected with their projects.

(4) Application of common sense by the inspector. This requires a little logical thinking on his part and involves the very important ingredient of careful observation.

(5) Emphasis on record keeping, especially a notebook or a diary. Besides providing a job record, the act of writing down things helps the inspector learn and remember.

(6) The studied practice of common courtesy by the inspector.

(7) Increasing knowledge by taking full advantage of information and educational aids offered by manufacturers and trade associations.

(8) Continued perusal of available literature in conjunction with work on the job.

(9) A program developed and supported by some contractors' organization aimed at discussing with inspectors and their supervisors the contractors' problems and viewpoints.

Many of the things discussed in this presentation may seem completely idealistic. Undoubtedly, many of the sophisticated will ridicule and sneer at certain concepts. I submit, however, that honest effort along the lines discussed will be necessary not only to aid the inexperienced inspector but to elevate his position to a level commensurate with its importance.

1-1.4   Project Inspection Guidelines.

1-1.4.1   General.   At the outset of a new assignment as project inspector, the Public Works Construction Inspector must be prepared for his leadership role with knowledge and background material concerning the work to be accomplished, as a foundation to establish an effective working relationship with the contractor, other agencies, engineering personnel and to meet with representatives of the public who are interested in the project.

During construction, he must evaluate the contractor's operations and production with respect to quality and progress, as well as for construction safety and public safety and convenience. He must anticipate and recognize problem areas, exercise judgment, take action and make decisions literally hundreds of times before the project is completed.

If he has organized and administered his responsibilities to control the work in a logical, mature and efficient manner, his reward will be a high quality public improvement that will function and endure as the designer intended.

1-1.4.2   Project Inspector's General Check List.
The following information, in the form of a "check list", is designed to guide the Construction Inspector in his overall organization and approach to duties on any project assigned to him. (Refer to the detailed check list at the end of each major Subsection of Part 3, Inspection Procedures of this Manual, for specific types of work.):

PROJECT INSPECTOR'S GENERAL CHECK LIST

(a) **Review Job Plans, Specifications and all other Contract Documents.**

    1) Plan Notes.
    2) Standard Plans, Reference Specifications.
    3) Traffic Control Requirements.
    4) Special Phasing or Sequence.
    5) Unusual Methods and Materials.
    6) Utility Conditions.
    7) Encroachments, Obstructions, Removals.
    8) Soil and Boring Data.
    9) Shop Drawings and Other Submittals Required.
    10) Permit Requirements from Other Agencies.

(b) **Check Job Envelope for Supplemental Information.**

    1) Utility Notice and Report of Utility Meeting.
    2) Correspondence.
    3) Progress Schedule.
    4) Records and Reports.
    5) Grade Sheets.

(c) **Relate Requirements to Site Conditions.**

    1) Check Adequacy of Survey Staking.
    2) Note Adjoining Property "Conditions."
    3) Note Vehicular Traffic and Pedestrian Problems.
    4) Utility Interferences.
    5) Drainage Conditions.
    6) Work Space, Storage and "Stock Piling."

(d) **Review Project with Supervisor.**

    1) Apparent Problem Areas.
    2) Interpretation of "Gray" Areas.
    3) Apparent Plan Errors or Omissions.
    4) Public Relations.
    5) Contractor's Organization.
    6) Clarification of Inspection Procedures (unfamiliar and unusual materials and methods).
    7) Engineering Liaison.
    8) Inspection Supplies and Equipment.
    9) Street Maintenance Liaison.

(e) **Review Project with Contractor.**

    1) Contractor's Organization.
    2) Subcontractors.
    3) Important Job Conditions.

    4) Construction Safety.

    5) Public Safety.

    6) Construction Methods and Procedures, Sequence of Construction.

  (f) **Exercise Controls During Construction.**

    1) Coordination and Communication.

    2) Construction Inspection Procedures.

    3) Sampling and Testing.

    4) Safety and Convenience Procedure.

  (g) **Maintain Accurate and Complete Records and Reports.**

    1) Log Job Progress and Status. (Schedule).

    2) Report Special Conditions and Events.

    3) Log Important Request, Notifications.

    4) Maintain Orderly Filing System.

    5) Measure Completed Work to Verify Monthly Pay Requests.

1-2   INSPECTION POLICY

    1-2.1   General. Inspection of public works construction is a control exercised by a governmental agency over the materials, methods and workmanship used by contractors in the performance of their work. The purpose of inspection is to ensure compliance with the plans, specifications and other requirements of contracts, purchase orders and permits for public works construction, including compliance with the pertinent provisions of orders, regulations and laws of the Agency and the State and Federal government. It is essential that the Inspector read all the contract documents, and re-read them from time to time to insure complete familiarity with all provisions and requirements.

    Inspectors shall not prescribe or interfere with the contractor's methods of performing work. However, if, in the opinion of the Inspector, the methods of the contractor will not meet the requirements of the contract, purchase order or permit, the contractor shall be warned and, if the contractor's methods will produce a hazard to life, health or property, or will result in defective work which would be impractical to correct or replace subsequently, the Inspector shall stop the portion of the work involved and immediately notify his supervisor. (See Subsection 1-2.6.)

    The Inspector shall cooperate fully with each contractor and assist him in all practical ways to complete the work economically, expeditiously and satisfactorily.

1-2.2 Relations with the Contractor. While an Inspector does not generally have the authority to allow deviations from essential contract requirements, he must carefully avoid an inflexible attitude with respect to requirements in trivial construction details or technicalities. The Inspector should not interfere with the contractor's method of performing the work. Advise, but do not try to force him arbitrarily to a certain course of procedure where the specifications permit more than one method. Such interference may operate to release the contractor in whole or in part from the responsibility he has assumed under the contract to obtain specific results. If, however, a contractor's methods are obviously improper, inadequate, unsafe or likely to result in damage or future expense to the Agency, it should be called to the contractor's attention at once. If prompt objection is not made to unsatisfactory work, it will be difficult to prove later that it was not satisfactory.

Orders to the contractor should be in writing, or later confirmed in writing, so that instructions will be clear and no misunderstanding develop over controversial issues. (See Subsection 1-2.6.) Particular care should be taken that no instructions are given which could be construed as assuming superintendence of the work. Poor judgment in this respect could result in claims against the Agency.

Instructions or formal orders should be given by the Inspector directly to the contractor, his superintendent or foreman only. The contractor must provide a competent foreman who is more than a "pusher." A foreman must be able to read plans and perform the necessary layout for the work and is expected to oversee properly the many phases of the work. He is expected to **direct** the activities and operations of the workers in accomplishing the work. All of these activities are properly the contractor's business and the foreman's responsibility and not that of the Inspector.

Relations with the contractor and his employees should be agreeably maintained. Surliness or an overbearing attitude or abusive language on the part of the Inspector is uncalled for. The Inspector should enforce his decisions through his personality, and his judgment should be fair and impartial. His knowledge of the work and the codes under which it is to be accomplished should be so thorough that he will achieve respect and compliance. He should not give any directions which are not justified by the contract documents, but should insist on

compliance with such directions as he does give. A reputation of being slack or easy, though it is quickly attained, is difficult to overcome.

An order suspending any part of the work betrays a serious condition on the project. Public relations as well as economic loss may be involved. Consequently, such orders are never to be given lightly or in a spirit of punishment. However, situations will occasionally occur when orders suspending work must be issued. Certainly the work must be built to line and grade. Dimensions and quality must be as specified, and the finished work must be acceptable within specification tolerances.

1-2.3 Relations with Other Agencies. The closest co-operation should be maintained at all times with all other levels of government with which the Agency conducts business. Any suggestions or criticism of any of the functions or personnel of another governmental unit shall not be tendered directly to such unit but shall be reduced to writing and forwarded through the Inspector's supervisor.

1-2.4 The Inspector's Public Image. Inspection personnel are expected to conduct themselves at all times in such a manner as to reflect credit upon themselves and the Agency they represent. Consumption of alcoholic beverages, gambling, fighting, lotteries, games of chance, use of narcotics or conduct of similar degree of impropriety during working hours will not be condoned. Violations of this nature are cause for suspension or discharge. It is expected that employees will be suitably dressed for the work to which they are assigned. Reasonable judgment should dictate the proper clothing to wear, but in any case, the clothing should be clean and pressed. Employees shall be clean and neat enough to be a suitable representative of the Agency to the contractor and the public. Bizarre clothing is incompatible with the position.

The Public Works Construction Inspector is expected to be pleasant, courteous and business-like in meeting the public. Above all, his conduct must be governed by common sense. To the public, he represents the Agency. The people hold him responsible for accomplishing his work in a manner which will afford the greatest public benefit and the least public inconvenience. It is important to be helpful and considerate in answering questions asked by the public, and if the employee cannot definitely answer their questions, he should refer them to the proper authority or department for accurate information.

1-2.5 Public Information.

1-2.5.1 General. Information furnished by the Inspector to the general public should be restricted to construction details for the specific project involved. Inquiries from representatives of the press requesting data for publication and to representatives of Chambers of Commerce and similar groups requesting data for reports to their organizations, should be referred by the Inspector to supervisory personnel for reply.

The Inspector is cautioned not to furnish any information on the following matters:

    (a) Matters pertaining to claims or lawsuits involving the Agency. Such information shall be released only by the legal counsel for the Agency.

    (b) Estimates made by the Agency for future work to be done under contract.

    (c) Information as to policies, procedures and official actions of the Agency, and as to property and rights in property to be acquired by the Agency.

    (d) Results of tests of competitive materials and products. Employees are not to discredit any contractor, product or manufacturer.

1-2.5.2 Public Speaking. Employees should not engage in controversial activities in public, particularly if it involves public speaking, public debate, radio programs, etc., without the prior approval of the head of the Agency.

1-2.5.3 Writing for Publication. All compositions intended for publication that relate to the business of the Agency must be approved and in accordance with policies existing within the Agency.

1-2.6 Jobsite Communications and Instructions.

1-2.6.1 General. Important communications and instructions should be issued in writing. If a contractor, permittee or other agency performing work under the supervision or control of the Agency, fails to comply with or violates any contract provision, ordinance or lawful instruction, or causes any unsafe condition, written instructions are mandatory.

1-2.6.2 Verbal Instructions. Appropriate verbal instructions relative to non-compliance, safety violations, etc.,

shall be given at once by the Inspector or Supervisor to the representative of the contractor or permittee on the job. The text of these instructions shall be noted by the Inspector in the Job Report.

1-2.6.3 Job Memorandum. The Job Memorandum is intended for the purpose of permitting the Inspector to issue written instructions regarding routine matters or confirming verbal instructions to a contractor or permittee where a Notice of Violation or Non-Compliance may be inappropriate or where the circumstances are not of such importance as to warrant the issuance of the latter form.

An example of the use of the Job Memorandum would be to issue to a foreman instructions not to backfill a sewer trench until the Inspector returns from a second job assignment at a specified time to check the make-up of the pipe joints. While this particular situation will not always require the use of this form, it will prove useful in the case of a more unreliable foreman who demonstrates that he often misunderstands instructions or who later claims no such instructions were ever issued by the Inspector.

1-2.6.4 Notice of Non-Compliance. Verbal instructions regarding non-compliance shall be confirmed the same day by a Notice of Non-Compliance, except in those instances where instructions are complied with at once. When this notice is issued to a party on the job who is not the permittee or prime contractor, the notice will be addressed to both the party on the job and the permittee or prime contractor.

Job Inspectors are authorized to issue Notices regarding violations or non-compliance with plans, specifications and legal requirements of the project, and to stop work on any portion of the job if the contractor's methods cause unsafe conditions or will result in defective work which would be impractical to correct or to replace subsequently, while permitting other (conforming) portions of the work to continue. Notices stopping all work shall be issued only by or at the direction of the Supervisor having jurisdiction over the work, or higher authority. Issuance of a Notice stopping all or any part of the work shall be reported by telephone immediately to the Main Office of the Agency and the appropriate District Office.

1-3 RECORDS AND REPORTS

1-3.1 General. Keeping accurate records and reports is a very important function of the Field Inspector. These records

are necessary for a number of reasons. Some of the most common reasons for job records and their use as references are as follows:

(1) Time and material accountability, including quantities for periodic progress payments and extra work under cost plus change order procedures.

(2) Verify actions and decisions of the Inspector, contractor or engineer.

(3) Establish job status and site conditions in the event of an accident or liability claim.

(4) Verify time charges and justify inspection activities to the permittee who questions inspection fees.

(5) Clarify the continuity of a project (working days, delays, activities) when the contract time is in dispute.

(6) Prepare responses to inquiries and complaints.

(7) Evidence in legal actions.

(8) When there is a change of inspection personnel; progress or status of project to orient the newly assigned personnel.

These uses should be kept in mind and job records should be prepared accordingly.

1-3.2 Job Reporting Procedure. The record of activities on a construction job should be reported in the exact sequence that they take place.

The basic daily reporting medium, the Construction Inspector's Daily Report (Plate 1 in the Appendix), commonly referred to as the "Job Log." It is a continuing report of job progress and provides for the use of as much space as is necessary to adequately report each day's progress and activities. Each day's report begins on the line following the previous day's report and each page is numbered consecutively.

Each daily entry should be brief but at the same time be complete, clear and factual and include all work accomplished by the contractor as well as pertinent related information. In other words, the inspector should think "who did what, where, when, how and how much." Entries shall be made daily to avoid errors or omissions, and include the number of hours charged against the job and the Inspector's **legible** signature. Abbreviations are desirable as long as their meanings are not confusing and have a common acceptance.

On Permit projects, the Daily Reports are the only continuing job reporting medium utilized, except for the Inspector's personal diary or notes and "as-built" information recorded on the project plans.

On most large projects, especially those requiring more than one Inspector, the Project Inspector in charge will keep a daily Job Log and other assigned inspectors will assist him in keeping the Job Log current. He will use the Job Log to record all project activity.

On contract projects, the Job Log should include a daily record of all men and equipment working on the job. This information is not included when a special reporting form is utilized for this purpose.

1-3.3   Job Reporting Checklist.   Following is a general checklist of entry items applicable to all jobs:

DAILY REPORT CHECKLIST — GENERAL

(1) All entries printed in ink or typed.

(2) The first report in any series should begin with the job title, job number, contractor's (and subcontractor's on first working day) name, address and phone number; and the superintendent or foreman's name and job office phone number.

(3) Be brief, but include all work and activities and related information.

(4) Entries are clear, accurate and legible.

(5) Total regular inspection hours worked and signature for each daily entry.

(6) Overtime hours noted by the initials "OT" after the number of hours.

(7) Entries made the same day the work is performed to avoid errors or omissions.

(8) For each daily entry, include the pre-printed number of any Job Memorandum or Notice of Non-Compliance issued on the job and underline in red.

(9) If work being done is Change Order work, record the Change Order number and description of the work as part of the entry on the job report.

(10) Record any verbal instructions or authority from the Design Engineer on the job report on the day received, including the Engineer's name.

(11) All job related incidents must be noted on the job reports, such as men and equipment working, traffic accidents, damage to existing improvements or utilities, injuries, etc.

(12) On permit work, when inspection costs are charged to the permittee, and the contractor (after requesting inspection) does not show up on the job site, a Job Memorandum must be issued to the permittee and a note accounting for the time charge (usually two hours) entered on the job report.

(13) Job progress must be reported in terms of quantity, distances, stations and weight, as they are appropriate and applicable. Reporting must account for all bid item quantities including when, where and what was constructed by exact limits so as to establish an accurate audit trail.

(14) Mention important visitors to the project and the nature of their business.

OTHER SIGNIFICANT ITEMS TO BE REPORTED

For all types of construction, the following items are to be considered and reported where appropriate:

(1) Factors adversely affecting progress of the work, such as delay in utility work completion, delivery of materials and equipment, unforeseen conditions, strikes, plan changes, poor contractor management, severe weather and resulting soil conditions, etc.

(2) Unsatisfactory work performed by the contractor and corrective actions proposed or taken.

(3) Conditions that may require changes or extra work, or generate controversy or claims. The proposed methods of handling the situations should be described. Any indications by the contractor of his intention to file a claim should be reported along with pertinent job report.

(4) Unusual or difficult engineering, construction or traffic problems involved and their solution.

(5) Unusual conditions regarding safety. Precautionary measures taken with respect to protecting construction workers, the traveling public and abutting property from injury or damage as a result of the construction operations.

(6) Right-of-way, public utility and public transportation problems.

(7) Quality of the work produced.

(8) Provisions for movement of traffic, access to property detours and signing.

(9) Causes of retarded progress and delays. Contract time, percent of work completed and time extensions granted.

(10) Unusual material and equipment brought on project or removed from project when this is considered a significant effect in maintaining satisfactory progress.

(11) Documentation of actions taken and justification therefore.

(12) Field sampling, testing and laboratory test results, particularly failures and resolution.

(13) Developments regarding problems or undesirable conditions discussed in one inspection report should be followed up in a subsequent report indicating final solution or disposition.

(14) When shutdown periods occur, the dates of suspension and resumption must be included in the project records.

(15) Observations and conclusions concerning the overall review of construction operations with particular emphasis on the actual construction features.

1-3.4 Surface and Grading Project Reporting. Daily reports should be used for all common surface improvements, such as: rough grade, fine grade, curb and gutter, paving and sidewalk.

Typical entries for grading projects should include:

(1) Limits of slide or alluvial material removed.

(2) Name of soils Engineer or Geologist who checked area (if available).

(3) Methods and equipment used. Soil type and lift thickness.

(4) Size and limits of subdrains laid.

(5) Limits of fills placed.

(6) Compaction tests and results reported by the laboratory.

(7) All failures should be circled in red and be accounted for by a subsequent entry reporting "retest passed" or other resolution.

Typical entries for street subgrade jobs should include:

(1) Limits of roughgrade, cuts and compacted fill.

(2) Limits of roughgrade checked. Tests by the laboratory and results.

(3) Base material source, number of samples and test results must be noted.

(4) Limits and thickness of base material placed and compacted.

(5) Location and results of compaction tests taken on base material. (Failures resolved as indicated in grading, Item 6).

(6) Fine grade checked and approved for paving.

Typical entries for curb, gutter, walk and driveways should include:

(1) Name of subcontractor (if any) if not entered on first card.

(2) Station to station limits of forms placed when concrete is not placed the same day.

(3) Station to station limits of concrete placed, type of concrete and additives if any, number of cubic yards placed and source of the concrete.

(4) Type and size of curb and gutter.

(5) Width and thickness of walk; width and thickness of driveways together with the distance from curb face to top of driveway slope.

(6) Number of concrete test cylinders taken.

(7) Station locations of blockouts for catch basins, curb drains.

Typical paving entries should include:

(1) Name of paving subcontractor if not shown on first card.

(2) Source of material.

(3) Method of laying, type, thickness, base or wearing surface and tons of asphalt paving material laid (or cubic yards of concrete placed), limits such as station to station and width and square feet if payment is made on this basis.

1-3.5   Sewers and Storm Drain Project Reporting. Storm drain main lines are usually designated by a letter such as Line "B". Laterals are usually designated by the letter of the main line and a number such as Line "B-1 or B-2". A catch basin can be identified by the lateral associated with it. If main lines and laterals are not designated by letter or number, then laterals should be located by station and catch basins should be located by station and/or by distance to nearest intersection.

Typical entries for sewers and storm drains should include:

(1) Station to station limits of removals, excavation, main line pipe laid (including size and for storm drains, the D-load), bedding, backfill and water densification by jetting (or other consolidation).

(2) Station of sewer house connections excavated or laid, including backfill and jetting or other operations performed. Include numbers of any house connection change reports.

(3) Manholes or other structures completed (or partially completed) including backfill and backfill densification.

(4) Limits of all special compaction completed.

(5) When curved sewer lines have been balled, make note on job report and underline in red.

(6) Any sampling and field tests performed as well as the test results reported.

(7) When line has been air pressure tested, make note on job report and underline in red.

(8) Location of concrete collars (storm drains).

(9) Make note on job card when "Y" sheets are sent to main office.

Plate 9 in the Appendix has instructions regarding the "Job Inspector's Record of Sewer Construction" ("Y" Sheet) which must be completed and forwarded to the Main Office for all sewers constructed. Instructions are also included for the "Request for Change of House Connection Sewer," which is required whenever it is necessary to omit, add or relocate a house connection more than five feet.

1-3.6 Street Lighting and Traffic Signal Projects Reporting. Daily progress of construction should be recorded on the job reports as on other phases of construction, such as: removals, limits of conduit laid, backfilled or "jacked," cable pulled, pull boxes set, concrete for bases placed and equipment installed.

Other items that must be reported include:

(1) When working on existing circuits, record any streetlight "safety clearances" obtained with date, time, duration and reason for clearance.

(2) For equipment and material entries include types and other descriptive information such as manufacturer and model number.

(3) All receipts for salvage equipment should be recorded on job report.

(4) When traffic signal shut-down takes place, record location, date, time, duration and substitute traffic control utilized during shut-down.

(5) Refer to Subsection 3-9.10 for supplemental information regarding street light reports

1-3.7 Contract Time. With rare exceptions, the contract time for agency projects is specified in working days.

The Agency further specifies the assessment of liquidated damages when the contractor fails to complete the work within the contract time. Therefore, the accuracy and substantiation of work progress and delays must be thoroughly and accurately documented. Records, reports and communications with the contractor during the course of construction are of the utmost importance in accomplishing the enforcement of the contract provisions in this regard.

From the information reported by the Project Inspector and reviewed by the District Supervisor the contractor is apprised by mail of the number of days charged and days remaining on the contract by means of a form entitled "Recapitulation of Contract Time" (Appendix, Plate 7).

After notification of award of a contract and prior to start of any work, the contractor submits his proposed construction progress schedule to the Agency. The schedule, in the form of a tabulation, chart or graph (or critical path diagram, when required) must be in sufficient detail to show the chronological relationship of all activities of the project including the start and completion of various activities and the procurement of materials. The construction schedule must reflect the completion of all work under the contract within the specified time. If the contractor wishes to make a major change in his operations after beginning construction, he must submit a revised construction schedule in advance of the revised operations.

As soon as it becomes evident that the actual rate of progress will not be sufficient to complete the project as scheduled and within the contract time, the Project Supervisor must initiate written correspondence to the contractor to advise him of this likelihood and urge him to expedite the work. Written correspondence should follow in progressive steps, i.e. utilizing field correspondence first (Job Memorandum, Notice of Non-Compliance); and if necessary, the Supervisor should prepare a letter draft for issuance by the Division Chief. The ultimate action by Agency management is to recommend that the contractor be declared in default of the contract.

1-3.8 Progress Payment Reporting

1-3.8.1 General. Monthly progress payments are made to the contractor on all contract projects and on assessment act projects when general funds finance a portion or all of the project. The quantities of work accomplished are estimated and reported monthly by the Project Inspector on a progress payment estimate form (Appendix, Plate 8) which he submits to his Supervisor for review and approval.

The normal closing date for this report is the fifteenth of each month (or a different date when requested by the contractor, in accordance with the limitations indicated in Plate 8, Appendix). A report is not required if no progress is made and the Project Coordinating Section in the Main Office is notified.

1-3.8.2 Cost Plus Change Orders. The cost of extra work, for which unit prices or stipulated prices cannot be applied, is usually negotiated. When a negotiated agreement cannot be reached, the work is done under "Cost Plus" change order procedures established by the Standard Specifications.

It is imperative that complete and accurate records be maintained to substantiate the labor, material and equipment used on the cost plus change order work. To facilitate accuracy and agreement with the contractor, the following detailed procedure has been established for such work:

PROCEDURE FOR EXTRA WORK (COST PLUS) CHANGE ORDERS

The following accounting procedure shall be in effect whenever a change order for extra work requires that the cost of such work be based on the accumulation of costs as provided for by the provisions of the Standard Specifications.

The Project Inspector shall prepare a "Daily Report for Cost Plus Changes," in triplicate, for each day that work is performed and chargeable to the change order. The form "Invoice for Cost Plus Changes" shall be utilized for this purpose by deleting the word "Invoice" and writing in the words "Daily Report" (examples shown in the Appendix, Plate 66). Daily reports shall be numbered consecutively in the upper right hand corner and the last report shall include the word "Final." The daily report shall account only for the time and quantities of labor, equipment and materials used.

At the close of each working day, the Project Inspector shall review the daily report entries with the contractor's representative, obtain his signature and sign the document. In the event that a disagreement develops regarding an item, either the Inspector or the contractor's representative shall establish a record of the disagreement by entering appropriate notes on the form prior to signing the document. The Inspector's Supervisor shall attempt to resolve any disagreements noted on the daily report with the contractor prior to submittal of the invoice.

Distribution of the "Daily Report"

      Original—Main Office (via Supervisor)
      cc: Contractor's Representative
      cc: Job Envelope

Following completion of the extra work, the contractor shall submit to the Inspector the "Invoice for Cost Plus

Changes" (on the form supplied by the Project Inspector and prepared as shown in the Appendix, Plate 25B) showing the cost for each item agreed to and listed on the "Daily Reports." After verification, the Inspector signs and forwards the invoice to his Supervisor for transmittal to the Agency Engineer for the preparation of a change order.

In the administration and control of extra work change orders, the Inspector must be alert and accurate to the extent that he approves only those charges which are necessary to complete the change order work.

The following instructions are to be observed by the Inspector engaged in cost plus change order work:

1) He must have a thorough understanding of what the change order requires. If the limits of the work are not clearly defined or understood, he cannot be accurate with his accounting.

2) When the construction operations for contract work and the cost plus change order work are being pursued at the same time and they are closely associated or integrated with other work, special care must be exercised in accounting for the charges against the change order.

3) He must be thoroughly acquainted with the Standard Specification controls governing the cost of such work.

4) He must be prompt in recognizing and resolving any situations involving unnecessary or inefficient use of labor, equipment or material.

5) The daily report must be fully descriptive. Labor must be accounted for by trade, name, classification and specialty when applicable. Equipment must be identified by specific type, model, size and accessories where differences in these items will affect the rental rate. (See the following guidelines). It must also be clearly indicated as to whether the equipment is rented bare (in which case the operator would be listed under labor) or operated and maintained. Description of material items must be specific with units and quantities clearly indicated. For example, the class must be shown for concrete, and asphalt base materials must be listed

by type. Miscellaneous items of work may be involved (such as dump charges) which should be accounted for on the daily report by number of loads and dump location with dump fee receipts attached to the report.

6) The Inspector must also report daily construction activity on the cost plus change order work in the job log.

COST PLUS CHANGE ORDERS GUIDELINES FOR LISTING EQUIPMENT

Air Compressor. All types rated in accordance with the manufacturer's rated capacity in cubic feet per minute at 100 pounds per square inch gage pressure. Indicate hose length over 50 feet.

Jack Hammers. Rated by tool weight in pounds (other air tools not rated by pounds).

Asphalt Paving Machines. Rated by manufacturer and model, includes all attachments and accessories.

Road Brooms. Towed rental rates by broom widths. Street-sweeper type, self-propelled, rated in accordance with the hopper capacity in cubic yards.

Compactors (Impact and Vibratory Types). Hand-guided, gasoline powered, including all attachments and accessories. Rated by load weight or vibratory impact weight.

Light Plants and Generators. Rated in accordance with the manufacturer's continuous rating in kilowatts.

Barricades (Lighted and Unlighted), Delineators. Includes all servicing. Rate per unit per day. (List types).

Loaders, Crawler. Includes all attachments and accessories except for clam action buckets and auxiliary backhoe units. Rated by manufacturer and model.

Loaders, Rubber Tired. Same as crawler type.

Motor Graders. Rated by manufacturer and model.

Pumping Units. Manufacturer's rated capacity.

Rollers, Tamping and Grid. Rated by number of drums and drum dimensions (diameter and length).

Rollers, Street (All Types). Rated by manufacturer and model.

Rollers, Vibratory (Towed and Hand Guided). Rated in accordance with type and net horsepower of the engine mounted on the roller.

Rollers, Vibratory (Self-Propelled Types). Rated by manufacturer and model.

Saws, Concrete Cutting. Rated by the net engine horsepower of the gasoline engine. Indicate lineal footage and depth of cut.

Hydraulic Cranes and Excavators (All Types). Rated by manufacturer and model. Includes all attachments and accessories.

Shovels, Power Crawler or Truck Mounted. Rated by manufacturer, model type and use (shovel, backhoe, driving piles with leads, crane, clamshell, dragline or for driving piles without leads).

Tractors, Crawler. Listed by manufacturer and model. Includes all attachments and accessories such as power control units and push blocks (when needed) but does not include bulldozer and ripper units. Indicate accessories used.

Tractors, Rubber Tired Small Industrial and Farm Types. Rated by manufacturer and model. Indicate accessories such as loader, bulldozer, backhoe.

Tractors, Rubber Tired, Heavy Construction Type. Same as crawler tractors.

Trenching Machines. Rated by manufacturer and model. Includes all attachments and accessories.

Dump Trucks (On Highway Type). Rated in accordance with the total number of axles in the vehicle train. Includes all end dump, side dump and bottom dump, including all attachments and accessories.

Welding Machines, Arc. Rated by manufacturer's output rating expressed in amperes. Includes all attachments, accessories, helmets, rod holders and cable. (Diesel, gasoline or electric powered).

1-3.8.3 Cost Breakdown, Lump Sum or Bid Item Projects. In order to provide a measure of uniformity in estimating progress payment amounts, the following guidelines are furnished. These values (expressed in percent) can be used by the Supervisor in reviewing cost breakdowns of lump sum projects or lump sum bid items; and by the Inspector in the field to break down unit bid items.

PIPELINE CONSTRUCTION			PERCENTAGE
Open Cut (Trenching)	Storm Drain	Excavation and pipe laying	80*
		Backfill and jet. (or mech. comp.)	10
		Perm. resurfacing and cleanup	10
		*Where total project is lump sum, reduce this item by 10% to provide for structures and other work.	
	Sewer (Unlined Pipe)	Excavation and pipe laying	80
		Backfill and jet.	10
		Perm. resurfacing and cleanup	10
	Sewer (Lined Pipe)	Excavation and pipe laying	75
		Joint make-up and liner plate welding	10
		Backfill and jet.	5
		Perm. resurfacing and cleanup	10
Tunnel	Storm Drain	Tunnel excavation	50
		Shafts	10
		Pipe laying	20
		Concrete and earth backfill	15
		Resurfacing and cleanup	5

			Unlined	Lined
	Sewer	Tunnel excavation	50	50
		Shafts	10	10
		Pipe laying	20	25
		Liner plate welding	—	5
		Concrete and earth backfill	15	5
		Resurfacing and cleanup	5	5

PAVEMENT CONSTRUCTION

Pavement	Asphalt Concrete	Subgrade for select material base	20**
		Select material base	Per sq. ft.
		Asphalt concrete	Per ton
	Concrete	Subgrade for select material base	20**
		Select material base	Per sq. ft.
		Concrete	Per sq. ft.
		**To pay for subgrade for SMB, use 20% of the price per sq. ft. for SMB.	

STREET LIGHTING CONSTRUCTION (LUMP SUM CONTRACTS)

Street Lighting	Removals and relocations***	
	Service points	5
	Underground work	35
	Bases	5
	Conductors installed	10
	Electroliers erected and connected	35
	Resurfacing, caps and cleanup	10
	***Estimate the percentage for this item and and reduce all other items to compensate.	

There will be instances where the nature or complexity of a particular project will result in the need to modify these values to more properly reflect appropriate payment to the contractor. The Project Inspector is authorized to make such adjustments subject to review by his Supervisor.

1-4 SAFETY AND CONVENIENCE

1-4.1 General. A primary responsibility of the Agency Inspector is to have a working knowledge of the controlling regulations, codes and directives dealing with public convenience, public safety and construction safety. He must have the ability to apply this knowledge to the construction operations to which he is assigned. In the area of safety, there can be no hesitancy on the part of the Inspector to take immediate action to reduce or eliminate a hazard or an unsafe practice. He must make a conscientious and diligent effort to eliminate any conditions which, in his judgment, would be hazardous to the workers, the public or to himself.

It is the responsiblity of the Inspector to follow safe-practice rules, render every possible aid to the contractor in providing safe operations, and report all unsafe conditions or practices to the proper authority. The contractor's supervisory force must insist on employees observing and obeying every rule, regulation and order as is necessary to the safe conduct of the work, and take such action as is necessary to obtain compliance.

In 1970 Congress passed the Williams-Steiger Occupational Safety and Health Act which resulted in the creation of the Occupational Safety and Health Administration (OSHA) within the Department of Labor. The newly created OSHA safety rules and regulations take precedence over any conflicting or overlapping State or local safety regulations which are "not as effective."

The federal law provides for enforcement agreements with individual states that adopt regulations that are as effective as the OSHA regulations and which have a safety enforcement organization.

Approximately 20% of the 50 states have historically entered into agreements with the federal government which permit local state enforcement.

The State of California abandoned its long-standing local OSHA enforcement program in favor of federal enforcement in mid-1987.

Although the matter of safety at the jobsite is the contractor's legal responsibility, the Inspector may well encourage safe working practices by pointing out possible sources of danger. The Inspector must be safety-conscious and not hesitate to promote the safety of the job and the public.

If, in the informed opinion of the Inspector, the precautions taken by the contractor are found to be insufficient or inadequate in providing job or public safety at any time during the life of the contract, he must inform the contractor to take additional precautions. When the contractor has failed to take action on safety violations, after being advised of the unsafe condition, it is the duty of the Inspector to notify Agency management in order that the enforcing OSHA agency may be notified.

The Inspector can demonstrate interest in safety by establishing a firm, positive attitude toward the prevention of accidents. His knowledge of the construction safety orders is essential if violations arise.

1-4.2 Agency Personnel Safety.

1-4.2.1 General. Employees of the Agency at the site of construction work shall be safety conscious at all times and shall not work under any conditions that are in apparent violation of the OSHA regulations. It is mandatory that all Agency Inspectors conform to the performance standards of all safety regulations. In this regard, the Inspector, as an employee, has the same rights and is afforded the same protection as any other public employee within the State. These are:

(1) Any employee or his representative may call the State Safety Agency and report any unsafe working condition. The employee need not identify himself. If he does identify himself, his identity is kept confidential by the State.

(2) An employee may refuse to work under unsafe conditions.

(3) Any employee has the right to observe, monitor or measure employee exposure to hazards and has the right of access to accurate records of employee exposure to potentially toxic materials or harmful physical agents.

(4) The employee may not be harassed or disciplined in any way for the legitimate calls reporting unsafe conditions or for refusing to work under unsafe conditions.

1-4.2.2 Safety Rules For Inspectors. The following are the general employee responsibilities as prescribed in OSHA law. No person shall do any of the following:

(1) Remove, displace, damage, destroy or carry off any safety device, safeguard, notice or warning, furnished for use in any employment or place of employment.

(2) Interfere in any way with the use thereof by any person.

(3) Interfere with the use of any method or process adopted for the protection of any employee, including oneself, in such employment or place of employment.

(4) Fail or neglect to do every other thing reasonably necessary to protect the life and safety of employees.

Almost all injuries and accidents are caused by someone ignoring safety orders, not following safety practices, taking a chance or failing to correct dangerous conditions. Safety orders only establish standards of work safety. They are the framework in which work can be accomplished safely. The Inspector's complete safety on the job depends on his own efforts to be safe. All unsafe acts and work practices must be avoided for the benefit of all concerned.

To prevent accidents, the Inspector must have a great desire not to have them. Attitude is the keystone of accident prevention. The individuals with proper attitudes have few accidents, whereas the careless have many. The Inspector must be able to recognize accident hazards and to eliminate them. Rules are just as necessary in working, as they are in competitive sports. Safe practice rules are needed so that every employee can work as a part of the team, without fear of injury. The following set of rules should be complied with in order to prevent accidents and to enforce safe practices:

SAFETY RULES

*Be in good physical condition before starting work, with your alertness and ability unaffected by illness or lack of rest, which causes fatigue and decreased efficiency. Problems can lead to accidents if your mind isn't on the job.

*If you become ill when at work, report to your Supervisor or Dispatcher for replacement so that you may receive proper medical attention.

*Wear the right work clothes and shoes for the job. Your clothing should allow freedom of action and should not hang loosely. Wear shoes that fit well; loosely fitting shoes are dangerous. International Orange vests shall be worn when high visibility of personnel is advantageous.

*Wear your hard hat. Be sure the hat band and laces are in good condition.

*Wear safety goggles when near welding operations or near hazardous liquids or other materials which may spatter and impair your vision. Think about what you see, where to look and what to look for.

*Be sure the equipment you are using, or working near, is in safe operating condition, grounded, properly operated and contributes to a safe working atmosphere.

*Keep as clean as possible to prevent skin trouble when working with chemicals, oils, paints or cleaners. Wash thoroughly after handling anything that might be poisonous or injurious, especially before eating. Report and treat all injuries, no matter how small they may seem. Prevent serious infection by receiving first-aid treatment.

*Never act impulsively. Think about what you are going to do before you do it. Consider the hazards and take adequate precautions. Correct any unsafe conditions you can; report all others to your Supervisor. Always expect the unexpected.

*Don't attempt to handle more than you can control. Do your work the right way and safe way; taking short cuts is often dangerous. Work at a speed which is known to be safe, watch where you're walking, and never run.

*Use handrails on stairs or on elevated places. Never jump from platforms, scaffolds, loading docks or other elevations.

*Your job in fire prevention is to keep things that start fires away from things that burn. If you notice a fire hazard, see that it is corrected. Observe "no smoking" regulations where posted. You should become familiar with the operation and use of the various types of fire extinguishers provided and their locations.

*Always use safe practices and follow instructions. Help make the entire job safe. Watch out for the safety of other workers and help new employees learn safe work practices.

*Be your brother's keeper. Consider what you do in terms of the hazards it may create for others. Never leave a booby trap for the next person who may come by.

*Obey all traffic regulations while driving vehicles both on and off the job. Be courteous to other motorists. When not driving, be a safe pedestrian. Stay alert and don't jaywalk.

*The rules of safety you use at work are just as important for you and your family while you are at home. For safety 24 hours a day, teach and practice safety in your own home. Safety is a year 'round job, always in season.

*Plan your work ahead to prevent accidents, and take part in regular accident prevention programs. Preplanning of safety measures to meet known construction activity hazards will prevent accidents and promote efficient and economical construction. By utilizing proper attitude, basic skill, good habits, thorough knowledge, fair judgment, along with mental and physical fitness, the benefits derived will be worth the effort involved and in the final analysis will prove that safety makes sense.

The Inspector's cooperation is necessary for the protection of himself and others. It is important that he follow all safety rules, take no unnecessary chances, use all safeguards and safety equipment provided and make safety a part of his job. Accidents and fires hurt all of us in many ways. The Inspector and his family suffer if he is injured; all employees lose, because accidents are wasteful. This means lost production, higher operating costs and inefficiency. The Inspector must do his part by giving full support to all safety rules.

1-4.2.3 Inspector's Protective Equipment.

The Agency Inspector is expected to wear suitable clothing and protective gear to meet the needs of his employment. Specialized gear will be supplied from Agency headquarters as needed.

For his protection, the Inspector shall wear the hard hat issued by the Agency at all construction jobs where he is subjected to the hazard of falling and flying material. This will also serve to identify the Inspector on the job and set a good example for other people working on the project.

Protective vests of International Orange must be worn for high visibility when the Inspector is in close proximity to traffic or moving equipment. It is better to be seen by a vehicle than to be hit by one.

It is particularly important that the Inspector insure that closed or confined spaces (such as tunnels, pipelines, tanks, manholes and other underground structures) are safe before entering or allowing others to enter. Most Agencies provide portable equipment for the detection of oxygen deficiency, lower explosive limit and for toxic concentrations of methane, hydrogen sulfide and other chemical substances. It is essential that the Inspector learn when and how to use such equipment. If it is not readily available from his Agency, he should contact the local fire department for assistance (see Subsection 1-4.3.4).

In the demolition of existing structures or facilities, as well as with new construction in an open area, toxic waste materials may be encountered. The Inspector should immediately request professional investigation of the site if he suspects chemical contamination, uncovers strange odors, discovers asbestos-like materials or encounters any other condition that he considers potentially hazardous.

1-4.3　Construction Operations Safety.

1-4.3.1　General.　The enforcement of regulations for the protection and safety of construction workers is the responsibility of the Federal or State Agency delegated by law to enforce occupational safety and health rules.

Employees of the Agency are cautioned that their participation in a contractor's safety program is to assist in the recognition of safe and unsafe practices. As a general rule, the contractor alone is responsible for the safe conduct of the contract and Agency employees are to avoid giving instructions to the contractor that might be construed as directing the work.

1-4.3.2　Construction Safety Enforcement.　The following general instructions are intended to provide guidelines to inspection personnel:

(1) All inspection personnel, on projects administered by the Agency, shall exercise a conscientious and diligent effort to eliminate any conditions which, in their opinion, appear to be hazardous to the contractor's employees, the public or themselves.

(2) Construction safety shall be governed by the pertinent requirements of the various OSHA agency publications as they apply, such as: Construction Safety Orders.

(3) At the beginning of a project, the Inspector shall discuss the subject of safety with the contractor to establish the interest and concern of the Agency.

(4) The Inspector shall have a timely discussion with the contractor and his Supervisor regarding safety problems which can be anticipated during construction.

(5) Any conditions, practice or act which develops during construction, which in the Inspector's judgment is a potential hazard, must be called to the contractor's attention at once.

(6) Any unsafe condition, practice or act should be clearly identified and if the contractor responds promptly and the resulting condition appears to be safe, no further action is required.

(7) When the contractor fails to take satisfactory corrective action promptly, the Inspector shall issue a Notice of Non-Compliance to the contractor and request OSHA to make an investigation. The Notice of Non-Compliance shall state the hazard and questionable work area to be vacated pending the investigation.

(8) Every request for investigation shall be noted in the job record, including the:

(a) Time of call;

(b) Name of OSHA authority representative contacted;

(c) Name of OSHA authority field investigator, the hour and date of his arrival on the job and a summary of his report.

(9) Judgment should be exercised to avoid unnecessary involvement of OSHA in minor violations which have little urgency. The Inspector should consult with his Supervisor when there is doubt regarding the action to be taken.

(10) Deaths and serious injuries on the project, either to the public or the contractor's employees, shall be reported to Agency headquarters by phone and a "Job Safety Record Accident Report" (See Plate 6, Appendix) shall be prepared by the Inspector and forwarded to the Agency headquarters as soon as possible.

1-4.3.3 Excavations and Trenches. In order to prevent deaths and injuries from cave-ins, the Inspector should satisfy himself that the contractor is familiar with minimum safety standards and shoring methods to prevent cave-ins and that the employer has taken all necessary precautions to protect his workers. The protection of workers must be judged at least as effective as that provided for by the Construction Safety Orders.

Many states, such as California, have laws providing that all employers must have Division of Industrial Safety permits to make excavations or trenches five feet (1.5 m) or deeper.

Agency contracts valued at more than $25,000 or which call for excavations or trenching five feet (1.5 m) or deeper, should require that detailed plans of trench shoring systems be submitted by the contractor for Agency review.

1-4.3.4 Tunnels, Pipelines and Confined Spaces. Hazardous conditions may exist or be created in a variety of situations when work is performed in confined areas. The Inspector should be alert to recognize these situations in order to insure that the contractor takes the necessary safety precautions.

The first safety consideration in tunnel construction is protection from moving ground. Most of the tunnel construction done under contract to the Agency requires approval of the contractors' proposed shoring plans by the Agency. It is the Inspector's duty to enforce strict conformance with the minimum requirements of these approved plans. As tunnel construction progresses, mechanical ventilation must be provided in order to provide sufficient clean air and avoid the accumulation of toxic gasses. Also, a means of quick communication with personnel outside the tunnel is vital to the protection of personnel.

"Confined spaces," as defined by OSHA Construction Safety Orders, includes the interior of storm drains, sewers, utility pipelines, manholes and any other such structure that is similarly surrounded by confining surfaces which could permit the accumulation of dangerous gasses or vapors. Most of the safe practice provisions for tunnel construction also apply to confined spaces.

Tests for the presence of hazardous gasses and oxygen deficiency shall be made with an approved sensing device immediately prior to a worker's entering a confined space, and at frequent intervals to insure a safe atmosphere while a worker is inside. Although this is primarily the contractor's responsibility, the Agency provides such testing devices for use by its own personnel and the Inspector needs only to contact his Supervisor whenever the equipment is needed. In general, the Agency equipment should be used on all projects as a back-up system, to check on the accuracy of the test equipment supplied by the contractor.

Sources of ignition, including smoking, should be prohibited in any confined space. If the possibility exists that confined spaces tested and found not to he hazardous may become hazardous as construction proceeds, an approved safety belt with a life line attached should be utilized with at least one worker standing by on the outside, ready to give assistance in case of emergency.

Potentially hazardous confined spaces where inspection work is performed by Agency personnel, such as the larger diameter sewer pipe lines, particularly where there is a live sewer atmosphere or plastic liner work, should be checked regularly to detect any deterioration from a safe environment.

1-4.3.5 Explosives. When the nature of the work requires that a contractor use explosives, the contractor must first obtain a permit from the proper authority. Copies of such permits must be kept on the project at all times. Such permits usually require a qualified blasting operator and special blasting inspection from the permit authority.

1-4.3.6 Accident Reporting. Inasmuch as accidents and personal injuries may involve complicated litigation in connection with workers' compensation or damage actions, complete and accurate reports are of the utmost importance. The Inspector must file accident reports in accordance with Agency reporting procedure [See Subsection 1-4.3.2, Item (10)].

1-4.3.7 Jobsite Maintenance. Good housekeeping and sanitary provisions are important to the safety of the worker and the public. The Standard Specifications should be referred to for specific requirements.

In addition, the contractor is responsible for public and private property insofar as it may be endangered by his operations and is required to take every reasonable precaution to avoid damage.

Throughout all phases of construction, the rubbish and debris on a project shall be held to the absolute minimum and confined to organized disposal and storage areas. In the interest of a safe working environment, materials and equipment shall be removed from the worksite as soon as they are no longer needed. Excess excavated material should be removed from the site as soon as practical.

Dust nuisance is to be held to a minimum by cleaning, sweeping and sprinkling with water or other means as necessary. The use of water for sprinkling must be controlled so as not to generate other problems such as mud and slippery conditions.

The contractor's equipment and construction operations shall not contribute excessively to air pollution by discharging smoke, exhaust fumes, dust or other contaminants into the air in such quantities as to exceed the limits legally imposed by any local control authority (such as the local Air Pollution Control District). Likewise, severe noise pollution for protracted periods should be avoided or minimized as much as possible. Any contemplated operations of this nature, such as on-site pavement crushing, should be reported to the Supervisor.

Care should be exercised on each project that adequate drainage is maintained at all times. Existing gutters, ditches or other drainage devices are to be kept clear of spoil or debris.

Blockage of normal drainage avenues is not permitted, except in time of emergency for a few hours during the day to protect the work. The Inspector is cautioned to insure that a temporary dam does not create a nuisance or hazard to the public. Under no circumstances is a contractor permitted to drain water or other liquid into an existing sewer line, and only clear water may be channeled into the storm drain system.

Sewers through the worksite shall not be disrupted. However, if sewer lines are accidentally damaged, the immediate temporary repair shall involve the resumption of sewage flow by conveyance in closed conduits until disposed of in a functioning sanitary sewer system.

Construction materials are normally not to be stored in public streets for more than five days after unloading unless specifically located within a pre-designated construction area. Care should be exercised in the placement of materials to minimize traffic hazards or damage to existing plants, trees, shrubs or ornamental objects to which the property owner attaches significant value.

Vehicular access to residential driveways shall be maintained to the property line, except when necessary for construction activity for short, reasonable periods of time during the day. Safe and adequate pedestrian zones and public transportation stops, as well as reasonable pedestrian crossings of the work at frequent intervals, are to be maintained by the contractor. Whenever possible, existing sidewalks are to remain free of obstructions.

1-4.4   Traffic Safety and Convenience.

1-4.4.1   General.   Agency contracts on highways, major and secondary streets nearly always have special traffic control requirements, such as street or lane closures, detours and hours of work. The *Work Area Traffic Control Handbook* (a reference document in many Agency contracts) specifies general requirements and controls. Extracts from this handbook and information on its availability are to be found in the Appendix.

The *Work Area Traffic Control Handbook* sets forth basic principles and standards in order to provide safe and effective work areas and to warn, control, protect and expedite vehicular and pedestrian traffic through the construction project.

The responsibility of safe and proper handling of traffic rests with the contractor. The Inspector shall see that the contractor provides for traffic as required by the contract and shall direct the contractor to correct any potentially dangerous situation that exists. If necessary, the Inspector will instruct him in writing to take action to protect and warn the traveling public.

1-4.4.2 Street Closures. Agency management is normally authorized to close residential streets for certain periods, when necessary for construction work, subject to the following limitations:

(a) Authority is limited to residential streets normally carrying light vehicular traffic traveling only to residences within the blocks immediately adjacent to the construction area.

(b) Closure is confined to daylight working hours.

(c) Closure must be approved by the Division Chief or higher authority, after consultation and notification to Utility, Police, Fire and Traffic Agencies.

(d) The Division Chief is responsible to assure that the contractor has provided for adequate advance notification to all residents affected by the closed area.

(e) Suitable warning barricades and lights shall be placed. Refer to the Work Area Traffic Control Handbook for guidance in providing a safe and effective work area.

Requests from the contractor to close or restrict traffic on any major, secondary or other street (including residential streets), subject to through traffic, must be received in writing sufficiently in advance to permit adequate time for investigation and report to Agency authority. No such closing or restriction of traffic may be permitted prior to approval. The Agency Public Information Officer will be responsible for notifying the appropriate elected officials of all street closings by the Agency.

In general, the Traffic Agency will post and maintain all necessary detour signs to lead traffic through the detour, without cost to the contractor. The contractor shall place and maintain all barricades, lights and signs necessary to protect the public from hazards within his area of operations.

1-4.4.3 Barricades and Striping. The preponderance of the work inspected by the Agency is performed in public streets. Consequently, nearly every project creates some increased degree of hazard to the traveling public and the imminence of moving vehicles in the streets increases the hazards to the workers and the Inspector on the project. It is imperative that the degree of interference with the normal traffic flow be kept to an absolute minimum and that the working area is adequately defined with barricades and lights to warn the traveling public of the work area and to afford a satisfactory degree of protection to the workers.

The *Work Area Traffic Handbook* shall be used for guidance when barricades, warning devices or signs are required. Any temporary pavement marking required will be done by the Traffic Agency. Necessary removal of existing marking and the later removal of temporary marking to restore the permanent marking is the responsibility of the contractor.

1-4.4.4 Temporary "No Parking." At the request of the contractor, the Traffic Agency will post and remove temporary "No Parking" signs. The contractor is charged for this service.

1-4.4.5 Traffic Emergency Service. When the contractor fails or neglects to adequately barricade and light his work area, and does not respond to instructions to correct these conditions, the Agency Inspector arranges for Agency forces to perform the necessary emergency work and the contractor will be billed by the Agency for the costs incurred.

1-5 CONSTRUCTION SURVEY STAKING

1-5.1 General. All construction staking on contract projects is supplied by the Agency Survey Division. Construction survey staking services by private engineering firms or licensed surveyors on all permits administered by the Agency must conform in all respects to the quality and practice required of the Agency Survey Division. All grade sheets must be prepared on a grade sheet similar to the Agency grade sheet form.

The contractor is required to notify the Survey Division prior to starting work, in order that necessary measures may be taken to insure the preservation of survey monuments and bench marks. At the beginning of the job, the Inspector should verify with the Survey Division that this has been done.

Inspectors shall instruct the contractor to protect all survey stakes, witness markers, reference points and survey data painted on existing improvements.

Normally, stakes will be set for rough grade, curbs, headers, sewers, storm drains and structures. Stakes may be set on an offset with a station and a corresponding cut or fill to finish grade (or flow line) indicated on a grade sheet. The grade sheet may be issued on a standard form or be a copy of the Surveyor's completed field notes. In the case of structures, such as bridges, these stakes may serve as controls for checking the formwork prior to placing concrete. All other stakes will be set to finished grade with top colored with blue crayon (commonly referred to as "blue tops"). It is the option of the Agency as to whether grade and line are provided by blue tops or by marking the cuts and fills on pavement (or the stakes) or by referring to stakes, drill holes, chisel cuts, etc., on a grade sheet. If the Inspector is on the job when the blue tops are set, he will check all hubs (blue top reference stakes) set by the contractor before permitting the blue tops to be disturbed. To avoid damage these hubs should be set a minimum of four inches (10 cm) below subgrade. Blue tops are not to be driven down for use as a hub or other grade reference for the contractor due to the extreme possibility of error in setting and also the blue color could mistakenly indicate finished grade.

It is never permissible for a contractor to set stakes for the elevations shown on the plan unless he himself is, or employs, a registered engineer or a licensed land surveyor. However, he may set such auxiliary stakes for his own purposes as he desires and he is required to set "guineas" (usually small stakes) or intermediate grades and to transfer grades from offset stakes.

1-5.2   Survey Service Requests.   All requests for survey service must be made by the contractor. Extra survey service, for replacing lost or disturbed stakes, or for the contractor's convenience, may result in an extra charge against the contractor. When the Inspector is doubtful that the lines or grade are to plan, due to abuse of the reference points, or for any other reason, or the line or grade does not appear to check, he may request survey to recheck or to provide additional control points. Care should be exercised to keep these survey requests to a minimum.

1-5.3   Earthwork Stakes.   Rough grade stakes will generally be set parallel to and on an offset from the operation being performed. The interval between stakes will be 50 feet (15 m) or less if the project is less than 500 feet (50 m) long. An attempt is made to use a consistent and convenient offset, but this is not always possible due to interferences. A lath, serving as a witness marker, will be set adjacent to the stake marked to show identifying stations and offset distances. Along with the stakes and laths, a grade sheet is issued to the contractor and Inspector containing essential information such as: type of stake set, station, offset distance and cut or fill to a specific plan location.

For slopes, where heavy cuts or fill are to be construed, slope stakes and offset reference stakes are furnished to the contractor together with a rough grade sheet to permit him to utilize heavy equipment to economically approach the final grades to within approximately .20 of a foot (6 mm).

Witness marker laths identifying these stakes show the difference in elevation between the slope stake and reference stake; distance between slope stake and reference stake; station of slope stake and reference stake; cut or fill and distance from slope stake to toe of cut or shoulder of fill; and slope ratio.

In addition to the inevitability of these slope stakes being lost during construction and inaccurancies that develop as the contractor transfers these grades, another set of stakes and grade sheets are provided for final grading operations. The location and information for these stakes will vary depending on the requirements, such as proximity to final grades, proposed drainage bench and other improvements.

1-5.4 Street Improvement Stakes. After rough grading is accomplished, a survey party will set curb, gutter (or header) stakes and issue grade sheets. Except when specifically noted on the grade sheets, all elevations shown refer to the top of curb (or header). The contractor sometimes mistakenly uses such elevations for flow line data and the Inspector is cautioned to check the grade sheet against the construction to insure that the grade sheet is being properly interpreted and the plan requirements are being met. In case of a varying curb face, cuts of fills will be given both to the top of the curb and to the flowline. Stakes for curb construction or for monolithic curb and gutter are always set on a convenient offset [usually five feet (1.5 m)] for ease of construction. Unless otherwise indicated, the offset distance refers to the.top front face (street side) of the curb. A tack in the top surface of the stake is the exact point from which to measure. Intervals between stakes are generally 25 feet (7.5 m), but this distance will decrease if the overall length of the project is less than 500 feet (150 m) or the rate of grade is under one-half of one percent. A witness marker lath will be set adjacent to each stake.

The Inspector must be on the alert to see that driveway depressions on the curb are not overlooked. The centerline of driveways may not be staked but the centerline station will be indicated on the grade sheet and, except for some permit work, will also be shown on the project plans.

Flow line elevations will be necessary if concrete gutter is to be placed against existing curb. The survey party provides this by chisel cutting an inverted "T" or by triangle symbols painted on the curb face. These are usually set at a constant vertical offset above the flow line [usually three inches (8 cm)]. This dimension above the flow line will be painted on the curb face at suitable intervals.

After the concrete curb and gutter, or gutter only, has been placed and the concrete has set sufficiently to prevent damage to the surface, the flow line should be checked for proper drainage by running water down the gutter.

Subgrade stakes may be set by the survey party under certain conditions. These are referred to as "red tops" because the tops are colored with red crayon to distinguish them from finish grade stakes which are colored blue. When blue top stakes are set, the contractor must calculate the subgrade and set hubs besides the blue tops and far enough below subgrade to prevent them from being disturbed by the subsequent grading operations. These hubs must be checked by the Inspector for accuracy and dimension below blue tops so there will be no question as to their elevation.

When the roadway measures less than 40 feet (12 m) in width between curbs, stakes will generally be set only where elevations are shown on the plans. If the crown section varies between centerline grade changes, additional stakes will be set on the centerline of the roadway.

For roadways whose widths are more than 40 feet (12 m) between curbs, stakes will be set on centerline at specified intervals, in addition to plan elevations.

Stakes for "T" sections are not normally set by the Survey Division. Necessary stakes along the "T" section must be set by the contractor and checked by the Inspector. Consult the standard plan for street crown sections for information required to perform the calculations necessary to check this operation.

In intersections, "blue tops" will be set for all plan elevations. After the base courses of asphalt pavement are laid [on major streets, pavement thickness over four inches (10 cm)] the fills to finish surface of the wearing course will be painted on the base course to indicate the fill to finished grade. If the base course is to be laid in more than one lift, the Inspector may request that fills to finished grade be painted on the surface of each lift. The fill data provided by the Survey Division for paving will be at the same intervals and locations stated above for blue tops set for fine grading operations. Fill data required along "T" sections must be set with a string line by the contractor and verified by the Inspector.

In alleys, rough grade stakes will be provided on one side of the alley only where the cut or fill is extensive, except in those cases when the grades for the opposite side of the alley are substantially different. Generally these stakes will not be "tacked."

Where the cut or fill is not extensive, or after extensive cut or fill operations, tacked grade stakes or reference points, with a suitable offset, will be provided on both sides of the alley between the property lines at each end of the alley and at specified intervals, depending on the alley length and flatness of grade. A grade sheet will be issued indicating the cuts or fills for both top of header grades and the flow line of the longitudinal gutter.

If alley intersections are to be constructed, the curb returns will be staked at the time the stakes for headers are set. If the project includes the improvement of adjacent streets, the curb returns for alley intersections will be staked along with the adjoining curbs.

When requested by the contractor, after rough grade has been completed, a survey party will set blue tops for the longitudinal gutter flow line.

Many street lighting systems are construed as a portion of the work to be performed by the contractor as part of a complete street improvement project. If this is the case, the electrolier bases are usually located after the curb has been constructed. It is a simple matter and will expedite construction for the contractor to establish the location of the electroliers (and their locations) by utilizing the curb stakes. The difference in stationing between the electrolier and the nearest curb stake is used to obtain the required measurement between them.

When the street improvements exist, electrolier locations will be indicated by a "Y" painted on the curb. Where no curbs exist, electrolier stakes will be referenced to the proposed curb.

1-5.5 Pipelines, Utilities and Other Substructure Staking. Under normal conditions, mainline sewer and storm drain pipe will be laid from offset stakes. The offset will be determined by the contractor based on the equipment he intends to use, depth of cut and type of soil encountered. Line and grade must be transferred from these offset stakes by the contractor and checked by the Inspector. These stakes will be set at specified intervals, generally 25 feet (7.5 m) or less. Generally, at least three consecutive stakes should be used to establish line and grade, either in the trench or on the surface, to detect staking errors prior to laying pipe.

Other offset stakes along the mainline will be set at the following locations: existing joins, BC's and EC's of curves and inlets, outlets and stubs of manholes or structures. If the manhole stub is not on the sewer line produced, a stake will be set 10 feet (3 m) or more from the manhole and on the line of the stub. Offset and dimensional stakes are also used to locate other structures such as: lampholes, clean out structures and special structures. A grade sheet will be issued describing the kind of stakes, offset dimension or line indication, cut to flow line or special elevation, station and other special information.

For large diameter pipe [generally 60 inches (1.5 m) and over], sloped excavations, or cast-in-place structures, "blue tops" for line and grade may be used in the trench in addition to the offset stakes which would then be used for excavation only. Blue tops become necessary because of the high risk of inaccuracy in transferring grades from long offset distances.

As a rule, stakes for house connections are set one foot (30 cm) or more beyond the end of the pipe of the house connection line produced. Offset stakes may be set if the house connection is unusually long or is not on a straight line or straight grade. If a general note on the job plans calls for a uniform depth at property line then the stakes are set only for location. If a special depth is called out for any house connection, then both depth and location will be indicated. This and any other special information will appear on the grade sheet.

Staking for catch basins for storm drain systems are frequently included with the curb stakes. Usually one stake is set on the curb stake line opposite the center of the catch basin. For catch basins over seven feet (2.1 m) long, stakes are also set opposite the ends of the proposed structures. If the curb stake line is too close to permit excavation for this catch basin without losing the stakes, the stakes are set on a larger offset dimension. This will be noted on the marker lath and the grade sheet.

If there is no existing curb and no curb is to be constructed, stakes for small catch basins are set five feet (1.5 m) back of the future curb on the centerline, and five feet (1.5 m) or more on each side of the centerline of the catch basin in order that the catch basin may be constructed to be on line with the future curb. For catch basins over seven feet (2.1 m) long, stakes are set opposite the ends of the structure in addition to the centerline stake. If no stations are shown on the plans, the stakes will be identified with letters.

A third condition is frequently encountered: a curb may already exist which must be removed for catch basin construction. In this case, drill holes are set in the top surface of the curb at an appropriate distance each side of the center of the catch basin. These points are identified and referenced to the grade sheet by letters. Always review the appropriate standard plans and project plans thoroughly. The center stake may locate the center of the basin, the center of the opening or the width depending on which type of basin is to be built.

Normally, a lateral pipe extending from the catch basin to the mainline transition or junction structure which is less than 25 feet (7.5 m) in length, is not staked unless the grade is less than half of one percent or there is a major line or grade change point required by plan. Catch basin outlet elevations are determined either from the project plans or the standard plan. The project plans will also indicate the elevation difference between the mainline and the connection lateral inlet flowlines. The flowlines of the lateral pipes are normally on a straight grade with their connecting structures.

In most cases, the utility companies will use the contractors rough grade stakes for any relocation of services that are required. However, when approved, a separate set of stakes for utility purposes may be set before construction of the improvement begins. This staking generally follows pipeline staking procedure.

A series of offset stakes, with cuts to specified elevations, will be provided to locate the shaft for tunnel operations. Controls to establish line and grade from the shaft into the tunnel may vary depending on the contractor's excavation methods. One popular system is for the survey party to drive nails and tins on line into the timber shoring on both sides of the shaft, and above the bottom elevation of the intended crown shoring of the tunnel to be driven. The nails and tins must be out of the way of the contractor's equipment. Line and grade for initial tunnelling operations can be easily transferred into the tunnel by the contractor using plumb bobs hanging from these controls. As the tunnel is driven, periodic checks will be made by the survey crew and additional reference points established. The kind of points again may vary with the type of equipment and methods used by the contractor. One system is for the survey party to drive "spads" (hook type nails) on line in the soffit of the tunnel shoring. This provides a means of hanging a plumb bob and visually producing a line from some point previously set. A cut from the spad to a specified elevation is also given or a nail and tin driven into the tunnel shoring on one side of the proposed pipe at springline. After the tunnel excavation has been completed, the bedding placed (when required), and the pipe is ready to be laid, blue tops must be set by the survey crew.

When jacked casings are to be used in lieu of tunnelling, the jacking pits may differ from the tunnel shafts (principally in length) in order to accommodate the jacking equipment, etc. Prior to jacking operations, the equipment and first pipe may be checked by the survey party to insure correct alignment. Since the casing will be moving, adequate permanent reference points cannot be set, therefore, it will be necessary that periodic checks of the casing alignment be made by a survey party to insure that the required line and grade are being achieved.

1-5.6   Bridges, Buildings and Retaining Walls.   Retaining wall and bulkhead stakes are usually set on the upperside and at an offset distance great enough to allow for excavation. The offset distance will refer to a plumb face or other definite plane of the wall or bulkhead that is constant thoroughout its length. The Inspector must be alert to the calculations that may be needed for necessary checks, such as batter, etc. Stakes will be set opposite the ends and BC's and EC's, grade changes, angle points, changes of cross section in the wall or bulkhead, and at specified intervals in between. A grade sheet will be issued indicating the offset and will usually give two grades from each stake, one for the footing and the other for the top of the wall or bulkhead.

After grading has been completed, the original stakes may be unusable for construction due to the height of the wall or extensive offset distance. In such cases, footing stakes may also be set with offsets and grades to specific locations.

In the construction of major bridges and structures, many of the measurements are beyond the scope of the Inspector to witness and check using hand instruments and he must depend on the surveyor. On some projects, a survey crew is retained on a full time basis; on others, only periodic services are required.

Stakes are first set beyond the lines of excavation on the prolongation of the control lines of each abutment, pier or bent, which will be needed during construction. The contractor should decide on an offset that will be convenient and will not encroach upon his construction activities. After the stakes for construction are set, the Inspector and the contractor must jointly review and understand to what location each offset and cut or fill stake is referred. If piles are required, the location of the pile line is established and a temporary bench mark is set at each end of the structure at pile cut-off elevation. In some cases, pile stakes may be combined with foundation stakes. Foundation stakes may be set to subgrade if the grade has been made. Piling cut-offs may not be marked if it is feasible for the contractor to use the foundation stakes for this purpose. Temporary bench marks may be placed at some even foot (cm) above the foundation to facilitate the contractor's work. If starter walls are to be constructed as part of the foundation, it may be necessary for the survey crew to make a line and grade check of these forms prior to placing concrete.

If starter walls are not utilized, it may be necessary to have a survey crew locate the bottom of the pier or abutment wall prior to forming (or after forms are set-up) to check the top and bottom for line and elevation. A convenient elevation marked on the back of the form can be of value to the contractor and Inspector in setting and checking variable height rebar, embedded items and pour strips. Other items that may be critical should be located and checked by a survey party prior to placing concrete. These could include: bearing plates, expansion joints, grade changes and wall openings. On some projects, when warranted, the surveyor will make frequent checks during concrete placement to assure that the forms remain plumb, in line, on grade, and that no shift or displacement is taking place. The walls or other components may again be checked after concrete has been placed to verify that the plan requirements have been met.

Falsework bent lines and temporary bench marks should be staked by the surveyor for the contractor's use in building the falsework. The specifications usually require the contractor to submit detailed shop drawings of the falsework for approval. It is known that each joint in the falsework will settle when the concrete is placed; also, there will be a settlement of the bridge due to its own load when the falsework is removed. The falsework and dead load settlement and the design camber must be taken into account to meet the plan elevations when the work is completed. Therefore, elevation checks on the bridge deck forms and girder locations are usually beyond the scope of the Inspector and will require the services of a survey party.

Other controls that may require special survey service are: the perimeter formwork, reinforcing steel layout, anchor bolts for railings and other equipment and streetlight locations. After the reinforcing steel is in place, elevations of forms should be read and the necessary adjustments made to meet the required grade and camber. The Inspector must be sure to have the screeds checked to insure that the finished surface required by the plan elevations will be met.

When necessary, grade sheets will be issued in the field by the surveyor.

The above outline is a general guide to acquaint the Inspector with the information and checks that may be necessary from the survey party in staking bridges and other structures. Every project presents unique dimensional checking problems and each solution will depend on the design and existing field conditions. The Inspector, contractor and surveyor should maintain close communication so that the stakes and information supplied by the surveyor is adequate for the contractor's construction needs and for the purpose of verification by the Inspector so that the surveying services are not wasted.

1-6 PRESERVATION OF IMPROVEMENTS AND UTILITIES

1-6.1 General. Most public improvement contract projects are located in developed areas, either business or residential. Such areas always have public and private improvements and utilities which must be considered in the design and construction of the improvement.

Agency contracts provide that the contractor is generally responsible for preserving public and private property and utilities along and adjacent to the roadway insofar as they are endangered by his operations. The contractor must take proper precautions in performing the work to avoid damage to property. The contractor is obligated to repair or rebuild damaged property, or to make good any damage or injury by other means in an acceptable manner.

Contract plans for the project should show the type and location of the improvements within and adjacent to the construction area. In addition, the contract documents will provide for the treatment of such improvements (removal, replacement, relocation). However, the inaccuracy of available underground location records or the construction of improvements after the project plans were prepared, or other reasons, may lead to problems not provided for in the contract.

The Agency Inspector is responsible to assist the contractor as much as possible to avoid damage and further to coordinate the expeditious relocation of utilities which the construction operations require. In addition, the Inspector must see that all damage that does occur is properly repaired. One of the first duties of the Agency Inspector assigned to a new project is to walk the job with the construction plans and compare actual field conditions with those noted on the plans, making special notes on the plans where conflicts exist and where other problem areas are obvious which may result in damage to existing improvements during construction. Consultation with the contractor or design engineer to resolve potential problems prior to construction will expedite progress and avoid unnecessary expense and potential litigation at a later date.

Usually after award of the contract and before any work is done by the contractor, the Agency conducts a preview inspection of the project in considerable detail. The purpose is to insure that all damage done by the contractor during construction operations is repaired and to insure that the Agency, the contractor and the public are protected from false claims and litigation.

The preview consists of a video (or photographic) and audio (tape recorder) description of the condition of the jobsite and adjacent improvements such as walls, sidewalks, driveways, pavement, buildings, fences and landscape features. Disputes regarding the prior condition of adjacent improvements can usually be resolved by replaying the video tape on a video cassette recorder (VCR).

1-6.2 Encroachment and Salvage. Many times privately owned improvements need to be removed or altered because they encroach into the public right-of-way and interfere with the planned improvements. Written notice ahead of construction is given by the Agency to the property owner to remove the encroachment.

As required by the contract provisions, the Inspector should see that the contractor also gives notice for those encroachments that remain at the time of construction. The contractor may want to assist the property owner to salvage or relocate such items as a public relations gesture although he is under no obligation to do so after giving reasonable notice.

1-6.3 Utility Protection and Relocation. The importance of protecting existing service utilities from damage in the construction area cannot be too heavily stressed because of the possible hazard to life and property and disruption of other services should damage occur.

The Agency searches all known substructure records and furnishes location descriptions (usually on the project plans) of all utility substructures (except service connections) which may affect or be affected by the construction work required. Information concerning the removal, relocation, abandonment or installation of new utilities is furnished to all prospective bidders. After award of the contract, it is the contractor's responsibility to either call the area Underground Alert (USA) Service or request the utility owners identified in the bid documents to mark or otherwise indicate the location of their facilities (including service connections to private property).

Although the project plans or specifications may require the contractor to relocate or reconstruct certain utilities as a portion of the work required, such relocation or reconstruction is usually performed by the owner of the utility at the request of the awarding agency. Such relocations are ordered when it is known that the existing utility will interfere with construction of the project. When feasible, the owners responsible for such reconstruction will complete the necessary work before commencement of work by the contractor. When utility interferences are considered extensive, a pre-construction meeting is called by the Agency prior to the actual start of construction to plan the necessary coordination of utility protection and relocation during construction. Such meetings will be attended by the contractor and his interested subcontractors, the design engineer and utility representatives having installations within the project site and the Project Inspector.

Should any potential hazard exist as a result of accidental damage, the Inspector should immediately instruct the contractor to evacuate all personnel from the vicinity of the damage and to prevent anybody in the vicinity from entering the hazardous area until emergency crews from the affected utility agency have made necessary repairs and given a clearance that the potential hazard has been eliminated.

After the initial safety precautions have been taken, the contractor or the Agency Inspector shall immediately notify the owner of the damaged utility.

There is almost no limit to the variety of utility interferences which are likely to occur during construction, especially in older, heavily built-up areas for which records may not exist or are so inaccurate with respect to new improvements as to be practically worthless. It thus behooves both the contractor and the Inspector to be on the alert and cooperate with each other to the fullest in order to minimize the great hazard to life and property which can ensue from accidental damage to many hidden utility substructures.

1-6.4 Substructure Interference Reporting. Because jobsite interferences frequently result in claims for additional compensation by the contractor or utility owner which are often difficult to resolve and may end in court for final resolution, the accuracy and completeness of the Inspector's job records are of the utmost importance in establishing the facts surrounding the circumstances of the actual damage or extent of any claim. To this end, refer to the special "Interference Report" form in the Appendix, Plate 13.

1-6.5 Protection and Use of Sewers and Storm Drains. All mainline sewers and storm drains will be identified on the plans and their proximity to the proposed improvements will be indicated. The Agency Inspector must see that the contractor takes all reasonable precautions to protect these installations. Any major damage to such mainline installations should be reported immediately to the appropriate maintenance organization so that crews can be dispatched to alleviate any emergency situation which might exist or be imminent. All existing sewer lines (mainline and house connections) shall remain in service and if damaged shall be maintained by temporary means to permit continued operation until permanent approved repairs can be made.

Unless specifically provided for in the contract documents, the Agency Inspector should not permit storm water or any material other than sewage to be deposited in the existing sewer system. The contractor shall provide adequate desilting of water before it is deposited in the storm drain system.

Catch basins shall remain in service during project construction except as provided for in the contract documents during remodeling or reconstruction phases of the work. It is noted, however, that such reconstruction should not be scheduled during the rainy reason or when disruption of existing storm drainage facilities would create a hazardous condition.

1-7 WARRANTIES AND DISCLAIMERS

1-7.1 General. When an Agency furnishes a contractor a set of contract documents, they are generally held in law to have an implied warranty to the effect that the plans and specifications are both accurate and suitable for constructing the project. The accuracy of such warranty refers to the Agency's factual representations about the details and nature of the project. Should these representations subsequently be proven inaccurate or be seriously misrepresented, the contractor may recover his added costs due to a breach of warranty. An example of such a breach would be depicting deep soil borings on the drawings with no indication of rock substrata, while in actual field conditions, bedrock was encountered at a depth of a few feet.

Generally, the Agency cannot evade its implied warranty by including boiler plate disclaimers such as a statement that all warranties of the plans and specifications are disavowed and thus rendered ineffective should a disparity arise during construction of the project. Neither will the Agency evade responsibility by including a statement in the contract documents that the contractor must inspect the worksite and examine all the specification and plan details to verify their accuracy. Any attempt to convey responsibility for the suitability of the plans and specifications to the contractor are usually disregarded in legal actions. The rationale substantiating this position is that the bidding process would become virtually impossible to conform to if intelligent contractors could not rely on the accuracy and suitability of the Agency's contract documents.

Contractors are aware that some discrepancies and inaccuracies occur in plans and specifications for most large projects. They understand that these will be taken care of by interpretation or by change orders at the appropriate time; and if contract time or cost is affected, the Agency will make a proper adjustment. However, when obvious or patent defects appear in the contract documents, the contractor cannot recover damages for knowledge which should have been obvious to him at the time he signed the contract. Both the contractor and the Agency are held to a standard of reasonable care, and responsibility is imposed on both parties. This doctrine is based on what an intelligent contractor knows as well as what he should have known in his field of endeavor.

With respect to a contract clause requiring the contractor to visit the worksite to familiarize himself with the site conditions, a prudent contractor would be expected to make a physical inspection of the surface of the site, and from such an inspection and subsurface data available, draw conclusions regarding its impact on his proposed methods of construction. He would not be obligated to undertake expensive and time-consuming pre-bid subsurface investigation.

However, there is a doctrine that acts against an Agency that attempts to avoid responsibility by deliberate silence or omission in the contract documents. The Agency is obligated to disclose all facts in its possession which could materially affect the contractor's bid. Concealment of such facts by the Agency will subject it to liability for any subsequent claims for damages. These damages not only relate to the direct costs such as labor, materials and equipment, but for other more intangible costs such as delay costs, lost efficiency, cost escalations and extended overhead.

1-8 DIFFERING SITE CONDITIONS

1-8.1 General. Differing or changed site conditions are subsurface or latent physical conditions differing materially from those represented in the contract; or unknown physical conditions of an unusual nature differing materially from those ordinarily encountered and generally recognized as inherent in work of the character being performed.

A prudent contractor will include a sum of money in his bid to provide for possible unexpected costs or contingencies which might be encountered in the project. Should no problems arise, this contingency amount becomes a bonus to the contractor. Modern specifications attempt to minimize such contingency amounts by providing a "differing site conditions" clause. This is intended to induce bidders to reduce such contingency costs in their bids and to depend on the differing site conditions clause to negotiate with the Agency during the construction period when differing or unforeseen difficulties are encountered. In theory, the contractor is treated in an equitable manner and the Agency receives lower bids over a period of time, having reduced contractor contingency provisions in its bids.

1-9 PROJECT DELAYS

1-9.1 General. Delays are classified as excusable but non-compensable, excusable and compensable, and inexcusable as well as non-compensable. Excusable but non-compensable delays are provided for in the contract documents, and after negotiation, time extensions are granted without any compensation to the contractor. Examples of this type of delay are: labor disputes, fires, adverse weather conditions, etc., which conditions are beyond the control of the Agency or the contractor.

Excusable and compensable delays occur when a valid change in the work is required and equitable settlement to the contractor is made in time extension and costs. Inexcusable and non-compensable delays result from a contractor failure to prosecute or properly sequence the work, or his abandonment of the project. No time extension or compensation is granted by the Agency in such circumstance.

In some instances, work may be delayed for reasons attributable to both the Agency and the contractor. This is referred to as a "concurrent delay," and in such event, neither the Agency nor the contractor is entitled to recover damages for the period of delay.

The inherent dependency of the contractor on such items as weather, labor disputes and availability of materials or equipment, often results in delays in the scheduled progress of the work. Due to the domino or ripple effect on other phases or elements of the work, serious delays may completely disrupt job progress, resulting in inefficiency in deploying labor and equipment. Deviation from the most logical sequence of work may cause the project to be delayed until unsuitable weather develops, thereby extending a delay period.

In all cases, the Inspector should keep accurate records of the disposition of men and equipment during any delay. He should realistically assess the impact of rain or its effects. Often certain craftsmen (such as electricians) can be moved from outdoor to indoor work without experiencing any delay from wet weather. Conversely, cement finishers cannot work in the rain and not for days after a rain until the subgrade is dry and firm. In the latter instance, the contractor would be expected to remove standing water from forms to expedite preparations for the earliest possible placement of the concrete after a rain.

It should be noted that in some jurisdictions where wet or cold weather is commonly experienced, local Agency specifications may not recognize such conditions as "adverse weather," and delays from such conditions may not qualify for time extension or compensation.

1-10   SUSPENSION OF THE WORK

1-10.1   General.   The issuance of an order suspending all or part of the work can have a dramatic effect on the additional costs incurred by the Agency and the contractor. Such an order must be specified as to whether the entire project is to be suspended or that a clearly defined nonconforming portion of the work only is to be suspended. Suspension of the work for the convenience of the Agency should be utilized only when no other alternatives are viable or available. Most orders to suspend work are of an emergency nature involving safety or potentially hazardous situations. However, some orders to suspend work emanate from changes found to be necessary in the work or from unforeseen site conditions. The procedure for issuing an order suspending work is outlined in Subsection 1-2.6.4.

1-10.2   Constructive Suspension of the Work.   When the Agency does not issue an affirmative order suspending the work, but the facts indicate that such an order should have been issued, the contractor may be entitled to an equitable adjustment in time and compensation under the doctrine of constructive suspension of the work.

To establish entitlement, the contractor must demonstrate that the Agency did something (or failed to do something) to accommodate the forward progress of the work that a prudent owner, faced with the same issues, would have done in administration of that contract. The costs to which the contractor may be entitled include the increased direct and indirect costs caused by the delay, disruption or suspension, but does not include profit.

Failure of the Agency to respond in a timely manner to requests for information or to process shop drawings, can act in such a manner as to delay fabrication and delivery of equipment to the extent that the project is delayed. This concept can also be reversed when the contractor fails to submit or resubmit shop drawings in a timely manner.

1-11   CLAIMS AND DISPUTES

While the plans and other contract documents establish the standards for materials and construction details for the project, they constitute the minimum acceptable to the Agency. On the other hand, these specified materials and details are the most the contractor has to furnish to comply. This usually results in a narrow band of contractor performance hovering between what he has to provide and the least the Agency will accept. Thus the contractor and Agency personnel are automatically placed in an adversary position at the outset, with the constant potential for dispute.

Such disputes most often arise from ambiguities in the contract documents or differing interpretations of plan or specification details. While the Inspector has little or no authority to change a contract document, or to impose his interpretation as a final decision, he is responsible to bring such problems to the attention of those who are responsible to clarify or resolve the matter.

Most disputes are quickly resolved, some by agreement as to the intent, and some by change order when additional cost or time is involved. When agreement cannot be achieved, some disputes result in claims, which if not resolved, can lead to arbitration or litigation.

Therefore, it is essential that disputes be quickly resolved to avoid stoppage of the work, or other costs to the contractor. If the contractor is correct in his position, he is entitled to any cost or time extension associated with the dispute. In the interests of the Agency, such costs must be avoided or minimized. When engaging the services of a consultant or construction manager, most large public agencies give considerable attention to the extent of experience professed by the applicants in claims avoidance.

Claims avoidance is best achieved by the Inspector (and contractor) planning ahead, looking for problems or conflicts that could arise and result in contractor delays or disputes. By this means, there is usually time to resolve the problem before the work reaches the stage that a delay will result.

Of course there will be times when both the Agency and the contractor cannot reach agreement, and the contractor will be ordered to proceed (without prejudice) according to the Agency's interpretation, with the contractor subsequently filing a claim. The contractor will submit documentation to substantiate his claim for additional time and payment for his costs. It becomes immediately apparent how important the Inspector's records are in documenting the field conditions leading up to the incident that initiated the claim, as well as his records of the labor, materials, duration or other factors involved in the disputed portion of the work as it progresses.

This should emphasize that complete and accurate inspection records are essential in substantiating (or refuting) contractor claims, particularly when the contractor belatedly files a claim for extra compensation for something that he claims happened in an earlier phase of the work. Good records and progress photographs (or video coverage) of the work become useful tools for assisting in resolving most disputes and claims during the course of the work and are invaluable in the event of subsequent litigation.

1-12 CONSTRUCTION SCHEDULING

1-12.1 General. When contractors bid a project, they expect to complete the project in the least possible time at the least cost. They traditionally approach the bidding process by listing all the cost items involved such as labor, materials and equipment, then add a percentage for overhead, profit and contingencies.

One of the cost factors best controlled by the contractor is the construction time. By his estimate of the extent of the work and the size of the work force he intends to use, the contractor can arrive at a close approximation of the time required to complete the work. Since time and labor costs are directly related, the contractor can prepare his bid accordingly. If he should by good management of time and work force, and by utilizing innovative methods, complete the work in a shorter period, the resulting cost savings accrue to him, thereby increasing his profit margin. Reducing the time for completing the work means less interest charges on cash invested during construction, less supervision and overhead expense, earlier availability of equipment for use in other work, and earlier release of funds traditionally retained by the owner.

All of this emphasizes the importance of developing a realistic schedule to assist in controlling construction time, which is one of the most critical elements of consideration during the bidding process. Prior to World War II, most construction contracts were scheduled using bar charts or similar devices to graphically depict major construction operations. As the size and scope of projects increased, particularly during the war and immediately thereafter, it became obvious that a better system was needed to control the vastly larger projects. Early systems such as the Gantt chart, the Line Of Balance (LOB) and Integrated Project Management (IPM) were principally graphic. Procurement and construction projects for the

U.S. Navy late in the war resulted in the development of a line and arrow diagram system to depict activity and time relationships. This system was called the Program Evaluation and Review Technique (PERT).

While this system worked well for Navy procurement contracts, improvements were developed in the private sector, principally in the chemical manufacturing industry and the emerging computer industry, evolving into the critical path method of scheduling known as CPM. This method of diagram scheduling (called networking) has many attractive features. It can be programmed into a computer to take the drudgery out of processing data or schedule revisions. Also, the CPM can graphically depict the time and cost elements of each activity and subactivity, show the impact of early or late start dates, develop logical sequencing of events, and most important, define the critical path. The critical path is the least time in which a project can be logically completed.

Any factor, such as a delay or the elimination of a portion of the project, will almost always impact on the critical path to shorten or lengthen it. Thus the diagram can be used to accurately estimate the effect of changes in the project with respect to cost and time.

1-12.2 Initial Schedule Development. The first step the contractor must take in preparing an estimate for bidding a project is to make a time schedule to fit into the project time constraints and set up a tentative plan for doing the work. This schedule should show all of the items affecting the progress of the work including the impact that the weather (seasonal) could impose. Such factors as: when delivery of critical items can be realistically anticipated; or what physical restraints may be imposed by the contract, such as keeping major traffic arteries clear near major shopping centers during the holiday shopping season, must be accurately evaluated. From these and other controlling factors, production rates for the major items of work are decided and the number, type and size of the contractor's plant, labor force and equipment needed to complete the work within the contract time, is determined.

From this schedule, the contractor should be aware of the indefinite, hazardous or other features that could affect his cost or time estimates. He can determine the total man-hours of labor and total machine-hours for major equipment required in doing the work, peak labor requirments, and controlling delivery dates for important items of equipment or materials. In addition, it can show him his cash requirements based on scheduled income and expenditures during the contract period. This is referred to as "cash flow."

1-12.3   Bar Charts.   The most common form of scheduling, particularly for smaller projects, is the use of bar charts. They are almost always used, even in larger projects, to initially phase the major elements of the work to keep them within the contract time. Since they are graphic, they reflect logical sequencing of work, and indicate the obvious need to accelerate certain items of work, or to adjust lead times for procurement.

Bar charts are best when they are kept relatively simple, reflecting only the major items of work or administrative processing. An example of a bar chart for the construction of a $300,000 steel-framed warehouse with an overhead crane is shown in Figure 1.

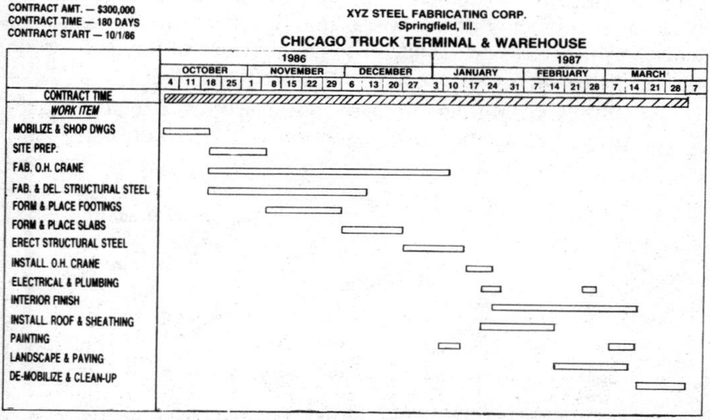

FIG. 1 — BAR CHART CONSTRUCTION SCHEDULE FOR WAREHOUSE IN SUBSECTION 1-7.3. OF PUBLIC WORKS INSPECTOR'S MANUAL

In graphing construction sequencing and showing construction time required for each major item of work, bar charts are of invaluable assistance in developing PERT or CPM diagrams. Even with a CPM schedule available, construction superintendents often use a bar chart in the field to measure and record actual progress against planned progress.

1-12.4 Critical Path Method of Scheduling (CPM).

This tool of management is very useful for larger or complicated projects and is required by many governmental agencies on some types of construction. CPM is based upon planning and job analysis that goes far beyond that needed to bid a project. Besides knowing the detailed breakdown of the work into its elementary operations and graphing the sequential relationships, the planners must know the duration of each operation, lead time for procurement, shop drawing preparation and approval times, fabricating and delivery times for procured items and methods that the contractor intends to utilize.

Activities are generally represented on the network by arrows or nodes connected by sequence lines. Analysis may be manual or by electronic computer for establishing realistic time relationships, selecting these operations whose completion times would be responsible for establishing overall project duration, determining the impact of changes and the operations affected (including the effect on project duration), establishing realistic sequencing of the work, and determining the status of work in progress with relation to the number of days ahead or behind schedule.

A simple CPM diagram is shown in Figure 2 for the warehouse project described in Subsection 1-12.3. Events are usu-

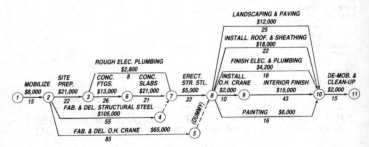

FIG. 2 — TYPICAL CPM DIAGRAM FOR WAREHOUSE IN SUBSECTION 1-7.3. OF PUBLIC WORKS INSPECTOR'S MANUAL

ally designated by circles (referred to as "nodes") and activities are indicated by arrows connecting two nodes. Activities can be tabulated for computer analysis by using the appropriate node numbers such as: 2-5, "fabricate and deliver overhead crane," or 7-8, "erect structural steel." In Figure 2, the time in days is indicated under the arrows and the activity described above the arrows. This diagram has been cost-loaded with the cost of each activity noted above the arrow, the sum of which must equal the contract amount of $300,000. Cost-loaded networks should be carefully evaluated to prevent the contractor from front-end loading his progress payments. Note that this diagram shows $8,000 for mobilization and only $2,000 for demobilization and clean-up. These figures are sometimes unrealistic because the contractor attempts to put bidding, bond and insurance premium costs in the first few items of work in order to recover his initial expenses and obtain a favorable cash flow. This practice is acceptable provided the contractor uses realistic costs for his upfront expenditures. The Inspector should be alert to scrutinize cost-loaded diagrams to discover and disallow unreasonable activity costs designated by the contractor so as to keep the progress payments more in line with the actual work completed.

Work items that are performed concurrently often have float time in them. Float is the difference between the time it actually takes to do the item of work and the time in which it must be completed. For example, the rough electrical and plumbing work is indicated in Figure 2 to take eight days between nodes 3 and 7, yet the placement of concrete footings and slabs between nodes 3 and 7 is estimated to take 47 days. The difference of 39 days is called float in the electrical and plumbing activity. Similarly, the fabrication of the overhead crane will take 85 days, but the project will not be ready to install it until node 8, 91 days after mobilization is completed at node 2. The difference of six days is float time and the dotted line arrows are called dummy activities which are used to complete the network.

"Free float" is the maximum time of slippage of an activity that can be tolerated without affecting the completion date of any other activity, assuming all activities start at the earliest possible times. "Total float" is the maximum slippage of an activity that can be tolerated without affecting the completion date of the overall project.

Each node represents the completion of the preceding activity and the start of the following activity. By the sequence of operations that will require the most time to complete the project utilizing normal work forces and equipment, the critical path is determined, which establishes the duration of the project. The critical path is indicated by darker (heavier) arrows or by double lines. The critical path is commonly shown on a horizontal line (as in Figure 2), but may be shown on contiguous arrows any place in the network. There is no float on the critical path.

Generally, CPM networks are evaluated to determine early and late starts with respect to each activity and its completion time. The early start dates are the earliest any activity can start, each in its own proper sequence. The late start dates are worked backwards from the specified project completion date and indicate the latest date that each activity can begin and still complete the project on time.

When the cost-loaded activities in the diagram are plotted against contract time and scheduled progress, a set of curves for the early starts and late starts result in a set of curves called the "banana curves" (see Figure 3). These curves are used to predict the cash flow requirements for the contractor and the owner, and can be useful in assessing the contractor's performance. When the contractor's progress is plotted on the banana

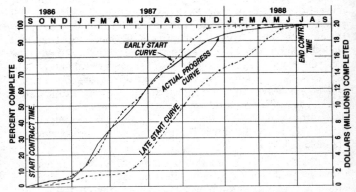

FIG. 3 — EARLY & LATER START CASH FLOW CHART
(Typical "Banana" Chart)

curves, it becomes obvious whether or not he is meeting his schedule. Should his progress curve fall below the late start curve, it is an indication that the contractor may be in trouble and he may need to accelerate the work to avoid exceeding the contract time. A speed-up of the work would presumably be accomplished only by more outlay for labor and equipment since the cost-loading of the normal network is presumed to be minimum.

A computer is frequently used to analyze the normal times of each activity on the critical path and compute the maximum time schedule. Then the activity is selected on the critical path which offers the least cost increase in relation to any time decrease, after which a new schedule is computed with the activity "crashed" (taken from the late start date). Under this procedure, the normal start date is considered to be the maximum time. Since these attempts are made to reduce it, the crashed time can represent a substantial reduction of time and produce a new critical path. The computer continues to "buy time" along the latest critical path as cheaply as possible. Once a final schedule has been decided, the contractor and owner are provided with sufficient information to insure adequate control over time and costs.

CPM schedules must be up-dated (usually monthly) to reflect the contractor's progress (or lack of it), change order work, delays or any other factors that may impact the schedule. The cost-loaded network, when compared to the work actually completed, gives the Inspector the best means of measuring progress for payment purposes on large and complex projects.

1-13 CONSTRUCTIVE CHANGES IN THE WORK

Any conduct by an Agency representative authorized to issue change orders, but which are not construed as formal change orders and have the effect of requiring the contractor to perform work different from that prescribed by the original terms of the contract, constitutes a constructive change order. This could entitle the contractor to equitable compensation and time extension.

An example of a constructive change occurs when it originates from a difference of opinion as to the interpretation of the specifications or plans. An Agency representative refuses to issue a formal change order for work in question because it was, in his opinion, already required under the terms of the contract. Should he later prove to be incorrect, the result is a constructive change order.

Proof that a constructive change has occurred lies with the contractor. The Inspector must be aware of the consequences of his interpretations of contract documents and avoid actions which would inadvertently trigger a constructive change.

1-14 CONSTRUCTIVE ACCELERATION. In the absence of an acceleration order, a constructive acceleration order would exist if (1) the contractor is entitled to an excusable delay under the contract documents, (2) the contractor has notified the Agency of a delay and requested an extension of time for an excusable delay which is improperly denied by the Agency, (3) the Agency issues an order or implies an acceleration order to meet existing contract dates, (4) the contractor notifies the Agency that he considers an informal order to alter his schedule to be a constructive change, and (5) the order to accelerate incurs additional costs related to the constructive change order.

It should be emphasized that the Inspector must assess all time delays and cause valid extensions of time to be issued based on the contract documents. Failure to do so in a timely manner can result in sizeable acceleration claims presented by the contractor.

1-15 CONSTRUCTIVE SUSPENSION OF THE WORK. When the Agency does not issue an affirmative order suspending the work, but the facts indicate that such an order should have been issued, the contractor may be entitled to an equitable adjustment in time and compensation under the doctrine and constructive suspension of the work.

To establish entitlement, the contractor must demonstrate that the Agency did something (or failed to do something) to accommodate the forward progress of the work that a prudent owner, faced with the same issues, would have done in administration of that contract. The costs to which the contractor may be entitled include the increased direct and indirect costs caused by the delay, disruption or suspension, but does not include profit.

Failure of the Agency to respond in a timely manner to requests for information, or to process shop drawings, can act in such a manner as to delay fabrication and delivery of equipment to the extent that the project is delayed. This concept can also be reversed where the contractor fails to submit or resubmit shop drawings in a timely manner.

PART 2

CONSTRUCTION MATERIALS AND MATERIALS CONTROL PROCEDURES

2-1 GENERAL. The Standard Specifications prescribe the standards which construction materials must meet to be acceptable. All materials of construction are subject to inspection, testing and approval by the Agency. Unless otherwise specified, all materials incorporated into the work shall be new and unused in previous construction.

It is the objective of the Agency to determine whether the quality of materials proposed for use are within reasonable conformity with the plans and specifications prior to their use on the project. This must be done on a timely basis with as much lead time as is practical to minimize delay and unnecessary expense to the Agency and the contractor.

All materials originating from or fabricated at some location other than the jobsite, are subject to inspection upon delivery to the jobsite, even through the material has been inspected by the Agency, or its agents, at the source.

The Inspector must determine, in advance, the sources which the contractor intends to utilize in furnishing construction materials and fabricated items. Where those materials will originate from sources not normally inspected on a routine basis, timely arrangements shall be made with the construction materials control group in order that shop fabrication inspection or sampling, testing and approval of the source may be made without interference with the contractor's schedule of operations.

Particular attention should be given to inspecting for damage which may·have occurred in transporting the materials to the site of the work. Where defective materials are discovered, the Inspector must give prompt notice to the contractor of such deficiency and, unless satisfactory corrective measures are taken by the contractor, the Inspector shall reject the materials and order them removed from the site of the work as provided in the Standard Specifications.

2-1.1 Offsite Materials Controls. Many types of materials delivered to the jobsite are premixed, fabricated, pretreated or otherwise partially or completely readied for use. Examples of such materials are: bituminous pavement mixtures, ready-mixed concrete, welded structural steel assemblies, laminated and glued wood truss members, pressure-treated wood piling, metal castings and reinforced concrete pipe.

Since it is neither practical nor desirable to require the Project Inspector to determine whether such materials conform to the specifications upon arrival at the jobsite, inspection must be provided at the source during the fabricating or mixing operations. In many cases, it is virtually impossible to determine whether a product is acceptable unless it is fabricated or mixed under continuous inspection.

Notwithstanding any prior inspection or approval, the Project Inspector shall reject any material which is damaged or otherwise does not conform to the specification requirements. All materials furnished by the contractor must be new, unless otherwise provided in the specifications. The contractor must furnish such samples and certificates as may be required, at no cost to the Agency.

Components such as motors, clocks, pumps, valves, pressure vessels and commercially available manufactured articles or equipment, are not generally inspected at the source. These are usually accompanied by a guarantee or a record of performance test.

The Inspector has the right of free access to such parts of a plant as are concerned with the manufacture or production of materials for any project.

Offsite control of asphalt paving mixes, portland cement concrete mixes and reinforced concrete pipe are described under these headings in other sections that follow in this part of the manual. Shop fabrication procedure is described in the subsection that follows.

2-1.2 Shop Fabrication Inspection.

2-1.2.1 **General.** Shop fabrication inspection is one of the most highly specialized types of inspection related to public works. It consists of the inspection, during manufacture or processing, of electric panels, prestressed concrete units, structural and miscellaneous steel fabrication, welding, metal castings, bridge rocker-plates, galvanizing, creasoting of lumber and wood piles, precast concrete piles, and many other construction materials or subassemblies fabricated at a location other than the jobsite. This class of work so frequently involves the inspection of welding or of precast and prestressed concrete units that specially qualified registered Deputy Inspectors are assigned to the work.

2-1.2.2 Acceptance of Standard Materials. Materials and components which are commercially available as standard or catalog items, manufactured by well-established and reliable companies, are not inspected at their point of origin. They are accepted if they comply with the specification with regard to size, rating, catalog, number, etc., and satisfactorily pass any performance test conducted by the Testing Agency when required or deemed necessary. Examples of such materials are lumber, electrical components, pumps, valves, plumbing fixtures, etc.

2-1.2.3 Materials Not Locally Produced Which Must Be Inspected. The contractor sometimes purchases materials from sources more than 50 miles outside the geographic limits of the Agency. If the Agency does not elect to furnish inspection, procedures are set up in the Standard Specifications for approval of the private inspection or testing agency which the contractor proposes to employ to inspect the work at the place of manufacture.

2-1.2.4 Materials Fabricated Locally. Most materials are manufactured or fabricated locally and are subject to shop inspection by the Agency. Before the Inspector can permit any fabrication work to proceed, he must have approved shop drawings and a copy of the plans and Special Provisions under which the manufacturing will be performed. The Special Provisions may make reference to one, or several, of the nationally recognized reference specifications, such as those of the American Society for Testing Materials, American Association of State Highway Officials, American Railway Engineering Association, American Society of Mechanical Engineers, American Welding Society, etc.

Shop fabrication inspection is so diversified and highly specialized that a description of the detailed inspection procedures will not be presented here. Inspectors assigned to this type of work will be given the specialized training required to enable them to perform satisfactorily.

2-1.2.5 Sampling and Materials Certifications. Frequent reference is made to sampling and testing procedures in

most specifications for shop work. Inspectors should give careful attention to the preparation of samples in accordance with
the Sampling Schedule. (See Plate 28, Appendix). Some samples require special preparation, as in casting test ingots,
machining test specimens, development of galvanizing test
coupons or taking test specimens by trepanning.

If the specifications permit, certain materials may be
accepted on the basis of mill test reports or certificates of analysis, provided they each bear an affidavit by a competent testing
authority.

2-1.2.6 Coordination of Shop Inspection. Project
Inspectors shall advise contractors whose work will involve
shop fabrication of certain materials, that such fabrication must
be performed under inspection. As soon as the manufacturer is
known, this information should be furnished to the Agency Dispatcher, together with the tentative date that fabrication
will begin. This procedure is essential to permit the proper
scheduling and coordination of the work of the Shop Fabrication Inspectors.

2-1.2.7 Evidence of Shop Fabrication Inspection.
Since inspection of materials at the source is often performed
well in advance of delivery to the jobsite, evidence that it has
been previously inspected must be provided for the benefit of
the Project Inspector.

A yellow-colored adhesive-backed paper sticker (illustrated below) bearing the word "Inspected" and the Agency
name, is affixed to the article or to a tag which in turn is tied to
the article or component.

CITY OF ANYWHERE
BUREAU OF CONTRACT ADMINISTRATION

N⁰ 26502

INSPECTED

Inspector   Date
DEPARTMENT OF PUBLIC WORKS

The Shop Fabrication Inspector will enter his name and the date in the spaces provided and enter the serial number of the sticker in his daily report. The Project Inspector will examine each shipment and then record the serial number of the sticker in the job log along with the name or a short description of the fabricated item. Tags should be detached and placed in the job envelope. Stickers applied directly to the article (when a tag is not used) need not be salvaged.

Treated lumber is marked on the end of each piece by an embossing hammer, and wood piles are marked on the butt end. The impression made by the hammer indicates approval for the Agency. A typical inspection stamp impression is shown following:

2-1.2.8 Reports. Inspectors assigned to shop fabrication work are required to keep records of all inspection performed.

All records, reports, certifications, affidavits and similar communications must bear the job title, job number, contractor's name and other pertinent information, and be forwarded to the Supervisor of the Materials Control Group for disposition.

2-1.3 Sampling and Testing.

2-1.3.1 **General.** In order for the testing program to be valid and objective, the following five elements of sampling should be carefully adhered to:

(1) The sampling by the Inspector must be truly representative of the material to be tested.

(2) The method of sampling must be consistent and avoid affecting detrimentally the test results.

(3) The sample must be properly identified so that the correct tests are performed and the test results are properly identified as to material and project.

(4) The sample must be properly packaged, protected and transported to prevent damage, distortion or contamination of the sample, which might create false test results.

(5) Test sample requests and sample pick-up must be executed promptly by expeditious notice to the contractor and testing laboratory to prevent construction delays.

The Appendix (Plate 28) lists materials and the frequency of sampling and testing in specific detail. The Agency Inspector must consider the particular characteristics of the project to provide a meaningful testing program. Thus, the sampling and frequencies listed become useful guidelines for the experienced Project Inspector charged with the responsibility of obtaining the general construction quality required.

It is essential that the Inspector recognize these important factors and utilize the appropriate procedure in the selection and processing of samples to be tested. This is emphasized in the following subsections.

2-1.3.2 Representative Sampling. Samples are obviously of little value if they do not represent the material which is to be incorporated into the work. It is therefore essential that samples be taken from materials delivered to the jobsite and intended for imminent use in the work. Some materials are sampled elsewhere for convenience, but in general, materials are to be sampled at the jobsite. (See Sampling Schedule Plate 28, Appendix). Samples of aggregate, soils and like materials are obtained by the quartering method. All samples of materials are to be selected by a representative of the Agency. To avoid the possibility of "salting" (deliberate misrepresentation of), materials sampled by a vendor, contractor or other entity cannot be accepted for testing. All samples must be taken by, or in the presence of, a representative of the Agency and must not pass from continuous possession by the Agency, thus precluding the possibility of loss or substitution by others.

2-1.3.3 Proper Method of Sampling. The size and frequency of samples are prescribed in the Sampling Schedule (see Plate 28, Appendix). However, due to apathy or carelessness, samples which would otherwise have been satisfactory are often rendered useless by improper sampling procedures.

For example, concrete test cylinders taken from the first part of the discharge of concrete from a transit-mixer truck will very likely be the wettest part of the load and the test cylinder may reflect a strength considerably less than the major part of the mixer load.

Special care must be taken to insure that the sample is not affected by the sampling method in any manner which will alter the characteristics or properties of the material tested.

It is also imperative that materials be sampled and forwarded promptly to the laboratory for testing. Even in those instances where the contractor appears to be lax in obtaining delivery of the materials to the jobsite, it is incumbent upon the Agency to process such samples promptly to minimize any delay in the contractor's program to utilize such materials.

2-1.3.4 Sample Identification.   To be of any value, a sample must be properly identified. All of the following items are necessary in marking a sample for identification:

> Name of the material
> Source of the material
> Name and number of the project
> Date sampled
> Name of individual sampling the material

Sample identification data should be securely attached to the sample to prevent separation. Tags should be attached with wire or strong binding twine. Labels should be attached with adhesives or adhesive tapes which will not be affected by moisture or other conditions to which the sample may be subjected prior to its receipt at the laboratory. Some samples collected in containers may have the sample identification data enclosed in the container.

2-1.3.5 Packaging and Protection of Samples.   All samples should be packaged in such a manner as to prevent any damage or contamination to the sample prior to its testing. Steel reinforcement bars should be *wired* together to prevent their separation and loss as effective samples, as may be the case if they were bound together with twine. Cement samples should be collected in cans with moisture-tight lids instead of paper sacks which may be easily damaged and offer little protection from moisture.

Special care is to be observed in packaging all samples so that the sample is retained in a state which is representative of the material during any unavoidable storage period, and while in transit to the laboratory.

2-1.3.6 Processing of Samples. Samples must be processed in time for testing, so as not to delay the use of the material when it is needed.

Once sampling has been done, every effort shall be made to expedite the pickup and testing of the material. Where time is critical, special arrangement for sample pickup can be made by telephone with the Testing Agency.

2-1.3.7 Test Results. The general determination of the quality of materials of construction and the test results rendered by the Testing Agency are binding in the acceptance or rejection of materials intended to be used in the work. Sampling and testing of construction materials by private laboratories or engineers is not accepted by the Inspector except when specifically authorized by the Agency.

When materials are to be supplied from sources located more than 50 miles outside the geographical limits of the Agency, the Agency may assign inspection and testing to an independent Agency to represent its interests as provided in the Standard Specifications.

2-2 AGGREGATES

2-2.1 General. The Agency materials control program provides for the routine sampling and testing of aggregates at the source of producers regularly supplying materials for Agency projects. Other sources are tested on a special request basis as needed.

The Testing Agency is responsible for the sampling, testing and publication of test results. The Materials Control Group is responsible for being familiar with the sources of rock materials, quantities and types of material supplied by the various producers and for maintaining a coordinated and effective materials control and testing program particularly for those rock materials that are combined or mixed prior to delivery to the jobsite such as for portland cement concrete and asphalt paving mixes.

The Materials Control Group assists the Testing Agency by recommending rock sources for routine sampling, requests special investigations of such materials as required and reviews test results before distribution to Agency project inspection personnel.

The special handling of rock materials as they relate to their use in mixed materials such as portland cement concrete and asphalt paving mixes is mentioned in subsections dealing with these products. Untreated base materials are discussed in Subsection 2-3.

2-2.2 **Sand.** Sand is a loose granular material resulting from the disintegration of rocks. Natural sands are usually made up of rounded particles which are the product of weathering combined with the action of running water, and they are obtained from stream deposits, glacial deposits and alluvial fans. Stone sands are produced by crushing and screening natural rock. Stone sands consist of more angular particles and when used in concrete, it is essential that thin, sharp and slivery particles be avoided. Sands for concrete should consist of clean, hard, strong and durable particles free of chemicals or coatings of clay or other fine materials that may affect the bonding of the cement paste. The contaminating materials most often encountered are dirt, silt, clay, coal, mica, salts, humus and other organic matter. These may occur as coatings or as loose, fine material, but with proper washing, many of them can be removed.

The grading of sand is very important because of its effect on water and cement proportions, workability, economy, porosity and shrinkage. Very fine sands or very coarse sands are objectionable; the former are uneconomical in that more cement is required, the latter give harsh, unworkable mixes. In general, sands which do not have a large deficiency or excess of any size and give a smooth grading curve, produce the most satisfactory results. Beach sands, with their consistently uniform particle size and normally present salt contamination, are entirely unsuitable for concrete mixtures.

(a) **Washed Concrete Sand.** This sand, intended for use especially in concrete, is in general a coarse sand. The particles are carefully washed to remove any coating and to reduce the amount of fine particles. This sand is required to have a smooth grading curve which provides the proper proportion of various particle sizes to fill the voids between the aggregates in the concrete. It is intended to provide a grading which will require the minimum amount of cement paste to coat the aggregate particles and to fill the voids between them. It is apparent that an excess of fines or dust coatings on the sand particles would require a greater amount of cement paste to coat these fine particles and that a well-graded sand and rock mixture would require less cement paste.

(b) **Plaster Sand.** Plaster sand is used primarily for exterior stucco plasters, interior plaster undercoats and in cement mortars. Coarse and harsh sands are undesirable for this purpose because of the reduced workability. Plaster sands are screened to produce a finer grading than washed concrete sand, and the percentage of fines is greater to increase the workability of the mix.

(c) **Gunite Sand.** Specifications require that sand for gunite conform to the grading established for washed concrete sand. Soft particles in gunite sand are undesirable because they crumble as they pass through the discharge hose and form fine powder, which may reduce the bonding value of the cement. The amount of rebound is less and a smoother surface texture is obtained by using sands graded with an excess of fines. If the sand is deficient in fines, the addition of diatomaceous earth (when approved by the Engineer) will improve the plasticity of the mix and decrease the amount of rebound. However, this finer grading will have a higher water requirement and a correspondingly increased drying shrinkage.

Sand for gunite should contain a minimum of three percent and a maximum of five percent by weight of uncombined water. If the sand is too dry, there is difficulty in maintaining uniform feeding; also increased rebound occurs because of a greater tendency for the sand and cement to separate. If the sand is too wet, there will be frequent plugging of the equipment and the discharge hose. Use of moist sands also avoids discomfort to the nozzle operator from discharge of static electricity.

(d) **Alkali-Reactive Sand.** Some sands are chemically unsound and will react over a long period of time with the alkalies in cement to produce excessive expansion, resulting in premature deterioration of concrete. Some of the subtances known to be alkali-reactive are opaline chert, chalcedony, volcanic glasses, zeolite, dactites, andesites and their tuffs. The reaction generates alkali silica gel which expands to create enormous pressure, resulting in cracking and spalling of the concrete.

In Southern California, for example, only two commercially developed sources of alkali-reactive aggregates are known to exist. Both are in the Monterey formation which lies in the coastal mountains. One area includes Ventura-Oxnard-Piru and the other is the Palos Verdes Hills in the Los Angeles area. These materials are usually subject to limitations in their use by the specifications.

Sand from the Palos Verdes area is easily recognized by its light yellow cast and contains pea-gravel size particles that are usually navy bean white in color.

2-2.3 Rock.

(a) **Gravel.** Gravel is composed of loose, rounded fragments of rocks, which are the product of weathering, the action of water or glacial movement. Gravels are usually obtained from stream deposits, glacial deposits and alluvial fans. The rounded particles are particularly suitable for concrete aggregates in that they present less surface area than irregular rock fragments and therefore are more economical in demand for cement paste. Because gravel is the result from wear of larger rocks in being moved by water or glacial action, only the harder and more sound particles remain in gravel deposits and this characteristic is an advantage over crushed rock aggregates. Also the semi-spherical shape of gravel lends a structural advantage to resist crushing or shear over the angular shape of crushed rock fragments.

(b) **Crushed Rock.** Crushed rock is obtained by crushing and screening of quarried materials having the principal characteristics of hardness, soundness and chemical stability to produce satisfactory concrete aggregates. Rock which is weak, friable or laminated is undesirable, as are shale and most cherts. Very sharp and rough aggregate particles or flat and elongated particles require more fine material to produce workable concrete than when aggregate particles are more rounded or cubical. Excellent concrete can be made from crushed rock but the particles should be more or less cubical in shape. Stones which break up into long slivery pieces should be avoided. In general, crushed rock aggregate, as compared with gravel, requires more sand and cement to compensate for the sharp, angular shape of the particles in order to obtain a mix comparable in workability to one in which no crushed material is used.

(c) **Rock Dust.** Rock dust is a product of crushing rock and is used as the binder in crushed aggregate base material. It is frequently used in asphalt concrete paving mixtures to make up for deficiency of fines in the aggregate blend.

2-2.4 Special Purpose Aggregates.

(a) **Lightweight Aggregates.** The lightweight aggregates are usually produced by expanding clay, shale, slate, diatomaceous, shale, perlite, obsidian and vermiculite through application of heat; by expanding blast furnace slag through special cooling processes; from natural deposits of pumice, scoria, volcanic cinders, tuff and diatomite; and from industrial cinders. These aggregates are porous and absorptive and must be wetted thoroughly before they are used. A larger proportion of fine aggregate is generally required because of the rough surfaces and irregular shapes of lightweight aggregate particles.

Concrete weights varying from 40 to 110 pounds per cubic foot can be obtained by utilizing lightweight aggregates as compared to an average weight of 150 pounds per cubic foot for concrete made with natural aggregates. Lightweight aggregates are used in some structural concrete where it is desired to reduce the weight of the structural member as in cantilevered slabs, roof slabs, etc.

(b) **Heavyweight Concrete Aggregates.** For making heavyweight concrete, steel rivet punchings are utilized. It is not practical to mix steel punchings with the concrete in the mixer due to the high degree of wear that would be experienced on the mixer blades. The punchings are usually added to the premixed concrete by placing them carefully in layers as a low slump concrete is placed. Care must be exercised to maintain any degree of homogeneity with respect to the steel punchings since they tend to settle from excessive vibration and working of the concrete. Use of external type vibrators is preferred and the minimum of vibration necessary to produce a dense concrete should be utilized to avoid settling of the punchings.

Heavyweight concrete is used in underwater structures to overcome buoyance problems and in similar circumstances where additional weight is required.

(c) **Aggregates for Nailing Concrete.** Sawdust, natural pumice and perlites are used to make concrete into which nails can readily be driven and still hold firmly. Equal parts by volume of portland cement, sand and one of the foregoing "aggregates" are used to produce nailing concrete. Such concrete is usually used for constructing cants to which roofing material, flashing, siding, corrugated metal or gypsum sheets can be nailed.

2-2.5 Alkali-Reactive Aggregates. Certain aggregate materials which contain opaline silica (amorphous, hydrous silica), siliceous limestones, chalcedony, certain cherts, andesites, dacites, rhyolites and phyllite, cause expansive deterioration of the hardened concrete by osmotic swelling of alkali silica gels, which are produced by chemical reaction of the susceptible material in the aggregate with the alkalies released by the hydration of the cement. [Also see Subsection 2-2.2 (d)].

Experience has demonstrated that this destructive action can be controlled by the selection of nonreactive aggregates or by using low-alkali cement (total alkali computed as $Na_2O + K_2O$ does not exceed 0.6 percent) or by the use of certain types of pozzolanic materials (see Subsection 2-4.3.7).

Other unsuitable and deleterious materials such as iron pyrites are also unacceptable.

2-3 UNTREATED ROADWAY BASE MATERIAL

2-3.1 General. Whenever the native soil in place is of an unstable nature or otherwise unfit for a foundation for a pavement subgrade, the plans for the improvement usually require that an untreated base material be imported and used as a base or subbase under such improvements. This material is processed as required to conform to certain limitations in grading and physical properties.

Several kinds of untreated base material are locally available in commercial quantities. They have widely different physical properties and grading characteristics, but all must compact to a hard, unyielding surface when rolled during the process of base construction, and thereafter remain stable. In general, five classifications of untreated base materials are used in Agency work: crushed aggregate base (CAB), crushed slag base (CSB), crushed miscellaneous base (CMB), processed miscellaneous base (PMB) and select subbase (SSB).

2-3.2 Crushed Aggregate Base (CAB). Crushed aggregate base is obtained from crushing stone or gravel and is often referred to in the construction industry as "crusher run." This material is available at most local commercial rock producers' plants and may be made available at any producer's quarry who will provide the necessary plant, such as crushing, screening, storage and blending facilities. Inasmuch as this material is produced only from quality rock, crushed, screened and reblended in desired proportions, it is considered to be the highest quality untreated base material available. For this reason it is used extensively as base on highways, freeways and major traffic arteries.

2-3.3 Crushed Slag Base (CSB). Either blast furnace slag or open-hearth steel slag, conforming to the requirements for crushed aggregate base, is considered to be equal to crushed aggregate base if it also conforms to the special processing and placing requirements of the Standard Specifications.

2-3.4 Crushed Miscellaneous Base (CMB). Crushed miscellaneous base is produced from varying combinations of asphalt pavement, portland cement concrete, railroad ballast or other rock. The material must be processed to produce the gradation, crushed material and fine materials to bind the coarser materials together to form a firm and unyielding subgrade when watered and rolled. The use of CMB is to be encouraged because of its relative economy and the fact that the sources of natural base materials are being exhausted. CMB is usually obtained by crushing existing pavement, curb, gutter and sidewalk found on a street improvement project. However, there are several commercial enterprises that manufacture CMB from pavement and other suitable materials removed from various construction sites and then stockpile it for future sale. CMB is also produced from quarried materials.

When CMB is produced on-site from existing materials, there are two types of crushers presently employed: the gyratory crusher and the impact-beater type. The pavement is broken, usually by stompers, and graded into windrows which the towed gyratory crusher will elevate, crush and deposit in a windrow behind itself. The impact-beater type of crusher will crush the improvements in place after stomping with several passes of the crusher. The crushed materials are then blended and moved into place by the use of a motor grader.

The tendency to pick up and incorporate too much clay material in the processing of this type of base should be guarded against since it will result in a poor quality base which will fail to meet the Standard Specification test requirements.

2-3.5 Processed Miscellaneous Base (PMB). Processed miscellaneous base is similar to CMB in that it is produced from broken or crushed asphalt, portland cement concrete, railroad ballast, glass and crushed rock, except that rock dust and some soils free of deleterious materials may be included. The principal difference is that PMB may have a coarser grading. CMB may not have more than 15 percent gravel particles retained on the No. 4 sieve, while PMB may have as much as 75 percent retained on the No. 4 sieve.

2-3.6   **Select Subbase (SSB).**   Large quantities of native soils meet the requirements for a select natural base. When properly mined and carefully checked to insure that the quality is maintained, these materials make excellent base and subbase for pavement.

SSB is usually mined from a quarry-face against a hill, either using a power loader or by dozing the material from the top of the face. It is apparent that soil strata of several types may be encountered and that blending of these soils may not be uniform and the characteristics of the material will vary widely between truck loads. Added to this problem is the difficulty in completely stripping off all of the overburden which includes the undesirable top soil, vegetation, etc. Some pit operators attempt to incur a savings to themselves by omitting removal of the overburden and attempting to mix it in with quantities of the "good" material. Such operators must be informed of the importance of careful stripping and disposal of all undesirable materials.

Another source of SSB is disintegrated granite. This is a disintegrated igneous rock, the principal constituents of which are orthoclase feldspar and quartz and is mined generally in the manner described above. Some sources may not have reached the advanced state of disintegration necessary to develop a uniform grading in the sizes required. This increases the cost to the contractor in the labor necessary to pick up and cast out the hard, over-sized lumps and in the subsequent reloading, haul-away and disposal operations.

2-4   PORTLAND CEMENT CONCRETE AND RELATED PRODUCTS

2-4.1   **General.**   The production and delivery of quality concrete on a consistent basis is dependent on the active control of the quality, handling and storage of the individual ingredients and the proper measurement or proportioning of the ingredients, the mixing of the ingredients, and the subsequent transport and handling of the resulting concrete mixture until it is placed.

One of the more important factors in producing quality concrete is the maintenance of the lowest water content consistent with the placing conditions to be encountered. It has been said that "the more a form is filled with the right combination of solids and the less it is filled with water, the better will be the concrete." Under these conditions the strength and durability will be the best that can be expected.

Cement in concrete is the chemical binding agent and should be only enough to achieve the desired strength and durability. The aggregate is the filler or bulking component and must be graded to fill the voids between particles and to develop the workability for the placement, consolidation and finishing of the concrete.

Every effort must be made in the handling and batching of aggregates to stabilize the moisture content. The fluctuation of the amount of "free water" in the aggregate is the major source of slump variation in the concrete. This effort should be coupled with moisture meter indicators and batch weight adjustments to minimize variations in the moisture content of the aggregate.

In the following subsections, only the components of concrete, admixtures and curing agents which are in common usage locally are discussed.

2-4.2   Portland Cement.

2-4.2.1   General. Portland cement is a finely pulverized mineral product consisting of a mixture of hydraulic silicates and aluminates of calcium and a small amount of calcium sulphate (gypsum), which is added to control setting time. In addition to these compounds, it always contains small amounts of nonessential, or actually detrimental constituents, derived from the raw materials used in the manufacturing process.

Portland cement is manufactured by intergrinding a properly blended mixture of siliceous, aluminous and calcareous materials, burning the mixture in a rotary kiln to the point of incipient vitrification, and regrinding the resulting clinker to which a small amount of gypsum has been added. This finely ground mixture is portland cement and it possesses the property of combining chemically with water and hardening into a coherent mass. This chemical reaction will continue almost indefinitely as long as the cement is kept wet but the rate of reaction diminishes steadily with time.

The principal compounds of portland cement are:

Name of Compound	Abbreviation
Tricalcium silicate	C_3S
Dicalcium silicate	C_2S
Tricalcium aluminate	C_3A
Tetracalcium alumino-ferrite	C_4AF

The nonessential compounds are magnesium oxide (MgO) and the alkali sodium oxide (Na_2O), and potassium oxide (K_2O). Sodium oxide and potassium oxide are always present in cement, generally in amounts less than 1.2 percent. They react chemically with certain kinds of aggregates and produce cracking, expansion and spalling in the concrete. It has been found that if the amount of the combined alkalies is kept below 0.6 percent, portland cement can be safely used with alkali reactive aggregates, and such cements are classified as "low alkali". It is well to remember that the specification of any of the five types of cement does not guarantee low alkali cement. If such is desired, it must be specified in addition to the cement type.

Cement in storage silos must be protected from the weather and be properly vented to prevent moisture absorption by the cement.

2-4.2.2 Type I Cement (Normal Portland Cement). This is the usual portland cement of commerce and is suitable for use in general concrete construction when the special properties specified for other types of cement are not required. It is not uncommon for the normal product of certain cement producers to conform to the requirements of both Type I and Type II.

2-4.2.3 Type II Cement (Moderate Sulfate Action and Moderate Heat of Hydration). This type of cement is used for greater resistance to the attack of sulfate or alkali waters, alkali soil or sea water. The moderate heat of hydration results in smaller volume changes in the concrete as it hardens. Type II cement is generally specified for use in connection with sewer pipelines and structures because of its higher resistance to sulfate and alkali corrosion.

2-4.2.4 Type III Cement (High Early Strength). Type III cement is manufactured for the specific purpose of producing high early strength in concrete. The principal characteristics of this cement are high tricalcium silicate content and a very fine grind.

2-4.2.5 Type IV Cement (Low Heat of Hydration). This is a special cement for use where the amount and rate of heat generated from hydration must be kept to a minimum. The development of strength is also at a slower rate. It is intended for use only in large masses of concrete such as large gravity dams where temperature rise, resulting from the heat generated during hardening, is a critical factor.

2-4.2.6 Type V Cement (High Sulfate Resistant). Type V cement is a special cement intended for use only in structures exposed to severe sulfate action, such as in some western states having soils or waters of high alkali content. While it has a slower rate of hardening than normal portland cement, it attains a higher ultimate strength.

2-4.2.7 Special Cements. In addition to the foregoing types of portland cement, there are special purpose cements such as:

(a) White portland cement for use as cement paint bases, white concrete ornamental objects, white mortar, cement paste for terrazzo work, etc.

(b) Plastic cement for use in cement mortar mixes to avoid the use of hydrated lime or fire clay to obtain plastic workability.

(c) Waterproof cement, obtained by grinding water-repellent materials with the clinker, for use in concrete walls and slabs to inhibit water flow through the concrete.

(d) Oil well cement, which is made to harden properly at the high temperatures prevailing in very deep wells.

2-4.2.8 Cement Samples. Cement samples are to be taken daily by the Inspector at the concrete proportioning plant or by the Inspector at the mixer when proportioning is done on the project. A sample of cement shall be obtained by using a sampling tube when sampling cement through a port in a silo or a bunker. When sampling cement in sacks, a composite sample shall be taken from several previously unopened sacks. A sufficient amount of cement shall be taken to fill a sample can. These sample containers will be furnished by the Testing Agency. A sample identification slip must be filled out completely showing the brand of cement, job title, project number, kind of work for which the cement is intended, date the sample was taken, and the name of the Inspector. The sample identification slip shall be placed inside the sample can. The sample shall then be stored in a dry, sheltered place until picked up by the Testing Agency. If the sample is stored in a location that is not a regular collection point, the Inspector shall advise the Testing Agency of its location.

2-4.3   Admixtures.

2-4.3.1   **General.**   A concrete admixture is defined as any material added to a portland cement concrete other than portland cement, rock, sand and water. The indiscriminate use of admixture in concrete is discouraged. On the other hand, the purposeful use of some types of admixtures is often desirable and may be specified. The use of admixtures is not permitted unless required in the specifications or authorized by the Engineer. Among the purposes for which admixtures are commonly used are to: improve workability of fresh concrete, improve durability, accelerate hardening, waterproof, disperse cement particles, retard setting, reduce shrinkage, increase hardness, produce a lightweight product, impart color, reduce bleeding, reduce evolution of heat, etc. (Also see Plate 19, Appendix).

2-4.3.2   Accelerators.

(a) **Calcium Chloride.**   Calcium chloride is used to accelerate setting time and to reduce the time necessary for the concrete to reach its specified strength. Calcium chloride shall be added to the concrete mixture in solution form only at the rate of four pints per 100 pounds cement, not sooner than 45 minutes before placing the concrete. Calcium chloride should never be used in the same concrete mix with an air-entraining agent of the vinsol resin type since it will precipitate the vinsol resin in the mixture. There is evidence that calcium chloride reduces the resistance of concrete to attack by sulfate gases, acids or aggressive soils and ground waters. In addition, it accelerates the alkali-aggregate reaction between high alkali cements and reactive aggregates. Calcium chloride is not used when the concrete will be in contact with steel or other metal surfaces.

(b) **Patented Accelerators.**   There are many patented accelerators available today for use as concrete admixtures. In general, these accelerators are used to shorten the time of set and increase the rate of hardening. The purpose for using an accelerator is usually to: permit earlier removal of forms, shorten the curing period, advance the time when the concrete can be placed in service, offset the retarding effects of low ambient temperatures, or compensate for the retarding effects of some other admixture.

2-4.3.3   **Retarders.**   Admixtures designed to offset the accelerating effect of hot weather on the setting of concrete and to delay the stiffening of concrete and grout under difficult conditions of placement, are known as retarders. Usually the commercially available retarders are compounded with additional gypsum to produce the retarding effect. Where extreme temperatures are encountered (as in cementing oil wells), sugars, starches and cellulose products are employed as retarders.

2-4.3.4 Plasticizers. Admixtures which are employed to increase the plasticity and workability of concrete mixtures are known as plasticizers. Materials commonly employed for this purpose are hydrated lime, fly ash, diatomaceous earth and bentonite. Powdered admixtures generally tend to require a higher water-cement ratio, so that appropriate adjustments must be made in the mix to avoid any adverse effect upon the strength, durability or shrinkage of the concrete.

Air-entraining agents and dispersing agents are also used to increase workability of concrete mixtures.

2-4.3.5 Air-Entraining Agents. Foaming agents which cause air to be entrained during the mixing of the concrete or agents which, by reaction with constituents present in the cement, produce a gas, are called air-entraining agents. A number of organic compounds are used for this purpose including natural resins, tallows and sulfonated soaps or oils.

This aeration, in the form of finely divided bubbles uniformly distributed throughout the concrete mass, produces the effect of reduced segregation, increased workability, decreased density, decreased strength, reduced bleeding and increased durability under freezing and thawing conditions. Admixtures used to entrain air must be carefully controlled and it is essential to make field tests of the concrete to make certain that enough air is being entrained to accomplish the desired results. However, if too much air is entrained, it will reduce the strength of the concrete unnecessarily.

Air-entraining agents make possible the reduction in the sand content in the mix in an amount approximately equal to the volume of the entrained air. Also, a reduction in mixing water is possible with no loss in slump and some gain in workability.

The maximum amount of air-entrainment resulting from an admixture permitted by the Standard Specifications is six percent by volume for general use and four percent by volume for structural concrete. The loss in compressive strength of concrete from air-entrainment is five percent for each one percent of air entrained. Entrained air in excess of six percent results in a precipitous loss in compressive strength. Some bulking of the concrete mixtures utilizing air-entrainment occurs, resulting in a greater yield which must be taken into account in designing the concrete mix. To offset the losses in compressive strength, the cement factor is generally increased. (See Subsection 2-4.5.8).

When a vinsol resin air-entraining agent is used, calcium chloride should never be used in the concrete mixture for it will precipitate the vinsol resin.

2-4.3.6   **Dispersing Agents.** There are many patented admixtures on the market known as dispersing agents intended to increase workability. Many of these agents have as their base calcium lignin sulfonate, a by-product from paper manufacturing. Stearates, calcium chloride, some oils and such proprietary powders as "Plastiment" and "Protex" are included in this class of admixture.

These are all wetting agents which break the surface tension of water and permit a significant reduction in the water-cement ratio with an increase in workability. A higher percentage of hydration of the cement particles is realized, resulting in early strengths considerably in excess of those in normal concrete. Dispersing agents result in some retarding effects on the setting time, which provides increased placement time and there is consistent entrainment of about four percent of air to lend the characteristics of an air-entrainment agent to the mixture.

2-4.3.7   **Pozzolanic Materials.** Pozzolanic materials are minerals utilized in a finely divided state as a replacement for cement and other special purposes. A number of naturally occurring materials such as pumicite, opaline shales and cherts, diatomaceous earth, certain shales and clays, and some materials resulting from manufacturing processes (such as fly ash), have been employed as pozzolans.

While a pozzolan in itself possesses little or no cementitious value, in the presence of water in a finely divided state, it will react chemically with calcium hydroxide (lime) at ordinary temperatures to form compounds possessing cementitious properties. Pozzolans are sometimes specified when it is desired to achieve a definite purpose such as to reduce the amount of heat liberated from hydration and thermal volume change in mass concrete structures. In concrete structures exposed to aggressive waters, the use of pozzolanic admixtures tends to lessen the attack of the salts and sulfates. In addition, these admixtures improve workability, increase impermeability and reduce bleeding.

However, the use of pozzolans may increase the normal water-cement ratio with a resulting decrease in compressive strength. In such cases, the pozzolanic admixture should be added to the normal concrete mix instead of being used as a replacement for a portion of the cement requirement.

Caution must be exercised in the selection and use of pozzolanic materials as their properties vary widely and some may introduce adverse qualities into the concrete, such as excessive drying shrinkage and reduced strength and durability.

Certain pozzolans, such as diatomaceous earth, opaline chert, some volcanic glasses, some calcined clays, and certain siliceous industrial products like Pyrex glass, are effective in controlling alkali-aggregate reactions, even where reactive aggregate and high alkali cement are used. These admixtures are utilized in a powdered form and the alkali-aggregate reaction is offset by creating a great excess of reactive particles for the amount of alkali present, and which combine with the alkalies while the concrete is still plastic, thus reducing their concentration and preventing later expansive reactions within the hardened concrete.

Fly ash, the major source of which is coal-fired steam generating plants, is becoming more frequently utilized as a concrete admixture for projects involving large quantities of concrete. While its use may also serve a special purpose (such as reducing the heat of hydration), the principal purpose for its use is to reduce the cost of the concrete by replacing a part of the more expensive cement content. In the Standard Specifications, only Class C and Class F fly ash can be used in concrete mixtures and then only when approved in advance by the Engineer.

Fly ash shall not be used with portland-pozzolan cement Type IP (MS) or Type III cement. The reason stems from the fact that fly ash would be a contributing factor to neutralizing the effect of the special properties "built in" to these cement types. When Type V (high sulfate resistant) cement is specified, fly ash may be used in conjunction with Type II cement to replace the Type V cement up to 25 percent of its weight. In all other instances when fly ash is authorized as a cement substitute, the maximum amount of portland cement replaced shall not exceed 30 percent by weight; but at least an equal weight of fly ash is required as a substitute for the replaced portland cement.

2-4.4   Concrete Mixtures.

   2-4.4.1   General.   Concrete mixtures for Agency work are specified by either class or compressive strength.

   For concrete specified by class, the mix proportions, including cement content, aggregate gradation and strength are designed in the Standard Specifications. See Subsection 2-4.4.2 for the typical classes of concrete used in Agency work.

   For concrete designated by compressive strength, the contractor, within the limitations imposed by the special provisions, is responsible for the design of the mix. The contractor's design is verified by test cylinders from full load batches. A compressive strength of 4,000 psi or more is usually required for the structural members, such as concrete bridge girders and columns. The full load batches required for verification of the design need not be wasted but can be utilized in the footings and other locations on a project requiring concrete of lower compressive strength.

   Controls and procedures exercised over the sources of concrete supplying Agency projects are described in Subsection 2-4.5.

   2-4.4.2   Concrete Mixtures Specified by Class.   The concrete class and maximum slump for typical types of public works construction are shown in the following table. Concrete is specified by class, for example: 520-A-2500. The first three numbers represent the pounds of cement required per cubic yard of concrete, the letter designates the grading of the aggregate, and the last four numbers specify the minimum 28-day compressive strength (psi). The exact proportions of aggregates and water to be used in the concrete are determined by the Agency Inspector from tests of the material to be used (See Subsection 2-4.5.8).

CONCRETE CLASS USE TABLE

Construction	Concrete Class	Maximum Slump (Inches)
Street Surface Improvements		
Concrete Pavement (not integral with curb)	520-A-2500	3
Curb, Integral Curb and Pavement, Gutter, Walk, Alley Aprons	520-C-2500	4
Extruded Curb, Curb & Gutter	520-C-2500	2
	520-D-2500	2
Sewer and Storm Drainage Facilities		
Pipe Collars, Beam Support for Pipe, Pre-Cast Manhole Components, Catch Basins, Sidewalk Culverts	560-C-3250**	5
Sidehill Surface Drainage Facilities	500-C-2500	3
Pipe Bedding and Encasement,* Anchors and Thrust Blocks, Wall Support for Pipe	420-C-2000**	4
Tunnel Backfill	480-C-2000	5
Trench Backfill Slurry	100-E-100	5
Reinforced Structures		
Bridges, Buildings, Retaining Walls	560-C-3250**	4
Cast-In-Place Piles	560-C-3250**	4
Channels and Boxes		
Invert	560-B-3250**	4
Walls and Deck	560-C-3250**	5
Miscellaneous		
Street Light and Traffic Signal Foundations, Survey Monuments	560-C-3250	4
Fence and Guardrail Posts Foundations	500-C-2500	5
Concrete not Otherwise Specified	560-C-3250	5
Air Placed Concrete, Method B	600-E-3250	4

* Use limited to bedding concrete over which backfill will be placed not less than 40 hours after placement. For backfill after 24 hours, add 3 pints (1.4l) of calcium chloride. For backfill after 16 hours and removal of sheeting after 18 hours, use 660-C-3750 with 3 pints (1.4l) calcium chloride solution.

** Use B Aggregate gradation when placing conditions permit.

COMBINED AGGREGATE GRADINGS (% PASSING)

Sieve Size	Grading A	Grading B	Grading C	Grading D	Grading E
2″ (51mm)	100	100			
1½″ (38mm)	95-100	95-100	100		
1″ (25mm)	64-80	80-96	95-100		
¾″ (19mm)	55-71	64-80	77-93	100	100
⅜″ (10mm)	37-53	40-52	50-70	92-100	90-100
No. 4	32-42	35-45	39-51	42-60	60-80
No. 8	25-35	28-38	31-41	33-47	50-70
No. 16	18-28	21-31	22-32	22-38	33-53
No. 30	10-18	10-20	12-22	17-25	19-35
No. 50	3-9	3-9	3-9	6-12	5-15
No. 100	0-3	0-3	0-3	1-5	2-6
No. 200	0-2	0-2	0-2	0-2	0-2

2-4.4.3 Sampling and Testing Fresh Concrete.

(a) **General.** The Project Inspector shall make slump tests and concrete test cylinders in accordance with the Sampling Schedule (Plate 28, Appendix) and Specifications Requirements.

Test specimens shall be made according to the latest ASTM standard. To accomplish this, each Inspector needs the following equipment: a slump cone, a cylinder mold and a ⅝-inch diameter rod with a rounded end.

(b) **Procedure for Making Slump Tests.** The Inspector shall obtain a sample of the concrete that is representative of the batch. The composite sample shall consist of not less than one cubic foot in order to obtain a sample that is representative.

The following procedure will be followed for obtaining samples of fresh concrete from mixers, hoppers or transporting units:

From Mixers Used in Construction, Other than Truck Mixers. The sample shall be obtained by passing a receptacle through the discharge stream of the mixer at about the middle of the batch. Care shall be taken not to restrict the flow from the mixer in such a manner as to cause the concrete to segregate.

Paving Machines. Paving mixes discharged upon the subgrade shall be sampled from a sufficient number of points in the batch on the subgrade to be representative.

From Revolving Drum Truck Mixers or Agigators. The sample shall be taken in three or more regular increments throughout the discharge of the entire batch. To permit sampling, the rate of discharge of the batch shall be regulated by the rate of revolution of the drum and not by the size of the gate opening.

From Open-Top Truck Mixers and Agitators. The sample shall be taken directly from the mixer and shall consist of portions from not less than three points in the batch.

From Receiving Hoppers, Buckets, etc. Samples shall be taken by whichever of the procedures described in paragraphs (a) or (b) above is most applicable under the conditions.

The composite sample shall be mixed with a shovel sufficiently to ensure homogeneity and immediately used for the slump test.

Moisten the inside of the slump cone and the top of the mold board or whatever flat surface is being used. Place concrete from the composite sample in the slump cone with a circular motion of a scoop or trowel, so that it will be well distributed as it falls. Fill the slump cone in three layers, each one filling one-third of the volume of the cone. The bottom layer should be about 2½″ thick, the center about 3½″, and the top 6″. Rod each layer of concrete with 25 uniformly distributed strokes which penetrate into the underlying layer, or in the case of the bottom layers, to the mold board. When the cone has been filled, strike off the top of the cone with a trowel to a smooth surface. Slowly lift the slump cone straight up when removing it, placing the cone along side the slumped concrete. Place the rod on top of the slump cone so it extends over the concrete and measure the slump from the bottom of the rod to the center or axis at the top of the concrete.

(c) **Procedure for Making Concrete Cylinders.** Concrete which has been used for making the slump test may be used for preparing the concrete test cylinder, provided it is again mixed with the original composite sample sufficiently to ensure homogeneity. Place the concrete in a cylinder mold (furnished by the Testing Agency) by rotating the scoop around the mold to secure uniform distribution. Fill the mold in three layers of equal volume. Rod each layer of concrete with 25 strokes with the rod, uniformly throughout the cross-section of the layer, and penetrating the underlying layer. After the top layer has been rodded, strike off the surplus concrete and smooth the top with a trowel. After the test cylinder has been made, it is to be labeled with the date the cylinder was made and the number of the lowest numbered Record of Test in the possession of the Inspector. Cover the cylinder with damp sand or earth and select a location for its storage where it will be protected from injury and which will be easily accessible for collection by the Testing Agency.

The corresponding Record of Test is to be filled in completely. Note on the back of the Record of Test the location where the cylinder is stored; draw a map, if necessary, for clarity. All Records of Test made in one day must be mailed to the Main Office that same day.

2-4.5   Concrete Proportioning Plant Inspection.

2-4.5.1   General. Most concrete used in Agency work is supplied from ready-mix plants, commonly referred to as concrete bunkers (See Plate 48, Appendix), and delivered to the job site in transit-mix trucks. When special design or structural concrete is to be produced, an Inspector is required at the plant to inspect the proportioning and other processes which affect the concrete mixture. For other classes of concrete mixtures, no Plant Inspector is required, but the plant must have been previously approved to supply Agency concrete mixtures as outlined in Subsection 2-4.5.5.

While small quantities of concrete (not exceeding 10 cubic yards) may be proportioned by volumetric methods, all quantities over 10 cubic yards must be proportioned by weight.

Inspectors assigned to the inspection of concrete proportioning plants should expect the plant operating personnel to be aware of all of the factors contributing to the production of acceptable concrete. Poor housekeeping, shoddy operation, poor equipment or careless storage and handling of materials cannot be tolerated, and the Inspector must not hesitate to insist upon compliance with specifications, irrespective of resistance he may encounter from plant operating personnel.

The responsibility for placing an order for concrete with the producer rests with the contractor. Agency Inspectors are not authorized to order concrete for the contractor. It is the responsibility of the Project Inspector to insure that the concrete delivered is the specified class, and to discuss the class of concrete to be used with the contractor before the order is placed.

2-4.5.2   Field Laboratory. One of the conditions for approval of a bunker is that a field laboratory be provided immediately adjacent to the plant. This laboratory is for the use of the Plant Inspector in making moisture tests, air-entraining tests, storing samples, etc., and provides a weatherproof facility in which to maintain his records and perform the administrative duties required. (See Subsection 2-4.5.5).

The use of the laboratory is extended to the Inspectors of other agencies provided they perform a fair share of the cleanup and care of the facility. Loitering by unauthorized personnel in the laboratory is not to be tolerated.

2-4.5.3   Field Communication Procedure. For structural and special design concrete mixes, the Plant Inspector will prepare one copy only of "Plant Inspector's Report to Field Inspector," entering the required information and any other pertinent data relating to the mixture and transmit the form to the Field Inspector with the first load of concrete delivered to the project. The examples on the following page illustrate typical entries to be made by the Plant Inspector and the Field Inspector.

An Inspector assigned to a concrete bunker to inspect structural concrete proportioning should also inspect such other classes of concrete as are being proportioned for Agency work during the time he is there and report the general performance characteristics to the Materials Control Group Supervisor.

2-4.5.4   Plant Equipment.

(a) **General.** All of the equipment for handling materials for concrete must be kept in such repair and condition as to fully maintain these materials in a clean and segregated state throughout the storing and proportioning operations.

(b) **Scales.** All scales must weigh accurately within the limitations stated in the Standard Specifications.

Scales must be sealed by the County Sealer of Weights and Measures: (1) at intervals of not more than one year, (2) each time the plant is moved, (3) after each overhaul of the scales or the scale mechanism, or (4) at any time the Supervisor of the Materials Control Group has reason to doubt their accuracy.

The certification of a reputable scale maintenance company will be acceptable for periods up to six months in case the County Sealer of Weights and Measures is delayed in checking the scales.

(c) **Water Measurement and Control.** The Standard Specifications require a water meter which is accurate to within one-half of one percent. The meters at most plants are checked and sealed by the County Sealer of Weights and Measures.

The Inspector must not only check the measurement of added water by meter, but he must also determine the amount of moisture in the aggregate and compensate for it in his calculations of the mix design. The greatest variations in water content in aggregates result from the free water — particularly in the sand. (See next page)

When transit-mix trucks are utilized, some water is required to wet the inside surfaces of the drum. To keep these surfaces wet, a fixed amount of water is permitted to be retained in the drum when the truck is returning empty to the plant, but this quantity of water must be known to the Plant Inspector in advance and the same quantity retained in every truck loading from that plant for a specific project. The Plant Inspector then considers this as part of the water to be added to the next load.

It should be noted that the water meters on transit-mix trucks are subject to abuse and tampering and must be periodically checked by the Plant Inspector for accuracy. This is done simply by discharging a quantity of water into a container of known volume and noting the reading on the meter or gauge.

2-4.5.5 Plant Approval Procedure.

(a) **General.** Concrete proportioning plants will be inspected on a periodic basis, the frequency of which is determined by the volume of concrete furnished for Agency work, the type and efficiency of the plant, the reliability of the plant personnel, etc. The frequency at which plants are to be inspected is determined by the Supervisor of the Materials Control Group.

(b) **Checking a Plant for Compliance with Agency Requirements.** Upon receiving a request from a plant owner for approval of his facility, the Inspector initially checking the plant for compliance with Agency requirements will consider the pertinent portions of the Standard Specifications, this Manual and the Inspector's Check List in Subsection 2-4.5.11. He may use the short form "Concrete Bunker Check List" for convenience in making routine reinspections of a plant. (See Plate 5, Appendix.)

2-4.5.6 Types of Concrete Mixers.

(a) **Central Wet-Mixing Plants.** Plants with stationary drum-type mixers, in which the concrete is thoroughly wet-

FRONT

City of Anywhere
DEPARTMENT OF PUBLIC WORKS
Bureau of Contract Administration
PLANT INSPECTOR'S REPORT
TO FIELD INSPECTOR

INSTRUCTIONS TO PLANT INSPECTOR:
Fill out, attach to load ticket and send to Field Inspector with first load.

PLANT NAME: Spalling Ready mix   DATE 4-21-87

PLANT LOCATION North Hollywood

FOR CONCRETE MIXTURES:

CLASS OF CONCRETE	SOURCE OF ROCK
520-C-2500	Consolidated

BRAND OF CEMENT	TYPE	SOURCE OF SAND
Colton	I	Consolidated

BRAND OF ADMIXTURE   AMOUNT OF ADMIXTURE PER BACK.

FOR BITUMINOUS MIXTURES:

TYPE OF MIX   GRADING

PENETRATION OF ASPHALT   SOURCE OF BITUMEN

PLANT INSPECTOR Frank Jones

REMARKS Running tomorrow?

INSTRUCTIONS TO FIELD INSPECTOR: FILL OUT REVERSE SIDE AND RETURN TO PLANT INSPECTOR IMMEDIATELY.

BACK

INSTRUCTIONS TO FIELD INSPECTOR:
Fill out this side and return to Plant Inspector immediately.

JOB TITLE Hody St & Berry Dr. I.D.

JOB NO.	LETTER CODE	SPECIFICATIONS
B-6087	CF35H6	170

(CONCRETE) (ASPHALT) USED FOR Curb & Gutter

GALLONS WATER ADDED AT JOB

FIELD INSPECTOR C.F. Smith

NOTES: Approx. 50 yds. to be used tomorrow.

mixed and then transported to the jobsite in a transit-mix truck or special-body truck, are commonly called central mixing plants. Portable plants of this type are frequently set up at jobsites requiring a large volume of concrete coupled with a need for a high rate of delivery, such as for slip form paving. Such plants, whether located on the jobsite or at more remote locations, must be approved in advance of their use for Agency projects.

Special-body trucks which do not agitate the mix must be approved prior to their use. Factors which must be considered are the haul distance, slump of the concrete, admixtures used to reduce segregation, baffle plate arrangement, extent of remixing to be expected in discharging the load and remixing equipment contemplated to be used at the placement site. The greatest problems arise from segregation of the aggregate and in the crusting of mortar in the bed of the truck.

When all of the materials for concrete (including water) are partially mixed for at least 30 seconds in a stationary mixer, then transferred to a transit mixer to complete the mixing, the method is known as "shrink-mixing." The principal advantages are for short hauls where insufficient time would elapse during the haul to permit complete mixing in transit; and it permits transit mixers to haul up to 12½ percent more than their normal rated capacities.

(b) **Dry Batching Plants.** Dry batching of concrete to a jobsite is often desirable where low-slump concrete is required which would be difficult to discharge from a transit-mix truck. This method involves the proportioning of the dry ingredients into small batches which are hauled in dump trucks having several compartments, each capable of being dumped individually. The water is added at the mixer in this method.

Ordinarily, the aggregates are loaded in a compartment of the truck and the cement charged separately into a closed container attached to each dump gate. This prevents the caking of the cement from the moisture it may pick up from contact with damp aggregates, and the closed container prevents the cement from blowing away during transport.

Where the cement is to be added at the jobsite by sacks, the dry batches are to be computed on the basis of full sacks for each batch, as no sack-splitting is permitted at the mixer.

(c) **Towed or Self-Propelled Mixers.** All concrete mixers must produce a thoroughly homogeneous mixture within the specified mixing time and be capable of discharging the mixture without segregation. Towed and self-propelled paving mixers are typical of this class.

Mixers that are charged from a skip and have a boom and bucket type of discharge are sometimes used for placing concrete pavement. Inspectors assigned to projects using this type of mixer must insist upon the skip being kept in a vertical (charging) position long enough to completely empty the contents into the mixer drum. The skip can be "banged" several times against the skip stop to insure complete discharge or it can be equipped with a vibrator. For the protection of personnel, a mechanical safety device must be provided to keep the area clear under the skip while it is elevated. Transit mixers or on-site central mixing plants are most commonly used for placing concrete for pavement.

(d) **Transit Mixers.** The Standard Specifications describe the requirements for transit mixers in detail. However, there are several things which the Plant Inspector must check to insure that the desired quality of concrete is maintained when using transit mixers. The pickup and throw-over blades must be examined for wear and build-up of mortar inside the drum, leaky water valves corrected, the quantity of retained wash water checked, and each truck's rated drum capacity must be rigidly observed.

It is well known that a slump loss will be experienced between the batching plant and the project. This reduction is attributable to the following possible causes:

(1) The grinding action of the mixer generating additional fines, resulting in increased surface areas of aggregate.

(2) Higher temperatures of the mixture from the chemical and frictional heat generated.

(3) High atmospheric temperatures and low relative humidity.

The Project Inspector should keep this in mind, so that he will not permit water to be added to the extent that the designed water-cement ratio will be exceeded.

2-4.5.7 Fundamentals of Mix Design. Considerable research has been done in the field of portland cement concrete which has resulted in data useful in designing a concrete mixture and predicting, with a reasonable degree of accuracy, the performance of that mixture. The following tables have been derived from this information.

COMPRESSIVE STRENGTH FOR VARIOUS WATER-CEMENT RATIOS
(The strengths listed are based on the use of normal portland cement)

WATER/CEMENT RATIO		PROBABLE 28-DAY STRENGTH	
WEIGHT	GALS./100#	PSI	MEGAPASCALS*
.40	4.8	5000	34
.45	5.4	4500	31
.50	6.0	4000	28
.55	6.6	3500	24
.60	7.2	3000	21
.65	7.8	2500	17
.70	8.4	2000	14

* International system equivalent.

APPROXIMATE CONTENT OF SAND, CEMENT AND WATER PER CUBIC YARD OF CONCRETE

Based on aggregates of average grading and physical characteristics in concrete mixes having a water-cement ratio (W/C) of about .65 by weight (or 7.8 gallons) per sack of cement; 3-in. slump; and a medium natural sand having a fineness modulus of about 2.75.

COURSE AGGREGATE MAX. SIZE	WATER		CEMENT	% SAND
	POUNDS	GALLONS		
3/8	385	46	590	57
1/2	365	44	560	50
3/4	340	41	525	43
1	325	39	500	39
1 1/2	300	36	460	37

It can be noted from the above chart that, for a given slump, the amount of mixing water increases as the size of the course aggregate decreases. The size of the course aggregate controls the sand content in the same way; that is, the amount of sand required in the mix increases as the size of the course aggregate decreases.

Other typical examples are contained in the pamphlet published by the Portland Cement Association entitled "Design and Control of Concrete Mixtures."

The Standard Specifications control the water content by designating the maximum slump and maximum water content for the various aggregate gradings. The Standard Specifications also provide that "the amount of water used in the concrete mixture shall not exceed the amount necessary to permit the practical placement and consolidation of the concrete."

Utmost precautions must be taken by the Plant and Field Inspectors in every step of proportioning, placement, consolidation and curing of concrete to assure that the concrete meets the specified strength and that the test cylinders truly represent the concrete placed.

The batch weights of concrete mixtures are developed from combined aggregate limits designated by the Standard Specification or Special Provisions. The weights are generally based on absolute volumes. (Absolute volume is defined as that theoretical volume which a given amount of material would occupy if no voids existed between the particles.) For all practical purposes, the following data may be assumed to be adequate for the calculations necessary to determine the batch weights of a concrete mixture:

Material	Specific Gravity	Weight per Cubic Foot At Absolute Volume
Rock	2.65 ±	165.36 lbs.
Sand	2.65 ±	165.36 lbs.
Cement	3.15	196.56 lbs.
Water	1.00	62.40 lbs.*

*Water weighs 8.34 lbs. per gallon and there are 7.48 gallons per cubic foot.

2-4.5.8 Determining Concrete Mix Batch Weights. Upon arriving at a plant and determining what type of concrete is required, the Inspector is to initially permit the proportioning of the specified concrete using the Table of Tentative Batch Weights published as Plate 49, Appendix. These batch weights are later adjusted by the Inspector to reflect actual moisture content and the latest screen analysis of the aggregates.

The weights shown in the Table of Tentative Batch Weights are saturated surface-dry weights (meaning material which has absorbed its full capacity of inherent moisture but having no additional moisture on its surface). Therefore, the weight of any additional moisture in the materials must be added to the Batch Weights of each primary aggregate and deducted from the allowable water permitted in the mix.

In order to permit the batching plant to commence operations, the Inspector is to use judgment as to the additional percentage of weight to allow for free water in the aggregates. (Pending the making of actual moisture tests, six percent additional weight of sand and one percent additional weight of the No. 4 rock only are reasonable estimates.) These percentages are predicated on the materials being damp; if the material seems drier, reduce the allowances for free moisture accordingly.

As soon as the moisture characteristics of the aggregate become uniform (after the fourth or fifth batch), the Inspector is to make moisture tests of each primary aggregate size. Meanwhile, commence the computation of batch weights based on the sieve analyses of the materials being used.

Assume a mix containing 520 pounds of cement, aggregate designated as Type "C" and a strength requirement of 2500 pounds per square inch. The Standard Specifications designation for such a mix is 520-C-2500. The maximum water is 35 gallons or 292 pounds.

The absolute volume of the ingredients in this mix for one cubic yard (27 cubic feet) is calculated below:

$$\text{Cement } \frac{520}{196.56} = 2.65 \text{ cu.ft.}$$

$$\text{Water } \frac{292}{62.4} = 4.68 \text{ cu.ft.}$$

$$\text{Aggregate } 27-(2.65+4.68) = 19.67 \text{ cu.ft.}$$

$$\text{Total} = 27.00 \text{ cu.ft.}$$

(Absolute Volume)

Total weight of aggregate in the mix would be:
$19.67 \times 2.65 \times 62.4 = 3253$ lbs.

The chart below shows the percentage limits set up for Type "C" grading and a typical actual grading distribution of material on hand as determined by sieve analyses of samples taken from the bins.

The percentages indicated on the "% of Mix" line are the final results of trial-and-error calculations, and adjustments are made until all of the percentages in the "Combined Grading" column fall between the minimum and maximum "Specification Limits."

Sieve Analysis, Primary Aggregates				Actual Comb. Grading	Specific Limits		
	No. 3 Rock	No. 4 Rock	Conc. Sand		Mini-mum	Ideal	Maxi-mum
% of Mix	50%	4%	46%	100%			
% Passing							
2 inch	100	100	100	100	100	100	
1½ inch	100	100	100	100	100	100	
1 inch	95	100	100	97.5	95	97	100
¾ inch	70	100	100	85.0	77	85	93
⅜ inch	14	95	100	56.8	50	60	70
No. 4	2	7	97	45.9	39	45	51
No. 8		2	83	38.2	31	36	41
No. 16		1	65	29.9	22	27	32
No. 30			40	18.4	12	17	22
No. 50			17	7.2	3	6	9
No. 100			5	2.2	0	1.5	3
No. 200			1.5	0.7	0	1	2

The "Dry Weights" of the primary aggregates can now be calculated.

	Total Weight of Aggregate		Percent	Weight of Each Aggregate Size
No. 3 Rock	3253	×	50	1627 lbs.
No. 4 Rock	3253	×	4	130 lbs.
Concrete Sand	3265	×	46	1496 lbs.
			100	3253 lbs.

After allowing one percent for absorption, assume six percent additional weight of sand and one percent additional weight of No. 4 rock to compensate for the free water each contains. (No allowance is made for No. 3 and larger rock, which are considered to be "saturated surface dry.")

The final one-cubic-yard batch weights will then be as follows:

	Batch Weights
No. 3 rock, 1627 lbs. (no moisture)	= 1627 lbs.
No. 4 rock, 130 lbs. + 1lb. (1% moisture)	= 131 lbs.
Concrete sand, 1496 lbs. + 90 lbs. (6% moisture)	= 1586 lbs.
Cement, 520 lbs.	= 520 lbs.
Added water (total water less water in aggregates, 292 − 91)	= 201 lbs.

The Inspector then instructs the batch operator to change the batch weights to reflect the weights as adjusted for free water and the latest sieve analysis.

If an air-entraining agent is added to the mix, a loss of strength will result and extra cement must be added to compensate for this loss. This has been determined to be 10 percent and this quantity of cement should be added to the mix design without altering the recomputed proportions.

The addition of an air-entraining agent increases the workability of the concrete mixture and permits the mixing water to be reduced by ¼ gallon per 100 lbs. of cement while retaining the same plasticity.

In a mix containing 520 lbs. of cement, this would amount to 1.3 gallons (11 lbs.) of water per yard, or .17 cubic foot. On the other hand, air-entrainment increases the volume of the mix by an average of four percent. It can be anticipated that such concrete will contain four percent of 27 cubic feet (or 1.08 cubic feet) of minute air voids. While these two physical properties tend to compensate for each other, the increase in volume due to air-entrainment is usually larger than the decrease in volume due to the reduction in the mixing water. In this case, the net increase in volume is the difference between 1.08 and .17, or .91 cubic foot.

It is necessary to compensate for this net increase in volume by reducing the dry weight of the sand in the mix by .91 cubic foot ($.91 \times 165.36$ lbs./cu. ft. at absolute volume) or 149 lbs.

The new Batch Weights for the air-entrained concrete mix would be:

No. 3 rock (no change) . . . .   1627 lbs.
No. 4 rock (no change) . . . .   131 lbs.
Concrete sand (— 149 lbs.) . . . .   1437 lbs.
Cement (+ 10%, 52 lbs.) . . . .   572 lbs.
Water (— 11 lbs.) . . . .   190 lbs.
Air-entraining admixture . . . .   3.12 oz.
   (0.602/100 lbs. cement)

The volume of the recomputed mix design using four percent entrained air would be:

		Absolute Volume (Cubic Feet)
Cement (520 + 52)	$\dfrac{572 \text{ lbs.}}{196.56 \text{ lbs./cu. ft.}}$	= 2.91
Aggregate (3253 lbs. — 149 lbs.)	$\dfrac{3104 \text{ lbs.}}{165.36 \text{ lbs./cu. ft.}}$	= 18.77
Water (292 lbs. — 11 lbs.)	$\dfrac{281 \text{ lbs.}}{62.4 \text{ lbs./cu. ft.}}$	= 4.49
Entrained Air		= 1.08
Yield (Absolute Volume)		27.25

If the entire amount of estimated water is not added at the plant, the Plant Inspector should use "Plant Inspector's Report to Field Inspector" to inform the Project Inspector, who must know how many gallons remain to be added before the specification limit is reached. If the contractor desires additional workability beyond the water allowance specified, he may add more water and more cement, provided he maintains the specified water-cement ratio for the class of concrete being used.

The Plant Inspector adjusts the proportions of the mixture when required by any of the following conditions:

(a) Changes based upon rock or sand having specific gravities other than 2.65.

(b) Changes in the gradation of the coarse aggregates.

(c) Variations in the moisture test results.

(d) Increases or decreases in total water actually being used.

2-4.5.9 Sampling and Testing. All sampling must be as prescribed in the Sampling Schedule (Plate 28, Appendix).

2-4.5.10 Daily Reports. A daily report for each job is required on "Concrete Plant Inspector's Daily Report," showing the concrete mixture, the number of cubic yards produced and the aggregate grading used. (See Plate 4, Appendix.)

2-4.5.11 Concrete Plant Inspector's Check List.
(a) **Cement.**
Is the cement the type specified?

Is the brand approved?

Have the certificates of analysis been checked?

Has a cement sample been taken?

Do the storage and handling facilities protect the cement from the weather and contamination?

Are air jets or vibrators used to cause the cement to flow freely?

Can the cement in storage be inspected easily and sampled without danger?

Is the cement used in the same order it is received?

Is the cement batching equipment in good repair and does it operate consistently without variation?

Is the cement weighed on a separate scale?

Are the controls interlocked to prevent filling the weigh hopper before it is empty and the scale balanced?

Have the scales been sealed by the County Sealer of Weights and Measures within the past 12 months?

Is the cement scale clean and kept in good operating condition?

At an automatic plant, is the weight of cement recorded as it is batched?

Can the cement weight be read accurately on the batch ticket?

Is the mix designation (i.e. 520-C-2500) on the batch ticket?

Is the discharge of the weighed cement from the weigh hopper into the mixer properly protected to prevent loss?

(b) **Aggregates.**

Is the aggregate from an approved source?

Are the aggregates properly stored and handled to prevent segregation, contamination and degradation?

Are the bin separators in satisfactory condition?

Is the fine aggregate stored to permit free draining of water?

Is the aggregate transferred from stockpiles to batch plant bins in a satisfactory manner?

Does the aggregate distributor head function satisfactorily?

If the coarse aggregate is not screened over the batching plant bin, does any appreciable amount of rock chips or under-size particles accumulate in the rock bins?

Do aggregate bins discharge freely?

Has the moisture meter on the fine aggregate bin been checked for accuracy?

Is a supply of pea gravel maintained at the plant?

(c) **Water.**

Is the water from a potable source?

Is water measured by weight or by volume?

If water is weighed, are the scales checked at the same time as the other scales?

If water is measured by volume, is the dispenser calibrated by the County Sealer of Weights and Measures?

Is all leakage of water prevented after measuring?

Is the water dispenser control interlocked to prevent discharge before reservoir is full or to prevent filling before discharge is completed?

(d) **Batching and Weighing.** (See Plate 49, Appendix).

Is the batching and weighing equipment in good condition, adequately housed and protected?

Are aggregates weighed separately or cumulatively on the same scale?

Are the scales springless dial, or beam with over-under indicator?

Can the operator and Inspector see the dial or indicator easily?

Are the scale parts clean, tight and free of any binding?

Have the scales been sealed by the County Sealer of Weights and Measures within the past 12 months?

Can batch weights be conveniently changed?

Do the weigh hoppers empty completely?

Are all batch weights based on the latest sieve analysis?

Are the tentative batch weights kept at the plant?

Does the load ticket indicate the amount of cement, the bin weights, water data and the time of loading?

Is a qualified operator in charge of the plant at all times?

(e) **Transit Mixers.**

Is there adequate control of the amount of wash water retained in the mixer drum? Is it uniformly maintained?

Is the operation of the mixer satisfactory?

Are water-metering devices on the mixer trucks in good condition?

Are the manufacturer's standard rating plates kept legible?

Are trucks being loaded within their rated capacity?

Is the inside of the drum free of encrusted material and is the condition of the mixing blades satisfactory?

(f) **Dry-Batching.**

Are batches completely separated at all times when handling and dumping?

Is the cement hauled in a separate waterproof compartment?

Are precautions taken to prevent loss of cement during transport?

Where cement is to be added at the jobsite has the batch size been computed so that full sacks only will be used?

(g) **Field Communication.**

Has a "Plant Inspector's Report to Field Inspector" form been sent with a truck driver to the jobsite?

Has this form been completed by the Field Inspector and returned to the Plant Inspector?

(h) **Admixtures.**

Has the use of an admixture been approved?

Are the dispenser controls interlocked to discharge automatically?

Can the dispenser be easily adjusted?

Has the dispenser been calibrated and is it checked regularly?

Is the operation of the admixture dispensing equipment satisfactory?

(i) **Operational.**

Has a moisture determination been made for the aggregate?

Have the batch weights been adjusted accordingly?

Has a Concrete Plant Inspector's Daily Report, been completed for each job every day, showing the concrete mixture, the number of cubic yards produced and the aggregate grading used? (See Plate 4, Appendix).

Do the load tickets include data showing the total water allowed in the mix, free water and water put in at the plant?

Has the amount of water added at the jobsite by the truck driver and the contractor been recorded separately?

Has corrective action been taken promptly on deficiencies previously noted?

Is the field laboratory being maintained in conformance with the Standard Specifications?

2-4.6 Mortar and Grout. Mortar is a plastic mixture composed of portland cement, sand and water. For special purposes, such as bedding mortar for masonry, lime putty may be added for plasticity.

Grout is a cement mortar to which sufficient water has been added to obtain a fluidity which will permit it to flow readily. Neat cement grout is portland cement mixed with water to a fluid consistency.

The excess water in mortar results in considerable shrinkage of the mortar when it has hardened. To offset this characteristic, aluminum powder (when approved by the Engineer) can be added (about one teaspoonful per sack of cement) which will generate hydrogen gas in the wet cement mortar and cause expansion of the mortar mass in approximately the same magnitude as the expected shrinkage from excess water.

Nonshrink grout can be produced with a mixture of one part of Type II cement to two parts sand with a water-cement ratio of 0.55. Aluminum powder equal to .005 percent of the weight of the cement is added to complete the mixture.

2-4.7 Concrete Curing Compounds.

2-4.7.1 General. Fresh concrete contains more than enough water for complete hydration of the cement, but under most job conditions much of this water will be lost by evaporation from the surface of the concrete unless certain precautions are taken. One means for obtaining a high moisture retention in the concrete is accomplished by applying a liquid which hardens over the surface of the concrete to form a thin impervious membrane. These liquids are known as sealing or curing compounds and are available as colorless and black, white or light gray pigmented coatings. Curing compounds are never used on the surface of concrete construction joints since they would inhibit bond of fresh concrete to the treated surface of the existing concrete.

2-4.7.2 Clear Curing Compounds (Paraffin Base). Clear concrete curing compounds usually consist of paraffin emulsions. In order to assist in obtaining a uniform application of the compound, a fugitive dye is utilized in the mixture which rapidly loses its color upon being exposed to sunlight or is readily soluble in water and is removed by washing. Such curing compounds are considered to be clear and they leave no lasting stain or discoloration on the concrete. "Hunt's Process" is one example of this type of concrete curing compound. However, concrete surface treated with such curing compounds have a paraffin residue remaining which must be thoroughly removed from any concrete surface intended to be painted. Where such surfaces are to be painted, other curing methods should be used.

2-4.7.3 Black Pigmented Curing Compounds. Where staining of the concrete surface is not a consideration, bituminous emulsions and coal tar cutbacks are sprayed over fresh concrete surfaces to form membranes to prevent evaporation. These compounds are less expensive than paraffin compounds and are generally used on concrete base for bituminous pavements, wall surfaces below finish grade and as primers for membrane waterproofing of concrete walls.

2-4.7.4 White and Light Gray Pigmented Curing Compounds. Pigmented curing compounds consist of a finely ground pigment of high hiding quality, dispersed in a vehicle of oils, waxes, or resins and a solvent. When applied to concrete surfaces, a coating of the pigmented compound, usually white or gray, presents a uniform color and effectively conceals the natural color of the concrete. The light color of the pigment reflects a considerable amount of the heat which would be otherwise absorbed from direct sunlight if the concrete were untreated or if it were coated with the clear or black compounds described above. The resulting lowered temperature (as much as 40°F. in hot weather) materially reduces cracking caused by thermal expansion and contraction.

Both the white and gray pigments weather and wear off in time. Where appearance is a consideration, such as a building or slab subject to public inspection, the gray pigment presents a better appearance in the later stages of weathering.

2-4.8   Reinforcement for Concrete.

2-4.8.1   **Bars.**   The most frequently specified material for reinforced concrete material is steel bars of intermediate grade, rolled from open-hearth or electric furnace billet steel. Intermediate grade billet steel is used because it has a relative high tensile strength and at the same time has sufficient ductility to be relatively easy to fabricate. The number of bars to be taken as samples is given in Plate 28, Appendix.

The deformation on the bars increase the bond (resistance to pulling out) of the steel to the concrete. It is possible, in most cases, to identify the steel as to manufacturer by examining these deformations (See Plate 15, Appendix). Bar sizes are indicated by numbers, sometimes embossed on the bars, representing the number of ⅛-inch increments included in the nominal diameter of the bar. (See Plate 15, Appendix).

Yield Point of a test bar is the stress at which there occurs a marked increase in strain without an increase in stress. In simple words, the yield point or yield load is the load (stress) at which a material exhibits a permanent set. **Stress** is the internal forces within a material that tend to resist deformation. **Strain** is the deformation caused by the application of an external force. **Yield Strength** is the limiting load used in design, because a member stressed beyond this point will not return to its original length.

Tensile Strength is the maximum load that a specimen will sustain. Yield Point and Tensile Strength are reported in pounds per square inch (psi).

Percent Elongation is a measure of ductility, reported as percent elongation of an eight-inch length of bar.

Bend Test is another measure of ductility and is important in determining whether a given lot of bars can be bent to shape without cracking or breaking.

Phosphorus is the only chemical constituent limited in reinforcing steel specifications. This is because it is the most undesirable of all elements commonly found in steel because it reduces the toughness, shock resistance and ductility of steel.

2-4.8.2 Welded Steel Wire Fabric. Welded steel wire fabric is to conform to the latest adopted Standard Specifications. To minimize the number of splices, wire fabric should be furnished in full rolls only. Splices are to be made by lapping the fabric two full mesh openings.

Wire fabric is usually designated by stating the opening size in inches followed by the gage of the wire. For example: a designation of 4x12-6/10 means the spacing of the longitudinal wires is four inches and the spacing of the transverse wires is 12 inches; and the longitudinal wires are 6-gage with the transverse wires 10-gage. This kind of wire fabric is referred to as a "one-way" type because the principal reinforcement is in one direction.

"Two-way" types of wire fabric are usually designed as: 6x6-10/10 which means that the mesh opening is six inches square and the wire gage is number 10 in both directions. The "two-way" designation specifically means that the cross-sectional area of the transverse steel is greater than the minimum required by the Engineer by reason of the transverse wires either having a spacing which is less than the permissible maximum, or being of a larger size than the permissible minimum.

2-4.8.3 Prestressing Rod, Strand and Wire. High-tensile steel is the universal material for producing pre-stress tendons and supplying resistance to the tensile forces in prestressed concrete. Such steel can be manufactured in any of three forms: wire, strand or bar. The most widely used shape is at present wires grouped in parallel into cables. Strands are fabricated in the factory by twisting wires together, thus decreasing the number of units to be handled in the tensioning operations. Since 1954, strands have been adopted by the majority of pretensioning plants in the United States. Steel bars of high strength have also been developed and successfully applied to prestressed concrete, often resulting in considerable economy.

2-4.8.4 Supports for Concrete Reinforcement Bars.
Bar supports may consist of concrete, metal or other approved
materials. Standardized factory-made steel wire supports are
most widely used. Wire bar supports may be made of plain
wire, pre-galvanized wire or stainless steel wire. The lower
portions in contact with the forms may be provided with special
rust protection such as a plastic covering or by being made of
stainless steel. In certain areas, precast concrete blocks (plain
or provided with embedded tie wires) and dowel blocks are
commonly used to support bars in footings and slabs on ground.
The production of these precast concrete supports should be
controlled to assure that a high strength concrete mix is used
and that they are cured properly.

2-4.9 Miscellaneous Concrete Related Products.

1-4.9.1 General. There is a variety of products produced and used with concrete in order to facilitate and tailor
its use for specific purposes and conditions.

Reinforcing steel (Subsection 2-4.8), admixtures (Subsection 2-4.3) and Concrete Curing Compounds (Subsection
2-4.7) are taken up in other subsections as indicated.

2-4.9.2 Concrete Joint Material.

(a) **Joint-Sealing Compounds.** Joint sealers are used to
form a resilient and adhesive seal in cracks as well as in expansion, construction or contraction joints. They must be capable
of effectively sealing concrete against the infiltration of moisture and foreign material through repeated cycles of expansion
and contraction due to temperature changes.

Standard Specifications provide for four types of liquid
applied sealants: polyurethane, asphalt-latex emulsion, hot-
poured rubber-asphalt and polysulfide polymer type sealants as
well as rubber rod.

Preparation of joints for sealing, components, application methods and temperatures of material are described in
detail in the Standard Specifications.

(b) **Premolded Expansion Joint Filler.** Premolded
expansion joint filler material is intended to be of such character as not to be deformed or damaged by ordinary handling
when exposed to atmospheric conditions normally encountered

in the locality. It should remain plastic and should not extrude from the joint or become brittle. Commonly used types of pre-molded expansion joint fillers are:

Preformed Expansion Joint Filler (Bituminous Type). This type of filler consists of a bituminous (asphalt or tar) mastic composition formed and encased between two layers of bituminous impregnated felt. The mastic is comprised of mineral fillers and reinforcing fibers.

Non-Extruding and Resilient Filler (Bituminous Type). This product consists of preformed strips which have been formed from cane or other suitable fibers of a cellular nature, securely bound together and uniformly saturated with a suitable bituminous binder; or strips which have been formed from clean granulated cork particles securely bound together by a suitable bituminous binder and encased between two layers of bituminous saturated felt.

Non-Extruding and Resilient Filler (Non-Bituminous Type). Three types of strip filler are covered by this type of product: Type I, sponge rubber; Type II, cork; Type III, self-expanding cork.

Sponge Rubber. The joint filler consists of preformed strips of a durable elastic sponge rubber compound, using synthetic rubber or natural rubber as a base and containing no reclaimed rubber. Unless otherwise specified, the sponge rubber shall have a cement gray color to blend with concrete in appearance.

Cork and Self-Expanding Cork. The joint filler consists of preformed strips that have been pressed together from clean granulated cork particles securely bound by a synthetic resin of an insoluble nature.

Dimensions of all preformed joint filler strips shall conform to the dimensions specified or shown on plans, standard plans or Special Provisions, within the permissible variation of $+ \frac{1}{16}$ inch in thickness, $\pm \frac{1}{8}$ inch in depth and $\pm \frac{1}{4}$ inch in length.

2-4.9.3 Waterstops. Waterstops are metal, rubber or plastic devices which are intended to be installed in expansion or construction joints of concrete walls or slabs to stop the passage of water through the joint. They are installed so as to embed one-half of the waterstop in the concrete on each side of the joint. (See Subsection 3-12.6.3.)

Metal waterstops are usually fabricated of copper sheet with an accordion-type fold in it to fit into the joint and provide the necessary flexibility in the waterstop to allow for the movement in the joint from expansion and contraction of the concrete. Splices are made in metal waterstops by soldering.

Rubber waterstops are molded or extruded from natural or synthetic rubber. Plastic waterstops are made of polyvinyl chloride. The resilient characteristics of rubber or plastic provide the flexibility necessary to allow for any movement in the construction or expansion joint. The most commonly used types of rubber waterstops are the "dumbbell" type (so-called because of the likeness of its cross-section to a dumbbell) and the labyrinth type (named for the multi-cell embedments on each side of the joint).

2-4.9.4 Membrane Waterproofing Materials. Asphalt coatings for membrane waterproofing are generally air-refined asphalts which conform to Type A and Type B as prescribed in the ASTM Standards. Type A asphalt is a soft, adhesive, "self-healing" asphalt which flows easily under the mop and which is suitable for use below ground level under uniformly moderate temperature conditions, both during the process of installation and during service. Type B asphalt is somewhat less susceptible to weathering and has good adhesive and "self-healing" properties for use above ground level where not exposed to temperatures above 125°F.

Concrete surfaces which are to be membrane waterproofed with asphalt material are usually primed with a bituminous sealing compound compatible with the asphalt coating. Where the concrete surface is to be cured with a curing compound, the bituminous type of concrete curing compound may be used and considered to serve as the primer.

Other types of waterproofing membranes include polyethylene sheets, asphalt-plastic panels, roofing felts, butyl-rubber sheeting, rubberized asphalt-coated polyethylene and asphalt membrane sheeting in rolls.

2-5 ASPHALT PAVING MATERIALS

2-5.1 General. This subsection covers the basic types of asphalts and their uses in public works construction; asphalt paving mixtures, and more importantly, asphalt paving mixture plant inspection (frequently referred to as "hot plant" inspection).

Most asphalts are obtained from the refining of selected petroleum crude oils and the heavier or more viscous portions of these crude oils are the asphalts.

Three basic types of asphalt are used in pavement construction and maintenance: paving asphalts, liquid asphalts and emulsified asphalts.

All asphalts are graded on the basis of consistency.

2-5.2 Paving Grade Asphalts. Paving grade asphalts are specified exclusively for all asphalt concrete paving on Agency projects and are derived exclusively from the bituminous residue resulting from the distillation of petroleum. They shall not contain any residues obtained in the distillation of coal or coal tar.

Paving asphalts are thermoplastic, which means that their consistency or fluidity is affected by changes in temperature. They are ductile and tacky and will adhere well to most aggregates. The various grades of paving asphalts were formerly classified by penetration: the higher the penetration values, the softer the asphalt. The penetration value is determined by a standard laboratory procedure of measuring the penetration of a standard blunt-pointed needle into a sample of asphalt at 77°F. when loaded with a 100-gram load for five seconds.

Paving asphalts for Agency use are now graded by viscosity rather than by penetration. The viscosity grades and qualifying tests, for use in paving mixtures, appears in the Standard Specifications. The viscosity is in "poise" units, a measure of absolute viscosity (the higher the number, the harder the asphalt) and is determined by a test that represents the condition of the asphalt on the street after the finish paving has cooled to 140°F. This is implied by the term "Aged Residue" (AR) as compared to the former penetration tests which were made on the asphalt before mixing and paving. Since paving asphalts cure in different ways, depending on their source, specifying the asphalt characteristics needed in the pavement rather than in the raw material should improve the quality and uniformity of paving mixes.

There are five nominal grades of viscosity asphalt: AR-1000, AR-2000, AR-4000, AR-8000 and AR-16000. Their use in Agency work is described in Subsection 2-5.5.

2-5.3 Liquid Asphalts. "Cutback" liquid asphalts are prepared by blending paving asphalt of the desired grade with a relatively volatile solvent such as naphtha, gasoline or kerosene. The primary purpose of the solvent is to reduce the consistency (viscosity) of the paving asphalt to a point where application and coating of aggregates may be made at relatively low temperatures. The solvent evaporates after a period of time, leaving the heavy asphalt to act as a binder in the mix. There are three types of cutback asphalts, known as rapid curing (RC), medium curing (MC) and slow curing (SC). Naphtha or gasoline is used to produce a rapid curing asphalt, while kerosene is used for producing a medium curing asphalt and relatively low volatile oils are used to produce slow curing asphalt. With cutbacks, the basic desire of the Engineer is to secure, at the end of a relatively short curing period, an adhesive having the properties of a paving grade asphalt.

The grades of all cutbacks are based on the amount of solvent in the mixture. For example, SC 70 has the most solvent and is very fluid in comparison with SC 3000.

In other liquid asphalt, an asphaltic residual oil, or a blend of such oil, is combined with a destillate that will not volatize readily. (These liquid asphalts are so fluid that their consistency cannot be measured at normal temperatures by means of the penetration test.) In the Western United States, it is graded by its viscosity and is designated by the lower limit of its kinematic viscosity measured in centistokes at 140°F. There are four grades of liquid asphalt: 70, 250, 800 and 3000 with the least viscous (most fluid) being Grade 70. The other grades increase in viscosity up to Grade 3000, the most viscous (thick, syrupy).

In addition to these gradings, descriptive titles are utilized within each grade to designate the types and rate of curing, so that SC (Slow Curing), MC (Medium Curing) or RC (Rapid Curing) can be specified in each of the four grades. The lightest grades (70s) are commonly used for penetration treatments and dust palliatives. The two intermediate grades (250s and 800s) are used extensively for cold-laid road mixes and stockpile mixes, with the choice between the two being dependent on job conditions. The heaviest grades (3000s) are used principally for seal coats.

2-5.4   Asphaltic Emulsions.   Emulsified asphalt is a suspension of asphalt in water. Its manufacture is accomplished by heating the asphalt to a liquid consistency, after which it is mixed or agitated with water in the presence of an emulsifier. During the mixing process the asphalt is divided into minute droplets or globules which are suspended in the water and prevented from recombining by the emulsifier. The emulsifier is usually some type of soap. To prevent possible injury to such emulsions, it is necessary to protect them from freezing.

The purpose of an emulsion is to permit the application of paving grade asphalts at normal atmospheric temperatures, without the necessity of heating, to obtain workable fluidity. There are two main types of emulsion based on the rate of separation of the asphalt from the emulsion. This separation depends on the amount of stabilizer used in the emulsion and the weather conditions prevailing when it is used. The two types are known as penetration grade and mixing grade emulsions. The penetration grade emulsions are rapid setting (rapid separation of the asphalt from the water) and are used as tack coats and seal coats.

Mixing grade emulsions are highly stabilized and the rate of separation is very slow. These slow setting emulsions permit the mixing of the emulsion with aggregates or soil prior to separation. The soil stabilizer grade of asphalt emulsion differs from the fine aggregate mixing grade in that the latter has a higher penetration value when the residue is tested in accordance with standard procedure. Mixing grade emulsions may be diluted with water.

Under ordinary circumstances, penetration grade emulsions should never be diluted with water as they will probably separate (break) prior to application.

2-5.5 **Asphalt Usage Guidelines.** In general, the uses of the various types and grades of asphalts (either separately or combined in mixtures with other ingredients) is influenced by type of construction, conditions of use (such as traffic loads and climatic conditions), construction methods and equipment, and economics.

The higher viscosity (harder) paving asphalts are favored for hotter climates. The slower curing liquid asphalts are generally used under the same conditions. Construction considerations, including the weather at the time of use as well as the methods and equipment, influence the grade and viscosity of the asphalt. The general uses for various types of asphalt are discussed below.

(a) **Dust Palliative.** Asphalt dust palliative in Agency work is normally used only on unimproved streets. A light application of asphalt used to bind fine surface particles together to minimize their displacement by wind or traffic is very effective, and minimizes the frequency of attention. SC-70, MC-70 or SS type emulsions are used for this purpose.

(b) **Prime Coat.** This is a spray application of a low viscosity asphalt on an untreated base preparatory to construction of the asphalt pavement or surface treatment.

For tightly bonded base asphalt courses laid in hot climates, MC-70 or SC-70 liquid asphalts are used.

For open bases, higher viscosities are preferred and recommended. In cooler climates, RC-250 will speed curing.

(c) **Tack Coat.** A very light spray application of asphalt on an existing paved surface will promote bond between this surface and the subsequent course. For this purpose, a diluted SS type emulsion is recommended. A light application of RC-70 liquid asphalt is also satisfactory. AR-1000 hot asphalt is used for spot applications.

(d) **Fog Seal.** A very light spray application of SS-1h emulsified asphalt diluted with water is used on existing pavement as a seal to minimize ravelling and to enrich the surface of a dried-out pavement.

(e) **Sand Seal.** A spray application of asphalt to an existing surface followed by a cover of sand, functions as a seal coat.

For hot climates, either MC-800, RC-800 liquid asphalt, or RS-1 or CRS-1 emulsion is used.

Lower viscosity and more rapid setting material should be used in cooler weather.

(f) **Chip Seal.** A spray application of asphalt to an existing surface, followed by a cover of rock chips or screenings, functions as a seal coat.

The asphalt used for chip seals must be fluid enough to wet and adhere to the chips and yet develop sufficient strength to bind the chips to the pavement and retain them under traffic conditions. RS-1, RS-2 or CRS-2 is recommended for hot climates and good drying conditions. RC-3000, CRS-1 or CRS-H2 is recommended for cooler climates.

If proper construction practice is followed, MC-3000 or paving asphalt AR-2000 grade may be successfully used in hot climates.

(g) **Slurry Seal.** A slurry mixture of SS type emulsified asphalt, sand and water applied to an existing surface and squeegeed into place serves as an effective seal coat. It is not recommended for city streets subject to heavy traffic. The slow-setting emulsions should be used. Specialized kinds of additives are available to enhance the quality of this material.

(h) **Penetration Treatment.** A spray application of liquid asphalt can be applied to an untreated granular roadway to form a light duty wearing course by penetrating and binding the in situ roadway material.

The type and grade of asphalt should be selected to fit the climatic conditions and the gradations of the material in the roadway. SC-250 or MC-250 may be used for this purpose.

(i) **Waterproofing.** Air-refined asphalts are extensively used in the roofing industry and in connection with joint sealing, sub-surface sealing and waterproofing of concrete structures where it is necessary to insure minimum change in the asphalt consistency with temperature changes. Air-refined asphalts are produced by blowing air through a selected stock derived from the distillation of crude oil. The purpose of this process is to change the thermoplastic characteristics of this material. The change in consistency of this asphalt with variations in ambient temperatures is materially reduced by this process. However, this advantage is partially offset by the loss in ductile properties which causes the asphalt to become brittle in cold weather. Therefore, air-refined asphalts are not used for pavement mixtures.

(j) **Asphalt Concrete.** Asphalt concrete is used wherever high quality paving is required such as for major highways and city streets. It is also commonly used for parking lots, driveways and other paved areas.

It is mixed in a central plant, using heated aggregates and paving asphalt, and laid with paving machines or spreaders and compacted with rollers to obtain the required densification. The paving grade asphalts and their uses in aggregate mixtures are as follows:

AR-1000	Normally not used in Agency paving (used for Tack Coat-Spot Application).
AR-2000	Asphalt concrete paving mixes used in cold climates; hand laid or thin edged sections; and trench resurfacing.
AR-4000	Asphalt concrete base and wearing surface mixes for residential streets and alleys.

AR-8000   Asphalt concrete base and wearing surface
             mixes used on major streets; extruded curb;
             and on hillside residential streets and other
             locations where more stability and quicker
             set are required.

AR-16000   Not generally available. Can be used for ex-
             truded curbs or berms where fast hard set is
             required; parking areas subject to extensive
             turning movement by heavy vehicles; and
             industrial floors.

2-5.6 Asphalt Concrete Paving Mixtures. A properly
designed asphalt paving mixture should reflect the consideration of six desirable properties: stability, durability, flexibility,
skid resistance, imperviousness and workability.

The amount of asphalt that should be incorporated in the
mix should be as much as possible to provide a water resistant
flexible pavement but not so much that the stability is reduced
below the value necessary to support the loads involved. Insufficient asphalt in the mix exposes the pavement to water intrusion and ravelling, and too much asphalt in the mix produces
bleeding and instability.

The asphalt content of the mix is a function of the surface
area, roughness and absorptive qualities of the aggregate as
well as the type of asphalt used. Mixes containing finer aggregate gradations and using the higher viscosity asphalts will
tolerate larger amounts of asphalt.

The harder asphalts are recommended for major streets in
urban areas and for parking lots and the relatively warmer
climatic conditions.

There are a number of ways to determine the proportions
of asphalt and aggregate to be used in a mix: from experience;
soils theory or surface area theory; and by test. In actuality, all
three must be involved to some extent. The initial mix design
determination usually involves a combination of the second and
third methods. At the time of production, some adjustment of
the mix may be necessary. The Plant Inspector may, from observation of the full load batches, increase the asphalt in the
mix if it appears to be "dry" or decrease the asphalt if the mix
looks too "wet."

Laboratory tests of the plant mix and the in-place pavement are utilized to evaluate the acceptability of materials, the
effectiveness of quality control procedures and construction
methods employed.

The Agency provides "start-up" batch weights for its regularly used paving mixes at each plant serving Agency projects. This permits the plant to begin operations each day without delay. These weights are then adjusted to reflect the hot bin screen analysis which is performed by the Inspector as soon as possible after plant operations begin. Typical "start-up" mixes in the format issued by the Agency to the plant operator are shown in Plate 11, Appendix. These batch weights will vary from plant to plant as may be reflected by the differences in the aggregates. Refer to Subsection 2-6 for further details regarding asphalt plant inspection operations.

(Editor's Note: Some jurisdictions do not provide inspection at the asphalt plant, but require the Contractor [or producer] to furnish and guarantee materials that conform to the specifications. However, this subsection may help the reader to better understand the basic procedures for producing acceptable asphalt pavement materials.)

2-6 ASPHALT PLANT INSPECTION

2-6.1 General. The quality, appearance and durability of asphalt pavement construction depends more on the plant operation, and particularly upon the Plant Inspector, than any other individual concerned with its construction. He must have the right of free access to such parts of the plant as are concerned with the production of materials for any project. His work must be properly performed before anyone else in the series of construction operations can satisfactorily accomplish his work.

This subsection will deal only with the batch mix type plant inspection and operations. Although other types of plants, such as continuous mix plants, are capable of producing quality paving mixes, the batch mix plant is considered more flexible to accommodate the varying needs of Agency projects in types of mixes and quantities of material.

2-6.2 Field Communication Procedure. Close liaison is necessary between the Plant and Project Inspectors. When the Inspector at the jobsite detects changes in grading, temperature or bitumen content in a bituminous mixture, such information must be quickly relayed by telephone to the Plant Inspector so that immediate investigation is possible and the necessary corrections made.

The "Plant Inspector's Report to Field Inspector," illustrated on the following page, is to be used as a standard means

City of Anywhere
DEPARTMENT OF PUBLIC WORKS
Bureau or Contract Administration
PLANT INSPECTOR'S REPORT
TO FIELD INSPECTOR

INSTRUCTIONS TO PLANT INSPECTOR:
Fill out, attach to load! ticket and send to Field Inspector with first load!

PLANT NAME _Valley Asphalt materials_ DATE

PLANT LOCATION _San Gabriel_

FOR CONCRETE MIXTURES:

CLASS OF CONCRETE	SOURCE OF ROCK
BRAND OF CEMENT TYPE	SOURCE OF SAND
BRAND OF ADMIXTURE	AMOUNT OF ADMIXTURE PER BACK

FOR BITUMINOUS MIXTURES:

TYPE OF MIX _1_   GRADING _B_

PENETRATION OF ASPHALT _AR 4000_   SOURCE OF BITUMEN _Black Oil Co._

PLANT INSPECTOR _Frank Jones_

REMARKS _Running tomorrow?_

FRONT

INSTRUCTIONS TO FIELD INSPECTOR: FILL OUT REVERSE SIDE AND RETURN TO PLANT INSPECTOR IMMEDIATELY.

INSTRUCTIONS TO FIELD INSPECTOR:
Fill out this side and return to Plant Inspector immediately.

JOB TITLE _Wheat St & Miller Ave ID_

JOB NO _C-4/523_   LETTER CODE _DA & E & BC_   SPECIFICATIONS _NO. 170_

CONCRETE (ASPHALT) USED FOR _Base Course for Streets_

GALLONS WATER ADDED AT JOB

FIELD INSPECTOR _C. F. Smith_

NOTES: _Will need Approx. 800 Tons 1C - 85/100 tomorrow._

BACK

of daily communication between Plant and Field Inspection personnel to insure that the material produced for the project is as required for the work, that the material is being produced and placed in the presence of an Inspector, and to provide information to the Plant Inspector for time-reporting procedures. [See Subsection 3-4.3.4(b).] Instructions on the form clearly define its use and disposition. A separate form will be prepared by the Plant Inspector in the event that the type of bituminous mixture is changed during the course of a day's operation. (See opposite page)

2-6.3 Plant Equipment and Operation.

2-6.3.1 **General.** Asphalt batch plants (See Plate 47, Appendix) must be approved by the Agency prior to producing paving mixtures for Agency projects. The Supervisor, Materials Control Group or his assistant, must inspect the plant layout, equipment and storage facilities for conformity with the Standard Specifications. Production operations and the ability of the plant to produce paving mixtures of consistent quality and uniformity is evaluated from observation and tests.

Important operations to be evaluated are:

(a) Cold feed gates and overflow of aggregate in cold aggregate bins.

(b) Temperatures of hot aggregates, asphalt and mixture.

(c) Gradation of hot bin aggregate and its fluctuation during the day.

(d) Dryer operation.

(e) Batching and mixing operations.

(f) Mixture uniformity.

The various aspects of these operations are discussed in the subsections that follow.

2-6.3.2 **Field Laboratory.** The producer of bituminous pavement mixtures must furnish and equip a field laboratory for use by the Plant Inspector in accordance with the Standard Specifications. This facility is one of the requirements the plant must meet before it can be approved to furnish materials. The Inspectors for other agencies are permitted reasonable use of the field laboratory, provided they perform a commensurate portion of the housekeeping work and do not loiter or hinder the Inspector in the performance of his work. Any lack of cooperation in this respect must be reported to the Supervisor of the Materials Control Group, who will take necessary steps to remedy the situation.

2-6.3.3   Cold Aggregate Storage.   The Plant Inspector must frequently check the stockpiles of different sized aggregate to insure that they are kept separated in a manner that will preclude intermingling of the aggregates. Separation can best be accomplished by installing bulkheads between stockpiles or by placing the various sizes of aggregate in separate bins.

From a screen analysis of the primary sizes of aggregate in the storage bins, the Plant Inspector determines how much of each size must be fed to the cold feed conveyor belt to keep the plant in balance. (See Subsection 2-6.3.14.) Screening of the various cold storage bins is done primarily to ascertain that the materials on hand can be blended to a combined grading that will meet the job specifications. This is usually done only where a new source of materials or a new aggregate mixture is to be used. If one aggregate is accidentally mixed with other sized aggregates, or if an aggregate is carelessly dumped by a truck driver or crane operator into the wrong bin, or if the mobile equipment is operated in such a manner as to crush and grind the aggregate on the bin slab, the bins will be contaminated with outsized materials. This results in an erratic grading of the aggregates being fed from storage bins onto the cold feed belt.

2-6.3.4   Cold Feed.   The majority of the problems that occur in the dryer, on the plant screens or in the plant bins can be eliminated, or at least minimized, by controlling the uniformity of the cold feed. The Inspector must be alert to detect intermingling of the aggregate in the stockpiles, segregation of the material within a stockpile, degradation of the aggregate due to abusive or careless handling by equipment, non-uniform feed from the stockpiles to the cold feed belt, or a stoppage in the feeders.

In general, feeders from storage bins are the gravity type, but sand has a natural tendency to arch in a feed chute, especially when damp. To overcome this tendency, the shape of the feeder chute is made rectangular, since arching of damp sand is less in a rectangular opening than in a circular or square opening. In addition, a vibrator is often installed on the side of the chute to minimize this possibility. Most plants use a small belt feeder equipped with a variable speed motor to feed the sand onto the main cold feed belt.

The Plant Inspector must watch out for variations in the gradation of aggregate fed to the plant, which can be troublesome. Erratic feeding of fines to the cold feed would result in layers of variable grading in the fine bin of the plant. This could lead to alternate "wet" and "dry" batches of the pavement mix because the asphalt demand would vary as the gradation of the fine aggregate varies, due to the difference in surface area of the particles to be coated (See Subsection 2-6.3.16).

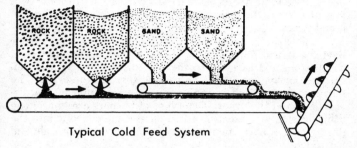

Typical Cold Feed System

When the total amount of aggregate in the cold feed varies, shortages and overages in the hot bins of the plant can result, caused by lack of aggregates being fed or unnecessary carry-over on overloaded screens. When the cold feed is in balance, it will sustain the hot storage bins with a supply of classified and heated aggregates sufficient to enable the repeated batching of the designed mixture. It will result in adequate bin levels of hot materials without having the difficulty of some bins discharging excess material through overflow chutes while other bins are running empty or "starved." When the bin levels of heated materials are properly maintained, no incentive exists for the mixer operator to "substitute bins;" that is, to take extra material from a full bin in substitution for the correct material which is momentarily in short supply. This is an undesirable practice, usually resulting in a variation of the mix.

A variation in the cold feed can cause fluctuation in the temperature of the aggregate going through the dryer and cause an overload in the dust collector system which will reduce the draft through the dryer. Reduced draft also adversely affects the aggregate temperature in the dryer. For these reasons, it can be readily understood that the cold feed is extremely important in the control of asphaltic paving mixtures.

The percentage by weight of each primary aggregate size to be fed to the cold feed belt is given to the plant operator as a guide, and it is his responsibility to adjust the flow (in pounds per minute) to produce the aggregate blend at the rate desired (usually maximum plant capacity).

2-6.3.5 Drying Aggregates. The cold feed usually discharges into a bucket elevator which lifts the aggregate to dryer. (See Plate 47, Appendix.) The purpose of a dryer is two-fold: to remove the moisture from the aggregate being fed into it and to heat the aggregate to the desired mixing temperature.

A dryer is essentially a continuously rotating cylinder having a series of lifting flights which pick up the material from the bottom and carry it to the top, discharging it in a veil through hot gasses and flame passing through the dryer. The burners, firebox and heating controls are located at the discharge end of the dryer. Two types of burners are in use: one utilizing steam to atomize a fuel oil and introduce it into the dryer, and a more common type using low-pressure air and natural gas.

The problems which commonly originate in the dryer are overheating, insufficient heating of the aggregate or fluctuation in the temperature of the aggregate. The principal causes for these problems are usually found in the cold feed. Moisture variation in the cold aggregate, feed variations, exceeding the dryer capacity or change in the character of the material being fed are contributing factors. Additional problems are caused by overcontrol of the dryer flame by the fireman, insufficient draft, incomplete atomization of the fuel, insufficient air for proper fuel combustion and an inaccurate heat-indicating device at the outlet chute of the dryer. Crowding excessive aggregate into the dryer beyond its capacity, particularly in the winter when aggregates may be wet, cannot be permitted by the Plant Inspector. In such cases, only the surfaces of rock particles are dried and heated, and the internal moisture and relatively low temperature at the center of the particle is virtually unaffected by the dryer. This moisture migrates to the surface and causes the asphalt-coated materials to become unacceptable. The condition is most readily discovered as the material leaves the mixer and is deposited in the truck. The color of the mix will quickly change to a dull, flat appearance, and the mix simultaneously undergoes a significant drop in temperature, usually to the extent that it is not hot enough to be acceptable for laying on the street.

Improper balance of air in the dryer will result in "puff-back," or black smoke being emitted from the stack. Puff-back results from a momentary back pressure because there is insufficient draft air for the volume of combustion air being introduced into the dryer. The most common cause of black smoke is insufficient secondary air in the dryer with which the fuel oil must combine to obtain complete combustion. These problems can be readily solved by reducing the amount of fuel being used or increasing the amount of air in the system.

To the Plant Inspector, black smoke coming from the stack of a dryer indicates an unsatisfactory situation in that the unburned fuel oil is not only being wasted out of the stack, but is also coating the aggregate particles. Fuel oil is a natural asphalt solvent, and if it clings to the aggregate in sufficient quantity, it prevents the asphalt from properly coating the particles during the mixing operation.

The temperature at which the aggregate leaves the dryer is extremely important. Excessive heating of the aggregate will materially reduce the service life of the bituminous mixture. If the aggregate temperature is too low, it is difficult to uniformly coat the particles and the mixture may be too cold to lay and compact properly on the street. For this reason, it is essential that a reliable heat-indicating device be installed at the outlet end of the dryer to register the aggregate temperature. This device is probably the most important single element in plant control and must be checked frequently by the Plant Inspector.

2-6.3.6 **Dust Collection System.** The purpose of the dust collection system is two-fold. First, it serves to collect the fine aggregate particles floating about in the dryer and other parts of the plant and, secondly, the blower for the dust collector is used to provide the draft which carries the flame through the dryer. The fine material in suspension in the air stream is collected in the bottom of a conical container (called a cyclone), where it is returned in a continuous manner to the hot elevator pit to be combined with the heated aggregates being elevated to the classifying screens. The amount of 200-mesh material permitted to be derived from the contents of the hot sand storage bin is limited, so the dust collector must have means of wasting the excess collected materials. Problems which occur in the dust collecting system are: insufficient capacity of the blower, a fouled damper or a choking-off in the duct system. Insufficient blower capacity can result from a partially blocked-off air intake screen, belt slippage on the fan or from the fan motor not performing properly. A damper fouled with an accumulation of dust will not open properly and will reduce the volume of air in the system.

The most common problem arises from condensation or "sweating" of the moisture in the air on the cold cyclone walls. It is more common for this to occur with very wet aggregates or when the plant is first started in the morning. Excessive condensation may cause the collected fines to turn to mud, which will completely plug the cyclone outlet. This condition will be evident from absence of dust flowing from the outlet. To control sweating, the Plant Inspector must insist that the rate of cold feed be reduced until the sweating stops. The cold feed can be gradually increased as the plant "warms up."

2-6.3.7 Smog and Air Pollution Control. From the foregoing paragraphs, it can readily be seen that an asphalt plant may be a major contributor to air pollution. The Plant Inspector should be alert to cause immediate remedies to be taken to control black smoke emission or excessive dust. (Many jurisdictions, such as Los Angeles County, require asphalt plants to burn natural gas in the dryer to comply with the smog control regulations.)

2-6.3.8 Classifying Screens. After the aggregate leaves the drier, it is elevated to the screen deck of the plant and deposited on the classifying screens. (See Plate 47, Appendix.) These must be of the flat, woven wire, vibrating type, with a vibration rate between 850 and 1000 cycles per minute. The size and type of screen for each hot storage bin is delineated in the Standard Specifications.

The screens must be regularly inspected to insure that they are clean and that the openings are not plugged or "blinded" by particles stuck in them. If these openings become plugged, the effective screening area is considerably reduced, causing material to bypass then bin it should enter and be carried over to the bin of the next larger size material. Conversely, holes worn in the screens permit oversize particles to enter bins for which they are not intended.

If either condition exists, the uniformity of the aggregate gradation which is stressed so much in bituminous pavement mixtures is, to a large extent, lost. The Plant Inspector suddenly finds that besides having fine material in the sand bin, he also has an undetermined amount in the next size aggregate bin. Since he has provided only for the withdrawal of a pre-determined size particle from one bin, any additional material of the same size coming from another bin will obviously upset the proportions of the aggregates in the mix. This will alter the grading of the mix, result in the loss of control of the feeding of the plant and degrade the quality of production in general.

The plants accepted for use by the Agency will have classifying screens adequate for normal plant operation, based on the rate at which material would pass over them to sustain the mixing periods specified. However, if more material is crowded onto the screen deck than the screen is capable of accommodating, for even short periods of time, it will result in carry-over and excessive bin contamination. Almost all plants are able to produce any mix specified, using the classifying screens called for in the Standard Specifications.

Uniform classifying characteristics of the screens over the various hot storage bins is possible only when the flow over the screens is uniform. The most efficient plant production occurs when the job mix formula (See Subsection 2-6.3.14) is accurate enough that the hot storage bins are supplied with materials at all times, the cold aggregates are fed to the dryer in accordance with the mix formula, and the material from the hot storage bins is used at a steady rate.

Other factors that can affect the efficiency and capacity of a screen deck are worn screens and the speed and direction of rotation of the eccentric shaft that vibrates the screens.

The batching and mixing operations reach their highest degree of efficiency only when all conditions are favorable.

2-6.3.9 Hot Aggregate Bins. One of the best indicators of the capability of a plant to produce uniform high quality paving mixes is in the consistency of the material in the hot bins. This can be determined from a comparison of screen analyses of their content on a regular basis.

It is important to see that the overflow vent in each bin is clear and functioning so that the material in one bin cannot flow into an adjacent bin. Intermingling of the aggregate sizes can also occur if for any reason a hole should develop in the partition separating two bins. Holes can develop from abrasion, failure of a weld seam or be deliberately cut by the operator in an attempt to balance materials in the bins. For these reasons, aggregate bins must be inspected frequently by the Plant Inspector.

Other problems develop from the tendency of fines to hang up in the corners of bins. This results in "slugging" a batch when this material lets go and overcharges the sand fraction in the weigh hopper. In turn, this results in too high a percentage of fines in the mix and yields a lean batch. Welding fillets in the corners of the bins and keeping the level of the material in the bin high will minimize this problem. Worn gates at the bottom of the bin may allow leakage of aggregate into the weigh hopper after the gate is closed. This poses a serious problem and must be corrected.

A natural phenomenon of any screening operation on a flat deck is that, in the direction of the flow of material over the screens, the finer particles will fall to the near side of the bin while the coarser particles fall to the far side, gradually changing from fine to coarse across each bin. The Plant Inspector should be careful to take samples across the entire discharge chute to get representative samples. This is of greatest importance in the case of the fine aggregate, since this material has the greatest surface area and the greatest asphalt demand.

2-6.3.10   The Weigh Hopper. The weigh hopper must be so oriented with relation to the mixer as to cause the complete and homogeneous blending of the various particle size groups of heated materials in the mixer. Any lack of uniform blending and distribution, particularly of the sand, must be corrected immediately. Changing the order in which the various materials are drawn from the hot storage bins into the weigh hopper will usually correct the problem.

Under most conditions, the coarse aggregate would be withdrawn first, followed by the middle-sized aggregate, then the sand. Under no circumstances should the sand be withdrawn first, for it would obviously be the first material to leave the weigh hopper and would fall directly to the bottom of the pugmill. If the pugmill paddles were worn and had excessive clearance, the sand could lie in a dead area beyond the reach of the paddle tips and never be mixed.

2-6.3.11   Asphalt Weigh-Bucket. All weighing devices, including the bitumen weigh-bucket, must be carefully inspected to insure independent suspension, clean knife edges and proper functioning of the other linkage and fulcrum components. No rocks or other foreign matter should be permitted to accumulate in the area of the scales. If a rock falls in the collecting cone under the weigh-bucket, it can partially support the bucket and result in over-weight of the bitumen without the scales indicating excessive weight.

2-6.3.12 The Pugmill Timer. The Standard Specifications require a device to indicate the length of time the material is mixed in the pugmill. Most plants are equipped with devices which start the timing cycle immediately upon opening the weigh hopper gate to charge the pugmill. It takes approximately five seconds or more for all the material to fall from the weigh hopper into the pugmill and this time should be taken into account in the total mixing time.

The time-lock for the mixer is the "governor" of the plant. By its very nature it establishes the rhythm of the operations described above. However, the mixer operator may trip the switch which controls it in an effort to "beat" the mixing time. This will upset the rhythmic production of heated aggregates and throw the whole plant operation into an unbalanced condition. The cold feed becomes erratic, the flow of materials over the classifying screens lacks uniformity, the materials in the hot bins vary as to sieve analysis, the mix being produced is not homogeneous, and the entire plant operation is unsatisfactory.

2-6.3.13 Mixing. The Standard Specifications establish fixed lengths of time for mixing, and this mixing cycle is intended to insure a homogeneous aggregate mixture. If, in the opinion of the Inspector, the mixture is not thoroughly blended and if the aggregate is not fully coated with asphalt, the mixing time shall be increased.

The pugmill mixer has but one function: to mix the materials introduced into it. However, some problems can develop if it is not properly maintained. Excessive wear on the paddles may cause a dead space to occur adjacent to the pugmill shell where the material will not become properly mixed. This condition is easily detected by the Plant Inspector when the pugmill gates are opened to discharge the material into the truck. The first material will be light in color, resulting from a deficiency in asphalt because of lack of proper mixing.

A similar condition occurs if the pugmill is overloaded. The material above the tips of the pugmill paddles has a tendency to float above that level and never get thoroughly mixed.

The Plant Inspector should check for leakage from the discharge gates of the pugmill mixer. In addition, the asphalt distribution system should have no leakage occur after the valve is closed. The seals on the ends of the pugmill shaft should be inspected for leakage of asphalt and repaired by the producer, if warranted.

Another duty of the Plant Inspector is to check the truck beds for excess diesel oil or distillate used to prevent the bituminous mixture from sticking. Excess oil must be drained before the truck is loaded, by raising the bed with the tailgate open.

During truck loading, the Inspector should observe the material being loaded for evidences of insufficient mixing time, improper aggregate grading, poor distribution of asphalt across the pugmill, insufficient or excessive aggregate temperature, and worn pugmill paddles.

2-6.3.14 Job Mix Formula. The job mix formula is usually developed at the discretion of the Supervisor of the Materials Control Group and will include such information as: date, job title and number, contractor's name, producer's name and plant location, sources of the various materials (primary aggregates, filler and bitumen), belt-feed proportions required to sustain the batching operation for the specified mix, tentative box weights upon which to commence batching operations and required mixing time per batch.

Plant Inspectors and personnel employed by the producers are familiar with the aggregate sources, their characteristics and the proportions required for various asphalt mixes. "Start-up" batch weights are provided at plants that frequently produce bituminous mixtures for Agency work (See Subsection 2-5.6 and Plate 11, Appendix).

However, batch weights for each mix must be developed if a plant is new or has not been used on Agency work for a prolonged period. Going first to the primary aggregate cold storage bins, the Plant Inspector must take representative samples of all available aggregates for which there may be a need in the proposed mix. A sieve analysis is then made from the samples.

The Inspector next determines the sizes and proportions of aggregates needed in order to meet the specified mix grading. Ability to do this efficiently generally comes through increased experience. It is done by a trial-and-error mathematical procedure, an example of which begins on the next page.

On Chart No. 1 (appearing on next page), the percentages entered on the horizontal lines marked "A" are from the Inspector's sieve analysis of the samples taken from the cold storage bins. These quantities are multiplied by the decimal fractions on lines marked "B" which represent the trial percentages entered in the horizontal spaces across the top of the chart labeled "Percent to Cold Feed." Each product is entered on line "C" and represents the net percentage to feed. All the entries on the several lines marked on "C" are added horizontally to yield the "Combined Analysis Percent." These quantities must fall within the "Specification Limits" shown in the columns at the right side of the chart.

When the available primary aggregate sizes are fed to the belt in the proportions shown as "Percent to Cold Feed," the resulting aggregate mixture entering the dryer should closely approximate the "Ideal" gradings shown. (See next page)

The Inspector then takes a sample from each hot aggregate storage bin after the materials have passed through the dryer and the classifying screens. (See Plate 47, Appendix.) After making a separate sieve analysis of each sample, the percentages obtained are entered as whole numbers in the appropriate places on the horizontal lines marked "A."

For the purpose of demonstration, it will be assumed that for a first trial the aggregates will be proportioned as follows:

> 8% from the No. 4 bin (¾″)
> 38% from the No. 3 bin (½″)
> 22% from the No. 2 bin (⅜″)
> 30% from the No. 1 bin (sand)
> 2% from the filler silo

These percentages are entered in the appropriate places on the horizontal line entitled "% of Mix" on the Tentative Batch Proportions form (Chart No. 2, below), and the decimal fraction representing each of these percentages is entered on all lines marked "B". (Example: 8% becomes .08.)

Each number shown on line "A" is then multiplied by the decimal fraction below it on line "B", and the product is entered

CHART NO. 1 — COLD BELT FEED FOR ASPHALTIC CONCRETE — C2 GRADING

PRIMARY AGGREGATES		3/4"	1/2"	3/8" PEA-GRAVEL	COARSE SAND	FINE SAND	COMMERCIAL FILLER	COMBINED ANALYSIS	SPECIFICATION LIMITS		
PERCENT TO COLD FEED		6%	26%	26%	20%	20%	2%	PERCENT	MIN.	IDEAL	MAX.
3/4" SCREEN	A	100	100	100	100	100	100	100.0		100	100
% (dec. frac.)	B	.06	.26	.26	.20	.20	.02				
NET % FEED	C	6	26	26	20	20	2.0				
1/2" SCREEN	A	95	87	100	100	100	100	96.3	95	97.5	100
% (dec. frac.)	B	.06	.26	.26	.20	.20	.02				
NET % FEED	C	5.7	22.6	26	20	20	2.0				
3/8" SCREEN	A	4	51	95	100	100	100	80.2	72	80	88
% (dec. frac.)	B	.06	.26	.26	.20	.20	.02				
NET % FEED	C	.2	13.3	24.7	20	20	2.0				
NO. 4 SCREEN	A	2	1	41	100	100	100	53.1	46	53	60
% (dec. frac.)	B	.06	.26	.26	.20	.20	.02				
NET % FEED	C	.12	.3	10.7	20	20	2.0				
NO. 8 SCREEN	A			1	89	78	100	35.6	28	35	42
% (dec. frac.)	B			.26	.20	.20	.02				
NET % FEED	C			.2	17.8	15.6	2.0				
NO. 30 SCREEN	A				58	42	100	22.0	15	21	27
% (dec. frac.)	B				.20	.20	.02				
NET % FEED	C				11.6	8.4	2.0				
NO. 50 SCREEN	A				28	30	100	13.6	10	15	20
% (dec. frac.)	B				.20	.20	.02				
NET % FEED	C				5.6	6.0	2.0				
NO. 200 SCREEN	A				6	12	90	5.4	2	4.5	7
% (dec. frac.)	B				.20	.20	.02				
NET % FEED	C				1.2	2.4	1.8				

PERCENT PASSING

CHART NO. 2 (First Trial) — TENTATIVE BATCH PROPORTIONS — C2 GRADING
Plant rated capacity — 4000 Lbs. — Liquid Asphalt 5.4%

PERCENT PASSING

Bin No.		Rock #4	Rock #3	Rock #2	Sand #1	Commercial Filler	Combined Grading	Spec. Min.	Spec. Ideal	Spec. Max.
% of Mix		8%	38%	22%	30%	2%				
3/4" Screen		100	100	100	100	100	100	100	100	
1/2" Screen	A	50	100	100	100	100				
	B	.08	.38	.22	.30	.02				
	C	4	38	22	30	2	96.0	95	97.5	100
3/8" Screen	A	4	58	100	100	100				
	B	.08	.38	.22	.30	.02				
	C	.3	22	22	30	2	76.3	72	80	88
No. 4 Screen	A		4	65	100	100				
	B		.38	.22	.30	.02				
	C		1.4	14.3	30	2	47.7	46	53	60
No. 8 Screen	A			4	98	100				
	B			.22	.30	.02				
	C			.8	29.4	2	32.2	28	35	42
No. 30 Screen	A				58	100				
	B				.30	.02				
	C				17.4	2	19.4	15	21	27
No. 50 Screen	A				40	100				
	B				.30	.02				
	C				12.0	2	14.0	10	15	20
No. 200 Screen	A				10	90				
	B				.30	.02				
	C				3	1.80	4.8	2	4.5	7

Key: A = % Screen; B = (dec. frac.); C = Net % Feed. Specification Limits columns: Min., Ideal, Max.

BITUMINOUS PAVING MATERIALS BATCH MIXING PLANT
(SCHEMATIC ONLY — NOT TO SCALE)

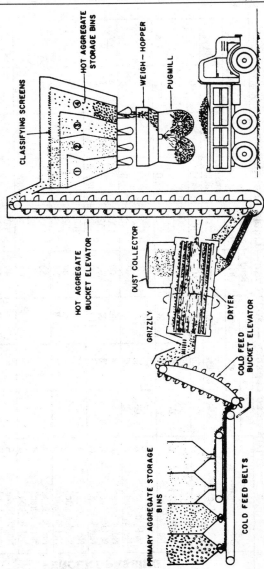

on line "C." The entries on each line marked "C" are added horizontally and the sum is listed under the column headed "Combined Grading."

A comparison of these combined grading values with the corresponding "Ideal" grading figures under "Specification Limits" will show that, although this trial mix is above the minimum limits, it is somewhat low on coarse aggregate and high in the small aggregate sizes. An adjustment of proportions for a better balance is illustrated in Chart No. 3 which follows Chart No. 2 shown on page 153.

To achieve better balance, a second trial mix is attempted after reducing the "% of Mix" by three percent in Bins 3 and 4 and simultaneously increasing Bins 1 and 2 by three percent. This is shown in Chart No. 3 on page 156.

The entries on lines "B" and "C" are adjusted and recalculated and the form completed as before. It will be noted that the entries in the "Combined Grading" column now very closely approximate an ideal grading, particularly in the numbered screen sizes.

It is good practice to set the total of sand and filler from two to three percent under the ideal grading desired. This will allow for the generation of a small amount of fines from the dry mixing in the pugmill as well as for carryover of some sand from the classifying screens into the No. 2 Bin.

With a known plant pugmill capacity of 4000 pounds, the batch weights can now be computed. Depending upon the procedure utilized by the plant, these weights can be "inside" or "outside" weights. This means that the weight of the required liquid asphalt (bitumen) is included in the total of 4000 pounds for "inside" weights, and added to the total of 4000 pounds when "outside" weights are used. Both of these weights are included in Chart No. 3 on page 156. The calculations on the following page show how these quantities were derived.

CHART NO. 3 (Second Trial) — FINAL BATCH PROPORTIONS — C2 GRADING
Plant rated capacity — 4000 Lbs. — Liquid Asphalt 5.4%

Bin No.			Rock		Sand	Commercial Filler	Combined Grading	Specification Limits		
		#4	#3	#2	#1			Min.	Ideal	Max.
"Outside" box weights		200 Lbs.	1400 Lbs.	1000 Lbs.	1320 Lbs.	80 Lbs.				
"Inside" box weights		189 Lbs.	1324 Lbs.	946 Lbs.	1249 Lbs.	76 Lbs.				
% of Mix		5%	35%	25%	33%	2%				
3/4" Screen		100	100	100	100	100	100	100	100	
1/2" Screen	A	50	100	100	100	100				
% (dec. frac.)	B	.05	.35	.25	.33	.02		95	97.5	100
Net % Feed	C	2.5	35	25	33	2	97.5			
3/8" Screen	A	4	58	100	100	100				
% (dec. frac.)	B	.05	.35	.25	.33	.02		72	80	88
Net % Feed	C	.2	20.3	25	33	2	80.5			
No. 4 Screen	A		4	65	100	100				
% (dec. frac.)	B		.35	.25	.33	.02		46	53	60
Net % Feed	C		1.4	16.3	33	2	52.7			
No. 8 Screen	A			4	98	100				
% (dec. frac.)	B			.25	.33	.02		28	35	42
Net % Feed	C			1	32.3	2	35.3			
No. 30 Screen	A				58	100				
% (dec. frac.)	B				.33	.02		15	21	27
Net % Feed	C				19.1	2	21.1			
No. 50 Screen	A				40	100				
% (dec. frac.)	B				.33	.02		10	15	20
Net % Feed	C				13.2	2	15.2			
No. 200 Screen	A				10	90				
% (dec. frac.)	B				.33	.02		2	4.5	7
Net % Feed	C				3.3	1.80	5.1			

PERCENT PASSING

(a) Computation of "Outside" Batch Weights. Total Weight of Batch = Aggregate (94.6%) + Asphalt (5.4%)

$$W = \frac{4000}{.946} = 4,228 \text{ lbs. Total Weight of Batch}$$

Then 5.4% of 4,228 lbs. = 228 lbs. Bitumen

Check:

$$
\begin{aligned}
\text{Aggregate} &= 4228 \times 94.6\% &=& 4000 \text{ lbs.} \\
\text{Bitumen} &= 4228 \times 5.4\% &=& 228 \text{ lbs.} \\
\cline{1-4}
& 100.0\% &=& 4228 \text{ lbs.}
\end{aligned}
$$

Proportions from line entitled "% of Mix" on Chart No. 3, using decimal equivalents:

Bin No. 4 = $4000 \times .05$ = 200 lbs.
Bin No. 3 = $4000 \times .35$ = 1400 lbs.
Bin No. 2 = $4000 \times .25$ = 1000 lbs.
Bin No. 1 = $4000 \times .33$ = 1320 lbs.
Filler   = $4000 \times .02$ =   80 lbs.

Total Weight of Aggregate = 4000 lbs.
Bitumen = $4228 \times .054$ = 228 lbs.

Total Weight of Batch = 4228 lbs.

(b) Computation of "Inside" Batch Weights. Inside batch weights are computed with the 5.4 percent bitumen inside of a total batch weight of 4000 pounds. The total weight of aggregate is calculated as follows:

$$
\begin{aligned}
\text{Bitumen} &= 5.4\% \text{ of total weight of batch} \\
\text{Aggregate} &= 94.6\% \text{ of total weight of batch} \\
\text{Total Weight of Batch} &= 4000 \text{ lbs.} \\
&\quad \text{(rated capacity of} \\
&\quad \text{pugmill)}
\end{aligned}
$$

Using decimal equivalents:

$$
\begin{aligned}
\text{Bitumen} &= 4000 \times .054 &=& 216 \text{ lbs.} \\
\text{Aggregate} &= 4000 \times .946 &=& 3784 \text{ lbs.} \\
\cline{1-4}
& && 4000 \text{ lbs.}
\end{aligned}
$$

Proportions from line entitled "% of Mix" on Chart No. 3, using decimal equivalents:

Bin No. 4 = $3784 \times .05$ = 189 lbs.
Bin No. 3 = $3784 \times .35$ = 1324 lbs.
Bin No. 2 = $3784 \times .25$ = 946 lbs.
Bin No. 1 = $3784 \times .33$ = 1249 lbs.
Filler   = $3784 \times .02$ =   76 lbs.

Total Weight of Aggregate = 3784 lbs.
Bitumen = 4000×0.54 = 216 lbs.

Total Weight of Batch = 4000 lbs.

2-6.3.15 **Asphalt Content.** The asphalt content of asphalt concrete mixtures is specified within general limits in the Standard Specifications. The Plant Inspector must hold the liquid asphalt content in the job mix within a narrow range to suit the actual characteristics and gradation of the aggregate. An excess of asphalt is not beneficial. It is usually detrimental in that it can result in the liquid asphalt "bleeding" to the surface and otherwise contribute to instability in the pavement mixture. Insufficient asphalt results in lack of cohesion between the aggregate particles. This causes ravelling, increases susceptibility of the pavement to water erosion and contributes to early structural failure.

Once the first screen analysis of the hot bins is made and the job mix batch weights have been adjusted from the "start up" weights (see Subsection 2-5.6), the problems described above develop if hot bin material fluctuates, especially in the #1 bin and to a lesser extent in the #2 bin (See Subsection 2-6.3.8).

2-6.3.16 **Plant "Trouble Shooting."** A partial list of problems commonly encountered at asphalt plants are tabulated here together with their probable causes:

Problem	Probable Cause
General appearance of mix on the "lean" or "dry" side. (Having too little liquid asphalt in the mix.)	(a) Full amount of asphalt not in the mix. (b) Sand grading is too fine. (c) Too much total sand in mix. (d) No. 2 bin is fouled by sand carrying over into it. This is caused by feeding the plant too fast or by the sand screen being partially blocked with sand particles stuck in the openings. There may also be a hole in the bin wall between No. 1 and No. 2 bins.
General appearance of mix is too "rich" or "fat." (Having too much liquid asphalt in the mix.)	(a) Asphalt is being overweighed or scales are defective. (b) Sand grading is too coarse.

Problem	Probable Cause
	(c) Not enough total sand in mix.
	(d) Filler is not being put into the mix by mixer man.
	(e) Hole in the sand screen, permitting rock to get into the sand bin, thus reducing actual amount of total sand in mix.
	(f) Hole in a bin wall permitting rock to get into sand bin (No. 1).
"Dry" material on top of batch in truck.	(a) Weigh hopper is leaking while the mixer gate is open or the mixer bottom is leaking.
	(b) There are "dead spots" in the mixer where the paddles do not reach the aggregate.
	(c) Mix is too cold.
	(d) Bitumen is too cold.
One side of load too "rich" — the other side too "dry."	(a) Asphalt is not being evenly distributed across width of mixer from the asphalt weigh bucket.
	(b) Sand is being weighed in one side of the weigh hopper and does not work over to the other side in the mixer. (Usually corrected by changing the rotation in which the bins are weighed, so as to throw the sand evenly into the weigh hopper and mixer).
	(c) Cold filler not being dry-mixed with hot aggregate before putting asphalt in the mixer.
1-inch and smaller rocks in sand bin.	(a) Hole in sand screen.

Problem	Probable Cause
Small rocks (¼″ and ½″) in sand bin.	(a) Hole in sand screen. (b) Hole in bin wall between No. 1 and No. 2 bins.
Excess of ½-inch rocks in No. 4 bin	(a) Hole in bin wall between No. 3 and No. 4 bins. (b) Plant being fed too fast, causing carry-over of ½-inch rock to No. 4 bin. (c) No. 3 bin screen partially blocked by rock particles stuck in the openings.
1-inch rock in No. 3 bin	(a) Hole in No. 3 bin screen. (b) Hole in bin wall between No. 3 and No. 4 bins.
Rocks larger than 1-inch in No. 4 bin when running fine mixes.	(a) Mesh openings of screen on No. 4 bin are too large. (b) Hole in No. 4 bin screen. (c) Reject chute is tilted wrong way, throwing reject material back into No. 4 bin. (d) Reject material, in falling off the No. 4 bin screen, is hitting chute, or top of bin wall, and bouncing back into No. 4 bin.
Heat of mixture fluctuating.	(a) All of the aggregates are not being fed evenly to match the heat of the dryer burners. (b) Moisture in the materials is not even (more heat is required for drying wet materials). (c) Moisture in sand not constant — some wet, some dry. (d) Fireman not giving close enough attention to matching the fire to the flow of materials.

2-6.4 Procedures on Tonnage Contracts. See Subsection 3-4.3.8.

2-6.5 Plant Inspection Waived. Asphalt driveways and other small paving projects constructed under revocable permits are considered to be temporary and will be removed when permanent street improvements are constructed. For this reason, plant inspection is not required for such construction.

2-6.6 Daily Reports. A daily repot is required on the form entitled "Asphalt Plant Inspector's Daily Report," for every project to which material is shipped. (See Plate 61, Appendix).

Reports are to be filled in completely, except that when the rate of production would not exceed 75 tons for the day (such as for narrow trench resurfacing, berms, patching and the like), the report need not include the bin analysis information. On such days, when specification material is produced at infrequent intervals, the Inspector's time is best occupied in careful observation of the general plant operation in an effort to assure a high quality product.

The daily reports must show the total tonnage of each mix produced each day for each project. Two or more mixes shipped to the same project in one day require separate reports.

2-6.7 Sampling and Testing.

(a) **General.** The Plant Inspector is responsible for taking representative samples and for identifying all liquid asphalt samples taken at the plant. However, the responsibility for using the specified asphalt in the bituminous mixes rests with the producer. All samples of liquid asphalt are to be taken by the Inspector or by authorized plant personnel under the direction of the Inspector. To eliminate any question as to the sampling procedure used, the Plant Foreman (or another authorized person representing the producer) is required to be present.

Samples of asphalt, aggregates and paving mixtures must conform to the Sampling Schedule, Plate 28, Appendix. However, there are precautions, described below, that must be observed by the Plant Inspector in obtaining representative samples.

(b) **Sampling.** The Standard Specifications require that samples be taken from a suitable valve on the asphalt supply line. Make certain that sufficient liquid asphalt is flushed through the valve to cleanse it and eliminate the possibility of

contamination. In addition, make certain that sufficient asphalt
has passed, or passes, through the feed line to flush the pipeline system.

Where a tank sample must be obtained, the sample should
be taken near the midpoint of the asphalt remaining in the tank.
If a doubt arises that a sample is truly representative of the
asphalt in the tank, the sample should be discarded. Sample
devices and containers must be thoroughly clean and dry before use.

The prescribed manner for making the identification card
for a plant sample is illustrated below. The sample identification card is used to identify various kinds of construction
materials which must be sampled. Typical entries for a sample
of liquid asphalt are shown. If the sample is not taken from a
tank, the card should include a notation: "From direct line."

BUREAU OF STANDARDS – SAMPLE IDENTIFICATION

JOB TITLE			R/T #
			SAMPLE #
OFFICE #	INSPECTOR	SAMPLED BY	DATE SAMPLED
CONTRACTOR		SOURCE, VENDOR	PLANT
LOCATION (STREET, STATION)			TYPE SAMPLE
TYPE OF MATERIAL, GRADE, BRAND, SPECIFICATION, OTHER IDENTIFYING NUMBERS, ETC.			

PLEASE USE OTHER SIDE FOR ADDITIONAL INFORMATION

FORM 601

Unless additional asphalt is added to a tank, only one plant
sample from each tank used each day is ordinarily required.
Where bituminous materials are being produced from one tank
for several projects, separate sample identification cards must
be made for each project and securely attached to the proper
plant sample can.

There are a number of undesirable factors which can cause
contamination or change the grade of asphalt in storage tanks.

Truck drivers delivering liquid asphalt to the plant may discharge their loads into the wrong tank, or the plant personnel may pump the asphalt in storage from tank to tank in an attempt to blend various grades of asphalt to meet specification requirements. Some contamination is experienced when the Plant Operator changes from one type of oil to another and permits some of the oil in the pipeline system to drain back into the wrong tank. Truck drivers may flush the truck valve system and filler hose with diesel oil and discharge this waste into the storage tanks.

Extended storage time, particularly when the amount of asphalt in a tank is low, tends to increase the viscosity grade of the asphalt due to the effects of prolonged heat. Unless the producer of a bituminous pavement mixture can furnish a test report indicating that specification viscosity grade asphalt existed in the plant tank within the last 18 hours, asphalt from that tank may not be used on Agency work if it has been in storage for more than seven days. If the producer furnishes such a test report, the Plant Inspector must also obtain a copy of the refinery test certificate which represents the last load of asphalt placed in the plant storage tank. These conditions having been met, the Plant Inspector will make the following entries on the reverse side of his daily report:

(1) Date the last load was delivered into the storage tank.

(2) Refinery certificate number.

(3) Certified viscosity.

(4) Refinery supplying the asphalt.

(5) The viscosity of the asphalt sample taken by the plant.

2-6.8 Asphalt Plant Inspector's Check List.

Has the setting of all box weights been checked?

Are the plant scales clean, calibrated, in good condition and in compliance with the Standard Specifications?

Has the cold feed operation been checked for proper aggregate sizes, aggregate storage, proper feed, clogged or "dry" feeders, etc.?

Have the temperatures of the dry materials and the paving mixture been checked for compliance with the Specifications and for reasonable uniformity?

Have bin analyses been made with enough frequency to insure the quality of the mixture, the uniformity of the cold feed and the efficiency of the classification of the hot aggregates?

Are the hot bin classifying screens clean and free from holes?

Are the hot bin overflow chutes in working order?

Is the rejection chute for oversize material operating properly?

Does the weigh hopper hang free?

Is the bin withdrawal in proper sequence?

Is the proper size batch being mixed?

Do any valves or gates leak?

Is the mixer operator consistently batching the materials exactly as designed, and is he allowing the proper "dry-mixing time" before the addition of bitumen to the mixture?

Have the mixing cycle period and the efficiency of the time-locking device been checked? Is the time-lock circuit light operating? Is the mixing time light operating?

Have the mixed materials in the truck been examined for uniformity, homogeneity, distribution of bitumen, thorough coating, temperature, etc.?

Are loads covered with a tarpaulin when required before they leave the plant?

Has a form or note been sent to the Project Inspector?

Have samples been taken in accordance with the Sampling Schedule?

Are safety precautions being observed?

Have the daily reports been made as required?

2-7 PIPE

2-7.1 Clay Pipe. Clay pipe is manufactured by blending various clays together, milling, mixing, extruding and firing in a kiln to obtain vitrification. The physical properties of the pipe can be changed by varying the proportions of the several clays used. The Standard Specifications provide that all clay pipe used in Agency work be extra strength. The pipe is supplied in two basic styles: spigot and socket; and plain end.

Spigot and Socket Pipe has a spigot on one end and a socket on the other, and is commonly referred to as "bell and spigot" pipe. The plans generally specify the type of joint to be used from the several types of jointing methods provided for in the Standard Specifications. For Agency work this type of pipe is manufactured with matching polyurethane gaskets molded on the spigot and socket which form a tight seal when the pipe is jointed.

Plain End Pipe is without a socket on either end and is joined with special couplings. The coupling consists of a circular rubber sleeve, two stainless steel compression bands with tightening devices and a corrosion resistant shear ring. Sometimes this joint is supplied with a cardboard form, open at the top, which is filled with portland cement mortar to resist shear and prevent future corrosion of the bands.

2-7.2 Concrete Pipe. The Standard Specifications provide for unreinforced and reinforced concrete pipe manufactured by casting in stationary or revolving metal molds. At the present time, the design practice is to specify reinforced concrete pipe for all purposes.

Unreinforced Concrete Pipe is cast in vertical steel molds, usually in pipe sizes of 21 inches or less, and is of the spigot and socket type. No steel reinforcement is used and the pipe is usually intended for use in irrigation systems and under light loading conditions.

Reinforced Concrete Pipe (RCP) is made in a number of different manufacturing processes and for a wide variety of pressure and non-pressure classes. It is available in standard sizes or it can be made to order to any diameter desired. Some of the larger diameters include diameters of 12 and 14 feet. A large variety of joint details are used with RCP. Tongue and groove joints are used for storm drain pipelines.

Reinforced concrete pipe for wastewater pipeline projects is supplied with gasketed joints and a polyvinyl chloride (PVC) plastic liner cast into the pipe.

(a) **Cast Pipe** is cast vertically in steel forms with the reinforcing cage securely held in place. The reinforcement is generally elliptical in shape to provide the maximum structural strength to resist the loads imposed on the pipe by the backfill and other stresses. Consolidation of the concrete is obtained by the use of external form vibrators.

(b) **Centrifugally Spun Pipe** is manufactured by introducing concrete into a spinning horizontal steel cylinder into which the reinforcement cage has been previously installed and which is equipped with end dams to provide the proper pipe wall thickness. The speed of rotation of the mold is increased and the centrifugal force produces a smooth, dense concrete pipe.

(c) **Pressure Pipe** may be cast or centrifugally spun pipe but it usually has a circular steel reinforcement cage (or cages) designed not only to resist the trench loading, but also the internal pressures exerted on the pipe from the fluid under pressure in the line.

2-7.3   Concrete Cylinder Pipe.   This class of pipe is generally used for high pressure water lines and sewer force mains and is available in sizes ranging from 10 inches to 60 inches and larger in special cases.

A sheet steel cylinder is wrapped with the designed steel reinforcement and a concrete lining is centrifugally spun in the interior of the steel cylinder. An exterior coating of concrete is applied generally by the gunite process, while the cylinder is slowly rotated. These coatings vary in thickness from ½ to ¾ of an inch. The joints are commonly of the steel ring and rubber gasket type, but are generally designed for the special purpose for which the pipe line is intended.

2-7.4   Reinforced Concrete Pipe Shop Inspection.

2-7.4.1   General.   The Agency requires shop inspection, by its personnel, of all reinforced concrete pipe supplied to Agency projects. Small quantities of storm drain connector pipe is occasionally approved to be supplied out of stock.

Inspection by Agency personnel gives reasonable assurance that all pipe is uniformly produced to Agency standards. A strength test is only one indicator in this regard. The quality and consistency of the concrete, placement and cover of the reinforcing, and the curing of the pipe all have a bearing on the durability of the pipe and its life expectancy in use.

Consequently, inspection personnel assigned to inspect the fabrication of this pipe must consistently demand that the specifications for the pipe be rigidly adhered to and that the workmanship be of the highest quality. Since the Standard Specifications set forth in considerable detail the manufacturing, inspection and performance standards, they will not be repeated here. Only those inspection functions which are not delineated or which require emphasis and amplification will be included in this subsection.

2-7.4.2   Definition of Terms.   In general, the terms used to designate types of reinforced concrete pipe refer to the process used in manufacture.

Cast RCP (Cast Reinforced Concrete Pipe). A concrete pipe having one or more cylindrical or elliptical cages of reinforcement steel embedded in it, the concrete for which is cast with the forms in a vertical position.

CSRCP (Centrifugally Spun Reinforced Concrete Pipe). A concrete pipe having one or more cylindrical or elliptical cages of reinforcement steel embedded in it, and cast in a horizontal position while the forms are spinning rapidly. This type of pipe may be designated as Spun RCP or as CCP (Centrifugal Concrete Pipe).

RCP (Reinforced Concrete Pipe). A reinforced concrete pipe manufactured by either the casting or spinning method.

Mitered Joints. Pipe lengths which have one or both ends manufactured at a predetermined angle with respect to the longitudinal axis of the pipe, to facilitate laying the pipe on a curve.

Liners. Vitrified clay plates or special plastic sheets placed in the forms prior to casting, to provide a protective lining for the interior of the pipe. They are usually held in place by integral lugs on the back of the liner which are embedded in the concrete.

D-Load. Design nomenclature for specifying strength of pipe where the load is expressed in pounds per foot-length of pipe per foot of internal diameter of the pipe. (Example: 2100-D).

2-7.4.3 Plans and Drawings. Reinforced concrete pipe will be designated on plans by size, type, strength and type of bedding. For example, a typical designation would be "39-inch RCP, 1750-D, Case II bedding."

The Inspector cannot permit the manufacture of pipe to proceed until he has plans in his possession approved by the Engineer. Pipe manufacture may be commenced prior to the receipt of signed plans only upon the approval of the Supervisor of the Materials Control Group. The Inspector at the pipe yard must call the Dispatcher to check whether a job has been cleared to start and to verify the work order number and project title. when no signed plan is available, the Inspector must prepare a Job Memorandum clearly stating that all work performed prior to the issuance of a signed plan is the sole responsibility of the pipe manufacturer and may be subject to later rejection.

Shop drawings must be submitted by the contractor and approved by the Engineer for all reinforced concrete pipe used for sewer conduits. Similarly, approved shop drawings are required for pipe to be jacked or for pipe having joint details which differ from standards previously approved by the Engineer. An approved line layout diagram is required for any portion of a sewer or storm drain conduit utilizing mitered pipe for laying on a curve. The Inspector must number each mitered pipe to correspond to the pipe numbers on the laying diagram.

If the manufacture or installation of plastic liner plate varies from the details specified on the Standard Plan a shop drawing is required to be submitted to the Engineer for approval.

2-7.4.4 Steel Reinforcement. Steel for reinforcing concrete pipe is generally furnished in large coils which will permit the use of machines to fabricate the "cages." The continuous steel rod is wound spirally at a prescribed pitch on a drum of the proper diameter. Where the rod crosses a longitudinal spacer rod, it is electrically welded to it so that the complete cage is relatively rigid. The Inspector must check each cage to insure that the welds are adequate and that the heat or pressure used for welding does not crater or flatten the principal reinforcement.

The Inspector must see that the reinforcement cages for all of the pipe of a given size and D-Load are identical, so that pipe selected at random for testing will be representative of the lot.

Reinforcement cages for pipe designed for external loading are generally elliptical in shape to take full advantage of the steel in tension. Pipe to be used with relatively small external loads or pipe designed for pressure lines will have circular cages. (See Plate 44, Appendix).

The Inspector must check the fabricated cages to insure compliance with the required effective area of steel per lineal foot of pipe. This is accomplished by counting the number of spirally wound rods in a one-foot length of the cage and multiplying this number by the cross-sectional area of the rod used. In addition, the pitch of the principal reinforcement must be checked for uniformity. Erratically wound cages are to be rejected.

Reinforcement cages must be rigidly fixed in the forms so that the placement of concrete or the effects of centrifugal spinning will not result in distortion or displacement of the steel. The orientation of an elliptical cage must be marked on the forms to assure that the minor axis can be located after the concrete is placed.

For design pipe, reinforcement steel will be sampled in accordance with the Sampling Schedule, Plate 28, Appendix.

All steel intended for incorporation into pipe for Agency projects must be identified as to heat number upon delivery to the pipe yard. For D-Load pipe, certificates attesting to the physical and chemical properties of the reinforcing steel are to be furnished to the Inspector by the pipe manufacturer.

2-7.4.5 Concrete for Manufactured Pipe.

(a) **General.** When pipe is specified by D-load, the manufacturer is responsible for the design of the concrete mixture and the D-load requirements although the Standard Specifications require that the mixture contain a specified minimum cement content. In some cases, the structural details of the pipe are shown on the project plans and no D-load bearing strength is required. In which case, the concrete strength is usually specified.

Details of mixing, placing and consolidating the concrete are given in the Standard Specifications. Test cylinders are to be made at frequencies determined by the rate of daily production or as specified by the Supervisor of the Materials Control Group.

(b) **Forms.** All forms for concrete pipe must be fabricated of steel plates and be of sufficient strength to prevent distortion in the casting process. The Inspector must examine the forms prior to their use to insure that they have the proper dimensions, are truly circular and are free from bulges or indentations. The faces of the forms must be clean and coated with a light film of form oil prior to the placement of concrete therein.

Pipe forms should have seams and parting lines neatly fitted to such tolerances that they are virtually watertight to prevent the loss of water with the resultant sand-streaking or rock pockets in the pipe. For cast pipe, the reinforcement cage is positioned around the inside form and securely held in place with supports against the inside and outside forms. The clearance between the forms and reinforcing steel cages is commonly checked by means of a plumb bob suspended from the top of the forms. If plastic liner plate is being installed, no chairs or other supports are to be used against the liner; all positioning supports are to be against the outside forms.

All forms are designed to fit machined steel end rings. Provisions must be made to lock the end rings and all parting joints together into a rigid assembly. Careless assembly of the forms or loosening of a locking device during the placement of concrete will result in non-conforming pipe dimensions. An offset in the bell or spigot may cause problems in matching the pipe when it is laid. Where this offset detrimentally affects the flow line and thereby the hydraulic efficiency of the pipeline, the pipe will be rejected by the Inspector.

(c) **Placing Concrete.** In cast RCP, the concrete is generally deposited over an inverted cone resting on top of the inside form. This permits an even distribution around the form and minimizes the problems of placing too much concrete on one side, thereby distorting the forms. The slump of the concrete should be maintained between two and three inches.

Internal or external vibrators may be used to consolidate the concrete continuously as it is placed. Excessive vibration as the pour nears completion will cause settlement of the coarse aggregate and an excess of water on the surface. This will result in the spigot end having a strength materially below that intended.

After the casting of a plastic-lined pipe is completed, the steel rods or bars holding the edges of the plastic sheets are to be pulled at once and the forms vibrated very briefly to cause the concrete to fill the resulting voids. If the forms are vibrated too long, mortar may creep between the plastic sheet and the forms and cause unacceptable embedment of the plastic liner.

(d) **Finish.** The finish of interior surfaces of concrete pipe should approximate a steel trowel finish. Spun pipe is finished with a roller or bar. Cast pipe has a nominally smooth surface resulting from the steel forms. However, all air or water pockets exceeding ¼-inch in depth must be pointed with mortar. In addition, holes which are less than ¼-inch in depth but exceed the size of a dime in diameter, are to be patched.

2-7.4.6 Curing and Handling. Curing procedures are set forth in the Standard Specifications in detail. Pipe over 54 inches in internal diameter shall not be stacked while in storage or while being transported. Smaller pipe may be stacked not higher than 11 feet provided all pipe with elliptical reinforcement cages are oriented so that the minor axis is within 20 degrees of being vertical.

The pipe manufacturer must not be permitted to damage pipe by improper stacking, rough handling, tipping, dropping, rolling against another pipe or by lifting it with a fork lift, tongs or sling not previously approved by the Inspector for such use. In the case of plastic-lined pipe, no equipment or lifting device may be used that comes in contact with the liner. Where large-diameter pipe is involved, wood or metal stulls may be required inside the pipe to prevent deflection during storage, lifting operations or from the weight of stacked pipe when loaded for delivery to the jobsite. Special pads are required on the ends of stulls to protect the lining of plastic-lined pipe. Pipe damaged in handling or in transit will be subject to rejection.

2-7.4.7 Joints. In general, any conventional type joint is acceptable in pipe to be used in gravity storm drain lines. Pipe to be used in gravity sewers and pressure sewer or storm drain lines must have the joint type specified or approved by the Engineer before it can be manufactured. Special joints, generally referred to as mitered joints, are sometimes required for pipelines laid on curves. (See Subsection 2-7.4.11.)

2-7.4.8 Defects and Repair. The Standard Specifications adequately define dimension tolerances, imperfections and variations in pipe which are causes for rejection and permit certain imperfections to be repaired.

Immediately after pipe is spun, the Inspector must examine the inner surface for evidence of reinforcing steel displacement. If the steel is exposed, no repair can be permitted; the pipe must be rejected. Driving the steel down into plastic concrete and plastering over the steel is not acceptable and the Inspector must be alert to prevent such unauthorized "repairs."

When the forms are stripped from cast or spun pipe after the preliminary steam cure, the Inspector must carefully examine the pipe in detail, inside and out, for dimensional conformity, surface imperfections, cracks or evidence of steel reinforcement displacement. All repairs permitted must be done in a workmanlike manner.

2-7.4.9 Marking Pipe for Identification. All reinforced concrete pipe shall be identified and marked in accordance with the following:

(a) **Batch Numbers.** The Inspector shall obtain from the Agency's testing laboratory a separate batch number for:

(1) Each 400 lineal feet, or fraction thereof, for each size and D-Load of pipe to be made.

(2) Each 50 pipes, or fraction thereof, in the case of internal pressure pipe, for each size of pipe and internal pressure specified on the plans.

Separate batch numbers shall be used whenever the manufacturer alters the design of the steel reinforcing, concrete mixture, curing method or the fabrication details in any respect. This applies to both D-Load pipe and internal pressure pipe. Batch numbers are to be used to identify pipe batches even when all the manufacturing details are shown on the approved drawings and described in the contract documents and no test is required. Compliance with all such details and contract documents is the basis of acceptance of these pipes.

Manufacture of all pipe in a batch shall be completed prior to the time of testing that batch. No pipe is to be shipped by the manufacturer until the required tests are completed. After a batch of pipe is tested, the further use of that batch number shall be discontinued.

If the batch fails to pass the specified test, the Inspector will add two digits to the three-digit number already stamped in the pipe to convert it to a five-digit batch number which will mark it as a rejected pipe. Batches which are tested and fail when no Inspector is assigned to the yard will be reported to the Agency by the testing laboratory. An Inspector will be immediately assigned to the pipe yard for the purpose of altering the existing batch number to a five-digit number as described above.

(b) **Pipe Marking.** Stamps for marking pipe are maintained in lockers under lock and key at each pipe yard. The Inspector is to permit no one else to use these stamps.

As soon as possible after pipes are taken out of the steam curing, the Inspector must check them for compliance with the dimensional tolerances. Acceptable pipe is to be marked with a circumferential line just inside the end of the pipe with a black permanent-type crayon. For pipe sizes 21 inches or larger, the exact location of the minor axis of an elliptical steel reinforcement cage must be marked on the inside of each pipe with a large letter "T." Areas to be patched are to be marked with red or yellow crayon. In addition, the date manufactured, batch number, pipe size, D-Load and the Inspector's name are to be written inside one end of each pipe in black crayon or felt pen.

Pressure pipe shall be marked "Pressure." Pressure pipe, and pipe having 100 percent of its internal surface covered with liners or liner plates, shall have the identification data written on the exterior surface of the pipe.

The placing of the large "INSPECTED — DEPARTMENT OF PUBLIC WORKS" stamp is to be withheld until immediately prior to loading pipe for shipment to the jobsite. The Inspector at the pipe yard will examine each length to insure that no damage has occurred during storage or in handling. This large stamp is the signal to the Inspector at the project site that the pipe was acceptable when it left the pipe yard. Pipe received on the jobsite not bearing this stamp must be rejected and returned to the manufacturer.

2-7.4.10 Pipe from Stock. Stockpiled pipe (pipe which was inspected during manufacture) may be used only for storm drain connector pipe in limited sizes and amounts. Such pipe must be properly identified and certified by the Inspector at the plant prior to shipment to the jobsite and must meet strength requirements when tested to 115 percent of the specified D-load, as well as other applicable requirements for the pipe.

The approval to use stock pipe must be received from the Supervisor Materials Control Group.

2-7.4.11 Mitered Pipe. Mitered pipe is manufactured to facilitate laying pipe on a curve. This eliminates the need for casting concrete collars around open pipe joints which would result if square-end pipe were used and the joints "pulled" vertically or horizontally to lay the pipe on a curve. The Inspector should give special attention to the accuracy with which forms are set to establish the proper miter angle. The Standard Specifications permit the mitering of one or both ends of a pipe having a conventional tongue and groove joint. If the magnitude of the miter angle is five degrees or less, only one end of the pipe need be mitered. If the miter angle exceeds five degrees, one-half of the total miter angle shall be applied to each end of the pipe.

Pipes with lock joints or steel joint rings are impossible to miter by depressing the joint ring or end ring. Plans calling for pipe with such joints to be laid on curves must indicate the method of obtaining the proper miter (or bevel) and designate the end (or ends) to which the bevel shall be applied. Such methods may involve welding steel extensions in the form of the mitered section to the standard lock-joint bell ring. If this is done, the interior concrete surface should be extended in the bell section so that the specified annular joint space will not be exceeded when the pipe is laid.

Miters for pipe (the amount the end ring must be dropped from the long side of the pipe to the short side) can be calculated by the Inspector and the calculation compared with the manufacturer's design criteria.

Mitering is accomplished by slanting one or both end rings. The degree that the ring is tilted is dependent upon the size of the pipe and the radius of the curve. For purposes of calculating miter angles, let

L = nominal length of one pipe in feet,
E = external diameter of the pipe in feet,
R = radius of the curve of the centerline of the pipeline in feet, and
M = the distance in feet that one side of the top ring is to be dropped below the opposite side.

When all of the miter is at one end of a pipe, then

$$M = \frac{LE}{R + \dfrac{E}{2}}$$

If the pipe is to be mitered at both ends, one-half the value of "M" should be applied at each end.

For example, a 72-inch (internal diameter) pipe with a wall thickness of 7 inches is to be laid in 8-foot lengths on a curve having a radius of 100 feet. If possible, it is intended to miter only one end.

L = 8 feet (given)
E = 72″ + 7″ + 7″ = 86″ or 7.167 feet
R = 100 feet

$$M = \frac{LE}{R + \dfrac{E}{2}} = \frac{8 \times 7.167}{100 + \dfrac{7.167}{2}} = \frac{57.336}{103.584} = .554 \text{ feet}$$

To complete the miter angle from this data,

$$\frac{M}{E} = \text{tangent of the miter angle}$$

Therefore: $\dfrac{M}{E} = \dfrac{.554}{7.167} = .0773$

From a table of natural trigonometric functions, .0773 is the tangent of 4°25′. Since this is less than 5°, the pipe may be mitered on one end only. If this angle had been 5° or more, it would be divided and one-half applied to each end of the pipe.

2-7.4.12 Sampling and Testing. One pipe from each 12 lengths shall be marked "sample" by the Inspector. The pipe manufacturer may segregate these pipes, making access easier to the test pipe when the batch is completed and ready for testing. When pipes are to be tested, a test pipe will be selected from the samples, either by the Inspector on duty at the yard or by a representative of the testing agency.

All requests for D-Load tests or internal pressure tests must be made by the pipe manufacturer directly to the testing laboratory and the Inspector will not act as the intermediary in such requests. The Inspector will assist the testing technician in making tests if his time and duties permit.

All testing shall conform to the requirements of the Standard Specifications for the class of pipe involved.

2-7.4.13 Records and Reports. A continuing, up-to-date record is to be maintained by the Inspector in a "Daily Record of Pipe Manufactured" form (See Plate 45, Appendix). This pipe record, which is to be kept in a loose-leaf book provided for the purpose, will indicate the pertinent data for each batch of pipe. This record is also used to note the authority given to accept pipe from stock and is referred to by personnel of the testing laboratory when they perform tests in the pipe yard. The "Remarks" column is used to record information pertaining to any particular length of pipe or to the batch in general. Typical entries would include data on rejected pipe, reasons for rejection, remanufactured pipe, the date when any particular pipe length of the batch is shipped, laying diagram pipe numbers for mitered pipe, etc. When the entire batch is ready for test, this will be noted on the bottom of the form, as well as the date the batch was tested and the last pipe stamped. A report of all batches tested for each project will be prepared on the form "Manufacture of Pipe" and forwarded each week to the Main Office for inclusion in the project file. (See Plate, 3, Appendix).

A pipe manufacturing log is to be maintained in the Inspector's office by the Inspector at the pipe yard to show at a glance the status of jobs that are in progress or completed. (See Plate 46, Appendix). Column 1 is a cross-reference to the factory order for the job which is issued by the pipe manufacturer. Columns 2, 3 and 4 are for listing the Agency work order number, letter code and project title, respectively. The name of the purchaser is listed under Column 5 while Column 6 is used to record the date on which any work is commenced on that order. When the last pipe is shipped to the project site, the date is entered in Column 7.

2-7.4.14 Concrete Pipe Plant Inspector's Check List.

Have approved plans been received prior to the start of pipe manufacture?

Has the Dispatcher been notified of the start of the pipe manufacture?

Have batch numbers been requested from the testing agency?

Have samples of the reinforcing steel been taken or have certificates attesting to the physical and chemical properties of the steel been obtained?

Have the reinforcing steel cages been checked during fabrication and again after being placed in the forms?

Have the cages been fixed rigidly in the forms with adequate chairs?

Have the forms been checked for length, diameter, straightness, roundness, and are the seams and parting lines tight?

Have the forms been cleaned and oiled?

If plastic liners are required, have the sheets been inspected at the place of manufacture and do they bear the Inspector's tag?

After being placed on the forms, have the liners been checked for subsequent damage and conformance to the area of coverage required?

Have all the conditions of the Standard Specifications been complied with in respect to the mixing, placing, consolidation and finishing of the concrete for the pipe being manufactured?

Are the proper curing procedures being followed after the pipe has been made?

After steam curing, has the pipe been inspected for imperfections, marked for repair or rejection, and have identification marks been placed on the pipe?

Are handling and storage techniques adequate to avoid damage to the pipe?

If a laying diagram has been furnished for the pipe line, have the pipe numbers been placed on the pipe?

Has the angle of bevel been checked on mitered pipe?

Has the pipe been given a final inspection just prior to shipment to the jobsite?

Are the daily records kept up-to-date and are the weekly reports submitted as required?

2-7.5   Asbestos-Cement Pipe. This kind of pipe is made from an intimate mixture of portland cement and asbestos fiber and is available in diameters ranging from four inches to 36 inches. A wide variety of pipe classes is available for special uses such as sewer lines, water lines, subdrains, etc. Many kinds of special and standard fittings are also available.

The ends of pipe lengths and the insides of fittings are machined to insure close tolerances for joint make-up. Pipe lengths shall be cut only with the special asbestos-cement pipe cutters designed for this purpose and cutting with a chisel must not be permitted. Field-cut ends of pipe should be reshaped for use with a standard coupling by using a machining and tapering tool. Otherwise a special adapter coupling should be used which is designed to accommodate field-cut ends of pipe.

Asbestos-cement pipe may not be used for main line sewer or house connection sewer construction unless it is so specified on the plans or in the specifications. It is authorized for use in house connections constructed under house connection permits, provided it is previously sampled, tested and reported by the Testing Agency as conforming to the requirements of the Standard Specifications.

2-7.6   Cast Iron and Ductile Iron Pipe. Cast iron and ductile iron pipe and fittings are cast in sand molds or centrifugally cast in sand-lined cast iron flasks. It is available in many different types and can be furnished for jointing by the following methods: bell and spigot, cast flange, screwed-on flange, mechanical joint, threaded joint, ball joint, victaulic or Dresser coupling.

2-7.7   Corrugated Steel Pipe (CSP) and Pipe Arches. Included in this class of pipe are: corrugated pipe, pipe arches, nestable pipe, slotted pipe and the coupling bands. It is rolled from galvanized steel or aluminum sheets by two methods: with transverse corrugations and a longitudinal riveted (or spot welded) seam or rolled with a continuously welded helical seam resulting in spiral ribs. The ends of spiral rib pipe are reformed to shape them to accommodate a coupling band that will result in a tight, concentric fit. Coupling bands utilizing dimples to lock into the spirals of unreformed pipe shall not be used without prior authority of the Engineer.

Nestable pipe is manufactured in half-circle sections and is used for flumes, surface down drains and for similar installations. Slotted pipe has a continuous slot framed by two angles that is used for shallow surface drains in pavement or gutters.

Pipe arches are fabricated as cylindrical pipe, then reformed to multi-centered pipe, having an arch-shape top with a slightly curved integral bottom. Its primary use is for shallow installation where little headroom or cover is available above flow line and where fast, unrestricted runoff is desired. It is more effective at low flow than round pipe.

CSP and pipe arches are available in a large range of sizes from 12 to 144 inches in round pipe and 15 to 120 inches (round equivalent) in pipe arches. For larger sizes, round or arch pipe can be fabricated in the field from plates rolled and punched for bolting together. This system is referred to as multiplate pipe or arches.

These CSP products are available with bituminous, asphalt mastic, polymeric or concrete coatings, and with optional paved inverts of bitumen or concrete. Paving for inverts must cover the crests of the corrugations to a minimum depth of not less than ⅛-inch, and the pavement shall extend to one-third of the periphery of pipe arches and one-fourth of the periphery of round pipe.

Pinholes, blisters, cracks, lack of bond or handling damage to coatings or paved inverts are cause for rejection. Procedures for repair must be approved in advance by the Engineer for minor deficiencies.

Corrugated steel pipe is measured for diameter (or span and rise in pipe arches) from the least inside dimension between ribs. Paved invert is taken to be the top of the corrugations at the flow line of the pipe.

Corrugated steel pipe is also furnished with other protective coatings such as asphalt coatings, asbestos bonded and with paved inverts. The invert of corrugated steel pipe is always taken to be at the top of the corrugations at the flow line of the pipe.

Corrugated aluminum pipe and arches are also available in shapes and sizes comparable to CSP. Its advantages are its light weight which facilitates handling and its resistance to corrosion in continuous contact with moisture.

2-7.8 Plastic Pipe and Conduit. Polyvinyl chloride (PVC) is one of a number of thermo-plastic materials used for the manufacture of pipe or conduit and has a wide range of uses. Acrylonitrile-butadiene-styrene (ABS) and polyethylene (PE) are also frequently used.

In use, plastic pipe offers numerous advantages not possible with other types of pipe. It is light in weight and therefore easy to install, low in cost and has a long life, resists corrosion and most acids, imparts no taste or odor and because of its smooth interior surface, has a high flow rate.

Pipe and tubing are made in a variety of grades and wall thicknesses and joint types, including threaded, solvent welded or heat welded. Flanged joints are also used, in which case the flanges can be secured to the pipe by either threaded, solvent weld or heat weld methods. Expanded bell end pipe is assembled by using a rubber ring seal.

Plastic pipe has a variety of uses including water and gas mains, irrigation systems and sanitary sewers. Thin wall plastic pipe is used for underground conduit for electrical power and telephone lines.

2-8 METALS

2-8.1 General. This subsection covers basic metal materials and manufactured metal products used in Agency work, except steel reinforcement for concrete which may be found in Subsection 2-4.8. Metal related processes and procedures such as galvanizing, welding, heat treatment and metal fabrication can be found in Subsection 2-9.

In general, most metal materials are accepted for use on Agency projects on the basis of certified mill test reports. Such material must be associated with test records and is referred to as "identifiable stock." Unidentifiable stock or stock that cannot be related to test records must be tested prior to use.

2-8.2 Metal Castings.

2-8.2.1 Cast Iron. Cast iron is a commercial variety of iron, containing more than 1.7 percent carbon, poured molten into a mold so as to solidify in a desired shape.

(a) **Gray Cast Iron.** Gray cast iron results from permitting the molten pig iron to cool quite slowly. The chemical compound of iron and carbon breaks up to a certain extent and much of the carbon separates out as tiny flakes of graphite, scattered everywhere through the metal. The graphitic carbon causes the gray appearance of the fracture which characterizes gray cast iron. Since graphite is an excellent lubricant, this metal is easy to machine. Gray cast iron, when molten, is very fluid and slow to solidify, thereby making it possible to produce castings of intricate design. It is used for automobile cylinder blocks, pump bodies, gears, pulleys, axle housing, etc., where weight and stiffness are required without very much strength or ductility. Most cast iron products used in public works are gray cast iron.

(b) **White Cast Iron.** White cast iron is produced by heating gray cast iron to a dull red, then cooling it rapidly. All of the carbon present in the gray cast iron is chemically combined with the iron and white cast iron is formed. It is very hard and brittle, has a silvery fracture and is often impossible to machine. It is used for castings where hardness is necessary or where good wear resistance is required. It is also used in the manufacture of malleable iron castings.

(c) **Malleable Cast Iron.** Malleable cast iron is produced by heating white cast iron to temperatures between 1400°F and 1700°F for about 48 hours in contact with hematite ore or iron scale. A portion of the combined carbon is thus transformed into the free or uncombined state. This combined carbon separates out in a different manner than in gray cast iron and is called temper carbon. It exists in the form of small, rounded particles, which give malleable iron castings the ability to bend before breaking and to withstand shock loads better than gray cast iron. These castings are high in strength, ductile, tough and resist shock. It is used to make small tools, pipe fittings and such automobile parts as steering gear brackets, clutch pedals, etc.

2-8.2.2 Cast Steel. Cast steel is any of the high carbon, medium carbon, low carbon, copper-bearing or tool steels cast into molds in a manner similar to the process applied to cast iron. Plain carbon steel castings contain, as a rule, not more than 0.35 percent carbon and a negligible amount of alloying materials.

2-8.2.3 Cast Aluminum. Aluminum castings are made from alloys of aluminum, the nominal composition of which contains varying amounts of copper, magnesium and silicon. Special physical properties can be obtained by including small amounts of zinc, nickel, chromium, titanium or manganese in different combinations. When castings are large, or when only a few castings are required, they are made as sand cast units. When a large number of castings of small or medium size are required, they are usually made as die castings. Other casting methods used for special purposes are: plaster molds, shell molds and centrifugal casting.

Castings are usually marked (or embossed) as follows with a letter and number code to indicate the temper of the metal:

- F as fabricated (no control of temper)
- O annealed (recrystallized)
- H cold-worked (strain hardened)
- T heat-treated (with numbers from 1 to 9, stating the physical properties of ductility, hardening, aging, stabilization, etc.)

Aluminum castings are used principally because of their light weight and resistance to corrosion. They are sometimes used for ornamental purposes such as handrail brackets, fence post caps, etc.

2-8.3 Wrought Iron. Wrought iron is made from pig iron in a puddling furnace. The carbon and other elements present in the pig iron are eliminated, leaving almost pure iron. In the process of manufacture of wrought iron, some slag is mixed with the iron to form a fibrous structure, that is, a structure in which long stringers of slag, running lengthwise of the bar, are mixed with long threads of iron. Wrought iron resists corrosion, oxidation and rusting because of the slag included in its structure. Its availability and use is becoming very limited, confined mostly to crane hooks, bolts, wire, ornamental iron work, etc.

2-8.4 Steel.

2-8.4.1 General. Steel is any commercial form of iron containing carbon in any amount up to 1.7 percent as an essential alloying ingredient and is malleable under certain conditions.

Low Carbon (Mild) steels have a carbon content of up to 0.30 percent and are soft and ductile. They can be rolled, punched, sheared and can be worked hot or cold. Low-carbon steel can be easily machined and welded and does not harden when cooled suddenly from high temperatures. It is used to make wire, nails, tubes, screws, plates and some structural members.

High Carbon steels contain from 0.50 to 0.90 percent carbon and are exceptionally hard. They are used in the manufacture of drills, taps, dies, springs, machine tools, etc. which are heat-treated after fabrication to develop the hard structure necessary to withstand high shear stress and wear. After manufacture in bar or sheet stock, it is annealed (or normalized and annealed) so as to be suitable for machining and fabricating into the desired shape. It is then heat-treated to restore the hardness characteristics. These steels are difficult to weld and must be pre-heated prior to welding, then stress-relieved after welding. Upon heating high-carbon steels to the critical temperature and quenching them, very hard steels are produced.

2-8.4.2 Structural Steel. Structural steel or rolled steel shapes such as beams, channels, angles or structural tubing are produced from a variety of steels including the basic carbon steels of which there are three strength classes: high strength (also produced in three strength classes); high strength low alloy of which there is a variety of grades and strengths; and corrosion resistant high strength low alloy or the so-called "weathering steels."

The most common shapes manufactured are: angles, channels, I beams, H beams and rails, although not all shapes are produced in every type of steel. The *American Institute of Steel Construction (AISC)* handbook covers the full range of available structural shapes and their properties.

The high strength steels have a number of advantages over the all-purpose basic carbon steels in certain applications. Lighter members can be used and the corrosion resistant or weathering varieties can be frequently used without coating.

See Plate 28, Appendix, for sampling and testing of structural steel.

2-8.4.3 Stainless Steel. Stainless steels are basically alloys of chromium and iron. When chromium, a metallic element, is added to iron in excess of 10 percent, it imparts to the alloy a remarkable resistance to corrosion and heat. Other elements may be added such as: nickel, molybdenum, columbium, titanium, sulfur and selenium to produce special characteristics. It is therefore apparent that there are many types of stainless steel, depending upon the alloy composition. In general, stainless steels are specified by the percentages of chromium and nickel they contain such as: 17-7, 25-12, 18-8, etc., the first numerals representing the percentage of chromium in the alloy and the second numerals the percentage of nickel.

Stainless steel can be welded by most of the commercial welding procedures such as the metallic arc, the inert arc, atomic hydrogen, oxy-acetylene, spot welding, line seam and flash welding. Special care must be taken during welding to avoid embrittlement or softening of the material near the weld, and annealing or heat treatment of the welded assembly is often required to restore the characteristics of the original alloy in the vicinity of the weld.

2-8.4.4 Processes for Making Steel.

Steel is made by refining pig iron and removing some of the carbon content from it. The process may start with the molten pig iron as it is discharged from the blast furnace or the solidified pigs may be remelted at some later time. In general, the carbon and some impurities are removed by any one of a number of processes described briefly in this subsection, and the carbon content is controlled by adding small amounts of scrap iron containing carbon or by adding pure carbon.

(a) **Open-Hearth Steel.** The name comes from the type of furnace used in making the steel. The open-hearth furnace is charged with pig iron and scrap steel, which are melted by a high temperature flame, usually gas. The silicon, manganese, and carbon are burned out and slagged off by adding mill scale, iron ore and limestone periodically. The molten steel is discharged from the furnace through a tap hole into ladles, where additions of various desired elements are made, and thence into molds.

(b) **Bessemer Steel.** Bessemer steel is made in a converter which is a tilting vessel, lined with siliceous material, having a perforated bottom. When the converter is on its side, molten pig iron is poured in. As the converter is righted, a blast of air is blown through the bottom holes and through the molten iron. This burns out the silicon, manganese and carbon, raising the temperature of the molten metal. Just as the carbon flame dies out, the converter is tilted, and the steel poured into a ladle where a small, controlled amount of carbon is restored by suitable additions, known as spiegeleisen and ferromanganese. These are irons containing high percentages of carbon and manganese. The steel is then cast into ingot molds for future working into shapes.

(c) **Basic and Acid Steel.** Basic steel is made in any one of several furnaces which must be lined with magnesite or dolomite. Acid steel is made in a furnace lined with ganister, containing a high percentage of silicon. The furnace lining imparts certain characteristics to the steel.

(d) **Crucible Steel.** Crucible steel is made from low-carbon steel cut into lengths and packed into crucibles with charcoal to make steel of a fairly high carbon content. The low-carbon steel asborbs the carbon as it melts, and the product is know as crucible steel, high-carbon steel or tool steel.

(e) **Electric Steel.** Electric steels are steels produced in furnaces in which the heat is furnished by carbon arc or by induction. Except for its higher purity and freedom from occluded gases, electric steel does not differ basically from other steels.

2-8.5   Bronze. Bronze castings for bridge expansion plates and bearing plates for Agency work must comply with the requirements of Alloy C ASTM B-22. This bronze is an alloy of copper, tin, lead and nickel. Traces of zinc, iron and antimony are permissible but the sum total of these metals must not exceed 1.5 percent.

Bronze is cast in a manner similar to that employed in casting iron or steel.

2-8.6   Aluminum Shapes, Tubing and Pipe. Aluminum shapes, tubing and pipe have a variety of architectural and structural uses in Agency work and are used most frequently for bridge railing and handrailing. Railings are usually fabricated by welding and the finished product is anodized for weather protection and architectural coloring.

This kind of work requires careful techniques in the handling, fabrication and treatment of the material to assure the architectural quality of the finished product. Quality standards and specifications for fabricated aluminum and anodizing are published by the Aluminum Association.

2-8.7   Chain Link Fence. This fence is made from wire pickets spirally wound and interwoven in the form of a continuous link fabric, without knots or ties except at the top and bottom of the fence, where it is twisted (barbed) or folded over in a single interlock(knuckled). This metal fabric is usually galvanized after it is woven, although some is initially made from galvanized wire. The Standard Specifications require the fabric to be galvanized after it is woven, and it can be readily recog-

nized by the irregularities in the coating at the wire intersections resulting from the dipping and draining operations.
Fabric woven from galvanized wire has a uniform coating
surface on the wire (often much thinner than hot dipped and
unwiped wire) and the cut ends of the wire at the barbs or
knuckles are uncoated. To avoid a thin coating and unprotected
end surfaces, this fabric must be hot dipped after weaving.

2-8.8 Bolts, Nuts, Washers and Rods. In general, this
subsection is intended to outline the manufacture and engineering use of bolts, nuts, washers and rods. While such hardware
can be manufactured from many different metals and materials, the most common materials used are wrought iron and
mild steel.

Bolts of the smaller sizes are usually formed as forgings
with the threads rolled on under heavy pressure in a cold forming operation. Larger bolts are generally shaped as forgings
and the threads machined in a lathe or cut in a screw machine
by special dies. For nomenclature of bolts in common usage, see
Plate 17, Appendix.

Nuts are usually cut from square or hexagonal wrought
iron bar stock. Small nuts have the holes punched and tapped,
while larger sizes are drilled and tapped.

Washers are usually stamped from sheet stock in punch
presses. Machined washers are cut from round bar stock and,
because of the high cost, are seldom used except in pre-
cision work.

Rods are wrought iron or rolled steel bars to which a nut
or special fitting is attached (usually by threads) in order to
obtain a slender but strong tension member. Rods are most
commonly used as a tie from a wooden bulkhead to a deadman anchor.

High strength bolts for specialized structural uses are
made by the hot forged or cold process, or are machined from
hot forged, hot rolled or cold-drawn bars and are heat treated
to meet the required physical properties. Precise tightening
procedures must be used when these bolts are specified to
produce tensions required to develop the full strength of the
connection. (See Plate 54, Appendix.)

2-8.9 Electrical Products.

2-8.9.1 Electrical Wire. Wire for use as an electrical
conductor is generally made of copper. It is manufactured by

drawing rods of copper through a die of the proper size. Since much heat is generated by the friction of the copper on the die, watercooling of the die is necessary. Lubricants, usually soap powders, stearates, tallows, soap solutions, soluble oils, etc., are also used to prevent the seizing of the drawn metal to the die.

There are many materials and combinations of materials which are used to insulate a wire conductor. However, only those specifically approved or provided for in the Standard Specifications may be used. The most commonly used insulating materials are Para rubber, polyethylene and polyvinyl chloride, which are applied to the bare conductor by the seam or seamless methods. The seam method consists of cutting the insulation material into long strips, passing the wire and strips over grooved rollers which press the strip closely around the conductor and the seam is then vulcanized. (See Plate 60, Appendix.)

The seamless method is more popular and consists of drawing the conductor through a pressure vessel containing the insulation material in a plastic state. As the wire emerges through the center of a die, the plastic insulation is extruded around the conductor. The thickness of the insulation is controlled by the size of the die opening. Depending upon the nature of the insulation material, the insulated wire is cured or vulcanized to harden the insulation before reeling.

The diameter or size of an electrical conductor is required by the Standard Specifications to conform to the American Wire Gage (AWG) sizes. (See Plate 18, Appendix.)

The principal factors taken into consideration by the design engineer in determining wire size for electrical conductors are the type of metal in the wire (copper or aluminum), its construction (stranded or solid), duty cycles of loads (continuous or intermittent operation), the design voltage and provision for sufficient oversize to minimize voltage drop and the effects of short-circuit heating.

In addition to these factors, he is equally concerned with effective insulation and its protective covering. To be effective, insulation must combine materials that contain insulating and physical characteristics that will provide resistance to environmental conditions, contribute to ease of installation and be economical to maintain. Rubber, including various butyl and mineral base materials, is a low-cost insulation material with good insulating properties. Thermoplastic materials, providing excellent protection against moisture, oils and chemicals, are specified for street lighting systems. They are tough, durable, and when lubricated with silicones, facilitate installation of the conductor. By varying the components in the insulation, different properties can be developed to meet the desired properties. (See Plate 60, Appendix.)

To protect insulation from physical damage or environmental deterioration, insulated conductors are often encased in a protective sheath. This minimizes the effects of impact, abrasion, corrosion, electrolysis, sunlight and other deteriorating agents. Since these sources of damage vary so widely, protective coverings are available in a wide range of products from metal and braids to resins and plastics.

2-8.9.2 **Conduit.** Rigid metal conduit is the most versatile of the many raceway materials for electrical wiring, although it is the most expensive. It can be used either exposed, concealed, embedded in concrete or used underground. It is fireproof, waterproof, resists damage from crushing under loading or from driven nails, and resists the normal corrosive action when embedded in concrete. The smooth interior facilitates the pulling of conductors through it.

Conduit is manufactured in a manner similar to steel pipe; that is, by extrusion as a tube or rolled from flat bar stock and continuously welded along the seam. Since the latter method is cheaper, most conduit is made by this process. Corrosion protection is provided by galvanizing, accomplished by electrolytic means or Sherardizing to insure a smooth coating free from peaks, blisters and irregularities which might damage the insulation of the conductors during the wire pulling operations. It is also supplied with a plastic coating for use in severely corrosive environments.

Threads on conduit differ from pipe threads in that no taper is used. This permits the ends of conduit to butt together in the coupling.

Conduit is readily available in standard sizes from ½ inch to 4 inches. While conduit can be easily bent to conform in some degree to the shape or dimensions required in an installation, certain minimum radii are always prescribed to prevent crimping or kinking the conduit and to insure long radius bends for ease of pulling wire through them. Sharp bends are accomplished through the use of conduit boxes and fittings. Rigid conduit bends (called factory bends) are also available in all standard conduit sizes. These elbows are generally formed to minimum radii and are used where bending of the conduit would be difficult or where turn-outs are required from embedded conduit.

2-8.10   **Wire Rope.**   Wire rope is manufactured from high grade steel wire. These wires are helically laid in strands and the strands laid into ropes around a core or center. When the wires in strands are laid in a direction opposite to the lay of the strands in the rope, the rope is called regular lay. When the strand wires are laid in the same direction as the strands are laid in the rope, the rope is called Lang lay. When the strands in a rope spiral upward from left to right, it is called a right lay rope. Conversely, when the strands in a rope spiral upward from right to left, it is called a left lay rope (See Plate 27, Appendix).

Wire rope is designated by the number of wires and strands and the lay of the wires and strands. For example: a wire rope having six strands of 19 wires each, with the strands laid counterclowise and the wires in each strand laid clockwise, would be designated as: 6 x 19, right lay, regular lay wire rope.

The greater the number of wires in each strand, the more flexible the wire rope becomes. Greater flexibility is also achieved by using wire rope which is Lang laid.

The diameter of a wire rope is always the diameter of a circle which will just enclose all of the strands. The correct diameter is the greatest diameter of the rope (See Plate 27, Appendix).

There is only one way to unwind wire rope from a coil. The end of the rope should be held and the coil rolled on the ground like a hoop. To remove wire rope from a reel, the reel must rotate as the rope unwinds, either on a horizontal or vertical shaft, or by rolling the reel on the ground. Unwinding wire rope from a stationary coil or reel will kink the rope — and once the kink is formed, the rope, at that point, is ruined beyond repair. Do not allow reels to be dropped and do not permit a bar to be used to roll a reel by prying against the wire rope.

Grooves in sheaves and drums should be slightly larger than the diameter of the wire rope. This avoids pinching, binding and unnecessary wear of the strands. However, grooves of too large a diameter to not properly support the rope and usually permit the rope to become elliptical. Never permit crosswinding of wire rope on a drum.

Some common causes of wire rope failures are:

Ropes of incorrect size, construction or grade are used.

Ropes are allowed to drag over obstacles.

Ropes are not properly lubricated.

Ropes are operated over sheaves of inadequate size.

Ropes are overwound or crosswound on drums.

Ropes are operated over sheaves or drums which are out of alignment.

Ropes operating over sheaves and drums with improperly fitting grooves or broken flanges.

Ropes are permitted to jump sheaves.

Ropes are subjected to moisture or acid fumes.

Ropes have improperly attached fittings.

Ropes are permitted to untwist.

Ropes are subjected to excessive heat.

Ropes have been kinked.

Ropes have been subjected to severe overloads.

Ropes have been exposed to excessive internal wear caused by grit penetrating between strands and wires.

There is only one correct method of installing wire rope clips. The base of each clip should bear against the live (or long rope end) and the U-bolt should bear against the dead (or short rope end). (See Figure 3, Plate 27, Appendix.)

2-9 METAL RELATED PROCESSES

2-9.1 Galvanizing (Zinc Coatings).

2-9.1.1 General. The process of applying a coat of zinc to the surface of iron and steel for the purpose of resisting corrosion is called galvanizing. There are four common methods of applying zinc to the surface of iron or steel:

> The Hot Dip Process
> Electrolytic or Zinc Plating
> Spraying Molten Zinc
> Sherardizing

2-9.1.2 Hot Dip Process. This process consists of three basic steps: surface preparation, fluxing and galvanizing.

It is essential that iron or steel articles to be galvanized be clean and uncontaminated if a uniform, adherent coating is to result.

Surface preparation is usually accomplished by dipping the article into a caustic (alkaline) solution to clean the surface of organic contaminants such as dirt, paint marking, grease and oil which are not readily removed by acid pickling in hot sulfuric acid (150°F) or hydrochloric acid at room temperature. This latter procedure removes scale and rust.

Surface preparation can also be accomplished using abrasive cleaning as an alternate to (or in conjunction with) chemical cleaning. Sand blasting, shot blasting or grit propelled against the article by rapidly rotating wheels are the most commonly used abrasive cleaning methods.

Final cleaning is performed by a flux. The method of applying the flux depends upon whether the "wet" or "dry" galvanizing process is used. Dry galvanizing requires that the steel be dipped in an aqueous zinc ammonium chloride solution, and then dried thoroughly. This procedure (called prefluxing) prevents oxides from forming on the surface of the article prior to galvanizing. Wet galvanizing utilizes a molten flux layer floating on top of the zinc bath. Final cleaning is accomplished as the article passes through the flux layer when it enters the zinc bath.

Actual galvanizing occurs when the article is immersed in the bath of molten zinc at about 850°F (See Plate 66, Appendix). The molten zinc (consisting of 98.76 percent zinc, 1.20 percent lead, 0.03 iron and a trace of aluminum) is contained in wrought iron or mild steel pots and kept at the required temperature by the application of heat to the vertical sides of the pot. This molten zinc is called spelter.

The time of immersion in the galvanizing bath varies, depending upon the dimensions and the chemistry of the base materials in the coated article. Thick sections take more time to galvanize than thin sections. If the silicon content of the article is high, this will produce a thicker coating than a low silicon content.

The galvanized article is removed from the pot and the surplus spelter drained off. This coating of zinc is called the spelter coat and the thickness may be varied by preheating the article, varying the dip time in the molten spelter, successive dipping, post dip wiping (or rolling) and by varying the temperature of the spelter.

The zinc coating resulting from hot dip galvanizing often assumes a spangled appearance, particularly on sheet stock and on the smooth surface of castings. Differences in appearance of the coating can vary with the immersion time, bath temperature, rate of withdrawal, removal of excess zinc (wiping, shaking or centrifuging) or by controlling the cooling rate (air cooling or water quenching).

Test coupons used to verify the thickness of the spelter coat must always be wired to the top of the article to be galvanized so that the coupon will enter the spelter last and emerge first, thereby assuming that the galvanized article has a spelter coating as thick or thicker than the coupon.

2-9.1.3 Electrolytic or Zinc Plating Process.
This method employs the electrolytic process for depositing zinc on iron articles. There are many advantages of this process over the hot dip process which include: complete control over the coating thickness, greater economy of zinc, purity of the coating, elimination of distortion or buckling of the article from the heat and the elasticity of metal springs is not affected adversely. However, it is very difficult to obtain a thick, nonspongy coat.

2-9.1.4 Sherardizing Process.
In this process, the articles to be coated are heated in metal drums or boxes while completely surrounded with metalic zinc dust. Sherardizing is particularly suitable where a thin protective coating is required such as on thin wall electrical conduit.

2-9.1.5 Metallic Spraying Process.
Metal spraying consists of applying a fine spray of molten zinc to the surface of steel, which has been previously cleaned and preheated. A specially designed metal spray gun is used to produce the spray. This method of galvanizing is used for coating articles too large or complex to galvanize by any other method or which are in a fixed position. The zinc coating does not alloy with the base metal but simply adheres to it, much the same as with paint.

2-9.1.6 Repairing Galvanized Surfaces.
Galvanized surfaces which have been abraded or otherwise damaged must be repaired if the effectiveness of the original coating is to be maintained.

All galvanized areas to be repaired must be thoroughly cleaned and dried before effecting any repairs. Under no circumstances shall an aluminum paint be used to repair damage to a galvanized surface.

Zinc oxide-zinc dust paint conforming to DOD-P-21035 and 8 mils in thickness may be used to repair damaged areas.

Besides touching up such areas by metal spraying as described in Subsection 2-9.1.5, there are many patented materials on the market which can be used for this purpose. However, all such materials must be submitted to the Testing Agency for testing and be approved by the Engineer prior to their use.

Some methods previously tested and currently approved follow:

(a) **Galvalloy.** A patented zinc alloy bar, called Galvalloy, which resembles a bar of solder, is currently available. The abraded galvanized area is preheated with a blow torch or with the bright flame of an oxy-acetylene torch and the Galvalloy rubbed over the damaged area until a satisfactory coating is built up. Some difficulty is encountered in effecting repairs on irregular surfaces, in re-entrant angles and other areas having problems of accessibility.

(b) **Galvicon.** This patented process is intended for use in a manner similar to paint. It consists of two separate components which must be mixed together in the desired quantity shortly before it is applied. It may be applied cold with a brush or spray gun or the article may be dipped into the mixture. One major advantage in the use of Galvicon is its ease of application, even to irregular surfaces and areas which may be inaccessible by other mehods. Also, the problem of applying heat and risking damage to existing galvanized surfaces or other materials is eliminated.

2-9.2 Welding Processes and Materials.

2-9.2.1 General. Most welding commonly encountered in construction employs the metal arc process. In the metal arc process, a flow of electrical current passes through an electrode having a shielded arc and deposits metal from the electrode into the area to be welded. Automatic welders are commonly used in fabrication shops. These automatic welders usually operate on the metal arc principle and mechanically follow the joint to be welded. Some automatic welders deposit a flux on the joint just ahead of the arc from the electrode which is continuously fed from a reel.

Other manual and automatic processes employ carbon electrodes, inert gas shields, electric resistance fusion and special alloy electrodes. Special welding techniques are used for stainless steel and many non-ferrous metals.

2-9.2.2 **Types of Joints.** Welded joints utilized for various types of work and the principal welding positions are shown on Plate 24, Appendix. Basically there are four welding positions: flat, horizontal, vertical and overhead.

Joints welded utilizing the vertical and overhead positions are called "freeze" joints. The weld metal must freeze quickly to keep the molten metal from spilling from the joint. Flat and horizontal fillets as well as lap welds in plate over ³⁄₁₆-inch thick, are called "fill" joints. They require fast fill electrodes with high deposit rates and are used only on level or slightly inclined joints. Joints in sheet metal less than ³⁄₁₆-inch in thickness requires an electrode that will weld at a high travel rate with a minimum of skips, slag entrapment or undercut. Such joints are called "follow" joints.

2-9.2.3 **Polarity.** In the metal arc process, an electric current (generally direct current) is passed through the electrode. There is a decided difference in welding characteristics when using "straight" or "reverse" polarity in a welding circuit. In "straight" polarity, the negative terminal of the generator is connected to the electrode holder, the positive terminal to the work. Conversely, in "reverse" polarity the negative terminal is connected to the work, the positive terminal to the electrode holder. Bare or lightly coated electrodes give better results using straight polarity because more heat is generated on the positive side of the circuit. However, electrodes with heavy coatings generally give better results using reverse polarity.

For overhead and vertical joints requiring a fast freeze, DC positive, reverse polarity is recommended. Similarly, when welding sheet steel under ³⁄₁₆-inch thick, DC negative, straight polarity results in best performance. For fast fill in horizontal or flat joints, AC for high speeds results in the best operation characteristics. Direct current (DC) can be used, but arc blow and control of the molten puddle are often problems.

2-9.2.4 **Classification of Electrodes.** Electrodes are classified by the American Welding Society (AWS) and the American Society for Testing and Materials (ASTM) by use of standard numbers. For example, in the designation E-6010, "E" means arc welding electrode. The first two digits of four digit numbers (and the first three digits in five digit numbers) indicate the minimum tensile strength in the stress relieved condition. Therefore the E-6010 electrode will have a minimum tensile strength of 60,000 psi. The next to last digit indicates the welding position best suited for the electrode: 1 for all position and 2 for flat and horizontal positions. The last two digits, taken together, indicates the type of coating, its polarity and current to be used.

In addition, many electrodes are for special purposes and a suffix is added to the designation such as: E-7010-A1. This suffix refers to the percentage of alloying metals in the electrode per the following listing:

– A1	½% Molybdenum (Mo)
– B1	½% Chromium (Cr), ½% Molybdenum (Mo)
– B2	1¼% Chromium (Cr), ½% Molybdenum (Mo)
– B3	2¼% Chromium (Cr), 1% Molybdenum (Mo)
– C1	2½% Nickel (Ni)
← C2	3¼% Nickel (Ni)
– C3	1% Nickel (N), 0.35% Molybdenum (Mo)
	1.25% - 2.00% Manganese (Mn)
– D1 & D2	0.25% - 0.45% Molybdenum (Mo)
	1.25% - 2.00% Manganese (Mn)
– G	[one of the following:]
	0.50% Nickel (Ni) minimum
	0.30% Chromium (Cr) minimum
	0.20% Molybdenum (Mo) minimum
	0.10% Vanadium (V) minimum
– M	1.30 - 1.80% Manganese (Mn)
	1.25 - 2.50% Nickel (Ni)
	0.40% Chromium (Cr)
	0.25 - 0.50% Molybdenum (Mo)
	0.05% Vanadium (V) maximum

2-9.2.5 Welding Symbols. To simplify the plans where welding is required, certain symbols are used. These symbols are shown on Plate 26, Appendix.

2-9.3 Heat-Treatment of Metals.

2-9.3.1 General. Heat-treatment is accomplished by specially controlled heating and cooling of a metal or alloy in solid state in order to obtain certain desirable conditions or properties.

2-9.3.2 Annealing. Metals which have been rolled, drawn, hammered, forged (work hardened) or which have been hardened by heating and quenching, can be made soft and ductile by annealing. This process involves heating the metal to about 100°F above the critical temperature range and cooling slowly in a confined space.

2-9.3.3 Hardening. When heated, iron passes through a critical temperature range (about 1350°F) changing from a form which has a low solubility for carbon to a form which has a high solubility for carbon. Upon cooling, the reverse transformation occurs, but since the changes are progressive and require time for completion, they may be arrested if the rate of cooling is increased.

If the cooling is very rapid (as in water quenching), the transformation takes place at temperatures far below the critical temperature range and the carbon is held in a finely divided state with the result that the steel becomes hard and brittle and a great deal stronger than steel that has been cooled slowly. Increasing the carbon content increases the degree of hardening possible.

2-9.3.4 Tempering. When a steel is hardened by a quenching process, it is usually too brittle for ordinary purposes. Therefore, some of the hardness can be removed by reheating the steel to a temperature lower than the critical temperature (which is known to produce the toughness characteristics desired in the steel) and the steel requenched. The tempering temperatures vary with the carbon content and the alloy composition of the steel.

2-9.3.5 Case Hardening. This process consists of causing the surface of a piece of steel to absorb carbon. A thin shell having the properties of tool steel is formed on the surface of the piece. This hardened case or shell can be heat treated as though it were tool steel. Only the case (which has a high-carbon content) becomes hard, while the core remains soft, tough and ductile. This case can be varied in thickness from a few thousandths of an inch to an eighth of an inch or more, depending upon the process used.

In the pack hardening process, the steel to be case hardened is packed in charred bone or charred leather in a closed iron container and heated for a considerable time in a forge or furnace. In the cyanide process, the parts are heated in a bath of molten potassium cyanide. The longer the time, the thicker the case.

2-9.4 Metal Fabrication Shop Inspection.

2-9.4.1 General. Shop inspection, in general, is discussed in Subsection 2-1.2. The Agency policy is to inspect all specially fabricated metal work at the shop. Structural steel receives the most attention with the effort varying from continuous to timely periodic inspection.

Miscellaneous metals are generally inspected after fabrication but before shipment to the jobsite. Some architectural metal fabrication such as anodized aluminum railings may warrant additional attention to minimize problems. In some cases, continuous inspection in the early stages will be helpful especially where a new fabricator is not familiar with Agency quality standards.

The Agency requires all welders, welding operations and welding procedures to be qualified in accordance with standard qualification test procedures. In most cases, American Welding Society standard welding procedures may be utilized without further qualification.

All materials utilized for metal fabrication must be identified and certified by mill test reports prior to being cut.

In most cases, shop drawings approved by the Agency are required for metal fabrication. However, when the project plans are sufficiently detailed (such as weld sizes, welding sequences and procedures) shop drawings may not be necessary. When the shop drawings include changes from plan requirements, the fabricator or the contractor is obligated to note such differences in his submittal. In the absence of direct evidence, the Inspector should verify that significant deviations from plan requirements have been considered by the Design Engineer.

2-10 TIMBER

2-10.1 General. The Standard Specifications provide that all lumber and structural timbers to be used shall be as indicated on the plans or in the Special Provisions. Piling shall be Douglas fir. All lumber shall be selected as to grade and shall conform in all respects to the standard Grading Rules for Western Lumber, published by the Western Wood Products Association and approved by the American Lumber Standards Committee. Redwood shall conform to the grading rules published by the California Redwood Association.

Douglas fir is well adapted for structural uses because it is strong, moderately hard and heavy. The heartwood (between the pitch and the outer, still-growing sapwood) is moderately resistant to decay. It is for this reason that the Standard Specifications require that sapwood be kept to a minimum. The strength of timber depends on the density, which is indicated by the number of annual rings and summerwood growth; the greater the number of rings per inch the greater the density.

2-10.2 Standard Dimensions. The traditional finished sizes of dressed lumber have undergone some changes in the new grading and dressing rules. The old 2 x 4 used to dress out, after being surfaced on four sides, to dimensions close to 1⅝ by 3⅝ inches. This was because the rough-cut members was two by four inches and ³⁄₁₆ of an inch was lost on each side and edge in the planing operation. When it is considered to be dry, the new 2 x 4 will dress out to 1½ by 3½ inches under the new grading rules. The unseasoned surfaced 2 x 4 would be ³⁄₁₆-inch larger in each dimension to allow for shrinkage upon drying.

Dry boards eight inches and wider are dressed to ¾-inch less than the nominal size instead of the ½-inch for narrower boards and timbers.

For the actual sizes and tolerances permitted, it is necessary to consult the Grading Rules. Some of the timber and framing members commonly referred to by their traditional "size" in the past as 2 x 8, 2 x 12, 4 x 4, and 6 x 8, when dry and surfaced on four sides are actually 1½ x 7¼, 1½ x 11¼, 3½ x 3½, and 5½ x 7½ inches respectively.

Lumber can be furnished rough or dressed. Rough lumber is saw cut only (unplaned) with saw marks normally showing on the longitudinal surfaces. Dressed (or surfaced) lumber has been processed through a planing mill. Lumber can be surfaced on one or more sides and the symbols S1S, S2S and S4S mean surfaced on 1 side, 2 sides or 4 sides respectively. Similarly S1E or S2E means surfaced on 1 edge or surfaced on 2 edges. Combinations of surfacing are available, such as S2S1E (surfaced on 2 sides and 1 edge), S1S2E (surfaced on 1 side and 2 edges), etc.

2-10.3 Grading. Grading of Douglas fir is to be strictly in accordance with the standards established in the current Standard Grading Rules for Western Lumber, published by the Western Wood Products Association and approved by the American Lumber Standards Committee.

For general engineering public works construction, the grades of Douglas fir most commonly used are listed in the following table:

DOUGLAS FIR GRADING

Type of Lumber	Grade	Typical Use
Select Structural Joists and Plans	Select Structural	Used where strength is the primary consideration, with appearance desirable.
	No. 1	Used where strength is less critical and appearance not a major consideration.
	No. 2	Used for framing elements that will be covered by subsequent construction.
	No. 3	Used for structural framing where strength is required but appearance is not a factor.
Finish Lumber	Superior	For all types of uses as casings, cabinet, exposed members, etc., where a fine appearance is desired.
	Prime	
	E	
Boards (WCLIB)*	Select Merchantable	Intended for use in housing and light construction where a knotty type of lumber with finest appearance is required.
*Grading is by West Coast Lumber Inspection Bureau rules, but sizes conform to Western Wood Products Assn. rules. These boards are still manufactured by some mills.	Construction	Used for sub-flooring, roof and wall sheathing, concrete forms, etc. Has a high degree of serviceability.
	Standard	Used widely for general construction purposes, including subfloors, roof and wall sheathing, concrete forms, etc. Seldom used in exposed construction because appearance.
	Utility	Used in general construction where low cost is a factor and appearance is not important. (Storage shelving, crates, bracing, temporary scaffolding, etc.)

DOUGLAS FIR GRADING (Continue)

Type of Lumber	Grade	Typical Use
Structural Light Framing Joists and Planks, Beams and Stringers, and Posts and Timbers	Select Structural	Used where high strength, stiffness and good appearance are required.
	No. 1	
	No. 2	Used for most general construction purposes.
	No. 3	Used in general construction where appearance is not a factor.

2-10.4 Grade Stamps. Grade stamps are intended to label the quality of lumber for ready identification. They are distinctive and denote grade, species, moisture content, mill number and the applicable grading rules. (See Plate 20, Appendix.)

2-10.5 Moisture Content. The moisture content of wood is the weight of the water in the wood, expressed as a percentage of the weight of wood from which all water has been removed, either by air-drying or in special kilns. Lumber having a moisture content of 19% or less is defined as "dry." Lumber having a moisture content of 20% or over is defined as "unseasoned" lumber. Lumber may be surfaced when dry or when it is unseasoned. Allowances are made in the size to permit lumber surfaced with a moisture content (MC) above 19% to permit it to shrink to the standard sizes. Such lumber is stamped "S-GRN" (surfaced green). Stamps containing a legend such as "MC-15" indicate that the lumber had a moisture content of 15% when it was surfaced.

2-10.6 Redwood. Redwood is a fairly strong and moderately lightweight material. The heartwood is red but the sapwood is white. One of the principal advantages of redwood is that the heartwood is highly resistant (but not entirely immune) to decay, fungus and insects. Standard Specifications require that all redwood used in permanent installations shall be "select heart." Grade marking shall be in accordance with the standards established in the California Redwood Association. Grade marking shall be done by, or under the supervision of the Redwood Inspection Service. (See Plate 21, Appendix.)

Redwood is graded for specific uses as indicated in the following table:

REDWOOD GRADING

Type of Lumber	Grade	Typical Use
Grades for Dimension Only Listed Here	Clear All Heart	Exceptionally fine, knot free, straight-grained timbers. This grade is used primarily for stain finish work of high quality.
	Clear	Same as Clear All Heart except that this grade may contain sound sapwood and medium stain.
	Select Heart	**This grade only is to be used in Agency work, unless otherwise specified in the plans or specifications.** It is sound, live heartwood free from splits or streaks with sound knots. It is generally used where the timber is in contact with the ground, as in posts, mudsills, etc.
	Select Construction Heart	Slightly less quality than Select Heart. It may have some sapwood in the piece. Used for general construction purposes when redwood is needed.
	Construction Common	Same requirement as Construction Heart except that it will contain sapwood and medium stain. Its resistance to decay and insect attack is reduced.
	Merchantable	Used for fence posts, garden stakes, etc.
	Economy	Suitable for crating, bracing and temporary construction.

2-10.7 Methods of Mill Sawing Lumber. Saw mills try to get as many boards as possible from a tree with minimum waste. At the same time, careful consideration is given to the slant of the grain which will result from the method of sawing so as to obtain lumber having the characteristics of the grade desired. Boards with vertical grain are generally stronger and are suitable for finish types of work. Boards with flat grain are susceptible to splintering and cupping but may result in highly desirable grain patterns for stain finishing. The usual methods for laying out and sawing timber are shown in Plate 23, Appendix.

2-10.8 Glossary of Lumber Terms. Some of the words and terms used in the grading of lumber follow:

Bow. A deviation flatwise from a straight line drawn from end to end of the piece. It is measured at the point of greatest distance from the straight line.

Checks. A separation of the wood which normally occurs across the annual rings and usually as a result of seasoning.

Crook. A deviation edgewise from a straight line drawn from end to end of the piece. It is measured at the point of greatest distance from the straight line.

Cup. A deviation from a straight line drawn across the piece from edge to edge. It is measured at the point of greatest distance from the straight line.

Flat Grain. The annual growth rings pass through the piece at an angle of less than 45 degrees with the flat surface of the piece.

Mixed Grain. The piece may have vertical grain, flat grain, or a combination of both vertical and flat grain.

Pitch. An accumulation of resin which occurs in separations in the wood or in the wood cells themselves.

Shake. A separation of the wood which usually occurs between the rings of annual growth.

Splits. A separation of the wood due to tearing apart of the wood cells.

Vertical Grain. The annual growth rings pass through the piece at an angle of 45 degrees or more with the flat surface of the piece.

Wane. Bark or lack of wood from any cause, except eased edges (rounded) on the edge or corner of a piece of lumber.

Warp. Any deviation from a true or plane surface, including crook, cup, bow or any combination thereof.

2-10.9   Plywood. Plywood is a built-up board of laminated veneers in which the grain of each layer is at right angles to the one adjacent to it. Plywood is made in two types: interior and exterior. Grading and marking shall conform to the rules of the American Plywood Association and Product Standard PS 1-83 for all construction and industrial plywood.

In general, the quality of the surface lamination is shown in the grading stamp, with A being the highest quality and D the lowest quality. Grade A-A (Int) means an interior grade of plywood with front and back faces of the highest quality. Grade B-C (Ext) means an exterior plywood with one good face and the back face of fair quality. Typical grade stamps, which are stamped on the edge or back of the panel, are shown on Plate 22, Appendix.

Plywood is commonly stocked in 4'x8' or 4'x10' panels. Other stock sizes of plywood (which may not be readily available) vary from 30 inches to 60 inches in width, and lengths vary from five feet to 10 feet.

2-10-10   Timber Piles. Timber piles are required by the Standard Specifications to be Douglas fir because of its great strength and its availability in long tapered lengths. Treatment with a preservative is generally specified. Western red cedar exhibits good resistance to decay but is considerably weaker than Douglas fir. It is available only in shorter lengths and since it crushes easily, it is not favored for use as piling.

2-10.11   Preservative Treatment. In general, the purpose of treating timber is to protect it against decay-producing fungi or against marine borers. Mild temperatures, dampness and sluggish circulation of air are conditions conducive to decay. Marine borers are found in all coastal waters in Southern California.

Preservative treatment shall conform to the standards established in the American Wood-Preserver's Association. The principal types of preservatives used are creosote, pentachlorophenol, chromated zinc chloride, tanalith, ammoniacal copper arsenate or chromated copper arsenate. Creosote treatment is accomplished by placing the lumber or piles in a heated, high-pressure retort. Subsequent to pressure treatment, cut ends, bored bolt holes and notches in creosoted lumber are painted with hot creosote.

Lumber treated with water-borne preservatives can be pressure treated, dipped, brush-coated or sprayed with the preservative, dependent upon the supplier and the circumstances attending the construction. When possible, such lumber should be treated in advance by the supplier and cut ends, holes and notches brush-coated or sprayed with the preservative during construction. When treated lumber is inspected by the Agency at the plant, it is identified as described in Subsection 2-1.2.7.

2-10.11.1 Creosote. This preservative is the most effective and long lasting of all and is most commonly used for treating piling and bridge timbers. Its principal advantages are: high toxicity to fungi and borers, insolubility and low volatility, ease of application, ease with which penetration can be determined, availability and low cost. Disadvantages are: fire hazard when still fresh, objectionable odor and tendency to irritate the skin. It is also very difficult to paint over creosoted surfaces. Pressure treatment of piles and lumber is accomplished in a large cylinder so constructed as to permit easy charging, usually on tracked dollies. The cylinder is equipped to heat the contents to permit the introduction or withdrawal of creosote, and to vary the internal pressure in the vessel from vacuum to pressure conditions. Lumber or piles to be pressure treated should not be taken directly from mill ponds, but must be thoroughly air seasoned or kiln dried. Excess moisture in the timber results in cracking during treatment. These timbers should be pre-inspected and all pieces which do not fully meet the specifications as to grade and condition should be rejected. In order to secure a more uniform penetration of the preservative, lumber measuring three inches or over in thickness by four inches or over in width should be incised by a machine having power-driven rolls designed to incise to a uniform depth and a continuity of pre-determined pattern. Lumber four inches or over in thickness should be incised on all four sides. Lumber less than four inches thick shall be incised on the wide faces only. The incisor teeth should be chisel-shaped and so designed that a separation and spreading of the wood fibers is accomplished upon their entering or leaving the wood. Pressure treatment of timber is accomplished by the two methods: full cell and empty cell processes.

(a) Full Cell Process (Bethel or Burnett Process). After the retort cylinder is charged with air-seasoned timber, it is subjected to 22 inches of vacuum for not less than 30 minutes.

Without breaking the vacuum, the cylinder is filled with creosote heated to between 180°F and 210°F. The pressure is then raised to 150 psi and these conditions maintained until the volumetric injection is obtained that will insure the stipulated retention, or until the wood is treated to refusal. This may take as much as six hours.

After pressure treatment is completed, the cylinder is rapidly emptied of preservative and a vacuum of 22 inches is applied promptly and maintained until the timbers can be removed from the cylinder free of dripping preservative. An expansion bath may be applied after pressure treatment or the treated timbers may be cleaned with steam.

(b) **Empty Cell Process (Lowry or Rueping Process).** After the retort cylinder is charged with air-seasoned timber, the pressure is raised to exceed atmospheric pressures. While maintaining this pressure, the cylinder is filled with creosote heated to between 180°F and 210°F. The pressure is increased to 150 psi and these conditions are maintained until the largest practicable volumetric injection is obtained that will insure the stipulated retention.

After pressure treatment is completed, the cylinder is rapidly emptied of preservative and a vacuum of 22 inches is promptly applied until the timber can be removed from the cylinder free of dripping preservative. The treated timber is generally steam cleaned prior to shipping.

2-10.11.2 Chromated Zinc Chloride. This waterborne preservative is frequently used for timber intended for use in contact with the ground. It has moderate toxicity, good paintability, good appearance, is readily available and is low in cost. It is not favored for wet locations as the preservative is soluble in water and may leach out of the treated piece.

2-10.11.3 Tanalith (Wolman. Salts). This is a proprietary water-borne preservative containing sodium fluoride, sodium hydrogen arsenate, dinitrophenol and certain chromates. The advantages and disadvantages are similar to those of chromated zinc chloride.

2-10.11.4 Ammoniacal Copper Arsenate (Chemonite). This is a water-borne copper arsenite solution in ammoniacal water. Arsenic compounds are toxic to many fungi but not to all. Arsenic preservatives should be used only where ventilation will be adequate. Lumber treated with this compound is moderately toxic, paintable, has good appearance and has a low treatment cost. The preservative tends to leach out when subject to wet conditions.

2-10.11.5 Chromated Copper Arsenate (Boliden Salt). This is a water-borne solution which, like other arsenic preservatives, is highly toxic to some fungi, but leaches out in wet locations. Lumber treated with this solution is similar in most respects to lumber treated with Chemonite in its toxicity, paintability, appearance and cost of treatment. Its advantages and disadvantages are also similar to those of Chemonite.

2-10.11.6 Pentachlorophenol. Pentachlorophenol (commonly known as Penta) is a chemical that can be carried in either solvents or liquid petroleum gas (LPG). Generally, five percent of the solution is comprised of the chemical Penta.

Wood treated with Penta is used for poles, posts and millwork. Penta in LPG (commercially known as Cellon) gives a clean dry surface which can be painted or stained.

The chemical retention of pentachlorophenol is LP4 above ground and LP-44 at ground contact. (Chemical retention is the weight of the chemical retained per cubic foot of wood after treatment; the larger the number, the more chemical retained.)

2-11 PAINT

2-11.1 General. Paint is composed of a pigment (or pigments) and the vehicle. The pigment component is provided to color the paint and to enable it to form a film on the painted surface to which it is applied. The liquid portion of the paint is the vehicle, which in turn includes components which serve as binders and volatile constituents known as thinners. (See Subsection 3-14 for painting inspection.)

2-11.2 Pigments. Pigments can be divided into three classes: natural, organic and synthetic pigments. The principal pigments provided for in the Standard Specifications are: red lead, red iron oxide, aluminum paste, white lead, zinc dust, zinc oxide, titanium dioxide and alkyd resin solids.

When paint vehicles and pigments are thoroughly mixed for painting, the pigments tend to settle out rapidly and it is necessary to remix frequently to obtain a uniform paint film application. To reduce this tendency for the pigments to settle out, aluminum stearate is compounded in most paint formulas. Aluminum stearate is added in very small amounts (.3 to .4 percent by weight) and tends to gel the paint without thickening it beyond painting consistencies. Aluminum stearate also imparts a flatting effect and water-resistant properties to the paint film.

2-11.3   Vehicles.   Paint vehicles are intended to keep the pigment in suspension until the paint is applied to a surface, after which it must "dry" to leave a pigment film. This "drying" occurs through evaporation, oxidation or polymerization of the vehicle. Where oxidation of the vehicle is intended, dryers are often employed to hasten the drying process. The principal vehicles provided for are: linseed oil, petroleum or mineral spirit thinners, turpentine and a special varnish used as an aluminum paint vehicle.

2-11.4   Paint Uses.   Each kind of paint is intended for a specific purpose or particular use. Red lead-iron oxide pigments in linseed oil-alkyd resin vehicles are particularly adapted for use in priming structural steel subjected to long exposure without topcoats. Structural steel not subject to much rehandling can be primed satisfactorily with red-lead linseed-oil paints. Galvanized metal can best be painted with a zinc dust-zinc oxide primer. Aluminum finish coats are generally applied only to provide a finished appearance to the work.

Since the sulfides of titanium are also white, titanium dioxide pigments do not discolor as do lead base paints in an sulfur-bearing atmosphere. This makes them particularly useful in painting wood.

2-12   ENGINEERING FABRICS

2-12.1   General.   In the past decade, many new products known as engineering fabrics have been introduced into the construction industry, each intended for a specific purpose. Most are plastic products of polyester or high density polypropylene materials and vary from open mesh and web configurations through permeable woven or permeable non-woven materials to impermeable films.

The mesh and web types with larger openings have a wide range of uses from snow fences, safety nets and industrial screening to mesh for reinforced concrete, and these types are commonly referred to as "netting." Special types of webs are three-dimensional so it can be used to provide drainage within its plane as well as transversely through its face. These are used as down drains behind walls and abutments as well as for

French drains under pond liners to relieve the hydraulic pressure of ground water against the side slopes or bottom of the pond. Other types of nettings are used to control erosion along shorelines and on steep slopes as well as for gabions, slide maintenance and in revegetation of slopes.

Some types of engineering fabrics are impermeable and are intended to prevent the migration of water and are commonly used for pond liners, drainage channels and pavement fabric.

Engineering fabrics are available in rolls up to 300 feet in length and vary in width from 36 inches for silt fences up to 15 feet wide for other applications.

2-12.2 **Geotextiles.** Woven and nonwoven fabrics manufactured of polyolefin, polyester or fiberglass fibers which are permeable and used in geotechnical applications are referred to as geotextiles. Those classes of fabrics such as nettings, woven needlepunched or slit film fabrics, woven monofilament films, and those made of randomly oriented petrochemical fibers heat bonded into a fabric, are the most common types of geotextiles. Their primary use in engineering construction is for soil stabilization, embankment stabilization and for sedimentation control (silt fences). They are frequently used to protect revegetated slopes when stapled or staked over the seed bed and mulch. Since they are essentially chemically and biologically inert and often ultraviolet light (UV) stabilized, they are very effective in protecting slopes from wind or rain erosion and disturbance of the seed bed for several seasons until the vegetation is well established. Rain or sprinkler watering readily passes through the netting to soak the seed bed, and the vegetation will grow through the netting.

Some fabrics are needlepunched, slit punched or otherwise manufactured to be permeable to the slow migration of water while restraining the fine grained soil particles. These fabrics are used as silt fences and where soil separation is necessary such as minimizing subgrade pumping of fine particles upward into railroad ballast.

Geotextiles are becoming more popular in the construction of roads and runways upon foundation earth that is unstable. The fabric, placed directly upon the unstable surface (such as in a swamp area) or on highly plastic silts (such as muck), tends to prevent rotational or wedge-type failure of the unstable foundation. In addition, it helps to minimize excessive vertical displacement by providing the strength and friction necessary to prevent lateral sliding, and it separates the fill from the underlaying muck.

2-12.3 Pavement Fabric. Pavement fabrics are most commonly nonwoven polypropylene sheets and are used on prepared subgrade for a roadway structure or upon an existing pavement prior to an asphalt overlay.

The primary purpose of the fabric is to prevent water from migrating through the pavement into the base and subgrade. This, however, cannot be a substitute for a proper roadbed design that provides for adequate drainage. In addition, the use of a pavement fabric on an old pavement will not eliminate reflective cracking entirely, but it does reduce the number of cracks and their severity.

2-12.4 Pond Liners. Pond liners are impermeable petrochemical sheets that are bonded together at the seams to form a non-permeable liner for such installations as ponds, reservoirs and toxic waste disposal sites. There are other proprietary products available, one of which consists of a layer of sodium bentonite bonded to a propylene mat. When installed and the pond filled with a liquid, the wetted bentonite swells to provide the impermeability of the lining.

2-12.5 Storage and Handling. Fabric is delivered from the manufacturer in rolls having a heavy-duty cardboard core with the roll sealed in a black plastic envelope, generally made of polyvinylchloride (PVC). Care must be exercised in handling these rolls (which can weigh up to 900 pounds) so as not to tear the envelope or damage the fabric.

Fabric rolls must not be rolled from the truck to the ground when unloading, but must be unloaded and transported to storage by hand or by using power equipment with slings under the roll or a pipe through the core and lifted from both ends. No hooks, tongs or other sharp tools shall be used in handling fabric.

It must be stored in a clean, dry building or, when stored outdoors, on supports at least one foot above the ground. The fabric must be kept in its protective covering until it is ready for installation. Opened rolls must be re-covered with a waterproof cover to protect the fabric from rain, dust and the effects of sunlight.

PART 3

INSPECTION PROCEDURES

3-1 GENERAL. The policies and procedures set forth in this subsection and in Part I apply generally to all classes of work.

Refer to Part I for General Inspection Policy (1-2); Records and Reports (1-3); Safety and Convenience Including Traffic (1-4); Construction Survey Staking (1-5); and Preservation of Improvements (1-6).

Information regarding procedures, inspection responsibilities concerning construction materials and their control are contained in Part 2.

3-1.1 Inspector Responsibility. It is the Inspector's responsibility to contact the Dispatcher for his daily job assignment during the afternoon of the preceding workday. On the first day of a new job assignment, a conscientious Inspector would report to his job assignment at a time sufficiently in advance of the contractor's regular starting time to permit him to introduce himself to the contractor's representative, determine that the plans for the project are in order and signed by the Engineer, insure that survey stakes are set and grade sheets available (where applicable), acquaint himself with the special conditions indicated on the plans or in the specifications for the project, review the standard plans referred to on the plans, determine what phases of construction are contemplated by the contractor for that day, and proceed to check those portions of the work for compliance with plans and specifications that will permit the contractor to commence the work at the regular starting time. During the course of each day on the job, the Inspector should prepare himself for the contractor's operations for each subsequent day. In these days of fast moving construction, it is too late to wait until the contractor starts the work before beginning preparatory inspection functions. (Refer to Subsection 1-1.4, Project Inspection Guidelines.)

Inspection of forms, subgrade for pavement and similar classes of work should be made immediately prior to the placing of concrete or pavement by the contractor. For certain other classes of work, inspection must be simultaneous with the contractor's operations, as in placing structural concrete, laying of sewer pipe, and pile driving. The Inspector must coordinate his activities to match those of the contractor, anticipating the need for his services far enough in advance to permit him to make an adequate check of the work for compliance without delaying the contractor's operations.

For some classes of work, the contractor must temporarily suspend operations at certain stages to permit the Inspector to check the work. Typical examples would include the mirroring of a sewer line to evaluate the pipe laying operations and determining the bearing capacity of a pile during driving operations. In other cases inspections must be timed to avoid unnecessary stoppage of the work. For example, the alert Inspector would be on hand and complete his check of wall reinforcement so that wall forms could be "buttoned up" without any delay. By close cooperation between the Inspector and the contractor these periods of work suspension can be minimized in length and frequency. In some cases the contractor may choose to shift his crews temporarily to proceed with another phase of the work.

The Inspector must determine the source of all materials intended to be incorporated into the work and, where plant or shop inspection is required, insure that such inspection has been made. (See Subsection 2-1.2.7.) When sampling of materials is required, samples must be taken promptly in accordance with the Sampling Schedule (Plate 28, Appendix) and expeditiously forwarded to the Testing Agency for testing. (See Subsection 2-1.3.)

The Project Inspector must identify and check all materials received on the project before they are incorporated into the work. He must see that the tests and inspections that are necessary at the site are carried out and verify that all tests and inspections required of materials prior to delivery have been satisfactorily completed. He must be sure that all test results are recorded, that any failures have been properly resolved, and that any required certifications of material have been received and filed. Finally, he must see that the materials are integrated into the construction in a satisfactory manner. Refer to Part II for detailed information concerning specific materials.

It is important that the Inspector is present at the project site during the contractor's regular working hours unless he has assigned duties elsewhere. In addition to his other responsibilities, the Inspector must remain available to the contractor to answer questions regarding the work or to respond to request for inspection service.

In cases of multiple assignments, the Inspector must exercise good judgment by dividing his time and setting his priorities so that all required inspection activities are carried out at each location. Good communication with the contractor and knowing his sequence of operation and construction schedule will avoid most problems in this regard.

The level of inspection service provided by the Inspector will be determined by a variety of conditions and circumstances. Examples where continuous inspection will be required are: laying and backfilling of a main line sewer, placing structural concrete, and reinforced concrete pipe manufacturing.

Semi-continuous inspection will be required for operations, such as laying and backfilling of house connection sewers, fine grade for pavement, and street light and traffic signal conduit installation.

Only intermittent inspection is required on noncritical work, such as removals, demolition projects and landscaping.

In determining the level of service required, the Inspector must also consider other factors, such as difficulty and complexity of the work, location and the character of the contractor's organization. Availability of the Inspector to answer the contractor's questions must also be taken into account.

The Inspector has the primary function and responsibility to inspect the work for compliance with the plans and specifications and this is a full-time job. He should direct all of his attention to the discharge of these responsibilities, and must avoid any circumstances which would make him appear to others to be idle, disinterested or display any other attitude that would reflect unfavorably on the function of inspection. Reading periodicals or engaging others in conversations not related to the work operates to discredit the image of the Inspector and will not be tolerated. The Inspector must create and maintain through his performance a public image which represents the highest standards of integrity, efficiency and proficiency.

It is the responsibility of each Inspector to keep himself and his superior fully informed with respect to matters affecting the project to which he is assigned. He should insure that he has received and is familiar with the applicable specifications, all changes of plan, approved shop drawings, and other documentation affecting the work. A chronology of the progress of the work and a brief summary of the events which occur on the project (which may later prove to be very important) should be carefully entered in the job records. (See Subsection 1-3 for detailed job reporting procedures.)

When problems arise which may be beyond the experience or authority of the Inspector to resolve, he should immediately consult his Supervisor for advice. It is emphasized that an Inspector is never permitted to guess. He must know that he is right in his judgment or he must consult with his superior for a resolution of the matter as expeditiously as possible.

The Agency provides each Inspector with small hand tools, measuring tapes, safety helmets, special clothing, sampling devices and special tools and devices as required. Except in rare circumstances, the contractor is not required to provide any item for the Inspector to use in the performance of his work. It is a policy of the Agency that the Inspector shall not request the contractor to furnish him any gauge, rule, tool, device or article of clothing which is not specifically provided for under the contract for the project. For example, undesirable inferences can be drawn by one who observes an Inspector wearing a safety helmet which bears the contractor's name or insignia.

Similarly, the Inspector is prohibited from operating vehicles or equipment belonging to the contractor, except in the case of extreme emergency. Not only would unfavorable impressions result, but the Agency would be liable in the event that an unjury or damage resulted from the operation of such vehicles or equipment by an Agency employee.

The most important character trait of an Inspector is his integrity. Unless the unquestioned integrity of the man is behind every decision, every action, every report, they all become meaningless, and the usefulness of the man to the Agency as an Inspector ceases.

3-1.2 Pre-Construction Conference. For major or complex construction projects, it is usually advisable to schedule a pre-construction conference to be attended by representatives of the contractor, his principal subcontractors, the Design Engineer, other design agencies that may be involved, affected utility agencies and other parties that may be concerned such as: flood control districts, school districts, adjacent municipalities, bonding agent, major material suppliers, etc.

The conference should be scheduled after the bid is awarded but at least 10 days prior to the start of construction and at a location central to most participants. There is sometimes an advantage to holding this conference at the jobsite, but it is often too noisy, windy and difficult to communicate and hold the interest of a moderately large group in the outdoors. Much more can be accomplished in a quiet indoor conference room. The meeting agenda is prepared by, and the conference conducted by, the Project Inspector or his Supervisor.

Agenda items can be solicited in advance by the Project Inspector from the participants and should include such items as: self-introduction, exchange of telephone numbers and opening remarks by the Project Inspector. The agenda will also include information on the notice to proceed, the responsibilites of the Agency and its representatives, the chain of communications, traffic considerations, plant operation involvement, submittal procedures, site layout and control, safety, scheduling requirements and CPM, payment request procedures, regular weekly meetings with the contractor, and other participant items that may be relevant to the project.

The discussion should be kept within the agenda by the individual conducting the meeting, keeping progress moving and tactfully discouraging commentary not relevant to the matter under consideration. Items involving utilities and other agencies should be covered early in the meeting so that they may leave.

Those present are encouraged to raise questions and to resolve questions as each item is discussed. When all agenda items have been covered, each participant is asked for additional input or questions until all matters of interest are settled.

Minutes of these preconstruction conferences should be taken and a copy provided to each participant.

3-2 SOIL TYPES AND TESTING

3-2.1 **General.** There is no more universal and ever-present construction material than soil. However, the complexities of soil behavior demand that sufficient investigation and research be undertaken to permit a rational analysis and prediction of the stability of each soil type or mixture under anticipated loads. Soils vary greatly from one place to another, often only a few feet away, and their performance may radically change with a small change in their moisture content.

A typical soil mass is composed of three constituents: soil grains, air and water. In soils consisting largely of fine grained material, the amount of water present in the voids has a pronounced effect on the soil properties. On soil composed largely of coarse grained material, this effect is materially reduced. Soil can be classified into three main states of consistency which are easily recognizable: liquid state (will flow like a viscous fluid), plastic state (can be molded like modeling clay) and solid state (will crack when deformed or will exhibit elastic rebound). (See Plate 30, Appendix.)

Rounded soil particles over three inches in diameter are referred to as cobbles, and boulders if they are larger than 12 inches. Solid material over one cubic yard in volume is classified as rock. In general, specifications usually limit or prohibit the incorportion of these materials in embankments of fills. The range of soil particle size extends from cobbles down to fine sands or clays which may easily pass a No. 200 sieve.

It is important for the Inspector to learn to identify general soil types and be familiar with their behavior under all conditions.

For most construction purposes, the following table lists the presumptive bearing capacities of various soil types:

Material	Capacity In Tons/Sq. Ft.
Hard sound rock	40
Medium hard rock	25
Hard pan overlaying rock	10
Soft rock	8
Gravel	6
Coarse sand	4
Fine dry sand	3
Sand & clay, mixed or layered	2
Firm clay	2
Fine & wet sand (confined)	2
Soft clay	1

3-2.2 Soil Classification. There are many different methods of soil classification in use today. However, only those classifications which can be easily understood and applied by persons unskilled in soil mechanics are included here.

3-2.2.1 Classification by Origin.

RESIDUAL	Cumulose	Rock weathered in place: wacke, lacterite, podzols, residual sands, clays and gravels. Organic accumulations: peat, muck, swamp soils, muskeg, humus, bog soils.
TRANSPORTED	Glacial	Moraines, eskers, drumlins, kames: till, drift, boulder clay, glacial sands and gravels.
	Alluvial	Flood-plain deltas, bars: sedimentary clays and silts, alluvial sands and gravels.
	Aeolian	Wind-borne deposits: blow sands, dune sands, loess, adobes.
	Colluvial	Gravity deposits: cliff debris, talus, avalanches, masses of rock waste.
	Volcanic	Volcanic deposits: Dakota bentonite, volclay, volcanic ash, lava.
	Fill	Man-made deposits: may range from waste and rubbish to carefully built embankments.

3-2.2.2 Classification by Particle Size. Soils can be classified in general terms by the nature of their predominant particle size or the grading of the particle sizes. These particle sizes are usually grouped into gravel, coarse sand, medium sand, fine sand, silt, clay and colloids.

The major divisions of soils are:

Coarse-Grained (Granular)		Fine-Grained		Organic	
Gravel	Sand	Silt	Clay	Muck	Peat

Soils comprised primarily of sand particles are referred to as "granular soils," while fine-grained soils are commonly called "heavy soils." It is accepted practice in the field to refer to a particular soil as a coarse sand, or silt, or by any of the particle size groupings which describe the soil generally from a visual examination.

3-2.2.3   Classification of Soil Mixtures.

Class	% Sand	% Silt	% Clay
Sand	80-100	0- 20	0- 20
Sandy clay loam	50- 80	0- 30	20- 30
Sandy loam	50- 80	0- 50	0- 20
Loam	30- 50	30- 50	0- 20
Silty loam	0- 50	50- 80	0- 20
Silt	0- 20	80-100	0- 20
Silty clay loam	0- 30	50- 80	20- 30
Silty clay	0- 20	50- 70	30- 50
Clay loam	20- 50	20- 50	20- 30
Sandy clay	50- 70	0- 20	30- 50
Clay	0- 50	0- 50	30-100

3-2.3   Soil Identification.   For most purposes, soils can usually be identified visually and by texture, as described in the chart that follows. For design purposes, however, soils must be formally identified and their performance characteristics determined in a laboratory by technicians skilled in soil mechanics.

Classification	Identifying Characteristics
Gravel	Rounded or water-worn pebbles or bulk rock grains. No cohesion or plasticity. Gritty, granular, and crunchy underfoot.
Sand	Granular, gritty, loose grains, passing a No. 4 sieve and between .002 and .079 inches in diameter. Individual grains readily seen and felt. No plasticity or cohesion. When dry, it cannot be molded but will crumble when touched. The coarse grains are rounded; the fine grains are visible and angular.
Silt	Fine, barely visible grains passing a No. 200 sieve and between .0002 and .002 inches in diameter. Little or no plasticity and no cohesion. A dried cast is easily crushed. Is permeable and movement of water through the voids occurs easily and is visible. Feels gritty when bitten and will not form a thread.

Classification	Identifying Characteristics
Clay	Invisible particles under .0002 inches in diameter. Cohesive and highly plastic when moist. Will form a long, thin, flexible thread when rolled between the hands. Does not feel gritty when bitten. Will form hard lumps or clods when dry which resist crushing. Impermeable, with no apparent movement of water through voids.
Muck and Organic Silt	Thoroughly decomposed organic material often mixed with other soils of mineral origin. Usually black with fibrous remains. Odorous when dried and burnt. Found as deposits in swamps, peat bogs and muskeg flats.
Peat	Partly decayed plant material. Mostly organic. Highly fibrous with visible plant remains. Spongy and easily identified.

3-2.4 Properties of Soil as Affected by Water.

3-2.4.1 **General.** Nearly all of the major soil problems revolve around the impracticality of maintaining a constant moisture condition in the soil. The principal difficulties result from the fact that both volume and bearing value can vary as the moisture content of the soil changes. Everyone knows from observation that a clay soil varies from a plastic condition when in a relatively wet state to a firm, brittle mass when dry. Excess water tends to lubricate the soil particles, permitting them to move readily over one another, yet when this "free water" is removed, the small fraction of the remaining moisture (termed cohesive water) assists in locking the same clay particles together into the characteristically brittle mass.

Water moves through the voids in soils as a vapor as well as a liquid. The ease with which this movement occurs is called the permeability; i.e., the higher the permeability, the greater is the quantity of water that can flow through the soil in a given period of time. Generally speaking, the coarser the particles the greater the permeability since the void spaces are greater. When a soil is uniformly (long) graded (having the right quantity of successively smaller particles needed to fill all the voids), its permeability is greatly reduced.

Water which moves as a liquid under pressure through a soil is termed seepage. If at some distance below the surface of the ground the soil becomes saturated, the top of the saturated soil strata is referred to as the water table. For example, when an excavation is made to a depth penetrating into saturated soil, the hole will fill with water to the approximate water table level. Moisture will also move vertically through fine-grained soils by capillary action. (See Subsection 2-12 and 3-15, Geotextiles and Pavement Fabric.)

Some soils, such as adobe, are highly expansive when they contain an excess of moisture. Every precaution must be taken with such materials when used for embankment or fills to provide for a design in the improvement to maintain a constant moisture content in the soil mass. One method for providing constant moisture in soils is to provide subdrains. Other methods include interception of surface water with pavement, impermeable subbase, gutters, drainage ditches, storm drains or seal coats.

Most soil problems generally fall into one of three categories: stability, settlement or permeability. Water is a factor in all of these categories.

3-2.4.2 Liquid Limit of Soils.

The liquid limit of a soil is the water content at which the groove formed in a soil sample by a standard grooving tool will just meet when the dish into which the soil sample is placed is lifted and dropped through one centimeter distance by a standard crank and cam device at a rate of two drops per second for 25 cycles. A 100-gram sample is used in a 4½-inch diameter brass cup. The sample is weighed, oven-dried and reweighed, and the loss is weight represents the moisture centent of the original sample. Several trials are made and the data plotted on a graph from which the liquid limit can be taken. The liquid limit is expressed as that percentage which the moisture content represents of the oven-dried weight of the sample.

3-2.4.3 Plastic Limit of Soils.

The plastic limit is the lowest water content at which the soil can just be rolled into a thread with a diameter of ⅛-inch without cracking, crumbling or breaking into pieces. In the laboratory, this test is performed by rolling the sample into a thread between the fingers and a ground-glass plate or unglazed paper. The specimen is weighed, oven-dried and reweighed, and the moisture content expressed as a percentage of the oven-dried weight of the sample.

Rough approximation of the plastic limit of soils may be obtained by rolling a soil specimen into a ⅛-inch diameter thread between the palms of the hands. The plastic limit is an indication of the lowest moisture content below which a soil can no longer be readily molded. The plastic limit, however, does not have a constant relationship to optimum moisture from one soil type to another.

3-2.4.4   Plasticity Index of Soils.   The plasticity index is the numerical difference between the liquid limit and the plastic limit of a given soil specimen. For example: a soil having a liquid limit of 29 and a plastic limit of 25 would have a plasticity index of 4. Soils which lack cohesion, such as coarse sands and gravels, are reported as non-plastic.

3-2.4.5   Shrinkage Limit of Soils.   The shrinkage limit of a soil is the water content at which there is no further decrease in volume with additional drying of the specimen, but at which an increase in water content will cause an increase in volume. A soil specimen is molded into a special form with a known volume and weighed, air-dried, then oven-dried to a constant weight. The oven-dried specimen is immersed in mercury to determine its volume in the dry state. The shrinkage limit is expressed as

$$SL = W - \frac{V - V_o}{W_o} \times 100 \text{ where:}$$

SL = Shrinkage limit
W = Water content of wet soil specimen expressed as a percentage of the oven-dried weight,
V = Volume of wet soil pat (in c.c.)
V_o = Volume of dry soil pat (in c.c.)
W_o = Weight of oven-dried soil pat (in gms.)

3-2.4.6   Atterburg Limit Test.   The liquid limit, plastic limit and shrinkage limit tests described above are known as the Atterburg limit test. They are named for the Swedish scientist who developed this series of tests in 1911.

3-2.4.7   Mechanical Analysis.   In general, mechanical analysis is understood by soil mechanics to mean the sieve analysis and hydrometer analysis of soils.

A nest of sieves ranging from .25-inch openings to .007-inch (approximate) openings are used to separate the oven-dried soil specimen into its various particle sizes. From this analysis, it is possible to determine a deficiency or excess of any particular particle size which may result in excessive voids, instability, permeability, etc. A sieve analysis is of value only to determine the grain size of the particles larger than No. 200 sieve size. To obtain the percentage of the smaller sizes present, a hydrometer analysis is used.

The hydrometer analysis is based on Stoke's Law that larger particles settle in water at a more rapid rate than smaller particles. The dried soil passing the No. 200 sieve must be completely broken up (if clustering occurs) and soaked in water overnight. The dispersed soil and water are poured into a glass cylinder and a specially graduated hydrometer immersed in the solution and readings taken at the ends of 1, 2, 5, 15, 30, 60,250 and 1,440 minutes (24 hour = 1,440 min.).

3-2.5   Soil Density and Strength Tests.

3-2.5.1   General.   In most cases, the strength of a soil (load carrying capacity) and resistance to movement or consolidation is important. These properties are greatly affected by the degree of compaction and moisture content.

Moisture density relationships are utilized in soil analysis to evaluate a soil's structural properties and to determine the quality of earth fill construction.

3-2.5.2   Optimum Moisture.   The soil density obtained by a given compactive effort depends upon the amount of water contained in a known volume of soil. For a given soil and a given compactive effort there is but one water content, called optimum water content (or optimum moisture content), which will result in a maximum dry density of the soil. Water content, both greater and smaller than this optimum value, will result in dry densities less than the maximum.

The optimum moisture content determined by the successive trial method in the laboratory is used to prepare the maximum density specimen to which subsequent compaction tests are compared. It therefore follows that the objective in constructing all earth fills is to accomplish all compaction with the soil having a moisture content as near to optimum as possible.

3-2.5.3   Soil Compaction Tests.   A variety of methods are utilized to compact earth and base materials for construction purposes, and is discussed in further detail in subsequent subsections.

Compaction tests within certain limits measure the quality of earthwork and base construction. If the earthwork has been constructed uniformly (compactive effort, lift thickness, soil type, moisture content), then relatively few tests are required to evaluate the quality of the work.

The compaction test (or relative density test) compares the compacted, in-place soil with the maximum density of the same soil determined in the laboratory (See Subsection 3-2.5.2), and is expressed as a percentage. For example, a mechanically compacted fill is generally considered to be stable, for most construction purposes, when it has been compacted to a relative density of 90%. Roadway subgrades are required to have a relative density of 95%, and 100% is sometimes required for special purposes such as airport landing runways. Natural ground is frequently found to have a relative density of less than 90%. This may be the case even though the in-situ soil tested is considerably below the existing ground surface.

· A brief description for making a compaction test (relative density test) follows:

All loose soil from an area approximately two feet square is removed from the site selected for testing. This can be done with a bulldozer or motor grader blade or with a square-pointed shovel; but in any event, the surface upon which the test is to be made should be below the level which has been disturbed by track-laying equipment or the tamping feet of sheep foot rollers. A sheet metal tray or pan with a hole cut in the center is laid on the prepared surface and a soil specimen is carefully excavated from the compacted fill through the hole. Every particle loosened in this excavation is removed from the test hole and placed in a clean, dry container with a tight lid. This test hole is then carefully filled with a dry sand having a known unit weight from a container having a known weight of dry sand in it.

Determine the moisture content of the soil sample, expressed as a percentage of its dry weight. The volume of the sample taken is computed by dividing the weight of the sand used to replace the soil by the known unit weight per cubic foot of sand. The moist and dry densities can be derived as follows:

$$\text{Moist density} = \frac{\text{Weight of wet soil sample}}{\text{Volume of soil}}$$

$$\text{Dry density} = \frac{\text{Moist density}}{1 + \dfrac{\% \text{ of moisture}}{100}}$$

The relative density (compaction) is determined as follows:

$$\% \text{ compaction} = \left.\frac{\text{Dry density}}{\text{Maximum density}}\right\} \times 100$$

Under some circumstances, relative compaction tests may be made in the field by the Inspector. Normally all formal testing of soils is performed by technicians from the Testing Agency.

3-2.5.4 Stabilometer Test. The stability of a soil can be determined by means of the Hveem Stabilometer, which measures the transmitted horizontal pressure due to vertical load. The stability, expressed as the "Resistance (R) Value," represents the shearing resistance to plastic deformation of a soil at a given moisture and density.

The R-Value may vary from 0 (representing a liquid) to 100, representing a material that transmits no horizontal pressure from an applied load. Organic clays may have values approaching 20 and untreated base and sub-base materials range from 60 to 80 (see Subsection 2-3).

3-2.5.5 Triaxial Compression Test. A soil specimen is encased in a rubber membrane and subjected to a constant lateral pressure through a liquid or gas around the specimen. A vertical axial load is then applied and increased until the specimen fails. The test is then repeated with different lateral pressures. The test data are analyzed graphically by use of Mohr Circles to determine the cohesion and internal friction of the soil. The results are used to determine the load-carrying capacity of the soil and base for pavements, buildings, dams and other structures. Several types of equipment and variations in test procedures have been developed.

3-2.5.6 Sand Equivalent Test. This rapid field method has been developed to detect the presence of undesirable claylike materials in soils, aggregate and base materials. This method tends to magnify the volume of clay present in a sample somewhat in proportion to its detrimental effects.

The sand equivalent test is a sedimentation-test in which a sample of the test material, in a prepared solution, is thoroughly agitated in a 100 ml. glass cylinder. After setting for 20 minutes, the sand and clay fractions settle into layers. The heights of these layers are measured by taking readings with a specially calibrated rod. The sand equivalent is determined by dividing the sand height by the clay height times 100.

3-3 EARTH WORK CONSTRUCTION

3-3.1 General. Earth work construction involves the movement and processing of earth to make it suitable as a foundation for a variety of purposes such as housing tracts in undeveloped areas, new highways, street improvements, bridges, buildings and trenching and backfilling of sewer and storm drain installations.

A close relationship among the operations of inspection, design and construction is required for earthwork. The processes by which an acceptable fill is produced are performed under field conditions as compared to the carefully controlled procedures that can be maintained in the laboratory. The requirement for knowledge, experience, judgment, responsibility and authority of the Inspector assigned to this class of work cannot be over-emphasized. Earth fill construction using careless and shoddy construction procedures, could ultimately result in the failure of the structure or other improvement placed upon it.

The adequacy of earthwork construction is determined from visual examination, measurement and by testing. Conditions of each project will tend to determine the extent and types of inspection required. During the initial construction stages, frequent tests should be made until the adequacy of the contractor's equipment and methods is determined. The method and equipment determined to be adequate by testing must be consistently and uniformly applied throughout the construction of the fill. Otherwise, tests will not be representative and the fill will be unsatisfactory. Under no circumstances should testing be eliminated entirely.

The Inspector should determine the precise requirements for the work he is to inspect and that his interpretation of the requirements is accurate. While his function is primarily to determine whether the work is acceptable or not acceptable, it is highly desirable for the Inspector to indicate to the contractor to what extent the work is not acceptable. Typical inspection functions for earthwork include the determination that the material is uniform and free from organic matter or trash, that the compaction equipment complies with the specifications, that the thickness of lifts and the number of passes by compaction equipment are according to specifications, and that the proper amount of moisture was distributed uniformly through each layer. The Inspector should identify unsuitable (perishable or unsound) materials during the stripping or excavating operations, as well as seepage conditions, and determine the extent the project is affected by such materials of doubtful suitability.

Regardless of the extent of prior investigation, it is the responsibility of the Inspector to make certain that any soil condition that develops or is discovered, which is not compatible with the design criteria for the project, is immediately brought to the attention of his Supervisor. Such action should be promptly taken in order to minimize the time required for additional investigation and design of the necessary corrective measures.

Standard Terms for Earthwork and Grading. (Also see Plate 31, Appendix.)

Backfill—Refilling of holes excavated below the ground surface or in confined spaces against rigid structures.

Base—A layer of untreated base or stabilized material immediately below the pavement.

Cut—Original ground removal to reach prescribed earth slopes or subgrade.

"Daylight"—Point at which a cut slope intersects the existing ground.

Embankment—A laterally unsupported fill built on top of the original ground surface.

Fill—Placement of earth on top of the original ground surface.

Finish Surface—The surface of earthwork or pavement which is specified on the plans as the elevation of the final surface.

Foundation—That body of undisturbed natural soil lying below the limits of excavation or the first lift of a fill.

Pavement—A layer or layers of portland cement concrete or plant-mixed bituminous material in place on a roadway.

Right Of Way—An area acquired or reserved for street, sewerage or drainage construction, or for utility installation.

Roadbed—The body of soil immediately below the rough grade elevation which supports the structural section, median, gutter and curb.

Roadway—That portion of a street intended for use by vehicular traffic.

Rough Grade—The approximate surface at the elevation of the lowest subgrade to be prepared for the placement of subbase, base or pavement. It can be either at the bottom of an excavation or at the top of a fill.

Slope Easement—An area acquired to permit the construction of the slopes of cuts or fills indicated on the plans but which extend outside the right of way.

Structural Section—That section of a roadway between rough grade and finish grade elevations, including the pavement and any base or subbase.

Subbase—Untreated base or stabilized material immediately below a base.

Subgrade—The surface upon which a pavement, base or subbase is to be placed.

3-3.2 Clearing, Grubbing and Removals.

3-3.2.1 **General.** The purpose of clearing and grubbing is to provide an unobstructed area for subsequent grading operations and to remove trees, brush, stumps, roots, other vegetation, surface improvements, structures, fences, rubbish debris and other objectionable material as well as the removal of topsoil deposits which are unsuitable for foundation purposes. Topsoil should be stockpiled for use in subsequent landscape installation. No excavation, grading or fill operations should be permitted in any area until the full extent of the clearing and grubbing has been completed. Scattered piles of debris within the fill area may be easily covered up by fast moving construction equipment unless the Inspector is alert to prevent it.

Care should be exercised to protect trees or existing improvements which are not designated on the plans for removal. Trees which are to remain in place, with certain trimming specified, should be trimmed at once to avoid serious damage to the trees from subsequent equipment operation.

Usually, clearing or grubbing is accomplished by a bulldozer pushing the surface materials and vegetation into piles. Larger trees may be cut in advance and in some cases brush is hand cut and piled. Buildings may need to be demolished and existing concrete slabs or footings broken up in advance. Roots 1½ inches in diameter or larger must be removed.

When clearing and grubbing operations are completed, a clean cut with a bulldozer blade over the cleared area will reveal roots, brush, debris or other conditions that may have been overlooked. The Engineer is to be advised at this stage of construction as it provides an opportunity for a visual examination of the foundation soil for unconsolidated fills, water seepage (see Subsection 3-6.7), changes in soil types and substructures not indicated on the plans. Conditions which differ materially from those anticipated for the project should be reported by the Inspector to his Supervisor immediately.

Materials cleared and grubbed from the right of way must be disposed of by the contractor as provided for in the Specifications.

During clearing and grubbing operations the Inspector should be alert to existing conditions in the foundation soil which would preclude the construction of any improvement upon it. Typical examples would be the presence of hidden inclined slippage planes, soft or saturated material, unconsolidated fill, buried debris, peat deposits, high water table or seepage, abandoned tunnels or large conduits. The Inspector must report such conditions immediately to his Supervisor.

Disposition of the problem resulting from such conditions will be made by the Engineer. Since these matters usually involve additional cost to the Agency, the Inspector is cautioned against directing a correction to be made except when the condition is minor in nature and the contractor does not intend to claim additional compensation.

3-3.2.2   Clearing and Grubbing Checklist.

(1) Review plans and preview Inspector's report for all site conditions. Check for encroachments to be removed and notices to property owners.

(2) Check limits of area to be worked and make sure it is clearly staked in accordance with plans.

(3) Check for location and protection of survey markers and monuments.

(4) Determine what structures, trees and other improvements are to remain (See Subsection 1-6). Utilities and other substructures should be noted and pipelines or tanks containing hazardous substances (such as gasoline or natural gas) should be uncovered by hand at frequent intervals to determine their length and depth, so as to avoid damaging them.

(5) Local depressions or holes caused from grubbing or removals must be filled and compacted before any subsequent grading or fill operations begin.

(6) Check for proper haul roads and permits.

(7) Check for contractor's authority to stock pile or dispose of material on private property. Secure copy of owner's letter of approval. Check for spillage and dust on public streets and take corrective measures.

(8) Check for drainage, erosion control and protection of adjoining property from damage or loss of lateral support.

(9) Has an herbicide or soil sterilent been applied to the finish surface in the proper proportions and rate of application, when required by the Specifications?

3-3.3 Excavation.

3-3.3.1 General. Most excavations can be classified under one of three categories: structural (See Subsection 3-3.3.3), roadway, or trench (pipeline) (See Subsection 3-5 and unclassified (See Subsection 3-3.3.2 below).

With very few exceptions, soil behavior problems in excavations are concerned with lateral stability such as caving trench walls, water or saturated soil and unstable ground at structural footings.

Another factor of concern in excavating is the presence of rock strata, boulders or hard pan. These materials increase the difficulty of excavation and often involve the use of costly oversize excavating equipment, heavy-duty impact stompers, drilling or blasting.

Each type of excavation differs in the type of equipment employed, methods of handling excavated material and safety requirements.

3-3.3.2 Unclassified Excavation. Excavation is unclassified if it is not otherwise defined by the specifications and may include sidehill cuts or through cuts when establishing a rough grade for a new street improvement. It may also include excavation of the entire roadbed area to permit installation of base materials. This type of work is generally accomplished with mobile power equipment such as scrapers, dozers and graders, or a combination of elevating graders, loaders, truck loading stages and trucks. Occasionally, large and deep face cuts will permit the economic use of power shovels or draglines.

The sides of roadway excavations are always sloped to the final slope grade as the cut gets progressively deeper until rough grade elevations are reached.

Pipelines are usually installed in excavated trenches, utilizing trenching machines, backhoes, draglines or clams. The width of the trench is critical below the top of the pipe to be installed and where caving or over-excavating occurs in this part of the trench, additional bedding or higher type of bedding as shown on the Standard Plans may be required. In some cases, the Engineer may approve a higher strength pipe in lieu of another type of bedding. In general, narrow trenches are excavated, utilizing trenching machines; wide or deep trenches, with a backhoe or dragline. (Also see Subsection 3-5, Sewer Construction, and 3-6, Storm Drain Construction.)

Walls of excavations and trenches, which may be unstable and collapse if not supported by bracing, tend to fail in shear along a more or less concave surface. The cost of bracing excavations and trenches is high and there may be a tendency on the part of the contractor to provide the absolute minimum that will be tolerated by the Inspector.

3-3.3.3 Structure Excavation.

Although most excavations are unclassified as to type or purpose, structure excavation is usually specified for construction of structures such as buildings, bridges, retaining walls, etc. In structure excavation, pay lines for excavation are usually specifically defined on the plans. Material which is excavated by the contractor outside such pay lines is not paid for by the Agency, either as excavation or backfill. Draglines, clams, power shovels, backhoes, and loaders are usually employed to make structure excavations.

3-3.3.4 Borrow Excavations.

Borrow excavations are usually off-site excavations made to supply earth materials imported for jobsite fills when the on-site cut areas are insufficient to supply the required amounts of fill dirt, or when the cut material is unsuitable. Borrow excavations are also used to supply subbase for roadway subgrade. The distance the earth material must be transported between the borrow site excavation and the fill site is termed the overhaul.

3-3.3.5 Excavated Soil Weights and Swell Factors.

It is well known that soil volume and density both undergo considerable change when earth materials are excavated, hauled, placed and compacted. When the volume of earth increases because of loosening through excavation from a soil deposit, the increase is defined as swell. Earth compacted in a fill under modern construction methods will often have a smaller volume than it had in its original state. This reduction in volume resulting from increased density is defined as shrinkage.

The following table lists approximate in-bank weights and swell factors for common materials:

Material	Approx. In-Bank Weight (lbs. per cu. yd.)	Percent Swell
Clay, dry	2300	40
Clay, wet	3000	40
Granite, decomposed	4500	65
Gravel, dry	3250	10-15
Gravel, wet	3600	10-15
Loam, dry	2800	15-35
Loam, wet	3370	25
Rock, well blasted	4200	65
Sand, dry	3250	10-15
Sand, wet	3600	10-15
Shale and soft rock	3000	65
Slate	4700	65

3-3.3.6 Disposal of Excavated Materials. Unsuitable materials and surplus excavated earth must be disposed of by the contractor. The Inspector should determine for himself what disposition the contractor intends to make of such materials. If his haulaway is made to a commercial disposal site, or in the case of suitable materials, if disposal is made to another construction site where control of its disposal will be regulated by others, no further action is necessary. However, if the disposal of any material is to be made on private or public property, the contractor must secure the necessary permits from the governmental agency regulating the deposit of such materials, together with a waiver of damages signed by the owner of the property on which disposal will be made, absolving the Agency from all damage claims arising out of such disposal.

A copy of the fully executed waiver is to be provided to the Inspector who will make a record of it on the Daily Job Card and file it with the job records. Waiver forms can be obtained from the Supervisor or hand written to conform to the following:

PERMISSION TO DUMP DIRT ON PRIVATE PROPERTY

(Agency) . . . .

(Address) . . . .

Date: . . . .

Permission is hereby given to . . . .
                                          (Contractor's name)
. . . . to dump excavated materials from his job

known as . . . .
              (Job No.)   (Job Title)
on my property located at . . . .
                                          (Address)
legally described as Lot No. . . . . . Block No. . . . . . Tract

No. . . . . . .

Signed: . . . .
                              (Property owner)

3-3.3.7 Excavation General, Checklist (also refer to Subsection 3-3.2.2, Clearing and Grubbing).

(1) Check project requirements for existing conditions, special shoring or lateral support; and for stockpiling required, such as for top soil or selected subbase.

(2) Check method of payment and make arrangements for survey if necessary to establish quantities for payment purposes.

(3) Check boring logs for soil type and the presence of water.

(4) Review plans and utility notices for existing pipelines and other substructures. Fuel lines are hazardous and should be located by hand at frequent intervals (See Subsection 1-6).

(5) Contractor must have written authority to dispose of or stock pile material on private property.

(6) Check for unsatisfactory haulage conditions on public streets such as spillage or dust, and order corrective maintenance and clean up.

(7) Contractor must provide water control including well points, drainage and erosion control. Ponding must be avoided.

(8) Arrange for inspection by soils engineer if material at bottom of excavation differs from soil borings or appears unstable.

(9) See that all vertical sides of excavations are shored; otherwise they must be laid back to a safe slope.

(10) Watch for earth movement and damage to adjacent property.

(11) Are excavation clearances adequate to permit construction?

(12) In cases of over-excavation, obtain approved method of correction from the Engineer.

(13) Blasting for rock excavation requires a permit.

(14) Be alert to potential hazards to the traveling public. See that satisfactory conditions are maintained for vehicular traffic and pedestrians.

3-3.4 Excavation Permits.

3-3.4.1 **General.** There are various types of construction carried on in the public way or immediately adjacent thereto (or both) for which excavation permits are required and which require varying degrees of control by the Agency. Examples are excavations (for footings, foundations and basement walls) which may imperil the lateral support of existing public improvements; trenching operations for oil and gas pipelines, telephone and television cables; and removal for abandoned tanks and basements.

It is the permittee's responsibility to protect existing improvements, substructures and utilities in the public way. He must not disturb such improvements except as authorized by the permit or by the owner of the utility involved. In the event of damage to a substructure resulting in an emergency situation, the contractor must immediately notify the affected agency and the Inspector. Specific procedures to be followed in case of damage to sewers, storm drains, street lighting and traffic signals are described elsewhere in this Manual. The Inspector should familiarize the permittee with these procedures and, if damage occurs, fully report all pertinent information in the job records. The permittee is responsible for the repair of all damage occurring as a result of his operations and the Inspector will withhold acceptance of work until all damage has repaired.

In general, any deviation from the permit requirement must be approved in advance by the Engineer, and major changes are required to be submitted by the permittee in writing. Changes of a minor nature addressed to the Inspector in the field should be discussed with the Supervisor. If any question remains as to the acceptability of such change, it must be forwarded to the Engineer for his approval. The resulting decision by the Engineer shall be transmitted to the permittee and recorded in the job records, listing the change and Engineer involved.

The following important aspects of construction should be considered by the Inspector.

(1) Excavation (sloping and special treatment of slopes). (See Plate 52, Appendix.)

(2) Temporary structures supporting the public way.

(3) Permanent structures supporting the public way.

(4) Sequence of operation.

(5) Backfill and compaction.

(6) Resurfacing.

(7) Repair of damage to improvements in the public way other than pavements (street lights, traffic signals, conduits, sewers, storm drains, etc.).

(8) Safety precautions for pedestrian and vehicular traffic.

Continuous, semi-continuous and periodic inspection may all be involved during construction of this type of work. The frequency of inspection and the length of time spent at any one project each day should remain flexible and should be determined by the special requirements and conditions of the project.

3-3.4.2 Application/Permit. Shown on following pages are examples of the APPLICATION/PERMIT FOR EXCAVATIONS filled in as:

(1) A typical Special Inspection Permit, with special deposit included to cover resurfacing charges by Agency street maintenance forces. The permit fees include charges for inspection, testing and plan checking. This method is used when the fees can be determined in advance and inspection charges do not exceed $100.

(2) A typical Special Inspection Permit, with a "work order" number included. This is for a larger project of longer duration. The amount of inspection and the number of tests cannot be determined in advance, so progressive charges are made against the work order. If restoration of surface improvements by Agency street maintenance forces is required, a "special deposit" fee will be included.

The pink copy shown is retained in the files of the Agency, while the yellow copy (not shown) is utilized as a Resurfacing Request to the Agency street maintenance forces. The appropriate information for the request is to be entered on both copies, utilizing the first five lines under RESURFACING RECORD.

City of Anywhere DEPT. OF PUBLIC WORK Bureau of Engineering	**APPLICATION/PERMIT** FOR **EXCAVATIONS** IN OR ADJACENT TO PUBLIC STREETS UNDER CHAPTER 0, ARTICLE 0, ANYWHERE MUNICIPAL CODE			12014

JOB ADDRESS
740 S. Rampart Blvd.

STREETS AFFECTED
Alley south of 7th St.

ARE STREETS NOW BEING IMPROVED?
☐ YES   ☒ NO

PURPOSE OF EXCAVATION
Basement footing encroachment into alley

PLAT FILED?
☒ YES   ☐ NO

APPLICANT/PERMITTEE
Better Builders, Inc.

ADDRESS
1000 Main St.

CITY OR TOWN Long Beach   **ZIP CODE** 90046   **TELEPHONE** 823-4601

I hereby agree to observe all requirements of the Municipal Code of the City of Anywhere and all amendments thereto.

Sam Bordon
AUTHORIZED SIGNATURE

WORK ORDER NO.	LIAB. INS. C.A. NO. 168279	MISC. CASH BOND NO. 15316
"A" PERMIT NO.	SURETY BOND C.A. NO.	MISC. RECEIPT NO.
WAIVER REC. NO. 6814	REPORT NO.	

APPLICANT/PERMITTEE
Better Builders, Inc.

JOB ADDRESS
740 S. Rampart Blvd.

SPECIAL INSPECTION NO. 12014	SPECIAL DEPOSIT PERMIT NO. 12015

RESURFACING RECORD

INSPECTOR *J.R. Doe*	DATE OF REPORT 3-24-87

EXCAVATION

SIZE	SURFACE
2' X 65'	☐ CONCRETE ☒ A.C. ☐ R & O ☐ DIRT ☐

DISTRICT ASSIGNED TO | **DATE**

AREA RESURFACED SQ. FT.	TYPE OF SURFACE
SQ. FT.	

DATE WORK COMPLETED | **CHARGE SHEET NO.**

BY *R. Smith* 3-8-87
BUREAU OF ENGINEERING   DATE

EXCAVATION SIZE AND TYPE

CON. CURB .... AT $ .... LIN. FT.		
CONC. WALK .... AT $ .... SQ. FT.		
CONC. GUTTER ...... AT $ .... SQ. FT.		
PAVEMENT 130 ...... AT $ 3.50 SQ. FT.	455	00
DIRT .... AT $ .... SQ. FT.		
ROCK & OIL .... AT $ .... SQ. FT.		
TOTAL SPECIAL DEPOSIT	455	00
SPECIAL INSPECTION		
1 HOURS AT $80. PER HOUR DAY DAY	80	00
TESTING		
RELATIVE COMPACTION 1 AT 15 EA.	25	00
STANDARD DENSITY 1 AT 22 EA.	30	00
PLAN CHECK	20	00
TOTAL SPEC. INSP., etc.	155	00
TOTAL AMOUNT	610	00

THIS PERMIT IS NOT VALID UNLESS RECEIPT ATTACHED OR REGISTER VALIDATED

RECEIPT NUMBER _____

CONTRACTOR	*Blank Const. Co.*
JOB FOREMAN	*J. M. Green*
EXCAV. START	*3-10-87*
BACKFILL START	*3-22-87*
METHOD TO CONSOLIDATE FILL	*Vibrating plate, 6" lifts*
FILL COMPLETED	*3-24-87*
APPROVED	*3-24-87*
INSPECTOR	*J. K. Doe*
REMARKS	*Footing encroachment as per plan.*

During the period of excavation for cut slopes, daily visits of short duration will generally provide necessary control of the operation. Operations involving vertical cuts and installation of temporary supporting structures most often require one or more timely vists of longer duration as well as brief daily inspections.

3-3.4.3 Soil Conditions. It is of vital importance that the Inspector carefully observe the excavation operations and report any unstable ground conditions to the Engineer for his consideration. Exposure of sub-soil conditions at this stage of work, which differ from the information on which the Engineer based his original approval, may result in a major change from the approved plans.

3-3.4.4 Methods for Supporting Excavations. Permits frequently specify a method and sequence of operation

| City of Anywhere
DEPT. OF PUBLIC WORK
Bureau of Engineering | **APPLICATION/PERMIT**
FOR
EXCAVATIONS
IN OR ADJACENT TO PUBLIC STREETS
UNDER CHAPTER 0, ARTICLE 0, ANYWHERE MUNICIPAL CODE | 13006 |

JOB ADDRESS

    3662 Alcan Ave.

STREETS AFFECTED

    Adjacent to Alcan Ave. and Rover St.   ARE STREETS NOW BEING IMPROVED? ☐ YES ☒ NO

PURPOSE OF EXCAVATION

    Basement excavation and building footings   PLAT FILED? ☒ YES ☐ NO

APPLICANT/PERMITTEE

    Jackson Const. Co.

ADDRESS

    1226 Weston Rd.

CITY OR TOWN	ZIP CODE	TELEPHONE
Los Angeles	90034	744-3211

I hereby agree to observe all requirements of the Municipal Code of the City of Anywhere and all amendments thereto.

K. A. Jackson
AUTHORIZED SIGNATURE

WORK ORDER NO.	LIAB. INS. C.A. NO.	MISC. CASH BOND NO.
11888	180732	31780
"A" PERMIT NO.	SURETY BOND C.A. NO.	MISC. RECEIPT NO.
21968	88695	2263
WAIVER REC. NO.	REPORT NO.	
---	C.E.#2	·12-18-87

APPLICANT/PERMITTEE

    Jackson Const. Co.

JOB ADDRESS

    3662 Alcan Ave.

SPECIAL INSPECTION	SPECIAL DEPOSIT PERMIT
NO. ---	NO. 13006

RESURFACING RECORD

INSPECTOR	DATE OF REPORT
J. R. Doe	6-22-87

EXCAVATION SIZE AND TYPE

CON. CURB ...... AT $ ...... LIN. FT.			
CONC. WALK ...... AT $ ...... SQ. FT.			
CONC. GUTTER ...... AT $ ...... SQ. FT.			
PAVEMENT 200 .. AT $ 3.50 SQ. FT.		700	00
DIRT 1400 .... AT $ .02 SQ. FT.		28	00
ROCK & OIL ...... AT $ ...... SQ. FT.			
TOTAL SPECIAL DEPOSIT		728	00

EXCAVATION

SIZE	SURFACE
	☐ CONCRETE
2.5 X 70'	☒ A.C. ☐ R & O
4' X 320'	☒ DIRT ☐

DISTRICT ASSIGNED TO	DATE

SPECIAL INSPECTION			
HOURS ...... AT ...... HOUR			
...... DAY PER DAY			

AREA RESURFACED SQ. FT.	TYPE OF SURFACE

SQ. FT.	

DATE WORK COMPLETED	CHARGE SHEET NO.

TESTING			
RELATIVE COMPACTION .... AT ...... EA.			
STANDARD DENSITY .... AT ...... EA.			
PLAN CHECK			

BY

R. Smith   1-6-87
BUREAU OF ENGINEERING   DATE

TOTAL SPEC. INSP., etc.			
TOTAL AMOUNT		728	00

THIS PERMIT IS NOT VALID UNLESS RECEIPT ATTACHED OR REGISTER VALIDATED

RECEIPT NUMBER _____

involving a sloping cut along the entire length of one side of an excavation and construction of footings and permanent walls in alternate sections. The Engineer's decision relative to the spacing and length of section increments is based on the soil conditions as they are reported by the private soils engineer. The alternate sloping sections remaining in place are calculated to provide the necessary temporary support during construction of the alternate sections.

CONTRACTOR	
JOB FOREMAN	
EXCAV. START	
BACKFILL START	
METHOD TO CONSOLIDATE FILL	
FILL COMPLETED	
APPROVED	
INSPECTOR	
REMARKS	*For details, see job reports for Work Order 1888.*

Temporary supporting elements for vertical cuts in close proximity to property lines often involve one or a combination of the following support elements: soldier beams, drilled and filled concrete caissions, walers and knee braces, or specially designed "tie backs." Solid sheeting may or may not be utilized. Soldier beams are generally standard wideflange structural steel shapes positioned vertically at a specified spacing in holes pre-drilled prior to excavation. They are most frequently used in conjunction with solid sheeting, where the sheeting is installed in the channels formed by the flanges of the beam as excavation progresses. "Tie backs" or knee braces and walers are specified where the soldier beams do not act as a cantilever from the base of the excavation because of insufficient size and penetration. "Tie backs" consist generally of high strength steel rods installed in slant-drilled holes from the face of the excavation and terminating in a belled-out hole. A special expandable mechanism is provided on the end of the steel rod in the belled-out hole and the entire drilled hole us then filled with concrete. From this anchorage, walers are pulled up tight against the soldier beams, caissons or the vertical bank, using a special stressing device on the exposed end of the rod . This method offers the advantage of very little or no interference with the contractor's operations during the construction of the permanent on-site improvements. Knee braces often interfere with the construction and for this reason, more frequent checking by the Inspector will be necessary to see that such supports are not disturbed or prematurely removed.

Exposed surfaces of excavations, vertical or sloped, are very often sealed with chemicals to prevent the soil from drying out and to prevent penetration of the surface by moisture, either of which could cause unstable conditions. Chemically stabilized or gunited surfaces are subject to minimum erosion from wind and rain.

3-3.4.5 **Permanent Support.** Retaining walls or building walls, which will provide the permanent support of subsurface improvements in the public way, are required to be inspected for compliance with the requirements of the permit, even though such support is on private property. The inspection procedure should incorporate the practices normally applied to this class of construction in the public way. However, such construction on private porperty is also under the jurisdiction of another division of the Agency and is inspected by others for compliance with the Building Code. A Deputy Building Inspector is often required to provide continuous inspection of such construction. In these instances, copies of test reports for both reinforcing steel and concrete must be obtained through the job superintendent or the Deputy Building Inspector. Under these conditions, inspection during this phase of construction can be reduced to periodic visits.

3-3.4.6 **Encroachment of a Structure into a Public Way.** The permit may allow portions of a private structure to encroach into the public way. In such instances, the approved plans will show the details of the allowable encroachment. Reinforced concrete walls are often constructed by forming only on the private property side, the concrete being deposited against the excavated bank on the side facing the public way. The Inspector should carefully observe the excavated bank for any irregularities which would cause the permanent structure to encroach in the public way. Only very minor encroachments are acceptable without a permit being issued therefor by the Engineer. Conversely, any irregularity must not reduce the required wall thickness or cover for the reinforcing steel.

3-3.4.7 Backfilling Excavations.

Backfilling shall be accomplished in accordance with the requirements of the Standard Specifications unless otherwise specified in the permit. The contractor generally utilizes mechanical methods of compacting the native material. Pea gravel or saturated sand placed by approved methods need not be tested for relative density. Compaction tests of backfill will be made by the testing Agency at the request of the Inspector.

On many projects, the owner will employ a soils engineer and private testing laboratory with earthwork. This could permit a reduction in the number of requests for tests by the Testing Agency and such tests would be for the purpose of verification only. The Inspector should bear in mind that private laboratory soil testing is frequently based on methods differing from the Standard Specifications, often producing a lesser maximum density standard.

3-3.4.8 Resurfacing.

Temporary resurfacing shall be placed by the permittee in accordance with the Standard Specifications.

Permanent resurfacing is accomplished by either of the following procedures:

(1) By the permittee under a separate Class A Permit, issued along with the Excavation Permit, or

(2) By the Agency street maintenance forces, the permittee having deposited at the time of issuance of the Special Deposit Excavation Permit, an amount of money to cover the cost of such work.

In each instance, the permit or approved plans will indicate the applicable procedure. There are some instances where neither procedure has been specified on the permit at the time it was issued, because it was not known whether any pavement existed, and resurfacing was not anticipated. Subsequent construction operations will often result in damage to adjacent improvements, requiring removal and replacement of additional pavement. In such instances, the Inspector will instruct the permittee to apply for a permit to cover such work and he will not accept the work until the permit has been obtained and the repairs completed.

3-3.4.9 Excavation Permit Check List.

(a) **Excavation.**

Did the excavation expose any unusual or unstable conditions requiring consideration by the Engineer? Is the slope within plan limitation?

Is any special protective treatment of slope required? (Pliofilm, chemicals, etc.)

Are vertical cuts performed in proper sequence and within permissible limit? (Length and depth)

Is there any evidence of movement of adjacent improvements? (Separation cracks, settlement, etc.)

Check for adequate or required traffic or pedestrian provisions.

(b) **Temporary Supporting Sturcture.**

Are the components of the supporting system of the size, dimension, weight and detail required by the plans?

Are the borings for soldier beams of the required diameter, depth and spacing?

Are walers at the required location and spacing?

Are knee braces installed with required thrust blocks, kick plates and at the proper angle?

Are tie-backs installed to the required penetration and at the required angle, and proof-tested to a specified load?

Are support connections in accordance with requirement? (Size and spacing of bolts, welding, etc.)

Are the various elements promptly installed and in proper sequence?

Is the temporary supporting structure being satisfactorily maintained in undisturbed condition during subsequent construction operations?

Are periodic inspections performed to detect movement or other evidence of possible failure of the supporting structure?

Is any overcutting behind lagging, backfilled with native material or grout to provide for full bearing?

Are excavated holes for soldier beams dewatered or is a mix method of depositing concrete under water approved? Is the concrete up to design strength prior to tensioning tie-backs?

In case of tie-back failure during tensioning, has an approved shop drawing showing corrective measures been received?

(c) **Permanent Supporting Structure.**

Is any encroachment into the public way in accordance with the approved plans?

Have you reviewed inspection procedures for structural concrete in Subsection 3-12?

(d) **Backfill.**

Have you reviewed inspection procedures for backfill in Subsection 3-5.5?

Has the structural concrete attained the required strength prior to backfill?

Are walls properly supported by floor construction or temporary bracing as designed or otherwise required?

(e) **Miscellaneous.**

Have repairs to improvements been completed prior to project completion and "sign-off"?

If tie-backs (which are required by the permit to be removed) are left in place because of extenuating circumstances, has the permit section been notified to bill the permittee? Has payment been received before signing off permit?

Upon completion of the project, have the records been reviewed and placed in good order before transmittal to the Main Office? (Cards must be titled and numbered, and all entries must be clear and legible. The final entry should indicate that the project is completed, including any repairs.)

3-3.5 Earth Fill and Backfill.

3-3.5.1 General. "Unclassified earth fill" is a term sometimes used to designate general types of fill construction. The compaction of earth fill in confined spaces or in trenches is described as backfill. Backfill is divided into two major classes: structural and trench.

3-3.5.2 Unclassified Earth Fill. Unclassified earth fill construction consists of depositing, conditioning and compacting earth, including the preparation of the areas upon which it is placed, where the major portion of the work is accessible to large or heavy hauling and compacting equipment. It may include embankments, sidehill fills, buttress fills and dikes; also the placing and compacting of material in holes, excavations, depressions or other low areas. It may also include earthwork required to fill excavations made in roadways for the purpose of removing unsuitable materials from the roadway foundation.

Fills should be placed on sound foundation soil cut to a plane as nearly level as possible. If it is necessary to excavate material of questionable bearing value or install subdrains (as determined by the Engineer), such work should be completed in advance of any fill operations. When necessary, suitable benches should be graded out before fills are begun. Particular attention should be given to obtaining the best possible interlock between sloping original ground sufaces and the new material. Since one of the most frequent areas of subsidence occurs where the roadway changes from fill to excavation, it is important that benching should be extensive enough to insure solid foundation when building against an existing sidehill. This usually can be accomplished by cutting into the sidehill to a depth of four feet and preferably the full width of the equipment used to deposit and compact the fill material.

Springs, subsurface water or spongy soils which may not have been evident during the clearing or grubbing operations may be disclosed when the initial operations of the fill begin and the Inspector should be alert to observe the performance of the prepared foundation under the initial loads of heavy construction equipment.

To insure a good bond between the foundation soil and the fill, the foundation surface should be scarified to a depth of six inches and watered to the approximate optimum moisture before the first lift of fill is placed. The Standard Specifications prescribe that fills be placed and compacted in layers not exceeding that which will provide the specified relative compaction through the full depth of the lift by the specific compaction equipment being utilized. However, soils vary widely as to the amount of compaction effort necessary to reach the specified degree of compaction. When difficulty is encountered in obtaining the required compaction, the first remedial action to be taken is to reduce the thickness of the lift since soils compact more readily in thin layers.

Uniform compaction is very much dependent upon the even distribution of moisture throughout the soil. Some soils, such as dry fine-grained soils, do not take up moisture as others. Often, moisture penetration and distribution can be improved by watering the soil in place in the borrow area and taking advantage of mixing resulting from the loading and dumping operations. Dispersion of the water through the soil can sometimes be improved by adding a commercial detergent. Additional watering of the fill material (and mixing if necessary) must be prior to compaction operations in the fill.

Adobes and clays appear to be soft after rolling at optimum moisture and will readily show heel marks when the heel of a shoe is stomped on fill.

A fill that has been compacted too dry, that is substantially below the optimum moisture content, will be misleading since it appears be firm and a sheepsfoot tamper will walk out in a few passes, but the density will usually be below the specification requirements. Soil that is "hard as a rock" immediately after compacting at low moisture content is usually questionable as to density and referred to as a dry fill. These "dry fills" later assume the higher moisture content of the soil in the native state, which reduces the friction coefficient between the soil particles and results in sinking and displacement under traffic loads.

Where possible, poorer classes of soils should be placed in the lower reaches of a fill. Where street fills are made in conjunction with other fills that are outside the jurisdiction of the Agency, it is desirable to dispose of the grades of soil in lower areas outside the right of way that are not expected to support structures.

Only suitable material complying with the Standard Specification shall be placed in the fill. Large rocky material, hard lumps and other materials which cannot be readily broken up shall be incorporated in the fill only as provided for in the specifications.

Considerable compactive effort is obtained from the construction equipment transporting the fill material. In order to insure uniformity of compaction throughout the fill, the Inspector should require such construction equipment to distribute its travel uniformly over the fill area insofar as possible.

Care should be exercised to preserve, where possible, line and grade survey stakes for fills, particularly top of slope or toe of slope stakes where slope easements are in effect.

3-3.5.3 Trench Backfill. For trench backfill, the Inspector should consult the Special Provisions and Standard Specifications for specific requirements and refer to Subsections 3-5 and 3-6, Sewer Construction and Storm Drain Construction, respectively.

A dozer is an excellent piece of equipment to use for backfilling trenches because the backfill material may be pushed directly ahead of the machine into the trench. Angle dozers are more efficient for this purpose than dozers equipped with a normal blade. Small cranes, equipped with a rectangular blade (called a mormon board), are sometimes used for this operation by trenching contractors. The mormon board is cast over the spoil bank and dragged toward the trench, with a second cable rigged to provide a horizontal pull on the blade. Where pipelines or box structures have been installed, particular care must be exercised to protect such conduits against damage from the backfill material as it is being placed in the trench.

3-3.5.4 Structure Backfill. Structure backfill is a special classification and is nearly always very critical. It requires the highest standards for compactive effort and efficiency. Such backfill is specified adjacent to exterior walls of concrete buildings, bridge abutments, retaining walls, vaults, box-section drains and similar structures. Compaction requirements are often specified to be higher for this class of backfill than for other classes because surface improvements may be designed to be supported by this backfill. Examples of this would include concrete pavement slabs constructed on bridge abutment backfills, or concrete steps or walks adjacent to a concrete building.

Only suitable materials free from lumps or free of hard materials exceeding four inches in greatest dimension, may be used within 12 inches of a structure. Occasionally, the material removed from an excavation for a structure is not suitable for use in backfill against such structure and must be disposed of and suitable material furnished by the contractor for the backfill.

Structure backfill is usually accomplished utilizing relatively small compaction tools and equipment. This is made necessary by the restricting nature of the confined or narrow space to be backfilled or because of its inaccessibility. Equipment commonly used includes: hand tampers; pneumatic or gasoline-powered impact tampers; truck-mounted pavement breakers with a tamping shoe attachment; small vibrating steel-tired (or pneumatic-tired) rollers; vibrating plates; and internal vibrators (for certain inundated soil conditions). Free fall tampers, some of which are guided in a tube, may be used under certain conditions, but caution must be exercised to avoid damage, displacement or undue strain being placed on the adjacent structure from the heavy impact loads developed by this type of tamping equipment.

3-3.6　Compaction Equipment and Methods.

3-3.6.1　**General.**　The method used for obtaining compaction in fills and backfill is usually controlled by the specifications, either by establishing minimum requirements and limitations on compaction equipment or by specifying end results. Sometimes a combination of method control and end results is used. The Inspector should familiarize himself with the Special Specifications for the project with respect to limitations and special condition.

The size of area to be backfilled will determine the type of equipment to be used. If the area is small, the equipment listed under structure backfill can be used. For larger areas, heavy compaction equipment such as tamping rollers, pneumatic-tired rollers, or vbarious vibrating-type rollers would normally be utilized.

The principal factors involved in compaction operations are: the type of soil to compacted, the type of equipment used, the amount of moisture present during compaction, the thickness of the lift being compacted, and the number of passes of the equipment on each lift.

The type of material to be incorported into the fill is critical from the viewpoint of the equipment used to compact it. This is obvious when one considers the wide differences in characteristics between granular and cohesive soils. With granular, rocky material (short on fines), vibration is the most effective means to achieve high densities. To some extent, heavy weight plus vibration results in achieving greater densities than by vibration alone. Moisture content is not too critical with such granular materials unless long-graded sandy or gravelly material is involved. For one-sized sand or gravel, water can be used if flooding or ponding technique is permitted by the specifications. On the other hand, clays are not affected significantly by vibration but are responsive to added weight. They can be most readily compacted with "sheepsfoot" or other tamping rollers.

3-3.6.2　**Compaction Equipment.**　Common types of compaction equipment, exclusive of vibrating types, are listed in the following table:

Types of Rollers and their Recommended Uses

Roller Type	Weight In Tons	Recommended Lift Thickness (Loose In.) for 8 Passes		Operating Speed (M.P.H.)	Most Suitable Soil Type
		Lighter Units	Heavier Units		
Pneumatic	3-12	4- 6	6- 8	1-15	Sandy, sandy clay, silts
Super-compactors	20-50	12-18	12-24	5-10	All types
Tamping (sheepsfoot)	2-20	6- 8	8-12	5-10	Clay and silty clays
Tandem (2-axle)	3-16	4- 6	6- 8	1- 5	Granular, particularly
Tandem (3-axle)	12-20	4- 6	6- 8	1- 5	where crushing is desirable
Three Wheel	5-20	4- 6	6- 8	1- 5	

Smooth steel-tired rollers for earth fills are the least effective of all compactors, but satisfactory compaction can be obtained if the lift thickness is reduced. A smooth surface results from the use of this type of equipment which will tend to reduce the bond with the next lift and produce layering. Consequently, the surface of each lift must be scarified before a subsequent lift is placed.

Rollers are usually designed to permit their weight to be easily increased by filling hollow wheels, drums, tires or tanks with water. Where weight is required and critical, the Inspector should check such equipment for water loss. The wheels or drum of a roller standing in the sun will feel cool to the palm of the hand below the level of the water contained inside. The name plate attached to the equipment or its model number will provide a means to determine the net and gross weights of different rollers.

It is important to insure that all of the tires of pneumatic-tired rollers, including wobble wheel rollers, be inflated to 90 psi or such lower pressure as may be designated by the Engineer, and that the treads of tires indicate approximately the same degree of wear. For most compaction purposes, smooth tread tires are preferable.

Tamping rollers are most widely used in fill construction. Numerous designs of tamping feet are in use and such tampers are available as self-propelled or towed models. Compaction by tamping rollers somewhat simplifies the problem with respect to the moisture content of the material to be compacted, in that satisfactory results can be obtained with a greater range of moisture content over and under the optimum.

The holes made by a tamping roller in the surface of a fill being compacted with an excess moisture content generally increase the surface area of the fill material and permit more rapid aeration. Conversely, the same holes trap water added to material which is too dry and permit more efficient distribution of the moisture through the soil. Additional passes over the fill serve to increase the rate of aeration or added moisture through the fill material. If a lift is too dry, a tamping roller will quickly "walk out" and this is an indication to the Inspector that the fill is questionable. The feet of tamping rollers penetrate the lift and tend to compact from the bottom up. If a lift is too thick, the roller will tend to ride on the drum and the tamping action of the tamping feet will be ineffective. The Inspector should check to see that the drum of such rollers is clear of the fill material on the first pass over a new lift.

The following table summarizes the types of compaction equipment used for various soil classifications:

Types of Soils and Recommended Compacting Equipment

Materials	Type of Compaction Equipment
Fine-grained embankment and subgrade soils	Sheepsfoot rollers Segmented steel-wheeled rollers Pneumatic-tired rollers Vibratory steel-wheeled rollers
Granular base, subbase and improved subgrade courses	Pneumatic-tired rollers Vibratory compactors (both shoe and steel-wheeled type) Segmented steel-wheeled rollers
Coarse aggregate base courses	Shoe-type vibratory compactors Steel-wheeled vibratory rollers Steel-wheeled rollers Pneumatic-tired rollers

Plant-mix base, leveling or surface courses	Breakdown rolling:
	  Steel-wheeled three-wheel rollers
	  Steel-wheeled rollers (two-axle tandem rollers)
	Intermediate rolling:
	  Pneumatic-tired rollers (self-propelled)
	  Two- and three-axle tandem rollers
	Final rolling:
	  Steel-wheeled rollers (two- or three-axle tandem rollers)

3-3.6.3 **Moisture.** Moisture is critical for most soils while being compacted in a fill. (See Subsection 3-2.4.) The Inspector should know the optimum moisture values for the various soils involved in the earthwork on the project, and acquaint himself with how those soils look and feel at optimum moisture content. Frequent spot checks by the Inspector, who examines a handful of the soil and squeezes it into a ball, will generally disclose significant departures from the optimun moisture content. Once a method or combination of procedures is determined which results in a fairly stable moisture content, at or near optimum, the problem of varying moisture content is minimized and the Inspector's job made easier.

3-3.6.4 **Lift Thickness.** The depth of the lift being compacted is another important factor in fill construction. Each layer of soil to be compacted must be no thicker than that which the type of compactive effort intended to be used can effectively compact. Maximum of each thickness of each lift is stated in the Special Provisions or Standard Specifications, which may also provide for the laying of greater lift thicknesses if it is successfully demonstrated that the equipment to be used will produce the specified densities.

When the maximum lift is specified or determined, the Inspector should continuously check to insure that the loose lifts deposited do not exceed the maximun. Several methods may be used by the Inspector to check lift thickness. He can observe and measure the thickness at the edge of the loose lift as it is spread, or scrape a hole through the loose material to the compacted surface below and measure thickness. A small diameter probe of metal or wood with the lower end calibrated in inches can be easily pushed through the loose lift to the compacted surface below and the thickness observed on the probe.

While each lift is being spread, the Inspector should look for large stones, organic or other unsuitable material, and be alert for changes that may occur in soil types. He should watch for spongy or unstable compacted material under the wheels of hauling and spreading equipment in motion, and should advise the contractor to instruct the equipment operators to distribute their loaded and empty equipment travel uniformly across the fill.

Uniform density cannot be expected when excessively thick lifts are used, since the lower few inches of the lift will tend to be or near the specified density and the upper few inches will be significantly greater.

3-3.6.5 Compactive Effort. The last major factor in obtaining satisfactory compaction results is the number of passes that the compacting equipment makes over the lift being compacted. In general, as the lift thickness increases, the number of passes required to produce a specified density with a given roller increases. If the lift thickness is maintained constant and the compactive effort increased by utilizing heavier rollers, usually fewer passes are required to obtain desired density. When it has been determined how many passes over each lift will produce the specified density, the roller equipment operators should be so instructed and frequent checks made by the Inspector to insure that the operators are making the required number of passes before subsequent lifts are placed.

3-3.6.6 Earth Fill Quality and Testing. Compaction tests should be arranged for by the Inspector on a routine basis as well as for special reasons. On large fills that rise slowly, several compaction tests taken daily in representative areas may prove sufficient. Special tests should be provided for doubtful areas or for rechecks of areas where previous tests indicate a failure and the area has been rerolled or the fill has been removed and recompacted. (See Subsection 3-2.5 for soil density test methods).

The Inspector should be confident that the compacted lift throughout the surface of the fill is equal to or better in quality than that represented by the test. He must have observed that the compactive effort used, the lift thickness, the number of passes made and the moisture content of the soil were the same as at the test location. The elevation and horizontal location of every compaction test must be accurately recorded in the job records by the Inspector for future reference.

In any event, compaction tests should be provided at such frequency that density failures are discovered before the contractor has constructed more than several vertical feet of fill. It is unreasonable to slow down an efficient contractor's production or to require him to remove vast amounts of compacted fill because of infrequent or untimely compaction testing, or through delays in reporting test results.

In summing up methods of compaction, only two criteria are essential — that the final density is adequate and the required degree of uniformity is produced.

A field density report indicates the moisture content of soil in place, optimum moisture (See Subsection 3-2.5.2), dry weight per cubic foot in place, and maximum standard dry weight. If a particular test fails to meet density requirements, a comparison of the moisture content of the test specimen with the predetermined optimum moisture for that soil, may disclose a deficiency or excess of moisture that could account for the failure. If the moisture content is close to optimum, other reasons for the failure must be determined. Assuming that roller weights were checked and found adequate at the start of operations, the cause of failure can be placed in one or more of the following categrories: excessive lift thickness, insufficient number of passes by the compacting equipment, or insufficient care exercised in making the compaction test.

By excavating through the local area of the compaction failure with a shovel or bulldoze blade, the side of the excavation may be examined for indications of failure. Wet and dry streaks may indicate insufficient mixing of water in the soil or excessive lift thicknesses. By noting the condition of the fill at the test location, the depth and extent of unsatisfactory fill can be determined. If the contractor elects to add water, cultivate aerate or provide additional rolling in an attempt to improve the fill to an acceptable density, he should be permitted by the Inspector to do so. Unless the soil moisture content is considerably higher than optimum, removal is not generally necessary, and aeration by scarifying, tilling or discing and later recompacting the soil will usually be sufficient. If the soil is wet or too dry, it is usually more economical in time and costs to remove and recompact unsatisfactory portions of fills.

It is a policy of the Agency to investigate every soil compaction failure, correct the compaction deficiency in the area, and retest the reworked fill at or near the same location and elevation as that of the original test failure.

3-3.6.7 Earth Fill Checklist.

(1) Refer to related checklists; Subsection 3-3.2.2, Clearing and Grubbing; Subsection 3-3.3.7, Excavation, General; Subsection 3-3.4.9, Excavation Permits.

(2) Check for seepage and other latent conditions that might affect the foundation of the fill.

(3) Report unsuitable foundation conditions to the Supervisor for investigation.

(4) Order survey to establish ground line for payment purposes.

(5) Are foundations prepared prior to depositing fill? Are organic materials removed and surfaces scarified? Are benches cut into existing slopes to tie in new fill?

(6) Check for adequate drainage. Do not permit ponding of water in fill area.

(7) Check for haulage conditions on public streets; spillage and dust control.

(8) Test for optimum moisture content range for adequate compaction.

(9) See that compaction tests are performed at an early stage to verify the contractor's method.

(10) Observe the operations and verify the uniformity of spreading, mixing, lift thickness and moisture control.

(11) Check for uniformity of compactive effort, equipment used, coverage and number of passes.

(12) Evaluate adequacy of equipment; quantity, type and condition.

(13) Be sure the mixing equipment (plows, discs, etc.) are adequate to break up and mix soil and distribute moisture uniformly.

(14) Observe earth under the roller for movement and signs of excess moisture. Have contractor rip and aerate, if necessary.

(15) Watch for changes in the fill material.

(16) Order sufficient compaction tests to evaluate the quality. Remember that good fill construction results and fewer tests will be required when the material is uniform, the moisture is uniform (at or near optimum) and the compacting method and procedure are uniform.

(17) Have all areas and lifts that have failed been reworked and retested satisfactorily?

(18) Observe the finished surfaces, contours and slope-rounding for appearance, drainage and other requirements.

(19) Order survey to check for conformity and payment quantities.

3-3.7   Erosion Control.

3-3.7.1   **General.** Any grading activity being done under a permit in designated hillside areas during the period of October 15 to April 15 must proceed under strict erosion control. In some instances the grading may be completed but the surface improvements have been not constructed. Areas being developed and adjacent property must both be protected against the hazards of erosion.

In order that the Agency may exercise proper control of temporary and permanent erosion control measures, close cooperation must be maintained wth representatives of other governmental agencies concerned with the project.

3-3.7.2 **Plans.** Grading plans for grading operations in hillside areas are to be filed with the Engineer for approval by September 15. The temporary erosion control methods and devices proposed to be used are to be indicated thereon. Permanent type retention basins for control of flood water, when required, will normally be indicated on the storm drain plans for the improvement.

After receipt of the approved temporary erosion control plan, the permittee will be required to install desilting basins not later than October 15, and other temporary erosion control devices not later than December 1. If the grading has not progressed to a point where all or part of the devices shown on the plans can be constructed, sandbags and other devices must be used to control erosion and protect adjacent improved private and public property. Temporary expedients must be provided by the permittee which will be expanded or revised as the grading progresses. In these instances, it must be a joint effort of the permittee, his contractor and representatives of the Agency.

3-3.7.3 **Construction Requirements.** The major types of erosion control devices are shown in the Appendix, Plate No. 33, "Typical Pipe and Wire Revetment," and Plate No. 34, "Typical Desilting Basin Outlet." The following general notes apply to the construction of desilting basins:

(a) Outlet pipe, weir, spillway and apron shall be placed as far as practicable from the basin inlet and shall be placed on all desilting basins and retarding basins with dikes.

(b) Desilting basin and retarding basin dike walls shall be no steeper than two horizontal to one vertical and must be compacted to 95% density under the direct supervision of the Inspector.

(c) Inlet wingwalls to basins shall be paved with two inches of asphalt concrete. Paved berms and inlet slope shall be equal to or steeper than the slope of the carrying surface immediately above the inlet.

(d) All basins built on lots adjacent to dwellings must be completely lined with asphalt concrete or gunite.

(e) All basins and check dams shall be pumped dry, and all debris and silt removed within 24 hours after each storm.

(f) All weirs shall be flat across the invert; semi-circular or "V" weirs are not permitted.

(g) Sizes of basins and weirs shall be as shown on the plans or of a capacity to service the watershed affected.

(h) All spillways from basins shall be paved to existing paved street or existing storm drain catch basin.

(i) Desilting basins required for temporary erosion control will not be permitted in the street area unless specifically authorized by the Engineer.

(j) A stand-by pump, of sufficient capacity to empty the basin within 24 hours, shall be provided at each retention or desilting basin and a guard shall be on continuous duty while the basin contains water. In lieu of the guard, an approved fence shall be constructed simultaneously with the basin.

(k) Retention or desilting basins may not be removed or made inoperative, without prior approval of the Engineer, until all surface improvements have been completed.

Additional general rules for temporary erosion control measures which may not be indicated on the grading plans, but which are to be complied with by the permittee and enforced by the Agency, are as follows:

(a) All devices shall be in place and maintained during the rainy season (December 1 to April 15).

(b) Sandbags shall be stockpiled in the parkway at intervals shown on the erosion control plan, or at intervals shown under subparagraphic (i)(1) below, ready to be placed in position when rain is forecast or when directed by the Inspector.

(c) All loose soil and debris shall be removed from the tract upon starting operations and periodically thereafter as directed by the Inspector.

(d) The temporary erosion control devices shown on the plan shall be revised when the Inspector so directs.

(e) A 12″ berm shall be maintained on the tops of those fills on which grading is not in progress, and all fills shall be graded to promote drainage away from the edge of the fill.

(f) Earth dikes may not be used in lieu of sandbag dikes.

(g) Brush and ground cover may not be removed more than 10 feet above fills between December 1 and April 15.

(h) Stand-by crews shall be alerted by the permittee or the contractor for emergency work during rain storms.

(i) Check dams in unpaved streets and unpaved graded channels: Velocity check dams may be constructed of sandbags or other erosion-resistant materials approved by the Inspector, and shall be in place at the end of each working day when rain is forecast. They shall extend completely across the street or channel at right angles to the centerline.

(1) Provide velocity check dams in all unpaved street areas at the intervals indicated below:

Grade of the Street	Intervals Between Check Dams
Less than 4%	100 feet
4% to 10%	50 feet
over 10%	25 feet

(2) Provide velocity check dams in all unpaved channels at the intervals indicated below:

Grade of Channel	Intervals Between Check Dams
Less than 3%	100 feet
3% to 6%	50 feet
over 6%	25 feet

(3) Provide velocity check dams across the outlets of all lots draining into the street.

(j) Trench Protection: Prior to backfilling, all trenches in the unpaved street area shall be blocked with a double row of sandbags at the intervals prescribed below. Where practicable, the sandbags shall be placed with alternate header and stretcher courses.

Grade of the Street	Intervals Between Blocking
Less than 4%	100 feet
4% to 10%	50 feet
over 10%	25 feet

(1) Utility trenches shall be blocked from top to bottom.

(2) Sewer and storm drain trenches shall be blocked extending downward to sandbags from the graded surface or the street.

(3) After trenches are backfilled and completed, the surfaces over such trenches shall be mounded slightly to prevent

channeling of water in the trench area. Care should be exercised to provide for cross flow at frequent intervals where trenches are not on the centerline of a crowned street.

3-3.7.4 Erosion Control Check List.

(1) Have erosion control plans been approved by the Agency?

(2) Are erosion control devices being installed as required?

(3) Have sandbags been placed where required when rain is forecast?

(4) Have sandbags been placed in trenches where required?

(5) Has the contractor provided for standby crews for emergency work?

(6) Have retention and desilting basins been promptly dewatered and cleaned of silt following a rain?

(7) Do you have contractor's emergency telephone number?

3-3.8 Earthwork Measurement and Payment.
Methods of payment for removals, excavation, backfill, soil stabilization and subgrade preparation are prescribed by the Special Provisions or Standard Specifications. Measurement of the quantities of these classes of work is usually a function of the Inspector to determine or verify. Where large earth fills or cuts are made which are beyond the capability of the Inspector to measure, survey crews must be requested to provide initial and final cross-sections from which quantities can be computed.

Particular care should be exercised by the Inspector in measuring work for which the contractor will receive additional compensation. The contractor should be advised frequently of the quantities determined by the Inspector as the work progresses. This will keep the contractor informed of his progress and bring to attention any serious discrepancies that might arise.

3-4   STREET SURFACE IMPROVEMENTS

3-4.1 General.
This subsection describes the typical components that make up a street surface improvement including the curb, gutter, walk and driveways constructed of concrete; and the roadbed pavement structure for vehicular traffic. The roadbed structure is described in Subsection 3-4.3.1, Asphalt

Pavement Construction, which is the typical system used for most Agency projects, although concrete paving is sometimes utilized for selected projects.

When cut and fill earthwork is completed on a project (See Subsection 3-3), the street area should be at a rough grade elevation, within ± 0.2 foot (60mm). The standard nomenclature for street construction is shown in the typical cross-section of a street improvement. (See Plate 31, Appendix.)

3-4.2   Subgrade and Base Courses.

3-4.2.1   **General.**   The street roadbed structural section includes the pavement, base courses and subbase, if required, and the foundation soil.

Definitions and Uses of Materials:

Base — The layer immediately below the pavement used in a pavement system to reinforce and protect the subgrade or subbase.

Subbase — The layer used in the pavement system between the subgrade and base course.

Subgrade — The prepared and compacted existing below the pavement.

Soil Foundation — The prepared and compacted existing soil below the pavement.

Structural Section — The pavement and base, subbase and processed layer of existing soil below the pavement.

The procedure for building up the structural section requires some processing of the subgrade (foundation soil). This processing usually provides for ripping and discing the soil to a specified depth; removing large rocks; bringing the soil to optimum moisture by aerating the soil if it is too wet or adding moisture if it is too dry; and recompacting the soil to the uniform density required by the specifications.

When subbase or base courses are involved, less processing of the subgrade is required. Conversely, if the pavement is to be placed on native soil, more processing and compaction is required.

Subbase and base courses (See Subsection 2-3) are composed of selected or treated soils, aggregate mixtures and reprocessed pavement or concrete. Properly installed, these materials increase the strength of the structural section and its ability to support the traffic loads. How well this is done also affects the long term maintenance economy and length of service.

In building construction, a poor soil foundation will ultimately result in the destruction of the building. The same is true of roadway pavement and its substructure. It must be capable of supporting all loads placed upon it. Compaction of all elements of the structural section is a key word in producing the desired strength and economy. The compaction effort compresses soils and base materials into a more solid mass to reduce water and air to acceptable amounts in the soils and thus minimize the effects of the traffic loads. Also, the more solid soil mass resulting from compaction resists water movement and volume change which can in time cause the deterioration of the pavement structure.

3-4.2.2 Subgrade for Pavements. Subgrade is the surface upon which a pavement, base or subbase is to be placed. The type of subgrade is designated as "subgrade for base," "pavement subgrade" or smilar terms. When the structural section below the pavement is composed of several courses of base and subbase, several intermediate grade tolerances are also involved. The intermediate grade tolerance is ±0.4 foot (12mm) for base and subbase, and ±0.02 foot (6mm) for pavement.

Compaction of subgrade increases its strength properties and, as a result, less strength is required in the pavement. Almost invariably the cost of achieving this additional strength by compaction is materially less than the cost of added pavement thickness. Higher subgrade density also means higher bearing values and less probability of settlement.

Another important factor in subgrade preparation is the smoothness of the completed surface. If this subgrade surface is not constructed to plan elevations, true cross-section, and within the specification tolerances for smoothess, the surface of the pavement will usually be adversely affected. In particular, bituminous pavement laid by a mechanical paver operating on the subgrade will tend to reproduce the irregularities of the subgrade in the finished surface of the pavement.

Dry rough-grade surfaces should be watered prior to processing. Scarifying is required to a depth of six inches, with all rocks over three inches in diameter removed from the loosened material. Such rocks, if left in the top six inches of subgrade, would later introduce problems in obtaining uniform compaction and in maintaining the pavement, since these hard spots tend to "pierce" flexible pavements under heavy traffic loads and vibration. Sand or gravel subgrades do not require this scarifying operation unless the presence of such rocks is known to be in the top six inches of the subgrade.

After rolling, the Inspector should not permit low areas to be filled with loose material and rerolled unless the smooth rolled surface of the low area has been scarified to a depth of at least two inches and watered (if necessary). This scarifying operation helps to prevent laminations of the soil.

When first reporting to an assignment to inspect subgrade preparation, the Inspecter should examine the construction site in the presence of the contractor's representative to note the condition of the existing improvements in the area. The conditions inside storm drain and sewer manholes should be checked. Manhole locations and utility installations in the roadway area should be noted. Manholes should be raised to grade or covered with a plate for resetting later as provided by the specifications. Wet or soft areas of the subgrade may indicate a damaged water main or service. The Inspector should determine that the contractor has provided access to driveways, has protected street name signs, has provided for traffic in accordance with the plans and specifications, and has obtained permits and waivers for excess materials to be exported from the construction site and disposed of on private property. In addition, the exact locations of all drainage outlets through curbs (roof drains) are to be recorded in the job records so that they can be reconnected through any new curb to be constructed.

Grade stakes will be set by survey crews in accordance with the procedures outlined in the Standard Specifications and Agency policy (See Subsection 1-5). All checking of line, elevation and cross-sections will be accomplished by the Inspector from these stakes, blue tops or hubs referenced from blue tops. Most grade checking by the Inspector is done with a fish line and pocket rule. It is preferable that such checking be done with the help of one or more of the contractor's representatives. With the contractor's men stretching the line taut and the Inspector measuring and locating high or low areas, grade can be quickly checked or rechecked. By the time any significant amount of grade is checked, the contractor's reprensentative is made aware of quality or lack of quality in a prepared subgrade and he can then take the necessary action to correct any deficiencies. Usually this involves the instruction of his equipment operators in the proper techniques of preparation of subgrade to improve the quality of future subgrades. While the Inspector can check subgrade by himself by utilizing steel pins to hold the fish line, this method is much slower and the Inspector often has to repeat the check in the presence of the contractor to prove any deficiency.

Rolling of subgrade is normally accomplished with a roller weighing not less than 10 tons. Pneumatic-tired rollers may be used to produce the required densities but steel-tired rollers are usually required to smooth the surface to the cross-section and tolerance required. Soft spots discovered during rolling usually necessitate some removals and refilling with suitable material. If such excavation is due to the fault of the contractor, the excavating and refilling shall be at the contractor's expense. If it is not, the Engineer will direct the necessary corrective measures, and in the case of contract work, the contractor will be reimbursed. Areas inaccessible to rollers must be tamped to acceptable densities and shaped to the proper section by hand methods.

Sufficient compaction tests are arranged for by the Inspector as subgrade is completed to insure that the specified densities are attained. After subgrade is accepted, the contractor must protect it from damage until it is covered with a base or pavement. Subgrade which has been prepared too far in advance of the subsequent paving operations is likely to be damaged by traffic or rain and may require rerolling and rechecking.

3-4.2.3 Soil Stabilization.

(a) **General.** Research is continuing to improve soil properties by the use of minor quantities of selected admixtures. There are four methods commonly used: namely, cement, lime, emulsified asphalt and mechanical stabilization. Improvement of soils by stabilization requires extensive processing and careful selection of materials. It is specified where the subgrade soil will not otherwise support surface improvements and the location and soil type is satisfactory for stabilization using a stabilizer. The extensive processing requirement usually precludes its use on city streets where access to property and traffic problems are involved.

Inspection requirements are comparable to those required for concrete construction and extensive testing is required. The primary construction problems are insuring the proper rate of application of the admixture and obtaining complete mixing, in the particularly fine-grained soils that may be involved.

Stabilized soil subbases add strength to subgrades and this added strength in turn permits a reduction in design requirement for structure footings and pavements.

(b) **Cement Treated Soil.** The method which develops the greatest bearing value is soil-cement stabilization. In a sense, weak concrete is produced. Soil-cement stabilization is accomplished primarily by one of three methods: central batch-mixing plants, jobsite mixers or dry application to soil in windrows. Mixing at central batch plants or at the jobsite is usually accomplished in batch or continuous type concrete mixing equipment, with the water added during mixing, and the soil-cement mixtures placed and rolled or vibrated in a manner similar to concrete. The Inspector must check the proportions of cement, soil and water used, the mixing time and the placement procedures.

More extensive inspection is required when the windrow method is employed. Dry cement is added at a predetermined rate to windrows which are sized to a uniform cross-section. After the moisture content of the windrowed soil is determined, additional water is added at a constant rate to bring the total moisture content of the soil up to the specified amount. The windrows are thoroughly mixed and spread over the area to receive the stabilized mixture and then compacted to the required density. Inspection of this class of work is supplemented by extensive laboratory work to determine moisture content of soil, cement requirements and final densities. In addition, careful checking of cement meters, rates of application of cement and water, and determination that satisfactory mixing is achieved all require the alert attention of the Inspector. This class of work is completely described in the Standard Specifications.

Where a small quantity of soil is required to be cement stabilized, the contractor may find it to be more economical to remove and waste the in-place soil and replace it with commercially available cement-treated crushed aggregate base (See Subsection on Cement Treated Base, Standard Specifications).

(c) **Lime Treated Soil.** Fine-grained native soils can be stabilized by lime treatment. Subgrade preparation by scarifying and windrowing is similar to that described for cement treatment. The soil must be tested before construction to determine the effective amount of lime to be mixed with the soil. During construction sufficient testing must be carried out to determine that the actual lime content is at the specified level.

Lime may be applied dry, or as a slurry from a tank truck equipped with a distributor, the soil and lime mixed by a traveling mixer, and the grade shaped and compacted. Hydrated lime or quicklime may be used but special safety precautions must be taken with quicklime. The Standard Specifications require a detailed safety program to include protective equipment for eye, mouth, nose and skin protection. Dry lime treatment of soils should not be attempted on windy days.

After lime-treated materials are spread and compacted, the surface must be sealed by the application of emulsified asphalt, or the surface kept moist until covered by other base materials. No equipment or traffic should be permitted on lime-treated material for 72 hours after a curing seal is applied.

(d) **Emulsified Asphalt Treated Soil.** Bituminous asphalt stabilized base, often referred to as emulsified asphalt stabilization, is also described in the Standard Specifications and is accomplished in a manner similar to the windrow method for soil-cement. The bituminous stabilizer used can be emulsified asphalt or rapid, medium or slow-curing grades of cutback road oils between the grades of 70 and 800, as required by the plans or specifications for the project. The techniques for inspection of this class of work are similar to those described in the preceding paragraph. Bituminous stabilization is not generally recommended for soil unless at least 50 percent of the particles are sand-size or larger, since the difficulty of achieving complete mixing increases immensely with the decrease in the particle size of the soil. The end product of bituminous stabilization of granular material is basically a weak bituminous road mix, providing the soil mixture with increased waterproofing and resistance to shear.

(e) **Mechanical Soil Stabilization.** Mechanical stabilization is simply the development of a uniformly-graded material. The gradation is so designed as to have a minimun of voids after compaction. A certain amount of cohesion appears to develop between the soil particles, due principally to aggregate interlock. Hygroscopic materials such as rock salt and calcium chloride add to the durability of such mechanically stabilized soil by causing moisture to be retained, thus adding materially to the strength of interlock.

3-4.2.4 Untreated Roadway Base.

(a) **General.** The Standard Specifications establish the specific requirements for the use of selected materials as base for pavement. If untreated base is required without specifying type, the contractor shall supply crushed aggregate (CAB). When a specific base material is specified, the contractor may substitute any higher classification of base material, following the order of preference listed in the Standard Specifications. Untreated base materials for roadway construction are described in Subsection 2-3.

Many factors adversely affect the quality of base materials. Poor grading, excesses or deficiencies of fines, unsound particles and adulteration by unsatisfactory material are the most frequently encountered problems in producing a uniform quality base material. Where base materials are processed or manufactured, many of these problems can be overcome. Crushed aggregate, for example, is processed from clean crushed rock, screened into standard particle sizes and combined again in a uniform manner in the proper proportions to meet specification grading. On the other hand, selected natural material and disintegrated granite are usually mined from sidehill excavations, the face of which commonly reveals strata of several different types of earth in varying thicknesses. Care must be exercised in this type of mining operation to prevent the mixing of unsuitable overburden soils with the base material.

The designer usually specifies the better classes of base materials, such as crushed aggregate or crushed slag, for use under pavements in arterial streets having high traffic densities. The cost of such materials is understandably higher due to the additional processing involved, but the quality of the base is correspondingly increased and the additional cost is warranted where heavy wheel loads can be expected.

The less expensive base materials (such as disintegrated granite and selected natural materials) which are mined and placed on the subgrade without further processing are normally utilized for base under pavement for secondary and residential streets.

When crushed miscellaneous base is used, haulaway and disposal costs are reduced, and the expense of importing base material is eliminated. Therefore, bituminous and portland cement concrete pavements processed for base by crushers on-site should be encouraged when it is a suitable procedure on a project. Also removals can be hauled to a processing plant offsite for crushing and return to the jobsite.

Crushing of the existing pavement removals on-site to produce processed miscellaneous base may pose problems of noise and dust. Noise can seldom be reduced but it can be controlled to the extent that crushing operations should not be commenced in residential areas in early morning hours or near noise-sensitive areas (such as movie studios or hospitals) during critical periods. Dust can be controlled effectively by wetting the material to be crushed in advance of the crushing operations and by the continuous introduction of water into the crusher.

The Inspector should carefully observe the base material as it is deposited on the subgrade for evidence of organic material such as: clumps of grass, twigs, rubbish or discoloration of the material by the normally darker organic top soils.

Where obvious changes are observed in the grading or composition of base material as it is delivered, the Inspector should notify the contractor that the material has changed and order further hauling stopped until additonal investigations, sampling and testing can determine that the new material meets the specification requirements.

In some instances where untreated base material is required for a street improvement, a deposit of material may be encountered elsewhere on the project which will qualify for the untreated base specified. After stockpiling is completed, the Testing Agency will sample it and, if satisfactory, it will be approved for use on that specific project only.

(b) **Spreading and Compacting.** The Standard Specifications control the method of spreading and compacting untreated base material. When the thickness of the untreated base material is more than six inches, it is to be placed in multiple layers of equal thickness, none of which exceed six inches. Any faulty method used by the contractor to deposit and spread the material on the subgrade, which tends to leave a non-uniform quality of material or cause segregation, is to be corrected before further spreading of the base is permitted. Blading of crushed aggregate or crushed slag, especially when the material is on the dry side, tends to segregate the material resulting in the fines gravitating to the bottom and the larger particles rising to the top. This undesirable condition is minimized by a delivered material that is pre-mixed and moist and by spreading the loads by tailgating; then using a motor grader for the minimum number of passes needed to level the course before rolling operations. Compacting this material by rolling densifies the course and tends to lock the particles together so that subsequent passes with a motor grader over the material to shape its surface to plan section do not result in such serious segregation.

Large clods, rocks and other foreign material adversely affecting the quality of the base must be remove. Hard lumps or rocks, which do not crush under the roller, will cause the roller to bridge adjacent areas and result in non-uniform and possibly low densities.

Watering of untreated base material is too frequently considered of little importance, yet all successive operations may depend indirectly on the amount of water used. Overwatering may cause segregation of the base material or soften the subgrade to the extent that it may become plastic under the action of the construction equipment and have to be removed. Insufficient watering, on the other hand, may result in unsatisfactory compaction. Where the material tends to be water-critical (as may be the case where silts are present in the base material) it may be to the contractor's advantage to provide for some watering at the borrow pit or mining operation.

(c) **Sampling and Testing.** The Inspector should anticipate when the subgrade will be ready for placement of untreated base material and advise the contractor to have a load or two delivered in advance so that a representative sample can be taken for testing. Results of the sand equivalent test can usually be obtained the day after sampling. However, if the sand equivalent is not within the minimum range, it may be necessary to test for the "R" value, which takes an additional day or two. (The "R" value test is a measure of the material's resistance to deformation.) The necessity for further testing is determined from the screen analysis and the amount of No. 200 mesh material in the base. It is therefore best to request testing of the base material three days in advance. If the material fails to pass the specified requirements, new material must be brought on the job and tested. For this reason, the Inspector should discourage the contractor from importing and placing untreated base on the subgrade prior to receiving the test results. If he disregards such advice, the Inspector should issue him a Job Memorandum stating that placement of untreated base material prior to approval is done at his own risk and is subject to removal if tests indicate that material does not meet the specification requirements. Sampling of untreated base material shall be in accordance with Plate 28, Appendix. Addi-

tional samples may be taken at any other time that the Inspector observes or suspects a change in the color, gradation or
texture from the original approved sample.

(d) **Measurement and Payment.** Untreated base material is normally shown on the plans to be a specified thickness
and placed in definite areas. It is customary to pay for such
material either on a square foot basis for a specific thickness, or
on a tonnage basis, as indicated in the proposal. The price bid
for untreated base material is considered to include full payment for all materials, labor and equipment used to prepare
the subgrade for the untreated base material as well as to place
and compact it. It does not include payment for grading and
shaping the material to pavement subgrade, which is considered to be included in the price paid for pavement.

Measurement of untreated base material on a unit area
basis should be determined from the plan dimensions taken in a
horizontal plane. Where untreated base material is furnished
on a tonnage basis, the Inspector must be provided with delivery tickets accompanying each load, on which is indicated the
weight of the material in each load as determined on a public
scale attended by a certified public or private weighmaster.

3-4.2.5 Roadway Subgrade and Base Checklist.

(1) Check for completion of prior construction requirements. Underground completed (utilities, sewers)? Curb and
gutter?

(2) Locate manholes to be brought to finish grade or to
be plated over during subgrade and base construction.

(3) Check plan requirements for existing soil foundation
preparation and stabilization, subbase and base. Thickness?
Density?

(4) Grade stakes set? Check for protection and setting of
hubs by contractor.

(5) Review requirements and procedure with contractor.
Sources of base and subbase; soil stabilization method; material
tests and approval; compaction tests.

(6) Check for soil movement under rollers and hauling
equipment to detect soft spots. Backfilled trenches may not
be sufficiently dried out and ready for base and subgrade
construction.

(7) Are all pockets of soft or yielding material ripped up
and dried out or replaced with suitable material? Evaluate for
contractor or Agency responsibility.

(8) Is existing soil processed to required depth and at subgrade for base? Watered; ripped; disced and mixed; large rocks removed; rolled to required density; cut to required grade and cross section and smoothness tolerance; and tested?

(9) Imported base or subbase sampled from material delivered to jobsite? Test results okay?

(10) Check for too much dirt pickup when pavement removals are crushed on site for reuse as base. Order sampling and testing as soon as processing has developed a representative stockpile.

(11) Maintain adequate dust and noise control during all grading and crushing operations.

(12) Watch for changes in grading of the material and appearance for all types of base material (imported or jobsite processed); and if warranted, order additional sampling and testing.

(13) Watch for segregation during spreading operations.

(14) Check for adequacy and uniformity of operations; moisture control and mixing; lift thickness; compaction effort (coverage and number of passes of equipment).

(15) Collect delivery tickets for tonnage payment (from certified weighmaster).

(16) Test for compacted density of subbase; base.

(17) Check finished subgrade for grade, cross section and surface smoothness. $\pm \frac{1}{4}''$ (6mm) (which must be compensating) is the usual tolerance of subgrade for pavement.

(18) Check contractor's provisions for protecting finished subgrade. Do not permit subgrade to dry out prior to being covered with the finish surfacing.

3-4.3 Asphalt Pavement Construction.

3-4.3.1 **General.** The durability, smoothness and general quality of asphalt pavements depend to a great extent upon the experience, knowledge and effective performance of the Inspector assigned to this class of work. Much of the technique of laying bituminous pavements is not contained in specification or text books, but is learned only from years of experience and observation. The material included in this subsection is intended to supplement the specifications and provide some of the fundamental knowledge required to adequately inspect the placement of bituminous pavements.

The Inspector must take an active part in asphalt paving operations and equip himself with the tools necessary to accomplish his function. A fish line, straight-edge, pocket rule and thermometer are essential to his work. He should also have a working knowledge of the construction equipment being used by the contractor and should be capable of determining by visual inspection of equipment performance and the condition of the pavement laid, whether the equipment is in good mechanical condition, properly adjusted and is doing its job.

By checking each detail performed by the crew and the performance of the equipment, the Inspector can often obtain an improvement in workmanship that makes the difference between a good job and a superior job.

Upon arriving at the jobsite, the Inspector should immediately familiarize himself with the project plans and specifications and the type of pavement mixture that is to be laid. Before paving operations are begun, he should make certain that the base or subgrade upon which the pavement is to be laid is at the proper elevation, true to cross-section, and has been compacted to the required density. Irregularities must be corrected before placing the first course of pavement.

The smoothness of the finished surface depends to a large extent upon the care exercised in obtaining a smooth, firm subgrade.

The Inspector should determine that all of the grades needed for checking the elevations of the finished pavement have been set. If no gutter exists, a chalk line should be snapped on the curb face between flow-line chisel cuts which will exactly indicate finish flow-line elevation. The Inspector should familiarize himself with the standard methods of checking elevations by measuring down to the desired crown section from a taut fish line stretched a known distance above flow-line elevation or between curb tops. Accuracy of the completed work depends to a large measure upon the ability of the Inspector to check crown sections of subgrade, base and finished pavement.

Unless otherwise specified, where asphalt concrete pavement does not terminate against a curb, gutter or other pavement, the contractor shall install a header on the line of termination. Such headers shall remain in place upon completion of the improvements. Headers must always conform to plan line and grade and be rigidly installed. Unless otherwise specified on the plans or in the specifications, headers are always 2-inch (nominal size) boards, the top edge of which is set to the plan elevations and line. These headers must be set with full bearing on firm subgrade. Where the subgrade is low, the area must be filled, thoroughly compacted and trimmed to true subgrade before the header is set. If the Inspector discovers headers which do not have full bearing, he must order these headers removed and the subgrade brought up to the proper elevation and the header replaced.

He must not permit wood shims or earth to be tamped under headers which lack bearing, nor should he permit additional stakes to be installed as a substitute for bearing. These make-shift repairs permit the header to depress under the weight of the roller and the plan grade is thereby distorted near the header line. Stakes are used to add rigidity to headers and to add resistance to lateral movement. They are not intended to hold up the header.

Side stakes are required to be 2-inch by 3-inch (nominal size), 18 inches long, or longer, and spaced not over four feet apart. To prevent them from projecting above the top of the header, they are to be driven on the outside of the header to a depth of one inch below the top edge and securely nailed to the header. Splices are to be made with 1-inch thick boards of the same height as the header and not less than 24 inches long.

Preparatory to paving operations, the interior of sewer and storm drain manholes should be cleaned out, the ring and covers removed and the holes covered with steel plates at approximate subgrade so that the paving operation can proceed without interference. This is the best procedure to avoid rough and low density pavement adjacent to the structure. Manholes are raised to finished street grade after paving and it is therefore the Inspector's responsibility to see that the contractor uses a witness mark or stake and records the offset distance so that manholes can be located accurately after paving without damaging paved surfaces outside the immediate vicinity of the manhole.

Prior to paving, clearance must be obtained by the contractor from all utility companies who have underground facilities such as power, water, gas, telephone, TV cables, petroleum lines, street lights and traffic signals in the area to be paved. The Agency provides a "Utility Notice" indicating the specific clearances required. All clearance replies by the utility companies are telephoned to the Agency's dispatcher on the day prior to paving the project. Before the end of the working day, the Inspector should contact the dispatcher to see that all clearances have been received, and if not, advise the contractor that paving operations cannot proceed.

Samples of asphalt mixtures are taken at the plant by the Plant Inspector and forwarded to the Agency's laboratory for testing. Thickness and density of the pavement material compacted in place are obtained from core samples cut from the finished pavement. Cores are normally requested by the Supervisor, but the Project Inspector may request cores at locations where he suspects that the pavement thickness is deficient or the required specific gravity has not been obtained. (See Plate 28, Appendix for sampling details.)

3-4.3.2 Transporting Asphalt Pavement Mixtures. Asphalt pavement materials should be transported only in trucks provided with tight steel beds which have been coated with a thin film of distillate or light oil before loading. The truck beds should be coated as often as required but not less than once each day. After each such coating, the truck bed should be raised to drain thoroughly, with no excess oil permitted.

To maintain the pavement mixture at the proper laying temperature, it may be necessary to cover each load with a tarpaulin when being hauled a long distance or during cold weather. The Standard Specifications should be checked for specific requirements.

3-4.3.3 Tack Coating. One source of asphalt pavement failure arises from improper tack-coating procedures, making it necessary for the Inspector to understand the need for the use of tack coats as well as the problems that can develop. The purpose of a tack coat is to assure a good bond between the new paving material and the surface of existing pavement upon which it is to be laid — and also where the asphalt pavement mixture contacts the vertical faces of curbs, gutters, cold pavement joints and the like. The tack coat covers the individual particles on the surface of the existing pavement and prevents these particles from later taking asphalt from the paving mixture and creating a slippage plane. If this tack coat is too scant, part of its effectiveness may be lost and the pavement may ravel or peel off. When the tack coat is applied in excessive amounts, it tends to lubricate the surface to which it is applied and create a slippage plane. Too much tack coat can also result in bleeding and instability of the new pavement. As a rule of thumb, a tack coat should be applied only in such quantity as to fog coat or speckle the surface to be paved.

Needless to say, all areas to be tack-coated must be thoroughly cleaned by brooming and washing if necessary. Emulsion-type tack coats may be applied to damp surfaces but hot asphalt tack coats can be applied only to dry surfaces. Work should be planned so that no greater area is treated with tack coat in any one day than will be covered by the paving mixture during the same day. All traffic not essential to work should be kept off the tack coat.

A tack coat of either AR-1000 paving asphalt, applied at an approximate rate of 0.05 gallon per square yard, or Type SS-1h emulsified asphalt at an approximate rate of 0.5 to 0.10 gallon per square yard, is required by the Standard Specifications, to be used where the asphalt concrete pavement being constructed makes contact with cold pavement joints, curbs, gutters and the like. Emulsified asphalt tack coats can be used during hot or cold weather. When applied, the tack coat has a characteristically dull brown color and should not be paved over until its combined water evaporates and it turns black and is tacky to the touch.

3-4.3.4   Spreading Asphalt Pavement Mixtures.

(a) **Laying Equipment.** In general, mechanical pavers are equipped with a hopper, spreader screws, screed and tamper mechanisms, and are self-propelled. Some tractor units are mounted on crawler tracks, other on rubber-tired wheels. The most common types used are the Barber-Greene, Blaw-Knox, Cedarapids, Adnum and Pioneer. Improvements are continuously being made in these pavers such as the introduction of an automatic leveling device to control the lift thickness.

No attempt will be made to describe the operating characteristics of these pavers, but the cause and correction of the most common deficiencies in pavement resulting from improperly adjusted (or worn) components or undesirable operating techniques will be enumerated, along with corrective measures.

When a paver is operated at high paving speeds, it tends to magnify or aggravate any worn or out-of-adjustment condition which may exist in the paver. In most cases, the screed bar will tend to drag the surface and pull numerous transverse cracks into the pavement or drag the larger rock particles along the surface. Reducing the travel speed will correct this deficiency and restore a smooth pavement suface. Little is gained by having a paver place bituminous mixtures at a faster rate than the supplying plant can produce it. This results in the paver operating at a high rate of travel for a few minutes, then a period of waiting for the next truck to arrive. During the waiting time, the working parts of the paver will cool off and the mix remaining in the machine will stiffen. When the paver starts again with another load of material, the resisting forces will have increased. The paver must overcome these forces before it can settle down again to a smooth spread. During the period that it takes for this adjustment to occur, the quality of the finished surface will be inferior.

If the tracks on the crawler portion of a paver are not snug, the sprocket wheels tend to climb the tracks with a rhythmic bumping movement. This movement is reflected to the screed mechanism and results in a ripple effect on the surface of the pavement. A simple adjustment of the tracks will remedy this condition.

Except with the Adnum paver, immediate correction of lift thickness cannot be effected. The paver must travel from 8 to 15 feet to reflect a change in the screed setting. This is often misunderstood by contractors as well as Inspectors and explains why an inexperienced screed operator is sometimes found measuring the lift and frantically operating the screed controls in an attempt to compensate for excessive or thin lifts. If the subgrade is properly prepared and true to cross-section, these screed controls can be set and adjusted at the start of paving operations and the pavement laid with only slight adjustments made subsequently as they may become necessary. Frequent manipulation of these controls results invariably in a rough pavement surface.

If the tamper bar ahead of the screed is out of adjustment and does not come down far enough, the screed must strike off the material. This tends to drag the material, particularly the rock particles at the surface, and cause a poor appearance. If the tamper bar comes down too far, a scum of oily material will build up behind it on the screed face and create a scuffing appearance on the pavement surface.

When the tamper bar becomes worn to a knife edge with use, it is no longer effective in tamping the material to a plane slightly below the leading edge of the screed, and the screed will drag the rock particles forward in the surface, leaving small voids behind each particle.

If the adjustment for clearance between the tamper bar and the screed is too great, oily scum will accumlate between them. This scum will contain sand particles, which are abrasive, and will tend to cause additional wear and increase the space even more. As this condition becomes worse, the build-up of material may become so severe that it can slow down the tamper bar, resulting in clutch slippage and erratic performance of the machine.

When this adjustment between the tamper bar and screed is too close, the tamper bar has a tendency to burr the nose of the screed plate, causing small projections to extend from the bottom of the screed. These projections drag the surface of the pavement and cause a scuffing action.

Care should be exercised to minimize the impact between the paver and trucks backing up to dump their loads. Heavy impacts tend to rock the paver backwards, impressing the screed into the hot pavement surface and causing a transverse indentation. A similar condition results if the paver operator starts the paving machine in high gear after it has been stopped.

The hopper of the machine must not be overloaded and paving material allowed to spill in front of the hopper or on the adjacent pavement. This material, when spilled on previously laid pavements, is hard to clean up and mars the appearance of the pavement.

The Inspector should never permit a spreading machine hopper to empty completely except at the end of the day. Even though these machines are on crawler tracks and ruggedly built, when the hopper is completely emptied, the paver will "ride up" at the front end. When a new load is dumped into the hopper, it is depressed from the weight of material, causing the spreading end to elevate slightly. This results in an offset in the permanent surface at the spreader bar which is difficult to correct.

The Inspector can often determine from his experience what operating conditions result in substandard pavement textures and must call such conditions to the attention of the contractor for correction.

(b) **Condition of Paving Mixture.** A Plant Inspector may be assigned to inspect several plants in the same day. When several plants start up simultaneously, it may be necessary to waive the requirement for a signed load ticket to accompany the first load of asphalt materials delivered. However, the Inspector should check the contractor's delivery ticket to identify the type of material being delivered. Job Inspectors are to accept materials even though no signed ticket accompanies the first load. The Plant Inspector will send a form, "Plant Inspector's Report to Field Inspector," with the first load dispatched after his arrival at the plant (See Subsection 2-6.2, Field Communication Procedure).

The Inspector shall, however, reject any materials which are observed to be defective. Some of the reasons for rejecting a mix follow:

Too hot. Overheated mixes can often be identified from the blue smoke rising from the mix in the truck or when the material is being emptied into the hopper of the paving machine. The temperature should be checked with a thermometer and if it exceeds the maximum placing temperature prescribed by specifications, it must be rejected.

Too cold. If the mix is too cold, it will appear to be "stiff," or the larger aggregate particles may be improperly coated. It should be checked with a thermometer and rejected if it is less than the minimum specification requirement.

Too much asphalt. When too much asphalt is incorporated in the mix, the load will tend to slump and level out in the truck. Properly mixed bituminous pavement materials are usually stiff enough to heap or pile up in the truck and resist this slumping. In addition, excess asphalt is easily detected behind a paver by the slick surface appearing on the pavement.

Too little asphalt. A pavement mixture having a brownish, dull appearance and lacking the shiny black luster typical of an asphalt mixture, generally contains too little asphalt. The lean, granular, brownish appearance results from lack of proper coating of the aggregate. It can be easily detected while the mix is still in the truck and should be promptly rejected. If the mix is erroneously incorporated in the pavement, it will retain its lean appearance and will not satisfactorily compact under the roller. In this case, the unacceptable mix must be removed from the subgrade and disposed of by the contractor.

Non-uniform mixing. Sometimes an improperly mixed batch can be detected while in the truck. It will display non-uniform, patchy areas of lean, brown, dull appearing material intermixed with areas having a shiny, black appearance and should be rejected.

Excess coarse aggregate. A mix containing too much coarse aggregate will appear to have too much asphalt, displaying a rich, black appearance and having a tendency to slump in the trucks. It can be detected by its coarse texture, particularly when it has been laid on the subgrade.

Excess fine aggregate. Asphalt pavement mixtures having excess fine aggregate will have the total surface of the particles so greatly increased that the proper amount of asphalt will not adequately coat them and the mix will appear to contain insufficient asphalt. It will also appear to be poorly graded with an obvious excess of fines.

Excess moisture. Steam will rise from a mix when it is dumped into the hopper of a paver if excess moisture is present in the mix. It may also appear to be rich and dark as if it had too much asphalt.

Miscellaneous. Segregation of the aggregate or contamination of the mix with organic or other debris, trash or dirt will render the pavement mixture unacceptable. These mixes are usually easily identifiable.

The Plant Inspector should be immediately notified of any abnormality in the quality or appearance of the paving mixture.

(c) **Spreading Operations, General.** Asphalt pavement mixtures should not be laid at atmospheric temperatures below 40°F. At the time of delivery to the site of the work, the temperature of the paving mixture should not be less than prescribed for the material in the Standard Specification.

Except when utilizing "thick-lift" construction procedure, asphalt paving mixtures should not be laid more than four inches thick. Ordinarily, when asphalt concrete base is to be more than four inches thick, it is laid in two or more courses of equal thickness.

The Inspector should check the project plans and specifications for the type of pavement to be laid. The mixes normally called for are listed in a Standard Plan and in Plate 11, Appendix. Coarser mixes are used for base and for machine laying; finer mixes are specified for wearing surfaces and for hand laying. (See Subsection 2-5.6.)

The harder asphalts (AR-8000) are used for major streets and on hillside streets laid in hot weather. Softer asphalt (AR-4000) is used for residential streets (See Subsection 2-5.5).

All "feather-edge" joins on existing paving must be tack coated (See Subsection 3-4.3.3.). A four to six-inch wide strip should be painted with bitumen on the old pavement side of the join line. This is to provide a bond between the old pavement and hot paving material along the edge. The balance of the area of the old pavement to be overlaid should be tack coated for the same reason. All feather-edges and thin areas should be rolled immediately after laying, before the paving mixture chills.

All joints in bituminous paving should be staggered approximately six inches between courses, both in longitudinal and transverse joints. At the beginning of each day's work, all edges of joints in wearing courses are required to be neatly trimmed to a vertical face for the full thickness of the course.

A leveling course should be laid to fill low places in existing pavement before laying the required pavement material. This is for the purpose of having a uniform thickness and density in the completed work and obtaining a smooth riding surface. Asphalt pavement which does not terminate against a curb, gutter or another pavement, must be constructed against headers, as described in Subsection 3-4.3.1. The exceptions to this requirement are for buildings that project into alleys, or at places where the pavement may be constructed beyond pavement lines indicated on the plan through arrangements between the contractor and a property owner, in which case the headers affected may be omitted.

Sometimes new pavement is to join existing pavement having a header still in place. These old headers must be removed before the existing pavement is joined. Asphalt pavement shall not be laid against new gutters until the gutters attain the age of seven days, except that if additional cement, calcium chloride or other approved accelerator was used in the gutter concrete, the new pavement may be constructed after three days have elapsed.

Laying operations should commence with the first pass adjacent to curbs or gutters. A subsequent pass is then laid adjacent to the first pass and this procedure repeated until the center or high point of the area to be paved is reached. Where a street with the crown in the center is to be surfaced, paving operations should begin at each gutter and progress toward the center.

Placement of a second course of asphalt concrete will be permitted when the first course has cooled to the extent that it does not displace under the contractor's equipment, such as a loaded truck.

Before laying, the thickness of each course of paving should be determined. This would appear unnecessary but there are many cumulative factors which can affect the thickness of the course being laid. The Inspector should never assume that, because the base course was four inches, a 2-inch finish course will produce a required thickness of six inches over-all. Some factors which can cause variations in the pavement thickness are: human error, subgrade and pavement variations, improper rolling and the occasional contractor who is trying to save on materials. When paving, a conscientious Inspector should be continually observing the various operations involved and correct any procedure that may cause a variation of the lift being laid.

In streets not exceeding 40 feet in width, the Inspector and the contractor should stretch a string from top of curb to top of curb and measure down to the surface of the base course and calculate the fills necessary to bring the second course to the required finish grade. This procedure should be repeated every 25 feet and the fills marked on the base pavement with yellow keel in numerals large enough to be readable by the screed operator from some distance. Where no curb exists, the string can be held a known distance above the gutter or header in a manner similar to checking subgrade. When the street is wider than 40 feet, the survey crew must be requested to mark the amount of fill along the center of the street, from which points the street can be strung, one half at a time. Any finished surface elevations shown on the plans should be set by the survey crew.

On streets over 40 feet in width, the Agency survey crew will paint fills on the last course of base at frequent intervals to indicate the thickness of the wearing course to assure the accuracy of the finish surface. These fills are increased by 12.5 percent for the machine laid thickness to allow for compaction.

When surfacing over existing pavement and hand-raking methods are employed, wooden blocks should be cut to the thickness of the pavement plus an additional 25 percent to allow for compaction. The block should be dipped in hot asphalt and stuck to the pavement at the location for which it was made. The location of each grade block should be noted and, as the raking is completed, the rakers must remove them. When over-laying existing pavements with new pavement of varying thickness, the survey party should paint the amount of fill on the existing pavement at locations shown on the plans or at such intervals as may be required to insure adequate control.

To allow for compaction of the paving material, the Inspector should add to the required pavement thickness 25 percent, if the material is being hand-raked, and 12½ percent, if the material is to be laid with a paving machine equipped with a tamping bar.

Except for asphalt concrete by the "thick-lift" method, which results in slightly less densities, asphalt concrete weighs 12.5 pounds per foot per inch of compacted thickness and this figure is useful in computing the rate of spread. Example: A four-inch compacted thickness of AC base would weigh 50 pounds per square foot (4 inches × 12.5 lbs.). From this it can readily be seen that an eight-ton load of material (16,000 pounds), divided by 50 pounds per square foot, would cover an area of 320 square feet. If the pavement is being laid in 10-foot passes, the load would cover an area 10 feet wide by 32 feet long, or one eight-ton truck load would permit the paver to travel 32 feet.

Based upon the foregoing methods for computing rates of spread, frequent checks should be made of the area which has been covered against the total tonnage of material which has been delivered to the job. If the rate of spread is less than it is calculated to be, the Inspector should take immediate action to determine that the pavement is not being laid too thin, or that loads are not being diverted to other work.

No greater amount of paving material shall be delivered in any one day than can be properly placed and rolled during daylight hours, utilizing the rollers the contractor has on the jobsite. The Standard Specifications establish the number of rollers required with respect to a given tonnage to be laid per hour. (See Subsection 3-4.3.5.)

New pavement should be barricaded against vehicular traffic during its construction and until the pavement has thoroughly set and cooled.

(d) **Mechanical Spreading.** It has been conclusively demonstrated that pavement laid by mechanical pavers is far superior in quality of finish to that laid by hand. It is the intention of the Standard Specifications to require mechanical pavers for all bituminous paving except where the work is inaccessible to such equipment.

Stakes, blocks, guide lines or the shape of the subgrade are used to establish grade for the finished pavement surface. When the first load of paving mixture is spread, and before rolling, the Inspector should check to determine its uniformity as to texture, grade and thickness. When laying bituminous pavement material with a mechanical spreader, the lift thickness prior to breakdown rolling, shall be the thickness specified on the plans plus ⅛-inch per inch of lift thickness to allow for compaction. All necessary adjustment in the paver should be made before paving operations commence. If a condition exists which results in substandard work and which cannot be immediately corrected, the spreading operation must be suspended until the cause is determined and a remedy found.

Spreading machines have a wide range of paving speeds, work best when operated continuously and produce the best riding qualities in the pavement. Stopping and starting the paver tends to leave transverse marks caused by the screed settling in the mat, which can be minimized by matching paver speed with plant output.

It is very important that the wheels of each truck delivering paving materials make firm contact with the truck rollers of the paver. If the truck is at a skew so that the rollers are pushing only against one set of dual wheels, the spreader will tend to skew and irregular, poorly compacted joints will result. The skill of the paver operator and truck driver have tremendous influence on pavement quality and daily tonnage. Pushing the truck while it is dumping its load is the paver operator's job. The truck should back up to the paver and stop, keeping a slight pressure on the brakes. The paver then engages the truck smoothly. Some pavers have a truck hitch device which couples the truck to the paver so the truck brakes can be released. When empty, the truck can pull out, allowing the paver to empty the hopper.

The contractor should provide a man to keep paving mixtures from building up on the side of the hopper. This material, if permitted to accumulate and cool, will eventually scale off onto the slat conveyor and pass into the pavement as a semi-cold mass, resulting in non-uniform surface texture.

When surface tearing or transverse cracks are observed in the pavement surface, the Inspector should investigate whether the mix is too cold or has too high a filler content.

A cold screed plate can also cause surface tearing because of mix sticking to the screed. This temperature problem can usually be traced to either improper screed warm-up or mix below the proper temperature. In normal weather, a few minutes taken to warm the screed is all that is needed. If the mix is arriving below temperature, super heating the screed will not correct the problem. That's a plant problem and should be corrected there. Normally, the heater should not run continuously. If the mix is the proper temperature and the rate of delivery is adequate it will maintain the heat in the screed.

Hand raking of joints or high areas in connection with mechanical spreading should be kept to a minimum to achieve a uniform texture. Sometimes a worker will needlessly scratch at the surface of the pavement material for the sole purpose of appearing busy. The Inspector should be alert to prevent this unnecessary blemishing of the surface texture.

To minimize the blemish effect on surface texture, all irregularities left by the paver should be corrected by hand directly behind the machine and before breakdown rolling. A lute or the back of a rake should be used immediately to dress longitudinal joints, pushing lapped material from the previously laid pavement to obtain a true line and vertical edge of the proper height to result in a smooth, tight joint when the material is compacted. Irregularities in the surface of the pavement course should be corrected at the same time. Excess material should be removed with a lute or shovel and low areas filled with hot mix and smoothed with the back of a shovel pulled over the surface. "Broadcasting" of the material over such areas should not be permitted.

All raking must be done with lutes or rakes, and rock particles that are collected by the lute in this operation should be dragged clear of the new pavement surface and discarded to avoid rocky textures.

If the operations ahead of the paver are properly performed and the equipment is in good condition, in adjustment and properly operated, there should be little need for repair work.

(e) **Hand Spreading.** Where spreading with a paver is either impractical or inaccessible, hand spreading is permitted. The paving material may be dumped on the grade, spread with a motor grader or shoveled into place and leveled with lutes to the thickness specified on the plans plus ¼-inch per inch of lift thickness to allow for compaction. Care should be exercised in spreading the paving mixture to avoid segregation of the coarse aggregate.

In spotting the loads to be dumped, it is good practice to locate them so as to avoid the need for workers to stand on the material while shoveling. Any footprints in the loose material should be re-raked to the full depth of the course. The proper technique in shoveling is to load the shovel, carry it to the place to be deposited, lower the shovel to the grade, and turn it over as the material is placed. The workers should never be permitted to cast or "broadcast" hot paving mixtures since extensive segregation of the coarse and fine portions of the mix will result. The small piles deposited from shovels should be spread only with lutes or rakes. If the material tends to form into lumps, they should be loosened. Should these lumps be hardened to the extent that they do not crumble easily, they must be removed and discarded.

When hand raked material is in place, and after breakdown rolling is completed, doubtful surfaces should be checked for irregularities with a template or straightedge.

Heated tamping irons should be used to compact pavement mixtures in areas inaccessible to rollers, and they must be of sufficient weight to produce pavement densities approaching that compacted by rollers. Hot smoothing irons, which are designed to be skidded on the material to compact by their weight and heat alone, are not to be used for any purpose other than smoothing joints. Tamping irons should weigh not less than 25 pounds and have a tamping face not exceeding 48 square inches.

The contractor is required to provide a means to heat tampers, shovels, lutes and rakes before they are used and to keep them hot during the paving operations. The temperature of tools should be no greater than that of the material being laid and care should be exercised not to overheat hand tools and thereby burn the pavement mixture. Only heat should be used to clean hand tools; the use of distillate or light oils should not be permitted.

3-4.3.5　Rolling Asphalt Paving Mixtures.

Rolling the asphalt paving mixture develops its strength and resistance to abrasion, develops cohesion and stability, and reduces voids which would permit air and water intrusion.

There are several critical but fundamental principles to be observed when rolling asphalt paving mixtures: rolling with the pavement mixture at the proper time and temperature; using a roller of the appropriate type and weight to achieve specified densities and produce a smooth surface; and proper roller operator technique.

The following are typical minimum temperatures for asphalt pavement rolling. The oil content and aggregate size will change these values which will range ± 15°F. (8.3 C.) from those given. Atmospheric conditions, mix viscosity, and equipment characteristics will have a lesser effect on these temperatures.

(1) Breakdown   260° (127 C.) min.
(2) Intermediate   200° (93 C.) min.
(3) Finish   175° (79 C.) min.

The initial or breakdown pass with the roller should be made as soon as possible after laying the pavement mixture, and yet not crack the mat or pick up the mix on the roller wheels. If the pavement mixture is too hot to roll, transverse cracking or hair checking will result. While this does not seriously affect the structural quality of the pavement, the appearance is unsightly and should be avoided. Pneumatic-tired rollers will heal "heat checks" and "hair checks." The greatest percentage of compaction that is ultimately achieved occurs during the breakdown pass. This usually requires one complete coverage of the mat utilizing steel tired rollers as provided in the Standard Specifications.

Breakdown and subsequent rolling should always be accomplished with the drive wheel forward in the direction of paving. The principal reasons for this are that there is a more direct vertical load applied by these larger wheels than by the smaller tiller wheels, and in addition, a greater proportion of the weight of the roller is on the drive wheel. There is also a tendency for a driven wheel to tuck the pavement material under it as it moves ahead. The tiller wheel tends to shove the pavement material ahead of it when it is used to lead, but when it is pulled behind the driver wheel, it displays the same tucking characteristics as the driven wheel. When the roller is reversed after a breakdown pass utilizing this rolling technique, the tiller wheel can move on compacted material, and the effect of displacement of the paving mix is minimized. An exception to this rolling technique is sometimes made to roll uphill on steeper grades or in laying "thick-lift" pavements. In this instance, advantage is taken of the partial compaction of the material under the tiller wheel in order to provide a more stable foundation upon which the drive wheel can move the roller along with minimum disturbance of the mat.

The rolling sequence should give top priority to thin edges or "feather edges" after which the order for lane paving should be:

(1) Transverse joints.

(2) Longitudinal joints.

(3) Outside edge.

(4) Breakdown of mat. Complete coverage from low side to high side.

(5) Intermediate rolling. Complete coverage from low side to high side.

(6) Finish rolling.

Rolling should commence at the gutters, or low side, and progress toward the high side or crown. Asphalt mixtures, when hot, tend to migrate under the action of the roller, and if the rolling is started at the high side, this migration is more pronounced and tends to crowd the paving material toward the edges, often squeezing it over headers or gutter edges.

When laying a pass adjacent to a previously laid pass or existing pavement, the longitudinal joints should be rolled immediately behind the paver, with a rear wheel of the roller extending across the joint onto the new paving mixture not more than six inches. If the edge has been properly prepared by hand operations to provide a standing edge of uncompacted paving mixture, with the large aggregate either properly imbedded or raked out, the pinching action of the roller will result in a smooth, tight joint.

Finish rolling, to produce a smooth finished surface, should not be started until the material has cooled sufficiently to avoid leaving marks from the roller tires. The proper temperature to accomplish finish rolling is when the bare hand can be placed on the surface of the pavement without experiencing excessive discomfort.

Asphalt pavements can be adversely affected by too much or too little rolling at the wrong time. Care should be exercised to avoid excessive rolling during breakdown or second rolling while the material is still relatively hot. Excessive breakdown and intermediate rolling of thin layers with steel-tired rollers tends to break the bond with the underlaying layer. Conversely, finish rolling should be extensive and must be performed before the material has cooled to the extent that the rollers would be ineffective.

Roller types and minimum weights for use on Agency projects are fully described in the Standard Specifications. Similarly, the number of rollers for the tonnage to be laid per hour are also prescribed. These rollers should be in good mechanical condition, run smoothly and be capable of being reversed without jerking. The rolls should be smooth and unpitted. A roller with a tiller wheel having worn bearings that permit it to wobble or steer erratically, must not be used on the work. Rollers should not be reversed suddenly, reversed at the same point on the mat, or permitted to stand in one place on hot pavement. These procedures cause indentations in the mat which are extremely difficult to remove.

Pneumatic-tired rollers and vibrating rollers are very effective in compacting asphalt pavement mixtures. They are particularly effective in compacting thick lift base courses. Pneumatic-tired rollers are desirable for intermediate rolling following breakdown rolling with steel-tired rollers for any pavement course. Pneumatic rolling duplicates or exceeds the compactive effort of traffic loads thus minimizing the in service rutting from such loads.

Pneumatic-tired rollers should be operated with tire pressure in the range of 85-100 psi (586-690 kPa) contact pressure and when used for breakdown rolling of base, the rubber tire should stay 6-8 inches (152-203mm) from the outside edge of the mat. The highest pressure should be used which will prevent rutting or shoving of the mixture. Rolling should continue until the tire marks are relatively shallow and the residual temperature will permit the steel wheel roller to compact the outer edge and iron out the tire marks.

Vibrating rollers usually permit thicker lifts to be compacted with fewer passes and they are particularly effective with larger aggregate base course mixtures. The roller should be in motion before the vibrator is placed in operation and it should be disengaged when the roller is reversing direction. Otherwise, surface irregularities will occur. The frequency, amplitude and speed of the vibrating roller must be correct to prevent surface irregularities and achieve proper density.

Roller speed should not exceed 3 MPH for steel-tired rollers or 5 MPH for pneumatic-tired rollers.

Failure to observe any of the principles of proper rolling described in this subsection will result in inferior pavements.

3-4.3.6 Trench Resurfacing. (Also See Subsection 3-5.12.) The paving techniques described in the foregoing portions of this subsection also apply in general to trench resurfacing.

The operation of heavy trenching and backfilling equipment often results in damage to paved street areas adjacent to the trench. A difference of opinion sometimes arises between the contractor and the Inspector over the method of repair and the thickness of pavement to be replaced in damaged areas which are outside the limits of the trench, but immediately adjacent to it. The following policy shall govern:

(a) Where existing pavement (adjacent to a trench or other construction) has been broken by the contractor, it is to be replaced with pavement of a thickness equal to the existing pavement, regardless of the thickness specified for the trench resurfacing on the plans; provided, however, that such resurfacing is placed upon a subgrade which has not been disturbed by the contractor.

(b) In those cases where the subgrade has been disturbed by the contractor (as would result from a cave-in of trench walls), the resurfacing of both the trench area and the caved-in area shall be of the thickness specified on the plans for the resurfacing.

(c) Resurfaced areas should have a cross-section at finished elevation to match the crown section of the existing roadway.

(d) Feather-edging shall be done over areas where existing adjacent pavement is unbroken but slightly depressed.

3-4.3.7 Asphalt Pavement Failures. The Inspector should learn to evaluate existing pavements for causes of failures, particularly where new pavement is to be laid against or over the old pavement. Such knowledge may help him to avoid the source of failure in the new work. (See also Subsection 3-15, Geotextiles and Pavement Fabric.)

Some of the common causes of failure in bituminous pavements are listed here:

(a) **Edge failure.** This is a result of insufficient mat thickness, excessive wheel loads, lack of lateral support (header displaced or removed) or base saturation resulting from high shoulders which trap water run-off. To prevent edge failure, the contractor should blade down high shoulders adjacent to the pavement to restore run-off. Check base permeability, repair headers or restore lateral support with compacted earth.

(b) **Weathered or dry surface.** This condition can develop as a result of age, but when it appears on relatively new pavement, it can generally be attributed to insufficient asphalt in the mix. Overheating a plant mix or use of absorptive aggregates can also create this effect. Seal or fog coats can be applied under certain conditions to renovate such pavements to avoid this condition. To avoid this condition, insure that sufficient asphalt has been provided in the mix and do not permit overheating.

(c) **Pot holes.** Nearly every cause of pavement failure will result in pot-holing. Water infiltration, insufficient asphalt to maintain a bond, open or segregated mix and unstable base are the most common causes of pot-holing.

(d) **Alligator cracking.** Lack of base support, usually from water saturation, is the principal cause of this type of pavement failure. Insufficient pavement thickness, even on a firm base, can also result in alligator cracking. To prevent this, the Inspector should insure that the subgrade is firm and well drained and a pavement thickness is provided which will support the anticipated wheel loads.

(e) **Bleeding and instability.** Almost always this type of pavement failure is caused by an excess of asphalt, either in the pavement mixture or from the cumulative effects of the asphalt in the pavement mixture with asphalt in tack coats, seal coats or fog coats. Where bleeding occurs, the excess of asphalt will tend to overfill the voids in the compacted mixture and act as a lubricant. Such pavement will lack stability and have an inclination to creep. Excessive amounts of silt, clay or rounded gravel lacking interlock will also result in an unstable paving mixture, but will show no indications of bleeding. Moisture accumulating beneath a pavement surface will migrate upwards through the paving material, gradually destroying the bond and permitting traffic to push the pavement into waves or ridges. To prevent this, insure that the proper mixing proportions of asphalt are maintained and do not permit the use of silts, clays or rounded particles in the mix in excess of the limits set forth in Standard Specifications. Proper drainage of the subgrade is essential.

(f) **Ravelling.** Ravelling is a result of a lean or overheated mix, or may occur where a skin patch is laid over a dirty, wet or improperly tack-coated area. Proper plant and field procedures will prevent this deficiency. Skin patching should be avoided, but where it is permitted or provided for on the plans, proper tack coating and use of a fine mix to feather the edges will prove to be the most satisfactory method. Care must be exercised during skin patching operations to avoid ravelling caused by lack of proper bond due to cold laying ro rolling.

In some cases ravelling can be inhibited by seal coating. The Inspector should discuss the problem with his Supervisor before ordering the removal of ravelling pavements.

(g) **Erosion of the surface.** This condition is caused by water running or standing on pavement surfaces for prolonged periods of time while subjected to traffic. Water destroys the bond between the asphalt and the aggregate particles, wheels of traffic displace the particles in the surface, and the area is eroded in a relatively short period of time. Often this condition can be eliminated only by the construction of storm drain systems and concrete cross gutters. Avoid construction of new bituminous pavements which will obviously impound water by providing for run-off, or if it is a design problem, refer it to the Engineer.

(h) **Longitudinal and transverse cracking.** These indications of distress occur as random cracks, seldom close together. They are generally caused by the contraction of the base or subgrade, and almost always correspond to the cracks existing in old pavement which is overlaid with bituminous pavement. It is almost impossible to prevent this type of failure, but it is helpful to clean and reseal cracks in existing base or pavement to be overlaid.

(i) **Distortion and depression.** These failures result from inadequate compaction of the subgrade or the base. Proper compaction of the base or subgrade will prevent this type of failure.

3-4.3.8 Measurement and Payment.

(a) **General.** Payment is made for asphalt pavements at the contract unit price per square foot or at the contract price per ton. This price includes full compensation for subgrade preparation, furnishing and placing all materials, labor, equipment and incidentals including headers and tack coats. Where payment is made on a square-foot basis, measurements to determine the pay area are to be made horizontally.

(b) **Tonnage Contractors.** When the amount of paving material to be laid on a tonnage basis is 200 tons or less per day, all scale-checking, signing of the weighmaster's certificates and receipting for the material shall be done by the Inspectors normally assigned to the plant and jobsite inspection.

Except at batch plants having an approved automatic batch weighing system, when the amount of material to be laid per day exceeds 200 tons, an additional Inspector shall be assigned to the plant scales and another Inspector assigned to receive and receipt for the material at the jobsite. The Inspector assigned to the plant scales shall be responsible for the following:

(a) Determine that the weighmaster holds a valid certificate as a Public or Private Weighmaster.

(b) Insure that the scales have been sealed by the County Sealer of Weights & Measures within the past year.

(c) Arrive at the plant one-half hour in advance of the plant starting time to observe the tareweighing of all trucks each day. This tareweight check shall be made again at noon or at any other time that there is reason to believe a change in the truck weight has occurred.

(d) Observe all weights registered on the scales to the nearest 20-pound increment and check the recording of these weights on the certificate. The certificate furnished to the Agency must be a clear legible copy.

(e) Verify the accuracy of the subtraction of the tare weight from the gross weight and the conversion of the net weight from pounds to tons and decimal fractions of tons.

(f) Sign all certificates and initial all erasures or corrections made on the certificate.

(g) When asphalt concrete is being produced for a tonnage contract, indicate on the weighmaster's certificate whether it is base or wearing surface.

(h) At the start of each day, verify the total accumulated tonnage for the previous day with the Inspector at the jobsite. Any discrepancy discovered must be reconciled immediately.

In addition to the Inspectors assigned to the various functions of pavement construction on tonnage contracts, an Inspector shall be assigned to collect the weighmaster's certificates from each truck as it prepares to deposit the bituminous paving materials in the spreading machine. He shall be responsible for the following:

(a) Check the certificate for accuracy of the mathematics, sequence of load numbers, signature of the plant scale Inspector and initialing of all erasures or corrections.

(b) Report to the plant Inspector immediately any error discovered.

(c) Insure that the material is laid only in tonnage areas. If it is not, the Inspector shall write in large letters the word "VOID" across the face of the certificate and deface his signature as well as the signature of the plant Inspector. Notify the plant scale Inspector when a certificate is "voided."

(d) Carefully estimate the portion of any load that is not laid in tonnage areas or that portion left over at the end of a day and deduct this amount from the tonnage reported for payment. Make the necessary change on the certificate and initial the alteration.

(e) Sign all tonnage certificates for the material that was received and laid in tonnage areas.

(f) Calculate from the plan dimension how much grade the accumulated tonnage should cover as a check against the actual tonnage delivered and laid in the calculated area, using 12½ pounds per square foot per inch of compacted thickness of the bituminous pavement. Inform the Inspector in charge of the paving operation if a significant difference is discovered.

(g) At the end of each week, recapitulate the tonnage certificates and prepare a form, "Summary of Tonnage Certificates," and forward with the corresponding certificates to the Agency.

Both the Plant Inspector and the plant scale Inspector must also forward an Asphalt Plant Inspector's Daily Report showing the tonnage of material shipped each day, as well as all other information required to be shown. (See Subsection 2-6.6.)

Tonnage laid must closely match the computed tonnage. A significant disparity must be immediately brought to the attention of the Supervisor.

3-4.3.9 Asphalt Pavement Checklist.

Preliminary

(1) Check plans and specifications for pavement type, thickness, method of payment, number of courses and other project paving requirements.

(2) Inspect subgrade. Has subgrade been checked for grade, cross-section and compaction?

(3) All underground construction completed? Clearances received?

(4) Manholes, valve boxes marked?

(5) Contact surfaces and joins prepared? Existing pavement trimmed? Surfaces cleaned? Tack coat applied to gutter edges, pavement joins?

(6) Review procedures and requirements with contractor.

(7) Check contractor's preparations? Source of paving mix? Condition of equipment?

(8) Check for required types, weights and numbers of rollers?

(9) Check condition of spreader. Is screed contour set properly?

(10) Overlay of existing pavement required? Check fills for variation and thickness to determine necessity for leveling course. Check for broken pavement that should be removed.

(11) Gutter and other concrete strength OK to lay pavement against (seven days or three days if accelerator used)?

Delivery of Paving Mixture

(1) Check for report from Plant Inspector sent with one of the first few loads.

(2) Does delivered mixture meet the requirements of the job? Truck beds free of holes and depressions? Equipped with tarpaulins (when required)? Compatible with the paver? (Too low or too wide for the hopper; bed insufficient overhang at the rear to permit dumping into the hopper without spilling on the grade.) Beds coated with distillate and properly drained?

(3) Check for truck spillage of mix on subgrade.

(4) Collect copies of weight tickets for tonnage payments. Check yield by measuring areas and coverage of loads.

(5) Check temperature of mix periodically. If bottom dump tracks are delivering and windrowing the mix, check the temperature in windrow ahead of pickup by paver. Stop windrowing if temperature drops below minimum for laying.

Spreading Operations

(1) Is direction of spreading satisfactory (normally same direction as traffic)?

(2) Check operation of spreader. Thickness of mat being laid? Lane width OK? Joint overlap?

(3) Are longitudinal joints staggered with respect to joints in the previous course?

(4) Check surface appearance of mat behind the spreader. Uniformity of texture; evidence of segregation or poor mixing?

(5) Check handwork at joints. Is overlapped material being laid pushed back into mat with a lute?

(6) Check for source of irregularities in surface and require correction. Try to minimize hand raking. When depressions are to be corrected, surface must be loosened and material added and graded, preferably with a lute. High spots loosened, excess material removed and area regraded.

(7) Is the speed of spreading machine matched to the rate of delivery of the material?

(8) See that wings of spreader are cleared of material between loads.

(9) Stop delivery from plant if weather conditions warrant. Permit pave out of remaining material if possible.

Rollers and Compaction

(1) Check that type, weight and number of rollers meet the requirements and are adequate for the job on hand.

(2) Determine the mechanical condition of rollers. Smooth stop, start and reverse action. Surface condition of rolls and tires. Water tank filled and sprinkler system operable? Inflation pressure of pneumatic tires?

(3) Evaluate operator performance. Is roller being operated smoothly at proper speed? Stops, starts and reversing action not causing surface irregularities? Turns made on cooler previously compacted pavement? Not standing on hot pavement?

(4) Rolling sequence pattern and coverage satisfactory? Thin edges and feather edges ironed down before cooling? Overlapping passes?

(5) Temperatures OK for rolling? Breakdown as soon as temperature permits? Look for surface checking, excessive displacement.

(6) Check longitudinal joints and gutter edge following breakdown. Joint between passes flush? Material at gutter edge preferably slightly higher after finish rolling; $\frac{1}{8}''$ to $\frac{1}{4}''$ (3-6mm).

(7) Check mat for irregularities and obtain correction immediately after breakdown rolling. (See Spreading Operations, Item 6, of this subsection.)

(8) See that intermediate rolling follows breakdown closely to assure maximum density. Use of the three axle tandem at this point will improve smoothness and riding

qualities. Keep in mind that the pneumatic roller (if used) begins to lose its effectiveness as the mat temperature falls below 150°.

(9) Finish rolling must be done while mat is sufficiently workable to remove roller marks and leave a smooth pavement surface.

(10) Check final finish of pavement for surface smoothness. Take action to obtain correction of major deficiencies. List other deficiencies requiring correction in the "Notice to Final Inspector."

Miscellaneous

(1) Is an Inspector present at the plant?

(2) Are additional Inspectors provided at the plant and jobsite for tonnage contracts?

(3) Is proper traffic control being maintained?

(4) Are safety measures being observed?

(5) Is the housekeeping and clean-up of the jobsite satisfactory?

(6) Are all surface irregularities being properly corrected?

(7) Are sufficient samples being taken?

(8) Are samples representative?

(9) Are records complete and up to date?

(10) Have you prepared form entitled "Report of New Paving, Guard Rails and Warning Rails" for transmission to Agency street maintenance headquarters?

3-4.4   Concrete Pavement.

3-4.4.1   **General.**   The placement and finishing of concrete base and pavement is described in detail in the Standard Specifications. However, there are many other factors which require the careful attention of the Inspector to assure that a satisfactory pavement is obtained.

Review Subsection 3-11 for the general requirements for transporting, placing, finishing and curing concrete.

The quality of the pavement is the responsibility of the contractor. Satisfactory quality can very often be traced to the competence of the Inspector who reviews the job requirement with the contractor; knows where problems are likely to develop and recognizes deficiencies and gets them corrected.

Before any concrete is placed, he should examine the pavement subgrade, check the forms, agree on joint spacing and approve the placing and finishing equipment that the contractor intends to use. The source of concrete and provisions for standby mixing facilities should be pre-arranged when warranted.

The subgrade and the line and rigidity of the forms should be continuously rechecked ahead of the placement of concrete. Soft spots in the subgrade are to be repaired. Construction debris and loose material must be removed. Manhole frames and covers, utility vaults, valve boxes and similar embedments must be reset to grade in advance of concrete placement.

The Standard Specifications allow the use of both wooden and metal forms. Wooden forms shall be 3-inch nominal lumber not less than 16 feet long except at changes in alignment or grade. The height of forms shall be within ½-inch of the thickness of the pavement slab. Metal forms shall be not less than the thickness of the specified thickness of the pavement slab. Staking of forms is described in detail in the Standard Specifications. Forms should have full bearing on subgrade that has been compacted and is unyielding, and should never be supported on shims.

For all types of concrete construction, contractors proposing to place concrete are required to notify the Dispatcher before noon of the work day preceding the day the concrete is to be placed. However, an Inspector will not be assigned to the concrete bunker for a specific day, except in the case of structural concrete and special-design concrete mixes. (See Subsection 2-4.5.3.)

Field Inspectors will be required to examine the plant delivery ticket that arrives with each load of transit-mix concrete to determine if the concrete mixture, time of loading, water and admixture are as required for the project.

The drum of the transit-mix truck should speed up from agitator speed to mixing speed for several minutes before starting to unload. The rate of discharge should never be controlled by pinching the gate of the mixer drum partially shut, as this will result in the last part of the concrete in the load being very rocky. Instead, the gate should be fully open and the rate of discharge controlled by the rate of rotation of the drum by the truck driver.

The concrete should be of the specified slump and within the water-cement ratio required. There should be no appreciable segregation of the mixture during discharge nor any segregation due to the equipment used in spreading. Particular attention should be given to the edges to see that sufficient mortar, compaction and vibration are applied to make the concrete dense, homogeneous and free of "honeycomb."

3-4.4.2 Spreading and Finishing Concrete. All operations of spreading and finishing should be carefully observed and checked at the initial stages to determine the need for machine adjustments and personnel performance. Checking should include stringing to identify high or low areas in the surface, and the necessary corrections made. Spreading machines should carry a nominal amount of concrete ahead of the strike-off blade at all times. Too much will make the machine "ride up;" too little will leave low spots behind the machine that are hard to detect and difficult to correct.

The tops of headers should be kept free of concrete ahead of finishing machines. The proper sequence, following the spreading, whether by machine or by hand template is:

(a) The concrete is struck off to cross-section.

(b) The tamping template tamps the aggregate below the surface. Tamping templates should not drive the aggregate too deep, causing excessive mortar to accumulate on the surface. If permitted to occur, this will lead to "scaling" of the surface later on.

(c) The concrete is floated longitudinally, overlapping each time at least half the length of the float over the area previously floated.

(d) The bull-floating is applied transversely to correct any irregularities.

(e) The final operation is burlap finishing and edging of the work, including joints.

Workers should not be permitted to walk on the screeded surface. This leaves footprints which will be floated full of mortar, causing problems to develop in the finished work. Similarly, workers spreading concrete must be careful that their boots do not track dirt into the concrete.

All finishing operations, including transverse edging, must be performed from outside of the forms or from bridges spanning the slab.

To provide a non-skid surface, a burlap drag (consisting of a long pole to which a length of wet burlap is attached) is dragged several times along the pavement parallel with the center line of the roadway.

Two to four passes of the drag are usually required. Texturing should be halted as soon as the desired texture is obtained, since additional passes may tend to reduce the depth and grittiness of the surface. However, dragging should be continued until the desired texture is obtained.

Timing is particularly important in producing a highly skid-resistant surface. Texture depths obtained with a burlap drag vary considerably with the time of finishing. The practice of waiting until the sheen of moisture is gone from the surface before starting texturing operations is not advisable. In general, the best burlap textures are obtained by dragging while the pavement is fairly moist, closely following the other finishing operations.

Two or more layers of burlap with an open weave usually provide deeper striations. Seamed burlap in contact with the pavement surface may also help provide a good texture. Fraying the end of the burlap for about 6 to 12 inches also has helped produce a better and more uniform texture.

The old idea of keeping the burlap clean and free of grout accumulation is not necessarily good. Very small particles of sand and grout that collect on the burlap drag actually help provide a deeper texture. However, the uniformity of the texture should be carefully watched and large grout buildups should be removed.

Flow lines should be checked with water and corrected if necessary. Stake holes must be filled with mortar.

3-4.4.3 Concrete Pavement Joints. All formed joints must be properly aligned and secured into position before concreting operations. It is very difficult to remove and replace them properly after concrete is placed.

Expansion, contraction, contact and weakened-plane joints must be constructed in strict conformity with plans, Standard Plans and Standard Specifications.

The practice of constructing joints during finishing operations is not desirable due to the difficulty in obtaining good riding qualities for today's high speed traffic. For small or handfinished jobs where high-speed traffic is not a factor, its use is not objectionable. In the construction of joints in pavement, during finishing, particular care should be taken by workers to avoid depressions or humps at the joint. Such practices as exerting too much pressure on edging tools (which depresses the edges of the joint) and floating too much mortar to the joint, results in poor riding qualities in the pavement. The Inspector should carefully lay a straight-edge across all joints, including longitudinal joints, while the concrete is still green enough to permit a correction.

Weakened-plane joints, when specified, should be sawcut in accordance with the Special Provisions or Standard Specifications. However, the specific timing, if specified, may need to be modified to compensate for variations in atmospheric temperatures, relative humidity and rate of set of the concrete. The depth of sawcut is also critical to the development of the controlled cracking at the sawcut and should be checked frequently during sawing operations.

Random spacing and angling the transverse joints is often specified to reduce the hypnotic drumming effect on motorists produced by uniformly spaced perpendicular joints. Sawing too soon is indicated by objectionable ravelling of the concrete. The correct time for sawing may produce slight ravelling that is not objectionable and will not detract from the quality and riding qualities of the pavement. If sawing is delayed too long, random cracks will develop which could have been controlled by earlier sawing.

3-4.4.4 **Slip Form Concrete Paving.** The slip form method of concrete paving permits construction without the use of pre-set headers. It is particularly suitable on large, high production type highway and freeway projects with uniform widths, thicknesses and grades and where the construction is free of traffic and adjoining private property restrictions.

Widths of 48 feet or more have been constructed utilizing this method which depends on a high operational efficiency and a high volume source of concrete. For these reasons, the method usually provides for a concrete source on the jobsite which includes centralized mixing and delivery of concrete using special bodied dump trucks to the paving train.

The Inspector with a well versed background in concrete construction and experience in conventional concrete paving construction should have no problem in adjusting his inspection techniques to provide adequate quality control of this method.

The Agency Materials Control Group will provide the necessary quality control of the concrete at the source, including on-site production facilities. All other quality control operations are the responsibility of the Project Inspector and his staff.

The quality control and inspection procedure for conventional concrete pavement construction is generally valid and applicable to slip form paving operations and should be utilized.

Particularly close coordination is required between the concrete placement and the speed of the paver. The mixture consistency and delivery rate should be uniform so that the paver moves at a steady rate without stopping on the fresh concrete.

The Inspector should periodically check for thickness and for evidence of edge slump in the unsupported edge as the paving train passes.

The concrete mixture for slip forming is usually air entrained and contains more sand than normal paving concrete.

3-4.4.5 Curing and Protection. Curing should conform to the requirements of the Standard Specifications and Subsection 3-11.12. All headers can be removed after 24 hours and the exposed edges should be sealed immediately with an approved curing compound.

3-4.4.6 Concrete Pavement Checklist.

(1) Review plan specification requirements; thickness, type of joint and spacing, lane widths.

(2) Has subgrade been approved for paving? Is base required? (See Subsection 3-4.2.5 for subgrade checklist.)

(3) Check contractor's paving equipment; spreading and finishing machines, strike-offs, screeds, floats, vibrators and compactors. Does equipment meet specification requirements?

(4) Source of concrete approved?

(5) Check side forms. Strength? Alignment and grade? Full bearing on subgrade?

(6) Is all equipment and material on hand for joint details? Curing (spray equipment and curing compound)?

(7) Any blockouts required for utilities?

(8) Steel reinforcement required? Other embedded items?

(9) Subgrade dampened before depositing concrete?

(10) Concrete deposited without segregation?

(11) Spreading, consolidation and screeding without delay?

(12) Check operation of equipment and results obtained?

(13) Concrete adequately vibrated or compacted? Along sideforms?

(14) Strike-off operation satisfactory? Full head of concrete against screed? Is surface proper following strike-off?

(15) Check surface after first floating operation for highs or lows. Use straight edge and fish line.

(16) Check edging. Edging tool operated without tilt or other faulty manipulation?

(17) Properly adjusted finishing machine should be producing a surface requiring minimum handwork. Otherwise, concrete consistency is the major suspect.

(18) After observing initial finishing operations, does concrete mix need adjustment? Rate of concrete delivery adequate to keep paving train moving at steady rate?

(19) Check finish and texture obtained with the burlap drag. (Burlap must be moist and operated by skilled personnel familiar with the technique and the critical timing involved in obtaining a good skid-resistant texture.)

(20) Check application of curing compound. Applied immediately after texturing operation? Rate and even coverage OK?

(21) Completed pavement barricaded to protect from traffic?

(22) Check joint sawing operation. Joint layout and sequence? Timing of sawcutting (without excessive ravelling of concrete)? Width and depth of cut per plan? Sawcut flushed out or cleaned of residue?

(23) Is joint sealing compound required?

(24) Core tests of completed pavement requested?

3-4.5 Concrete Curb, Gutter, Sidewalk and Driveway.

3-4.5.1 **General.** Concrete curb, gutter, sidewalk and driveway are competents of any street improvement project and give definition, permanence and stability to the overall improvement. In sequence, the curb or integral curb and gutter is constructed first and provides the line and grade reference for all other subsequent construction on the project. Depressions left in the curb mark locations where aprons will be constructed to complete driveway and handicap access ramps.

Conduit for the street lighting system is installed in the space behind the curb before it is backfilled. Walk and roadbed paving are referenced to the curb in both dimension and grade.

In alleys, the gutter is constructed first and is the line and grade reference for subsequent construction.

Curing of all concrete work is required in accordance with the Standard Specifications.

3-4.5.2   Concrete Curb and Gutter.   Unless otherwise specified, all curb and gutter is aligned by the top front edge of the curb. All other dimensions for the curb and gutter section are taken from this edge which is carefully set as to alignment and grade.

This curb grade is set by transferring both line and grade from an offset stake set by surveyors for this purpose. The line of stakes is carefully stationed on an offset line back of the curb (usually five feet) and each stake registered on a grade sheet with appropriate cut or fill to the plan grade from a tack in the stake. The top edge of the front curb form is carefully set to this grade and alignment by several simple methods — usually by using a carpenter's level. The face plank must be the exact height for the curb to be constructed so that critical flow line grade can be maintained. The back form is set from the front form, as is the outer gutter form, and held securely by stakes and spacers. While the gutter form must be full height, the top of the back curb form need not be set to finish grade as long as the contractor demonstrates that he can produce a finished curb with a uniform ¼-inch cross-fall. Batter of forms and spacing of expansion and contraction joints must conform to the appropriate Standard Plans. Unless rigid metal forms are used, all curb forms must be fabricated of 2-inch thick lumber, except that 1-inch lumber may be used for curves when necessary.

After curb forms are set, the Inspector should check them for accuracy as to line and grade, curb height, proper batter and cross-section, rigidity and form condition. He should sight down the front curb plank to discover any departure from the desired alignment. Blockouts or inserts for roof drains or fire sprinkling system drains should be placed with their inverts one inch above gutter flow line. Where a catch basin is to be constructed with the improvement, headers are to be used to terminate the curb and gutter on each side of the future basin. Driveway depressions should be marked and checked for alignment adequate curb face width, and the radius of curb return verified. (See Subsection 3-4.5.5 for driveway layout and width details.)

To add rigidity to the forms and prevent the concrete from leaking under the forms, earth should be bladed or pushed against them from the outside. On the other hand, when constructing new curb and gutter adjacent to existing bituminous pavement, the concrete should be permitted to extrude under a 2-inch deep outer gutter header to form a concrete base for pavement. Otherwise, it would be difficult to compact a bituminous base course in the narrow space usually encountered.

Concrete should be placed first for a short distance in the gutter portion of integral curb and gutter. It should be spaded thoroughly, particularly adjacent to the gutter header to prevent rock pockets on the gutter face. To avoid cold joints, the concrete should be placed in the curb portion shortly thereafter. However, excess spading of this concrete will result in slumping under the front face form and swelling of the gutter. Too little spading may cause rock pockets, in which case the contractor may be required to place curb concrete in 6-inch maximum lifts to reduce the consolidation effort required.

A baffle board is useful to deflect concrete as it is deposited in curb and gutter forms from transit-mix trucks. The use of a baffle board avoids the impact and thurst of the stream of concrete, which can move forms out of line, and segregation is considerably reduced.

Locations of all wooden spreaders used should be marked on the form or have a wire attached to facilitate removal after the concrete is placed. The Inspector should check that the curb forms remain in vertical and horizontal alignment after concrete is placed and that the top width of the curb is uniform. Curb which is out of line must be immediately restored to proper alignment while the concrete is still plastic. Driveway depressions, previously marked on the curb plank, are formed by a template dragged between the forms.

After the forms are filled and the concrete spaded and struck off, the top of the curb is dressed with a curb planer consisting of a 2-inch × 6-inch board approximately four feet in length, angled at both ends, and with a handle on top. This planing removes high spots, fills low areas and develops the ¼-inch cross-fall. The gutter surface is floated on a straight grade form the outer gutter form to the bottom of the curb face plank. The front and back edges of the curb and the outer edge of the gutter are edged as prescribed by applicable Standard Plans.

When the concrete has attained sufficient strength to retain its shape without slumping, the curb face plank is removed. The Inspector must check the curb alignment at this stage and cause any misalignment to be corrected by adjustment of the back form while it is still in place. Trimming of bulges or plastering indentations to correct alignment is not permitted. All stakes used to support the face plank and all spreaders used for lateral restraint of the forms must be removed and the holes filled with mortar.

A fluid mortar, commonly called "butter," is used to coat the top and front face of "green" curb and is troweled smooth using special curb finishing tools. At the approprate time, the gutter is given a wood float finish except that it is troweled smooth for a distance of four inches from the intersection of the curb and gutter. Troweling and edging are repeated as necessary to produce the required surface planes and edges. The troweled surfaces of the curb are finally given a hair broom finish except for those portions of the tops of curbs within driveway depressions, which are finished with a wood float to a cross-fall of ¾-inch. All joints in curb and gutter must be vertical and at right angles to the face of the curb.

Gutters built on nearly flat grades must be checked with a small amount of water to detect low spots and to insure that the water will flow. This must be done after the concrete has hardened, to permit water checking without damage to the surface, but soon enough that the flow line can be reworked to obtain proper drainage.

Curing of concrete curb and gutter should be accomplished as described in Subsection 2-11.12.

3-4.5.3 Extruded Curb and Gutter. Curbs and gutters are more and more being constructed by the extrusion process without the use of forms by using a machine designed for this purpose. The concrete is received into a hopper, conveyed by auger into the mold end of the machine. As the pressure builds up, voids are squeezed out, and the mold fills up and acts as an abatement and the machine moves away exposing the completed curb behind it.

Several variations of this type of equipment are available. Some machines operate directly on the subgrade and line and grade is maintained using a pre-set wire line and a sensor on the machine. Other types operate on pre-set metal tracks. The concrete mixture varies depending on the type of machine.

Some use a heavily sanded pea gravel mix and others use the normal mixture with air content (See Subsection 2-4.4.2). The Agency deletes the requirement for expansion joints when this method is used and weakened plane joints are installed by use of a special saw or other device.

Prior to extrusion, the Inspector should check the shoe, make frequent checks of the curb face dimension and batter; top of curb slope and dimension; the gutter width and hike-up; and the batter of the gutter to detect discrepancies. Vertical surfaces should be checked for sag. Improper operation of the machine or the consistency of this concrete mixture are the usual sources of problems.

3-4.5.4 Concrete Sidewalk and Driveways. Forms for concrete sidewalk and concrete driveway approaches shall be 2-inch (nominal) thick lumber. They should be straight, clean, free from warp, and held securely in place by stakes at intervals of five feet or less. Tops of stakes must be sawed off flush with the top of the form. If a mechanical screed or tamper is utilized, the forms must be provided with such additional stakes as may be required to support the weight and vibrating forces exerted by the device.

Where existing sidewalk is to be removed, saw cuts 1½ inches deep must be made along scoring lines, if they exist, and the concrete removed to a neat, vertical face. Existing sidewalk to be joined must be in good condition. Otherwise, removal may be required to secure acceptable grade or alignment with the new work. Monolithic construction of curb and sidewalk should be avoided. If the adjacent curb and sidewalk are constructed the same day the curb should be constructed first, after which a sheet of building paper extending the full thickness of the sidewalk shall be used as a separator to prevent a bond. Driveway aprons may be constructed monolithically with the depressed portion of the curb.

Unless otherwise specified on the plans (or permit), the forms for sidewalk shall be set to place the finished surface in a plane sloping up from the top of the curb at a rate of ¼ inch to one foot when measured at right angles to the curb. Where this grade does not meet existing improvements such as private driveway slabs or building entrances, the Engineer may permit some adjustment of the grade of the headers for the sidewalk. In such cases, the adjusted slope must always be on a straight grade from the curb to the revised grade at the building line. Ramping or warping of sidewalks should be kept to a minimum and resorted to only after consulting the Engineer.

Coloring of sidewalk or driveway is permitted only when authorized by the plan. The same solid color shall extend along the full frontage of the lot, including driveways (if any). Partial coloring or checkerboard patterns of two or more colors are not permitted.

Coloring of full-height curb will not be permitted, but colored depressed curb may be constructed monolithically with a colored driveway.

Colored sidewalk or driveway may be constructed in one or two courses. If constructed in one course, the coloring shall extend throughout the full thickness. Dusting the top surface of the concrete with the coloring material will not be permitted. If construction is to be in two courses, the second or top course shall be of colored mortar ½-inch thick (one part cement to one-half parts sand, with color added to suit). This mortar must be mixed in a concrete mixer. The second course shall be placed on the first course within one hour after placing the first course.

When reconstructing portions of a colored sidewalk or driveway, the existing color shall be matched as closely as possible.

Care should be exercised to prevent concrete from splashing on existing improvements such as buildings, curbs, street lighting electroliers, fire hydrants, etc. When this occurs, the contractor must be required to clean such surfaces before the spatter hardens to the extent that removal is difficult.

Water meter boxes, gas shut-off valve boxes, street lighting and traffic signal pull boxes are frequently encountered in sidewalk and driveway construction. The appropriate agency having jurisdiction should be consulted. Some installations may have to be relocated. Others may be allowed to remain in place but may require different boxes with metal covers. All such boxes must be set or adjusted so that the top surface of each one will match the slope and elevation of the adjoining sidewalk or driveway to be constructed.

Roof drains shall be constructed as required of 4-inch bell and spigot cast iron pipe, asbestos-cement pipe, PVC pipe, ABS pipe or fiber duct and shall be laid on a straight grade from the property line to the curb. Where any portion of the roof drain extends above the sidewalk subgrade (to a maximum of one inch), a strip of welded wire mesh 18 inches wide must be centered over the roof drain and embedded in the sidewalk. Fire sprinkler drains must also be installed where required.

Street name signs, traffic regulatory signs, fire signal boxes and similar devices must be installed in advance of placing concrete. Fire hydrants must be adjusted by the utility owner so that the assembly flange is free from embedment in the concrete.

The minimum thickness for sidewalk is three inches. New sidewalk to be constructed in line with a new or existing driveway shall be the same thickness as required for a new driveway at that location. Existing sidewalk in residential areas, in line with new or existing driveways, may be left in place, provided it lies on the standard slope and is in good condition. Residential driveways shall be constructed four inches thick, commercial driveways six inches thick.

3-4.5.5 Layout of Driveways. No portion of a driveway shall be constructed between prolonged intersecting property lines at any street intersection or between the points of curvature of any curb return having a radius of 20 feet or less. Exceptions will be noted on the plans or permit, or will be authorized by a Change Order. Under certain conditions, a driveway may be merged with an adjacent alley intersection. No driveway shall be located where only partial ingress or egress of vehicles onto private property is possible. The intent is to prohibit the use of the sidewalk for parking vehicles for loading or unloading, thereby obstructing use of the sidewalk by pedestrians.

Abandoned driveways and depressed curbs shall be removed and replaced with full-height curb and sidewalk on standard slope. Existing curb depressions which do not conform to the minimum standards of the latest Standard Plans shall be reconstructed to the latest requirements when constructing a new driveway slab. Where Standard Plans cannot be followed because of existing conditions, the Engineer may authorize deviations from standard construction.

Where side lot lines are not at a right angle to the curb line, the driveway should be laid out at a right angle to the curb from the point of intersection of the side lot line and the frontage lot line. The side slopes may be constructed beyond the point of intersection of lot lines.

For a residence or apartment building, the width of a driveway approach (exclusive of side slopes) shall be nine feet minimum, 18 feet maximum. For commercial use, the driveway width shall be 12 feet minimum, 30 feet maximum. Exceptions to such limits may be granted only by the Engineer. Any such exception granted will be noted on the plans or permit. Not less than 20 feet of full-height curb shall be retained between driveways located to serve the same lot. Not less than 20 feet of continuous curb space shall be retained in front of each lot where the street frontage of the property served is greater than 40 feet. Where such frontage is 40 feet or less, continuous curb space shall be retained in front of each lot equal to one-half the length of the frontage, except that this provision shall not be applied to prevent the construction of one driveway having a width of nine feet. Where driveways serve separate lots, and are so located that at least two feet of full-height curb cannot be constructed separating said driveways, then the two driveways shall be merged into one. This necessitates removal of the entire existing side slope. The permit shall enumerate any exceptions.

3-4.5.6 Joints in Curb, Gutter, Sidewalk and Driveway. Joints in sidewalk and driveways should be either expansion joints, weakened plane joints or score lines as prescribed by the plans and specifications. The Inspector should review requirements with the contractor and assist in laying out the joint pattern to comply with the requirements. The joint layout is facilitated by a joint layout plan as shown in Plate 12, Appendix.

Expansion joints are constructed with a pre-molded joint filler (See Subsection 2-4.9.2) and should extend to the full depth and width of the concrete being placed. Sleeved dowels or keyways are usually installed to maintain the concrete at the same level on either side of the joint.

Weakened plane joints are constructed by pressing a T-shaped plastic strip into the concrete at least one inch deep and extending the full width of the concrete being placed. The top of the "T" holds the strip straight and is pulled off at an intermediate stage of the finishing operations in time to edge and finish adjacent to the embedded strip. Installation is facilitated by channeling the fresh concrete with a metal straight edge before pressing the strip into the concrete.

Concrete joints (prescribed by some agencies as weakened plane joints) are constructed with a special grooving tool or "T" bar and, when finished, should be one-half inch deep and not wider than one-eighth inch and should extend for the full width of the concrete being placed.

Joints for sidewalk and driveways, should be transverse to the line of work and at regular intervals not exceeding 10 feet. At walk returns they should be laid out radially and installed at the BC, MC and EC except at the BC of alleys and the EC of alleys if the walk is not placed against the curb. The Inspector should review the specifications carefully because some agencies require expansion joints at the EC and BC of walk returns and a score line at the MC, whereas other agencies specify weakened-plane joints, exclusively.

Joints should also be installed at the top of driveway slopes where the walk thickness changes to that required for driveways. Additional joints should be installed as transverse continuations of the sides of vaults, pull boxes, catch basins and other structures 30 inches or more in width. For circular structures the joint should be laid out through the center of the circle. When the concrete within the walk area is blocked out for tree wells or installations of street light or traffic signal facilities, transverse joints should be installed at each side of the block-out.

Occasionally, a block-out is necessary because a structure has not been raised to the required sidewalk grade. In this case, it is best to stop the placement of concrete for the full width of the walk at the nearest transverse joint on both sides of the structure which will allow sufficient room for excavating to raise the structure to grade. This procedure will also eliminate the creation of a patch-work of joint lines. When concrete is placed in these blocked out areas, the joint is called a cold joint and the edge need only be tooled to the required radius. If this is the normal location of an expansion joint it should be deleted.

In lieu of weakened plane joints and score lines, a one inch deep saw cut may be used. Sawing should take place within 24 hours after concrete has been placed.

Sidewalk 20 feet or wider should have a longitudinal center score line.

Pre-molded expansion joint filler should be tightly wrapped around the base of all utility poles encased in concrete.

On parkway fill-in projects, expansion or weakened-plane joints shall be located in line with those in the existing sidewalk. If none exist, weakened-plane joints in the new parkway fill-in shall be located at intervals not exceeding 10 feet, and in line with existing scoring lines in the adjacent sidewalk.

Templates should be used to insure that all joints are truly transverse or radial.

3-4.5.7 **Finishing Sidewalks and Driveways.** The procedures for finishing concrete slabs described in Subsection 3-11.11 generally apply to sidewalk and driveway finishing. Care should be exercised by the cement finishers to insure that the edging tools are not depressed below the headers, causing the edges to be low and out of the normal plane of the slab. This condition develops at an early stage of finishing operations and is difficult to correct at a later stage.

Sidewalk surface finishes vary with the slope of the walk. These and the finish for driveways are as follows:

WORK	FINISH REQUIRED
Sidewalk finish on level or nearly level streets (where slope is less than seven inches in 10 feet) (less than 6% grade)	Fine hair broom finish (transverse to the work)
Sidewalk on streets (where slope is over seven inches in 10 feet) (over 6% grade)	Wood float finish .
"Y-slope" area of driveways, including surface of depressed curb and top surface of side slopes	Wood float finish

When required, scoring lines are ¼-inch deep with a ⅛-inch radius. Longitudinal center scoring is required in all sidewalks 20 feet or more in width.

3-4.5.8 **Curbs, Gutter, Walk And Driveway Checklist.**

General, Before Placing Concrete

(1) Know the plans and specifications and review with contractor.

(2) Check subgrade. Firm and on grade? Any base required? Elevation proper for thickness required?

(3) Check forms and headers. Rigid? Straight? Elevation? Contour?

(4) Joints laid out and expansion joints installed, if required: material on hand for weakened plane joints (See Plate 12, Appendix).

(5) Curing compound and spray equipment on job.

(6) Check finishing tools. Is edger and inside corner tool radius as required?

Curb and Integral Curb and Gutter

(1) Check integral curb and gutter forms for batter·of curb and gutter cut. Height of curb face? Top of curb width? Gutter width; thickness and hike-up?

(2) Sleeves for roof drains installed in curb forms?

(3) Driveway and handicap ramp depressions located and marked? Is the "X" slope dimension proper?

(4) Radius of curb returns per plan?

(5) Keys or dowels required for adjoining sidewalk?

Gutter

(1) Check gutter side forms for width, thickness, batter?

(2) Headers securely staked? Continuous bearing on sub-grade? Set for proper gutter hike-up?

(3) Flow line stakes installed?

(4) Forms for low flow channels installed, if required?

Extruded Curb and Gutter

(1) Check extruding machine and mold; does the mold shape correspond to the standard plan?

(2) How will grade be maintained? Check wire line for sensor or track setting.

(3) If a crawler type is used, check smoothness of sub-grade (machine sensor cannot correct for rough subgrade); check the transverse grade (should be level for the operating width of machine).

(4) Check extruded shape for accuracy (use level and rule); check for sag before concrete sets; check alignment.

Sidewalk

(1) Side forms 2-inch lumber staked securely with full bearing on subgrade?

(2) Thickness checked (use scratch template across headers to check grade if big job is involved)?

(3) Joints laid out and material on hand for types of joint specified?

(4) All vault, meter boxes and pull boxes set to grade and parallel with curb?

(5) Tree wells blocked out?

(6) Blockouts for street light and traffic signals, if required? Other blockouts required for uncompleted work?

Driveways and Handicap Access Ramps

(1) Is depression in previously constructed curb proper? "X" slope? Bottom width? Lip at gutter (check precise tolerance for handicap access ramps)?

(2) Apron forming for commercial driveway or residential driveway as required?

(3) Check for thickness, commercial or resident as required?

(4) Is "X" slope and lip forming set with top to finish grade when driveway is constructed in existing work to avoid freehand rodding of concrete during placement of apron?

Concrete Placement and Finishing

(1) Subgrade dampened prior to concrete placement?

(2) What finishes are required?

(3) Finishers and equipment on job are sufficient for work to be done?

(4) Check delivery tickets and observe concrete mixture as it is being placed. Is type of concrete correct? From approved source? General appearance and consistency satisfactory?

(5) Check slump and prepare compression test cylinders as required.

(6) Is concrete being deposited properly? Without segregation? Spaded, tamped or vibrated?

(7) Spreaders being removed as concrete placed in curb?

(8) Curb alignment checked after front face is stripped and curb straightened while still plastic? Check back edge for alignment (poor back edge alignment is accentuated when adjoining walk is placed).

(9) Expansion joints located and edged?

(10) Weakened plane joints installed and edged?

(11) Check sidewalk finishing sequence; spaded at face of form or header; screeded and tamped; bull floated and edged; steel floated (hand trowel or long handled fresno)? Check for surface humps and hollows? Edges sloped down?

(12) Additional trowelling of sidewalk after water sheen has disappeared? Hair broom finish timed for proper texture?

(13) Check final finish of curb and gutter. Crossfall of top of curb? Gutter hike-up and finish (woodfloat, 4″ trowelled flow line)? Gutter cut, edge not bent down? Curb finish (fine hair broom)? Joints edged?

After Placing and Finishing

(1) Curing compound applied with proper coverage?

(2) Work properly barricaded to protect the finished concrete?

(3) Residents cautioned to avoid vehicular access to property over fresh concrete?

3-4.6   Class "A" Permits.

3-4.6.1   General.   Class "A" permits are issued by the Engineer for the construction, reconstruction or repair of concrete curbs, sidewalks, driveways and gutters, along with work appurtenant to the foregoing, such as roof or area drains through the curb. The Inspector should review the requirements in Subsection 3-4.5 for curb, gutter, sidewalk and driveway inspection procedure. Inspectors assigned to Class "A" permit work should be thoroughly familiar with that subsection. Repair work is generally done as the result of a "Notice to Repair" served upon the property owner by a local governmental authority. New construction or reconstruction of these items generally occurs due to the building of new homes, apartments, commercial buildings, gasoline service stations, parking lots, etc.

Any person may apply for a Class "A" permit. The permittee need not be a licensed contractor. Many are issued to property owners who then employ others to do the work, but occasionally a property owner will do his own work. A completion bond is not required and there is no requirement for liability insurance.

Inspection of Class "A" permit projects is under the jurisdiction of the Supervisor of the District where the work is located.

Inspection of work done under Class "A" permits requires initiative, good judgment, knowledge of good construction, tact and diplomacy. The Inspector rarely has a plan or a sketch to guide him. He must quickly review the many varied conditions encountered at each job location and decide which rules, regulations and standard plan requirements should be applied to the particular situation. Alterations in forming and grading are frequently found necessary, and in order to obtain corrections, the Inspector must often resort to tactful persuasion and a display of a thorough knowledge of the requirements.

Most of the rules and regulations governing driveway, curb, gutter and sidewalk work are included in the pamphlet entitled "General Information Concerning the Construction of Curbs, Driveways and Sidewalks under Class 'A' Permits." The Inspector should use this pamphlet for quick reference and to assist in explaining to contractors and property owners the standards for Class "A" permit construction.

The Standard Plans most frequently applicable are those entited "Standard Driveways" and "Types of Curb and Gutter."

3-4.6.2   **Inspection Procedures.**   The Inspector should report to each assigned location from 10 to 30 minutes early. If corrective work is required, it often can be completed prior to arrival of the concrete or asphalt at the jobsite.

Determine from the contractor where he plans to start placing concrete. Then inspect that portion of the work which will be constructed with the first truckload of concrete. Obtain necessary corrections, if required; then permit the material to be placed in this portion while proceeding to inspect the balance of the work.

(a) **Permit Requirements.** After introducing himself, the Inspector must ask the contractor for the white copy of the Class "A" permit. If it is not at the jobsite, he must telephone the appropriate District Office and verify the existence of a permit for the work at the location in question. The Supervisor, the Senior Inspector in charge or the Dispatcher will attemp to locate the pink copy of the permit in the office files and advise the Field Inspector of any special information thereon. If the pink copy of the permit is not on file in the District Office of the Agency, the contractor or permittee must be informed that inspection cannot be provided for the work. When the white copy of the permit has been located, the contractor or permittee may make a new request for inspection of the work.

It is often found that permit requirements do not correspond to the job conditions, usually for the reason that inadequate or incorrect information is furnished to the Engineer when the application for the permit is made. In that event, the Inspector must disregard the non-conforming instructions on the permit and see that proper requirements are applied. For example, an incorrect curb height shown on the permit should be disregarded and the actual measurement used as a basis for determining the correct length for side slopes of a driveway. In some cases, it may be advisable to telephone the Supervisor, the Senior Inspector in charge or the Permit Office, in order to review the proposed changes from the permit requirements and the reasons therefor.

(b) **Forms and Subgrade.** Make a visual inspection of the forms for line, grade and general condition. Form lumber showing excessive warping or bowing must be corrected, either by additional staking and bracing or by replacement with acceptable lumber. Alignment and elevation of curb and sidewalk forms should be checked with a thin but strong nylon or linen line pulled tightly along the forms. Watch for disturbed subgrade or dry, uncompacted fills, particularly in areas where curb has been removed. Such areas should be made firm and unyielding, either by tamping or by removal and replacement with sand, gravel, disintegrated granite or other suitable material. Puddles of water and mud must be removed from the subgrade before placement of concrete or asphalt. Existing improvements to be reconstructed must be removed to their full depth. Burying of broken concrete and other paving materials in the parkway or beneath a driveway or sidewalk is not permitted.

All new curb shall be constructed using full-depth forms, both front and back. Do not allow a wall of dirt or broken concrete to be used as a back form. The only exception is where new curb is built adjacent to existing concrete pavement or concrete gutter, in which case the front form should match the height of the curb face.

(c) **Asphalt Removals.** Where depressed curb for a driveway or full-height curb is to be constructed at a location where the gutter area is bituminous material, a strip of gutter six to eight inches wide must be removed to permit the erection of full-depth front forms for the curb. After removal of the front forms, see that the curb face is finished to at least four inches below the gutter flow line. Include on the inspection report a notation, "Asphalt repairs required." The Agency street maintenance office should then be notified to make the necessary repairs. This service is rendered without charge to the permittee.

(d) **Street Light and Traffic Signal Pull Boxes in Driveway Areas.** (See Subsection 3-9.)

When it is necessary to relocate a pull box out of a driveway area, the relocation and alteration to the conduits must be done before the driveway is constructed. Notify the appropriate agency prior to commencing the work.

(e) **Measurements.** After a general visual inspection, several spot-check measurements should be made, using a straightedge and a rule, to ascertain that thickness for sidewalks and driveways will be at least equal to the minimum requirements. The length of the side slopes and Y-slope areas of driveways should be verified. Sidewalks and driveways should be measured for length and width. The standard sidewalk slope of ¼-inch rise per foot should be checked with a straightedge, a rule and a level. Thoroughness by the Inspector in making these measurements is essential. Areas to be joined should be checked for proper elevation and acceptable condition. Information regarding dimension tolerances, construction of warped sections or ramps in order to join existing off-grade areas and other variances can best be obtained by consultation with the Supervisor or the Senior Inspector in charge.

In checking driveways for compliance with minimum and maximum width limitations (but not for measuring areas), the following rules should be observed:

(1) Driveway width is measured from the bottom of one side slope to the bottom of the other side slope. The side slopes are not included in measuring the width.

(2) The three-foot radius of the curb return of a Case 3 or Case 4 driveway is excluded from the width measurement.

(3) If a new driveway is to be merged with an adjacent driveway, the division between the two lots is established by a line passing through the common lot corner at right angles to the curb line, regardless of the direction of the side lot line. The width of the driveway is then measured from this division line to the bottom of the side slope.

(f) **Concrete Placement.** Before allowing any concrete to be placed, see that the delivery ticket shows the correct concrete mix from an approved concrete proportioning plant. In placing the concrete for a driveway, the best work is obtained if the concrete is placed from one side only, progressing across the driveway to the side opposite. By follow this method, rodding is made easier, tamping of the concrete is accomplished while it is still plastic, and mortar is floated up readily to facilitate finishing the concrete as the work proceeds.

3-4.6.3 Homeowners' and Contractors' Qualifications. It is important to determine the workers' qualifications before the work is commenced. Examination of work previously completed by them on nearby or adjacent private property will often give a good indication of the quality of their work. Observe what quality of finish was obtained. Inspect their tools for concrete finishing. Experienced concrete finishers carry a full assortment of steel trowels, wood floats, edging and scoring tools, as well as a tamper and longhandled float. Be wary of workers with essential tools missing or with new tools showing little or no evidence of previous use.

A check of previous work done and the tools on hand will help the Inspector to determine the amount of instruction he must give the workers and the extent of follow-up inspection required later if his other assignments require his leaving the site before the concrete finishing is completed.

3-4.6.4 Revocable Permits. Revocable permits are sometimes issued for driveways or sidewalks constructed of bituminous paving materials. These permits are subject to being revoked at a future date if the work authorized therein later interferes with construction of any permanent improvements in the public right-of-way. For construction of temporary driveways or sidewalks composed of bituminous mixtures the following deviations from the specifications are normally approved by the Agency:

(a) Type I-D-AR-4000 asphalt concrete is to be specified.

(b) An Inspector is not required at the asphalt plant where the mix is manufactured.

(c) Minimum thickness is to be four inches unless otherwise specified on the permit or plan.

(d) The mixtures may be rolled with a roller weighing not less than three tons.

3-4.6.5 Reporting Work Inspected. Furnish in detail all the required information in the spaces provided on the reverse side of the white copy of the permit form.

(a) As the permittee may be a property owner or a general contractor rather than the concrete contractor, it is necessary to obtain the name, address and telephone number of the contractor actually doing the work.

(b) Report each day's work on a separate line. If work abuts a corner lot, use a separate line for each street and write in the name of each street. Measure the area constructed — do not rely on the quantites shown on the permit.

(c) If the work will be completed in one day, retain the white copy of the permit and transmit it and other completed permits to the appropriate office of the Agency.

(d) If the work will not be completed in one day, make out the report as above and leave the permit with the contractor for completion by the next Inspector. The Inspector must not assume that he will be reassigned to the job. If he leaves the permit with the contractor, he must also make out a "Class 'A' Permit Daily Inspection Report" (See Plate 2, Appendix), reporting all work inspected by him so that a record of his inspection will be on file if the permit should be lost.

(e) This report is also to be used in the absence of the white copy of the permit, provided the required information has been obtained by telephone as instructed in Subsection 3-4.6.2(a). Indicate on the form whether the work is completed or whether additional work remains to be done. If the work is completed, instruct the contractor or permittee to locate the white copy of the permit and mail it to the appropriate office of the Agency or give it to the Inspector on his next job. If the work is not completed, issue instructions to have the white copy at the jobsite for use by the next Inspector. Transmit the completed report to the appropriate office of the Agency.

If the quantities constructed are in excess of those shown on the original permit an additional permit must be obtained if the excess quantities involved will result in a permit fee of $8.50 or more. The permittee is notified as to the amount due either by telephone or by letter.

3-4.6.6 Permit Completion or Continuation. If the work is to continue the next day, inform the contractor during the morning to call the Dispatcher before noon to arrange for inspection for the next day. The Inspector must not assume that he will be reassigned to the same job, since assignments are made by the Dispatchers on a daily basis.

When the Inspector is required to leave the job in order to go to another assignment, he must instruct the contractor or permittee as to the concrete finish and the scoring requirements. He should also advise the contractor that he expects to return later in the day to check on the progress of the work. Concrete and surplus dirt is to be removed from the street area or adequate lights and barricades provided to insure public safety if such material is to remain overnight. The contractor is to be instructed to remove form lumber not earlier than 24 hours after construction and to backfill with dirt where necessary.

3-4.6.7   Class A Permit Check List.

(1) Review Subsection 3-4.5.8 for detailed checklist for curb, gutter, walk and driveway inspection.

(2) Check permit requirements first upon arriving at the job location.

(3) Check form set-up, grade and thickness.

(4) Measure actual quantities and enter on permit. Are the quantities shown on the permit less than those installed?

(5) Review finishing and other completion requirements with contractor or permittee (stripping forms, surplus material removal, clean-up, barricades and lights) before leaving job. Also that additional inspection must be requested from Dispatcher for permits not completed the first day.

(6) If minor pavement (street) repair is required, note on permit.

3-5   SEWER CONSTRUCTION

3-5.1   General.   Sewer construction represents a large proportion of the construction which is inspected by most agencies. It requires the assignment of high caliber inspection personnel because it involves many of the problems encountered in inspection which are critical in nature, namely: traffic control, protection of property, utility interference, access to property, public relations, trench safety, backfill compaction, accurate records and nuisance problems of dust, mud or noise.

Effective public relations can operate to reduce the number of complaints and keep the job moving smoothly. Careful attention to matters which are in the best interests of the traveling public, adjacent property owners and the workers will pay dividends in good public relations: proper traffic control, maintenance of access to driveways and business establishments, and precautions to minimize or eliminate unnecessary damage to existing improvements or planted areas. These factors result in an attitude on the part of those affected which contributes toward a tolerance for the inconvenience they suffer. Sewer construction usually results in the least possible inconvenience to all when it is diligently prosecuted. (See Subsection 1-4.)

The Inspector should be alert to insure that problems do not arise from the obstruction of fire hydrants, or by the contractor's equipment, construction materials or spoil banks. He must see that gutter flow lines are kept unobstructed or that a plank is leaned against the curb to prevent earth spoil from blocking water flow. Where necessary, pedestrian bridges should be provided over excavations. Proper placement and lighting of barricades is essential to protect the pedestrian as well as the motoring public from the hazards involved in the work.

Streets may be closed to traffic only as provided by the plans, Special Provisions or in strict compliance with the provisions of the Standard Specifications. While street closings may expedite the work and reduce the time of inconvenience, the degree of inconvenience is considerably increased to property owners residing on a closed street. Mail service, deliveries, garbage and rubbish pickup, school bus pickup and other vital services are either curtailed or suspended by the closing of a street. In addition, the property owners may experience hardship in such elementary areas as marketing for groceries, use of baby strollers and getting invalid patients to medical care. The contractor must always conduct his operations in such a manner that an emergency traffic lane in a closed street will be available for such emergency vehicles as fire equipment, police cars or ambulances. Prior notice by the contractor to the property owners affected by a street closing will greatly reduce such problems and permit them to make other arrangements during the period the street is closed. (See Subsection 1-4, Safety and Convenience).

Sewer construction in easements or rights-of-way across private property often poses special problems for the Inspector and contractor, particularly where the property owner has landscaped the area or constructed other improvements. The contractor should be requested to conduct his operations so as to minimize or avoid entirely any damage to such improvements. By pot-holing with short tunnels or excavating by hand methods and exercising care, much can be done to protect small buildings, slabs, walls, trees and other significant improvements from damage. Some ground cover may be lost, but the property owner should be given adequate notice so that he can salvage and replant as much as possible. Good public relations in these situations is essential.

Before permitting the contractor to proceed, the Inspector should check the plans to insure that they have been approved and signed by the Engineer. Preliminary unsigned plans which the contractor might have used to prepare his bid may be significantly changed in the final approved plans. It would not be uncommon for there to be an increase in the size of pipe for the sewer, restationing of manholes, relocation of the entire sewer, change in the depth of the sewer, change in the type of joints, or other major change. The plans should be carefully examined for special conditions and notes as well as the references to Standard Plans under "Notice to Contractors." Grade sheets must be on the jobsite before excavation is commenced.

In the performance of his duties, there are four major problem areas in sewer construction which can cause future functional problems and expense: poor pipe subgrade, poor joints, poor flooding or compaction of backfill, and poor records. Poor subgrade and joints result in cracked and broken pipe, infiltration of ground water, or exfiltration of sewage. Poor consolidation of backfill causes pavement failures and costly maintenance. Poor records may lead to needless costs to the Agency in locating "lost" sewer connections or saddling the main line when none can be found.

The usual procedure in sewer construction in built-up areas is to construct the main line first, backfill the trench, build all structures and construct the house connections on one side of the street. When this part of the work is completely flooded and cleaned up, traffic is diverted to that side of the street before constructing the house connections on the other side of the street.

The upper ends of new house connections are capped where they terminate at property line. Actual connections to private house sewers are made under individual sewer connection permits issued at a later date after final inspection and acceptance. (See Subsection 3-7, Sewer and Storm Drain Connection Permits.)

3-5.2 Definition of Sewer Construction Terms. Some terminology in sewer construction may not be in common usage and is listed here:

Balling a Line. The operation of passing an inflated rubber ball, which is slightly less than the diameter of the pipe, through a sewer line. The purpose of balling a line after its completion is to insure that no obstructions exist, no pipe has collapsed or partially collapsed, joint fins have been removed, and to clean the line of dirt or other foreign matter. Water introduced by the contractor at a manhole is used to force the ball through the line between manholes.

The outlet pipe in each successive manhole downstream should be blocked with a pick to prevent the ball from continuing down the line and into the existing sewer system. A sandbag dam should also be placed in the manhole to prevent rocks and dirt being washed into the existing sewer system. Balling is mandatory for lines that are curved between manholes in order to prove continuity.

Chimney. A vertical riser constructed on a vertical tee in a main sewer, the riser having open or more branches at the top to permit the construction of future house connection sewers at a shallower depth. Chimneys are usually required where the main sewer is constructed in trenches exceeding 15 feet in depth.

A circular section of 16-inch diameter concrete reinforcemain sewer, the riser having one or more branches at the top to 16-inch square sections shown on the Standard Plans. Prefabricated cylindrical cardboard forms are commonly used for this purpose.

Cradle. Concrete reinforcement used between a pipe line and the walls of a trench to increase the load-bearing capacity of the pipe.

Crown. The top quadrant of a pipe or cast circular section.

House Connection Sewer. A 6-inch sewer that connects the property to a main line sewer. The term "house connection sewer" is generally used, even though the connection may involve a commercial structure, apartment building, school, church or any other improvement requiring a sewer connection. House connections may be larger than six inches, or two or more 6-inch lines may be required, depending upon the quantity of sewage expected to originate from such establishments. House connection sewers are sometimes referred to as "lateral sewers." (Also see Subsections 3-5.8.2 and 3-7.)

House Sewer. A 4-inch (or larger) sewer on private property that connects the plumbing at the building line to the house connection sewer at the property line.

Interceptor Sewer. A sewer that receives flow from a number of transverse main sewers. Interceptor sewers discharge into outfall sewers.

Invert. A line on centerline at the inside bottom of a pipe or conduit, also commonly referred to as the flow line.

Lamp Hole. A vertical riser similar to a chimney but brought to the surface of the ground or pavement and provided with an appropriate cover. It is intended to be used by maintenance forces to lower an electric light to the main line for inspection purposes. It is usually specified at the end of a line expected to be extended in the near future, but is never specified more than 200 feet distant from the nearest manhole.

Main Sewer. A sewer which receives the flow from house connection sewers, or from one or more tributary sewers. A main sewer is also referred to as a main line sewer.

Outfall Sewer. A sewer that receives sewage from a collecting system and conducts it to a point of final discharge such as a disposal plant.

Relief Sewer. A sewer which provides additional capacity in a sewered area to relieve overloaded sewer systems.

Saddle. A connection to a main sewer where no wye or tee exists, made by breaking into it and attaching a specially fabricated spur pipe.

Spring Line. The line formed along the sides of a circular or elliptical conduit by the intersection of the conduit walls with an imaginary plane passing horizontally through the conduit on its longitudinal axis. A circular pipe filled with water to its spring line would be half full.

Soffit. The inside top of a pipe or box-section conduit.

Swab. A cloth bundle securely attached to a handle and used by a pipelayer to pull through pipe laid with mortar joints, in order to smooth mortar fins which may result from the jointing operations.

Tee. A prefabricated pipe fitting intended to permit connection of two pipe lines at right angles.

Terminal Cleanout Structure. A structure consisting of placing a long-radius vertical curve in the main sewer to bring its end to the surface of the ground or pavement. It is used to permit cleaning of the main line sewer from an otherwise dead-end sewer which does not terminate in a manhole. Terminal cleanout structures are used at a maximum distance of 200 feet to the nearest manhole where future extension of the sewer is not anticipated.

Wye. A prefabricated pipe fitting intended to permit connection of two pipe lines at a 45-degree angle.

3-5.3 Shop Drawings. In most cases, the Special Provisions for sewer projects involving large diameter reinforced concrete pipe require that the contractor submit shop drawings to the Engineer for approval. These drawings are prepared by the pipe supplier and represent a refinement of the contract drawings, since the contract drawings usually provide for more than one option with respect to pipe details. The shop drawings will include line layouts, joint details and tolerances and related information. Sometimes the location of structures is changed on the shop drawings from the location shown on the contract drawings. It is important therefore that the surveyors and Inspector check the approved shop drawings very closely with the contract drawings.

3-5.4 Traffic Control. The effective movement of traffic through and around construction projects is essential. Where a traffic control plan is indicated on the plans or Special Provisions for the project, it must be rigidly enforced. Otherwise, the provisions for traffic control outlined in the Standard Specifications must be placed into effect. It should be kept in mind that these requirements are minimum standards and do not entitle the contractor to obstruct traffic any more than his operations reasonably require for prudent prosecution of the work. Barricades and other traffic control devices must operate to **lead** traffic through or around the work site with no confusion to the motorist. It must be rememberd that such devices may look adequate to the contractor placing them, but may be perplexing to the motorist. The Inspector should drive both directions through the worksite to determine for himself the sufficiency of the warning devices and then require the contractor to make any adjustments found to be necessary or desirable. (See Subsection 1-4.4)

3-5.5 Removals. Where the removal of existing pavement is necessary before excavating for sewer installations, pavement cutting or breaking machines are customarily used. The Inspector should be alert to prohibit the use of high-impact types of pavement breakers where damage to nearby structures or substructures may result. The pavement to be removed should be cut slightly wider than the digging width of the equipment intended to be used, so as to prevent hooking and raising the adjacent pavement by such equipment.

It is highly undesirable to break pavement great distances ahead of excavating operations because it presents an unnecessary nuisance to motorists and, in some cases, a hazard. The contractor should be permitted to break pavement ahead to the extent that trenching will follow in one or two days.

Broken pavement can be rolled and sand spread and broomed into the voids to present a smooth and more stable riding surface. Dirt and fragments of broken pavement originating from the pavement breaking operation must be cleaned from the street immediately.

The edges of existing concrete pavement adjacent to a trench are to be saw cut to a depth of 1½ inches in accordance with the Standard Specifications. Saw cutting of bituminous pavement is desirable but not required.

3-5.6 Sewer Materials. (See Subsection 2-7 for additional information.) Vitrified clay pipe is checked and tested at the pipe yard by the Testing Agency and reinforced concrete sewer pipe is inspected by inspection personnel at the point of manufacture. However, this does not relieve the Inspector from rechecking it for defects which may have been overlooked or damage that might have occurred in subsequent handling. Broken spigots or bells are obvious, but invisible cracks can be disclosed by tapping each joint of vitrified clay pipe with a metal object as it stands in a vertical position on its bell. A clear bell-like tone results when a sound pipe is struck, as compared to the dull, toneless sound produced when a cracked pipe is struck. This procedure, however, when applied to pipe with mechanical compression joints, is not conclusive due to the dampening effect of the joint components.

Concrete pipe is inspected at the point of manufacture by the Agency materials control group (See Subsection 2-7.4) and accepted pipe is stamped for identification. Pipe should also be checked after it is delivered to the jobsite. Plastic-lined concrete sewer pipe should be inspected for damage to the lining. The gasket groove on the spigot and the gasket contact surface on the bell or socket end of concrete is particularly subject to damage and should be carefully examined. It is important that this pipe be stored or stacked using wood spacers, cradles and sleepers, or by standing the pipe on the bells so that there is no bearing on the gasket components.

Clay pipe wyes, tees or other fittings which are fused during vitrification, may be coated inside and outside at the junction of the intersecting elements with a clear epoxy compound to reduce porosity. Pigmented or opaque coatings which may obscure cracks, perforations or other imperfections in the fittings are prohibited.

Flexible pipe is supplied in several materials, types and joint configurations. The Standard Specifications provide for reinforced thermosetting resin (RTR), reinforced plastic mortar (RPM), polyethylene (PE) and polyvinyl chloride (PVC) solid wall pipe; and acrylonitrile-butadiene-styrene (ABS) in solid wall and composite wall pipe. Such pipe and fittings should not be stored in sunlight for extended periods of time. Also, in storing plastic pipe, irregular support or long spans should be avoided to minimize bends in the pipe, which will slow the subsequent laying operations by the work necessary to block or shim the pipe against the trench walls to a straight line and grade.

Manhole rings and covers should be checked for conformance to the type and and size required by the plans and to see that no casting projections or disfiguring imperfections exist. Manhole covers must seat tightly, with the top of the cover flush with the ring. Manhole covers that rock must be rejected.

Brick for manholes must be clean, sound, hard burned and give a clear ringing sound when struck together. Whole bricks only are permitted in manhole structures except for such bats as may be necessary to fill a space less than the dimension of a full brick when completing a course. Chinking of brick pieces in small voids or under manhole rings is not permitted.

Precast concrete manhole components are supplied from sources approved by the agency materials control group. The project Inspector should check the components as they arrive at the jobsite for source, type, size required and condition.

In those instances where the plans or specifications require the contractor to deliver manhole ring and cover sets to the Agency for credit, he should be advised to obtain a receipt therefor and have it available to the Final Inspector during final inspection.

Joint components for mechanical compression-type clay pipe joints are manufactured of polyurethane materials.

Store neoprene joint components away from heat and long exposure to sunlight, and check for cuts and abrasions. Sleeve type couplings (which include stainless steel compressor bands and shear ring components) and "O" ring gaskets are frequently made of neoprene.

Lubricants must be compatable with the materials. Lubricants from a source other than the pipe supplier must be tested.

While the smaller diameters of pipe may be joined without the use of a lubricant, a lubricant greatly facilitates the jointing operation when using mechanical compression joints. However, as the diameter of the pipe increases, a joint component lubricant becomes increasingly essential.

3-5.7 Excavating.

3-5.7.1 **General.** One of the first duties of the Inspector, upon arriving at the jobsite, is to determine from the contractor that he has an excavation permit issued by the appropriate agency. Permits are issued for individual projects or may be obtained on a yearly basis. In either case, the permit number should be recorded in the job records. The contractor is not allowed to proceed with any excavation work over five feet deep until such permit has been obtained and a copy is available at the jobsite.

The Inspector should review the presence of utilities and other important existing conditions with the contractor. The plans will specify the type of bedding and a standard plan reference. The Inspector should note the details of bedding and maximum trench width for the type of bedding required.

The soil type and stability, traffic requirements, depth of trench, proximity of existing improvements and substructures, and costs of resurfacing are all factors taken into consideration by the contractor when determining what type of excavation he will make and equipment he will use.

The Inspector must remain alert during trenching and flooding operations to detect settlement of adjacent surface improvements and must bring such matters to the attention of the contractor. Trees, poles and street lighting electroliers may require special support to prevent them from subsiding or falling into the trench. Careful records of damage to surface improvements resulting from the contractor's operations must be maintained by the Inspector.

Test borings are sometimes made along the line of a sewer and the date, stations and findings of such borings are shown on the plans. The Inspector, as well as the contractor, will find this information valuable in planning the work, taking into account poor ground conditions, water table, rock formations and trench support methods. It should be kept in mind that test borings made in the summer months may not disclose any evidence of ground water which may be present during the rainy season of the year.

The Inspector should review Subsection 3-3.3 for general information concerning excavations and the checklist for excavations in Subsection 3-3.3.7.

3-5.7.2 Trenching. The pipeline must be staked by the Agency survey party with grade sheets on the job before trenching begins. (See Subsection 1-5.5 for Agency survey procedure.)

The Inspector should check to see that the trench is centered on the plan line for the sewer and that the width is acceptable (refer to the Standard Plan for pipe laying in trenches and this subsection regarding maximum trench width).

One of the most important elements of excavating for sewer construction is to maintain the specified width of the trench at the top of the pipe. Where the specified maximum width is exceeded, even for a short distance, the backfill load may cause the pipe to fail. Above the top of the pipe, extra trench width does not increase the load on the pipe . The maximum load occurs on pipe when the trench width below the top of the pipe exceeds two and one-half to three times the pipe diameter (refer to the Standard Plan for exact limits).

Although pipe off-center in the trench is not desirable, it is permitted provided the maximum allowable trench width is not exceeded and the minimum side clearance is maintained. The side clearance must be provided to permit backfill under the haunches and for working room. If additional excavation is necessary to provide proper side clearance, it may cause the trench to be overwidth; in which case, a concrete bedding will be required in accordance with the Standard Plan for pipe laying in trenches.

While most trench cross-sections are shown on plans and Standard Plans with flat bottoms, trenching machines do not cut them flat. It is not necessary to require trimming the trench to square corners if the subgrade is undisturbed and correct bedding depth has been obtained.

Loose material in the bottom of the trench must be removed to solid, undisturbed ground before pipe bedding is placed. This is best accomplished by hand labor close behind the excavating equipment so that the materials can be easily thrown ahead and be picked up by the excavator. For the protection of the laborer, it is imperative that the trench shoring be maintained as close to the excavating equipment as feasible.

Several trench types are in common usage: the vertical wall trench, sloping (or vee'd) trench, or a combination of both with the top portion sloped and the bottom portion a vertical-walled trench. All trenches and excavations must be adequately braced. Even where the excavation appears to be stable and safe, jacks and shores, must be installed in accordance with the OSHA Construction Safety Orders. Failure on the part of the contractor to conform to these requirements cannot be permitted (See Subsection 1-4.3, for Agency policy regarding construction safety operations).

TRENCHING PRECAUTIONS

OSHA **Construction Safety Orders** give **minimum requirements only,** but distinctly specify that trenches in all types of earth must be guarded against the hazard of moving ground.

It is the contractor's responsibility to see that employees are not injured from caving ground. Experienced construction men offer the following advice, which will be helpful in deciding how much sheeting, **in addition to the minimum specified,** is required:

1. **Beware of disturbed ground.** Ground that has been filled or disturbed will require additonal sheeting and bracing. So will hard compact ground if there is filled ground nearby. A trench wall that is near another recently filled trench, for example, is unstable, even though it appears to be hard compact material.

2. **Take special precautions where moisture is present.** Provide extra sheeting where there is water or seepage. Keep the excavation pumped out at all times, and avoid any accumulation of water, day or night, until the work is done.

3. **Guard against caving hazard created by vibration and load from highway traffic.** Trenches located near highways and streets are more likely to cave than similar trenches in locations not exposed to moving loads. Extra sheeting is necessary, and loose rocks and chunks of earth that could fall on men in the excavation should be removed.

4. **Install upper trench jacks first.** When trench jacks are used to hold uprights in place against trench walls, the top jack should be installed first. The next lower one should be held in position with hooks from above before a man enters the trench at that point to place the lowest jack. Shoring does not serve its purpose if men expose themselves to hazard while installing it. Most of the installation work should be carried on from a safe position outside of the trench.

5. **Protect all men in trenches.** If a man is needed at the bottom of the trench near the boom-end of a boom-type trenching machine, he should be protected by metal shields attached to the boom-end. These shields should be of adequate strength and design to serve as a substitute for shoring and bracing.

Jacks and struts must always be horizontal, with both ends seated firmly on the shores and nailed or cleated to prevent slipping. Jacks usually have patented ends with a limited ball-and-socket action to permit firm seating, and are provided with projections or prongs which become embedded in the shores when under pressure and thus prevent slippage. These ends need not be nailed or cleated except when the shores are sloped to the extent that the jack might slip. It is never permissible to use only one jack or strut between two shores, since any movement of ground would tend to rotate the shore and cause the system to collapse.

Excavations in wet or running sand must be sloped or tight-sheeted with timber or steel sheet piling. Where this is not practical or economically feasible, the contractor may pothole and tunnel. This method consists of drilling or excavating a series of vertical shafts from the surface to the laying depth along the line of the sewer. Short tunnels are excavated between shafts to complete the excavation.

Because of the high cost of excavation, sewers are seldom constructed in tunnels except when required by the plans or specifications or the depth precludes the open trench method. Under some conditions the contractor may elect to tunnel under surface (or subsurface) structures or improvements to avoid traffic interference or expensive replacement of the interfering obstruction.

3-5.7.3 Dewatering. Control of water is another problem encountered in trenching in some areas. Most project Special Provisions require the contractor to submit to the Engineer for approval a written program for effective control of water pollution. Water should be drained to sumps and pumped out, or well points used to lower the water level below the laying depth of the pipe. Where this is not possible because of severe ground water or tidal conditions, pipe with mechanical compression joints (or other approved type of pipe joint) can be utilized and the pipe laid in or under water. Ground water may be pumped and discharged into a storm drain or street gutter. Where silt is carried by the water being pumped, a means for desilting the water is required when discharging such water in a street gutter or storm drain. Where practical, and space permits, the contractor can construct dikes to impound the silty water, either letting the water percolate into the ground, or allowing the silt to settle out and discharging the water from the pond with a crude low-velocity siphon. Several ponds are required for this method because too much agitation of the water occurs in the pond receiving the water from the pumps to permit any degree of settling.

Where small quantities of water are involved, two oil drums can be used effectively by discharging the silty water into one drum with the overflow passing through a pipe which extends down two feet into the second drum. Relatively clean water will result from the overflow of the second drum. Clear water will not be obtained by either method, but the water will be practically free of the larger silt particles which would settle out in flat gutter grades and present a cleaning problem for maintenance forces.

3-5.7.4 **Protecting Utilities and Substructures.** (See Subsection 1-6 for general information and Subsection 3-5.7.5 for special reporting requirements.) Trenching for sewer construction in an existing roadway almost invariably results in interferences with utilities and other types of substructures. Such installations must be protected by the contractor during trenching, pipe laying and backfilling operations. He may arrange with some utility agencies to cut and reconnect services (usually water and gas) but many must be maintained in service. This may involve some means of support across the trench, the most common method being to place a heavy timber to bridge the trench and suspending the utility from it with wire or cable slings. High pressure water or gas transmission lines, telephone ducts and other special or heavy substructures must be supported by a means which is adequate to prevent damage to the substructure. The supports for these substructures must not be disturbed until all backfilling and flooding operations are completed and all settlement of the backfill material has occurred. Suspension wires and cables should then be cut off below pavement subgrade elevation.

Existing sewer and storm drain piplines crossing trenches must be supported by a concrete beam or concrete wall constructed beneath the exposed length before backfilling operations are begun, as provided for on the Standard Plans for such conditions.

No substructure (or other hard object such as a rock) should be permitted to touch the sewer line and develop a point-loading situation which may crush the sewer pipe. A small cushion of earth fill (approximately six inches) should be provided between them, or the entire crossing encased in concrete to the bottom of the trench. Where concrete encasement is used, the contractor must furnish and install a cushion of expansion joint filler around the utility, or provide a sleeve or other opening in the encasement. This is to prevent embedment of the utility or "freezing" it with the concrete, and facilitates its subsequent maintenance or replacement.

3-5.7.5 Unforeseen Conditions. During excavation, utilities or other substructures may be encountered which are not indicated or are shown incorrectly on the plans. Damage or interference with the new improvement may occur in either case. Also, the delay, design change or change in the contractor's method that may be involved could result in extra work and cost. The Supervisor or Engineer must be notified immediately and instructions obtained as to how to proceed. Examples of such obstructions may be buried debris, abandoned walls or footings, rock strata or similar unforeseen conditions. Similarly, unconsolidated fill at the pipe laying depth may be discovered which will require a determination as to what corrective measures must be taken. Emergency Change Orders are normally issued in these cases to avoid delays to the contractor and to authorize additional work.

In all cases of unforeseen conditions, the Inspector must keep accurate records to verify the extent of the interference and any delay or extra work resulting therefrom. This is necessary to protect the Agency in case of dispute and litigation. See Plate 13, Appendix for a typical reporting form for this purpose.

3-5.7.6 Line and Grade. Survey procedures are established to set stakes for sewer construction on an offset line at intervals of 25 feet. In difficult trenching conditions where long trenches cannot be maintained, it may be necessary for the contractor to request stakes at 12½-foot intervals. Wood stakes are used where possible, with all horizontal offsets and vertical cuts measured from a tack in the top of the stake. In paved areas, a spike and tin is set in the pavement. Stationing is marked on a lath driven next to the stake or is painted on the pavement. All offset distances are shown on the grade sheet. Right and left offsets are established by facing upstream and are set far enough off the centerline of the proposed sewer line to permit trenching without the need to disturb the stakes. Grade stakes for each manhole are set on an offset at the inlet, centerline and outlet stations. Stakes for most house connections are set on the centerline of house connection ends, one foot beyond the end of the pipe to be laid. However, in some cases the ends are staked on an offset rather than on the centerline produced. Grade sheet details should be read with extreme care.

The station of any pipeline, house connection, manhole, tee, chimney, lamphole or terminal clean-out structure may not be changed without authority of the Engineer or as otherwise provided in this subsection.

All grade stakes must be checked by the Inspector to determine that none have been disturbed and that the contractor has planned his operations to preserve the stakes in an undisturbed condition. There are several methods for transferring grades from the grade stakes to the bottom of the trench, and some patented devices have been developed which are widely used. The most common method for smaller pipe in dry trenches is the bottom line method shown on Plate 36, Appendix. The top line method is better for laying pipe in trenches which are wide at the top or which are difficult to dewater satisfactorily. (See Plate 38, Appendix).

Where the pipe diameter is large, it is sometimes advisable to request the stakes to be set in the trench by the surveyor. While special conditions may sometimes warrant this procedure, it should be resorted to only if the contractor cannot accurately transfer the grades himself with honest effort, for this may result in greatly increased utilization of a survey crew and increased costs to the Agency or permittee. Large pipe can be easily and accurately set with another form of the bottom line method shown on Plate 37, Appendix.

With some exception, it is Agency policy to require that larger pipe for sewer pipelines (48″ and larger) be laid to blue tops set in the trench by Agency survey crews. This is due to the inherent inaccuracies of transferring line and grade from the greater offset distances that are involved. This policy should be discussed with the Supervisor at the beginning of a project where it might be applied.

The transfer of all grades, whether top or bottom line methods are used, will be done by the contractor and checked by the Inspector.

3-5.7.7 Bedding for Pipe. The surface upon which sewer pipe is to be laid must be true to grade, firm and thoroughly compacted. Where the trench bottom consists of hard compact material with a low sand equivalent, imported bedding material is required. If the native material at the bottom of the trench is granular or sandy, the pipe may be bedded in the material found in the trench. Otherwise, the trench must be excavated to an additional depth to provide for the imported bedding material. (Refer to the Agency Standard Plan for pipe laying in trenches.)

If excessively wet, soft, spongy, unstable or similarly unsuitable material is encountered at the pipe bedding depth, the unsuitable material shall be removed (when ordered by the Engineer) and be replaced with imported bedding material to provide a stable foundation.

Granular bedding material serves two purposes: it insures a uniform support along the bottom quadrant of the pipe to give it good load-bearing characteristics, and it provides a subdrain if ground water is present, which reduces the infiltration head on the sewer.

Imported granular material, if required, consists of pea gravel or sand for the smaller clay pipe sizes. Graded crushed stone is preferable for the larger concrete pipe sizes.

Mechanically excavated trenches have a fairly flat bottom. If pipe is laid directly upon such a surface, it would rest on the bells or along a narrow area of contact with the surface of the barrel. This would result in a very large reduction in load-carrying capacity and possible failure of the pipe during backfilling operations. Granular bedding material permits easy excavation for the bells and easy shaping in order to cradle the pipe barrel firmly and continuously over its full length.

Some types of bedding conditions specify additional granular bedding material alongside and under the haunches of the pipe. The additional bedding is deposited after the pipe is laid. The Inspector must assure himself that the material is spaded or rodded or densified by other methods to eliminate all voids. For larger pipe, two or more lifts may be required.

Some pipe installations provide for concrete bedding or a combination of granular and concrete bedding.

When the bedding includes concrete below the pipe, the preferable method of construction is to lay the pipe on a previously placed concrete slab, shimming the pipe to grade, and then placing the remaining concrete under the haunches, alongside and over the top of the pipe as required for the type of concrete bedding specified. To avoid floating, the pipe should be

blocked down from trench shoring jacks or held down by wire
anchored in the invert slab. The pipe can also be laid on concrete cradle blocks or block masonry units and the pipe wedged
in place with wood chocks installed at approximately 45 degrees
from the pipe to the walls of the trench. Adequate measures
must be taken to avoid floating the pipe or to deflect it laterally
when placing and consolidating the concrete. A tremie tube and
hopper should be used and the stream of concrete placed on
both sides of the pipeline at the same time. Filling the pipeline
with water reduces the tendency for it to float, but care must
still be taken to prevent lifting the pipe while consolidating
the concrete.

3-5.8 Pipe Laying and Jointing.

3-5.8.1 **General.** The Inspector must check the setting of the grade line in the trench for correct line and grade
shown on the grade sheet. If there is any deviation from a
straight line noticeable from sighting along the grade line for
three or more points, the contractor must adjust the line. While
pipe is being laid, the Inspector should observe the activities of
the pipelayer, making sure each pipe has full bearing and is
cradled in the subgrade or bedding material. (See Subsection
3-5.7.7 for bedding details.) When large diameter pipe is involved a template cut to the outside barrel of the pipe will facilitate preparation of the cradle in the bedding.

The Inspector must check the plans for locations of tees
and wyes for house connections. Tees should be located at the
station or to the nearest joint downstream of the house connection end. Wyes for house connections should be laid at the
nearest joint downstream of the house connection. When
specified on the plans, tees or wyes can be laid flat to provide
additional fall for long house connections.

All bell and spigot pipe should be laid upgrade, with the
bell ends of the pipe pointed upstream. If pipe laying is suspended for long periods of time (or overnight), the open ends of
the line must be temporarily capped until pipe laying is resumed.

Most types of mechanical compression joints require
thorough lubrication of the gasket and gasket contact surfaces
to reduce friction and facilitate closure of the joint or to avoid
damage or displacement of the gasket in gasketed joints. Loose
gaskets should be lubricated before installation. A gasket
should be installed by stretching it uniformly around the
circumference of the spigot and seating it in the groove. The

gasket should then be "relieved" by running a suitable tool under the gasket around the entire circumference of the pipe to be sure the gasket is of uniform volume around the circumference. It should be emphasized that gasketed joints are designed to very close tolerances, therefore cleanliness is essential. Surfaces of the bell and spigot in contact with the gasket during jointing should be thoroughly cleaned before application of the lubricant. The lubricant should be maintained free of any foreign matter.

The steel ring components of steel ring joints are sometimes required to be protected from exposure both inside and outside the joint. This is accomplished by the application of a fillet of an approved mastic type compound on the inside corner of the bell and spigot prior to the application of lubricant. The size of the fillet should be sufficient to allow bell and spigot to plow into the material during jointing to the extent and depth necessary to seal the bell ring from outside exposure and the spigot ring from inside exposure.

For larger diameter concrete pipe, joint spacing may be critical. Hardwood or metal spacers placed on the inside shoulder of the bell will facilitate control of the joint gap within the limits of the joint design and the line layout (usually shown on the shop drawings) during the laying operation.

The line layout must be utilized by the Inspector during construction to check the accuracy of the contractor's laying operation. Since all the pipe is pre-cast ahead of laying, joint spacing within the tolerance permitted must be controlled between manholes to avoid creep that will allow the pipe to encroach on the structure at the upper end. In addition, the pipe must be laid accurately to orient the invert of the pipe axially when elliptical steel cage reinforcement is involved.

Although large diameter pipe may be joined by swinging the boom of the crane, this method is not recommended especially for the all-concrete joint. One recommended method is by means of a "come-a-long" and "deadman" placed in a previously laid pipe. Initial entry of spigot into the bell may be facilitated by slightly raising the bell end of pipe being laid. After the initial entry of the spigot into the bell, the pipe should be brought straight home and not at an angle. One other, and equally recommended, method which will minimize the possibility of damage to the pipe or gasket during jointing is described as follows:

The cable sling is permitted to remain on the previously laid pipe. The new pipe is lowered into the excavation and with the bell (upper end) in an elevated position, the spigot is started into the previously laid pipe. A no-slack cable connection is made between the slings of the two pipes which, as the bell end of the new pipe is lowered to grade, effects a pull sufficient to compress the gasket and complete the full entry of the spigot into the bell of the previously laid pipe. If a substantial shock impact of bell face and spigot face occurs during initial entry, the Inspector should require an examination of the contact surfaces for fractures or spalls before jointing is allowed to continue.

After jointing is completed, a thin flexible L-shape metal feeler gauge may be used to check the position of the rubber gasket. The necessity for this operation is dependent on the method of jointing and conditions observed during the closure. It is possible to cut the gasket or roll it out of the spigot groove during the jointing operation and inspection at this point is important.

Line and grade of the outer end of the pipe and joint gap should be checked after completion of the jointing operation. A line should be pulled across a minimum of three pipes or stations for the line and grade check.

For steel ring joints, the outer joint space is frequently required to be filled with cement mortar. This is accomplished by first placing a band of waterproof paper or cloth diaper around the joint, then drawing it up tight with box strapping, thus providing a retainer for the mortar. A hole is cut at the top, slightly to one side of center. The joint should then be moistened and the mortar mixed to the consistency of thick cream poured into the joint recess on one side only and rodded into place until it appears on the opposite side. During the operation, check for leakage and settlement of mortar and require refilling if necessary. Backfill may be performed at once but flooding or jetting of the backfill should be delayed until mortar has set, about three hours.

The inside joint space of both steel ring and concrete bell and spigot pipe for sewers is usually filled with mortar and should be done after backfill and flooding has taken place. Mortar should be mixed to a stiff consistency, forced into the joint and finished flush (or slightly recessed) with a trowel.

The following precautions taken during the construction of a sewer pipeline will minimize the occurrence of poor joints and other defects and assure the performance and longevity of the improvements.

(1) Each length of pipe is checked for cracks and other damage and imperfections before laying. Reject pipe with any of the imperfections listed in the Standard Specifications.

(2) Insure that ends of the pipe are clean and joint components and contact surfaces are free of defects.

(3) When laying pipe having gasket joints, check to see that the type or shape, size and material is as specified or required.

(4) Insure that the allowable joint gap is not exceeded or that joint closure is made to the home mark or full depth of the socket, as applicable.

(5) Check to see that the pipe has full continuous bearing and cradling in the bedding or subgrade as it is laid.

(6) Allow no backfilling operation to proceed until the pipe is laid, bedded and jointed in accordance with the requirements and concrete has reached the age or strength requirements specified.

(7) See that care is used during the backfill operation to insure that the pipe is not disturbed.

(8) If the top of the pipe of any part of a sewer system is within 42 inches of the surface of the ground or roadway, it must be reinforced with concrete.

3-5.8.2 **House Connections.** House connection sewer laterals are usually included as part of the work to be done in addition to main line sewer construction under contracts and permits; and the requirements for excavation, laying, bedding and backfill shall be the same unless otherwise specified. Information in the following paragraphs applies to such construction. Individual house connection sewers may also be built under separate House Connection Permits issued by the Engineer. (See Subsection 3-7.)

All house connections are Type "A" (straight grade from mainline to upper end as designated by the Standard Plan), unless conditions warrant otherwise. Where a main sewer is 14 feet deep or over, the policy has been to permit a Type "C" house connection, with a chimney at the main line at least eight feet below the existing surface and a depth of at least four feet at the property line.

Pipe may be vitrified clay, cast iron or asbestos-cement (when tested and approved prior to use), and six inches in diameter. In easements across private property, pipe must be cast iron or vitrified clay with flexible joints.

Unless otherwise shown on plans, house connection sewers should be laid on a uniform grade of not less than two percent. The depth of the invert of the house connection at the property line shall be not less than four feet below the elevation of the top of the existing curb (or the proposed curb) unless a greater depth is required to serve the property. (See Plates 50 and 51, Appendix).

The upper end of each new house connection is sealed with a cap at property line. Actual connections to private house sewers are made under individual property line sewer connection permits issued at a later date after final inspection and acceptance of the main line and laterals. (See Subsection 3-7, Sewer and Storm Drain Connection Permits.)

Some project plans call for immediate connection to be made to existing house sewers, in which case separate house connection permits are not required. For example, a project may call for construction of a new main line and laterals, along with abandonment of existing main line and laterals, due to new freeway construction interfering with the sewer system. If the pipe diameters of the house sewer and the lateral differ, a proper fitting must be used. Connection must not be made by telescoping the smaller pipe into the larger pipe.

After the Inspector approves the pipe installation, the trench must be backfilled as soon as possible. After backfilling, the surface of such trenches in improved roadways and in driveway areas must be temporarily paved with two inches of bituminous premix material. In sidewalk areas the premix must be not less than one inch thick after compaction. The temporary pavement must be maintained by the contractor until the trench areas are permanently resurfaced.

Where house connections are constructed under a contract or permit, the Inspector must check to see that the plans indicate that a house connection is provided for every lot. All changes in house connection lengths must be accounted for and authorized by the Engineer. This is very important for assessment district projects in determining the correct amounts for assessment.

The letter "C" shown on plans near the lot number indicates that the Engineer has sent a postal card to the property owner and it has been returned with an approval of the location of the upper end of the house connection as shown on the plan. The Inspector cannot always rely on the card, however, as there may be a change of ownership. All house connection locations should be discussed with the property owners to insure that each location is to the best advantage for the owner. By his own authority, an Inspector may move a house connection up to five feet to avoid an object such as a tree, driveway or water meter. If a house connection is added, omitted or relocated more than five feet, the Inspector must get the owner (not a tenant) to sign a form entitled "Request for Change of House Connection Sewer," commonly called a "waiver." Relocation of a house connection is to be indicated on the form by omitting the house connection from the plan location and adding the house connection at the new location. A blind tee or wye must be installed in the main line, even if the house connection is to be omitted.

For all contract projects or permit construction, house connections may be added, omitted or relocated at distances greater than five feet from their plan stations only by a Change Order. Advance approval of the change by the Engineer may be secured by telephone, but it must be obtained prior to construction. In all instances a Change Order will be issued.

No more than three house connections on a single line may be relocated more than five feet from plan stations by waivers. Otherwise, the tracing for the plans must be revised to show the correct locations.

To indicate the property parcels participating in the sewer construction or assessment district, the designer encloses such parcels in a heavy dotted or solid black boundary line. Where this boundary line divides a single parcel into several parts, only that portion within the indicated boundary is participating. Portions of lots which cannot be served by the sewer provided by the plans or which are to be served by some future sewer, are sometimes excluded from the sewer district. The Inspector cannot permit the construction of a house connection to any property parcel which is not within the district shown, except by special arrangement with the Engineer's office.

A property owner MAY NOT on any type of project pay the contractor privately for an added house connection. For assessment district projects, the cost of such house connections will be computed for the Change Order by the Engineer at unit prices, and assessed or credited against each parcel affected. Similarly, house connections to property parcels not within the participating boundaries of subdivision permit construction may be subject to special fees or conditions.

The depth of each house connection invert at the property line should be accurately checked. If it is laid higher than called for by the plans, a building at the rear of a deep lot may not be provided with proper drainage.

All house connection sewers 10 feet long or longer, shall be laid by means of a taut grade line at the tops of the bells from the ⅛ bend to the upper end of the lateral. Inspectors should check line with a level before any pipe is laid, to see that there is at least ¼ inch fall to the foot.

A swab must be pulled through a house connection laid with mortar joints, and then the upper end tightly capped so that it will not leak. The method used for capping is described in the Standard Specifications.

Where running sand, ground water or other difficult laying conditions are encountered, the contractor may be permitted to lay the ⅛ bend and the first pipe of the house connection when the main line is laid.

The Project Inspector must not record the laying of any house connection unless he personally has seen and approved it before it was backfilled.

In addition to careful inspection during construction, the Inspector should use mirrors or lights to examine completed lines. He should instruct the contractor to wash the lines to clear them of dirt and other construction debris.

A subdivision permit will occasionally include a few feet of house connection sewer, presumably to be installed to an existing main line sewer in the street. This case usually arises when the unimproved half of an already partially improved street is being constructed. Usually no sewer plan for these house connections is prepared and the connections are not shown on the street plan. In the absence of any plan requirement, it may appear that there is no obligation on the part of the Inspector to insure that such house connections are installed. As a matter of good policy, however, the Inspector should check to determine whether or not the house connections are actually required. If so, he should see that they are installed either as a part of the permit or under separate house connection permits. This policy follows the general obligation to see that all underground construction is completed prior to paving the streets.

3-5.8.3 Saddles. When no wye or tee exists on a main line sewer and a house connection is to be constructed, a special pipe fitting called a saddle is utilized to make the connection. As the name implies, the spigot end is especially shaped to fit snugly against a hole cut in the main line sewer. These saddles are plastered with cement mortar on the inside and outside of the pipe junction.

As a general rule, when saddles are required in new or existing main line sewers, they are to be installed by the contractor only when continuous inspection is being provided the Agency, as would be the case for cash contracts, assessment district projects or permit projects. Agency sewer maintenance forces install saddles whenever required for work being constructed under a sewer house connection permit.

Experience has demonstrated that care must be exercised in constructing saddles to eliminate projections into the main line, such as extruded mortar or jointing compound, which would collect debris from the sewage and ultimately obstruct the sewer.

Where saddles are to be installed in conjunction with sewer house connection permits, the contractor must excavate to the main line at the location where the connection is to be made and make the excavation safe in accordance with the applicable State Safety Orders before Agency forces will install any saddle.

Saddles are readily available in pipe sizes ranging from four to eight inches and may be obtained for larger pipe sizes from the pipe manufacturer on special order.

When cutting the opening into main line pipe for the installation of a saddle, care must be taken to prevent cracking or breaking the pipe. If the pipe is cracked or broken, that length of pipe must be removed and a new wye or tee branch fitting installed in its place. It is standard procedure to use a core drill or rotary masonry drill to cut a series of holes in a circular pattern or to use a masonry saw to cut a "V" notch in the pipe. These openings are carefully dressed to fit the saddle by gentle trimming with small chisels or special dressing tools. All pipe chips must be removed from the bottom of dry main line pipe. If the saddle is being installed on a live sewer, a means must be provided to prevent the chips from falling into the sewage.

3-5.9 Manhole Construction.

3-5.9.1 **General.** The two basic types of manhole structures used in Agency work, either brick or pre-cast concrete, are detailed on Standard Plans and the Inspector is cautioned to review such Standard Plans before inspecting manhole construction. He should not attempt to rely on his memory for details.

As a general rule, concrete bottom slabs for manholes will be placed at least 24 hours before any brick is laid thereon. If a large quantity of ground water is encountered, this requirement may be varied to suit the existing conditions. With the water level kept below the bottom of the base by continuous pumping, the base slab is laid, using concrete with a slump of two inches or less or containing an approved accelerator. As soon as the concrete has set, three or four feet of the manhole may be built and plastered, and the second bottom constructed. The water level must be kept down below the manhole bottom while the plaster and concrete are setting. The remainder of the manhole should not be built until the next day.

Close attention should be given to every detail on the Standard Plans. Channel details should be constructed with care for depth, slope of the shelves toward the channel and dense troweling. Brick arches must be turned over the inlet and outlet pipes to protect the embedded pipe from crushing from the weight of the manhole walls. Excavation for manhole structures must be at least six inches greater in all dimensions to permit the plastering of the exterior brickwork. When the depth exceeds 22 feet, the diameter of the manhole and the wall thickness are increased and a larger bottom slab is required. (See Standard Plans.)

The Inspector should closely watch the plastering of the outside of manholes. The Inspector should insist upon dense, full ½-inch thickness of plaster coating.

All brick should be well moistened with water before being used in manhole construction. When mixing mortar for manhole construction, the cement and sand may be carefully measured into a mortar box in lieu of a requiring one-cubic-foot measuring box.

When installing a pipe stub in a manhole for future extension of the sewer line, the Inspector must carefully check the alignment and invert grade of the stub. Improperly placed stubs require expensive manhole remodeling when future sewers are constructed.

Steps are usually not required in Agency work and maintenance forces use portable ladders.

Manhole frames and covers may be adjusted to pavement elevation either before or after the trench resurfacing pavement is laid. The manhole must be constructed so that the center of the cover is exactly on the plan station and centered over the center line of the sewer. Changes in station or offset distance from the center line can be made only upon the prior approval of the Engineer.

3-5.9.2 **Precast Concrete Manholes.** Precast concrete manholes are usually specified for local (residential) sewers where it is unlikely that corrosive conditions will develop in the sewer. Listing of the standard plans for both types of manholes on the project plans will be sufficient to allow the contractor the option of providing either type.

Concrete bottoms are placed as described for brick manholes except that in most cases the channels are constructed integrally with the bottom (base slab), thus eliminating the usual second bottom (channels and shelves) procedure.

Where the entire bottom is to be cast as a single unit and it is intended that channels not be stripped for finishing, the forming and the resultant concrete surfaces shall be equal to the quality of a trowelled finish. Irregularities, such as holes, fins and offsets projecting or indented from the finished surface, must be corrected by grinding or patching with approved epoxy or epoxy-bonded mortar.

All precast manhole components should be checked for configuration, dimension, thickness and damage as they are delivered and before they are set.

The following general criteria should guide the Inspector in making a judgment relative to damage:

(1) Components, with the exception of flat-tops, are essentially unreinforced. Therefore, cracks through the wall shall be cause for rejection.

(2) Any spall of such an extent that a proper joint seal between components cannot be accomplished shall be cause for rejection.

(3) Minor spalls (less than one inch in depth) on the interior may be repaired with epoxy-bonded mortar patches finished to match the contour and surface texture of the original unit. Minor spalls on the exterior need not be repaired.

Precast manholes are stacked in sections with a bedding of mortar between each section. The sections are four feet in inside diameter and can be supplied in various lengths so that the top of the manhole can be set to approximate surface grade. An off-set, tapered cone, reducing the diameter from 48 to 30 inches, is then set and the fine grade adjustments are made with precast 30-inch diameter rings so that a 30 to 24-inch reducer, when set at the top, will bring the frame and cover to exact surface grade. Other reducing components are available to accommodate 27- and 30-inch manholes.

The correct assembly of a pre-cast manhole involves the establishment of a level base and the proper jointing of the components which will result in a plumb and watertight structure.

A level base is best accomplished by placing and finishing the concrete to a base ring established at the proper elevation in the trench. The difficulty of installation is increased and the quality deteriorates where dependence is placed on mortar to correct major irregularities in the base. All contact surfaces involved in the jointing should be thoroughly cleaned prior to the application of joint sealing material. The base should be moist prior to the application of the mortar leveling bed.

3-5.10   Trench Backfill and Flooding.

3-5.10.1   **General.** The contractor must take the necessary measures to protect his work at all times, particularly during backfilling operations. Backfill shall be considered as starting one foot over the top of the pipe or at the top of the concrete bedding over the pipe. Below this point is bedding.

For pipe 24 inches in diameter or smaller, the pipe should be covered by hand methods one foot over the top of the pipe, using soft earth that is free of large rocks. This operation, referred to as "shading the pipe," is done to avoid damage or breakage of the pipe from rocks or other hard objects falling into the trench.

Rocks greater than six inches in any dimension will not be permitted in backfill placed between one foot above the top of any pipe or box and one foot below pavement subgrade. When the trench is wider than three feet, rocks not exceeding 12 inches in greatest dimension, which originate from the trench, will be permitted in the backfill from one foot above the top of any pipe or box to five feet below the finished surface. Rocks greater than 2½ inches in any dimension will not be permitted in the backfill within 12 inches of pavement subgrade. Broken concrete and asphalt pavement originating from the trench may be placed in the backfill, subject to the same size limitations as rock.

Backfill may be made in one or more lifts, depending on the depth of trench and method of flooding or compaction to be used. Trenches may be backfilled in lifts not exceeding 15 feet for jetting. (See Subsection 3-5.10.2.) Before backfilling is begun, the Inspector should measure and enter in his records the extent of cave-ins under the sidewalk or pavement for future repair by the contractor.

Trench shores must remain in place during backfilling operations. Jacks or struts may be removed from the bottom as the top of the backfill material threatens to cover them. Under certain conditions, especially in heavy ground, it may be necessary to leave some timbering in place until the flooding or compaction is completed. In heavy ground, where structures such as manholes are not yet constructed by the time the main line trench is backfilled, sets of timbers and jacks should remain on both sides of the manhole excavation while the manhole is being constructed.

Caution should be taken when backfilling tunnels, whether they are to be flooded and the top barred down, vee'd and flooded, mechanically tamped or backfilled with gunite. Regardless of the backfill method, after compaction the entire excavation for tunnels must be completely filled and free of voids. Whenever the project plans, Special Provisions or encroachment permit requires special compaction of trench backfill, the contractor shall apply in writing to the Engineer for approval of the compacting equipment he proposes to use. Compaction of trench backfill shall not proceed until such approval is received by the Inspector.

After the trench has been backfilled, the contractor should remove the excess spoil dirt and clean the street as soon as possible, especially if the job is in a business or residential area.

3-5.10.2 Trench Jetting. Trench backfill must be consolidated by jetting unless other methods of compaction are required by the plans or Special Provisions. During jetting operations, jets must be used at close intervals along the trench in such a manner that sufficient water to lubricate and consolidate the fill reaches all parts of the backfill, and all of the backfill material is saturated and caused to settle. Care must be exercised so that the sewer pipe is not damaged by the jetting operation.

A jet ordinarily consists of a pipe to which a 2-inch diameter hose is attached at its upper end, utilizing conventional pipe fittings or swivel fittings. The jet pipe should be not less than 1½-inch steel pipe and its length should be approximately two feet shorter than the depth of the lift of backfill being compacted. It should be used with a continuous supply of water.

The jet pipe should be kept at least two feet away from the pipeline since the bedding may be washed from under the pipe, causing settlement or breakage. The probability of this kind of damage decreases as the size of the pipe increases. Only that amount of water should be used which is necessary to consolidate the backfill. The intention is to flood the trench from the bottom, controlling the water so as to keep it under ground until an area has been saturated, before moving the jet.

Different soils require different methods of compaction. A problem in jetting is sometimes created by unconsolidated backfill that has been exposed to traffic or rain. The surface may have been wetted and packed while the lower portion of the backfill might not have been affected by the rain water or traffic. Those crusts which develop at the top of the trench must be broken down. The Inspector must examine the trench as flooding progresses to see that all of the backfill material has settled and that no crusts or "bridges" remain.

Covers of downstream manholes should be removed when jetting so that the amount of water that enters the sewer lines and structures from the jetting operations may be observed. All visible leaks must be repaired.

When water is observed passing through the manholes during jetting, the Inspector should determine where the leaks are in the pipeline system. Common sources of leaks are cracked pipe, faulty joints, poorly sealed caps in tees or house connection ends and permeable walls of manhole structures. All visible leaks, detected by the Inspector, must be repaired by the contractor. Repair of small diameter pipe almost invariably involves re-excavation. Excess sweating or visible leaks in manhole walls must be repaired by excavating outside of the structure to the depth necessary, thoroughly cleaning the surface and replastering the area.

Cracked or broken pipe must be replaced.

If the source of the infiltration is not discernible and the quantity of infiltration water appears to be in excess of the maximum prescribed in the Standard Specifications, the Inspector should consult with his Supervisor for instructions.

Final Inspectors are provided with weirs for measuring infiltration in sewers and, upon request, will determine the acceptability of sewers in this respect during jetting operations. Sewers in wet ground will be checked with a weir as routine procedure during final inspection of the work.

3-5.11 Air Testing Sewers. After backfilling and jetting operations have been completed and the lines have been balled and cleaned, an air pressure test is made to determine if the sewer is serviceable and has not been damaged during installation. The contractor should provide all materials, equipment and labor for making the test. Each section of the sewer should be tested between successive manholes. The method for air testing is outlined in detail in the Standard Specifications.

Serious defects in the system are quickly revealed by a rapid drop in pressure or inability to attain any pressure at all. These defects are usually due to broken pipes or bells, or a poorly installed house connection plug. Slow leaks which permit a more rapid decrease in pressure than allowed by the specifications are usually due to cracked pipe, poor joints or joints which have been pulled too much in curves.

The exact location of these defects can be detected by a double diaphragmed device which is pulled through the main line and which can pressure test each length of pipe between manholes. The pull rope is graduated so that the exact location of a defect can be determined by taking the distance indicated on the pull rope and adding or subtracting this distance to the manhole station.

Defects must be repaired before the line can be accepted by the Agency. If a defect appears to be at a wye or tee, it is more than likely due to an improperly installed plug at the end of the house connection.

Procedural Requirements

(1) Permanent resurfacing will normally be withheld pending completion of the air test.

(2) Job record entries of air test results shall be underlined in red.

(3) It is not intended that a new pipeline be air tested if it is installed as an extension of an existing pipeline or if other live line conditions exist between manholes.

(4) The gauge utilized for the test shall be of a scale and range equivalent to 2.5 inch diameter, 0-10 psi range (0.2 psi maximum increments). Gauges supplied by the contractor shall be tested for accuracy by the Agency or shall have a current certification of accuracy from an approved testing agency and shall be carefully examined for damage.

3-5.12 Resurfacing. Trench resurfacing is usually accomplished in two phases: the placement and maintenance of temporary resurfacing until all settlement has occurred and the replacement of the permanent pavement. Ordinarily, temporary resurfacing is placed after jetting or after the backfill is compacted by other methods.

Sometimes it may be necessary to place some temporary resurfacing before any jetting has been done, such as in providing access to business establishments where the backfill material may not adequately support the traffic without rutting. These reaches of trenches must be temporarily resurfaced again after jetting. It is the duty of the Inspector and the responsibility of the contractor to insure that all trench areas are maintained in good condition for traffic until the permanent resurfacing has been installed.

Heavy equipment used for trenching or backfilling often damage paved street areas adjacent to the trench. A conflict sometimes arises between the contractor and the Inspector as to the type and thickness of pavement to be replaced in the damaged areas which are outside the limits of the trench but immediately adjacent to it. Where existing pavement, either adjacent to a trench or within the area of his operations, has been broken by the contractor, it must be replaced with pavement of a thickness equal to the existing pavement; provided, however, that such resurfacing is made upon a subgrade which has not been disturbed by the contractor. In cases where the subgrade has been disturbed by the contractor, such as a cave-in of the trench walls, the resurfacing of both the trench area and the caved-in area shall be of the thickness specified on the plans. (See also Subsection 3-4.3.6 Trench Resurfacing.)

Dirt and debris are occasionally deposited in the manhole structures and to some extent in the adjacent reaches of sewer and storm drain pipe, usually as a result of the resetting of manhole frames and covers to pavement grades or from grading operations prior to the paving of streets. The following procedure is to be observed in an attempt to eliminate the damage to these installations and the problems arising from a stoppage therein.

The Inspector responsible for the subgrade operations will cause the contractor to remove all manhole covers within the grading area and will personally inspect each manhole in the presence of a responsible representative of the contractor. All dirt or debris found therein shall be removed prior to acceptance of the grade for paving. Should such debris not be removed at the time the grade is completed and checked, the Inspector will issue a Notice of Non-Compliance to the contractor and promptly advise the Dispatcher of this condition by telephone. Paving inspection will not be provided until the manhole structures are satisfactorily cleaned.

The Inspector assigned to paving or resurfacing operations will determine for himself that all manholes have been cleaned by verifying with the Dispatcher that the grade has been approved for paving and by spot checking the structures himself upon arriving at the jobsite.

After paving or resurfacing is completed, the Final Inspector will check each manhole structure to insure that there is no dirt or debris in the manhole structures or reaches of pipe between structures.

When bituminous trench resurfacing is placed in more than one course, the base course shall be constructed with a uniform surface to a minimum of one inch below the elevation of the finished surface, to insure uniform compaction and eliminate unnecessary "skin patching."

The Inspector must require that the contractor use equipment and methods which will result in a good riding surface when resurfacing is completed.

3-5.13 Records and Reports.   The preparation of sewer records and reports is described in Plate 9, Appendix. However, there are several standard procedures utilized by the Agency to provide continuity between the several Inspectors who may be assigned to a single sewer project during its construction.

First, an approved plan signed by the Engineer must be on the project before work can be started. A yellow crayon or pencil is used by each Inspector to color the appropriate portion of the mainline, house connection or manhole on the plan as the pipe is laid or structure built. In a similar manner, jetting can be recorded with a red crayon or pencil. The Inspector will note on the plans the stations at which the tees, blind tees and upper ends of house connections are actually laid.

This procedure discloses at a glance what pipe or structures remain to be constructed or jetted. The date on which the work is done is also recorded on the plan.

It is also standard procedure for an Inspector being relieved (or who is taken sick, etc.) to have his marked plan delivered to the Inspector who relieves him. The relief Inspector can pick up the work intelligently and effectively from an up-to-date, properly marked laying plan. Similarly, work copies of record sheets should be kept up to date and delivered to a relief Inspector.

3-5.14   Sewer Construction Checklist.

General and Preliminary

(1) See Subsection 1-1.4.2, Project Inspector's checklist.

(2) Check plan requirements, utilities and other substructures, pipe materials, joints, bedding, traffic requirements. Are shop drawings required?

(3) Are utilities located and marked at the site (actual location of pipelines containing hazardous materials such as natural gas and gasoline) determined by potholing at frequent intervals?

(4) Has an excavation permit been issued to the contractor by CAL/OSHA?

(5) Construction survey staking complete? Grade sheets on job? Off-set distance sufficient for protection?

(6) What do soil borings indicate? Groundwater? Wellpoints required? Proper provisions for disposal of water? Soil stability for shoring?

(7) What are access to property requirements? Temporary bridges required?

(8) Are street closures authorized? Interested agencies (police, fire, other) notified? Property owners?

(9) Temporary traffic signs, delineators and barricades in place?

(10) Pipe stored properly?

(11) Provisions for surface drainage? Gutters clear?

(12) If joint is made to existing pipe or structure, what provisions are made for: 1. Preventing debris from entering existing system? 2. Protection from sewer gas?

Trenching

(1) See Subsections 3-3.2.2 (Clearing and Grubbing Checklist) and 3-3.3.7 (Excavation, General Checklist).

(2) Check for maximum trench width.

(3) Line and grade control satisfactory?

(4) Does actual soil condition agree with plan? Is approved shoring method adequate for actual trench condition?

(5) Is spoil bank clear of trench? Is it encroaching into required traffic lanes or private property?

(6) Have dirt waivers been received for stockpiling on private property?

(7) Check subgrade. Is it firm? Is it granular or will imported bedding material be required?

(8) Check trench for evidence of unconsolidated fill. (If in the trench bottom, it may require additional excavation. If located above pipe invert, it may require mechanical compaction in lieu of jetting.)

(9) Is temporary support of existing utilities and improvements being provided? In event of damage, are owners promptly notified?

(10) Are sufficient ladders being provided?

Pipe Laying

(1) All loose soil removed from the trench?

(2) Required granular bedding material and thickness provided? Shaped to cradle the pipe?

(3) Excavation provided for projecting bells?

(4) Method of transferring line grade into trench accurate? Checked through 3 points for grade and alignment?

(5) Provisions for increased bedding at location where maximum trench width is exceeded?

(6) Pipe handling satisfactory? Not being damaged?

(7) Is each pipe checked for damage before lowering into trench?

(8) Is ground water being controlled adequately (maintained below rock bedding invert until any concrete bedding has set)?

(9) Jointing of pipe satisfactory? Gaskets and contact surface of mechanical compression joints lubricated as necessary and required? Maximum joint gap not exceeded? Joint closure to homemark or full depth of socket (when applicable)? Sleeve type coupling bands tightened to required (or recommended) torque? Is joint mortar or mastic seal required?

(10) Wyes and tee's accurately located and measured? All lots or properties provided for?

(11) In-place pipeline checked for line and grade regularly during laying with light or mirror?

(12) Has additional bedding (if required) been placed alongside and under the haunches of the pipe after laying? Is the bedding (concrete or granular) rodded or spaced so that it completely fills all the space in the trench?

(13) Is pipeline "shaded" with finer soil material, carefully placed? (Backfilled to one foot over top of pipe with sand if trench backfill is mechanically compacted.)

Trench Backfill and Jetting (or compaction)

(1) Does concrete and brickwork have sufficient set to avoid damage (special concrete mix for "early backfill")?

(2) Are all support walls or beams for existing utilities or other improvements installed?

(3) Are abandoned pipes and conduits bricked up or sealed (if required)?

(4) See pipe laying item (12) above.

(5) Check for maximum lift thickness for jetting or mechanical compaction.

(6) Is jet pipe size and length satisfactory? Is water supply adequate?

(7) Spacing of jet pipe adequate? Is trench backfill saturated from top to bottom (last two-three feet dry, mounded and rolled)?

(8) Is lower manhole open to check for leakage during jetting?

(9) Is required thickness of temporary paving spread and rolled?

Manholes and Structures

(1) Is excavation size sufficient for working room? Sloped back or shored?

(2) Is grading for bottom or invert slab, completed before reinforcing steel is placed (if required)? All loose earth removed, firm and unyielding?

(3) Is concrete not less than 24 hours old before brickwork is laid or pre-cast units are set?

(4) Review requirements with manhole builder.

(5) Do pipe and pipe joints at the manhole provide for flexibility as required (see Standard Plan)?

(6) Are pipe stubs required and installed accurately?

(7) Is brickwork laid with full head and bed joints? Arches turned over all pipes? Shape of manhole satisfactory; vertical wall height, taper (without "bottleneck")? Opening size at top?

(8) Check channels and shelves for dimension, slope and finish.

(9) Check pre-cast manhole assembly. Correct shape, size, concentric or eccentric as required? Mortar joints between unit and at bottom?

(10) Check frames and covers for compliance. Does cover seat in frame properly without rocking? Inner cover required? Locking cover required?

Miscellaneous and Testing

(1) Are all house connections completed? Depth and location at property line checked?

(2) Is air pressure testing required? Completed prior to permanent resurfacing?

(3) Are temporary paving, lights and barricades adequate for traffic maintained until completion of permanent resurfacing?

(4) Have sewer wye records been completed and forwarded to the office?

(5) Restoration and repair of improvements completed? Curbs, walks, paving, parkway lawns?

(6) Manholes, catch basins and sewer clean and free of debris? Sewer bypasses and plugs removed?

(7) Has notice to Final Inspector, listing uncompleted work, been prepared?

3-6 STORM DRAIN CONSTRUCTION

3-6.1 General. As the name implies, storm drains are constructed primarily to collect and control water resulting from rainfall. However, these drains perform a useful function all year long by intercepting other intermittent sources of water such as lawn sprinkling, broken water lines or other water wasted or pumped into a street gutter, thereby preventing much damage to pavement and the nuisance of wet gutters and intersections.

In this subsection, several types of substructures will be discussed, including pipe systems, cast-in-place concrete box (or channel) systems, culverts and subdrain systems.

The Inspector should have a thorough understanding of Subsection 3-5 Sewer Construction and particularly the subsections dealing with excavation and bedding; pipe laying and jointing; and backfill and jetting; all of which apply to storm drain pipelines.

The structures and catch basins utilized for storm drains are generally unique to the type of construction. Box conduits are frequently utilized because of the demand for large capacities and to solve installation problems involving limited vertical dimensions.

Corrugated steel pipe (CSP) and pipe arches and corrugated aluminum pipe (CAP) and arches are used for all types of drains including down drains, subdrains and culverts. The flexibility of CSP and CAP requires installation techniques and precautions that differ from those associated with concrete pipe.

Information concerning storm drain connection permits may be found in Subsection 3-7.

3-6.2   Definition of Terms.   (See also Subsection 3-5.2.)

Terms and nomenclature common in the construction of storm drain installations are defined here:

Catch Basin. A rectangular concrete box constructed below grade to collect surface water and discharge it into a drain system.

Culvert. A drain intended to convey water under an improvement (such as a roadway or sidewalk).

Local Depression. A warped surface of gutter or pavement which diverts water flow more efficiently into an adjacent catch basin inlet.

Stulls. A wood or steel strut placed inside pipe and wedged snugly to preserve its shape and to prevent damage to the pipe from handling or backfill stresses.

Subdrain. A drain intended to collect subsurface water through continuous perforations therein or open joints and convey it to a disposal point.

T. A mark in the form of a letter "T" painted or imprinted on the inside of a reinforced concrete pipe on the minor axis of elliptical steel reinforcement of the pipe.

3-6.3   Concrete Pipe Storm Drains.   Most storm drain pipe is fabricated of concrete. Cast concrete pipe can be reinforced or unreinforced and is usually supplied with tongue and groove, self-centering, joints; although it is available in many different joint designs. Reinforced concrete pipe is inspected at the point of manufacture and marked with a rubber stamp inside each length. The stamp indicates the name of the Agency, batch number, Inspector's name and the date the pipe was made (See Subsection 2-7.4.9).

Shop drawings and line layouts are not required for concrete pipe storm drains except for pipe on curves. On long radius curves, "pulled" joints may be used within the joint gap tolerances permitted by the specifications. Shorter lengths and mitered pipe may be necessary for short radius curves. The use of straight pipe and collars at the open joints is discouraged as a method of laying pipe on curves for Agency work.

Concrete pipe delivered to the jobsite should be examined by the Inspector for damage from handling or transporting. Such pipe must be carefully handled and not permitted to be dropped or rolled against other pipes when storing it on the site. Pipe which shows cracks or damage beyond the specification tolerances must be rejected. Concrete pipe must be lifted by one or more slings around the barrel of the pipe, never by threading a sling through the pipe.

When rock mattress, rock subdrains and concrete cradle are separate bid items, the Inspector must keep exact records of the amount used, its thickness and location by stations.

The minor axis of the elliptical steel reinforcement of reinforced concrete pipe over 18 inches in diameter, is marked with a "T." Such pipe must be installed with the "T" at the top or the bottom (flow line) of the pipe.

Catch basin hardware such as gratings, bulb angles, protection rods, manhole ring and cover sets, anchor bolts and steps should be checked for conformity to the requirements of the plans and Standard Plans. Non-conforming items must be rejected.

When laying lock-joint pipe (pipe having a steel ring forming the contact face of the bell and a rubber gasket in a groove on the spigot end), it is necessary to use a spacer between a previously laid pipe and the pipe being laid in order to gauge the correct caulking space indicated for the approved joint design. If the caulking space is too narrow, difficulty will be encountered in obtaining a satisfactorily caulked joint. Pipe should be laid to maintain a smooth flow line. All offsets resulting from slight diameter variances or shell thickness (within the specified tolerances) should occur at the soffit of the pipe.

3-6.4 Corrugated Steel Pipe (CSP) and Corrugated Aluminum Pipe (CAP) Drains. The trench for corrugated pipe should be kept as narrow as possible to allow for the alignment of the pipe, installation of band couplers and to permit tamping under the haunches and other backfilling operations.

Bedding conditions require that the pipe be cradled in the bedding as it is laid, which does not differ from the requirements for other types of pipe. (See Subsection 3-5.7.7.) However, except for shallow cover installations in easements, most installations require additional bedding or earth to be placed and mechanically compacted under the haunches and adjacent to the pipe as indicated in the above-mentioned subsections.

Care must be exercised in handling the pipe to keep the ends free of dents and to protect the pipes that have coatings and paved inverts.

Before installation, the Inspector should determine that the specified material is being supplied. The manufacturer must supply a certificate attesting to the gauge of the metal when the stamp on the pipe has been obliterated by coatings. There is a variety of corrugated pipe and types of joints available. In some cases, the pipeline will be under head pressure, such as in a siphon, in which case the Engineer might specify continuously welded pipe and band couplers with rubber gaskets or other provision for watertight joints.

When the pipe is to be installed in deep fills, the specifications may require that the pipe be elongated vertically (usually not to exceed 5 percent). This is accomplished by having the pipe fabricated in this manner or by strutting the pipe with stulls in the field as it is being installed.

If the contractor elects to jack the pipe, when it is not required by the plans, he must supply increased strength in the pipe to withstand the jacking loads.

During the pipe laying, the Inspector should observe that the gap between the pipe lengths does not exceed that allowable and that the band couplers are centered on the joints. Failure to observe either of these conditions will weaken the joint and make it susceptible to failure.

Laps of all circumferential seams should be installed so that the corrugations of the inside laps are pointed down stream. Longitudinal seams should be placed at the sides of the pipe, never on the bottom.

During backfill and compaction adjacent to the pipe, the Inspector should check that the pipe is not damaged or deformed in excess of the elongation required by the plans. Do not permit heavy equipment to pass over the pipeline until the cover over the pipe is adequate to distribute the load.

3-6.5 Cast-In-Place Storm Drain Conduit. The subgrade for cast-in-place conduits must be firm and unyielding and be made and checked with the same degree of accuracy that is exercised in making pavement subgrades. A templet of the required depth and shape should be used in checking the subgrade. Low places may be brought to subgrade elevation with pea gravel, compacted crushed aggregate base or concrete.

Where steel reinforcement is specified in drain walls or slabs, it should be carefully placed to plan requirements, rigidly tied and securely held in place to prevent its displacement during the concrete placing and consolidating operations. Care must be taken to insure that slab steel is adequately suspended or blocked up to prevent settlement of the blocks into the subgrade, with the result that the reinforcement steel will be out of plan location when embedded in concrete. The Inspector should be familiar with Subsection 3-12 reinforced concrete structures, which is directly applicable to reinforced concrete box conduit inspection. Subsection 3-11 also applies.

3-6.6 Storm Drain Structures. Storm drain structures such as manholes, catch basins and junction structures are usually cast-in-place. Details of these and other structures are set forth in the appropriate Standard Plans or on the project plans. Subsection 3-12 is generally applicable to cast-in-place concrete storm drain structures.

Depth of a catch basin outlet is shown on the plan as "V" and indicates the vertical distance from the top of the curb to the invert of the outlet.

A three-inch radius is required at the junction of the inside of a catch basin wall and an outlet pipe. A plaster fillet must be used to form this radius, and chipping or dressing of the concrete after casting is not permitted. A serious loss in hydraulic capacity of the outlet results if these edges are left sharp. The interior of all cast structures must be free of projections, fins, rough form texture and other irregularities which tend to increase the hydraulic friction factor and reduce the efficiency of the conduit.

The construction plans for a storm drain usually indicate (by a small circle) where to locate the manhole frame and cover for each junction structure and catch basin. If this is not shown on the plans, the Inspector will have it placed against the back wall or against one of the end walls and near the opening of the outlet pipe, but always so that an unbroken vertical line of steps can be placed without offsets. Additional steel reinforcement bars must be used under the manhole frames as shown on the Standard Plans.

The curved sections of the end walls and front wall at the inlet area of a side-opening catch basin must be constructed using curved forms. Omission of curved forms and subsequent chipping and plastering to the required radius is not permitted.

Catch basin construction should take place in the following sequence: first, the walls, with the back and end walls brought up to the elevation of the bottom surface of the top slab. If the top slab will be within the limits of a proposed sidewalk, the top slab must be constructed with the sidewalk rather than only to the perimeter of the catch basin. Transverse plastic control joints are placed in the walk in line with the outer edges of the end walls of the catch basin (see Plate 12, Appendix). The front wall must be constructed 10 to 12 inches below the gutter flow line grade, so that the curved section at the top of the front wall can be constructed with the adjacent concrete gutter or local depression area.

After removal of forms for the walls, the floor of the catch basin is constructed. It is possible to construct the walls and floor in one monolithic operation if the forms for the walls are constructed so as not to interfere with proper trowelling of the floor.

Top slab soffit forms for shallow cast-in-place culverts are often difficult to remove after the culverts are built. They must be supported on collapsible elements which can be easily removed, generally by using shims and wedges with wires securely attached to permit their easy removal.

Asphalt-impregnated building paper ("tar paper") must not be used to cover soffit forms to facilitate form stripping on shallow culverts. This material ultimately sags and blocks the culvert and is very difficult for Agency maintenance forces to remove. Such forms may be covered only with untreated paper which will soften and wash away when wet.

3-6.7 Subdrains and Culverts. Subdrains are commonly used to collect seepage that originates in filled ground or in areas where the water table is so high that it may endanger surface improvements. Perforated pipe, fabricated of corrugated metal, plastic or asbestos-cement effectively collects subsurface water and conveys it to a disposal system.

Unless otherwise specified on the plans, the pipe is to be installed with the perforations turned down to minimize the amount of silt which may filter in with the water, thereby silting up the conduit and clogging the perforations. To be most effective, perforated pipe should be laid in a gravel bedding which entirely surrounds the pipe.

Corrugated metal pipe is frequently specified for culvert construction or for installation on very steep grades. It is not uncommon for such pipe to be slightly curved (warped) due to the stresses built into it during fabrication. Where this occurs, the contractor must use struts against the trench walls or tamp backfill into the trench in such a manner as to remove horizontal curvature. Vertical curvature is frequently encountered with elliptical pipe sections. This curvature can be corrected by staking the high reaches down or by prudent placement and loading of the pipe with backfill material. (See Subsection 3-6.4 for additional details concerning corrugated metal pipe.)

Some large corrugated metal pipe sections are available for assembly in place, utilizing pre-formed plates which are bolted together. Bolt holes are pre-punched for the use of carriage bolts with the nuts on the outside of the plates. Stulls or struts are required to support the arch of such conduits during the placement and compaction of backfill over them.

3-6.8 Storm Drain Inspection Records. The records of storm drain construction are to be maintained on a form entitled "Construction Inspector's Job Report for Storm Drains."

3-6.9 Storm Drain Checklist.

3-6.9.1 General.

(1) It is important that the Inspector supplement this checklist with Subsection 3-5.14, Sewer Construction Checklist, which is applicable to storm drains, in most respects.

(2) Is tongue and groove pipe being laid with tongue end of pipe in the direction of flow?

(3) Is the "T" being oriented at the top (soffit) or bottom (invert) when concrete pipe with elliptical cage reinforcing is laid?

(4) Is concrete pipe being laid with proper joint space for caulking?

(5) Check for proper spur details for connection of laterals.

(6) Are curves being laid in accordance with the plan requirements? Is bevelled pipe required? Are pulled joints permitted? What is the maximum joint space allowed?

(7) Check for proper corrugated metal pipe (CSP or CAP) and joint materials. Gauge of metal? Band couplers, style, width, gaskets or other requirements for watertight joints (if required)? End pieces?

(8) Check laying of corrugated metal pipe for proper location of longitudinal laps (at side) and circumferential lap (inside lap in same direction as the flow). Is space between adjoining pipes within that allowable? Is band coupler centered on joint?

(9) Is corrugated metal pipe strutted or elongated before backfilling (if required)? Is backfill material compacted under haunches and along side of the pipe? Check that method of compaction does not deform pipe beyond the requirements for strutting or elongation.

(10) Check to see that heavy equipment does not cross over corrugated metal pipe or other pipe until there is sufficient backfill to distribute load.

(11) Check for proper catch basin hardware. Gratings? Manhole ring and covers? Are protection bars required?

(12) Is catch basin wall thickness per plan? Check slope of invert slab.

(13) Check concrete lateral connection and collars for complete stripping and finish on the interior.

(14) Is provision made for constructing catch basin deck with sidewalk construction?

(15) Are forms for sidewalk culverts and other shallow culverts designed for satisfactory removal after placing concrete?

3-7 SEWER AND STORM DRAIN CONNECTION PERMITS

3-7.1 General. Laterals branching from a main line sewer to individual lots are generally constructed under a subdivision permit or an assessment act contract. Each lateral is temporarily capped at property line. Subsequently, when the house sewer is to be connected to the lateral at property line, a sewer connection permit issued by the Agency is required. A permit is also required for the construction, remodeling or repair of all or any portion of a sewer lateral between the main line sewer and the property line.

Permits of this type are commonly referred to as "house connection" permits. The term "house connection" is used although the sewer lateral may serve a house, apartment building, factory, commercial building or any other type of building structure. The main line sewer may be in a public street or alley, a right-of-way or an easement. The construction standards and details are identical for all house connection sewers.

It is desirable that a House Connection Inspector have a background of experience inspecting the construction of new sewers and storm drains, both in tract developments and on assessment act projects in built-up areas. Terminology used in sewer and storm drain construction, details of pipe bedding, methods of pipe laying, types of pipe joints, methods of measurement, etc., will be familiar to him. (See Subsection 3-5 and 3-6 for construction generally and 3-5.8.2 for house connection sewers.)

The House Connection Inspector will obtain information as to the location and depth of the sewer lateral or storm drain connection from the copy of the connection permit which he receives from the Engineer. Sometimes it will be necessary for him to review the sewer record maps maintained by the Agency for additional information. Other information and criteria are contained in the Standard Specifications and in various Standard Plans.

Inspectors assigned to house connection permit construction should frequently review and become thoroughly familiar with these references.

Connections made to storm drains also require a permit. Any connection of a private drainage system to a storm drain pipe or to a structure (such as a catch basin) must be authorized by a permit issued by the Agency. Connections of this type are permissible if the purpose is to dispose of relatively clear water which is free of sewage or industrial waste. Roof drains, yard or area drains, and sumps emptied by electric pumps are typical sources of this type of drainage water. In most cases, a sketch (in duplicate) prepared by the Engineer will accompany the permit.

If the contractor wishes to deviate from the dimensions, materials or instructions included on the sketch accompanying the permit, the Inspector must consult the Engineer. After obtaining his approval, appropriate notes pertaining to the change must be made on both copies of the sketch, including the name of the Engineer approving the change. When the work is completed, one copy of the sketch is retained in the files of the Main Office, along with the permit, while the other copy is transmitted to the Engineer.

Except for property line connections, house connection permits are issued only to licensed contractors who have posted a cash bond with the Engineer and have a valid liability insurance policy on file with the Agency.

The applicable provisions of the Construction Safety Orders of the State of California must be enforced on all work done under house connection permits. Adequate lights and barricades are required to warn and protect the traveling public. (**Note:** The WATCH handbook is going to be published separately.)

Occassionally, a contractor will request assistance in locating a house connection, or he may ask for advice in handling an unusual field problem such as an interference with a structure or utility pipe. The Inspector should make an appointment to meet the contractor at a convenient time for this purpose.

3-7.2 Inspection Procedures.

3-7.2.1 **General.** On this type of "called" inspection, the contractor normally has previously excavated in the street, located the wye or tee on the main line, prepared the subgrade and bedding, laid the lateral pipe with an increaser fitting at the property line and is ready to backfill the trench upon receiving an approval. To make an adequate inspection of a house connection sewer, the Inspector must go into the trench for a close examination of the pipe, the joints and the subgrade. To avoid disturbing the joints or moving the pipe out of line or off-grade, care should be taken not to step or walk on the pipe.

3-7.2.2 **Subgrade.** It is customary for the Inspector to use a small-diameter rod as a prod to check for loose, uncompacted fill under the pipe. This condition may result from over-excavation of the trench below subgrade for the pipe (or bedding if the native material is not granular) and is most commonly encountered when excavation is done with a backhoe. If such a condition is found, the pipe must be taken up and the loose soil removed and replaced with compacted bedding material (See Subsection 3-5.7.7). Soil must never be used for this purpose. Machine excavation should be kept slightly above subgrade for the bedding or pipe and the fine grading, trimming and pipe bedding prepared with hand labor to avoid disturbing the support for the pipe. (See Plate 50, Appendix.)

Where the soil is granular and undisturbed, the bottom of the trench should be shaped to support the lower segment of the barrel of the pipe. Holes for the bells should be dug at the proper intervals so that the pipe is supported by the barrel. Bell holes should be no larger than necessary; otherwise, the support for a portion of the barrel of the pipe is lost. This would concentrate the load on a short section of the barrel of the pipe when the trench is backfilled and a cracked or crushed pipe may result.

Where the native material at the bottom of the trench is rocky or bedrock (and the flow line elevation of the pipeline cannot be raised to avoid this condition), it is necessary to excavate four inches or more below pipe subgrade and backfill to grade with granular bedding material. This will provide a firm and uniform support for the pipe and avoid point loading which can cause the pipe to fail.

The correct and incorrect methods of laying house connection sewer laterals are shown on Plate 51, Appendix. At each joint the spigot end should be properly centered in the bell to form a close, concentric joint. House connection sewers must be laid on a straight line and grade unless otherwise specified on the permit. Fall of at least ¼ inch per foot (about two percent is required. The depth of the invert of the house connection at the property line should be not less than four feet below the elevation of the top of the existing curb, sidewalk, alley surface or four feet below ground level in the case of a sewer in a right-of-way or easement.

3-7.2.3 **Joints and Fittings.** Pipe for sewer laterals must be manufactured of vitrified clay, cast iron or asbestos-cement (when tested and approved before use). The pipe diameter is usually six inches, but may be greater if the permit so specifies, for very large apartment buildings or commercial structures.

Pipe joints shall conform to the requirements of the latest provisions of the Standard Specifications. All changes in direction shall be made by using prefabricated pipe fittings such as quarter-bends, eighth-bends, tees, wyes, etc. No chipping of pipe is permitted.

Where pipe diameters change, a proper fitting must be used. Connection must not be made by telescoping the smaller pipe into the larger pipe.

All vitrified clay pipe must have been tested and approved in advance by the Testing Agency. Approval is indicated by a three-digit number stamped inside each length of pipe. Pipe stamped with a number having more than three digits will not be acceptable for use.

If no wye or tee exists on the main line sewer where a house connection sewer is to be constructed, a special pipe fitting called a saddle must be used to make the connection. These saddles must be installed by the Agency sewer maintenance forces.

3-7.2.4 Backfilling and Jetting. After the contractor has received a yellow "O.K." tag, he is permitted to backfill and jet the excavated areas. A notation on the tag requires him to temporarily resurface the trench with a layer of bituminous premix material two inches thick in a roadway or one inch thick in sidewalk areas within three days after backfilling.

It is the responsibility of the House Connection Inspector to return after three days to each jobsite where premix is required, to see that it is in place. To insure that further settlement has not occurred, these locations should be patrolled by the Inspector from time to time until permanent resurfacing is placed by the Agency. The Inspector will maintain the necessary communication with the contractor, informing him as to the maintenance requirements for temporary resurfacing.

3-7.3 Approval of Work and Materials. If materials and workmanship are acceptable, the Inspector will make out a yellow "O.K." tag ("Approval of Sewer Connection on Public Property or Right-of-Way") and wire it at a convenient and conspicuous location at or near the trench.

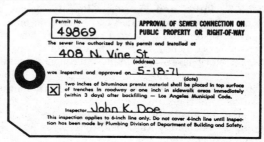

If unsatisfactory materials or workmanship are encountered, the Inspector will make out and leave at the jobsite a red tag ("Disapproval of Sewer Connection on Public Property or Right-of-Way"). When a contractor receives a red tag, he can telephone the Inspector the next morning for more details and instructions on corrections if the deficiencies are too extensive to be described on the tag.

When the red or yellow tag is used in connection with storm drain permits, cross out the word "sewer" and write in the words "storm drain."

City of Los Angeles
DEPARTMENT OF PUBLIC WORKS   Bureau of Contract Administration

**DISAPPROVAL OF SEWER CONNECTION
ON PUBLIC PROPERTY OR RIGHT OF WAY**

The sewer line authorized by Permit No. **49872**
and installed at **616 N. Main St.**
(Address)
was inspected and **"NOT APPROVED"** for reasons shown on
reverse side of this notice.

AFTER the corrections are completed, call for re-inspection.

NOTE: THIS INSPECTION APPLIES TO 6-INCH LINE ONLY. DO
NOT COVER 4-INCH LINE ON LOT UNTIL INSPECTION
HAS BEEN MADE BY PLUMBING DIVISION.

---

*Do not lay pipe on natural ground
with wedges. Lay on bedding of
pea gravel. Call for inspection
when ready.*
John K. Doe   5-18-71

The yellow or red tags mentioned above are used because the pipe is usually in place and is ready for inspection at the time the Inspector arrives but the workers have left for another job location. The tags are a convenient means of communication between the Inspector and the contractor. A yellow tag is often used by the contractor to show the property owner that his work has been inspected and approved.

3-7.4 Sewer and Storm Drain Permit Reporting.

3-7.4.1 Reporting Location. In addition to approving materials and workmanship, another important function performed by the House Connection Inspector is the verification and maintenance of the Agency records pertaining to house connection locations and depths. Each house connection is located by a measurement made over the main line sewer from

---

APPLICATION/PERMIT
FOR
SEWER OR STORM DRAIN CONNECTION

City of Anywhere
DEPT. OF PUBLIC WORKS
Bureau of Engineering

60040

UNDER CHAPTER 0, ARTICLE 0, ANYWHERE MUNICIPAL CODE

JOB ADDRESS		INTO
808 Oak St.		Oak St.

LOT	BLOCK	TRACT
21	2	6430

BUILDING TYPE
☐ COMMERCIAL   ☐ INDUSTRIAL   ☒ RESIDENTIAL

STORIES	DWELLING UNITS
1	1

CONNECTION TO
☒ SEWER   ☐ STORM DRAIN

PURPOSE
☒ NEW CONNECTION
☐ RELOCATION

☐ REPAIR
☐ RECONNECTION

CONTRACTOR
Best Plumbing Corp.

WILL THIS CONNECTION CONTAIN
Industrial Waste? ☐ YES ☒ NO
Swimming Pool Water? ☐ YES ☒ NO

STATE LICENSE NO.
1508

CLASSIFICATION
☐ A ☐ B-1 ☐ C-36 ☒ C-42

FOR OFFICE USE ONLY

ADDRESS
4052 Smith Ave.

PERMIT FEE	$	15	00

CITY
Los Angeles

ZIP CODE
90065

TELEPHONE
653-5213

TAP FEE

I hereby agree to observe all requirements of the Municipal Code of the City of Anywhere and all amendments thereto.

SPEC. INSP.

3-10-87
DATE   *Larry Jones*
            AUTHORIZED SIGNATURE

TOTAL	$	15	00

JOB ADDRESS
808 Oak St.

PERMIT NUMBER
60040

CONTRACTOR
Best Plumbing Corp.

INSPECTOR REPORT

INTO   Oak St.   SEWER MAP NO.   5524-3

DATE PIPE INSPECTED	TYPE	CONDITION	STATION	Y	CURB	PL.	DEPTH
3-15-87	VCP	O.K.	3+32	231			9

ALL MEASUREMENTS FROM LOWER MANHOLE

Y	CURB	P.L.	LENGTH
231		233/5	30'

NOTE:

LOWER M.H.   1+01

EXCAVATION
30 (WIDTH & LENGTH)   TYPE OF SURFACE

LOCATION   1st MS north of
Green St.

| 2.5' x 12' | AC |
| 2.5' x 6' | Dirt |

UPPER M.H.   3+86

DATE ES. MTCE. NOTIFIED   3-16-87

REMARKS   Terminal MH. Main line on C/L 60-ft. street.

INSPECTOR
J. K. Doe

BY   *R. Smith* 3-10-87 10:30 A.M.
BUREAU OF ENGINEERING   TIME AND DATE

THIS PERMIT EXPIRES 9/10/87 DAY FROM DATE OF ISSUANCE

THIS PERMIT NOT VALID UNLESS RECEIPT ATTACHED OR REGISTER VALIDATED

RECEIPT NUMBER _____

the center of the closest downstream manhole to a point at a right angle to the intersection of the sewer lateral with the property line. The location of the house connection indicated on each permit must be verified to the nearest foot by measurement with a tape. This information is to be recorded in the spaces provided on the Inspector's copy of the permit.

If unusual conditions are encountered, it is advisable to make a sketch on the back of the permit, showing distances to both upstream and downstream manholes, length of lateral, depth of lateral at property line, measurements to angle points, etc.

3-7.4.2 Reporting Areas to be Resurfaced. The House Connection Inspector is required to measure and report the type and extent of the excavation made by the sewer contractor. This information is used to assign street maintenance crews to do the necessary replacement of concrete curbs, gutters, sidewalks, driveways, concrete pavement and asphalt pavement. Excavations in unimproved areas are reported as "dirt." Spaces for recording this information are provided on the Inspector's copy of the permit. The cost of restoring the surface is charged to the permittee in addition to the permit fee.

At locations where new buildings are under construction, it is not unusual to find the house connection sewer trench is within an area where a sidewalk or driveway will be reconstructed under a permit when the building is completed. The existence of a permit should be verified and the areas in question reported as "dirt."

Connections that are made at the property line and require no resurfacing are to be reported as "no area."

Where existing concrete pavement is removed in connection with the construction of a house connection sewer, the edges of the removal area must be sawed to a depth of 1½ inches.

Concrete to be replaced in sidewalk or driveway areas shall be saw-cut along the nearest scoring line and removed.

The Inspector will leave a red tag at the jobsite to disapprove any work requiring concrete saw-cutting if it has not been accomplished.

3-7.4.3 Reporting Pipe Footage. Measurement will be made at the time of inspection in addition to the usual measurements made for areas to be resurfaced. It will be the duty of the

Inspector to measure and record the pipe footage in accordance with the following instructions so that the permittee can be billed by the Agency:

(1) To determine pipe footage, horizontal measurements will be made parallel with the house connection lateral. Record this footage to the nearest even foot.

(2) If an entire lateral is laid from a wye, a saddle or a chimney, the length of the lateral will be measured from the center of the main line, regardless of the diameter of the main line.

(3) If a portion of a house connection sewer is remodeled or repaired, the total length of new pipe laid, measured along the line of the work, shall be used in measuring pipe footage.

(4) The word "exposed" is not intended to include the last two feet of a lateral which may require exposure or alteration when a property line connection is made. There is no need to measure or report pipe footage of a property line connection.

(5) The word "exposed" will cover rare situations where, for example, pipe joints or sections are uncovered to determine condition of joints, root penetration, possible crushed or damaged sections, etc. At such locations the pipe footage exposed will be measured and recorded. In most cases, however, the pipe footage entry will show only pipe actually laid or relaid.

(6) Occasionally the permittee is a Department of the Agency. Agency Departments are required to obtain sewer and storm drain connection permits (for new work, for repairs and for remodeling), but they are issued on a "no fee" basis.

For the sake of uniformity in the various offices, the following procedures will be followed:

(1) On the pink copy of the permit, the pipe footage measured by the Inspector will be entered as usual under "Inspector Report" in the space entitled "length."

(2) On the yellow copy of the permit, the pipe footage measured by the Inspector will be entered under "Excavation" just to the left of the word "size."

(3) On both the pink and the yellow copies, the footage figure will be **circled in red.** This will call attention to the fact that the pipe length has been measured and that billing is required. The permittee will be billed accordingly in addition to the usual charges for trench resurfacing.

(4) On "no fee" permits issued to Agency Departments, the pipe footage circled in red will not be shown by the Inspector on the yellow copy of the permit.

3-7.5　Additional Inspection and Charges.　The fee paid for a house connection permit is generally understood to include the initial inspection of the house connection and one inspection of the placement of the temporary resurfacing, if required. A charge is authorized for each additional inspection required. Typical occasions for its use are as follows:

(1) If no temporary resurfacing is found in the trench area three days after completion of pipe laying and backfilling, the contractor will be instructed to place such resurfacing immediately and advised that a daily charge for inspection will be levied until it is in place.

(2) A charge for extra inspection is to be made when the Inspector returns to a jobsite for reinspection after notifying the contractor to saw-cut the edges of an excavation through concrete.

3-7.6　Sewer and Storm Drain Connection Permit Check List.

(1) Review Subsection 3-5 and 3-6 General Information; 3-5.8.2 for Sewer House Connections; 3-5.14 Sewer Construction Checklist; and 3-6.9 Storm Drain Construction Checklist.

(2) Check Standard Plan for type of house connection details.

(3) See Plates 50 and 51, Appendix. Is pipe bedded properly? Is overexcavation refilled with compacted bedding material? Is proper pipe increaser used? Is line and grade satisfactory?

(4) Has the distance from the downstream manhole to the house connection location been measured and recorded?

(5) Have the edges of excavations in concrete been saw cut?

(6) Have the dimensions of areas to be resurfaced by the Agency street maintenance forces been measured and recorded?

(7) Has the lineal footage of pipe laid, relaid or exposed been measured and recorded?

(8) Has a yellow or red tag been issued as circumstances require?

(9) Has the follow-up condition of temporary resurfacing in trench areas been checked three days after the excavation has been backfilled and flooded?

3-8 PILES AND PILE DRIVING

3-8.1 General. A pile is a column driven or jetted into the ground which derives its supporting capabilities from end-bearing on the underlying strata, skin friction between the pile surface and the soil, or from a combination of end-bearing and skin friction.

Piles can be divided into two major classes: **Sheet piles** and **load-bearing piles.** (See Plates 40 and 41, Appendix.) Sheet piling is used primarily to restrain lateral forces as in trench sheeting and bulkheads, or to resist the flow of water as in cofferdams. It is prefabricated and is available in steel, wood or concrete. Load-bearing piles are used primarily to transmit loads through soil formations of low bearing values to formations that are capable of supporting the designed loads. If the load is supported predominantly by the action of soil friction on the surface of the pile, it is called a **friction pile.** If the load is transmitted to the soil primarily through the lower tip, it is called an **end-bearing pile.**

There are several load-bearing pile types, which can be classified according to the material from which they are fabricated:

      Timber (Treated and untreated)

      Concrete (Precast and cast-in-place)

      Steel (H-Section and steel pipe)

      Composite (A combination of two or more materials)

Some of the additional uses of piling are to: eliminate or control settlement of structures, support bridge piers and abutments and protect them from scour, anchor structures against uplift or overturning, and for numerous marine structures such as docks, wharves, fenders, anchorages, piers, trestles and jetties.

3-8.2 Types of Piles. Detailed specifications for pile types are set forth in the Standard Specifications and will not be repeated here. Only the most commonly used types of piles will be discussed in this subsection. (See Plate 41, Appendix.) The Inspector must require the contractor to use only the type of pile (or alternate) indicated on the plans unless a Change Order is issued authorizing a substitution.

3-8.2.1 Timber Piles. (See Subsection 2-10.10.) Timber piles, treated or untreated, are the piles most commonly used throughout the world, primarily because they are readily available, economical, easily handled, can be easily cut off to any desired length after driving and can be easily removed if necessary. On the other hand, they have some serious disadvantages which include: difficulty in securing straight piles of long length, problems in driving them into hard formations and difficulty in splicing to increase their length. They are generally not suitable for use as end-bearing piles under heavy load and they are subject to decay and insect attack. (See Subsection 2-10.11, Preservative Treatment.) Timber piles are resilient and particularly adaptable for use in waterfront structures such as wharves, docks and piers for anchorages since they will bend or give under load or impact where other materials may break. The ease with which they can be worked and their economy makes them popular for trestle construction and for temporary structures such as falsework or centering. Where timber piles can be driven and cut off below the permanent ground-water level, they will last indefinitely; but above this level in the soil, a timber pile will rot or will be attacked by insects and eventually destroyed. In sea water, marine borers and fungus will act to deteriorate timber piles. Treatment of timber piles increases their life but does not protect them indefinitely.

3-8.2.2 Concrete Piles. Concrete piles are of two general types: precast and cast-in-place. The advantages in the use of concrete piles are that they can be fabricated to meet the most exacting conditions of design, can be cast in any desired shape or length, possess high strength and have excellent resistance to chemical and biological attack. Certain disadvantages are encountered in the use of precast piles, such as:

(a) Their heavy weight and bulk (which introduces problems in handling and driving).

(b) Problems with hair cracks which often develop in the concrete as a result of shrinkage after curing (which may expose the steel reinforcement to deterioration).

(c) Difficulty encountered in cut-off or splicing.

(d) Susceptibility to damage or breakage in handling and driving.

(e) They are more expensive to fabricate, transport and drive.

Precast piles are fabricated in casting yards. Centrifug-ally spun piles (or piles with square or octagonal cross-sections) are cast in horizontal forms, while round piles are usually cast in vertical forms. With the exception of relatively short lengths, precast piles must be reinforced to provide the de-signed column strengths and to resist damage or breakage while being transported or driven.

Precast piles can be tapered or have parallel sides. The reinforcement can be of deformed bars or be prestressed or poststressed with high strength steel tendons. Prestressing or poststressing eliminates the problem of open shrinkage cracks in the concrete. Otherwise, the pile must be protected by coating it with a bituminous or plastic material to prevent ultimate de-terioration of the reinforcement. Proper curing of the precast concrete in piles is essential.

Cast-in-place pile types are numerous and vary accord-ing to the manufacturer of the shell or inventor of the method. In general, they can be classified into two groups: shell-less types and the shell types. The shell-less type is constructed by driving a steel shell into the ground and filling it with concrete as the shell is pulled from the ground. The shell type is con-structed by driving a steel shell into the ground and filling it in place with concrete. Some of the advantages of cast-in-place concrete piles are: lightweight shells are handled and driven easily, lengths of the shell may be increased or decreased easily, shells may be transported in short lengths and quickly assembled, the problem of breakage is eliminated and a driven shell may be inspected for shell damage or an uncased hole for "pinching off." Among the disadvantages are problems encoun-tered in the proper centering of the reinforcement cages, in placing and consolidating the concrete without displacement of the reinforcement steel or segregation of the concrete, and shell damage or "pinching-off" of uncased holes.

Some shell type piles are fabricated of heavy gage metal or are fluted, corrugated or spirally reinforced with heavy wire to make them strong enough to be driven without a mandrel. Other thin-shell types are driven with a collapsible steel man-drel or core inside the casing. In addition to making the driving of a long thin shell possible, the mandrel prevents or minimizes damage to the shell from tearing, buckling, collapsing or from hard objects encountered in driving.

Some shell type piles are fabricated of heavy gauge metal largement at the lower end to increase the end bearing. These enlargements are formed by withdrawing the casing two to three feet after placing concrete in the lower end of the shell. This wet concrete is then struck by a blow of the pile hammer on a core in the casing and the enlargement is formed. As the shell is withdrawn, the core is used to consolidate the concrete after each batch is placed in the shell. The procedure results in completely filling the hole left by the withdrawal of the shell.

3-8.2.3 **Steel Piles.** A steel pile is any pile fabricated entirely of steel. They are usually formed of rolled steel H sections, but heavy steel pipe or box piles (fabricated from sections of steel sheet piles welded together) are also used. The advantages of steel piles are that they are readily available, have a thin uniform section and high strength, will take hard driving, will develop high load-bearing values, are easily cut off or extended, are easily adapted to the structure they are to support, and breakage is eliminated. Some disadvantages are: they will rust and deteriorate unless protected from the elements; acid, soils or water will result in corrosion of the pile; and greater lengths may be required than for other types of piles to achieve the same bearing value unless bearing on rock strata. Pipe pile can either be driven open-end or closed-end and can be unfilled, sand filled or concrete filled. After open-end pipe piles are driven, the material from inside can be removed by an earth auger, air or water jets, or other means, inspected, and then filled with concrete. Concrete filled pipe piles are subject to corrosion on the outside surface only.

3-8.2.4 **Composite Piles.** Any pile that is fabricated of two or more materials is called a composite pile. There are three general classes of composite piles: wood with concrete, steel with concrete, and wood with steel. Composite piles are usually used for a special purpose or for reasons of economy.

Where a permanent ground-water table exists and a composite pile is to be used, it will generally be of concrete and wood. The wood portion is driven to below the water table level and the concrete upper portion eliminates problems of decay and insect infestation above the water table. Composite piles of steel and concrete are used where high bearing loads are desired or where driving in hard or rocky soils is expected. Composite wood and steel piles are relatively uncommon.

It is important that the pile design provides for a permanent joint between the two materials used, so constructed that the parts do not separate or shift out of axial alignment during driving operations.

3-8.2.5 Sheet Piles. Sheet piles are made from the same basic materials as other piling: wood, steel and concrete. They are ordinarily designed so as to interlock along the edges of adjacent piles. The most commonly used types are indicated on Plate 41, Appendix.

Sheet piles are used where support of a vertical wall of earth is required, such as trench walls, bulkheads, waterfront structures or cofferdams. Wood sheet piling is generally used in temporary installations, but is seldom used where water-tightness is required or hard driving expected. Concrete sheet piling has the capability of resisting much larger lateral loads than wood sheet piling, but considerable difficulty is experienced in securing water-tight joints. The type referred to as "fish-mouth" type is designed to permit jetting out the joint and filling with grout, but a seal is not always effected unless the adjacent piles are wedged tightly together. Concrete sheet piling has the advantage that it is the most permanent of all types of sheet piling.

Steel sheet piling is manufactured with a tension-type interlock along its edges. Several different shapes are available to permit versatility in its use. It has the advantages that it can take hard driving, has reasonably water-tight joints and can be easily cut, patched, lengthened or reinforced. It can also be easily extracted and reused. Its principal disadvantage is its vulnerability to corrosion.

3-8.3 Types of Pile Driving Hammers. A pile-driving hammer is used to drive load-bearing or sheet piles. The commonly used types are: drop, single-acting, double-acting, differential acting and diesel hammers. The most recent development is a type of hammer that utilizes high-frequency sound and a dead load as the principal sources of driving energy.

3-8.3.1 Drop Hammers. These hammers employ the principle of lifting a heavy weight by a cable and releasing it to fall on top of the pile. This type of hammer is rapidly disappearing from use, primarily because other types of pile driving hammers are more efficient. Its disadvantages are that it has a slow rate of driving (four to eight blows per minute), that there is some risk of damaging the pile from excessive impact, that damage may occur in adjacent structures from heavy vibration and that it cannot be used directly for driving piles under water. Drop hammers have the advantages of simplicity of operation, ability to vary the energy by changing the height of fall and they represent a small investment in equipment.

3-8.3.2 Single-Acting Hammers.

These hammers can be operated either on steam or compressed air. The driving energy is provided by a free-falling weight (called a ram) which is raised after each stroke by the action of steam or air on a piston. They are manufactured as either open or closed types. Single-acting hammers are best suited for jobs where dense or elastic soil materials must be penetrated or where long heavy timber or precast concrete piles must be driven. The closed type can be used for underwater pile driving. Its advantages include: faster driving (50 blows or more per minute), reduction in skin friction as a result of more frequent blows, lower velocity of the ram which transmits a greater proportion of its energy to the pile and minimizes pile damage during driving, and it has underwater driving capability. Some of its disadvantages are: requires higher investment in equipment (i.e. steam boiler, air compressor, etc.), higher maintenance costs, greater set-up and moving time required, and a larger operating crew is needed.

3-8.3.3 Double-Acting Hammers.

These hammers are similar to the single-acting hammers except that steam or compressed air is used both to lift the ram and to impart energy to the falling ram. While the action is approximately twice as fast as the single-acting hammer (100 blows per minute or more), the ram is much lighter and operates at a greater velocity, thereby making it particularly useful in high production driving of light- or medium-weight piles of moderate lengths in granular soils. The hammer is nearly always fully encased by a steel housing which also permits direct driving of piles under water.

Some of its advantages are: faster driving rate, less static skin friction develops between blows, has underwater driving capability and piles can be driven more easily without leads. Among its disadvantages are: it is less suitable for driving heavy piles in high-friction soils and the more complicated mechanism results in higher maintenance costs.

3-8.3.4 Differential-Acting Hammers.

This type of hammer is, in effect, a modified double-acting hammer with the actuating mechanism having two different diameters. A large-diameter piston operates in an upper cylinder to accelerate the ram on the downstroke and a small-diameter piston operates in a lower cylinder to raise the ram. The additional energy added to the falling ram is the difference in areas of the two pistons multiplied by the unit pressure of the steam or air used. This hammer is a short-stroke, fast-acting hammer with a cycle rate approximately that of the double-acting hammer. Its advantages are that it has the speed and characteristics of the double-acting hammer with a ram weight comparable to the single-acting type, and it uses from 25 to 35 percent less steam or air. It is also more suitable for driving heavy piles under more difficult driving conditions than is the double-acting hammer. It is available in the open or closed-type cases, the latter permitting direct underwater pile driving. Its principal disadvantage is higher maintenance costs.

3-8.3.5 **Diesel Hammers.** This hammer is a self-contained driving unit which does not require an auxilliary steam boiler or air compressor. It consists essentially of a ram operating as a piston in a cylinder. When the ram is lifted and allowed to fall in the cylinder, diesel fuel is injected in the compression space between the ram and an anvil placed on top of the pile. The continued downstroke of the ram compresses the air and fuel to ignition heat and the resultant explosion drives the pile downward and the ram upward to start another cycle. This hammer is capable of driving at a rate of from 80 to 100 blows per minute. Its advantages are that it has a low equipment investment cost, is easily moved, requires a small crew, has a high driving rate, does not require a steam boiler or air compressor and can be used with or without leads for most work. Its disadvantages are that it is not self-starting (the ram must be mechanically lifted to start the action) and it does not deliver a uniform blow. The latter disadvantage arises from the fact that as the reaction of the pile to driving increases, the reaction to the ram increases correspondingly. That is, when the pile encounters considerable resistance, the rebound of the ram is higher and the energy is increased automatically. The operator is required to observe the driving operations closely to identify changing driving conditions and compensate for such changes with his controls to avoid damaging the pile.

Diesel hammers can be used on all types of piles and they are best suited to jobs where mobility or frequent relocation of the pile driving equipment is necessary.

3-8.4 **Accessory Pile Driving Equipment.** Most pile driving hammers are easily adaptable to being fitted to cranes for land work or to a suitable barge for work in water. For accurate positioning, the pile is fastened into a set of **leads** which can be held vertical to drive plumb piles or inclined to drive battered piles. Leads are parallel rails between which the pile is held and are so constructed that they can be extended as necessary to handle long piles.

The forged or cast steel seat of the hammer case which rides on top the pile is called the **driving head** (or driving cap). It holds the pile in position during driving and transmits the energy of the hammer uniformly over the head of the pile. Together with the cushion blocks, it absorbs the sharp impact of the hammer blow which could damage the pile. It is important that the seat of the driving head be shaped to fit the shape of the butt of the pile or sheet piling being driven.

Cushion blocks are utilized between the anvil blocks to absorb just enough of the inital impact of the hammer that damage to the pile is avoided. They can be made of many different materials, but wood is the material most commonly used. Soft woods absorb too much energy while hard woods split and splinter. Both should be avoided for use as cushion blocks. It is best to use a wood having the quality of toughness such as oak, maple or eucalyptus (gumwood). Cushion blocks should be cut to fit the driving head and to the proper length to fit between the anvil blocks. The grain of the wood should be vertical. Cushion blocks should be replaced when they heat up to the extent that they start smoking or are compressed from use more than half their original thickness. Layers of plywood are commonly used as cushion blocks when driving prescast concrete piles.

Followers are devices set in the leads to permit a pile driving hammer to drive piles to depths below the reach of the hammer. A follower must be used with drop hammers or uncased steam or air hammers for driving piling under water. An objection to the use of the follower arises from the fact that an additional mass is introduced between the hammer and the pile, making evaluation of pile bearing capacities by a dynamic formula somewhat doubtful. (See Subsection 3-8.7.)

To reduce the difficulty in driving piles, water jetting or predrilling is sometimes utilized. A **jet pipe,** which can range in size from two to four inches in diameter, is connected to a water source and sunk into the ground alongside the pile being driven. The water passes through a nozzle at the lower end of the jet and assists in loosening the earth ahead of the pile tip. The soil around the pile is kept in agitation, thereby reducing resistance to driving due to skin friction. Water pressure required at the nozzle varies from 100 to 300 psi. Jets are useful as an aid to pile driving in sand or fine gravel, but are virtually useless in coarse gravel. The last three feet of penetration of the pile must be obtained by driving without the use of the jet in order to permit the safe bearing capacity of the pile to be determined by conventional formulas. Jetting of piles on Agency projects can be permitted only when provided for in the Special Provisions or authorized by the Engineer.

Predrilling consists of drilling a hole with a continuous flight auger of smaller diameter than the pile. The depth of predrilling shall be approved by the Engineer.

A **spud** is a solid steel mandrel that is driven into soils containing large boulders, debris or other impediments to pile driving which might damage the pile or throw it off line. The spud pushes these obstructions aside in the proposed path of the pile and, after withdrawal, provides a pilot hole for the pile. In soils offering high resistance to driving, a similar pilot hole can be produced by earth drilling methods.

3-8.5 Inspection of Cast-in-Place Piles.

When driven shell type cast-in-place concrete pile are construced, the driven shells should be thoroughly examined to their full depth by the Inspector utilizing an electric droplight with sufficient cord length to permit lowering it to the bottom of the casing. A mirror can also be used for this purpose if sufficient sunlight is available. Indications of tearing or collapsing of the shell should be noted, and if a significant inward bulge is detected which would materially affect the cross-sectional area of the pile, the condition must be corrected. This can sometimes be accomplished by replacing the mandrel in the shell and striking it a few blows with the hammer. Pile shells which cannot be repaired in place or which were driven without mandrels, must be pulled and new shells driven.

All types of cast-in-place piles must be inspected to insure that the shell or bored hole is free of water and loose soil and that the reinforcement cage is centered and properly blocked to prevent lateral movement during the placement and subsequent consolidation of the concrete. Concrete should be placed in drilled piles the same day they are bored. In the placing of the concrete, methods must be utilized to insure that segregation of the concrete does not take place and in the case of drilled piles, that concrete is prevented from striking the sidewalls and causing the soil to dislodge and mix with the concrete. (In some cases, temporary casing in unstable or filled ground may be required.) Concrete placement utilizing tremies or a hose line and pumps should be utilized to avoid these conditions. Consolidation of the concrete can be achieved by rodding or puddling with long poles or by the use of internal-type vibrators. Care must be exercised to avoid having the vibrator strike the reinforcement cage or get wedged in the cage. Damage may result to the cage and the vibrator is usually very difficult to get loose. The maximum permissible slumps outlined in the Standard Specifications should be observed, but the use of high-slump concrete to avoid mechanical means of consolidation cannot be permitted.

While caissons are not classified as piles, it is convenient to mention that the precautions mentioned above for drilled piles apply also to caissons. They can be excavated by hand or with such equipment as cesspool diggers through strata of poor bearing value until reaching stable formations capable of supporting heavy loads. The resultant excavation is filled with concrete and generally is steel-reinforced. Some caissons are under-reamed or enlarged at the bottom to give greater bearing areas. Where the upper strata is unstable, temporary casings may be required to eliminate water or caving. After concrete is placed and while it is still plastic, casings for the caisson are usually withdrawn.

3-8.6 Driving Piles.

3-8.6.1 **General.** The first important element of inspecting a pile driving operation is the inspection of the pile itself. Piles which do not clearly meet the specification requirements should be promptly rejected by the Inspector. Timber piles are seldom perfectly stright, but unless they are within the tolerance established in the Standard Specifications, a bend will become exaggerated as the pile is driven into the ground and may result in a broken pile underground. Piles with a twist or spiral vertical grain exceeding specification tolerances tend to develop fractures in the twist as a result of driving stresses.

While precast concrete piles are usually within specification tolerances for length, shape and straightness, the Inspector should satisfy himself by a close inspection of each pile that no damage has occurred from improper curing, storing or handling. Concrete piles which have been abused in handling should be rejected. Steel H piles should be straight and free of any damage to the flanges. A damaged flange may cause the pile to twist or to deflect into a bend and thus alter its bearing capacity. Significant dents in steel pipe piles may result in collapsing or buckling of the pile at the dented area when it is driven, and could increase the difficulty in jetting out the interior and in performing inspection functions.

After a thorough inspection of the piles, the Inspector should check that the type of pile hammer that the contractor intends to use is adequate. As a general rule, the heaviest pile hammer that can be used without permanently damaging the pile should be employed. However, heavy hammers used for driving light piles in hard driving conditions will invariably result in pile damage. If too light a hammer is used, difficulty may be encountered in achieving the required minimum penetration of the pile, and the computed bearing value may not represent the actual bearing.

Removals, grubbing, excavation, fill and rough grading should be completed prior to drilling or pile driving operations. The Inspector should make an examination of the area in which piles are to be driven after it has been excavated to subgrade elevation. Where the Inspector believes conditions are changed from those indicated on the plans or in the Special Specifications for the project, the Engineer should be informed so that a re-evaluation of the pile length or spacing can be made.

Survey crews are to be used to stake the location of piles on the site and to mark the cut-off elevations of piles after they are driven.

The sequence with which piles or shells are driven in a pile pattern can also be very important. When a pile is driven, it displaces a volume of soil equal to the volume of the embedded portion of the pile. If a pile is driven between two previously driven piles which are reasonably close together, the soil between them will have been densified by this displacement effect and the new pile will, with less penetration, develop driving and bearing values materially higher than the existing piles. If pile shells are driven under these circumstances, the nearby unfilled pile shells may be collapsed or distorted by excessive impact vibrations or soil pressures.

If the driving sequence is not indicated on the plans, the Inspector should arrange for a sequence which will avoid the foregoing problems. In general, a satisfactory sequence can be developed by starting driving operations at the geometrical center of the pile pattern and progressing outwards.

3-8.6.2 **Driving Operations.** Once the driving of a pile is started, driving should not be interrupted until the proper penetration and bearing have been attained. After each blow of the hammer, static skin friction develops between the soil and the pile surface. The greater the interval between blows, the greater the frictional forces that are developed. If driving operations are suspended for a significant period of time, difficulty is usually experienced in overcoming this re-sistance in re-starting the pile. The resistance to driving is materially increased after a period of rest as short as 15 minutes.

This "freezing-up" effect is very pronounced when using drop hammers with their characteristically slow driving rate. It is practically negligible when using rapid-rate drivers, such as the double-acting or diesel hammers, unless driving is in-terrupted. The apparent success of the new hammer utilizing high-frequency sound is primarily attributable to the extremely high rate of vibration of the pile which practically eliminates static friction.

The contractor should exercise care in raising piles into the leads, particularly precast concrete piles which should be lifted only by their predetermined pick-up points. Pre-stressed piles are especially subject to failure if improperly lifted or handled. Long timber piles should have chain chokers or special clamps to hold them in the leads. This will minimize whipping of the pile in the leads, which absorbs hammer energy and may cause damage to the pile.

Piles driven into soft material should not be pointed. However, if piles are to be driven in very hard soils, through hard strata, or in ground containing boulders, steel shoes should be provided and securely attached to the tips of the piles.

While the pile is being driven, the Inspector should ob-serve the behavior of the pile and the hammer for signs of pile distress. Piles which strain to pull from the leads usually have the penetrated portion of the pile out of plumb as a result of: striking an underground obstacle, spiral grain stress, using a bent pile or from starting the pile out of plumb. If the pile meets extreme resistance to driving, the hammer will work harder with a reduced rate of penetration of the pile. This effect is created when a pile reaches an underground obstacle or hard stratum and the pile is at a point of refusal. Continued driving will result in failure of the pile through splitting or brooming the tip or head. The Engineer must be advised when a pile is driven to refusal and the desired minimum penetration has not been achieved.

Brooming and splitting of the head of timber piles can be reduced by several common methods: shaping the head to receive the seat of the driving head, utilizing forged steel rings around the head of the pile or wrapping the heads with length of cable.

After driving, piles should be reasonably in the position and line indicated on the plans. Those that are materially out of line should be pulled and replaced. Slight bending to pull a pile into line is permitted provided the pile is reasonably plumb and serious lateral or bending stresses are not developed. Piling must be driven to the minimum penetration required by the plans, even if the designated load-bearing value is obtained earlier. The required penetration is usually specified to provide sufficient embedment of the piles to resist lateral forces in a structure and sometimes to protect against loss of bearing through erosion or scour of the soil surrounding the piles. However, when piles are driven to refusal before achieving plan penetration, driving must be suspended and the matter referred to the Engineer for decision.

3-8.6.3 Driving Piles Under Water. Two methods are commonly used for driving piles under water. When using a drop hammer, diesel hammer or open-type steam or air hammer, the pile is driven to just above the water surface. Then a follower is placed on top of the pile and driving is resumed. If a closed-type steam or air hammer is used, driving may be continued below the surface of the water without a follower, provided an exhaust hose is installed to vent the exhaust steam or air above the water surface. In addition, compressed air must be supplied to the lower part of the hammer casing to prevent water from flowing into the housing around the ram.

3-8.7 Determination of Pile Bearing Values. Piles are to be driven to the penetrations and bearing values indicated on the plans. The bearing value of the pile can be accurately determined by loading a driven test pile. However, the bearing value is usually determined by dynamic pile bearing formulas, the most commonly used being the Engineering News formula and modifications thereof. While different jurisdictions may use variations of this formula (or another formula altogether), the

Standard Specifications for Public Works Construction promulgated by the APWA-AGC Joint Cooperative Committee require bearing values to be determined from the following formulas:

Pile Hammer Used	Formula
Drop hammer	$P = \dfrac{2\,WL}{s + 1}$
Single-acting steam or air hammer or diesel hammer	$P = \dfrac{2\,WL}{s + 0.1}$
Double-acting steam or air hammer	$P = \dfrac{2\,L\,(W + ap)}{s + 0.1}$
Single-acting or double-acting steam or air hammer; or diesel hammer (alternate formula)	$P = \dfrac{2\,E}{s + 0.1}$

P = Safe bearing load developed by the pile in pounds.
W = Weight of the hammer (or ram) in pounds.
L = Length of stroke or height of fall of the hammer in feet.
s = Penetration of the pile into the ground per blow in inches (decimal fraction) taken as the average over the last 10 blows.
a = Effective area of the piston in square inches.
p = Mean effective steam or air pressure in pounds per square inch.
E = Manufacturer's rating of energy developed by the hammer in foot-pounds.

When computing bearing values of piles, the weight of a follower is not considered to be included as a part of the hammer weight. Actually, some of the hammer energy is absorbed in overcoming the inertia of the follower, which introduces a problem not provided for in the dynamic pile bearing formulas.

While the mathematics of determining pile bearing value from the appropriate dynamic formula is relatively simple, it is important that the calculation be performed accurately, since errors can result in widely varying bearing values.

An example of calculating bearing value of a pile follows: a single-acting steam hammer is used to drive step-tapered steel pile shells (utilizing a mandrel) to a bearing value of 20 tons per pile. The ram of the hammer weighs 2,875 pounds and has a stroke of 2.33 feet. From measurement of the penetration of the pile over the last 10 blows, the average penetration per blow is determined to be 0.23 inches. From this data, it can be seen that $W = 2,875$ lbs., $L = 2.33$ feet, and $s = 0.23$ inches.

By substituting these values into the formula for single-acting steam hammers, the bearing value of the pile would be derived as follows:

$$P = \frac{2\,WL}{s + 0.1}$$

$$P = \frac{2 \times 2875 \times 2.33}{0.23 + 0.1}$$

$$P = \frac{13398}{0.33}$$

$$P = 40{,}600 \text{ pounds (or 20.3 tons)}$$

If this pile hammer is assumed to have a rating plate affixed to it by the manufacturer indicating that the hammer develops 6,700 foot-pounds, the pile bearing value could be determined by the following formula where $E = 6{,}700$ foot-pounds.

$$P = \frac{2\,E}{s + 0.1}$$

$$P = \frac{2(6700)}{0.23 + 0.1}$$

$$P = \frac{13400}{0.33}$$

$$P = 40{,}600 \text{ pounds (or 20.3 tons)}$$

To determine true bearing value, it is imperative that exact measurements be made of the penetration of the pile for each of the last 10 blows. When the proper penetration is reached and the pile appears to be approaching the specified bearing, a mark is made on the pile and referenced to a fixed elevation so that the amount of penetration per blow can be determined. If the leads are securely attached to the pile driver rig so that their elevation will not change, the pile can be referenced from a mark on the leads. Other methods may be employed, including the use of a surveyor's level or by setting up batter boards to support a taut string passing near but not touching a mark on the pile.

It is important that pile driving operations are not interrupted immediately before measuring the value of "s." If the pile has "rested" in the period immediately before determining its bearing value, the dynamic pile formulas will give inaccurate bearing values — always higher than would have been indicated from the sample pile if it had been driven without interruption.

Since all of the values to be substituted into the formulas are known prior to commencing pile driving operations, the Inspector should substitute them into the proper formula and solve the equation for the value of "s," the average sinking in inches per blow over the last 10 blows:

$$s = \frac{2E}{P} \; 0.1$$

By this procedure, he can determine (in the case of the example given above) that the value of "s" would be 0.23 inches maximum or that it would take between four and five blows to sink the pile one inch when the bearing value reaches 20 tons. This procedure of calculating the value of "s" in advance permits continuous driving and gives the Inspector better control over the driving operations as the piles approach required bearing values.

When specified bearing is attained, the Inspector should so advise the pile foreman immediately, so that the pile driving rig can be promptly moved to drive another pile. Since a major portion of the total pile driving operation is spent in setting up to drive or in moving, it is imperative that the Inspector cooperate with the pile driving crew in reducing the non-productive moving time to the minimum. On the other hand, the Inspector should take sufficient time to be sure that the pile bearing value is carefully determined and should not permit himself to be pressured by the crew to hurry.

When required by the plans or Special Provisions, exploratory piles may be required to determine the length, penetration and bearing value of the piling to be used for the project. The Engineer will establish the conditions under which exploratory piles are driven and test loaded. Exploratory piles are to be driven with the same pile driver that is intended for use in driving the remainder of the piles.

Exploratory piles are not to be load tested until 48 hours after the pile is driven; or in the case of cast-in-place piles, the concrete has attained a minimum compressive strength of 2000 psi. A load test consists of the continuous application of a load

to twice the design load required, and once begun, the loading
must be continuous on a 24-hour day, 7-day week basis until
completed. The test pile is considered to have a bearing value
equal to the design load if the settlement produced by the test
loading is not greater than ¼ inch measured 48 hours after loading is completed.

3-8.8 **Pile Driving Records.** The Inspector must complete a form entitled "Record of Pile Driving." (See Plate 39,
Appendix.) Unless the pile pattern is relatively simple, a separate card should be made for each pile group; that is, for each
abutment, pier, bent, structure or portion of a structure. It is
preferred that this record be developed in a rough-draft form
and transferred later to the form, in ink.

In completing the data required for his record, the Inspector should fill in **all** blank spaces in the top portion of the card.
It is emphasized that the make and kind of pile hammer should
be clearly indicated, for example: "Vulcan No. 2, single-acting
steam."

Make a sketch on the back of the card to show the pile pattern. Letter each row and number each pile consecutively (C-1,
C-2, C-3, for example). An arrow indicating north must be included in the sketch. Use short arrows to mark battered piles.

In the tabulating portion of the record card, the piles are to
be listed in the order in which they are driven. Record the date
each pile is driven and whether it is a vertical or battered pile.
Under the column titled "Location," furnish the station, bent,
row or other designation. Enter the pile number in the appropriate column. Record all pile lengths and hammer drop distance to the nearest one-tenth of a foot, but the average final
penetration of the pile is to be recorded in decimal fractions of
an inch. The safe bearing capacity is to be recorded in tons and
decimal fractions of tons. The ease or difficulty with which individual piles were driven, or other pertinent information, is to
be entered under "Remarks."

The completed pile cards are to be forwarded to the Design
Engineer immediately upon completion of all pile driving. They
if not to be kept with the job records until the project is
completed.

3-8.9 **Pile Driving Safety.** Additional precautions are
necessary around pile driving operations because of the increased hazard potential. Wrenches, bolts, nuts and other
objects can loosen from vibration and fall from elevated leads,

cables under strain can fail, steam or high-pressure air lines can break and whip, piles can be dropped, to name but a few of the hazards. Piles should never be lifted or swung over areas where men are working.

Safety helmets must be worn by all pile driving crewmen and inspection personnel during driving operations. Oils and greases spatter from the hammer parts or exhaust when it is operating and often this oil is hot. Safety goggles, gloves and coveralls must be worn to avoid burns and protect dress clothing.

The Inspector should insist that the pile foreman frequently examine cables for indications of wear, check steam boilers and lines and keep all overhead parts of the pile driving rig free from unsecured objects. Knock-down type of leads should be examined occasionally to insure that vibration has not loosened the connections.

Extreme caution must be exercised when driving piles near power lines. There is so much interest in the accurate location of the leads for pile driving, that the crew sometimes becomes careless about nearby power lines.

The tops of driven pile shells or drilled holes shall be securely covered immediately upon withdrawal of the mandrel or drilling equipment to eliminate the hazard to life and to prevent dirt or debris from falling into them. In addition, provision must be made to prevent surface water from entering the casing, shell or hole.

3-8.10 False Pile Bearing Values. There are numerous ways in which the pile driver operator can deceive the unwary Inspector into assuming that the specified bearing has been obtained. Some of the "tricks of the trade" are enumerated here, while others remain to be discovered:

1. The contractor will furnish a drop hammer which is too light for the work it is expected to do. A light hammer engaged in heavy driving will yield a false high bearing value when computed by the Engineering News formulas.

2. When using a double-acting hammer, a slight reduction in steam or air pressure will reduce the speed of the hammer, increase the skin friction, decrease the penetration per blow and distort the results of the Engineering News formulas.

3. Similarly, changing the steam parts or resetting of the slide bar on a double-acting hammer will slow the cycle rate or

increase the back pressure, thereby reducing the penetration per blow and yield higher bearing values when computed by the Engineering News formulas.

4. Cushion blocks of soft wood may be substituted for the tougher woods commonly used, thereby absorbing much of the energy of the hammer and distorting the calculated bearing values in favor of the contractor.

5. A single-acting hammer can be easily slowed down by the operator to reduce the stroke several inches. Unless this is noticed by the Inspector, he will unwittingly use the full stroke of the ram in his computations.

6. The operator may deliberately use a pile driving sequence that results in driving a great number of piles between other piles already driven. This practice yields unrealistically high bearing values for the reasons explained in Subsection 3-8.6.1.

7. Driving may be stopped for several minutes to permit skin friction to develop. Once driving is suspended on a pile, considerable energy must be utilized to start it moving again. If bearing readings are taken during this phase, erroneously high bearing values will be obtained. Bearing values should not be taken on a pile that has been "resting" until it has been driven an additional two or three feet.

A good Inspector will be alert to notice any change in driving rhythm, raising or lowering of the pitch of steam or air exhaust, changes in sound of the hammer impact on the pile or any other clue to indicate that conditions are changed from normal driving conditions. If these changes are not obvious, he should make a detailed check of all of the conditions which might affect a bearing evaluation. Intentional attempts by the contractor to deceive the Inspector should be immediately stopped by the Inspector and the matter reported at once to his Supervisor.

3-8.11　Sampling and Testing. Sampling of piling is not customarily performed on Agency projects since the Standard Specifications clearly delineate the causes for rejection based on defects which are visible to the Inspector. However, treated wood piles are inspected at the treatment plant and stamped with a die impression of the Inspection Agency within three feet of the butt end of each pile. (See Subsection 2-1.2.7.)

With precast or cast-in-place concrete piles, samples of reinforcing steel prestress tendons will be taken and concrete test cylinders will be made in accordance with the Sampling Schedule, Plate 28, Appendix.

3-8.12 **Measurement and Payment.** The Standard Specifications give complete instructions for measuring piling for payment. It is emphasized here that the contractor is paid in two ways: for furnishing piles and for driving piles.

3-8.13 Piles and Pile Driving Checklist
General

(1) Check general conditions in the area where piles are to be driven (or drilled) — Clearing, grubbing, removals completed? Existing improvements and utilities protected? Excavations or embankment to plan subgrade completed prior to driving piling? (Refer to checklist in Subsection 3-3.2.2.)

(2) Check for correct type and length of pile. Other pile requirements? Butt and tip diameter?

(3) Has pile been checked for damage and defects?

(4) Locations of piles staked by survey?

(5) Check for hazards and provisions for safety. Will overhead power lines be sufficiently clear of crane boom or pile driver leads (refer to CAL/OSHA Clearance Requirements)?

(6) Check soil borings for expected driving or drilling conditions. Ground water elevation?

(7) Obtain pile driver specifications and operating data. (Type, weight and stroke of ram, etc.)

(8) What is minimum penetration and bearing values required and formula for calculating the bearing value?

(9) What is the method of measuring penetration for calculating bearing during driving? Does method exclude introduction of deliberate error by the operator?

(10) Is the operation of the pile driver satisfactory? Continuous driving until penetration is attained? Check that ram is operating at full stroke, rated speed and fully recommended operating pressure. Check for slowing of hammer.

(11) Check for proper lifting and handling of pile in the leads.

(12) Check for proper alignment during driving, plumb or batter?

(13) Check for sequence of driving or drilling (inside piles in group usually driven first).

(14) For H-Beam piles: are welded splices permitted? Approved welding procedure, certified welder used? Check for bends in flanges.

(15) For step taper piles, check for treatment or sealing of joints in ground water. Water and soil removed before placing concrete? Inspected with mirror or light and checked for collapsing after driving? Reinforcing steel centered and concrete placed slowly to prevent voids?

(16) Watch for proper handling of precast prestressed concrete piles. Are proper cushion blocks used?

(17) Check for overdriving during driving (sound and vibration, bouncing of hammer). High driving resistance in upper portion may require pilot drilling or jetting (review with Design Engineer).

(18) Recheck low driving resistance in cohesive soils by driving next day.

(19) Maintain record of driving as required. Record of driving resistance, pile number, butt and tip elevation; notes regarding delays during driving, extent of jetting if permitted or required. Records kept current throughout operations?

Drilled Cast-in-Place Piles

(20) Check diameters and depth. Drilled vertically? Does soil from drilling agree with borings on plan (report differences to Design Engineer)?

(21) Is casing being used in unstable soil (pulled during concrete placement)?

(22) Check hole for loose soil and water with mirror or light (removed before placing concrete)?

(23) Reinforcing steel centered in hole? Oriented vertically?

(24) Concrete placed in hopper and tremie to avoid segregation and disturbing soil on sides? Consolidated by rodding or mechanical vibrator?

(25) Piles drilled and concrete placed same day?

(26) Report concrete mix slump and cubic yards placed in job records.

3-9 STREET LIGHTING AND TRAFFIC SIGNAL CONSTRUCTION

3-9.1 General. Street lighting and traffic signal installations are frequently constructed in connection with a street improvement project. The plans for such projects may require the installation of a new system, or the remodeling or relocation of all or portions of an existing system. When the street improvement exists and no remodeling is contemplated, contracts for street lighting or traffic signal installations may be awarded separately; for example, street lighting assessment district projects or the signalization of an existing intersection.

When the street lighting portion of a project is commenced, the Dispatcher will fill out the form "Street Lighting Construction Start Notice," entering the name of the street lighting contractor and the starting date of the street lighting work. Copies of the form will be transmitted at once to the Street Lighting Engineer and to the serving Utility Agency. (See Plate 64, Appendix.)

The Inspector has the responsibility to require that the contractor perform all work in strict accordance with the plans and Standard Specifications and to secure a high quality of workmanship.

At the begining of work on each project, the Inspector should review the project plans for the items required to be salvaged. Refer to Subsection 3-9.11 for detailed instructions.

Lists of approved materials are issued by the Agency Street Lighting Engineer and new materials and products are added as they become available. The street lighting contractor is required to submit a list of the equipment proposed for use from this list as soon as it is practical following the contract award. In no case should the contractor (or permittee on permit projects) be allowed to proceed with the work before the list has been received and a copy is at the jobsite for use in checking the equipment as it is being installed. This list must include complete catalog numbers for each item listed in order to serve this purpose. (See Plate 14, Appendix for sample.)

Sampling of electrical material shall be in accordance with the Sampling Schedule. (See Plate 28, Appendix.)

3-9.2 Definition of Terms. While the terms listed in this Subsection may have a wider application in the electrical construction industry, they are defined here only as they apply to street lighting or traffic signal installations.

Bond. Electrical ground continuity between the metallic appurtenances of an electrical system such as conduit, electroliers, metal cases of ballasts, etc., usually supplied by copper wire or copper strap.

Bushing. A cylindrical device which is threaded on conduit to cover the sharp end surfaces of the conduit and protect cable insulation from damage.

Cable. An insulated bundle of conductors.

Conductor. A wire or cable through which current is intended to flow.

Conduit. A metal tube in which electric conductors are installed for protection.

Circuit. The complete path of an electric current.

Cut-out Box. An enclosure, designed for mounting on a pole, containing an element which, when removed, will de-energize an electric circut.

Electrolier. Street light assembly complete, including foundation, electrolier standard, luminaire arm, luminaire, etc.

Electrolier Standard. The shaft or pole used to support the luminaire arm, luminaire, etc.

Factory Bend. A prefabricated conduit bend.

Film-disc Cutout. A flat circular piece of insulating material installed with individual lamps in a series circuit to provide circuit continuity when the lamp fails.

Ground. A connection to earth to make it a part of the circuit.

Hy Crab (Mole). An electrical connecting device consisting of a bus bar encased in a waterproof jacket with connectors for several conductors.

Lamp. A light source which may be one of several types, such as filament (incandescent), mercury vapor, sodium vapor or fluorescent.

Luminaire. The lamp housing including the optical and socket assemblies (and ballast if so specified).

Luminaire Arm. The structural member, bracket or mast arm, which, mounted on the electrolier standard, supports the luminaire.

Mole (Hy Crab). An electrical connecting device consisting of a bus bar encased in a waterpoof jacket with connectors for several conductors.

Multiple Circuit. A low-voltage parallel-wired circuit.

NEMA. The abbreviation for National Electrical Manufacturers Association.

PE (Photo Electric) Cell. A light sensitive switch inserted in the circuit that energizes the street light at sundown and de-energizes it at sunrise.

Pothead. A device attached to the end of a wire or cable, hermetically sealed to the sheath and making a moisture-proof connection.

Pull Box. A concrete or metal box in which conduit runs terminate.

Pull Wire. A flexible iron wire or nylon rope or cord used to pull a conductor or cable through a conduit.

Running Thread. An extra length of thread on one end of a conduit to permit the use of a standard coupling in lieu of a union for joining two conduits.

Series Circuit. The arrangement of the separate parts of a circuit, successively end to end, to form a single path for the electric current.

Slip-joint Coupling. A waterproof telescopic joint used between two conduits to permit longitudinal expansion and contraction.

Terminal Block. A point at which any conductor may be directly connected to one or more other conductors.

Transformer. A device used to change alternating current from one voltage to another.

3-9.3   Locating Electroliers and Traffic Signal Devices.

3-9.3.1   **Street Lighting Electroliers.** Locations for street lighting electroliers are planned by the Engineer to obtain a specific degree of illumination in an intersection or on a roadway. On contract and assessment projects, the Agency will mark locations for the electroliers by a "Y" painted on the curb or by a stake if no curb exists. On subdivision permit work this is done by the private engineer. (See Plate 42, Appendix.)

However, interferences are often encountered in the field of which the Engineer may be unaware. Sometimes, the problem can be resolved by simply relocating the electrolier. In other cases, it may be necessary to relocate the interfering surface installation or facility.

Common interferences are driveway approaches, catch basins, outlet basins, future storm drain facilities, fire hydrants, utility poles, overhead wires, guy wires, traffic signals, trees, etc. Determine what interference exists (or will exist later, as in the case of a small tree planted near an electrolier), identify it, measure the distance from the center of the interference to the electrolier, examine the area for an alternate location for either the electrolier or the interference, identify the owner of the interference, then contact the Street Lighting Engineer by telephone relating the foregoing information. (See Subsection 3-9.4, Authorized Changes.)

3-9.3.2 Traffic Signal Devices. Signal standards, controllers and appurtenances shall be located only as shown on the plans. All deviations must be approved in the field by the Traffic Engineer or his authorized representative, prior to the installation.

All requests for temporary traffic signals made necessary or desirable during construction shall be referred to the appropriate Engineering Office having responsibility for design of the project. The contractor is never permitted to utilize temporary traffic signals without prior authority.

3-9.4   Authorized Changes.

3-9.4.1 Street Lighting Projects. Inspectors are authorized to make certain minor changes in street lighting installations in accordance with the following procedures; however, in no case may an Inspector permit a change to be made which would result in a change of cost to the Agency without prior approval:

(a) Conduit may be moved not to exceed four feet from its intended location behind the curb without prior approval of the Street Lighting Engineer. Under sidewalk returns, conduit shall be placed as close to the curb as possible, depending upon the construction methods used by the contractor, but in no case shall conduit be placed closer than one foot from the property line.

(b) Similarly, prior approval of the Street Lighting Engineer is not required for changes in location not exceeding 10 feet for electroliers (except on major streets and at intersections of local streets) or 30 feet for a pull box not associated with an electrolier. The Inspector shall inform the Engineer of the contemplated change and obtain a verbal clearance that no interference with future surface or substructure installations will result from the change in location. All changes in locations of electroliers exceeding 10 feet, or on major streets, and at intersections of local streets, must be cleared in advance with the Street Lighting Engineer.

(c) Changes in location not included in the foregoing must be approved by the Engineer.

Prior to the release of a project by the Final Inspection Group, the Engineer will issue a Change Order covering all changes authorized in paragraph (c) above.

3-9.4.2   Traffic Signal Projects.   Minor changes in the location of traffic signal conduit may be made by the Inspector without prior approval of the Traffic Engineer as long as no change in cost is involved. Where radical changes in location of conduit are necessary or foundations cannot be placed where shown on the plans, call the Engineer for clarification.

3-9.5   "As Built" Plans.

3-9.5.1   Street Lighting Installations.   The first Inspector assigned to a street lighting installation will be furnished a set of plans for the project, which will be stamped "AS BUILT."

All entries shall be neatly made using red pencil on white prints or yellow pencil on blue prints.

The Instructions that follow appear on the first sheet of the As Built Plan for the ready reference of the Inspector.

STREET LIGHTING AS BUILT PLAN INSTRUCTIONS

CONTRACTOR'S NAME:	DATE FIELD WORK STARTED:
	DATE AS BUILT COMPLETED:

1. SHOW ALL CHANGES FROM PLAN AT PLAN LOCATIONS WHERE THEY APPLY (DESCRIPTION, CHANGE ORDER OR OTHER AUTHORITY AND DATE) INCLUDING ELECTROLIER & SERVICE POINT RELOCATIONS (DIMENSION FROM OLD PLAN LOCATION OR LOCATE BY OTHER SUITABLE MEANS); FOR EQUIPMENT CHANGES (ELECTROLIER, LUMINAIRE, LAMP SIZE) INDICATE CHANGE AT EACH AFFECTED LOCATION OR CIRCUIT (IF APPLICABLE TO ENTIRE CIRCUIT) AND CHANGE PLAN MATERIAL LIST TO REFLECT CHANGE.
2. RECORD DATE IN OR OUT OF SERVICE AT EACH POST OR AT EACH CIRCUIT DESIGNATION IF ENTIRE CIRCUIT IS IN OR OUT OF SERVICE ON SAME DATE. SHOW AS "(IN/2-25-86)" OR "(OUT/ 12-25-86)."
3. FOR ITEM ON THE MATERIAL LIST (ELECTROLIER, LUMINAIRE) INDICATE MANUFACTURER AND CATALOG NUMBER.

INSPECTOR(S) NAME:

This "As Built" plan is to be protected from handling wear and abuse, rain damage or sun fading, and no unnecessary marks are to be made thereon. It is imperative that this "As Built" plan be progressively marked by those Inspectors assigned to the various phases of the work as changes are encounted and authorized. Temporary ground locations should be marked lightly in pencil on the plan, noted "temp," and then erased when the ground is removed. During periods when the street lighting project is inactive, this plan must be returned to the office where the job records are normally filed.

When the Street Lighting Engineer specifies by a note on a permit that "conduit only" or "foundation only" is to be installed behind new curb being constructed, the "As Built" information must be shown on a sketch and attached to the permit or indicated on the street improvement plan for the permit. In this case the street improvement plan becomes an "As Built" plan and is to be protected and forwarded as provided herein.

The specifications may require the contractor to submit the "As Built" plan. If this is the case, the Inspector must continue to maintain the "As Built" plan in order to verify the contractor's submittal. The Inspector's signature on the contractor's plan will be evidence that this has been done.

Upon completion of the street lighting work, these "As Built" plans **must be forwarded** with the job records to the Final Inspection Group.

3-9.5.2 Traffic Signal Installations.

For traffic signal installations, the contractor must submit to the Traffic Engineer an "As Built" or corrected plan showing in detail all construction changes, a wiring diagram, locations and depth of conduit, and locations of standards and pull boxes.

The Inspector must maintain a smilar "As Built" plant to verify the accuracy and completeness of the plan submitted by the contractor. It must be forwarded to the Final Inspection Group when the work is completed.

A form entitled "Notice of Completion of Traffic Signal Work by Private Contractor" shall be utilized to provide information to the Traffic Engineer of all traffic signal work performed by private contractor as authorized by permit, contract or authorized by said Agency in the case of permanent repair of accidental damage. The form will be initiated by the Inspector having knowledge of the work done. Upon completion of information required on the form, it shall be immediately forwarded in accordance with the distribution stated thereon. (See Plate 53, Appendix.)

3-9.6   Construction Policies.

3-9.6.1   **General.** On contract projects, the Street Lighting Engineer verifies service point locations at the time the project is advertised. Any changes from the plan are included in a change order after the project is awarded. To minimize erroneous service point installations on permit projects, the Inspector should instruct the contractor to verify service point locations by calling the serving agency prior to installation. The contractor shall install the required individual circuit service equipment prior to construction of other components of that circuit.

After the contractor has completed installation of the service equipment for which he is responsible, the Project Street Lighting Inspector will prepare a request to the serving Agency to complete the service installation. The form entitled "Street Lighting Construction Record of Request" is to be filled out in quadruplicate and sent to the Dispatcher to be processed. (See Plate 42, Appendix.)

Street lighting and traffic signal conduit shall be installed prior to any subsequent work which will cover it, examples of which follow:

(a) The construction of concrete sidewalks.

(b) The construction of alley intersections.

(c) The construction of integral curb returns and spandrels.

(d) The construction of electrolier foundations.

Where portions of existing sidewalk must be removed for jacking pits, pilot holes and electrolier foundations, excavation must be made to saw cuts conforming to the dimensions and locations called for in the Standard Specifications.

The requirement that all utility installations in street areas be complete prior to paving is to be applied to street lighting and traffic signal conduit installations.

Street lighting conduit is generally installed behind the curb just after the curb is constructed. At curb returns the conduit is stubbed out under the concrete spandrels to provide for street crossings which are made after all other utility installations are complete in the street. Sometimes these stub-outs are installed at locations that may result in the concrete cross-gutter being constructed over a conduit crossing location. To avoid the circumstance of having such cross-gutters being constructed prior to the installation of the conduit, field personnel are instructed to insure that all conduit stub-outs for street crossings are marked by a painted "X" on the vertical face of the curb directly over the locations of the conduit at the time it is placed; and when the conduit crossing is completed, a circle is painted around the "X" on the face of the curb. (See Plate 42, Appendix.)

Inspection personnel assigned to inspect concrete cross-gutter construction are instructed to examine the curb in the vicinity of all cross-gutters for symbols indicating a conduit crossing. Make sure that the installation of the conduit is complete before allowing construction of the cross-gutter to proceed.

When plans require the top of curbs to be marked to indicate the location of traffic signal conduits, the letter "T" will be chipped on top of the curb.

Chief Inspectors may authorize deviations from this policy in cases where, in their judgment, the best interests of all concerned will be served.

3-9.6.2 Standard Specifications and Standard Plan Clarification. Clarifications of various portions of the Standard Specifications and standard plans are listed here for the information and guidance of the Inspector:

(a) Circular foundations, shown as alternates on most standard plans, may be used for any foundation unless it is specifically prohibited by the project plans.

(b) Locating a foundation, so that only one square of sidewalk need be removed, is authorized.

(c) On street lighting reconstruction contracts, the intent of the plans and specifications is that the existing painted steel electrolier bases be painted with the same paint as that required for the new portions of the electrolier.

(d) When the plan requires that certain lights be kept burning, the Inspector will ascertain the contractor's plan of operation and secure approval of this plan from the Street Lighting Engineer. Generally speaking, **all** lights on one side of the street are to be kept burning on **all-night** circuits.

(e) Conduit shall be installed around and in back of catch basins rather than through the top slab.

(f) Any electrolier standard having a bow or bend that is perceptible to the eye after erection shall be rejected.

(g) Compression connectors are required for all street lighting conductor splices. The Inspector should be familiar with the requirements for a good mechanical connection. The manufacturer's literature is a good source for the proper method to use. For example when using Nicopress sleeves, the sleeve is to be compressed twice (once at each end) as indicated below:

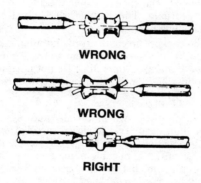

WRONG

WRONG

RIGHT

(h) Splices are authorized only in pull boxes and light standard bases. Interconnect conductors for traffic signals should be continuous from controller to controller unless splices are specifically authorized by the Engineer.

(i) When there is an urgent need, electroliers or traffic signals may be set after the foundation is 24 hours old provided Type III cement is used in the concrete mixture or Class 660-B-3750 concrete is used.

(j) When it becomes necessary to install a **traffic signal** pull box in a concrete driveway or other area subject to vehicular traffic loads, it shall be provided with a metal cover as required for an armored pull box. A ¼-inch steel non skid plate cover shall be used as shown on the Standard Drawing therefor. Pull boxes for **street lighting** systems shall not be installed in any driveway pavement.

(k) About two weeks prior to completion of the electrical system, the contractor should request that a "burn" test be scheduled. (See Subsection 3-9.9.)

(l) In series street lighting circuits the project plans normally call for use of No. 8 AWG solid copper conductors insulated with approved polyethylene compound rated for 5,000-volt operation. "Certified Performance Data" certificates for these conductors are to be made available to the Project Inspector by the contractor prior to their installation. Normally the conductors will not be sampled for physical testing. The Inspector will identify each conductor, and if the data contained in the manufacturer's certified performance sheet issued for each reel conforms to the specifications therefor, he can assume such data is acceptable. The Inspector's Daily Report should indicate that this has been done.

When the reel or the conductor is not identifiable, a sample should be cut from the reel and sent to the Agency's testing laboratory. (See Plate 28, Appendix.) Do not permit unidentifiable wire to be installed until satisfactory tests are completed.

3-9.7 Inspection.

3-9.7.1 **General.** All materials and system components of street lighting or traffic signal installations are to be inspected upon their delivery to the jobsite for conformance to the requirements of the applicable plans and specifications and the approved equipment list (see Subsection 3-9.1). Particular attention should be given to detailed requirements, such as the light distribution settings for street lighting luminaires. Notify the contractor of any non-conforming or otherwise unacceptable materials or equipment and do not permit their use. Materials which are found to be defective shall be rejected and immediately removed from the jobsite.

The techniques for inspecting street lighting and traffic signal installations are, in general, the same. Where differences in the specification requirements exist due to some inherent characteristics of each system, the procedures may vary slightly.

3-9.7.2 **Conduit Installation.** Conduit is to be checked upon its delivery to the jobsite for proper type, size, brand name and Underwriters Laboratories' label. The size of conduit is specified in the Standard Specifications or will be shown on the plans. Unless otherwise authorized, all conduit is to be rigid galvanized steel.

Threads on conduits are to be inspected to insure that they are not inadvertently cut too deep, creating a burr on the inside of the conduit which is likely to result in damage to the conductor insulation. Threads should be cut so as to extend far enough back from the end of the conduit to permit the conduit ends to butt together in the coupling. Threads should be painted with red lead or other approved material before joint make-up. There should be no more than two threads showing after the conduit is joined with couplings.

Water pipe is now being approved and used for conduit because of the favorable economical considerations. When water pipe is used the couplings should be replaced by conduit type couplings (non-taper threads). This will permit the pipe ends to butt together as required even though the threads on the pipe are tapered.

Conduit is usually cut with a pipe cutter or back saw which leaves a sharp edge on the inside of the conduit. This edge must be removed with a pipe burring reamer. Where a reamer cannot be used due to inaccessibility, a round file can be used. The ends of all lengths of conduit must be reamed even when threadless couplings are used. Slip joints or running threads are not permitted for joining conduit for traffic signal installations. Where a standard coupling cannot be used, a threaded union coupling may be used.

Conduit is normally installed behind and adjacent to new curb at a depth equal to that of the curb and to a minimum depth of 14 inches behind existing curb. In roadways, conduit is laid 30 inches below gutter flow line elevation. Trenches should be cleaned of concrete, dirt and other matter which will interfere with laying the conduit to the prescribed depth. It is important to maintain proper depth to prevent damage to the conduit from future landscaping operations in the parkway and to minimize the danger to the public from the high voltage carried by the conductors in the conduit. Where driveway approach slabs are installed, care must be taken to prevent the conduit from being imbedded in the concrete. If the conduit were to be embedded, any movement of the concrete slab from expansive soil loading deflections, thermal expansion or from future removal operations would probably result in conduit collapse or rupture with resultant damage to the conductors.

All damage to the galvanized coating of conduit or fittings and marks from wrenches and pipe tools must be painted with an approved rust-preventive compound and allowed to dry before backfilling of the trench is permitted. Care must be taken to prevent the compound from spreading to the inside of the conduit where it may cause a drag on the conductors, placing an unnecessary strain on them during pulling operations.

Conduit shall be drilled or jacked into place in 10-foot lengths, except that where conditions exist where shorter lengths must be used, five-foot lengths are permissible. Holes should be dug at 15 or 20-foot intervals to check that the drilled conduit is at the proper depth. The contractor should use a minimum amount of water for lubricating purposes when boring or jacking conduit. The Inspector should be alert to detect trouble from drilling conduit in hard or rocky ground. If much resistance to the rotation of the conduit is experienced, the couplings may turn and tend to thread themselves further onto the conduit. This may cause the butting ends of the conduit in the coupling to curl inward, often resulting in burrs which seriously restrict the opening and cause damage to the cable or conductor insulation during pulling operations.

Where existing conduit is to be incorporated into a new system, it should be cleaned with a mandrel and blown clean with compressed air.

No sharp bends are permitted in conduit since they tend to flatten the conduit and reduce the effective cross-sectional area. Factory bends may be used provided they meet the specifications for minimum radii and other requirements.

When making conduit bends at traffic signal and electrolier bases or pull box locations, the ends of the conduit should be carefully located and capped. Pipe caps must always be used on all stub-outs and, when shown on the plans, at tract boundary lines. Bushings with metal discs may be used to cap conduit ends in electrolier bases.

Conduits must be bonded with a copper ground strap equal in conductivity to a No. 8 copper wire in accordance with the Standard Specifications. Bonds are to be thoroughly secured by means of $\frac{1}{4}$-inch brass bolts and nuts at the time the conduit is installed, and before pull boxes are set.

Bonding of conduit, service equipment and neutral conductors at service points should be made with a strap or copper wire equivalent to No. 8 AWG. In addition, metallic conduit or bonding conductor system should be grounded at intervals not exceeding 500 feet as prescribed by the Standard Specifications. Non-metallic conduit should be bonded with a bare No. 8 copper wire running continuously in all circuits.

Conduit ends are not to be left open during any phase of construction. Pipe caps must be used to prevent debris from entering the conduit which might damage or prevent the pulling of conductors.

3-9.7.3 Pull Box Installation.

The Inspector must check the plans for the size and location of pull boxes. They should be approximately equally spaced, but not over 200 feet apart. The box is to be set so that the plane of the top is in the plane of the sidewalk (or future sidewalk) with one side parallel to the curb. Twelve inches of one-inch crushed rock is required under all pull boxes. Make sure that the proper depth and width of rock is supporting the box and that the box is not just being used as a bin to hold a few inches of rock in the bottom. If a larger opening has to be chipped in a pull box to accommodate larger conduit or to permit a misaligned conduit to enter, extra rock should be placed outside the box to prevent dirt from entering or rodents from filling the box with earth.

Conduit ends must be properly located in pull box installations in order to avoid transposition and to permit the installation of I.L. (individual lamp) transformers and cable loops, as well as to facilitate future maintenance. The Inspector must check the proper standard plan and insist on the conduit location specified together with any slope or angle needed on the riser end of the conduit. Where ballasts or transformers are installed in a pull box, a pull box extension should be installed to provide the additional space needed for the equipment.

3-9.7.4 Electrolier and Traffic Signal Foundations.

Before excavation, the Inspector must check each site to see that no overhead or other obstruction would interfere with the proposed installation. He must check the project plans and standard plans for foundation dimensions, and number and size of conduits required at each foundation. The project plans may require extra bends for future circuits. Care must be exercised to avoid transposition of conduit ends in bases or in the trench. Conduit stub ups in foundations must be set at the proper elevation so that they will not project above the hand hole of the pole to be installed. A drain hole must be formed from top to bottom of the base in an electrolier foundation by using a proper size pipe, tube or commercial forms as shown on the standard plans.

The excavation for the base must be dug to the full size and depth required. Tapering of the excavation is not permitted and the excavation should not be allowed to stand for long periods of time before the concrete is placed. Otherwise, the sides of the excavation may air slack and ravel into the hole. All loose dirt and debris must be removed from the hole before the concrete is placed therein.

Anchor bolts are to be set in a template which maintains each bolt in proper pattern, elevation, projection and vertical alignment as required for the specified electrolier or traffic signal device. Care must be taken to see that the bolt pattern is not rotated. Otherwise, the arm of an electrolier or mast arm of a traffic signal may not be perpendicular to the center line of the street as required.

Plumbing of standards shall be accomplished by adjusting the nuts on the anchor bolts before the foundation cap is placed. Shims or other similar devices for plumbing or raking will not be permitted.

A continuous copper bond strap is to be securely grounded to each conduit with brass bolts and nuts, and one end of the bond strap must extend 10 inches above the ends of the conduit. While this extension is not required where high-voltage conductors are to be spliced to I.L. or mercury vapor transformers in a pull box adjacent to an electrolier, the transformer metal case must be grounded by the continuous copper bond strap that is used to ground the conduit.

3-9.7.5 **Installing Conductors.** Before any cable or conductor is installed, the Inspector must check the wiring diagram on the plans. Conductors of the proper size and type, appropriately color coded, must be installed in the proper sequence.

Conduit bushings must be installed on all conduit ends before conductors are pulled through the conduits.

Conductors are to be installed in conduits by methods which will not damage the insulation. Sometimes a "snake" is pushed through the conduit first and is used to pull the conductor through. A more efficient method is to blow a leather "parachute" through the conduit with compressed air, which simultaneously pulls one or more conductors. New conductors may be pulled by hand but pulling with power winches is prohibited. Existing conductors which are to be removed and salvaged may be pulled, using power winches. In such cases, and where the condition of the conduit is such that cleaning will not be required, a new conductor may be installed by attaching it to the trailing end of the conductor being replaced. Only approved lubricants, such as talc or powdered soapstone, may be used for reducing the drag on the conductor as it is pulled through the conduit, and the contractor should be encouraged to use lubricants.

At least two feet of slack in each conductor should be left at each standard, and within each pull box sufficient slack should be left to extend 18 inches above the pull box grade. The ends of all conductors to be spliced are to have the insulation penciled and securely taped to keep out moisture. Oakum is to be tamped into each conduit around the conductors in pull boxes and electroliers to keep dirt and debris out of the conduit.

Special care must be exercised during the installation of conductors to protect the insulation. Under no circumstances should a conductor be dragged over the ground or exposed to any abuse which might damage the insulation, such as permitting vehicles to run over it or workers to walk upon it. Any damage to the insulation, although it may appear to be minimal in extent, often results in a subsequent short-circuit and costly replacement.

For these reasons, conductors must be pulled directly from the reels into the conduit, being careful to restrain each reel so that slack does not develop which would result in the conductor coming in contact with the pavement during the pulling operation.

Insofar as possible, conductors are to be installed between designated terminals without splices. A splice is never permitted to be installed in a conduit. Where a splice is unavoidable, it must be made in an electrolier base or a pull box. Where a continuous conductor is indicated on the plans to pass through a pull box or electolier base without terminating at a transformer or lamp, a splice is authorized in such instances in order to permit pulling the conductor directly from the reel.

A conductor extending beyond conduit ends at electrolier foundations, and which is intended for later installation in the electrolier, shall be neatly coiled, taped securely and placed over the foundation bolts to minimize damage to the insulation.

3-9.7.6 Installing Electroliers and Traffic Signals.
Electroliers are assembled (standard, mast arm and luminaire) prior to erection. The Inspector must check each assembly to see that all components are as specified and are securely mounted. Photo-electric cells must be oriented to the north. Each luminaire must be set to the required light distribution pattern.

Electroliers may be set after foundations have cured for at least three days, exccept that the electrolier may be set after 24 hours, as provided in Subsection 3-9.6.2(i). Washers are required on leveling nuts on the anchor bolts as specified on the Standard Plans. The electroliers are to be set plumb and with the arms aligned properly with the street. All nuts are to be tightened with wrenches of the proper size.

Targets are required on the "traffic side" of the electrolier arms to identify lamp sizes. (See Plate 43, Appendix.) The project plans are to be checked for correct socket position for mercury vapor-type luminaires. Film disc cut-outs are required in all bayonet-type sockets.

Insulation on the projecting ends of conductors should be checked for damage caused from the pulling operations. If insulation is scored or damaged, it may require replacement of the conductor and repair of the conduit which caused the damage.

Only after all other traffic signal equipment (including the controller) is in place and ready for operation, may the signal heads be installed at an intersection; otherwise, they must be covered or have the faces turned away from the traffic.

3-9.7.7 Safety Procedures. The contractor is required to comply with the provisions of all local codes governing safety procedures as well as all safety regulations issued by local electrical utility companies governing electrical installations.

3-9.7.8 Public Safety. All holes, including those for electrolier foundations, pull boxes, pilot holes and in-place concrete foundations prior to erection of electroliers, are required to be barricaded at all times when they are not immediately attended.

3-9.8 Safety Clearance and Engineering Service.

3-9.8.1 Routine Street Lighting Safety Clearance. Before a contractor can cut a conductor, or otherwise interrupt a circuit, or remove any electrolier or part of a street lighting system from service, he must first obtain a safety clearance. The procedure set forth herein for scheduling safety clearances must be rigidly followed:

(a) The contractor must first request a safety clearance from the serving Agency.

(b) The contractor must then notify the Dispatcher of the Inspection Agency, requesting inspection and informing him that the serving Agency will schedule a clearance.

(c) The Dispatcher will confirm with the serving Agency that the contractor has arranged for inspection and a safety clearance.

(d) The Dispatcher will then notify the Project Inspector of the time, place and date the contractor has requested the inspection and clearance.

(e) If there is no Project Inspector, the Dispatcher will assign an Inspector to the work at the time scheduled by the contractor.

3-9.8.2 Routine Traffic Signal Clearance. The contractor must notify the Traffic Engineer and obtain a clearance prior to performing any work on any existing traffic signal system. Unless otherwise specifically authorized by the Traffic Engineer, the contractor shall maintain existing traffic signals and electrically illuminated signs in effective operation at all times during the progress of the work.

3-9.8.3 Protection. On street improvement projects, the Inspector shall insure that the general contractor is aware of existing traffic signal and street lighting installations and that adequate measures are taken to protect them from damage.

Existing street lighting installations will be shown on the plans and, upon request of the contractor, the location of the street lighting conduit will be marked by the Street Lighting Engineer.

Due to the hazardous and highly technical nature of the work and the inherent details in coordinating clearances through the several agencies involved, the general contractor should not attempt to make repairs or perform work on street lighting or traffic signal installations with his own forces. He should make arrangements, prior to the start of any subsurface construction, for the services of a licensed street lighting contractor to temporarily disconnect street lighting circuits during the course of the work, to repair damage to these facilities arising from the construction operations, to make any permanent repairs required, and to perform all new street lighting and traffic signal construction or relocation required in the contract.

3-9.8.4 Interference. Where existing traffic signal or street lighting installations obstruct or otherwise interfere with specified improvements, the contractor shall notify the appropriate office of the Agency involved and he shall not alter or disturb such installations unless specifically authorized to do so.

Street name signs and roadside warning signs are under the jurisdiction of the Traffic Engineer. In the event that a sign interferes with construction operations or the permanent improvement, the following instructions shall apply:

Each sign shall be carefully removed by the contractor, appropriately tagged and stored in a protected location to await pick-up by the Traffic Engineer. If the removal is temporary, the tag should indicate its original location. Where the nature of the permanent improvement alters the conditions and cancels the need for the sign, the tag should read "For salvage — not to be reinstalled." The contractor shall call the sign foreman at the appropriate office of the Traffic Engineer and request that the sign be picked up. The Inspector shall enter a note in the job records for each such sign removed. Upon notification, the Traffic Engineer will reinstall signs without cost to the contractor. The contractor shall notify the sign foreman at such time construction operations have advanced to a point where this can be done.

3-9.8.5 Accidental Damage. When damage occurs involving street lighting or traffic signal installations, the contractor shall immediately notify the appropriate Agency. Prompt notification is very important, especially when traffic signals are accidentally rendered inoperative, as a serious traffic hazard may result.

The Inspector shall enter in his job record cards the nature and location of the damage, office and employee notified, date and time.

Service by the Street Lighting Engineer in connection with damage will be at the contractor's expense and limited to temporary repairs only. Permanent repairs or replacement of damaged portions of street lighting installations shall be the contractor's responsibility.

Service by the Traffic Engineer in connection with damage will either consists of:

(a) Permanent repair at the contractor's expense, or

(b) Temporary repair at the contractor's expense and instruction to the contractor to make the permanent repair under inspection.

Where (b) above is involved on permit projects, the contractor is required to obtain a separate Excavation Permit to cover the inspection costs involved in the permanent repair. Such permanent repairs must also be reported to the Traffic Engineer. (Refer to Subsection 3-9.5.2 for instructions.)

3-9.9 "Burn" Testing Street Lighting Systems.

3-9.9.1 General. When the street lighting contractor has completed his work to the point where he will be ready for testing new lights within a minimum of seven calendar days, he shall request the Project Street Lighting Inspector to arrange a tentative "burn" date with the serving Agency. (Large projects should be constructed and burned in multiples of four circuits or more.) The Project Street Lighting Inspector will prepare a "burn" test request, using the form entitled "Street Lighting Construction Record of Request," which he transmits to his Dispatcher. (See Plate 65, Appendix.) The Dispatcher will call the serving Agency and request a date for the "burn" test as close as possible to the contractor's indicated date of readiness. After entering the scheduled date and time of the test, the Dispatcher will sign the form and mail one copy to the contractor and one to the serving Agency. He will also advise the Project Street Lighting Inspector and the District Supervisor of the scheduled date and time of the "burn" test.

On State projects the State inspector arranges with the serving Agency for a tentative date for a "burn" test.

3-9.9.2 Confirmation of "Burn" Date. The contractor and the Project Street Lighting Inspector must make a final judgment regarding the readiness of the project for the "burn" test not later than the morning of the day prior to the day scheduled. Any notice to cancel shall be reported to the Dispatcher for transmittal to the serving Agency, after which a new date for the "burn" test will be initiated by the contractor through the Project Street Lighting Inspector.

The contractor should be reminded to have on hand a ladder truck and other equipment and materials that may be needed for the particular type job that is to be tested, such as connectors, tape, extra lamps, cable, etc., as the test will be cancelled if these items are needed and are not on hand.

3-9.9.3 Field Procedures for "Burn" Test. On the date scheduled, the Project Street Lighting Inspector, the contractor and the serving Agency's crew will meet at the jobsite to initiate the "burn" test.

Two procedures are followed, one for low-voltage multiple circuits and the other for high-voltage series circuits. On the former, the system is energized and if the project is small, the photo-electric cell on each electrolier is momentarily covered to check the operation of the cell itself and the condition of the lamp it controls. Spot checks are made on larger systems involving multiple circuits.

High-voltage circuits wired in series are first tested with an instrument known as a "megger" to check for open circuits or faulty grounds. The contractor makes corrections as needed during this operation. The system is then given a high-potential test at about 6,300 volts furnished by a portable transformer.

Since circuits of excessive length have higher resistance in comparison with those of lesser length, long high-voltage series circuits on large projects are cut in half with a temporary disconnection by the contractor and each half tested separately.

A defective or damaged conductor will cause a ground or an open circuit and must be replaced by the contractor before the test can continue.

After certain temporary connections are made, the system is energized for about five minutes. If all lamps remain lit and no grounds develop, the system is considered to pass the "burn" test. Permanent connections are then made by both the contractor and the Agency crew, after which the system is energized once more. The contractor replaces any burned-out lamps and the new system is ready for operation.

The specifications require a three-night operational test and the correction by the contractor of any inoperative equipment discovered during that period. The Agency's Street Lighting Night Patrol will report to the Dispatcher any inoperative equipment observed during the test period. The Dispatcher will in turn relay this information to the Project Street Lighting Inspector. Upon successful completion of the "burn" test, the new lights remain in service.

If the contractor has signed a "Maintenance Consent "Agreement" as part of the "burn" test request procedure (see Plate 65, Appendix) the Agency will assume all maintenance, as provided, when its terms have been satisfied. Otherwise, the Agency will assume maintenance responsibility only for renewal of lamps, replacement of vandalized glassware and repair of minor wiring. The contractor remains fully responsible for the correction of subsequent failures resulting from defective materials and equipment or from poor workmanship.

Following the "burn" test, the Project Street Lighting Inspector will fill out the form "Street Lighting Construction

Record of Lamp Changes" (see Subsection 3-9.10), indicating thereon the lamps placed in service following the "burn" test. The required entry can be added to an existing form if one has been previously started, having been made out to list lamps taken out of service or lamps previously placed in service on other circuits during construction of the project.

3-9.10 Street Lighting Construction Record of Lamp Changes. Either record the appropriate date on the as-built plans as selected from the check-list below or use form (See Plate 14, Appendix).

Report a "REMOVAL" whenever any of the following items occur:

(1) Any time a lamp is out of service, for any reason.

(2) Existing electrolier is taken out of service, either permanently, temporarily or for the purpose of relocation.

(3) Any equipment removed from an existing electrolier, such as ballast, luminaire or lamp.

(4) Schedule change, such as from M (midnight) to AN (all night).

Report an "INSTALLATION" whenever any of the following items is performed on the job:

(1) New electrolier placed in service.

(2) Equipment installed on existing electrolier and placed in service.

(3) Existing electrolier relocated and placed in service.

(4) Schedule change on existing electrolier left in service.

(5) Reactivation of an existing electrolier previously out of service.

Report changes chronologically as they occur during construction. Upon completion of the project the "Record of Lamp Changes" is to be forwarded to the main office in the job envelope.

Use separate lines to report removals and installations, even though both occur on the same date.

Use the remarks column to designate field changes, change orders, "schedule change only," as they are involved, and any other clarification of entries.

If existing electroliers were erected under two or more old plans, the new plans may identify existing electroliers by ap-

propriate enclosing symbols and will include a legend to match
the enclosing symbols with the existing plan number. Parenth-
eses (), brackets [ ], circle ○ and rectangles ▭ will be used in
that order depending on the number of existing plans involved.
If more than four plans are involved, additional symbols will be
indicated. These symbols must be utilized in reporting lamp
changes. In most cases this will involve the entry for electrolier
"removal."

Electrolier numbering is done consecutively when plans
are prepared. The Inspector is cautioned, however, that
changes during design may cause an electrolier to be eliminated
without re-numbering the entire system. Care must be exercised to avoid reporting an electrolier that does not exist.

Where electroliers have more than one luminaire, each
luminaire is designated by the electrolier number and a letter
commencing alphabetically. For example, an electrolier with
four luminaires would have luminaire designations 1A, 1B, 1C
and 1D.

New electrolier numbers are usually indicated for electroliers which are re-used. Plans will indicate new numbers for
existing electroliers which are involved in equipment changes
involving ballast, lamp size, electrolier type (including addition
of mast arms and other modifications), luminaire arm, luminaires or electrolier relocation.

The following sample form includes a number of typical
entries to indicate the correct reporting procedure. The
numbered paragraphs below refer to the numbers in the left-
hand column of the sample form:

#1 Existing post (4) removed and to be relocated. Note
that (4) does not appear as an installation item on subsequent
entries even though the post is to be relocated. This is
explained by the policy which requires the designer to give the
post a new number for the re-installation. #2 Represents new
85-post system placed in service. #3 Existing post schedule
change. #4 Existing post removed. Not to be installed. #5
Existing post replaced with new post and luminaire by change
order. #6 Four existing posts taken out of service temporarily.
#7 Four existing posts placed in service after installing new
conduit and wire between posts. #8 New 35-post system placed
in service. Three posts have four luminaires each.

When the street lighting portion of a project is commenced, the Dispatcher will fill out form, entering the

CITY OF ANYWHERE
DEPARTMENT OF PUBLIC WORKS
BUREAU OF CONTRACT ADMINISTRATION   Page ___/___ of ___/___

STREET LIGHTING CONSTRUCTION RECORD OF LAMP CHANGES

JOB TITLE **Pearl St & Barrington Ave LD**   JOB NO. **A 11 79118**

PLAN NO. **D-22193**

PATROL MAP NO. **136, 150, 151**

Existing Equipment—Legend of Symbol
( )—Plan No. _____   —Plan No. _____
[ ]—Plan No. _____   —Plan No. _____

Post No.	Removal Date	Installation Date	Schedule M	AN	Lamp Size	Post Type	Remarks	Inspector
(4)	3-28-87			1	400 MV	953C	to be relocated	J. Jones
	Thru 85	Inclusive						
		7-2-87	85		175 MV	851 A		
(12)	9-8-87			1	175 MV	851 A	Schedule	
"		9-8-87		1	"	"	Change only	J. Jones
(26)	9-8-87			1	400 MV	953C	Permanent	J. Jones
(14)	9-15-87			1	400 MV	953C	Equip Change	
"		9-15-87		1	175 MV	851 A	C.O. #2	J. Jones
(7)	Thru (10)	Inclusive						
	9-15-87			4	175 MV	851 A	Temporary	J. Jones
(7)	Thru (10)	Inclusive					Replace conduit	
		9-17-87		4	175 MV	851 A	& wire bet. posts	J. Jones
1	Thru 35	Inclusive					Luminaires on	
		9-25-87		44	175 MV	953C	posts 4,5,6)	J. Jones

Form 160 (Rev 12-69)

Original forwarded to Bureau of Street Lighting
Date **10-6-87** by **P. Smith**
Final Inspector

tion Start Notice," entering the name of the street lighting contractor and the starting date of the street lighting work. Copies of the firm will be transmitted to the Street Lighting Engineer and to the Serving Agency. (See Plate 64, Appendix.)

3-9.11 Salvaged Material. At the beginning of work on each project, the Inspector must review the project plans for items required to be salvaged. The condition of items to be salvaged should be checked prior to removal of the equipment.

The contractor must be aware of the salvage procedure and the need for a receipt from the Agency yard when salvage is delivered. The receipt shall be furnished to the Project Inspector by the contractor after delivery is made. Receipts to cover all salvage on the project will be verified by the Final Inspection Group.

When required by the specifications, items of salvage must be disassembled by the contractor. Traffic signal standards for example, must be dismantled into components. (Shaft, base casting, head and mast arms.) All individual pieces shall be tagged by the contractor to indicate the project title or the street location from which the material came.

The contractor will be held responsible for any damage to salvaged items resulting from his operations. However, the contractor's responsibility to salvage equipment need not extend beyond a reasonable attempt at disassembly by normally accepted methods which will not damage the equipment.

Disassembly of threaded shafts from base casting is best accomplished with these components in place prior to removal of the base from the foundation.

In the event the contractor cannot disassemble such equipment, he shall arrange for its delivery to the yard by prior appointment. The delivery of all traffic signal equipment salvage shall be between the hours of 9 a.m. and 2 p.m.

3-9.12 Job Envelope. A separate job envelope with a green title label and a supply of green inspection job record cards marked "Street Lighting" will be provided for each street lighting project. Street lighting job records shall be maintained on inspector's report which are separate from the traffic signal system job records. Record all entries for traffic signal installations on salmon-colored job cards marked "Traffic Signals."

3-9.13 Final Inspection. See Subsection 4-3.12 for procedures to follow for final inspection of street lighting and Subsection 4-3.13 for traffic signal work.

3-9.14 Inspector's Check List.

Have the necessary standard plans been obtained for use on the particular project?

Have samples been taken of the materials to be used in the project or have they been previously approved by brand name and number?

Have all electrolier locations been marked by a painted "Y" on the curb?

Do the project plans call for any items to be salvaged?

In case of an interference, have steps been taken to move the interference, or has an electrolier location change been approved and noted on the "As Built" plan?

Are conduits installed at the proper depth?

Is conduit terminated properly in pull boxes?

Are stub-ups in electrolier foundations at correct elevation to match hand hole in pole?

Are all stub-outs for street crossings located by a painted "X" on the curb face, and when the conduit is installed across the street, is a circle painted around the "X"?

Where required, is the letter "T" chipped on the top of the curb to denote the locations of traffic signal conduit?

Are the conductors of the proper size and type and are they color coded as specified or required?

Are conductor splices made only where authorized?

Have the threads and joint make-up on conduit been inspected?

Do all conduit bends comply with the minimum radius requirements? Is the conduit kinked or flattened?

Have the ends of all lengths of conduit been properly reamed?

Are the ends of all conduits capped?

Are all conduits bonded?

Are pull boxes placed on the required rock backfill and set to sidewalk grade?

Are the conduit ends entering pull boxes in the location specified on the appropriate Standard Plan?

Have anchor bolt templates been checked to insure that the bolt pattern has not been rotated and that bolt pattern is correct?

Are the electroliers set plumb?

Have the targets to indicate lamp size been affixed to the "traffic side" of the arm of each electrolier?

Have all conductors been checked before and after installation in the conduit for evidence of damage to the insulation?

Has the proper amount of conductor slack been left in all pull boxes and electrolier bases?

When pull boxes are imbedded in concrete sidewalk, have the boxes been set flush and the covers cleaned of mortar?

Have electrolier standards been cleaned of concrete?

Are the ends of all conduits inclined at the proper angle to facilitate maintenance through access plates in electrolier standards?

Are all safety requirements being carried out in accordance with the provisions of the applicable codes and ordinances?

Before a conductor is cut or a circuit interrupted, has the contractor obtained the required clearances?

Has an entry been made on the Street Lighting Record of Lamp Changes form and "As-Built" Plan when one or more street lights are taken out of service or put into service?

Are the "As-Built" street lighting plans kept up to date and all the necessary information posted thereon?

Have the plans and job record cards been returned to the office when the work ceases for an extended period?

For traffic signal installations, has the contractor been instructed to submit an "As-Built" plan to the Traffic Engineer and has the Inspector prepared such a plan?

3-10   LANDSCAPE AND IRRIGATION

3-10.1   **General.** Landscape and irrigation work involves walls, curbs, planter boxes, walks and other architectural structures and objects in addition to planting and irrigation. Since structural work is discussed in other sections of this manual, only planting and irrigation inspection will be considered in this section. It should be noted however, that structural work, unless otherwise provided, should generally be constructed after rough grading and before planting but not until the main pressure lines and laterals of the irrigation system have been installed and pressure tested in accordance with the specifications.

On landscape and street tree planting projects, the landscape architect or Street Tree Division representatives will be involved in the approval of topsoil, plants and other materials prior to installation. The Inspector should use these sources of expertise whenever necessary to resolve difficult questions of a technical nature such as the health or growing condition of a plant or tree.

The field Inspector should familiarize himself with the plans, Special Provisions, Standard Plans, and review the portions of the Standard Specifications that will apply to the project. This will eliminate unnecessary calls to the landscape architect for information, and also assist in minimizing error during construction of the project. Any questions regarding unusual job conditions should be brought to the attention of the Supervisor.

Special Provisions for landscaping projects, in general, will provide for specific call outs that relate to individual project conditions. Project plans will be detailed as to the type of plant material, irrigation system, automatic control system and water and power service points. The plans for landscape will usually locate important features such as walks, planters and headers by dimension. If not, the Inspector should seek clarification from the landscape architect.

The Inspector must check all materials and equipment promptly as it arrives at the jobsite and inform the landscape contractor regarding any deficiencies.

3-10.2 Topsoil and Amendments. Topsoil is designated as Class A (imported), Class B (selected) or Class C (unclassified). The type and thickness to be used will be shown on the plans or specified in the Standard Specifications.

Prior to designing a project, the Agency's landscape architect will have had the on-site soil tested to determine its agricultural suitability and boron content. Depending on the results of these tests, he will designate the use of the existing soil or specify its removal and replacement with selected or imported topsoil. Imported topsoil, unless otherwise specified, must be tested by a laboratory registered by the State and approved by the landscape architect. Imported topsoil test results, together with a written request for approval, is submitted by the contractor to the landscape architect prior to its use. Approval must be confirmed by the Inspector before allowing the topsoil to be brought on the job.

Topsoil should be transported from the source to its final position, unless stockpiling is permitted by the Special Provisions.

Processing of the native soil or topsoil material to a finely divided state in the area to be planted is required to make the soil horticulturally usable. The area must be graded to produce smooth uniform surfaces and contours. The Inspector should verify that the entire area to be landscaped has been water settled prior to finish grading after installation of sprinklers but before adjustment to grade of the sprinkler heads. This sequence will avoid subsequent settlement from the fininshed grades after planting and watering begins.

Fertilizers and soil amendments are added when the landscape area has been properly prepared and brought to finish grade. After spreading, the fertilizing and conditioning materials are cultivated into the soil to the required depth. Control of the proper distribution of these materials can present a problem to the Inspector. If these amendments are delivered in sealed sacks, sizes of the areas involved can be determined and the sacks can be laid out along the length of the job on a linear footage basis or on a subdivided area basis, as required, so that the proper quantities and uniformity of distribution is accomplished. Bulk delivery of materials can be handled in a similar manner by proportioning out the load based on the amount indicated on the delivery ticket. Indiscriminate borrowing and spreading from a bulk stock pile should not be permitted.

Mulch materials are similar to fertilizers and soil additives except that they are spread at a specified thickness on the surface of the finished grade after planting or seeding and are not cultivated into the soil.

The Inspector should obtain from the contractor copies of sales receipts and bills of lading to substantiate the quantities of soil amendments delivered to the jobsite and this information should be recorded in the project daily log. The Inspector should caution the contractor regarding removal of soil amendments from the project site after they have been accounted for, without the approval of the Inspector.

3-10.3 Irrigation System Installation.

3-10.3.1 **General.** Work on the irrigation system, including hydrostatic and coverage tests, preliminary operational tests of the automatic control system, and the backfill and densification of trenches and other excavations, should be performed after the topsoil work and before planting.

A detail sheet will be provided for standard sprinkler system items such as water meter, power service hook-up, gate valves, remote control valves, vacuum breakers, trench section (showing supply lines, laterals and direct burial wires), auto controller, notes and symbol legend. The details will show minimum and maximum dimensions for units being used. Architectural features such as walls, walks, steps, planter boxes and the like may be shown on a separate sheet or incorporated on the same sheet with irrigation or planting details.

The Inspector should verify that the contractor has requested electrical and water services, as required, well in advance of their need. The contractor must verify the exact locations of existing conduits and other utilities before the start of work and before installing the irrigation system. The electrical and water service points should be determined since the layout shown on the plan is normally only schematic. Field conditions may necessitate changes in the layout. Changes in the field must be approved by the landscape architect. The routing of pressure supply lines is diagrammatic and the lines should be installed to conform to the details shown on the plans. All pipe is to be installed in trenches and at depths specified in the Standard Specifications. The size and type will be shown on the plans. Trenches and excavations should be backfilled so that the specified thickness of topsoil is restored to the upper part of the trench. Backfill should not be placed in pipe trenches until automatic control wires or hydraulic control tubes are also installed. Couplings, joints, fittings and valves should not be covered until lines have been pressure tested in accordance with the specifications.

The contractor must submit to the Agency "As-Built" drawings showing the installed location of pipe, valves, tubing, wiring, controllers and electrical and water services. The Inspector should note in his records and on his plans any contract plan changes so that he can verify the accuracy of the "As-Built" drawings.

Irrigation systems are constructed of galvanized, threaded steel pipe and malleable iron fittings and couplings; or plastic pipe with solvent weld socket or threaded fittings of rigid unplasticized polyvinyl chloride (PVC). The weight or schedule for steel and plastic pipe, fittings and couplings is designated on the plans or in the Special Provisions.

Unless a large project is involved, the Inspector usually has other assignments and must inspect the work on a timely, periodic basis. The contractor should be properly informed so that the following inspection approvals of the irrigation installation can be performed.

(1) Open trench inspection and pressure test of the pressure supply mains between remote control valves upstream and the water meter, automatic control system wiring or hydraulic tubing.

(2) Open trench inspection and pressure test of all lateral lines between control valves and sprinkler heads.

(3) Sprinkler coverage test inspection after irrigation system installation is complete. (When the sprinkler coverage cannot be obtained with the prescribed number of heads specified, the Inspector should advise the landscape architect and request a change order to provide additional sprinkler heads.)

It must be made clear to the contractor that each phase of the installation must be approved in its proper sequence by the Inspector. If any work is covered without prior approval, the Inspector must require that it be uncoverd by the contractor so that required inspections can be made.

Pipe should be laid on a straight grade and supported continuously on the trench bottom at a depth to provide the minimum cover as shown on the drawings. Backfilled trenches are compacted by flooding.

Sprinklers are installed after the main and lateral pressure tests have been completed. After installation, the sprinkler coverage test should be performed. Sprinkler head spacing should not exceed the maximum shown on the plans or as recommended by the manufacturer. In new lawn areas, sprinkler rises are set above grade and reset to the finished grade just prior to the first mowing. In other areas, heads are set above grade as required by the project plan. The Standard Specifications should be referred to for the type of heads, clearances from curbs, vertical faces and the types of flexible and swing couplings for sprinkler risers.

The contractor is usually required to supply certain tools and equipment to the Agency as part of the contract (valve keys, spanner wrenches, etc.). The equipment must be received prior to acceptance of the work.

3-10.3.2 Jointing Plastic Pipe. Solvent welding is the preferred method of joining rigid PVC pipe and fittings, thereby providing a chemically fused joint. Solvent welding procedures are simple if each step is handled with reasonable care.

The Inspector should know what is required for the individual project. All plastic pipe and fittings are permanently marked with the manufacturer's name, nominal pipe size and SDR (Standard Dimension Ratio) and pressure rating or schedule. The Inspector should obtain the manufacturer's instructions and reference specifications for jointing pipe and determine that the joint cement is compatible to the pipe used. Light bodied, low viscosity (like pancake syrup) cements are used for pipe up to two inches. Heavy bodied, high viscosity (like honey) cements are used for large fittings and pipe.

PVC pipe to be jointed must be cut square and to the desired length. Ends of pipe should be chamfered approximately 10 to 15 degrees. The pipe and fitting socket must be free of dirt, grease and moisture. A home mark to the depth of the socket should be made on the pipe for reference. The dry fit of pipe into the fitting or socket should be at least ⅓ the depth. The inside socket surface to the depth of the shoulder, and the outside surface of the end of pipe to be inserted into socket, should be brushed with solvent cement (time is important at this stage). While both the inside socket surface and the outside surface of the male end of the pipe are soft and wet with solvent cement, the male end of the pipe is bottomed in the socket with a twisting motion to give the pipe approximately one-quarter (¼) turn before the pipe end penetrates to the socket shoulder. The pipe end must fully penetrate to the bottom of the socket. The joint must be held together until both surfaces are firmly gripped (usually less than 30 seconds) as there is a tendency for the pipe to extract itself from the socket in the first few seconds. After assembly, excess cement should be wiped off and the joint checked for any gaps that may indicate a defective assembly job. Permanent set up time varies from 30 minutes to 4 hours, depending on the temperature. The joint should be allowed to cure for an adequate time before pressure testing.

3-10.3.3 **Irrigation Control System.** The irrigation automatic control system usually consists of a number of electrically operated supply valves each serving a group of sprinkler heads, an automatic controller to operate the valves on a timed sequence, and an electrical service connection. Portions of the Standard Specifications, the electrical code, and the utility service company regulations are applicable to such work. Valves are usually specified to be housed in concrete boxes to permit easy access for servicing. The Inspector should see that the boxes are set on a foundation of rock so that they will not settle or tilt off grade.

The automatic controller location should be on a concrete foundation and outside the coverage pattern of the irrigation system. Service wiring is installed in galvanized conduit from the service point to the controller. Splices should be made with a packaged kit approved for underground use and only in

concrete pull boxes set to grade on crushed rock. Low voltage
control wiring or hydraulic control tubing is housed in conduit
between the controller and a concrete pull box, installed outside the limits of the controller foundation. Do not permit wires
or hydraulic tubing to be cast directly in concrete. Low voltage
control wires or tubing issuing from pull boxes are laid direct
burial, installed and taped to the irrigation pipe mains where
ever possible as prescribed by the Standard Specifications.
Low voltage wiring must be continuous without splices between pull boxes and all splicing methods must be approved for
underground installations. The Inspector must check all wiring
for ground and continuity, damaged insulation and color coding
before permitting trenches to be backfilled. Slack must be left
in the wire at connections to avoid strains.

3-10.4 Planting.

   3-10.4.1   **General.**   Trees and plants are inspected and
tagged at the supplying nursery by the landscape architect or
by a representative of the Street Tree Division prior to shipment to the jobsite. This nursery inspection may not always relate to the particular project and its specific requirements.
Therefore, upon delivery of trees and plants to the jobsite and
prior to planting, they should be checked by the Inspector to
verify the sizes and types required for the project as well as
their growing condition. The quality of plants is difficult to define since they are living things. They may vary in quality between delivery and installation and at time of acceptance. All
plants must be healthy and well-rooted, and plants should be inspected for evidence of having been restricted, deformed or
root bound during the growing period in the container, as well
as for the presence of pest infestation and disease. The Project
Specifications may require that plants be grown in nurseries
which have been inspected by the State Department of Agricul-
ture and which have complied with its regulations. All plants
must be of normal size for the container specified. Plants not
meeting the requirements should be considered defective
(whether in place or not) and be rejected.

   Plants must be set in holes so that after the soil has
settled, the plants will be at their natural growing depth. No
roots should show after planting. Mechanical tamping around
the roots during or after the planting operations should not be
permitted. Any plants that have settled below the normal
growing depth must be removed and replanted or be replaced
with a new plant if the existing plant cannot be salvaged.

Large specimen trees should be installed prior to the installation of the irrigation lateral lines.

In the event that irrigation line alignment conflicts with tree locations, the irrigation lines should be rerouted around the tree root ball. Specimen trees usually need to be guyed.

Plants should be watered immediately after planting and follow with regular watering, in sufficient quantities as seasonal conditions require. This must continue until final inspection and field acceptance following completion of the establishment period.

3-10.4.2 Street Tree Planting. The Agency has a continuing program to provide trees in street parkways, unimproved traffic medians and grade separations located within the street right-of-way. Street tree planting may be included as a portion of work performed by the contractor in connection with a general street improvement project or as a street tree project exclusively. Permits for private developments usually include a requirement for street tree planting. Trees planted in the parkway enhance a neighborhood generally and make the street more pleasing for the motorist and pedestrian alike. Landscaping gives off oxygen helping to purify the air we breathe, reduces noise, screens off unsightly objects, and generally, makes the community more liveable and desirable.

The Inspector should familiarize himself thoroughly with the project plans, Special Provisions and Standard Specifications for prior approvals and special requirements, observe field conditions and anticipate any changes that may be required.

Check each phase performed by the planting crew. Good planting methods are absolutely necessary to assure the vigorous healthy growth of the tree. Tree planting projects, by nature, require special attention by the Inspector. In addition to the planting inspection, the Inspector must check to see that barricades are maintained, the project is kept clean and safe and to maintain effective public relations.

Types, sizes and quantities of trees required for the project are listed on the plans or in the Special Provisions. When the contractor has arranged to purchase the trees to be planted on the project, the contractor must notify the Agency, Street Tree Division. A representative of that Division will inspect the stock at the nursery for identification of species, growing condition and size, with respect to container capacity, and will tag the trees for identification at the jobsite. Upon de-

delivery to the jobsite and prior to planting, the Inspector must verify that the trees meet the specific project requirements unless a change order is issued to modify such requirements.

It is highly desirable on the larger projects that a pre-construction conference be arranged by the Project Inspector to include the contractor, the Street Tree Division representative and the landscape architectural representative. The requirements of the plan and specifications should be reviewed and clarified at this conference. It may be advisable to walk the job and direct attention to any job conditions that warrant further consideration.

After preliminary layout of the trees, in accordance with the plan locations, the Street Tree Division is normally requested to verify the tree locations and to move or eliminate any location that conflicts with existing improvements.

Typical clearances between trees and other improvements are as follows:

Street Lights	20 feet
Electrical Power Poles	20 feet
Fire Hydrants	10 feet
Water and Gas Meters	6 feet
Driveway Aprons and Crosswalks	6 feet
Alley Entrances	20 feet
Intersections	45 feet
Parking Meters	4 feet

Consideration is also given to building entrances and homes. Trees should not be located in commercial and public transit loading zones.

The Street Tree Division representative will mark the actual locations where trees are to be planted by a blue dot, spray-painted on the street curb, for trees planted along street frontages.

Tree wells are specified on most projects where full width parkway walk exists, or will be constructed with the new improvements. When the tree well is to be constructed in existing walk, the Inspector should check the saw cutting of the concrete. Corners must be square and the dimensions and layout must conform to the Standard Plan for the proper installation of the tree well cover, grating or bricks (or blocks) as required. Grates, drains and covers vary in detail from one Standard Plan to another. When the drain is installed, the top of the pipe must be at the proper elevation and filled with clean rock to properly receive and store water when the trees are watered.

On new projects that require tree well construction, the Street Tree Division should be requested to mark tree well locations, as soon as the curb is constructed, so that blockouts in sidewalk for tree wells can be formed and walk construction can proceed without delay.

Planting of trees must be performed with materials, equipment and procedures favorable to the optimum growth of the trees. On projects that include irrigation systems, large specimen trees are planted prior to installation of the irrigation system.

Care must be exercised during the transportation, handling and storage of trees, prior to the planting. They must be protected at all times from physical damage and the effects of the sun and drying winds. Those that cannot be planted immediately upon delivery, should be kept in the shade, well protected and watered. Any plant with a broken or cracked root ball before or during planting, shall not be planted.

There are some basic rules to follow when planting trees. The old gardeners' observation: "It is better to put a 50¢ tree in a $5.00 hole, than a $5.00 tree in a 50¢ hole," might be kept in mind when inspecting tree planting. The size of the hole, subsurface drainage, preparation of the soil used in filling the hole, and proper placement of the tree, all have a major influence on the ability of the tree to develop healthy, vigorous growth after planting. A tree should be properly conditioned to reduce the shock of transplanting. The Standard Specifications require square planting holes with vertical sides. One reason for the preference of the square hole over the round hole is to avoid the circling of the roots which leads to girdling and the roots increasing in diameter. If the contractor prefers, the hole can be augered and then squared with a spade or bar.

The native soil at the bottom of the planting hole must be scarified. When planting, the trees should be lifted and handled from the bottom of the ball only and placed so that after settling, the soil line will coincide with the depth in the container. Allowance for settlement will vary according to the depth of the planting hole and materials mixed with the soil. The deeper the hole, the greater the settlement. This may be reduced somewhat by tamping the soil beneath the roots. Even when this is done, allowance of at least one inch for settling should be provided. If generous amounts of amendments have been added into the soil, it is well to allow two inches. With trees growing in boxed or metal containers, roots must be removed com-

pletely from the container. The Inspector should check and see
that the root system is established to the size of its container
and that it has not been in the container too long (root bound).
The roots should be free from deformation; a cause for rejection. All planting holes must be backfilled with the prepared
soil as specified for the project, using only freshly dug material.

Soil should be placed and firmed around the root ball
until the hole is from two-thirds to three-quarters full. Then the
hole is flooded. After the water is soaked into the soil, the
filling process is completed with loose soil. Air pockets must be
eliminated from under the ball and in the fill. A circular water
basin slightly larger than the planting hole, is left around the
plant. The bottom of the basin should be at approximate finish
grade or slightly lower. Unless tree wells are called for, mulch
is usually required in the basin.

The Inspector must insist on the proper size hole, and
trees should never be forced or twisted into holes too small for
the roots, for this is a primary reason for the "girdling" of roots
which later causes the mysterious decline of fine trees.

The trees shall be staked, as specified in the specifications, six inches away from the trunk and tied high enough to
give good support.

The amount of water to be given and the frequency of
watering, during maintenance, will depend upon the soil type,
the amount of humus incorporated in the mixture when filling
the hole, the ambient temperature and the exposure to the
wind. As a general rule, one good soaking a week should be
adequate.

The following checklist applies to street tree planting. Refer to Subsection 3-10.7 for landscape and irrigation
checklist.

(1) Has the Street Tree Division been notified to adjust
and mark actual tree locations?

(2) Do any tree locations conflict with other improvements?

(3) Have the plant materials been approved, checked and
recorded?

(4) Do fertilizer and soil amendments check for type and
class required?

(5) Does the preparation of topsoil meet specified requirements?

(6) Are the trees approved, tagged and of proper size?

(7) Are the tree holes the size, depth and shape required?

(8) Is the irrigation system, if required, complete?

(9) Is electrical work required?

(10) Are trees staked and properly tied as required?

(11) Is tree well 4″ pipe drain installed to proper elevation, with the proper amount of rock?

(12) Are tree well covers flush and tight to adjacent walk?

3-10.5 Maintenance and Plant Establishment. The contractor should maintain all areas planted prior to completion of work on the project. Upon completion of the project, including the sprinkler coverage and controller performance test, the contractor should request a final inspection. The Final Inspector will notify the contractor of the effective beginning date of the plant establishment period. The plant establishment period (30 calendar days minimum) is indicated on the plan but can be extended if the planted areas are improperly maintained, appreciable plant replacement is required or other extensive corrective work becomes necessary. The maintenance period is NOT included in the number of working days specified in the proposal for completion of the work.

During the maintenance period, the contractor should provide for watering, weeding, trimming, cultivating, fertilizing, spraying for insect, rodent and pest control, replacement or any other operation necessary to assure normal growth.

A final inspection for acceptance is made at the conclusion of the maintenance period.

3-10.6 Landscape Inspection Records. Keeping complete, concise and thorough records is very necessary. Records should be written so they are easily understood when read by others. Often, after the work has been completed, requests for information and use of the records are received by the Agency. Certain important information included in the records for future reference to another Inspector that may follow on the project or to final inspection should be underlined with red pencil or ink for their attention. Do not hesitate to put on record important information as related to approvals, plan changes, men and equipment, materials used to complete extra work, special dates, etc.

The Final Inspector must record dates of maintenance periods on the correction list and advise the Project Coordinator of any intermediate inspection dates (21 day check) and the end of maintenance period date, as well as any extension dates.

3-10.7 Landscape and Irrigation Checklist. (Refer to Subsection 3-10.4.2 for street tree planting checklist.)

(1) Is the area to be landscaped, excavated to proper depth for topsoil and scarified?

(2) Is the source of topsoil approved?

(3) Is the mixture and preparation of the topsoil in accordance with the requirements?

(4) Is the topsoil backfill consolidated with the areas to receive planting not excessively compacted?

(5) Verify that the required drainage conditions are provided.

(6) Verify layout of major plant materials and adjustment to field conditions.

(7) Check for installation of sleeves, raceways and piping that is required for irrigation, electrical, etc., in coordination with site improvements, paving and walks.

(8) Is the trench for feed line excavated to required dimension?

(9) Has the feed line been pressure-tested before backfill?

(10) Has the water meter, gate valves, remote control valves, vacuum breakers, etc., been placed at plan locations and per detail sheet call-out?

(11) Are sprinkler pipe lines set at proper depth?

(12) Has pipeline system been flushed before heads are placed?

(13) Has the sprinkler system in the open trench been inspected and tested (joints exposed during pressure test)?

(14) Has pipe trench backfill been compacted by flooding?

(15) Are sprinkler heads installed at plan spacing and are they the type specified?

(16) Are heads installed to required grade and required position with respect to walk or curbs?

(17) Are quick couplers installed at required location and grade?

(18) Has the sprinkler system been checked for proper coverage?

(19) Is power supply from service point to auto controller installed per detail? Are proper electrical conduit and wire size, pull boxes, hydraulic control tubing conduit and conduit ground installed per details?

(20) Is auto controller installed at plan location and orientation (doors faced away from sprinkler spray) with required pull boxes, power supply switch, base and power supply?

(21) Is 24-volt direct burial wire of proper type and size?

(22) Are splices of direct burial wire made per plan notes?

(23) Are splices of direct burial wire made in pull boxes?

(24) Are splices of direct burial wire to remote control valves made per plan notes?

(25) Is backfill of trench of direct burial wire made with sand and through plastic conduit when installed under sidewalk, curbs, etc.?

(26) Is area to be landscaped graded to required dimension below curb and/or walks?

(27) Are required soil amendments added to the topsoil and rotor tilled to minimum depth?

(28) Has rototilled soil been water settled?

(29) Are trees, shrubs, ground cover and lawn seeds approved?

(30) Are holes for trees backfilled with soil with required soil amendments?

(31) Has ground cover been placed at plan location and spacing, and have seeds been broadcast at required rate per sq. ft.?

(32) Are proper tree stakes installed and trees properly tied?

(33) Are pull boxes set to grade?

(34) Do all pull boxes have proper cover identification?

(35) Are all pull boxes installed with proper amount of rock for drainage?

(36) Have locks and keys been furnished?

3-11   CONCRETE CONSTRUCTION, GENERAL

3-11.1   General.   See the following subsections for additional information:

2-4   Portland Cement Concrete & Related Products.

2-4.4 Concrete Mixtures.

2-4.5 Concrete Proportioning Plant Inspection.

3-4.4 Concrete Pavement Construction.

3-4.5 Curb, Gutter, Sidewalk and Driveways.

3-12 Concrete Structures.

Inspection of concrete construction will generally include the following:

Identification and field sampling of materials.

Control of proportioning.

Examination of the foundation (or subgrade) and forms.

Inspection of the placement of reinforcing steel.

Inspection of the mixing, transporting, placing, compacting, finishing and curing of the concrete.

Preparation of concrete test specimens and making slump tests.

Observation of the contractor's equipment and methods.

Preparation of records and reports.

The quality of concrete depends largely on workmanship, and the function of inspection is to assure that the work is accomplished in accordance with the plans, specifications and good construction practice.

3-11.2 Water Content of Concrete.   The proportion of water used to the amount of cement in the paste is referred to as the "water-cement ratio" and is one of the most important factors in controlling the quality of the concrete. The hardening of the cement paste is a chemical reaction. Very little water is required to satisfy the reaction, as is evident from the partial hardening of cement from moisture in the air during prolonged storage in bags. However, concrete must be plastic to permit mixing, transporting and placing, so additional water is utilized to obtain a plastic state. Only that water should be used which is necessary to obtain the minimum slump at which the concrete can be placed. Excess water results in too much dispersion of the cement gel particles and drastically reduces the strength of the concrete, much in the same way household glues are rendered less effective by dilution with water. In addition, excess water increases bleeding, adds to shrinkage, extends the finishing time, and reduces the durability of the concrete.

Concrete mixes tend to stiffen shortly after mixing. If more than a slight amount of stiffening occurs during placement, corrective action must be taken. Usually this change in consistency can be traced to delays in placing after mixing, evaporation of the mixing water by high atmospheric temperatures or low relative humidity, excessive absorption of mixing water by the aggregate, sunheated aggregates, or "hot" cement which displays a flash set.

Indiscriminate retempering (addition of water) to increase slump and workability after the concrete is mixed should be prohibited. Small increments of water can sometimes be added, provided that allowable water-cement ratio is not exceeded, and the entire batch remixed at least half the minimum mixing time. Under careful supervision, more water can be added, provided additional cement is used to maintain the proper water-cement ratio.

3-11.3 Effects of Temperature on Concrete.

Concrete mixtures gain strength rapidly in the first few days after placement. While the rate of gain in strength diminishes, concrete continues to become stronger with time over a period of many years, so long as drying of the concrete is prevented. Its strength at 28 days is considered to be the compressive strength upon which the Engineer bases his calculations. The temperature of the atmosphere has a significant effect upon the development of strength in concrete. Lower temperatures retard and higher temperatures accelerate the gain in strength.

Most destructive of the natural forces is freezing and thawing action. While the concrete is still wet or moist, expansion of the water as it is converted into ice results in severe damage to the fresh concrete. In situations where freezing may be encountered, high early strength cement may be used. Also, the mixing water or the aggregate (or both) may be preheated before mixing. Covering the concrete, and using steam or salamanders to heat the concrete under the covering, will help prevent freezing. Air-entraining agents help to diminish the effects of freezing of fresh concrete as well as in subsequent freezing and thawing cycles throughout the life of the concrete.

Hot weather will present problems of a different nature in placing concrete. Concrete will set up faster and tend to shrink and crack at the surface. To minimize this problem, the concrete should be placed without delay after mixing. Avoid the use of accelerators (perhaps even use a retarding agent),

dampen all subgrade and forms, protect the freshly placed concrete from hot dry winds, and provide for adequate curing.
Crushed ice or chilled water can be used as part of the mixing water to reduce the temperature of the mix in extremely
hot areas.

Insofar as is possible, the moisture content should be kept
uniform to avoid problems in determining the proper amount of
water to be added for mixing. Mixing water must be reduced to
compensate for moisture in the aggregate in order to control
the slump of the concrete and avoid exceeding the specified
water-cement ratio.

3-11.4 Concrete Batching and Mixing (On-Site). Con-
crete for Agency work is usually supplied from central proportioning plants located off site. The Materials Control Group
provides inspection of these facilities and coordinates its activities with the project inspection personnel. (See Subsection
2-4.) However, concrete is sometimes batched and mixed at the
jobsite. When the concrete required is 25 cubic yards or less,
the materials may be measured either by weight or volume.
When volumetric measurement is used, sacks of cement may
not be split between batches, and each batch must contain one
or more full sacks of cement. A standard sack contains one
cubic foot of cement and weighs 94 pounds.

The proportioning and measurement of materials is described in detail in the Standard Specifications. However, it is
the Inspector's responsibility to check all measuring and weighing equipment to insure that the proportions of materials
specified are constantly maintained. Water measuring devices
must be accurate and dependable in use. The measurement of
water is so intimately related to the amount of moisture in the
sand and aggregate that it must be taken into account in determining the proper quantity of mixing water to be added.

There are other details that the Inspector must be alert to
check during the mixing operation. He should examine the
mixer before use for blade wear and insure that the inner surfaces of the mixing equipment are free of large accumulations of
hardened concrete or mortar.

Mixers should never be charged with more material than
that indicated by the rated capacity set by the manufacturer.
To avoid balling of the cement, it is preferred that it be charged
into the mixer with the aggregate. In this way, the aggregate
tends to disperse the dry cement into the mixture, and to some

degree provides a protective shroud enclosing the cement during charging. Approximately 10 percent of the mixing water should be introduced first and the remainder added continuously during the entire time that the solids are entering the mixer. No part of the charging time should be considered as part of the mixing time, and automatic time locks should be set to take the charging time into account.

Batch mixers should be checked frequently to determine that portions of the mix have not "hung up" on the blades. The mixer drum must be stopped and the blades cleaned when this occurs. All concrete should be mixed thoroughly until it is uniform in appearance, with all ingredients homogeneously distributed. (See Subsection 2-4.5.6 for Types of Concrete Mixers.).

3-11.5 Field Control Test. Under normal circumstances, only concrete test cylinders and slump tests (described in Subsection 2-4.4.3) will be required. When flexure test specimens are required, beams shall be molded in smooth, rigid, non-absorptive forms unless otherwise specified. Each beam specimen shall have a 6-inch x 6-inch cross-section and shall be at least 21 inches long. The beam is cast with its long axis horizontal. Concrete is placed in the form in approximately 3-inch layers and rodded 50 times for each square foot of area. The top layer must slightly overfill the mold before rodding. The concrete is to be spaded along the sides and ends with a mason's trowel (or similar tool) and the top struck off with a straightedge and finished with a wood float. (Refer to Plate 28, Appendix for Concrete Sampling.)

3-11.6 Handling and Transporting Concrete. Care should be exercised in the handling or transporting of concrete to avoid segregation of its components. For transporting concrete short distances, chutes, conveyors, buggies and buckets are most commonly used. Chutes should be metal-lined, round-bottomed, and have sufficient slope to be self-cleaning but not so steep that the material tends to segregate from the mortar clinging to the chute while the larger aggregate accelerates. Long chutes should not be permitted and shorter chutes should be wetted with a cement mortar slurry before each use. In any event, the condition of the concrete as it is discharged from the chute should govern its use. When chutes are used, water used for flushing or cleaning them should not be permitted to drain into forms.

Push or power buggies with pneumatic tires are useful for short hauls from central batching plants and storage hoppers to the point of deposit. Smooth and rigid runways should be provided to minimize any tendency for the concrete to segregate in the buggies. Such buggies should be capable of being discharged rapidly.

Cranes equipped with drop-bottom buckets are often used to move concrete from a loading point to the point of discharge. The buckets must be inspected to ensure that the gates operate freely and that they close properly to avoid loss of material. The bucket must be free of dried concrete so as to discharge all of its load.

Belt conveyors are popular for transporting low-slump concrete from a loading point to the point of discharge. Maximum efficiency is achieved with a 3-inch slump. Not only can they be used to move concrete horizontally, but most belt conveyors will deliver their rated capacities at a vertical inclination of 30 degrees. The capacity will be reduced if the slump is increased or if operated at a steeper angle up to a maximum of 45 degrees. Belts must be kept clean during operation through the use of belt scrapers. Otherwise, cement paste is lost through adherence to the belt, which is an undesirable loss of the most important constituent in concrete. Moreover, some loss in workability may result. Cement paste carried over on the belt can lead to jamming of the operating parts of the conveyor and damage to the belt. The total length of the conveyor should be controlled to limit transport time to not more than 15 minutes.

For longer hauls, trucks with a special body equipped with baffles or transit-mix trucks are commonly used to transport concrete.

Check the following for applicability in handling and transporting concrete:

Buggies should be operated to minimize jolting of the concrete. They should not run at high speeds over rough ground (especially power buggies).

Use buckets large enough to handle one batch load or a multiple thereof. Don't split batches.

Use round-bottom chutes with a metal inner surface.

No transporting method should be used which results in a loss in slump of more than one inch.

Don't permit buggies or wheelbarrows to ride directly on planks which lay on the reinforcement.

Insist that handling and transporting equipment be in good repair.

Long exposed chutes or belt conveyors should be protected from sun and wind.

Concrete pumping equipment should be checked for maintenance and capacity before starting operations.

Concrete with an air-entraining admixture, for greater cohesiveness and mobility, will help if there is a difficult handling problem.

Be sure that the maximum aggregate size is satisfactory for placement based on the reinforcement concentration.

Concrete should be handled as little as possible and discharged directly into forms where practical.

Placing conditions should provide organized traffic flow for concrete transporting equipment and continuity of concrete supply.

Inspect the mix frequently for segregation of concrete when transporting and handling.

Added water to ready mixed concrete at the jobsite should not exceed the allowable and not more than needed for placement conditions.

Don't permit the chute for concrete to be positioned at an angle so steep that segregation results — or at an angle so slight that the concrete must be pushed along.

Never allow concrete to free-fall more than 6 feet.

Don't pump very high slump concrete (it will segregate) or very low slump concrete (it will clog the lines).

Always use a baffle and downpipe when discharging concrete from a belt conveyor.

Concrete in buckets should be discharged so that segregated stones fall where they can be worked back into the concrete.

3-11.7 Handling Concrete by Pumping Methods. Transportation and placement of concrete by pumping is another method gaining increased popularity. Pumps have several advantages, the primary one being that a pump will high-lift concrete without the need for an expensive crane and bucket. Since the concrete is delivered through pipe and hoses, concrete can be conveyed to remote locations in buildings, in tunnels, to locations otherwise inaccessible on steep hillside slopes for anchor walls, pipe bedding or encasement, or for placing concrete for chain link fence post bases. Concrete pumps have been found to be economical and expedient in the placement of concrete, and this has promoted the use and acceptance of this development. The essence of proper concrete pumping is the placement of the concrete in its final location without segregation.

Modern concrete pumps, depending on the mix design and size of line, can pump to a height of 200 feet or a horizontal distance of 1,000 feet. They can handle, economically, structural mixes, standard mixes, low slump mixes, mixes with two-inch maximum size aggregate and light-weight concrete. When a special pump mix is required for structural concrete in a major structure, the mix design must be approved by the Engineer and checked and confirmed by the Supervisor of the Materials Control Group. The Inspector should obtain the pump manufacturer's printed information and evaluate its characteristics and ability to handle the concrete mixture specified for the project.

If concrete is being placed for a major reinforced structure, it is important that the placement continue without interruption. The Inspector should be sure that the contractor has ready access to a back-up pump to be used in the event of a breakdown. In order to further insure the success of the concrete placement by the pumping method, the Inspector should be aware of the following points:

(a) A protective grating over the receiving hopper of the pump is necessary to exclude large pieces of aggregate or foreign material.

(b) The pump and lines require lubrication with a grout of cement and water. All of the excess grout is to be wasted prior to pumping the concrete.

(c) All changes in direction must be made by a large radius bend with a maximum bend of 90 degrees. Wye connections induce segregation and shall not be used.

(d) Pump lines should be made of a material capable of resisting abrasion and with a smooth interior surface having a low coefficient of friction. Steel is commonly used for pump lines, and some of the new plastic or rubber tubing is gaining acceptance. Aluminum pipe should not be used for pumping concrete because a chemical reaction occurs between the concrete and the aluminum. Hydrogen is generated which results in a swelling of the concrete, causing a significant reduction in compressive strength. This reaction is aggravated by any of the following: abrasive coarse aggregate, non-uniformly graded sand, low-slump concrete, low sand-aggregate ratio, high-alkali cement or when no air-entraining agent is used.

Pump lines must be properly fastened to supports to eliminate excessive vibration. Couplings must be easily and securely fastened in a manner that will prevent mortar leakage. It is preferable to use the flexible hose only at the discharge point. This hose must be moved in such a manner as to avoid kinks or sharp bends. The pump line should be protected from excessive heat during hot weather by water sprinkling or shade.

(e) During temporary interruptions in pumping, the hopper must remain nearly full, with an occasional turning and pumping to avoid developing a hard slug of concrete in the lines.

(f) Excessive line pressures must be avoided. When this occurs, check these points as the probable cause: segregation caused by too low a slump or too high a slump; large particle contamination caused by large pieces of aggregate or frozen lumps not eliminated by the grating; poor gradation of aggregates or particle shape; rich or lean spots caused by improper mixing.

(g) Corrections must be made to correct excessive slump loss as measured at the transit-mix concrete truck and as measured at the hose outlet. This may be attributable to porous aggregate, high temperature or rapid setting mixes.

(h) Two transit-mix concrete trucks must be used simultaneously to deliver concrete into the pump hopper. These trucks must be discharged alternately to assure a continuous flow of concrete as trucks are replaced.

(i) Samples of concrete for test specimens prepared to determine the acceptance of the concrete quality are to be taken as required for conventional concrete. (See Subsection 2-4.4.3.)

Sampling is done before the concrete is deposited in the pump hopper. However, it is suggested that, where possible, the effect of pumping on the compressive strength be checked by taking companion samples, so identified, from the end of the pump line at the same time. The Record of Test must be properly noted as being a special mix used for pumping purposes.

This will enable the Materials Control Group to compile a complete history of mix designs and their respective compressive strengths.

The prudent use of pumped concrete can result in economy and improved quality. However, only the control exercised by the Inspector will assure continued high standards of quality concrete.

3-11.8 Placing Concrete. (See Subsection 3-12.7 for Additional Information on Concrete Placement for Structures.) Concrete is always placed — not poured. The former indicates a careful depositing of the mixture and consolidation without segregation; the latter infers an excessively wet mixture which may lack the required strength and which has such a fluid consistency that the larger particles tend to settle out. Segregation must always be prevented — not corrected after it occurs.

Forms should be clean, tight adequately braced and moistened before placement of concrete. Whenever possible, concrete should be discharged from the mixer directly into the forms. Concrete should be placed in forms and vibrated in level layers or lifts, preferably not to exceed two feet (three feet maximum). It should not to be placed in large quantities at one point and allowed to flow or be vibrated over a long distance in the forms. This practice results in segregation since the mortar tends to flow ahead of the coarse aggregate. In addition, these sloping planes are often discernible in the final concrete surfaces.

To reduce segregation, concrete should not be permitted to drop freely more than six feet. Metal or rubber tremies should be used to deposit concrete in forms where the free fall would exceed this distance, particularly where obstructions are encountered which would greatly increase segregation, such as the reinforcement steel in high walls. Tremies are also utilized to deposit concrete under water. A foot valve is attached to the lower end and the tremie lowered into the water as it is filled with concrete. With the lower end in the submerged form, the valve is opened. The lower end is kept embedded in the deposited concrete as more concrete is added at the top. This procedure allows the concrete under pressure in the tremie to flow outward and upward from the end of the tremie and fill the underwater form with the least agitation, and prevents dilution of the concrete mixture or excessive washing away of the mortar.

Other than that when placed under water, concrete should be compacted and worked into place by spading or vibrating. Care should be exercised to avoid over-vibrating since this can result in segregation of the concrete and damage to the steel reinforcement and forms. High-frequency vibrators may be internal or external types. Internal types have a vibrating element intended to be embedded in the plastic concrete. External types are of the clamp-on design to attach to the outside of forms or float on the top surface of the concrete. Clamp-on types should not be utilized unless the forms are specifically designed for such use. Ample standby vibrator units should be on hand to replace those which malfunction during concrete placement.

An internal vibrator should be inserted in fresh concrete in a vertical position at approximately 18-inch intervals and lowered so that it penetrates several inches into the previously deposited layer of concrete, except where this layer is no longer plastic. While some contact of the vibrator with reinforcement steel may be beneficial in increasing bond, prolonged contact should be avoided since it may break the ties and distort the steel placement pattern. Where the steel projects from partially hardened concrete which will not become plastic under vibratory action, precaution should be taken to avoid vibrator contact with the steel since this will operate to reduce the bond.

Where concrete is placed rapidly in high forms, the full depth of the concrete may become plastic under the action of a vibrator and exert excessive hydrostatic head pressures on the forms, causing form deflection or failure. (See Subsection 3-12.4.4 for Discussion of Concrete Pressure in Forms.)

Air Placed Concrete (gunite) is discussed in Subsection 3-11.9.

3-11.9   Air Placed Concrete (Gunite).

3-11.9.1   General. The gunite method of placing concrete, also referred to as sprayed mortar, consists of forcing a dry cement-sand mix through a hose by compressed air, adding water at a higher pressure at the nozzle and depositing the wetted mix in a continuous spray. The cement and sand are mixed in the desired proportions and introduced in batches into a pressure chamber where high-pressure air forces the mixture through the hose.

Gunite sand must not contain more than five percent by weight of uncombined water. Otherwise, the inside of the hose and the nozzle will tend to cake up and restrict the flow of materials. Even though the line does not completely plug up, this caking will cause the nozzle operation to be sluggish and uneven. Gunite is most commonly used to place concrete on sloping planes, to line excavations and to coat steel pipe, but can be used to construct reinforced concrete structures.

The Standard Specifications outline in detail the proportions of gunite mixes and mixing requirements. Several precautions must be taken by the Inspector to assure that the quality of the finished work is satisfactory. One of the most important factors is that the nozzleman must be experienced and competent and the Inspector should make this determination early in the work. Attention should be given to insuring that the subgrade (or forms) have been dampened but show no evidence of free water. Ground (or screed) wires should be properly set and pulled tight. Some rebound will normally occur but will become excessive if the mix is too dry or the air pressure in the hose is too high. Rebound must be cleaned up as the work progresses to prevent it from becoming buried in the mortar being applied. Its reuse as aggregate for remixing is not permitted unless specified. Some project specifications may permit as much as 25% of the rebound to be reused as aggregate.

3-11.9.2 Placing Gunite. In placing gunite, the nozzle must be held so that the stream of mortar is perpendicular to the surface to which it is applied. Gunite is usually built up in thin layers of from 1 to 1½ inches as the operator constantly plays the mortar stream back and forth over the area being covered until the desired thickness is obtained. The operator should not attempt to place mortar in any area larger than that which will always have a fresh surface upon which to apply successive layers. For steep slopes, vertical walls or overhead work, the thickness of each layer must be reduced to prevent sagging or fall-outs. The maximum thickness permitted to be deposited overhead is ¾-inch.

The amount of water introduced at the nozzle is regulated by the operator to obtain the proper consistency. Too dry a mix will not adhere, while too wet a mix will sag on steep slopes and result in excessive shrinkage.

When depositing gunite on surfaces of previously placed and hardened gunite, the old surface must be "opened" by scraping the entire surface with the edge of a steel trowel. This is important since it opens pores in the surface which provide excellent bonding characteristics.

Gunite structures are constructed by applying mortar against forms set on the side of the wall opposite the operator. Steel reinforcement, block-outs, embedments, etc., are attached securely to the wall form and grounds set to establish the wall thickness. Skill must be shown by the nozzleman to avoid entrapment of rebound, dispersion of the mortar stream by the reinforcement, shadows behind the steel bars which would reduce bond; and he must use care in the placement of the mortar around irregular block-outs.

3-11.9.3 Joints. Whenever a stoppage occurs in the application of gunite or at the end of a shift, the mortar must be sloped off at an angle of 45 degrees to the surface involved at all joints. No square joints are permitted except where specified on the plans. Joints must be cleaned with an air and water blast before additional mortar is applied for adjacent work.

3-11.9.4 Finishing Gunite. When the full thickness of mortar is developed, it should not be screeded since this will tend to cause the mortar to sag. Screed wires or grounds should be removed and, where applicable, the surface carefully planed to a true plane with a darby or wood float. When required, steel troweling should be delayed as long as possible, particularly on vertical or overhead surfaces.

3-11.9.5 Curing. Curing shall conform to the requirements of the Standard Specifications.

3-11.9.6 Shot Crete. Shot-crete is a method of placing concrete similar to gunite. The difference is that, instead of a dry mortar mix being pneumatically conveyed to the nozzle, a concrete pump is used to pump a special pea gravel concrete mix through the hose as compressed air at the nozzle, blows the concrete in place. Application conditions are similar to gunite except that the rebound is much greater. The gravel in the mix tends to rebound off the forms and reinforcing steel while the mortar has a tendency to stay in place. The nozzleman should be instructed not to apply the shot-crete directly at these surfaces.

3-11.10 Joints. (See Subsection 3-12.6.3 for Joints In Concrete Structures.) Concrete shrinks upon drying and will expand upon subsequent wetting. Similarly, concrete expands and contracts with atmospheric temperature changes. To control these forces and reduce the destructive effect on concrete slabs and structures, expansion and contraction joints are generally specified by the designer. For the sake of appearance, joints in concrete should be made straight, exactly horizontal or vertical, and placed at the locations specified on the plans.

Expansion joints are constructed at predetermined intervals to permit the expansion of the concrete and usually consist of compressible materials, such as bitumen-treated felt. These joints are provided with dowels or keyways to transfer loads without affecting alignment. It is important that all such dowels be carefully aligned and one end provided with a sleeve (or other means) to prevent bond and permit it to slide.

Contraction joints are weakened planes constructed into the concrete to control cracking as it shrinks. They are usually formed by the use of a tapered bar depressed into the wet concrete, by deep scoring, or by concrete sawing between four and twelve hours after the concrete has been placed but before shrinkage crack develop. (See Subsection 3-4.4.3 for Concrete Sawing and Subsection 3-4.5.6 For Joints in Curb, Gutter, Sidewalk and Driveways.)

3-11.11 Finishing Concrete. The quality of concrete work is universally judged by the quality of its surface finish. While the utility of the slab or structure may not be diminished by poor concrete finish, it is highly desirable not to skimp on obtaining good surface finishes.

For the best results, the slump for concrete that is to be finished should not exceed four inches and even lower slumps are preferable when vibrating type screeds are utilized. This will help to minimize the effects of excess water that appears on the surface shortly after placement (commonly referred to as "bleeding"). Water-reducing and air-entraining admixtures will also help to minimize bleeding.

If any finishing operation is done while excess moisture is on the surface, the ultimate result could be the scaling and dusting of the hardened concrete surface. It is therefore of great importance that the operations of spreading, screeding and darbying or bullfloating be done before bleeding occurs.

It is also important that none of the basic steps required to finish the concrete be omitted. These steps should precede almost any type of final surface finish to be applied including wood float, steel trowel or broomed finishes. The steps are spreading, screeding, tamping, bullfloating or darbying and hand or machine floating. If edging and jointing is required, some preliminary work is done following bullfloating or darbying and is completed during floating and final finishing operations. The steps are discussed in detail in the following paragraphs.

The first step in developing the surface finish in concrete slab work is to screed or strike off the excess concrete to the proper contour or elevation between headers. The screed (or templet) used may have the lower edge curved or straight, depending upon the requirements. It should be moved back and forth across the concrete in a sawing motion as it is advanced forward a short distance with each movement. A surplus of concrete should be maintained against its front surface so that low areas will be filled as the templet passes over them. Screeding is also done with power equipment called "Vibrating Screeds," "Oscillating Screeds" and "Roller Screeds."

Unless the screeding encompasses vibration, a grid tamper, usually constructed with parallel metal bars or expanded metal mesh, is used immediately after screeding to tamp the larger aggregate particles down into the plastic mass and bring mortar to the surface for finishing operations. To level the concrete surface after tamping, a long-handled wood float (bull float) or a darby is used. Care should be exercised to avoid overworking the mortar during this operation, as it may bring an excess of water to the surface, which may result in problems for subsequent finishing. Where required, an edging tool should be used along headers or forms to move aggregate into the plastic concrete and facilitate later edging operations.

If joints are required to control cracking, preliminary grooving or the installation of Plastic Control Joints should follow bullfloating. (See Subsection 3-4.5.6 for Installation Details of Control Joints.)

When the sheen has left the surface, all marking or grooving should be accomplished, followed by hand or machine floating. If done by hand, a wood float is used as a hand plane to cut down high spots, fill low areas followed by steel troweling. For this first troweling, the trowel blade is worked as flat as possible against the surface. Where a non-slip surface texture is desired, the concrete should be remarked and given a final wood float finish or broom finish using a soft bristle push broom, after the concrete has partially hardened, being careful not to obliterate the marking.

If a smooth finish is desired, one or more subsequent steel trowelings may be necessary to develop the desired finish. All markings should be re-marked as necessary to insure a sharp, clean score mark **before** the final steel trowel operation. It is essential that steel troweling operations be performed at the proper time as the concrete hardens. Unless delayed until the concrete hardens sufficiently, fine material and water will be worked to the surface and this may result in crazing, dusting or scaling of the surface. Too long a delay may result in difficulty in obtaining a proper finish. Spreading of dry cement on wet concrete surfaces to take up excess moisture should not be permitted. Rotary trowel finishes are obtained by troweling in a rotary pattern while the surface is still sufficiently wet to "sweat up" under the trowel. Hard, smooth surfaces are developed by delaying the final steel trowel operation as long as possible before the concrete hardens. Smaller trowels should be used on the final troweling to enable the finisher to use greater pressure on the concrete surface.

Care should be taken in all floating or troweling operations to avoid dragging concrete or mortar from the high side of slabs to the low side. Floating or troweling from the low to the high side tends to eliminate this problem.

The finishing of concrete is one of the most costly operations to the contractor in concrete construction. There is a tendency for him to cut costs by employing less cement finishers than can properly finish the work as it is placed. Since little can be done to improve poor or unsatisfactory finishes after the concrete is hardened (short of removal and replacement), it is essential that the Inspector regulate the rate of concrete placement to the capabilities of the cement finishers assigned to the work.

It is the policy of the Agency to permit the contractor to place concrete in slabs for the full eight hours of the working day, and to permit the finishing to be accomplished after the Inspector has completed his workday. The contractor must be informed that such finishing must meet the accepted standards of workmanship and that the finishing must be completed in daylight hours without the need for artificial lighting. If substandard work results, it must be removed and replaced and thereafter, with the approval of the Supervisor, the Inspector may remain on the work until all concrete finishing has been completed.

3-11.12   Curing and Protection of Concrete.   (See Subsection 2-4.7 for Membrane Curing Compounds.)

Proper curing helps to achieve the following important properties of concrete:

Strength. Compressive strength of properly cured concrete is substantially increased over concrete that has not been cured at all. Tensile strength is increased and this increases concrete's resistance to cracking and surface crazing.

Abrasion resistance. Properly cured concrete surfaces will wear well and poorly cured surfaces abrade rapidly.

Efflorescence. By preventing water from evaporating from the concrete, proper curing will considerably reduce efflorescence.

In thin sections, four inches or less thick, the following advantages of proper curing also apply:

Shrinkage. Drying shrinkage is greatly reduced. If the excess water in concrete is allowed to evaporate too quickly excessive shrinkage and resultant cracking is inevitable.

Impermeability. The hydration produces a gel which reduces the size of voids in the concrete. Proper curing, and thus full hydration, therefore assures greater water-tightness.

Since the hardening of concrete is a chemical reaction of water with the cement in the concrete, it is necessary for the moisture to be retained in the mix for a sufficient time to permit this reaction to take place. While this reaction occurs rapidly at first, it proceeds at a constantly diminishing rate after the first few hours. The strength of the concrete will increase with age as long as moisture is present. Premature drying stops the chemical reaction before it has had time to impart the desirable properties to concrete. Any process used to retard moisture loss from concrete is referred to as curing.

Two basic concepts for curing concrete are: retention of the moisture already in the mix or the addition of moisture to the hardened concrete. Chemical or liquid membranes sprayed on the surface, plastic membranes or waterproof paper coverings are used to retain existing moisture. Fresh concrete contains more than enough water for complete hydration of the cement if it is not permitted to be lost through evaporation from the surface.

Some of the methods used to cure concrete by adding water are: sprinkling, soaker hoses, ponding or by covering with wetted burlap or cotton mats, sand blankets, etc. Where sprinkling is utilized, care must be taken to prevent crazing or cracking of the concrete surfaces by alternate cycles of wetting and drying.

Curing should be continued for the periods required in the specifications, but as a general rule, not less than seven days under ordinary atmospheric conditions.

Check the following curing tips for applicability.

Don't neglect slab edges, column bases and other hard-to-get-at places when inspecting curing.

See that the edges of curing paper, film or burlap are secured against wind forces.

Curing paper and plastic film should be overlapped and the edges securely taped in place.

When a floor slab is to be cured, a technique should be used that will protect the slab from any construction activity that may take place on the slab or close to it.

To be effective, water spray and fog techniques depend on having a continuous supply of high pressure water.

Wind barriers may be necessary when curing by water spraying or fogging.

. Check for pipe leakage and nozzle clogging when spraying and fogging is used.

Check for proper coverage when using a membrane curing compound, and take particular note of the amount of curing agent to be applied.

Sprayed membrane curing compounds should be applied in two directions to ensure complete coverage of the concrete surface.

Burlap for curing must be kept continuously wet.

The curing medium should be protected from damage in heavily trafficked areas by wood planks for walkways and driveways.

Protection and curing are especially important during hot weather. See that the continuity of curing is not interrupted, continuous water curing is preferable. If this is not practicable, an opaque water barrier membrane should be used.

The rate of coverage of curing compound will be determined from tests by the Agency or approved laboratory.

3-11.13 Concrete Admixtures. Admixtures for concrete are not a panacea for concreting problems. They cannot make a poor concrete job good nor are they applicable in all concrete work. Advance approval by the Engineer is required prior to the use of admixtures.

The three basic types of concrete admixtures are accelerators, water-reducing retarders and air-entraining agents.

Some admixtures are now available which have modifications or combinations of these properties. Admixtures are discussed generally in Subsection 2-4.3.

The following table lists the available general types of admixtures and their purpose:

Admixture	Purpose	Effects on Concrete	Advantages	Disadvantages
Accelerator	Hasten setting.	Improves cement dispersion and increases early strength.	Permits earlier finishing, form removal, and use of the structure.	Increases shrinkage, decreases sulfate resistance, tends to clog mixing and handling equipment.
Air-Entraining Agent	Increase workability and reduce mixing water.	Reduces segregation, bleeding and increases freeze-thaw resistance. Increases strength	Increases workability and reduces finishing time.	Excess will reduce strength and increase slump. Bulks concrete volume.
Bonding Agent	Increase bond to old concrete.	Produces a non-dusting, slip-resistant finish.	Permits a thin topping without roughening old concrete, self-curing, ready in one day.	Quick setting and susceptible to damage from fats, oils and solvents.
Densifier	To obtain dense concrete.	Increased workability and strength.	Increases workability and increases waterproofing characteristics, more impermeable.	Care must be used to reduce mixing water in proportion to amount used.
Foaming Agent	Reduce weight.	Increases insulating properties.	Produces a more plastic mix, reduces dead weight loads.	Its use must be very carefully regulated — following instructions explicitly.
Retarder	Retard setting.	Increases control of setting.	Provides more time to work and finish concrete.	Performance varies with cement used — adds to slump. Requires stronger forms.
Water Reducer and Retarder	Increase compressive and flexural strength.	Reduces segregation, bleeding, absorption, shrinkage, and increases cement dispersion.	Easier to place work, provides better control.	Performance varies with cement. Of no use in cold weather.
Water Reducer, Retarder and Air-Entraining Agent	Increase workability.	Improves cohesiveness. Reduces bleeding and segregation.	Easier to place and work.	Care must be taken to avoid excessive air entrainment.

3-11.14 Subgrade for Concrete. There are three stages of subgrade inspection: the preliminary examination of the excavation or foundation; the semi-final check when forms (and reinforcement steel, block-outs or other embedments) are in place; and the final inspection for completeness, adequacy of forms and clean-up immediately before concrete is placed.

When properly prepared, subgrade for all concrete slabs or structures should be hard, smooth, uniform and to proper elevation and grade. Unless otherwise specified, it should be undisturbed natural earth or fill compacted to a minimum relative density of 90 percent. High areas must be be trimmed to the proper elevation. Low areas can be filled with concrete or, in the case of slab work, they can be filled with earth and tamped. Soft spots in the subgrade must be discovered and measures taken to correct them.

Wetting of the subgrade is essential to reduce the effect of taking up moisture from freshly deposited concrete. Sand subgrades should be thoroughly drenched with water and, when practicable, rolled. Highly expansive soils should be brought to a state of "no shrink, no swell" by compacting at the approximate moisture content of similar undisturbed earth. Other soils must be thoroughly dampened but not to the extent that mud or puddles develop.

More detailed information regarding subgrade may be found under specific headings such as Excavation, Street Improvement and Concrete Structures.

3-11.15 Forms for Concrete. (See Subsection 3-12.4 for additional information regarding forms for concrete structures.) The materials most commonly used for forms are wood and metal. Wood forms are the most versatile since they can be easily fabricated into any desired shape. By utilizing care in their removal, cleaning and re-oiling, wood forms can be used several times for repetitive work. Metal forms can be used indefinitely unless abused or damaged. While they are not so versatile, they are more quickly assembled through the use of patented stakes and fasteners.

Wood or metal forms are used to cast an endless variety of concrete improvements, from simple slabs to elaborate structures. The primary requirement for any form is that it retain its shape and elignment throughout the casting process. It must be rigidly braced and tied together to successfully resist all of the forces normally expected during the placement of concrete.

Forms should be mortar tight and free from holes, seams or blemishes which would result in mortar leakage and unsightly patterns on the surface of the concrete.

Warped (or bent) form elements should be discarded or properly repaired. All forms should be cleaned and lightly oiled with a non-staining form oil to prevent them from adhering to the fresh concrete.

A typical wood form assembly for a concrete wall is shown on Plate 35, Appendix.

Form ties and spacers should be approved types which will not result in any metal embedments remaining near the surface. Wire ties are not permitted in important work. Snap ties, plastic spacers and other accessories may be used only when approved by the Engineer. Form oils or coatings must be applied before the reinforcement steel is in place. Otherwise, it may coat the steel and prevent a bond with the concrete.

All foreign material such as chips, blocks, sawdust and dried mortar must be removed by air, water or steam blasting. It may be necessary to cut clean-out holes at the bottom of wall forms to remove this debris, particularly that which collects in corners and places of difficult access. Where possible, these clean-out holes should be cut on non-showing faces (such as ends of walls) and tightly closed and braced before concreting is begun.

3-11.16 Concrete Construction, General Checklist.
Also see the following related checklists:

3-4.4.6 Concrete Pavement Checklist

3-4.5.9 Curb, Gutter, Walk & Driveway Checklist

3-12.10 Concrete Structures Checklist

(1) Check for completion of site work and grading; completion of underground construction; and utility clearance before beginning concrete work. (See appropriate checklists for clearing, grubbing and removals.)

(2) Check for proper base and subgrade preparation for concrete.

(3) Is reinforcing steel properly stored at jobsite? Protected from rusting and distortion, and kept free from oil or grease?

(4) Check that all headers, screeds and forms are in place and securely staked and braced. Are forms oiled?

(5) Is reinforcing steel tied and supported above subgrade on concrete blocks or chairs?

(6) Are the locations of all construction joints and other limits of concrete placement determined and approved? Are keyways required?

(7) Check that preparations are completed and materials are available for joint installation during concrete placement. Is joint lay-out established?

(8) Is source of concrete approved? Is plant inspector required? (Structural concrete or special mixes.)

(9) When placing of concrete cannot be interrupted, has a standby concrete source been provided?

(10) Is the class of concrete correct for the work to be done?

(11) Have the problems caused by extremely hot or cold weather been considered?

(12) Is placing equipment and method satisfactory to avoid segregation of the mix? Is form alignment maintained during placement?

(13) Check plant delivery tickets to determine the time of loading, weights, water content, materials and admixtures to see if they meet the requirements for the project.

(14) Are slump tests and compression test cylinder specimens prepared according to sampling and testing schedule?

(15) Will concrete be placed in time to permit finishing during daylight hours?

(16) Is the number of finishers adequate?

(17) Is the class of finish correct for the type of work involved? Is the finishing procedure producing the required smoothness or texture; levelness within tolerance? Slopes for drainage? Trowel marks removed?

(18) Have provisions been made for curing the concrete? Is curing started promptly? Is curing compound thoroughly mixed and applied at the approved rate?

3-12 CONCRETE STRUCTURES

3-12.1 General. See the following Subsections for related information:

2-4   Portland Cement Concrete and Related Products

2-4.4 Concrete Mixtures

2-4.5 Concrete Proportioning Plant Inspection

3-11   Concrete Construction, General

3-11.9 Gunite Construction

3-13   Prestressed Concrete

In general, the basic principles involved in constructing reinforced concrete structures are common to the high-rise building and the simple storm drain catch basin. In relating these principles to a specific structure, the Inspector must be observant of its nature and critical features and exercise practical judgment in the application of tolerances.

When tolerances for the structure are not specified in the contract documents, the Inspector should discuss the Agency guidelines for acceptance with the contractor. Tolerance should never be set at levels any more exacting than needed to satisfy the structural, operational and aesthetic functions of the structure. Although they may not fit for every structure, the following tolerances are considered reasonable for most purposes:

(1) Variations from vertical and horizontal lines and surfaces of buildings, including columns, piers, walls, floors and beam soffits, except as indicated in item (2), below; ¼ inch in 10 feet, ⅜ inch in any story or 20 feet, ¾ inch in 40 feet or more.

(2) Exposed corners, columns grooves, joints, lintels and other conspicuous lines; ¼ inch in 10 feet, ½ inch in 20 feet.

(3) Variations in cross sectional dimensions or thickness of structure elements such as walls, columns, beams and slabs; minus ¼ inch, plus ½ inch.

(4) Footings: Minus ½ inch, plus two inches, provided starter wall location complies with item (1).

(5) For bridges, variations from horizontal and vertical lines and surfaces of structure; ½ inch exposed and one inch backfilled, in 20 feet.

(6) Variations of finished openings in walls and floors; ¼ inch.

(7) Tolerances should not adversely affect coverage of rebar.

3-12.2 Line and Grade. Work on a concrete structure should be commenced only after line and grade have been established by a survey party. For small subterranean structures, this may consist of two or more stakes, with cuts and offsets indicated on a grade sheet. On major structures, bench marks or reference points are generally established clear of the work area so that frequent checks can be made to determine that the building is plumb, on line, and the grades of the controlling features are at the proper elevation. Such reference points must be protected from loss or displacement by construction operations by marking them with suitable flags and barriers.

Forms must be inspected to determine that they are erected on line and are adequately braced to remain on line. Finish grade must be established before placing any concrete. Elevations are usually established by the use of pour strips for walls and columns and by screeds for floors and decks. These elevations should always take into consideration the settlement anticipated in the forms and falsework from the weight of the concrete. (See Subsection 3-12.4.5.) Agency construction survey standards for bridges, buildings and retaining walls may be found in Subsection 1-5.6.

3-12.3 Structure Foundations and Earthwork.

Subsection 3-3, Earthwork, contains important information for the Inspector concerning structure foundations, excavation and backfill. The Inspector should be familiar with soil borings for the project and note any differences in the excavated material. The soil base for footings should be free of loose soil or water and should be checked for soft areas. Unsatisfactory foundation conditions should be reported to the Design Engineer.

Excavation for structures must be carefully controlled to avoid disturbing the subgrade for footings or foundation slabs. This may not be possible in sand or where rock is present and requires blasting. All loose material should be removed before reinforcement steel is installed. Except in sand, wetting, flooding or tamping loose material is not permitted. It is usually necessary to keep sand moist until concrete is placed in order to maintain a firm stable foundation.

Such removals may result in the bottom of footings extending below the plan elevations. This over-break or over-excavation is to be backfilled with concrete, placed monolithically with the concrete in the footing unless otherwise approved by the Engineer.

Structural backfill is discussed in Subsection 3-3.5.4, and should be reviewed prior to inspecting the placing of backfill against concrete structures.

It is frequently necessary to perform backfill in confined spaces with equipment of limited size. It is best to use select material which is relatively less critical as to moisture content and compactive effort where such limited conditions occur. Pea gravel may become necessary as a backfill material if access is severely limited.

3-12.4 Forms and Falsework.

3-12.4.1 **General.** Formwork for concrete structures represents a very important part of concrete construction, both in terms of its effect on the finished structure and in terms of its erection cost. Formwork frequently costs more than the concrete and the reinforcing steel together. The Inspector should familiarize himself with the terminology of formwork and falsework as shown in Plates 35 and 56, Appendix, respectively.

Good formwork is essential where the showing faces of concrete are intended to reflect architectural or esthetic lines. the architect may detail wood (or other materials) to be attached to the face of forms in a pattern to result in projections or indentations in the finished wall face. This is called "rustication". Chamfer strips ¾″x¾″ cant strips nailed into the forms at inside and outside corners) are helpful in avoiding mortar leaks at corners and result in a neat finished appearance. The Inspector must keep in mind that every imperfection in the forms will result in a matching impression or projection in the surface of the concrete. Consequently, panel joints must be laid out by the contractor to give the most pleasing pattern. Patches, tears, holes, warp and other defects in form faces must not be permitted except below grade or on non-showing faces of structures. Similar requirements for smooth surfaces also apply to structures where fluids in motion are involved and minimum resistance to flow is desirable.

The Inspector must check the forms and falsework in some detail in order to determine that they are built to the correct dimensions and tolerances, architectural appearance requirements and strength to withstand construction loads and concrete pressure.

Among the properties that concrete form materials must possess are strength, rigidity, smoothness and re-usability. Because of their adaptability and workability, the most commonly used form materials are lumber and plywood.

Many patented form panels of steel or a combination of steel and plywood are manufactured today. They are available in various sizes so that virtually any conventional concrete element can be formed by bolting a series of panels together at their flanges, with little or no need for special filler strips. Such forms have the disadvantage in that they are expensive and must be reused many times to be economically practicable. As a result, frequently reused panels become worn and damaged, plywood facings deteriorate and metal facings become dented. Panels become difficult to assemble and align in the wall form, causing offsets and open joints with subsequent bleeding of the concrete at the panel joints. These and other characteristics have excluded most such systems from architectural work. On the other hand, they are normally acceptable and have been utilized extensively for below-ground portions of bridges, pumping plants and fluid-conveying structures. Where their use is contemplated, the Inspector should instruct the contractor, prior to delivery to the site, as to their acceptability for the various parts of the structure. Immediately after delivery the Inspector must determine that the condition of the panels is suitable to produce satisfactory concrete surfaces and then instruct the contractor accordingly.

Forms for round columns or caissons are available in fiber form tubes in sizes up to 48 inches in diameter and in lengths up to 50 feet. These tubes are manufactured by spirally wrapping and gluing successive layers of fiber sheets and coating the inside and outside surfaces with wax or a plastic material for waterproofing purposes.

Fiber form boxes, sometimes described as "egg-crate" boxes, are often used for waffle-type floor construction and as forms for pan-joist type floor construction. These cardboard boxes are fabricated of heavy fiber cardboard with glazed or waxed surfaces. They are generally reinforced inside by the type of cardboard separators used to compartmentize cartons for shipping fragile objects — hence the term "egg-crate."

Special purpose steel forms are fabricated for use where a large number of units of the same size and shape must be cast. These include forms for concrete piles, columns, precast beams and girders, slip forms for silos or stacks, and forms for electrolier standards, concrete pipe and pan-joist type construction. Plate 57, Appendix, shows a typical pan-joist installation as well as waffle slab form construction using steel domes.

New and special form materials are constantly being developed for casting special purpose concrete. Ornamental concrete or intricate geometric sections are frequently cast using plaster of paris molds. Plastic or fiberglass sheets joined with resins open the way for stain-proof forms of unlimited size and shape with no visible joints. Such materials and forms are generally expensive, but they often offer the best solution to the problem of casting concrete to meet the architectural details incorporated in modern structural design.

3-12.4.2 Wall Form Construction.

Good formwork is accurately dimensioned, constructed of material of sufficient strength to maintain deflection or distortion within acceptable limits, surfaced to reflect the degree of esthetic quality called for, and adequately braced and supported to withstand the weight and pressure of the concrete and superimposed construction loads. Irrespective of what materials are used to fabricate forms, the complete forms must have adequate rigidity and strength to withstand the concrete pressures without displacement. Where plywood is used on horizontal or vertical studs, the Inspector must determine that the spacing between studs is not so excessive as to cause a scalloped effect due to deflection of the plywood between the studs. Plywood installed with the long dimension of the sheet at right angles to studs furnishes the maximum strength for resisting deflection. For example: One manufacturer recommends a reduction of 27% of the recommended allowable load for ¾" plywood having its long dimension parallel with the studs. Panels should also be as long as possible. This is emphasized by the knowledge that the value for the stiffness of a panel spanning a single stud space is only half of the value resulting from a continuous panel spanning several studs.

Nails must be driven up tight, but hammer marks in the face of panel should be avoided. All nail heads, knots, panel joints, holes or other depressions must be filled in flush with the face of the panel with a quick-setting compound. Otherwise, these imperfections will be transferred to the concrete surface and be difficult to repair without leaving a blemish.

The spacing of wales depends upon the height of a wall, the anticipated rate of the concrete placement, and the spacing of the form ties. Before the concrete is placed, it is important for the Inspector to see that the studs are sized (checked to see that all have the same dimensions) and that the wales are straight so that every stud will have full bearing on the wales. Otherwise, the pressure of the concrete may move the forms and detrimentally affect the alignment of the surface of the concrete.

Strongbacks should be used to support the wales for high walls or long spans. Wood, concrete or patented steel spreaders should be used to keep opposing forms the proper distance apart. Each wood spreader must have a wire attached leading to a nail at the top of the forms. As the concrete is placed and approaches a wood spreader, it must be knocked loose with a pole and extracted by the wire. It is customary to throw the spreader over the side of the form, leaving the wire attached to the nail. The Inspector can thus check at any time to determine that all wood spreaders have been removed. Metal spreaders should be wired to the reinforcing bars. As the concrete level approaches these spreaders, they must be knocked lose from the forms and permitted to remain wired to the rebar and ultimately embedded in the concrete. Care must be exercised by the contractor to avoid breaking the wire tie to the reinforcing bars, or the spreader may float to the face of the form. Due to lack of sufficient cover, the spreader may rust and disfigure a showing face.

For showing faces, studs should never be spaced more than 16 inches on centers when used with one inch wood sheathing or ¾ inches and thicker structural grade plywood. Studs should be carefully plumbed and should not be spaced more than 12 inches on centers when used with ⅝-inch plywood. Wales should not be spaced more than 24 inches on centers and ties should not be spaced more than 27 inches on centers when double 2x4-inch wales.

For wood forms more than 10 feet high, double 2x6-inch vertical wales (sometimes referred to as strongbacks), spaced not more than 10 feet on centers and extending the full height of the forms, should be bolted to every other set of horizontal wales to maintain the forms in straight and true alignment.

It is imperative that forms be designed so that they are easy to strip without damaging the concrete. Similarly, form design should take into account the problems involved in placing the concrete.

The Inspector should give the following list points careful attention when checking the adequacy of wall forms:

(a) Proper spacing and splicing of studs and wales.

(b) Staggering of joints or splices in sheathing, plywood panels and bracing.

(c) Proper number and location of tie rods or clamps.

(d) Proper tightening of tie rods or clamps.

(e) Adequately tied corners.

(f) Form coatings applied before placing of reinforcing steel and not used in such quantities as to run onto bars.

(g) Details of control joints, construction joints and expansion joints.

3-12.4.3 Form Ties. Form ties are used to keep the two opposing forms from spreading under the pressure of the fluid mass of concrete. There are many types and sizes of form ties, ranging from slender rods and straps to heavy clamps and threaded bolts. The more conventional types are stud-rods, plain steel rod and clamp assemblies, coil ties and snap ties. Coil and snap ties are not permitted in Agency work when architectural structures are involved.

Stud-rod tie assemblies have certain advantages over prefabricated wire ties, primarily because of their more rugged construction and ultimate strength. If struck by a high-frequency internal concrete vibrator, they are not likely to break and transfer loads to adjacent ties.

Form ties for achitectural concrete should be adjustable to permit tightening of forms to the required dimension and to be of such type as to leave no metal closer than 1½ in. to the surface. They should not be fitted with lugs, cones, washers or other devices which will leave holes through the member larger than one inch in diameter or depressions larger in diameter than the depth at the exposed surface of the concrete. Ties should be tight-fitting to prevent leakage at the holes in the form. Ties that are to be pulled from the wall must be coated with nonstaining bond breaker to facilitate removal. The Inspector should obtain the manufacturer's pertinent data and recommendations for the type of form tie used. He should also know the contractor's methods and intended rate of placing the concrete to determine the maximum spacing of the of ties.

Snap ties and coil ties are satisfactory devices provided that they are used strictly in conformance with the manufacturer's recommendations. The most common problem with their use is that the contractor attempts to place them as he would form bolts and subject them to the same loads and construction abuse. Often their slender components, reduced sections or fusion-welded contact surfaces will not withstand excessive spacing, heavy concrete pressures or vibrator contact, and they will bend or break readily under impact.

3-12.4.4 Concrete Pressure in Forms. Freshly mixed concrete has properties similar to a heavy fluid. When placed in forms, the concrete gradually changes from this semifluid condition to a solid state as the concrete hardens. The rate which the concrete sets has considerable effect on the lateral pressure exerted on the forms into which the concrete has been deposited.

Other factors also affect the pressure produced on the forms, including the following: the depth of placement, the rate of placement, slump, the method of consolidating the concrete, the temperature, the amount of cement in the mix, type of aggregate, admixtures, impact effect from free fall of the mixtures, the size and shape of the forms and the amount and location of the reinforcing steel.

Rich concrete mixtures take longer to begin their initial set, as is also the case with high-slump concrete. In addition, high-slump concrete has less internal friction, thereby being a more fluid concrete which causes higher pressures on the forms. Impact of the falling concrete imposes additional loads on the forms, as does the method of consolidation, particularly where a high-frequency internal vibrator is used. The depth of placement and the rate of placement are related in that the greater the rate and depth of placement, the greater the pressure on the forms, since there will be a greater depth of plastic concrete. The shape and size of the forms and the amount the placement of the reinforcing steel provide baffles which partially support the plastic concrete, somewhat reducing the pressure on the formwork. Temperature has a significant effect on the initial setting time, with high temperatures accelerating the set and colder temperatures retarding it.

The following graph gives the pressure on forms for a typical concrete mixture (150 lbs. per cubic foot) with a five-inch slump, placed at temperature between 60° and 70° Fahrenheit:

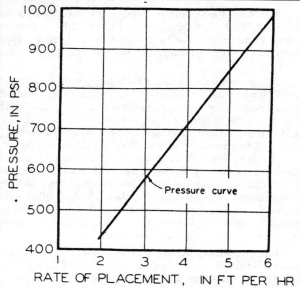

Concrete: 150 lbs./cu. ft.   Temperature: 60-70° F.   Slump: 5 inches

VARIATION IN PRESSURE WITH RATE OF PLACEMENT
(Civil Engineering — Dec. 1965)

(**Note:** Chart depicts a typical concrete mix with a moderately high slump. Structural concrete mixes are seldom permitted to exceed a slump of four inches.)

From this graph it can readily be seen that the pressure is a straight line function of the rate of placement and that an indiscriminate rate of placement of concrete, without regard for the depth of plastic concrete in the forms, may cause a failure of otherwise adequate forms. It should be remembered that the maximum pressure considered in the design of forms for walls is 2,000 pounds per square foot. Higher slumps or air temperatures cooler than 60° Fahrenheit rapidly increase the pressures indicated on the graph. For example: the same five-inch slump concrete placed at a rate of four feet per hour would exert 930 pounds per square foot at 45° Fahrenheit as compared to 715 pounds per square foot placed at 60° Fahrenheit, or an increase in pressure of over 30 percent.

The Inspector must examine the factors affecting concrete pressure in forms and, using the graph as a guide, control the rate of concrete placement to keep within safe limits and thereby eliminate form distortion.

3-12.4.5 **Falsework.** Temporary scaffolding used to support the forms for floor and deck slabs is commonly referred to as falsework. In special cases where it supports domes, arches or symmetrical bridge spans, it is called "centering."

It is important to obtain solid bearing for the footings and sills of falsework and for the heavy loads of major structures such as bridge decks. The same precautions must be applied to these footings as are applied to permanent footings. Excavation should extend to hard, firm earth which is leveled carefully to provide full bearing for each sill. Too often, the contractor will place falsework footings on spongy subgrade or disregard subsequent rain softening of the footing subgrade. If necessary, drainage ditches should be cut to keep water from collecting in the excavations or the excavations should be backfilled and consolidated to shed water away from the falsework footing. In some cases, where the bearing value is low, it may be necessary to drive piling for major falsework systems.

Falsework may be fabricated of timber, structural steel or patented tubular scaffolding units. For major structures, the contractor must submit plans of the falsework he proposes to use to the Engineer for approval prior to its erection.

Timber falsework (see Plate 56, Appendix) must be carefully fabricated so that every saw-cut is square and in one plane. This is necessary to obtain full bearing for all members. Otherwise, each post would take a load differing from its design load. This differential loading would cause overloading of individual posts and result in varying amounts of deflection in the falsework. Wood-to-wood joints are expected to close when the full weight of the concrete is placed on them. Consequently, the soffit form must be built deliberately high by adding 1/16 inch for each wood-to-wood contact surface, from the top of the sills to the bottom of the soffit form. This will allow for deflection of the falsework from concrete and construction loads. Additional hike-up is necessary in falsework to provide for the deflection from bending of the stringers and joists of the soffit forms from the weight of the concrete. Posts are usually adjusted to proper height by wedges or screw jacks which permit easy reestablishment of grade in case of settlement of the forms. They also facilitate removal of the falsework. Wedges may be used at the top or bottom of shores but never at both ends. During the placement of concrete, the forms can be adjusted to grade by the contractor with the assistance of a survey party.

When patented shores or methods of shoring are used, manufacturers' recommendations regarding load-carrying capacities should be verified by test reports of a qualified and recognized testing laboratory.

Lap splices constructed in the field should be limited to alternate shores under slabs or every third shore under beams. When spliced more than once, diagonal bracing should be provided at every splice point. To avoid buckling, splices should not be located near the mid-height of the shores without lateral support nor midway between points of lateral support.

Every splice must be reinforced to prevent buckling. The minimum length of splice material for timber shores should be 2'4". Shores made of round timbers should have three splice pieces and square timbers should have four splice pieces.

Deflection of forms can easily be observed by using a "tell-tale" rod. A long, slender square rod is pushed up against the soffit form and nailed to a joist. The other end is allowed to hang freely to about one foot above the ground where it is loosely tied to a stake driven into the ground. A horizontal index mark is drawn across the rod and stake and deflection can be determined by the separation of the index marks as the forms take the load. As many "tell-tales" should be used as is necessary for adequate measurement of deflection.

Similarly, plumb bobs hung on long lines attached at or near the top of a wall or column, with the bob indexed over a cross mark on a board nailed securely to the bottom of the forms, can be used to register any tendency for a wall to move out of plumb.

3-12.4.6 Causes of Failures in Falsework. A shoring system supporting the fluid concrete and superimposed construction loads for a bridge deck or other heavy, suspended slab is an awkward, top-heavy structure. Lateral bracing and continuous vertical support are mandatory. The principal cause of failure in falsework can be traced to inadequate lateral bracing of the shoring system. Placing concrete for vertical members such as walls and columns as soon as the deck forming is in place, and prior to placing rebar for the deck slab, will greatly enhance the lateral stability of the structure. To a lesser extent, many failures result from inadequate shores with respect to size and number. Other causes may contribute to the failure of a falsework system and the Inspector should be alert to detect the need for and order a remedy where the following factors exist which experience has indicated may contribute to a failure: excessive impact from dropping concrete on a wood falsework system; damage from inadequate blocking or bridging of stringers or joists; inferior quality of lumber; and unstable vertical loadcarrying members resulting from excessively extended jacks or from using more than two wedges to a post.

The Inspector should see that adequate procedures are employed by the contractor to permit frequent checks of the falsework to be made during the concrete placement to determine the deflection (see also Subsection 3-12.7) and to observe how the falsework reacts under the increasing load. Any deficiency must be called to the attention of the contractor for immediate correction.

In summary, the Inspector should be concerned with the following in connection with falsework:

(a) Adequacy of diagonal and horizontal cross bracing of shores.

(b) Adequacy of splicing and seating of shores.

(c) Proper control of the rate and sequence of placing concrete horizontally to prevent unbalanced loadings.

(d) Stability of soil under mudsills.

(e) Procedure to check falsework during and after concrete placement to detect abnormal deflections or other signs of imminent failure.

(f) Provisions for lateral pressures on formwork.

(g) Plumbness of shoring.

(h) All locking devices on metal shoring in place and secured.

(i) Resistance to vibration from adjacent moving loads.

(j) Adequate provision to resist overturning.

3-12.5 Reinforcing Steel (Rebar). Concrete has the property of withstanding very heavy loads in compression but is relatively weak in tension. Reinforcing steel bars, being long and slender, are ineffective in compression but very strong in tension. In reinforced concrete structures, the best features of both materials are combined.

Nearly every element of a structure, such as a wall, column, slab or footing is designed to resist bending, overturning, perforation or shear. The use of reinforcing steel to resist bending (placing the steel in tension) is best illustrated in the diagram below.

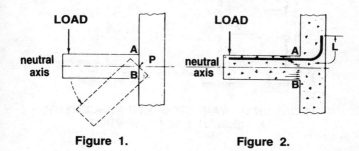

Figure 1.   **Figure 2.**

In Figure 1, the horizontal concrete member, when loaded vertically near its free end, would tend to rotate about point P, a point on an imaginary line drawn through the geometric center of the horizontal member called the neutral axis. It can be readily seen that the movement of the member to the position represented by the dotted lines will place the contact surface represented by PA in tension while simultaneously placing PB in compression. This is typical for all structural members under a bending load. The cross-sectional area on one side of the neutral axis will be in tension while the area on the other side of the neutral axis is in compression. The values of tension and compression increase in a straight line ratio from zero at the neutral axis to a maximum at the outer surface of the member.

By placing a steel bar as shown in Figure 2 in the area of maximum tension, the tension forces can be effectively resisted. The steel bar prevents rotation of the member, resulting in the maximum utilization of the compression resistance of the concrete in the lower portion (below the neutral axis) of the member. In many cases, steel is placed in compression areas where stresses are too high for the concrete to resist the compression forces alone.

The Inspector must be alert to detect the improper placing of steel reinforcement bars. It is possible for the ironworker to unintentionally reverse a steel pattern with regard to the principal reinforcement. The following diagram shows typical loading situations and illustrates the importance of the proper location for the reinforcing steel.

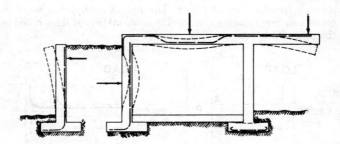

LOCATION OF MAIN STEEL REINFORCEMENT
ON TENSION SIDE OF MEMBER

Any bend near the end of a steel reinforcing bar is called a "hook" whether or not it is in the shape of an L or J. All other bends in the bar are referred to as "bends." Bars intended for use in beams or slabs are often bent for placement in the upper portion of the member over the supports and in the lower portion of the member at the center portion of the span. These bars are called truss bars. Bars transverse to the principal reinforcement in long slender horizontal members such as beams or girders are called stirrups. The purpose of stirrups is to resist shear and diagonal tension in these members. In rectangular or circular compression members such as columns, the vertical reinforcement is restrained with ties or spiral reinforcement. Dowels are the projections of embedded rebars which permit their extension by lapping correspondingly placed rebars in a subsequent concrete placement, thus maintaining the structural continuity of the member. (See Plates 58, 59, Appendix.)

It is known that concrete shrinks upon changing from a plastic to a solid state and that subsequently it will expand and contract from thermal changes. If not controlled, this shrinkage and volumetric change will tend to concentrate in several places in the member, resulting in "working" cracks which can critically affect the life of the structure. These may be difficult to waterproof and may cause distress in embedments passing through or straddling such cracks. To minimize this condition, reinforcing steel is usually placed in a uniform pattern in a member (often as a curtain on the side of a wall opposite from the pricipal reinforcement) and is referred to as temperature reinforcement.

Undesirable cracking and even failure of structural concrete can result if there is insufficient bond between the reinforcement steel and the concrete. For this reason, no coating of any nature is permitted on the rebar which will reduce its bond with the concrete. Rebar is deliberately rolled to produce deformations to increase the bond, and the bars are either bent into hooks or extended into slabs or beams to increase the anchorage effect.

Where considerable repetition of reinforcing steel requirements occurs, such as in multi-story structures, the steel is often specified on the plans by the use of schedules. The fabricator then utilizes detailers of steel reinforcement to detail the rebar and issue placing diagrams. The Standard Specifications require submission of placing diagrams to the Engineer for approval where reinforcing steel is paid for by weight or when required by the Special Provisions. The Inspector is cautioned that the contract drawings are of first priority in checking reinforcing steel for compliance. He should not refer to unapproved placing diagrams. The contract drawings must be clarified by the Engineer. The placement of all reinforcing steel must be checked and approved by the Inspector before the forms are "buttoned up," that is, before the erection of forms reaches such a state of completion that the reinforcing steel placement would not be readily accessible for the Inspector to check.

3-12.5.1 Placing Reinforcing Steel. The Inspector must see that bars are clean and sound, free of loose rust and scale, grease, concrete or any other coating or foreign substance that will destroy or reduce the bond. They must not be bent or straightened in a manner injurious to the material and bars with kinks and bends not shown on the plans must not be used. All reinforcing steel and wire mesh must be tested by the Testing Agency before being placed in a structure. (See Plate 28, Appendix.)

Bars must be fabricated to correct dimensions. The Inspector must carefully check the dimensions, lengths, depths and radii for compliance with plans and permissible tolerances.

Bars must be properly spaced. The minimum center-to-center distance between parallel bars is normally two times the diameter, one inch minimum. For bar splices in vertical columns, the minimum clear distance between pairs of bars is normally 1½ times the bar diameter.

Bars must be continuous. Splices cannot be made at points of maximum stress, and approval of the Engineer is required for any splices not shown on the plans. Splices must be lapped the minimum distance required by the drawings, the Special Provisions, or 30 diameters per the Standard Specifications.

Bars must be properly embedded with clear cover (not measured to the center of the bar) as shown on the drawings. Typical clear cover is represented by the following:

Concrete against earth – not formed	3″
Concrete against earth – formed	2″
Concrete exposed to weather	2″
Interior columns	1½″
Beams and girders	1½″
Interior walls	¾″
Suspended slabs	¾″
Joists	¾″

The Inspector must check to determine that bars are accurately located and firmly held in place to prevent displacement due to construction loads prior to or during concrete placement. All points of bar intersection are to be tied with No. 16 (BWG) annealed wire. Metal spacers are utilized to secure proper spacing between curtains of rebar. Concrete blocks or chairs with embedded tie wires are employed to maintain proper clearances of the reinforcing steel from the forms. Metal chairs are not acceptable for concrete exposed to weather. Stirrups must be secured at the top and bottom. Dowels must be secured in place, not stabbed into new concrete, and must not be bent or displaced after the concrete has hardened.

The following tolerances apply to the placement of rebars:

Longitudinal location in member	± 1 inch
Transverse location in member	± ¼ inch
Bottom bar in member	– ¼ inch
Top bar in member	+ ¼ inch, –0
Vertical terminations (in column)	± ¾ inch
Truss bar bends (location)	± 2 inches
Stirrups and ties (location)	± 1 inch
Minimum spacing between bars	– ¼ inch

All measurements of bar lengths and columns cores are made from out to out as shown below:

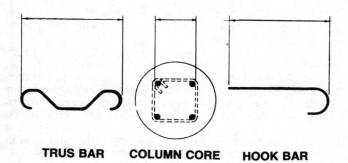

TRUS BAR   COLUMN CORE   HOOK BAR

A common problem occurs when slab reinforcing is assembled from the smaller bar sizes (#3 and #4) and trussed over beams. Where welded wire mesh is installed, it shall be pulled up with a hook into its proper position in the slab at the time that the concrete is placed and struck off. Even moderate foot traffic over such areas can dislocate and distort such bars or mesh which, if permitted to remain, would substantially destroy their effectiveness in the completed structure.

3-12.6 Embedments.

3-12.6.1 General. Almost every concrete structure has included in its design the need for some type of embedment. Manhole steps, electric pull boxes, pipe rail stanchion sleeves, anchor bolts, block-outs for mechanical equipment, inserts and pipe hangers and metal frames for doors and covers are typical examples. These embedments need to be accurately and securely located with respect to pattern, elevation, orientation and depth of embedment. Improperly located embedments are very expensive to relocate and result in second-rate installations as well as in unsightly repaired structural walls. For this reason most embedments must be installed in the forms and checked prior to the placing of the concrete.

The Inspector must always be concerned about the structural effect of embedments. In all cases, the integrity of the structure has priority over any other consideration. The Engineer should be consulted before reinforcing steel is shifted or cut to provide for embedded items.

3-12.6.2 Conduits, Piping and Raceways. The proper routing of conduits and raceways in reinforced concrete structures is generally left to the craftsmen and the Inspector to coordinate at the site of the work. It is important, therefore, that the Inspector be aware of the major problems encountered in this type of embedment.

The most frequently encountered problem occurs where conduits interfere with the steel reinforcement or with each other in walls and slabs. Direct routing is not always possible. The electrician may be required to install an extra pull box or completely relocate a conduit in a roundabout way to avoid displacing the reinforcement steel or to avoid conduit cross-overs. To avoid rebar displacement, the craftsman is tempted to pass conduits over or under the mats, thereby placing his conduit too close to the concrete surface. This alternative is unacceptable since it would very likely result in a crack in the concrete at that location. The ideal location for conduits and raceways is near the center of the slab or wall. The generally acceptable practice is to secure the conduit to the mat or curtain of rebar on the side opposite the least dimension of concrete cover, with local offsets to serve pull boxes and outlet boxes. In most situations, this procedure will provide adequate cover (¾″). If not, alternative solutions must be found.

Where conduits and raceways pass through expansion joints, a sliding sleeve must be installed to permit the joint to open and close without rupturing the embedment.

Except for radiant heating systems, plumbing conduits containing fluids under pressure are never cast into concrete. These installations are usually installed later by attaching them to the surface of concrete structures. Where necessary, plumbing conduits may penetrate walls and slabs by passing through oversized sleeves previously cast in place expressly for that purpose. Plumbing systems must be accessible for maintenance and ultimate replacement, and embedment of any part of the system (except drains) would make such work very difficult and unnecessarily expensive.

The Inspector must not permit piping or other conduit, sleeves and the like to be embedded in important structural members such as beams, girders or columns except as shown on the plan or approved by the Engineer. The above limitation does not include one inch and smaller trade-size conduit passing through the upper portions of beams and embedded in an adjoining slab or located vertically in a column.

3-12.6.3   Joints and Waterstops in Concrete Structures.   Three basic types of joints occur in concrete structures: contraction, construction and isolation.

Contraction joints are used to control shrinkage without random cracking. Isolation joints are used to separate one portion of the structure from the other and permit independent movement either vertically or horizontally. Construction joints are used for convenience to divide the structure into logical units for construction purposes.

Construction joints are installed in walls, slabs, beams, girders and columns at locations that will not be critical to the functional structural elements that make up the structure. For example, joints in beams and suspended slabs should be located near the midpoint of the span, not near the support where the maximum shear occurs. Unless shown on the plans, locations of construction joints must be approved by the structural engineer.

Where watertight construction joints and good bond between lifts of concrete are needed, the Inspector should be sure that the previously placed concrete is cleaned of laitance and any dirt or soft concrete. It is best done by wet sandblasting after the concrete has hardened or by high-pressure water jet after the concrete has reached its initial set. This operation need proceed only enough to remove the soft material to clean concrete surface without excessive cutting. Then the surface is preferably kept damp or wet (cured) until ready for the next placement. Prior to concrete placing the surface should be washed clean and any free water removed.

The specifications may require a mortar grout on the surface of a construction joint immediately before placing the first layer of concrete; or a richer mix with a slighly higher slump and sand content in the first layer. This can be accomplished by omitting part of the coarse aggregate (or the larger size coarse aggregate) from the mix. In any case, the Inspector should check that the first layer of concrete is thoroughly vibrated.

It is very desirable to minimize the lateral deflection of a construction joint in concrete members to reduce the shear effect. Of course, the reinforcing steel projecting through the joint will offer some resistance to shear, but the steel is placed in the member primarily to take up the tension forces. One method is to place a keyway into the wall or slab so that shear resistance can be developed in the concrete itself. Some typical wall keyway shapes are shown below. A keyway is made by forming or by embedding a special shape in the concrete as it is placed. It should be noted, however, that some structural engineers are currently not requiring any keys in wall construction.

Figure 4   TYPICAL KEYWAY TYPES

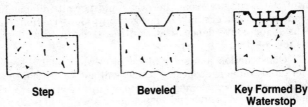

Step   **Beveled**   **Key Formed By
                                                      Waterstop**

TYPICAL KEYWAYS

Where keyways are to be installed, they should be pre-cut with hangers and splice plates already attached and stored adjacent to the walls in which they are to be placed. They should be pressed firmly into the plastic concrete to full depth and the hangers nailed down securely to the forms. If there is insufficient concrete in the forms to come to the top of the key-way, additional concrete should be placed and thoroughly consolidated by the vibrator along the sides of the keyway to fill this space, in order to give greater effectiveness to the key-way for resisting shear. Where a single curtain of steel reinforcement is used in a wall, the keyway form must be split to straddle the dowels unless a step-key or shear blocks are specified.

Unless the contractor elects to sandblast the keyway and the dowels before placing more concrete, these should be cleaned by wire brushing as the splattered concrete dries initially and while it will brush off easily. Keyway forms should not be removed until they dry out sufficiently to shrink slightly and permit their easy removal.

Waterstops are utilized where joints are subject to hydrostatic pressure and water percolation is undesirable. The installation of waterstops in forms often taxes the skill of the builder. Since part of the waterstop must be excluded from embedment so that it may be cast in the next concrete section, end forms of walls must be split, and this can result in a weakening of the forms and some mortar loss. The type of waterstop to be installed must be approved in advance by the Engineer. Various kinds of waterstops are shown below:

TYPES OF WATERSTOPS

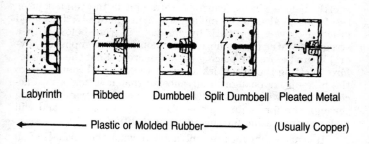

Labyrinth   Ribbed   Dumbbell Split Dumbbell Pleated Metal

◄———— Plastic or Molded Rubber ————►   (Usually Copper)

One of the crucial operations in the installation of waterstop is splicing. Splices must be made so that the integrity of the waterstop is maintained with respect to its tensile strength, flexibility and waterproofing quality. Splicing is accomplished by heat and fusion, vulcanizing, welding or soldering as may be prescribed in the Special Provisions.

Rubber waterstop should be prefabricated, when possible, to conform to the plan configuration. Joints may be made in the shop or in the field, but only by a vulcanizing process. Cemented sleeve-type connections are not acceptable.

The exposed portion of waterstop previously installed must be protected from damage until it is ultimately cast in place.

3-12.7 Placing Concrete. Many of the procedures, quality control methods, precautions and techniques of placing concrete are covered in Subsection 3-11.8 (see Subsection 3-11.7 for Pumped Concrete). In addition to these procedures, certain additional steps are essential for concrete structures and are outlined in this subsection.

The various methods of handling and transporting concrete are discussed in Subsection 3-11.6.

Where the volume of concrete expected to be placed is relatively large, the contractor must arrange in advance for a standby concrete proportioning plant to furnish the remainder of the concrete in the event of a breakdown at the original source of concrete. This is insurance against creating a cold joint in a critical part of the work.

After forms are erected, the Inspector must check to see that they are thoroughly cleaned of chips, dirt, nails and other debris that may collect on or in them. They must be wetted shortly before placing concrete to minimize the tendency for the forms to absorb the mixing water prematurely. It is good practice to wet falsework by spraying it from below with a stream of water from a hose. This should be accomplished several hours before the placing of the concrete if not the night before. Wetting the falsework allows it to swell and contribute to the hike-up far enough in advance so that it is taken into account. Otherwise, dry falsework will swell from water leaking through the forms during the placement of concrete and will make compensation for this movement difficult.

It is necessary for the contractor to wash the surfaces of all buckets, buggies, tremies, chutes and concrete transporting equipment to prevent their dry surfaces from extracting mortar from the first few batches of concrete placed. The same procedure must be used to coat the starter walls and the bottom portion of wall forms. This "washing" is done by using a grout mixture consisting of the regular concrete specified, but with all of the rock larger than one inch omitted and the slump increased to a fluid consistency. This is sometimes referred to as a "slush coat".

The contact surfaces of all construction joints must be properly prepared, prior to the commencement of succeeding concrete operations, by removing laitance so as to expose sound concrete. Laitance is a whitish scum consisting of very fine-sized particles of material which collects on the surface of wet concrete and is caused by too much water or excessive vibration. The most frequently used method for its removal is sand-blasting which simultaneously serves to clean rebar dowels. Other methods include jet washing (three to six hours after concrete placement), chipping, and using a set retarder applied immediately after placement which is jet-washed the day following placement.

The shrinkage of concrete upon its initial hardening poses certain problems that demand the attention of the Inspector. If the rate of placement is too slow, the concrete in the forms will begin to set and will shrink vertically as well as away from the forms. When this condition occurs, the mortar from fresh concrete placed upon it will squeeze down between the hardening concrete and the forms and will result in a lap effect on the surface of the concrete. This problem can be avoided by eliminating long lapses of time between lifts, by keeping the surface of the concrete in the forms plastic by occasionally topping it with fresh concrete, and by extending the internal vibrator into the last previously placed concrete when vibrating each subsequent lift. Experience has shown that a steady rate of pour results in the most production at lowest cost and produces the highest quality concrete.

Shrinkage raises another problem when casting columns, capitals and deep floor beams. If the lift extends above the top of a column into a capital or beam, the vertical shrinkage will cause a transverse crack in the column at the change in section. For this reason, girders, beams, columns and other vertical members should be filled on the last lift to the bottom of a change in section and allowed to set until vertical shrinkage has subsequentially taken place (about two hours). Only then should additional concrete be placed.

Precautions must be taken in topping out a reinforced concrete wall, particularly one that will be extended upward by a subsequent lift. Excess water may accumulate on top of the concrete in the forms which will result in laitance forming on top of the hardening concrete. Laitance can be effectively reduced by avoiding excess mixing water and by providing for a means of escape for the accumulation of water on top of the placed concrete.

The insertion of tremies and vibrators into wall forms often results in misaligned steel or broken tie wires at rebar intersections.

While the concrete is still plastic, the position of the reinforcing steel must be checked and misaligned bars moved into proper position and tied off, if necessary, to retain them in place.

3-12.8 Stripping Forms and Striking Falsework. The Inspector shall not permit forms to be stripped from walls or suspended slabs until the times as stated in the Standard Specifications have elapsed. Adjustments may be made in stripping time by the use of high early strength cement, approved accelerators or other methods approved by the Engineer.

If the forms are properly designed, wall forms can be removed independently of soffit forms so that their early reuse may be effected. Properly designed forms will not bind in the corners. When binding does occur, it not only increases the problems of stripping but often contributes to damage to the face of the concrete. Crow bars or large pry bars must not be permitted to bear on the concrete during form-stripping operations. Chamfer strips, wood inserts or block-outs which remain attached to the concrete after stripping should be permitted to remain until surface finishing operations begin. They can be best removed when the concrete attains a greater strength. If they are removed while the concrete is relatively weak, spalling may result which is difficult to repair satisfactorily.

Care must also be exercised by the contractor when striking centering or falsework. It must not be disturbed in any way until the concrete has attained a strength sufficient to sustain its own weight. If a time is not prescribed in advance, it may be determined by the Inspector requesting that the Testing Agency program a progressive testing of the concrete cylinders which were made at the time the concrete was placed.

Falsework should be first cut loose from any attachment to wall forms, then uniformly lowered by the screw jacks or wedges originally used to adjust it to proper elevation. Unless it is especially fabricated for rolling to another location for reuse on a subsequent span, the falsework should be carefully dismantled in place. Any method of dismantling proposed by the contractor which would result in the placing of any load or impact on the concrete structure is prohibited.

Centering must be removed uniformly and gradually, beginning at the crown and working toward the haunches, to permit the arch to take its load slowly and evenly. Centering for bridges having two or more adjacent arch spans must be struck simultaneously.

3-12.9 Curing and Protection of Concrete. (See Subsection 3-11.12 for more details concerning concrete curing.) Due to the configuration of most concrete structures, problems in effective curing often arise. Projecting dowels and sharp metal embedments tend to perforate plastic sheets. Blankets or burlap coverings are difficult to keep continuously wet and often result in the undesirable condition of alternate wetting and drying. Where approved chemical curing compounds can be used without objectionable effects on the appearance of such concrete structures or on subsequent painting, they are very effective. Forms may be left in place and kept wet, or a continuous sprinkling or misting water system can sometimes be economically and effectively utilized as a curing method. In the latter case, the water spray system must keep all of the exposed concrete surfaces wet continuously throughout the curing period. The Inspector must frequently check such systems to insure that they are functioning properly and not adversely affected by such factors as the wind or plugged sprinkler heads. Continuous curing is usually required during daylight hours, including weekends and holidays.

3-12.10   Concrete Structures Checklist.

Preliminary

(a) Has survey control been established?

(2) Are supplemental drawings required? (Anchor bolt setting plans for structural steel, mechanical equipment, falsework, shoring, form work.)

(3) Review Subsection 3-3.2.2 Clearing Grubbing & Removals Checklist.

(4) Review Subsection 3-11.16 Concrete Construction, General Checklist.

(5) Review Subsection 3-3.3.7 Excavation General, Checklist.

(6) Has the contractor excavated to the elevations and dimensions required? Has over-excavation occurred and has it been corrected?

(7) Is the subgrade for the footings stable?

(8) Do the plans require that the concrete be placed against undisturbed earth? If not, is there sufficient clearance to construct and remove the formwork?

(9) Has all loose material been removed prior to the placement of rebar?

(10) Is proper drainage provided to maintain a stable subgrade and allow for subsequent concreting operations?

(11) When required, is the excavation properly braced to comply with the Safety Orders?

Formwork

(1) Are there any special conditions or requirements affecting the type, quality and strength of the formwork?

(2) Are construction joints, contraction joints and expansion joints required (or permitted), and are they properly located?

(3) What are the specific conditions affecting the design of wall forms? (Exposed faces or concealed faces, intended rate of concrete placement, etc.) Are the form materials in good condition consistent with the architectural quality required?

(4) Is the thickness of plywood or other sheathing, spacing of studs, wales and ties consistent with good formwork design?

(5) Are block-outs for windows, doors, equipment, etc. installed to the correct dimensions and location? Blocked and cross braced to resist concrete pressure?

(6) Are chamfer strips required for exposed corners, walls, columns, beams, etc.? Joint patterns and rustication formed as shown?

(7) Are waterstops or keyways required? Have waterstops been properly spliced? Have wall forms been plumbed, aligned and properly braced? (Corners "log cabined" or otherwise braced.)

(8) Have adequate provisions been made for the removal of temporary spreaders?

(9) Are the forms sufficiently tight to prevent mortar leakage?

(10) Are pour strips installed to the proper elevation?

(11) Are dimensions of all members checked? Alignment?

(12) Are cleanouts and proper concrete placing conditions provided?

Falsework and Shoring

(1) Are the mudsills continuously supported upon a firm foundation with provisions for adequate drainage?

(2) Are shop drawings of the falsework required?

(3) Are the vertical posts adequate with respect to size and spacing? Are all posts plumb?

(4) Are post splices properly reinforced?

(5) Is sufficient diagonal and horizontal bracing provided?

(6) Are horizontal joints in vertical members cut square to provide full bearing?

(7) All locking devices on metal shoring secured?

(8) Are the connections of shores to joints, stringers and wales adequate to resist torsion and uplift?

(9) Are wedges or other vertical adjustment devices provided to correct for settlement and provide proper camber?

(10) Has the falsework been wetted at least two hours before the placing of the concrete?

Reinforcing Steel

(1) Is the grade of rebar correct and has it been tested? Is it in good condition (no kinks or unauthorized bends) and clean?

(2) Have the forms been oiled or treated with some other protective coating prior to the placing of the rebar?

(3) Is dowel projection in accordance with the plan requirements? Have the dowels been cleaned?

(4) In which direction is the main steel to be installed in the wall? (Vertical or horizontal.) Have the additional bars required around openings been placed?

(5) Check for proper location of temperature steel inside or outside (above or below) main steel.

(6) Have column dowels been offset to allow for the proper placement of column rebar?

(7) Does the size and spacing of the rebar agree with the plan requirements and the placing diagrams?

(8) Is the corner rebar in the walls properly spliced?

(9) Is the pattern and spacing of column ties correct?

(10) Are the locations and length of splices in accordance with the structural requirements? (Spaced to develop full bond.)

(11) Are welded splices required? Is preparation and welding in accordance with AWS procedure?

(12) Is the clear distance of the rebar, as spaced in the forms, sufficient to provide the concrete cover required by the plans? (Check cover of top bars in bridge slab with strike-off machine if used.)

(13) Are bar bends in beams slabs accurately fabricated and properly located?

(14) Are stirrups properly spaced with respect to supports?

(15) Is the rebar tied and adequately supported so that it will maintain its position during concrete placement? (No metal chairs for concrete that is to be exposed to weather.)

(16) Is all rebar installed within allowable placing tolerance?

(17) Do not permit wall and column forms to be "buttoned up" prior to inspection and approval of rebar installation.

Embedded Items. (Preparation of a checklist for the inspection of embedded items is sometimes a necessary procedure for intricate strutures.)

(1) Items should be fixed firmly in correct location before the concrete is placed. (Blocking out the concrete to permit subsequent grouted installation of embedded items is not permitted unless specifically called for by the drawings.)

(2) Cutting or omission of steel reinforcement to allow for the installation of embedded items should not be permitted except as approved by the Engineer.

(3) Check architectural, mechanical and electrical drawings and approved shop drawings for anchor bolts, piping, sleeves, conduits, frames and boxes that are to be cast in the concrete. Obtain the Engineer's approval for installations in structural members when not shown on structural plans.

(4) Are embedded items protected against damage during placement of concrete? (Bolt threads and machined or polished sufaces covered; light metal sleeves or boxes braced internally; open pipes or conduits capped or plugged.)

(5) Do not permit fluid carrying pipe lines to be cast into the concrete.

(6) Do not permit conduit to be installed on the other side of the rebar (the side nearest the face of concrete).

(7) Conduit should be spaced away from parallel rebar, the clear distance equal to $1\frac{1}{3}$ times the maximum size coarse aggregate in the concrete.

(8) Do not permit any embedded item to impede the proper placement and consolidation of the concrete.

Concrete Placement Operations

(1) Do not permit concrete operations to be scheduled until forms, falsework, reinforcing steel and embedded items have been completed, inspected and approved.

(2) Are the forms clean?

(3) Have construction joints and dowels been sandblasted or otherwise treated to remove laitance?

(4) Has a Plant Inspector been arranged for at the concrete batching plant?

(5) What class of concrete is required? Is the slump and size of aggregate selected consistent with the placing conditions? Is a slush coat of grout required on the existing concrete joint prior to placing concrete?

(6) Is the handling and the placing equipment adequate and in sufficient quantity? (Vibrators, tremies, chutes.)

(7) Are the handling and placing methods adequate to permit concrete placement without segregation of the mix?

(8) Is the concrete delivery, rate of placement, and placement sequence sufficient to avoid cold joints and to avoid exces-

sive fluid pressure in wall forms? Check for and obtain correction of displaced or deflected rebar during concrete placement.

(9) Are required slump tests and compression cylinders prepared?

(10) Are additional cylinders prepared for easy strength test to permit form removal?

(11) Has rebar moved from its proper position to permit placing the concrete, replaced in proper position?

(12) Is concrete placed in approximately level two-foot lifts (3 feet maximum)?

(13) Allow time for concrete settlement after placing walls and columns before placing beams and slabs.

(14) Are the forms and decks maintained to proper alignment and grade? (Continuously checked. Tell-tales utilized to detect movement.)

(15) Has the welded wire mesh been pulled up from the soffit forms?

(16) Are "topping off" operations adequate? Has the final lift been vibrated? Are keyways installed?

Form Removal and Curing

(1) Refer to Subsection 3-11.12 for review of curing details.

(2) What compressive strength of the concrete is required prior to the removal of the forms?

(3) Is the timing for form removal critical? Have sufficient cylinders been made to determine the concrete strength and to establish the earliest allowable date for form removal?

(4) Are forms designed to permit their removal in stages? (Consistent with strength requirements.)

(5) Are the methods and sequence of form removal adequate to prevent damage to the concrete surfaces and to avoid adverse structural loads on members?

(6) How many days of curing are required?

(7) Is the curing adequate? Is the water curing continuous, and is it providing full coverage during daylight hours, including weekends? Are the plastic and chemical membranes used for curing protected against damage from construction operations and, when damaged, properly repaired?

3-13 PRESTRESSED CONCRETE

3-13.1 General. The Inspector should be familiar with the general principles of reinforced concrete and the following references in this Manual:

Subsection 3-8 for prestressed piles
3-11 Concrete construction, general
3-12 Concrete structures.

Prestressed concrete is concrete that is held in compressive stress by highly tensioned steel. There are two basic types of prestress: pretensioning and post-tensioning, each offering its own particular advantage and adaptability in construction. In some cases, the methods are combined to advantage in the same member.

In the pretensioning method, the wire or strand is tensioned between end anchorages or buttresses before concrete is placed. The prestress is transferred to the concrete through bonding after the concrete reaches the desired strength. Pretensioning is particularly effective and economical in the casting of standard structural members in large numbers, usually manufactured in permanent production facilities. Several members are fabricated simultaneously in a casting bed that may be up to 500 feet in length. Reels of cable are stored at one end of the bed and as many as 100 strands (called tendons) are sometimes pulled into the bed at one time. Tendons are anchored to a "dead man" at one end and hooked up to a hydraulic jacking assembly at the other end. After each tendon is stressed individually a small amount to equalize tension, the entire assembly (all tendons in the bed) are jacked to the required elongation and tension. Bulkheads are installed in the beds at appropriate locations to divide the bed into the member lengths required. Conventional reinforcement, hardware, lifting lugs and other required embedments are installed and the concrete is placed. Accelerated curing, such as steam, is usually provided to avoid use of the beds for a prolonged period. When concrete reaches the required strength, the prestress is transferred to the members in the bed by cutting the tendons at the end anchorages and between the individual members in the same bed.

Post-tensioning is a prestressing method in which the concrete member is cast before stressing the tendons. Tendons are prevented from bonding to the concrete by suitable wrapping or tubing or they are inserted in prepared ducts after casting. Tendons in ducts are bonded after tensioning by grouting. After the specified strength of concrete has been reached, the tensioning elements are stressed by jacking against the ends of the member and then the tendons are anchored to special fittings. The post-tensioning method is particularly flexible and useful for cast-in-place construction of large or long span members in structures such as freeway bridges and grade separations.

3-13.2 Prestress Definitions.

(1) **Elongation** — The measured length of stretch needed to provide the required tension or load in the tendon.

(2) **Jacking Force** — The initial force as applied to the tendon by the jacks.

(3) **Stress-Strain Curve** — The relationship between the load or tension in the prestress steel and the stress or elongation which the tendon undergoes while it is being stressed.

(4) **Tendon** — Prestressing wire, strand, cable or rod.

(5) **Transfer** — The transfer of prestress force to the concrete. For pretensioned members, transfer takes place at the release of prestress from the end anchorages; for post-tensioned members, it takes place during the tensioning process.

(6) **Working Force or Working Stress** — The force or stress remaining in the prestressing steel after all losses, including losses allowed for in design such as creep and shrinkage of concrete, elastic compression of concrete, creep of steel; losses in post-tensioned steel due to sequence of stressing; losses due to friction and take-up of anchorages and other losses peculiar to the method or system of prestressing.

3-13.3 Materials.
There are two basic materials in a prestressed concrete member: concrete and steel. The high tensile strength, stress relieved, prestressing steel is used in three basic forms:

(1) High tensile strength single wire, applied in the form of assemblies made up of two or more substantially parallel wires. They may be used for either pretensioning or post-tensioning purposes.

(2) Small diameter (¼″ to ½″), high strength strand, factory made, usually made up of seven wires (six wires spiralled around a center wire). Small diameter strand is for both post-tensioning and pretensioning purposes.

(3) High strength alloy steel bars produced by a cold stretching or drawing process and then stress relieved. They are available with smooth or deformed surfaces in diameters ranging from ⅝ to 1⅜ in. Alloy steel bars are used principally for post-tensioned construction.

Detailed data concerning properties should be obtained from the manufacturer and samples should be obtained in accordance with the Sampling Schedule, Plate 28, Appendix. Test results must be known prior to use.

Anchorages for post-tensioning elements come in a variety of types and styles; or wedge anchors for bars; factory end fittings for large cable, button head, plate and conical wedges for multiple wire systems, and wedge anchors for 7-wire strand. Data regarding strength and losses during transfer and seating must be supplied by the manufacturer and verified by tests. At least one anchorage is usually supplied for testing if required by the Agency. A variety of ducts or tubing are used to house post-tensioning elements. However, the Standard Specifications provide only for rigid galvanized sheet metal.

The Inspector should see that prestressing steel is properly stored and handled. Careful protection from the weather is required since this material rusts easily. Rust spots that can be removed by rubbing with the thumb or scraping with a fingernail, even if light streaks or spots remain after rubbing, is acceptable if pitting is not present. No pitting of prestressing steel is acceptable and steel having bends, kinks and nicks must be rejected. Welding should not be permitted on or near the steel. Coiling of strand should be of sufficient radius to prevent kinking. The section of strand which has been in anchorage grips must not be reused in the structure.

Prestressing steel to be bonded in concrete must be free of form oil and lubricants and other impurities which are detrimental to bond. Positive methods should be devised to protect tendons which must necessarily be in position in many instances at the time forms are oiled. Strands to be tensioned in one operation should be from the same manufacturer since its physical properties may vary from one manufacturer to another. Excessive cold working of the strand may also alter the properties.

Concrete mixes for prestressed units are typically high compressive strength mixes. In the plant, manufacturing of pretensioned members, concrete compressive strengths of 5000 psi are regularly used; and for post-tensioned work on-site, 4000 psi strengths and above are used. Water-reducing, air-entraining and retarding admixtures are acceptable admixtures in prestressed concrete when permitted by the job mix specifications. Calcium chloride, or other admixtures containing calcium chloride, should not be permitted in prestressed concrete.

Attention should be given to the mixing equipment and its ability to handle low slump concrete as well as the size of the course aggregate for thin sections with congested and "bundled" tendons and ducts. The Materials Control Group will review concrete mixes and mixing equipment (either in plant or on-site) for prestress concrete prior to construction.

3-13.4 Construction of Prestressed Members. Forms for prestressed members should provide for the free movement of the member horizontally and vertically. Sideforms should be slightly tapered and soffits must be smooth and free of offsets and other irregularities that might restrain the free movement of the member laterally.

Post-tensioned members, constructed on-site, should be within the tolerances specified for concrete structures in Subsection 3-12.1. Pretensioned members should normally be constructed within the limits specified for precast members. Sectional dimensions under 18 inches should be within $\pm$ ⅛ inch and members over 18 inches within $\pm$ ¼ inch. Members should not vary from the specified length more than $\pm$ ½ inch for members under 50 feet and $\pm$ 1 inch for members over 50 feet. These tolerances should be modified to suit the actual use of the members in the structure.

The location and number of tendons must be checked after placement and before tensioning. It is much easier to correct errors before tensioning than after. Vertical and horizontal positioning of prestressing steel or ducts is important. Unless otherwise specified, the cross-sectional location of prestressing steel or post-tensioning ducts in the member should be within $\pm$ ⅛ to $\pm$ ¼ inch, depending on the size of the member. The location of the lateral deflection points ("harping points") of pretensioned strands should be within one inch.

Ducts for post-tensioning should be checked for location and smooth drape at several points; that joints, and ends are taped to prevent entry of mortar; and, that they are securely tied to stirrups or anchored by other means to avoid floating or other change from their correct location during concrete placement. Semi-rigid sheet metal ducts and wrapped tendons should be tied off at not more than 10-foot centers. Flexible type ducts should be tied off more frequently.

If voids or blockouts are to be built into the member, care must be exercised in securing the void forming material (such as waxed cardboard cells or plastic foam) to prevent flotation or other shifting during placement and consolidation of the concrete.

During concrete placement, the Inspector should observe that concrete is properly placed and vibrated. Vibrators are to be properly handled to avoid breaking the ties and joints of post-tensioning duct, and special attention must be given to placement locations where tendons and reinforcing steel are congested as well as the underside spaces between the soffit of the member and the void form.

Compression tests determine the time for transfer of stress. Therefore, care in preparation, handling and curing of test specimens is very important so that no delays occur because of faulty test specimens.

Standard 28-day compression test cylinders should be made for each day's concrete placement in accordance with the sampling schedule (Plate 28, Appendix). Additional cylinders to determine strength for transfer of prestress should be made and cured under the same conditions as the member.

Strengths are usually judged to be satisfactory if the average of any three consecutive strength tests of the laboratory cured specimens, representing the strength of concrete, is equal to or greater than the specified strength; and, if not more than 10 percent of the strength tests have values less than the specified strength with no single cylinder strength below 90 percent of the specified strength. The procedure of curing the structure member should be well-established and carefully controlled. For moist steam curing, concrete should attain its initial set before steam is applied. Otherwise, the elevated temperature may have a detrimental effect on the concrete strength. This delay period may vary from one to six hours and is dependent on many factors. The average delay is about four hours.

The usual rate of increasing concrete temperature is about 60°F per hour. The maximum recommended curing temperature is usually 165°F and its duration is dictated by the cylinder strength required for detensioning. The cooling rate of the curing concrete is not as critical as the heating rate.

3-13.5   Stressing Methods and Procedure.

3-13.5.1   **General.** All methods of prestressing use hydraulic jacks for the stressing operation. The jacks should be equipped with a pressure gauge having an accurate reading dial, accompanied by a calibration chart, approved by the testing agency, showing the relationship between gauge readings and load. The jack and gauge should always be calibrated and used together.

The Inspector should not permit the tensioning of steel in any post-tensioned member or the transfer of load to pre-tensioned members until tests on concrete cylinders, cured with the member, have attained the compressive strength required by the plans.

Both elongation and hydraulic pressure measurements should be used in any prestress operation to determine the amount of stress. One is used to verify the other.

In practice, hydraulic gauge readings are the primary method of measuring force.

The prestressing force determined from hydraulic jack gauge readings may be checked by measurement of the actual elongation of a representative number of tendons in a group or run and computation of the force from such data. The actual elongation is inserted in the formula:

$$P = \frac{AED}{L}$$

where:
P = Jacking force in pounds.
D = Measured elongation (inches).
L = Measured length of tendon between the grips at the jack and end anchorage (feet).
A* = Cross-sectional area of the tendon (sq. in.).
E* = Modulus of elasticity of the tendon (psi).

*Obtained from the manufacturer's data.

If the difference between the computed force as determined from elongation and the actual force as determined from the hydraulic jack gauge readings is more than five percent, the cause should be determined and corrected before the Inspector approves the member.

The Inspector must record all gauge readings and elongation measurements and computed forces for all members (See Plate 11, Appendix, for sample reporting form and procedure.)

3-13.5.2 Pretensioning Details. Single strand or multiple strand tensioning may be used. Each method is applicable to straight or deflected ("harped") strands. In both cases, several members are likely to be pretensioned in one operation and cast in a continuous line.

To minimize losses from temperature variation and creep in the pretensioned strands, concrete should be placed within three days after stressing. If delayed longer a representative number of strands should be rechecked. If the loss is over five percent, all strands should be retensioned.

When multiple strand pretensioning is used, each individual tendon is tensioned to some low specified value and anchored off before multiple strand tensioning begins. This procedure is necessary to insure that all strands will have as nearly as possible, the same final stress (the magnitude of this tension depends on the length of the strand). The strands are then mass jacked in a template to the full load.

To reduce the eccentricity of the prestress force at the ends of pretensioned members, deflected ("harped") strands are frequently required. There are several ways to tension deflected strands:

(a) Tension strands singly in the deflected position the same as for straight strands. In this case, hold-downs for harping must consist of low friction pulleys to permit large movement of strand.

(b) Tension the straight strands and the harped strands in separate operations. With this method, very long beds and a large number of deflection points may require that tendons be stressed symmetrically about both ends to equalize the stress and correct for friction losses at the "hold-down" points. Pulley type hold-downs are usually required to minimize friction.

(c) Tension straight or partially deflected strands with rams. The remainder of the stress is applied by pushing the strands down or pulling them up to final deflected position. This procedure will minimize friction at the points of deflection and can be used with the single or multiple tensioning unit.

The system and equipment for "harping" varies considerably throughout the industry. Any system that will carry the load and minimize friction should be satisfactory. Some systems provide for temporary rollers at the points of deflection during the stressing operations. In general, the location of deflection points in the longitudinal direction is not critical, but should be as shown on the plans ± one inch. The center of gravity of all deflected strands should usually be symmetrical about the midpoint of the member at the ends. A vertical tolerance of three percent is usually satisfactory.

Some plans may specify bond retarder coatings or strand sleeves at the ends of prestressed members. These coatings, like deflected strands, serve to reduce the concrete stresses at the ends of the member due to prestress. Whenever the process is used, the specified strands to be coated should not exceed the specified length shown on the plans with a minus tolerance of 10 percent.

The concrete strength required at time of prestress transfer should be as specified by the Engineer.

The cutting and release of prestressed steel in pretensioned members should be performed in an order that minimizes eccentricity of prestress.

There are two general methods of detensioning: cutting of the tendons in the bed by torch one at a time (used when tendons are tensioned individually) in which case tension cutting should be as symmetrical as possible about the vertical centerline of the member; or, release of the strands by the hydraulic jacks before the actual cutting of strands between members (used in the multiple strand tensioning system).

After release, the prestressing steel is usually cut off flush with the end of the member.

3-13.5.3 Typical Pretensioning Step Procedure.

(1) Pull strands into bed, cut to length, thread into jacking template and install wedge anchors.

(2) Support strands along bed to reduce the effect of strand weight on required load.

(3) Preload each strand an equal amount by jacking individually using a calibrated dynamometer and anchor off in template. The preload will be reduced by an amount due to slippage action of the wedge anchor at the jacking end during seating (commonly referred to as anchor set). No loss occurs at the anchor end since the load is indicated after slippage occurs.

(4) Determine required elongations. These are usually shown on the approved shop drawings but may be calculated as follows:

(a) Determine the required load for one strand (specified initial tension mutiplied by area of strand). Determine multiple strand jacking load (number of strands multiplied by load for one strand).

(b) Determine the elongation required to produce the specified initial tension from load/elongation data (PL/AE).

(c) Determine the elongation for the preload from the load/elongation data.

(d) Deduct (c) from (b) to determine the additional elongation required after preload to produce the full load (not counting anchorage losses).

(e) Add all anchorage losses to the calculated additional elongation in (d). This will include the loss from seating that takes place in the anchorage devices at each end when the additional load (the difference between preload and total load) is applied. (For most anchorage devices the losses due to slippage during seating are usually known as the result of prior testing and should not need to be determined for each member).

(5) Jack all strands in the template to the full multiple strand jacking load. The full load is the load for one strand multiplied by the number of strands in the template. A calibration chart is used to convert load to hydraulic jacking pressure.

As a check, the actual elongation can be measured and compared to the calculated elongation.

For further verification, jacking pressures can be converted to total load by multiplying the hydraulic line pressure by the area of the jack piston. This will not usually check precisely with the calibration chart due to frictional and other losses in typical hydraulic systems. Within 5% is usually considered acceptable.

Variation in procedure is required for harped or deflected strands. Also, in some cases, member design requires variable strand deflections as shown below:

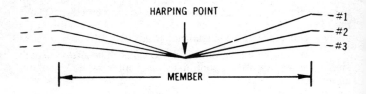

The procedure frequently used provides that the strands in the member be given varying amounts of preload individually, after which all strands in the member are mass jacked and then harped.

Harping causes additional tension which varies due to the variation in the depth of harping. By varying the preload tension all strands will have equal tension after they are harped. In the above case, strands are numbered in order of increasing preload required. If the strands were to be harped prior to stressing the reverse would be true.

3-13.5.4   Post-tensioning. Many post-tensioning systems provide for the tendon housing to be placed without stressing steel. The prestressing steel is then pulled into the housing after concrete is placed and just prior to stressing. This technique minimizes corrosion of the prestressing steel and at the same time facilitates tendon placement and alignment since the weight of the tendon does not need to be supported during the concrete placement.

Some systems to remain unbonded are shop fabricated as a complete unit. The assembled tendon is delivered to the jobsite cut to length. In this case, the prestressing steel is either greased and wrapped or placed in a flexible duct. Grouting of the duct is usually not required, and grease or other approved corrosion protection is essential.

The tendon unit or duct housing is assembled within the forms and tied to reinforcing steel in its specified location. The spacing of ties to maintain the position of the duct or tendon assembly should not exceed 10 feet. If the flexible type duct without tendon is used, this spacing should be reduced. Ties should be sufficient to prevent the duct from floating during concrete placement.

Prior to stressing, concrete strength must be in accordance with the plan requirements. The sequence of stressing should be as specified on the plan or established by the Engineer. The force applied to the post-tensioning tendon should be measured by both elongation of the tendons and hydraulic gauge readings. The gauge reading must be compared to a recent calibration chart to determine the corresponding jacking force. As indicated above, for pretensioned members comparison of actual and predicted elongation as shown on the approved drawings should be made to determine that the jacking equipment is functioning properly and that previously assumed values of friction between tendon and duct are correct.

The loss of prestressing force throughout the tendon length due to tendon-to-duct friction can be readily calculated using the appropriate formula approved for this use.

The apparent modulus of elasticitiy of prestressing steel may vary from coil to coil. This variation should be allowed for when comparing the force determined by gauge pressure and that determined by elongation.

3-13.5.5 Post-Tensioning Stressing Procedure. Some variance from this procedure may be required to suit the particular system or method in use for a given project.

(1) Prior to placing the forms for closing slabs of box girders to be pretensioned, the prestressing steel should be checked to see that it is free in the duct or, if prestressing steel has not yet been placed, that the ducts are unobstructed. Otherwise access to girder stems for required repair work is difficult.

(2) Stressing data should be recorded during the post-tensioning operation as indicated by the typical record sheet (See Plate 10, Appendix).

(3) The Inspector must determine that the total jacking force does not exceed the force shown on the plans and that the specified jacking sequence is observed.

(4) The Inspector must not permit tensioning until tests on concrete cylinders indicate the concrete has attained the design compressive strength.

(5) To compensate for slack, tendons should be stressed to 10% of the required load before marking reference points on each end of the stands for elongation measurements.

(6) Stress tendons to final jacking force and measure total elongation.

(7) Use the calibrated jack gauge pressure or load cell reading to measure force, and compare measured elongation with calculated elongation. If the difference exceeds the allowable (not more than 5%), the Inspector must order that the operation cease until the cause of trouble is eliminated.

(8) Measure final elongation at jacked ends. Measure anchor slippage at unjacked ends. Any slippage exceeding the allowable should be reported to the Design Engineer.

(9) Stressed tendons should be grouted without undue delay.

3-13.6 Grouting Post-Tensioned Members. The main purposes of grouting ducts in post-tensioned members is to protect the prestressing steel from corrosion and to create a bond between stressed tendon and the surrounding concrete.

Grout for post-tensiong ducts is usually a mixture of cement and water. Admixtures to provide good flow, low water content, minimum bleed and non-shrink qualities are usually required. Calcium chloride should not be used in any quantity because of its corrosive qualities. Water content should be the minimum necessary for proper placement (0.45 water/cement ratio by weight or 5 gallons/sack of cement). The U.S. Corps of Engineers flow cone method (CRD-C79) can be used to test consistency. A grout mixture should have a flow time of less than 11 seconds.

For best results, vents should be at high points and drain holes should be provided at the low points of the duct to dispose of flushing water. Duct should be at least ¼″ larger than the strand for tendons made up of a simple strand. For multi-strand tendons, the duct area should be at least twice the net area of the prestressing steel.

The grouting equipment should include continuous mechanical mixing and a positive displacement pump to produce pressures in the range of 150 psi or more. The equipment should also provide for screening the grout to avoid lumps in excess of 0.125 inches. Compressors and pumps should have seals or filters to prevent oil from being introduced into the duct.

Flushing of ducts is not necessary if ducts are known to be unobstructed and clear of foreign substances. If flushing is required, ducts should be purged of all water before grouting begins. All vents, seals and grout openings must be open when grouting starts and then be progressively closed as the grout reaches each vent and the air is purged. Avoid pressures that exceed 200 psi. At higher pressures the cement and water mixture begins to separate which in turn causes blockage.

Grouting Step Procedure.

(1) Verify that ducts are clean.

(2) Flush ducts prior to grouting only if required or when a foreign substance is known to exist in the ducts (such as anticorrosion powder). Purge ducts of all water and impurities prior to grouting.

(3) The initial pumping pressure should be small and should gradually increase due to friction between the grout and the duct (and grout head, if any) until the duct is filled.

(4) Grout injection pipes should be fitted with positive mechanical shut-off valves. Vents and injection pipes should be fitted with grout-tight caps, valves or other positive mechanical shut-off devices.

(5) All vents should be open when grouting starts. Grout should be allowed to flow from the first vent after the inlet pipe until any entrapped air has been removed, at which time the vent should be closed. This sequence should progress in the same manner from vent to vent.

(6) Whenever the flow of grout cannot be maintained and pressure exceeds the allowable, the grout should be immediately flushed out of the duct and the trouble determined.

(7) Grout should be pumped through the duct until no visible slugs of air or water are in evidence. The outlet pipe should then be capped and the pumping pressure maintained until the injection pipe is closed.

(8) Valves and caps should not be removed or opened until the grout has set.

3-13.7 Prestressed Concrete Checkist. (See also Subsections 3-11.16 and 3-12.10.)

Preliminary

(1) Is prestressing steel of the type specified and shipped to the job in sealed containers in a rust-free, uncontaminated condition?

(2) Are approved supplementary prestressing drawings on hand?

(3) Does framework and falsework provide for horizontal and vertical movement of the member during transfer of prestress?

(4) Does the path of the prestressing correspond to that shown on the plans?

(5) Are the ducts or tendons securely tied to prevent movement during placement of concrete?

(6) Are anchorages of the type specified and securely attached to the forms in the proper position?

(7) Is ductwork of the type and size specified and securely taped at all joints to preclude intrusion of mortar during placement of concrete?

(8) Are predicted elongations, anchor sets and prestressing forces for each tendon listed on the approved drawings?

(9) Are hold-downs of the proper type to minimize friction during tensioning?

(10) Is end block and other reinforcing as shown on the plans?

(11) Are all strands in each tendon pulled through the duct as a unit, fed in uniformly to preclude twisting or entanglement during installation?

(12) Are necessary lifting points installed at the location shown on the drawings?

(13) Are grout and vent pipes and drains secured in place as specified?

Prestressing Operation

(14) DO NOT STAND DIRECTLY BEHIND OR IN PATH OF JACKING EQUIPMENT DURING STRESSING — THIS IS EXTREMELY HAZARDOUS IF THE TENDONS SHOULD RUPTURE.

(15) Is concrete strength at time of transfer of prestressing force at least as great as required?

(16) Are hydraulic jacks and pressure gauges recently calibrated by an approved testing agency and are calibration charts available relating gauge pressure to jacking force?

(17) Are sufficient elongation measurements recorded to enable verification of initial and final elongations and anchor set?

(18) Are reference points precisely marked on prestressing steel at each end of tendons to facilitate elongation measurements and detection of slippage of individual strands?

(19) Does predicted elongation agree with measure elongation with ± 5%?

(20) Does predicted anchor set agree with actual anchor set?

(21) Are initial and final jacking forces as indicated on the plans?

(22) Is precast concrete sufficiently cured before cutting of strands or removal from the casting beds?

(23) Are pretensioned strands cut after cure in the prescribed sequence in a manner to minimize impact damage to the member?

(24) Is prestressing steel cut after anchorage in a manner to preclude damage to the steel inside the member?

Grouting Operation

(25) Are ducts free of obstructions and purged of all water, oil and debris and other impurities?

(26) Are ducts tightly capped to prevent leakage of grout at anchorage?

(27) Are valves at all vents and ends of ducts open at beginning of grouting?

(28) Is grouting equipment capable of developing the required pressure?

(29) Is the grout mixture as specified?

(30) Is grout screened before injection into ducts?

(31) Is grout flow continued for a sufficient time before closing each valve to insure ejection of air and water slugs?

(32) Is pressure held constant long enough after all ports are closed to assure that leakage is not occurring?

(33) Are all valves leak-free after removal of grouting equipment?

3-14 PAINTING AND PROTECTIVE COATINGS

3-14.1 General. The Inspector assigned to painting inspection must check the quality of surface preparation; acceptability of materials; the application methods and procedures; coverage or thickness; and the appearance of the painted surface.

The Inspector must familiarize himself with the project special provisions, Standard Specifications and reference documents prior to doing any painting inspection work. It is important to note the surfaces to be painted (and not to be painted), color samples, surface preparation, samples and material brochures that are required or needed prior to allowing the work to proceed. The Inspector should be aware that all painting requirements for a project may not be specified in the painting section of the specifications.

A pre-job conference for the more complex painting jobs, to include the project designer, painting contractor (material supplier when appropriate) and the Inspector can serve to uncover problem areas and settle differences regarding the intent and scope of job requirements. The Inspector should obtain the name of the painting contractors' supervisor in charge of the work at the site who can make decisions and who will be responsible for fulfilling the painting requirements.

The Inspector should see that the pre-job meeting includes a review of all surfaces to be painted. If possible, he should prepare a list of surfaces to be painted prior to the meeting. Once agreed upon, such a list that includes the surface preparation, color, type of paint and number of coats can be used as a ready reference to the Inspector and the contractor during painting operations and will avoid errors and disputes as the work progresses.

3-14.2 Painting Materials. A general discussion of paint materials may be found in Subsection 2-11.

The Inspector should check all paint materials as soon as possible after delivery to the jobsite. Sampling, if required, should be in accordance with the sampling schedule (Plate 28, Appendix). Architectural paint materials are usually accepted by brand name and label identity, delivered to the jobsite in sealed containers, without sampling. Industrial type paint coatings, supplied in large quantities for specific projects, usually require testing before use. When colors are involved, the Inspector should first check the color code number on the unopened can and subsequently verify the actual color by a match-up of the painted surface with a color sample.

3-14.3 Surface Preparation. The Inspector should have a clear understanding with the contractors' supervisor that all surfaces to be painted must be approved prior to the application of the first coat of paint.

In some cases, it is advisable that surface preparation samples be prepared ahead of time and be used for comparison as the work progresses. This is frequently done when sandblasting of metal surfaces is involved. To facilitate inspection, the contractor should, on the first day of sandblasting operations, sandblast metal panels to the degree called for in the specification. These plates should be standard plate stock and should measure a minimum of 8½ inches by 11 inches (200mm x 280mm). After mutually agreeing that a specific panel meets the requirement of the specification, it should then be coated with a clear non-yellowing finish. Panels should be prepared for each type of sandblasting specified and be maintained and utilized by the Inspector thoroughout the duration of sandblasting operations. In any case, the Inspector must see that the method, steps and degree of preparation are no less than the requirements specified for the project.

The Inspector should direct his attention to the contractor's provisions for the protection of surfaces and equipment not to be painted that might be damaged by the surface preparation or painting operations and stop the work if the contractor fails to provide adequate protection.

3-14.4 Application of Paint. The Inspector should review the specifications for any limitations and specific requirements regarding the application methods and equipment. Under certain conditions and locations the specifications may not permit spray application of paint materials and in other cases the type of spray equipment is specified. In any case, the Inspector must see that the equipment is of a suitable type and in proper working condition so as not to be detrimental to the paint material or its application.

Weather conditions may not be satisfactory or conducive to the application of the paint materials. Severely cold weather, rain, fog, mist and wind may require that paint operations be discontinued. It may be necessary to delay the beginning of coating operations until mid-morning or later so that surfaces are dry. The Inspector must see that the following good practices in this regard are observed by the painting contractor.

No coating should be applied when the surrounding air temperature, measured in the shade, is below 40 degrees F. Coatings should not be applied to wet or damp surfaces and should not be applied in rain, snow, fog or mist or when the relative humidity exceeds 60 percent. No coating should be applied when it is expected that the relative humidity will exceed 60 percent or that the air temperature will drop below 40 degrees F. within 18 hours after the application of the coating. Dew or moisture condensation should be anticipated and if such conditions are prevalent, coating should be delayed until mid-morning to be certain that the surfaces are dry. Further, the day's coating should be completed well in advance of the probable time of day when condensation will occur, in order to permit the film a sufficient drying time prior to the formation of moisture. Moisture meter tests of plaster, concrete and masonry surfaces should be made if necessary or required.

In most cases, timing is very important. Sandblasted metal surfaces should usually be covered by the prime coat during the same eight-hour day to avoid the formation of corrosion.

The Inspector should exercise adequate control to determine that paint materials are properly mixed. The need for thinning should be demonstrated before it is permitted. Paint thinned under cold conditions is likely to be too thin for application when the weather warms up.

Inspection during painting should cover "hard to get at" areas to be sure they are covered. Completed work should be checked for paint runs, drops, waves, laps, excessive brush marks and for variations in color, texture and finish. (See Subsection 3-14.5 for a discussion of various types of paint failures.)

When required, the thickness of coatings should be checked with a non-destructive magnetic-type thickness gauge. Coating continuity can be checked with a holiday detection unit. Care should be exercised that the unit used is properly calibrated and operated in accordance with the manufacturer's recommendations. All pinholes should be marked, repaired in accordance with the coating manufacturer's printed recommendations and retested. No pinholes or other irregularities should be permitted in the final coating.

3-14.5 Paint Failures. There is a cause for every paint failure, and in most instances the failure can be prevented by observing specific precautions. The most often observed paint failures are: cracking, flaking, scaling, alligatoring, bleeding, excessive chalking, blistering, fading, spotting, washing and discoloration. The probable causes, preventive measures and corrective measures are discussed in the following subsections:

Alligatoring. When a rupturing of the top paint coat causes the surface to break up into irregular areas separated by wide cracks in "alligator hide" fashion, the condition is called alligatoring. Its cause is due to applying paint to unseasoned wood or from applying a heavy coat of paint over a relatively soft undercoat before it has thoroughly dried. To correct, remove the entire paint film and repaint.

Bleeding. When the color of a previous coat is absorbed into the top coat, this condition is called bleeding. It is caused by the partial solubility of the pigment of the undercoat in the vehicle of the top coat. Asphalt or bituminous undercoats are particularly susceptible to bleeding. In order to prevent or correct bleeding, care must be exercised to select a vehicle for the top coats which is not a solvent for the undercoat pigments.

Blistering. Blistering is evidenced by blister-like irregularities on the film of a painted surface. The most common cause of blistering is the application of paint over a damp or wet surface. Under the action of the sun's rays, the moisture is drawn out of the wood (or vaporized on a metallic surface), raising the paint coating with it in the form of blisters. Blistering can also be caused by using too much dryer in the undercoats. To avoid blistering, do not paint damp or wet surfaces, green lumber or greasy spots. Avoid excessive amounts of dryers in undercoats. To correct, remove the paint film in the blistered area, let the surface dry and repaint.

Blushing. A surface in which blushing has occurred is characterized by a white discoloration in the paint film or a precipitation of an ingredient. It is caused by the condensation of moisture on the paint film or by improper composition of the vehicle or solvent. By applying paint under conditions which do not permit moisture to condense on the applied film, blushing can be avoided. Do not paint cold metal under humid conditions. Blushing can be corrected only by removing the paint film in the affected areas and repainting.

Chalking. Chalking of a painted surface can be detected by gentle rubbing which will disclose loose powder on the paint film. Slow, uniform chalking is a desirable quality in the paint, but excessive chalking is undesirable and indicates a paint film failure. It is caused by excessive rain, fog or high humidity during the application of the paint or during the drying period. Paints low in binder content or high in inert pigments have a tendency toward early and excessive chalking.

To prevent chalking, use a paint which is neither deficient in oil content nor high in inert pigment content and apply only under dry conditions. To correct chalked surfaces, remove all loose chalked substance from the surface with a wire brush and repaint the surface with a paint of good quality.

Checking. Checking of a painted surface can be detected by the appearance in the topcoat of small openings or ruptures which divide the surface into small irregular areas, leaving the undercoat visible through the breaks in the topcoat. It is usually caused by too soft an undercoat or by applying a coat over an underlying coat which has not thoroughly dried. To correct, wire brush or sandpaper to remove the loose film and apply a new coat of paint, making sure that it is as elastic as the previous coat.

Cracking. Cracks are breaks in a paint film which extend through to the surface to which the paint was applied. Where cracking is severe, flaking, scaling or peeling usually follows. It is usually caused by improper compounding of the paint, resulting in a hard and brittle paint film lacking in elasticity. Low-grade paints are often inelastic because they are deficient in oils or contain too much inert material. Cracking will also result from painting a surface upon which too many coats of paint already exist. To avoid cracking, use paint of proper consistency and elasticity, and remove heavy coats of paint from the surface to be painted prior to repainting.

Crawling or Creeping. This defect can be distinguished by the little drops or islands which are formed by the paint film. It often occurs when paint is applied on an oily, waxy or greasy surface or on a very smooth surface such as glass and polished metal. To correct, remove all greasy or oily spots from the surface. On glossy surfaces, wash with a mild soda ash solution or sand with fine sandpaper.

Dulling. Dulling is characterized by a loss in gloss which develops in high-gloss paints and enamels and is caused by improper compounding, use of very old stocks of paints and enamels or through the use of too much turpentine as a thinner. To avoid dulling, use fresh paint stocks of good quality. To correct, sand the dulled coat with fine sandpaper and repaint.

Flaking. Flaking is the dropping off of small pieces of a paint coat which has generally started with checking, developing into cracking, and finally the small cracked sections fall away from the surface. The causes and corrective measures are the same as for cracking.

Mildew. Mildew, a form of plant life, is a fungus frequently found on exposed surfaces in damp, warm locations, particularly on soft paint films. It is caused by soft paint films becoming sticky in the warm location and wind-blown spores and decayed and dried vegetation adhering to the surfaces. The oil in the paint becomes infected, and breeding of the mildew spores takes place in the damp, warm environment. Mildew can be prevented by using a hard-drying paint, applied under dry conditions. Paints which contain zinc oxide are resistant to mildew infections. To correct, remove the paint coat with a blowtorch, wash the area with an abrasive soap and water, or with a water solution of trisodium phosphate, rinsing the surface with clear water and allowing it to dry. The addition of one-half ounce of mercuric chloride per gallon of paint or the use of less oils and more turpentine is advisable where mildew is likely to occur. Exercise extreme caution in handling of paints with mercuric chloride or other fungicides to prevent poisoning of the skin.

Peeling. Peeling of a paint film is evidenced by large scales of the film curling and peeling off the painted surface. It is usually caused by the application of paint in the presence of moisture or from being applied over a faulty priming coat. It can be caused by moisture getting behind the paint film at a corner, or in the case of wood, at knot-holes which are not properly sealed. Painting unseasoned lumber will also cause peeling. To avoid peeling, seal knot holes and end grains of lumber with shellac before painting and insure that the edges and corners of steel shapes are thoroughly covered. To correct, remove all loose, peeled paint by wire brush or blowtorch, clean the surface of dust film, and repaint on a dry surface only.

Runs and Sags. Ripples, runs and sags on a vertical surface are caused by the application of too heavy a coat of paint, or by using a paint which has been thinned excessively. Other contributing causes are the use of stiff, inflexible brushes or incomplete brushing of the film. It can be prevented by applying a uniform coat of paint of the correct consistency, using a flexible brush and properly brushing out the paint. When runs or sags appear on spray-painted surfaces, it is also indicative that too heavy a coat was applied, or that the paint was excessively thinned. To correct, remove the runs or sags with sandpaper and repaint the area.

Scaling. Scaling is an aggrevated form of flaking. It is evidenced by large sections of paint coming loose and falling from the painted surface. Scaling is usually preceded by cracking, and like cracking, is usually caused by the paint drying hard and brittle and being unable to expand or contract as the painted object does with changes in temperature and moisture. Scaling frequently occurs when unseasoned lumber is painted. In some cases, previous coats of paint may have lost their elasticity and become "lifeless." This causes poor adhesion in the old coat and, in drying, the new coat shrinks and pulls the old film loose from the painted surface. To avoid, do not paint unseasoned lumber, or over a paint which dries hard and brittle, or over old lifeless paint films. Remove the paint with commercial paint removers, scrapers or blowtorch. Remove dust from the surface and repaint only when the surface is thoroughly dry, using a paint which dries with an elastic film.

Slow Drying. The drying time of a paint film varies with the inherent characteristics of the pigment or of the vehicle. However, certain faulty conditions may prolong the drying period and cause the condition to be termed a paint fault. Paints, which under normal drying conditions are tacky or sticky for 12 hours or longer after application, are likely to catch dust and dirt, promote mildew formations or fail by checking or alligatoring. It is usually caused by using paints to which a small amount of mineral oil has been added through negligence or error. Such paint may never dry thoroughly. Old linseed oil that has become fatty by exposure or inferior dryers and thinners frequently contribute to slow drying of paint coats. This condition can be avoided by painting when the temperature is above 50°F or by applying thin coats of paint in colder weather. Use less oil and allow ample time for each coat to dry before applying subsequent coats. Once paint is applied and fails to dry, the condition can be corrected by allowing sufficient additional time for drying, or by removing the paint with commercial paint removers or by scraping, and then repainting with the right type of paint under proper conditions.

Spotting. The appearance of discolored spots or craters in a painted surface is called spotting. It is usually caused by too few coats, such as painting on new work using only two coats, or painting old work with one coat. The lack of controlled penetration causes uneven fading in the pigments. Sap in wood may affect the paint and cause spotting. Spotting may be caused by improperly sealed nail heads, or rain or hail on a freshly painted surface. On plastered surfaces, an inferior primer or sealer may cause spotting as the alkali in the plaster burns through. To prevent spotting, apply sufficient coats of paint and avoid painting when rain is imminent. Insure that all old paint, plaster surfaces and nail heads are properly sealed with quality paint films. To correct, apply an additional coat of paint. Paint surfaces spotted from rain or hail must be sanded smooth before repainting.

Washing. Washing of paint is evidenced by streaks in the paint surface, the discoloration generally accumulating at the lower edges of boards, panels, girders, etc. Washing is caused by using paints having pigments which form water-soluble compounds or by painting under damp conditions. This defect often occurs when paints of inferior quality are used. To prevent washing, use only good quality paints. To correct, remove the paint film completely and repaint.

Wrinkling. Wrinkling of a paint coat is evidenced by the paint film gathering in small wrinkles. Wrinkling may be caused by the application of an excessively thick coat, or by failure to brush out the paint properly. It is frequently caused by too much dryer in the paint or by using paints which have been excessively thinned with oil and applied thick. To avoid wrinkling, do not apply thick coats or use excessive amounts of dryer or oil. To correct, remove the wrinkles with sandpaper and repaint with properly thinned paint which does not have excessive amount of dryer or oil in it. If the coat of paint is excessively wrinkled, strip off the old coat and repaint.

3-14.6 Painting Checklist.

(1) Is all paint material tested or approved?

(2) Should surface preparation samples for sandblasting be required?

(3) Are color samples required?

(4) Is the contractor required to submit a list of paint materials for approval?

(5) Are delivered paint materials as specified?

(6) Prior to painting, check each surface with contractor for preparation, type of paint, number of coats and color.

(7) Is pretreatment required?

(8) Is paint properly mixed? Not excessively thinned?

(9) Is coverage satisfactory? Surface appearance and texture? Color?

(10) Is adequate ventilation provided in confined space? Lighting conditions satisfactory?

(11) Are weather conditions satisfactory for painting?

(12) Is dry film thickness to be measured? Tested for holidays?

3-15 ENGINEERING FABRICS

3-15.1 General. Installation of geotextiles, including pavement fabrics, should be by experienced contractors and laid out according to previously approved plans. No deviation from the plans should be allowed without the approval of the Engineer. It is important to handle these fabrics carefully to avoid tearing or puncturing non-permeable fabrics. Insofar as it is possible, the fabric should be rolled into place or pulled from a roller supported on a mobile piece of motorized equipment as it backs across the prepared subgrade.

Fabrics for pond liners should not be installed in standing water, aqueous mud or when rain is falling. Each panel should be adjusted to eliminate large wrinkles and provide for a lap over the previous panel to facilitate seam welding called "seaming." These lap areas must be thoroughly cleaned prior to seaming. After placement, pond liners and drainage channel liners should not have any more foot traffic over them than is necessary to complete the seam welding operations.

3-15.2 Site Preparation. Subgrade for ponds or reservoirs must be shaped to the final configuration on the sides and bottom. If the soil is coarse-tectured or contains rock or cobbles which would cause punctures in the liner, the area must be overexcavated and the material replaced with clean soil and compacted. If native vegetation exists, particularly if it contains reed-like grasses, all vegetation must be stripped and the subgrade sterilized with a soil sterilant. If organic matter is not removed, gases will develop as a result of decomposition, and if not properly vented, could cause the liner to fail over a protracted period of time. It is important to remember that a liner is no more effective than its weakest part.

Pond liners are anchored into trenches dug several feet deep around the perimeter of the pond. These trenches must be at least 12 inches above the final liquid level in the pond, and 18 inches back from the finish waterline. As each panel is placed, the ends of the sheet are inserted in the trench and the panel temporarily held in place by 4x4 lumber or used auto tires. These facilitate the easy adjustment of each panel as it is positioned in the system.

After initial placement, each panel is pulled taut to align it with the previous panel and to remove the larger wrinkles. Care should be exercised to avoid pulling the panels too taut so as to allow sufficient slack to accommodate shrinkage. On the other hand, if large wrinkles exist that may later collapse into folds with sharp bends in the liner material, this can result in cracking and failure of the liner. When the liner panels are all in place and seamed, the 4x4s or auto tires are removed and the anchor trench is backfilled and compacted, being careful not to damage the liner ends in the trench.

Subgrade for movement fabric is similar to pond subgrade, being free of organic matter, rocks and stones that could result in punctures. It must be shaped to the proper crown section and compacted to the required densities. Fabrics laid on native subgrade do not require a tack coat unless specified by the Engineer.

3-15.3 Pavement Preparation. The surface of the distressed pavement intended to be covered by a pavement fabric followed by an asphalt overlay, must be clean and dry. Potholes and deep spalls should be repaired or a leveling course placed prior to tack coating. Cracks wider than ¼ inch should be filled with asphalt joint filler or broomed full of dry sand before the tack coat is applied.

A tack coat consisting of AR 4000 paving asphalt is applied uniformly in a width that is at least two inches, but not more than six inches wider than the fabric width. The temperature of the tack coat must not exceed 325°F and the ambient temperature must be above 50°F when the fabric is placed.

3-15.4 Placing Pavement Fabric for Asphalt Overlay.
It is a general practice to avoid placing fabric in areas where
the asphalt overlay will be less than 1½ inches because the
overlay will have insufficient structural strength and will tend
to fracture and spall.

Fabric should be placed in increments that can be handled
by the contractor's forces without crowding the several operations. The fabric is unrolled, stretched and aligned to lap the
adjacent edges from two to four inches. The fabric shall be
seated with brooms or pneumatic rollers after placing. No more
fabric shall be placed than can be covered by the asphalt overlay the same day; and the fabric shall not be placed more than
600 feet in advance of paving operations.

Care must be exercised to avoid tracking the tack coat onto
the fabric or distorting the fabric during seating of the fabric
when utilizing roller equipment. Turning of the paving machine
or other vehicles must be gradual and kept to a minimum to
avoid fabric damage. To prevent the fabric from being picked
up by construction equipment, a small layer of asphalt may be
spread over the fabric immediately in advance of placing the
asphalt overlay.

Public traffic must not be allowed on the bare fabric unless
it is under strict traffic control. The Engineer may require the
contractor to place a thin layer of asphalt concrete over the
fabric to protect it from traffic damage.

3-15.5 Placing Fabric on Unstable Subgrade. After
the area is cleared of vegetation, sharp objects, stumps and
debris, the subgrade surface should be shaped as much as possible to provide cross slope and surface drainage. The pavement
fabric is unrolled directly on the subgrade, pulled taut and
aligned. Laps will vary from 1½ to 3 feet, depending upon the
required load bearing capacity. If necessary, the laps may need
to be sewed to prevent expressive lateral shifting during subsequent operations.

Aggregate fill is then placed and compacted, the depth of
which is determined in advance by the Engineer to carry the
anticipated wheel loading (usually between 9 and 24 inches).
The aggregate is dumped on the fabric as the trucks back onto
it to distribute the wheel load of the trucks. The aggregate is
then spread and compacted. The aggregate must be spread in
the same direction as the fabric overlays to avoid separating
the fabric at the laps.

3-15.6 **Field Joints.** Joints at laps of fabric panels for ponds or reservoirs are seamed by one of two methods: heat seaming or solvent adhesive seaming. Heat seaming utilizes a hot air gun to fuse the lapped fabric together at the edge of the top sheet. For greater strength, a 2-inch cap strip is often required to be placed over this joint and both edges of the cap strip heat seamed to the fabric.

Lining materials which cannot be bonded by heat are often bonded by use of a bodied solvent adhesive or contact cements. In either case, the contact surfaces must be cleaned with a solvent wash prior to the application of the adhesive.

All holes, tears or cuts discovered in a liner after installation shall be patched with a piece of the same fabric with rounded corners that is three inches greater in all dimensions than the hole. The contact surfaces of the patch and the liner are then solvent cleaned, and the patch heat welded to the liner. Any lining that is scuffed, or in distress for any reason, should be replaced or covered and seamed with an additional layer of fabric.

3-15.7 **Testing.** All field joints should be randomly tested in tension to be at least equal to the original fabric in tensile strength. This can be accomplished by utilizing a hydraulic seam test tool that grips the fabric on each side of the seam and puts the welded seam in tension to the specified fabric strength. Seams are sometimes tested by directing an air jet of 50 psi at the leading edge of the seam. Any separation is a failure.

3-15.8 **Inspector's Checklist.**

(a) Preliminary.

(1) Is the fabric of the specified type and thickness?

(2) Is each lot clearly identified and accompanied with a test certificate from an approved testing laboratory?

(3) Is the fabric in good condition, free of shipping and handling damage, and is it wrapped in a protective envelope?

(4) Has the fabric been properly stored in a clean, dry place or if outdoors, stored at least one foot above the ground? Is it protected from exposure to ultraviolet (sunlight)?

(5) Have opened rolls been re-covered while in storage?

(6) Are fabric rolls being handled properly in transporting or while being installed in the field?

(b) Subgrade Preparation.

(1) Has the subgrade been shaped to the proper section? Is it free of rocks or other sharp objects that could puncture the fabric?

(2) Has all vegetation been removed from the area and the subgrade sterilized?

(3) Is there standing water or mud in any area where fabric is to be placed?

(4) Are anchor trenches properly located and of the proper depth?

(c) Fabric Installation.

(1) Has the fabric been stretched taut to eliminate major wrinkles, but not to the extent that there is no provision for shrinkage?

(2) Are the panels properly aligned with the specified lap at adjacent edges?

(3) Have the seams been heat welded and do they meet the specified tensile strength tests?

(4) Are all tears, punctures or scuffed areas properly repaired?

(5) Has aggregate fill over fabric been properly placed, spread and compacted?

(d) Preparation of Existing Pavement.

(1) Is the pavement surface clean and dry?

(2) Have potholes, spalls and major cracks in the old pavement been repaired?

(3) Is the proper tack coat material (AR 4000) being used?

(4) Is the hand application of the tack coat being kept to a minimum?

(5) Check that the tack coat is applied at least two inches but not more than six inches wider than the fabric.

(6) Does the tack coat temperature exceed 325°F? Is the ambient temperature below 50°F?

(e) Placing Pavement Fabric.

(1) Has the fabric been placed and broomed (or rolled) into place in the tack coat?

(2) Is the contractor crowding the work or extending the fabric placement more than 600 feet in advance of the paving operations?

(3) Is public traffic detoured around the fabric laying operation or otherwise under strict traffic control?

PART 4
PREVIEW, FINAL INSPECTION & ACCEPTANCE

4-1 GENERAL. The function of the Final Inspection Group is to make a final comprehensive check on all aspects of the completed work done under permit, assessment act improvement, cash contract and work order projects, as well as to preview the conditions existing prior to the start of the construction work on all Assessment Act, cash contract and other types of projects. Other types of projects may be previewed when it is considered advisable. In addition, this group makes an underground final inspection of sewer and storm drain installations prior to paving the surface over them, and performs certain other operational tests for street lighting and traffic signal installations, automatic sprinkler systems for landscaping, flumes, weir manholes, pumping plants, infiltration in sewage systems, etc.

The Final Inspection Group has other important functions to perform, including the completion of numerous administrative details which may not be completed at the time the job is released to the Group from the District, as well as the resolution of unsettled complaints from the general public. The Final Inspectors review job plans, specifications, office file and job envelope records, and all the signed copies of change orders. They obtain test reports from the Testing Agency for concrete, asphalt and other materials used in the work, and check for notices of non-compliance, sewer house connection waivers, waivers to dump waste materials on private property, certificates of performance, receipts for salvaged materials, etc., in the job envelope.

Final inspection frequently involves notification to and coordination with other governmental agencies interested in the completion of new projects. Joint final inspection is often made with engineers or representatives from such agencies as the State Department of Transportation, County Dept. of Public Works (Flood Control, Road Dept. or County Engineer's office), utility companies, the Board of Education, the Redevelopment Agency and neighboring cities.

Preview Inspectors and Final Inspectors having their headquarters in the Main Office, will notify the Chief Dispatcher by memo listing all projects scheduled for preview or for final inspection on the following day.

Preview and Final Inspectors having their headquarters in branch offices will similarly notify the appropriate dispatcher in the District Office, who in turn will transmit this information to the Chief Dispatcher in the Main Office.

4-2 PREVIEWS

4-2.1 General. Before the start of construction activities, the Final Inspection Group is responsible for previewing the construction area for all assessment act improvement and cash contract projects, including portions of dedicated streets which will be affected by permit projects and which may be damaged by the construction operations. The preview is a visual survey and photographic record of all existing damage (such as cracks in sidewalks and driveways, off-grade curbs, dead or barren lawn areas, broken window glass, cracks and chips in buildings and walls, fences in need of repair, etc.) as well as a log of those improvements which are in undamaged condition but which are likely to be affected by the contractor's activities.

In addition to the preview photographs, video tapes can be made to show details and over-all views before and after construction for all contract and assessment projects involving surface improvements.

4-2.2 Notification of Impending Work. The Final Inspection Group becomes aware of all new contract projects from several documents received each week form the Board of Public Works. The principal sources are "Bids to be Received" and "Contracts Awarded by the Board of Public Works," in which assessment act and cash contract projects are listed. In addition, this Group receives each day a copy of a form entitled "Assignment Report — Survey Division" which lists titles of jobs for which survey parties have been requested or are currently assigned. District Supervisors are charged with the responsibility of requesting a preview covering those portions of dedicated streets which will be affected by permit construction if the circumstances indicate a preview is desirable.

4-2.3 Notification of Completed Work. From the daily assignment sheet, the Final Inspector assigned preview responsibility can determine what projects are nearing completion and which jobs are scheduled for final inspection. He will be advised when "Project Completion Notices" have been issued. From this information he can then schedule the taking of "after" pictures.

4-2.4   Field Procedures for Previews. The Final Inspector assigned to making previews utilizes a television camera and recorder with audio to provide the audio-visual record of job conditions before construction.

The preview necessitates walking the entire job and taking pictures to properly reflect the conditions encountered.

The recorded tapes are listed on the form "Television Preview Sheet" in duplicate. They are coded to match the coded entries which appear on the form. One copy of the form is filed in the job folder and one in the job envelope.

Photographs before and after construction are to be taken on all cash contract and assessment act projects involving surface improvements. The "before" pictures are usually taken the same day the preview is made. "After" pictures are taken subsequent to project completion. On major streets, the "after" pictures are taken following the completion of traffic lane striping by the Traffic Department. In order that a comparison will be evident, it is important that the "before" and "after" pictures be taken from the same location.

4-2.5   Processing and Disposition of Photographs. The Inspector assigned to preview functions arranges for photo processing in his area. He orders and maintains a stock of film and orders development of exposed rolls of film. All negatives of photographs are filed in the Main Office files.

The Inspector making a preview will order three prints of each view of "before" and "after" pictures, assemble them for each project in three sets, provide information as to job title, photo location and compass direction, and turn them over to the Clerical Section for mounting and titling.

4-3   FINAL INSPECTION

4-3.1   General. When a project has been physically completed, the District Supervisor will sign and date the Project Record Card. He will then forward the job records to the Final Inspection Group, advising the latter by "Notice to Final Inspector" of any **minor** deficiencies in the construction that may remain to be corrected.

The Final Inspection Group will sometimes receive a request for final inspection before the job records have been signed and forwarded as outlined above. In such cases, it is the duty of the Final Inspection Group to obtain a verbal clearance

or release from the respective District Supervisor before
proceeding with the final inspection. Under these circumstances the correction list developed by the Final Inspector will
be noted: "Subject to review of job records." The correction list
is thereby held open for additional items if the job card entries
or a "Notice to Final Inspection" indicates additional corrective
work is needed.

   4-3.2 Scheduling Final Inspection. For assessment act
or cash contract projects, if the contractor does not promptly
request a final inspection, the District Supervisor will initiate
action with the contractor and Final Inspector to start final
inspection.

   For permit projects, the District Supervisor will initiate
action to insure that the permittee or his contractor requests
final inspection. In case of delay, he will initiate the necessary
correspondence to the permittee, suggesting that a final inspection be arranged at once.

   If no response is forthcoming, and if the completed project
is small, the District Supervisor will request the Supervisor of
Final Inspection to make a final inspection without the contractor or his representative being present. If approved, the Final
Inspector and Engineer will make the final inspection and
the correction list will then be mailed to the contractor or
permittee.

   If no response is forthcoming following final inspection, the
the Supervisor of Final Inspection will communicatate with the
permittee, private engineer or bonding company and request
that corrections be expedited.

   As soon as a final inspection has been scheduled, the Final
Inspector will make a preliminary review of the job plans and
the project records to familiarize himself with the nature and
extent of the work. Particular attention shall be given to all
special notes usually on sheet number 1 of the plans.

   4-3.3 Partial Final Inspection. On some projects, it
may be desirable or necessary to conduct partial final inspections of completed portions of the work. For example, it is
desirable to perform a final inspection of a sewer or storm drain
prior to construction of the permanent paving to avoid unnecessary removals and patchwork when corrective work requires re-excavation.

   In some cases, it may be necessary to place portions of a
project in service as they are completed. For example, placing

increments of a large sewer project in service as they are complete could relieve a critical local sewage disposal problem. On large street lighting projects, the contractor is encouraged to complete the project in increments so that circuits can be energized progressively.

A "partial final" is handled in the same manner as outlined herein for underground finals and full surface finals, including release by the District Supervisor, notification to interested bureaus, departments and agencies, preparation of a Final Inspection Correction List. The latter contains a space for indicating "partial final" under the heading "Type of Final Inspection."

When the Agency accepts all or a portion of a project as being physically completed prior to formal acceptance, a "Statement of Completion (or partial completion)" is issued to the contractor or permittee. The contractor or permittee is then relieved of responsibility for the maintenance of the portion covered by the statement.

Refer to Subsection 4-4.3 for information on the preparation of the form entitled "Statement of Partial Completion."

4-3.4 Notifying Other Bureaus and Agencies. A preliminary review of the job plans may indicate to the Final Inspector certain other governmental agencies may be interested in a particular job nearing completion. At least 24 hours before the appointed time for final inspection, the Final Inspector will notify all parties concerned that a final inspection has been scheduled which may be of interest to one or more of the following:

(a) All Design Engineers whose names are shown near the left-hand margin of the job plans, including those who gauge weir manholes and pipe flumes.

(b) Special Project Engineers for large outfall sewers.

(c) Special Project Engineers for sewers remodeled due to freeway construction.

(d) Structural Engineers for bridges, retaining walls, any span of 10 feet or more, sidewalk vaults, automatic sprinkler system, etc.

(e) The Street Tree Division, Bureau of Street Maintenance, for tree planting.

(f) The State Division of Highways.

(g) The County Department of Public Works (Flood Control, Engineer or Road Element).

(h) Other adjacent incorporated cities.

(i) Department of Building and Safety:

(1) For plumbing installations (Example: Sewer pumping plant).

(2) For electrical installations (Example: Sewer pumping plant).

(j) The Board of Education, if a school is involved.

(k) The Traffic Department, for traffic control devices, traffic lane striping, or the removal of temporary detour striping.

(l) The Bureau of Street Maintenance or Bureau of Street Lighting, if additional work is to be done beyond the responsibility of the permittee or contractor.

(m) Railway Company, if trackage, grade crossings, grade separation, railroad rights-of-way, etc., are involved.

(n) Rapid Transit Districts, if bus stops or routes are affected.

(o) Federal — Navy, Coast Guard, U. S. Army Engineers, Bureau of Reclamation.

(p) Private design engineers, when involved in the design of City contract projects.

(q) Manufacturers of products, such as switchboards, pumps, sprinkler system timers, etc.

One or more of the above may wish to participate either in a joint final inspection or to make an independent final inspection of the project. They may also desire advance notice of rechecks or subsequent final inspections after corrections have been made, or may wish to be advised when the project is ready to "sign off" and is recommended for acceptance.

4-3.5 Reporting Status of Jobs in Final Inspection. Every workday morning each Preview Inspector and Final Inspector of the Final Inspection Group will contact the Project Coordinator and report the status of each daily final inspection assignment.

On Tuesdays of each week, each Final Inspector of the Final Inspection Group will contact the Project Administrative Control Section and report the status of every assessment act or cash contract project then in process of final inspection.

A Weekly Recapitulation of Working Days is required on cash contract and assessment act projects when the time of completion of the contract is awarded on a workday basis. (See Plate 7, Appendix.)

On each project which includes a liquidated damages clause, the Final Inspector will ascertain the number of days remaining in the contract time, or the number of days the contract time is in arrears, and the amount of liquidated damages to be assessed, as provided in the contract. Both the number of days and the amount of liquidated damages per day will be entered upon **each** correction list made out for the project in question, with the exception of partial or underground final inspections.

When a project in the process of Final Inspection is in arrears more then 10 days, a Special Status Report to Agency Department Management must be initiated by the Supervisior, Final Inspection Group.

4-3.6 Final Clearances. If the project provides for the construction of a street lighting or traffic signal system, an investigation must be made as to whether this activity has been completed. This information is then noted in the appropriate spaces on the Final Inspection Correction List. If the job plans call for any items or materials to be turned in as salvage to an Agency yard, a receipt for these items should be in the job envelope. If no receipt is found, one shall be called for on the Correction List.

4-3.7 Core Test Results. After completion of paving operations and preceding final inspection, requests to the Testing Agency for asphalt and concrete cores should have been initiated by the District Supervisor in accordance with the following:

(a) Asphalt Concrete Pavement.

(1) All assessment act projects.

(2) Projects where approximately 400 tons or more of pavement are placed.

(3) Any paved area where doubt exists as to the pavement thickness or its specific gravity.

(b) Portland Cement Concrete Pavement.

(1) Where approximately 3,000 or more square feet of pavement has been constructed.

(2) Whenever it is necessary to resolve any doubt as to the thickness or the compressive strength of the concrete.

Cores need not be cut from pavement sections where the improvement consists of a pavement overlay or where the tonnage involved is so small (50 tons or less) that the expense of core testing would be unwarranted.

Core test results are often not available until the project has been released to the Final Inspection Group by the District Supervisor. Regardless of when the results are known, the tolerances specified and the procedure for resolution of failures are to conform to the policies established and published in the Administrative Orders issued to Supervisory personnel.

If pavement coring has not been done within 14 days after the request is made (due to a heavy workload in the Testing Agency), the core request will be cancelled (except on assessment act projects) and the job shall be processed and recommended for acceptance, if all other items have been completed.

4-3.8   The Final Inspection Correction List.

4-3.8.1   General. (See Plate 63, Appendix.) After reviewing the entire project, the Final Inspector will combine and condense his notes and transfer to the Final Inspection Correction List, making an original and sufficient copies of supply the need of all interested persons. It is necessary to list all corrective work to be done at this time. New items of correction are not to be added later at the time of recheck, unless they are of a serious nature or are due to unusual circumstances. Correction lists are valid only for 30 days, after which the project is subject to another final inspection and new items may be listed.

Upon completion of the list, the Final Inspector will review it with the contractor or his representative to make sure that all of the items are clear and understandable. The terms "repair" or "correct" are customarily used, with the method of repair being the responsibility of the contractor. However, the contractor should be cautioned not to resort to methods of repair which would be unacceptable. For example, the contractor should be advised that no asphalt skin patches are permissible and that any overlay repair must be made with one-inch minimum thickness. Items which must be repaired under inspection shall be so marked.

4-3.8.2   Distribution of the Final Inspection Correction List. The Final Inspector will send the original to the Project Coordinator, the first copy to the contractor and the second copy will be filed in the job envelope. Additional copies will be sent to the Engineer, the Permittee on "B" Permits, and the construction Division Chief. The Project Coordinator, after entering the receipt of the original correction list on his file card, will transmit this list to the Supervisor of Final Inspection who will review the list and distribute copies to the District Supervisor through the appropriate Division Chief. It is intended that pertinent items on the Correction List be reviewed with the appropriate job inspector previously assigned to the project.

4-3.8.3 Completion of Corrections.

(a) Major Corrections: If other than minor corrections are found necessary, the Final Inspector and the Supervisor of Final Inspection will so inform the appropriate Chief Inspector and the District Supervisor. Major corrections usually require that the job be returned to the District Supervisor for resolution, with corrections to be made under full-time inspection.

(b) Delinquent corrections on assessment act and cash contract projects: If corrections are not made within 10 days, the Final Inspector will report the uncorrected items to the Supervisor of Final Inspection. The latter will initiate a letter directing the contractor's attention to the remaining items to be corrected and to the date on which liquidated damages become effective. Every effort shall be made to expedite completion of the work so that the liquidated damages clause under the contract will not be invoked.

(c) Delinquent correction on permit projects: If corrections are not made within 10 days, the same procedure as outlined above will be followed, except that the orginal letter is sent to the permittee and a carbon copy to the Main Office files.

When all items on the correction list have been completed, the contractor will call in again and ask for a recheck. The Final Inspector will again notify the Design Engineer in case he may wish to see the corrected work. Once again the Inspector will meet the contractor or his representative and verify the completion of all of the correction items. Very minor items may not require the presence of the contractor or his representative.

When all corrections are completed the Final Inspector will "sign off" the project; make the appropriate entries on the Job Record Card and forward the project records to the Supervisor, Final Inspection group. Any unresolved complaints should be noted. Refer to Subsection 4-4.2 for additional policy, regarding recommendations for acceptance.

   4-3.9   **Final Inspection of Surface Improvements.**   The Final Inspector arranges to meet the contractor or his representative at the jobsite at a specific time and date. They may be joined by the Design Engineer, the permittee or others who have been previously notified that the final inspection will take place.

   The project area must be cleaned by the contractor, either by brooming or flushing with water, so that no surface areas are obscured from view and gutter drainage can be checked.

   Final inspection of a full-width street requires walking down one side and back on the other. As he walks, the Final Inspector must review the entire area for compliance with the plans, specifications and change orders. He must reread all special notes which usually appear on Sheet Number 1 of most job plans and note any discrepancies in the work such as: omissions, incorrect dimensions, broken sidewalks, chipped curbs, header boards to be removed, etc. Parkway and sidewalk widths must be measured as well as street crown and T-sections. The Inspector must compare the quality of texture and finish of the concrete and asphalt surfaces with established standards and check that guard rails and guide posts are installed where required. Any necessary repairs must be listed, and any work the Inspector considers to be not in strict conformance with the plans and specifications, such as incorrect construction, wrong location, poor appearance or improper functioning, shall be noted as not acceptable.

   The Final Inspector must be see that every sewer and storm drain manhole on the project is opened to check that no dirt, debris or paving materials have collected in them and to insure that the rings have not been knocked loose during the paving operations. He must also check for the proper replacement of the top step in manholes that have been adjusted to pavement grade. The contractor is required to introduce sufficient water to bituminous flow lines, flat concrete spandral and gutter areas, and any other flow line areas that the Final Inspector may deem necessary to check for proper flow and the absence of water pockets.

   When the job is found to be acceptable, the Final Inspector will make appropriate entries on the back side of the Project

Record Card. The dates shown by the Final Inspector for job completion shall indicate, as nearly as can be determined, the date on which the work was completed, including corrections, if any. Examples follow.

Example "A": A project completed with no corrections needed.

12-15-86. Job complete and recommended for acceptance 12-15-86. J. K. Doe

(In the example above, both dates are identical. Also, when the final inspection is initiated by the Agency without a final request from the contractor, both dates are identical, with the date of such inspection being considered as the completion date.)

Example "B": A project completed with no corrections needed.

12-15-86. Final. Job complete and recommended for acceptance on 12-12-86. J. K. Doe

(As in the example above, in the absence of evidence as to the actual completion date, the job shall be recorded as complete on the day the contractor requested final inspection.)

Example "C": A project completed after corrections.

12-10-86. Final. Correction list issued. J. K. Doe

12-15-86. Recheck. Job complete and recommended for acceptance on 12-16-86. J. K. Doe

(In the example above, the job has been found acceptable after recheck and has been recorded as complete on the day the request for recheck was made).

Note: Portions of some of above-described entries are pre-printed on the back side of the Project Record Card.

If a project includes street lights or traffic signals, the entries shown in the examples above are not to be made until these systems have been tested and found acceptable by the Final Inspector assigned to that type of work. (See Subsection 4-3.12 and 4-3.13.)

The final inspection report on the back side of the Project Record Card shall also contain the following entries:

(a) A complete list, by plan number, of all the plans used in conducting the final inspection. (Revised plans and revision date shall be noted, followed by the Final Inspector's name or initials).

(b) The current Standard Specifications shall be shown and Special Provisions (if any) shall be noted.

(c) Design Engineers notified of inspection shall be listed by name, together with the date they were notified and date the project was acceptable to the Engineer.

(d) If house connection laterals only are laid from a previously existing main line sewer as part of subdivision permit construction, the house connection permit numbers shall be listed.

(e) If one or more Class A permits are issued and the work is done in conjunction with subdivision permit construction, the Class A permit numbers shall be listed.

4-3.10 Landscape and Street Tree Planting Final Inspection. On projects involving the planting of landscape or trees, a final inspection is made to determine the acceptability of planting prior to the beginning of the establishment period.

The Agency Landscape Designer or maintenance representative attends the final inspection on street tree planting and landscape projects. These representatives also approve and tag plants and tree stock at the nursery for use on these projects.

On street tree projects, the Final Inspector checks the size and growing condition of the tree and the location and installation arrangement. Tree well covers are checked for the correct type and size and that they are installed flush with surrounding walk and so as not present any hazard to pedestrians. The number of trees planted must agree with the bid item quantity reported on the final payment estimate.

Similarly, on landscape projects the Final Inspector checks the size, spacing, location and growing condition of trees, plants, ground cover and grass areas; grading, ground contour and special mulches; irrigation system for number of heads and coverage, valves and the functioning of automatic equipment.

On permit projects, the permittee has the option of depositing the cost of the tree planting with the Agency, in which case the Street Tree Division will furnish and plant the required trees. The Final Inspector must determine that the deposit is for the required number of trees.

The starting date of the maintenance or establishment period is included on the Final Inspection Correction List. Subsequently, the Final Inspector checks the job as necessary during the maintenance period to determine that the contractor is watering, weeding, mowing and cultivating as required and that the growing condition is satisfactory. The Final Inspector may suspend the "plant establishment" or "maintenance" period at any time that the contractor fails to perform the required maintenance. At the end of a satisfactory maintenance period, he signs the job off with a notation to that effect and forwards the job to the Final Inspection Group Supervisor.

4-3.11   Final Inspection of Underground Installations.

4-3.11.1   General.   Final inspection is not always deferred until the project is completed. Sewer and storm drain installations are usually given a final inspection prior to any paving operations on the surface over them. This inspection is commonly referred to as an "underground final."

An "underground final" is necessary unless waived by the District Supervisor, as it is more economical and easier to do corrective work prior to construction of permanent paving of streets or permanent resurfacing of trenches. Temporary premix, where required, must be in place (unless waived by the District Supervisor) and improved areas cleaned before an underground final can be scheduled. Power sweeping may be required to achieve the degree of cleanup necessary.

4-3.11.2   Scheduling Underground Final.   Upon completion of the underground portion of the work, the District Supervisor should suggest that the contractor arrange for an underground final inspection.

Requests from contractors for underground final inspection are received and scheduled for a subsequent workday by the Final Inspectors. An estimate of the amount of time required to perform the final inspection should be made by the Final Inspector at the time the request is received, so that effective use can be made of the Inspector's time for the remainder of the day.

4-3.11.3   Release by District Supervisor.   Upon receipt of a request for an underground final, the Final Inspector will obtain verbal clearance from the District Supervisor. The District Supervisor will advise the Final Inspector that the required air test has been satisfactorily performed and that all sewers laid on a curve with pipe 18 inches or less in diameter have been "balled" (flushing an inflated rubber ball matching the inside pipe diameter through the sewer). The Final Inspector may ask for the job record cards or sewer record sheets covering the underground construction if the District Supervisor does not have full knowledge of these activities.

4-3.11.4   Functions Preceding Underground Finals. Before leaving for the jobsite, the Final Inspector will thoroughly review the job plans, Special Provisions and change orders affecting the construction. Notification to other bureaus, departments or agencies (as outlined in Subsection 4-3.4) may be required, depending upon the nature, extent and location of the work.

4-3.11.5   Field Procedures for Underground Finals. Manholes must be opened progressively throughout the job and a thorough examination made of the grade and alignment of the pipe, with the aid of a strong light; or mirrors to reflect a sunbeam through the pipe line. The pipe lines must have been flushed with water and be free of dirt and debris. Inlet and outlet pipes to structures are examined for evidence of cracks or settlement. Any portion of the pipe line which holds water and does not drain is subject to rejection. The Final Inspector may call for additional water to be introduced in the line, or he may require the line to be "balled" if conditions warrant. Manholes and structures are checked for dimensions, proper channel construction, taper, step embedment and spacing and for conformity to the appropriate Standard Plan or special detail on the plans.

If the sewer or storm drain pipe is 24 inches in diameter or larger, the Final Inspector will pass through the line, using a special four-wheel cart, examining the joints as he proceeds, looking for cracked pipe, evidence of settlement, damage to liner plate, etc.

Sewers 21 inches and smaller are required to be air tested. The Final Inspector should review job records for test reports or inspection log entries as evidence that a test has been performed for each reach of pipeline on the project and that acceptable results were obtained (See Subsection 3-5.11).

4-3.11.6   The Final Inspection Correction List. After inspecting the underground portions of the project, the Final Inspector will combine and condense his notes and transfer them to a Final Inspection Correction List, making an original and four carbon copies. (See Plate 68, Appendix). This form contains a space for indicating the type of final performed, "sewer underground only" or "storm drain underground only," in the case of an underground final.

It may be necessary to describe in writing any exclusions or items which will be subject to recheck at the time a full final inspection is given at a later date, so that there will be no misunderstanding. Typical exclusions are as follows:

(a) Reset manhole ring and cover sets to finished pavement elevations after permanent street paving or trench resurfacing.

(b) Remove by-pass in manhole at Station $7+00$, Line No. 3.

(c) Install inner cover and caulk.

Upon completion of the final correction list the Final Inspector will review it with the contractor or his representative to make sure that all items are clear and understandable.

4-3.11.7   Waivers for Connections Prior to Acceptance. If the permittee of a subdivision permit wishes to install house connection sewers immediately following an underground final inspection and prior to final acceptance of all work provided for under his permit, he must execute a waiver. A supply of the form entitled "House Connection Waiver" will be carried by each Final Inspector. The waiver, signed by the permittee, is to be transmitted to the Main Office by the Final Inspector or mailed by the permittee, so that the sewer records can be released to the Engineer and house connection permits issued.

Where sewer connections are urgently needed, the contractor may be requested to sign a waiver allowing the Agency to issue house connection permits without waiting for the contractor to complete permanent resurfacing and clean-up. The Final Inspector will obtain the contractor's signature when the underground final is complete, unless the contractor declines to sign, in which case no connections are authorized until such time as his signature is obtained or the project is accepted in its entirety.

4-3.11.8   Plugging of Sewers. The Final Inspector will examine the plans for notes to plug the lower ends of the sewers. If the tract or right-of-way is not recorded, or if the sewer system has no outlet, the lower end of the sewer system is to be plugged after all the work is completed and acceptable to the Final Inspection Group. A manufactured stopper or bricks laid in the end of the pipe and sealed with mortar are used for this purpose. The Final Inspector shall inform the Sewer Records Section regarding the plug. (See Subsection 4-3.11.10.)

4-3.11.9   Entry on Project Record Card for Underground Final. When the underground portion of a sewer or storm drain system is found acceptable, the Final Inspector will notify the Project Coordinator and make the appropriate entries on the back side of the Project Record Card as follows:

> 10-10-86. Sewer underground O.K. for H.C's
>
> > J. K. Doe
>
> 11-17-86. Storm drain underground O.K.
>
> > J. K. Doe

4-3.11.10   Entry on Sewer Construction Job Record Card. After an underground final inspection has been completed on the sewer portion of any project, the Final Inspector shall inform the Sewer Records Section so that an appropriate entry can be made on the Sewer Construction Job Record Card. If the lower end of the sewer is plugged as described in Subsection 4-3.11.8, the location of the plug by station and line number shall also be furnished to the Sewer Records Section. After a full final inspection, including completion of street paving, trench resurfacing, and resetting of manholes to finished pavement elevations, the Sewer Records Section will be furnished with the completion date and the name of the Final Inspector.

4-3.12   Street Lighting Final Inspection.

(Editor's Note: The procedures for final inspection of street lighting and traffic signal installations are described as they are performed in the City of Los Angeles. The procedures may serve as a guide for other Agencies, even though they may not have as many bureaus and departments involved in the acceptance process.)

4-3.12.1   General. Final inspection of street lighting construction is furnished on a wide variety of surface improvement projects. In addition, lighting systems for vehicular and pedestrian tunnels and railroad underpasses are subject to street lighting final inspection.

Street lighting work may also originate with construction of a new State freeway. The new installations on the freeway itself are inspected solely by the State Inspectors, but inspections of new street light installations or relocations on adjacent streets required by the construction of the freeway are made jointly by the State and Agency Inspectors. Large storm drain installations included in a County Flood Control project often require temporary disconnections and removals, circuit revisions and extensive alterations in the street lighting systems, with inspection furnished by the Agency under a service agreement with the flood control district.

In all of these cases, final inspection of the new or remodeled street lighting installations is required. It is conducted separately from a full final inspection given to the balance of the construction and, depending on the timing, may precede or follow the surface final.

Traffic signal construction and remodeling is often done in conjunction with street lighting work, either by the same electrical contractor or by an Agency crew. Information on final inspection of traffic signals can be found in Subsectional 4-3.13.

4-3.12.2   Request for Final Inspection of Street Lighting. On all projects or portions of projects involving street lighting, final inspection by a Street Lighting Final Inspector is required. Requests for final inspection are made by the contractor by a direct call to the Street Lighting Final Inspector.

In some cases, it may be desirable or necessary to schedule partial final inspections. On large assessment and replacement projects the contractor is encouraged to complete the project in increments of several circuits. On street widening projects, existing lighting is frequently maintained on one side of the street while it is being replaced by a new lighting system on the other side. In such cases, partial final inspections are in order.

4-3.12.3   Request for Street Lighting Energy Fee Requirements). On subdivision permit projects only, the Street Lighting Final Inspector arranges for the preparation of the form entitled "Request for Street Lighting Energy Fee Requirements." The entire set of the form, with carbons in place, is transmitted to the Bureau of Street Lighting for additional entries to be made on the form by that Bureau. Copies of the completed form are then sent to the Bureau of Accounting, and the Bureau of Contract Administration.

4-3.12.4 **Functions Preceeding Final Inspection of Street Lighting.** The Street Lighting Final Inspector receives the street lighting job records envelope and the "as-built" plan from the District Supervisor some time after the "burn" test, because the contractor's work often continues beyond "burn" date and the Project Street Lighting Inspector must retain the job records and the plans in order to inspect and record the stages of the work.

As the circumstances permit, the Final Inspector will check the contents of the job envelope and will review the "as-built" plan. He will ascertain that the closing entry on the last job record card reads "Ready for final inspection" with the date noted along with the Project Street Lighting Inspector's signature. He will check for the District Supervisor's signature and date on "Project Record" form or on the "Class B Permit Record" form or obtain his release of the project by telephone. He will review the job report cards to make sure that the entries are correct and complete and that entries pertaining to traffic signal construction are recorded on separate cards and not intermixed with street lighting entries. In addition, he will review change orders, supplementary circuit sketches, test results on conductors, sketches of temporary ground locations, delivery tickets for concrete used for electrolier foundations, and other pertinent job records. The form entitled "Street Lighting Construction Record of Lamp Changes" (See Subsection 3-9.10) must be reviewed with care to make sure it is accurate and complete.

Inaccurate, incomplete or missing reports, unresolved test failures or complaints and other questions should be referred back to the appropriate construction division, Supervisor and Inspector.

4-3.12.5 **Field Procedures for Final Inspection of Street Lighting.** The first final inspection of the day is usually scheduled for 10 a.m. This gives the Street Lighting Final Inspector time for review of the job records, discussion of the work with the District Supervisor and makes allowance for travel time to the jobsite from headquarters.

The Final Inspector will walk throughout the lighting district and check for compliance with plans and specifications, listing items needing correction or completion on the form "Final Inspection Correction List" (See Plate 63, Appendix). He may be accompanied by the contractor's representative, the Project Street Lighting Inspector or both.

If any materials are required to be turned in at the City yard for reuse, the Final Inspector will locate and review the carbon copy of the receipt issued to the contractor. If none is on hand, he will instruct the contractor to obtain a receipt or to arrange with the Bureau of Street Lighting to pay for the value of such materials.

The new system may tie into an electrolier or pull box in an existing system, or perhaps into a new pull box, or the plans may call for a new service point and cut-out box on a utility pole. In the latter case the Final Inspector will compare the constructed work with the sketch previously furnished by the serving Agency. The cut-out box must be 10 feet above ground level. It must be located on the correct side, or quadrant, of the pole as shown on the sketch. Unused holes in the cut-out box must be plugged.

The type and number of electroliers are verified. Electroliers must be plumb and not bent or otherwise damaged. Each extension arm must be at a right angle to the curb. The condition of the paint or the galvanizing is examined for defects.

The Final Inspector will check for correct lamp size targeting on each electrolier arm as specified in Subsection 100-1 of the Special Specifications of the Bureau of Street Lighting and in Plate 43, Appendix.

When electroliers have not been located exactly as originally planned, the Final Inspector should ascertain that there is proper authority for such change (See Subsection 3-9.4.1) and that the change and authority are included on the "as-built" plan. (See Subsection 3-9.5.1.)

Doors and hand hole covers on electroliers are removed to make sure that the concrete cap construction has been done properly and does not prevent the removal of the doors or covers. All metallic parts must be connected to each other with grounding straps to provide electrical ground continuity.

Concrete caps on street light bases are examined for good workmanship and to ascertain that they are on standard sidewalk slope. Variations in slope to meet existing conditions are sometimes necessary. Cuts made in the sidewalk or in the street areas are checked for permanent resurfacing and for sawed edges in concrete areas. Lawn areas in parkways may require additional backfilling, reseeding and suitable mulch.

Pull boxes must be flush and level with the sidewalk or the parkway grade. Each one is opened to see that it is set on a layer of crushed rock (one-inch rock size). No excessive amount of crushed rock should be in a pull box. The conduit bends must be in proper position and elevation and not transposed. Spot-checks are made of workmanship in conductor splices.

The Final Inspector may request the Project Street Lighting Inspector to advise him when minor corrections such as clean-up, touching up of paint, etc., have been completed. Otherwise, he may elect to make a recheck personally at a later date.

4-3.12.6 Functions Following Final Inspection of Street Lighting. After all corrective work has been completed and the job records are received in the Main Office by the Final Inspector, it may be necessary for him to review all or part of the records once more, depending upon the extent of the previous checking he has had an opportunity to do. He may review the "as-built" plan, revised plan (if any), change orders, post moves, conduit moves, change of service points according to the sketch furnished by the serving Agency, and deletions from plan requirements not yet covered by change orders.

4-3.12.7 Closing the Job File. When the Street Lighting Final Inspector is satisfied that the project is finished, all required change orders are on hand, and the records are complete, he will fill in the "Final Inspection Record" portion of the form "Construction Inspector's Job Report—Street Lighting".

The Final Inspector then initiates the issuance of the form entitled "Notice of Completion of Street Lighting Work" and transmits it to the Project Coordinator, together with the job records; and forwards the "as-built" plan and the Record of Lamp Changes to the Bureau of Street Lighting. Copies of the completion notice are mailed to the permittee and the contractor.

If the project involves only street lighting costruction, closing entries must also be made on the "Project Record" form or the "Class B Permit Record" form.

4-3.13 Traffic Signal Final Inspection.

4-3.13.1 General. Final inspection is furnished on all traffic signal installations made by private electrical contractors, with the exception of those built in connection with freeway construction performed under State inspection and thereafter maintained by the Agency. If a project includes traffic signal and street lighting work, the same electrical contractor ordinarily will make both installations.

Plans for some projects specify that the Traffic Department forces perform all or part of the traffic signal work. Any such work done by Agency forces is not subject to final inspection.

Existing traffic signal systems are sometimes damaged by a contractor engaged in construction activities in the street. After emergency repairs are made by Agency forces, permanent repairs must be made by a qualified electrical contractor employed by the project contractor. Inspection is furnished by the Agency for this work and is subject to subsequent final inspection.

Final inspection of traffic signals is preceded by an operational test witnessed by and participated in by a technician representing the Traffic Engineer. There may be a considerable lapse of time between the date of the operational test and the date of final inspection. Once the signals have passed the operational test, they continue in service, as the need for the signals is usually urgent. Details on the operational test are found in Subsection 4-3.13.5.

Final inspection of traffic signal installations is conducted separately and apart from the final inspection given to other items of the new construction.

4-3.13.2 Scheduling Final Inspection of Traffic Signal Construction. After all work pertaining to a traffic signal installation has been completed, including construction of concrete caps, permanent resurfacing of street and sidewalk areas, general clean-up, etc., the contractor will arrange with the Final Inspector for an appointment. The Final Inspector obtains the verbal release of the traffic signal construction from the District Supervisor and notifies a representative of the Traffic Engineer that a final inspection has been scheduled.

4-3.13.3 Field Procedures for Final Inspection of Traffic Signals. The contractor, the Final Inspector, a representative of the Traffic Engineer, and when warranted, the Project Traffic Signal Inspector arrange to meet at the jobsite. A complete inspection of the signal system is made. Construction must be in full compliance with plans, revised plans, change orders and traffic signal specifications and Standard Plans as supplied by the Traffic Department. Manufactured items used in the construction must agree with a list of items authorized to be used, said list having been submitted by the contractor to the Traffic Department for approval before construction. Substitutions (if any) must have had prior approval. The Final Inspector will verify that the insulation colors on the various conductors comply with the color code called out in the Traffic Department specifications. Or, if no color code is specified, identify the conductors with appropriate tags. Wiring in controller cabinets is checked for neat arrangement and proper harnessing. Concrete caps on bases will be examined for good workmanship and to ascertain that they are on standard sidewalk slope. Variations in slope are sometimes advisable. Cuts made in sidewalk or street areas are examined for permanent resurfacing. Lawn areas in parkways may require backfilling, reseeding or both. Signal heads must be mounted plumb and push button installations verified. Items required to be galvanized or painted are examined for compliance. Signal sequences and timing are observed for proper operation and signal heads are checked for visibility and freedom from visual obstructions.

Induction loops are checked for proper installation in sawcuts with approved epoxy caulking, correct configuration and location and optimum sensitivity.

Pull boxes must be flush and level with the sidewalk or the parkway grade. Each one is opened to see that it is set on a layer of crushed rock (one-inch rock size). No excessive amount of crushed rock should be in a pull box. The conduit runs must be in proper relative position without transposition.

Items to be corrected or completed by the contractor are listed by the Final Inspection on a "Final Inspection Correction List". An original and three carbon copies are required.

4-3.13.4 Functions Following Final Inspection of Traffic Signals. After all work including corrections (if any) has been completed and the job records are received in the Main Office, the Final Inspector will review the entire contents of the job envelope. All required items must be on hand, including change orders, receipts for salvaged materials turned in at an Agency yard, etc. He will make sure that entries pertaining to traffic signal construction have been entered on separate job record cards and are not intermixed with street lighting entries.

When the traffic signal work is complete and can be recommended for acceptance, the Final Inspector will make a closing entry below the Field Inspector's last entry on the job record card. A sample entry follows:

1-17-86. Traffic signals OK and acceptable per
*_____J. K. Doe, Inspector

*(Enter name of representative of Agency Traffic Engineer making joint final inspection.)

The records are then transmitted to the Project Coordinator for further processing.

    4-3.13.5 Policies Governing Operational Tests of Traffic Signals. An operational test of traffic signals may be made prior to the construction of those items of work which do not affect signal operation, such as construction of concrete caps, painting, general clean-up, etc. The operational test is not to be confused with final inspection. The traffic signal operational test may either precede or follow the street lighting "burn" test where street lighting construction is also part of the project, but the two tests are rarely scheduled for the same day.

    Complex installations at major intersections often require that portions of the traffic signal system be placed in operation progressively over a period of several weeks or even several months.

    (a) Scheduling an Operational Test of Traffic Signals. When a traffic signal installation is ready for an operational test, the contractor will call the Department of Traffic. A convenient date and hour will be arranged.

    (b) Field Procedures for Operational Tests of Traffic Signals. The Final Inspector normally does not witness an operational test. This phase of the work is conducted by the designated representative of the Agency Traffic Engineer, the contractor and Project Traffic Signal Inspector. The following tests are then made on all traffic signal circuits:

    (1) Test for continuity of each circuit.

    (2) Test for grounds in each circuit.

    (3) A "megger" test on the complete signal system (or portion thereof) when required by the representative of the Agency Traffic Engineer.

    (4) A functional test in which it must be demonstrated that each and every part of the system functions as specified or intended by the plans and specifications.

    Any fault in any material or in any part of the installation which is revealed by these tests shall be corrected by the contractor and the test repeated until no fault appears.

    The representative of the Agency Traffic Engineer adjusts the timing of the signals and the synchronization with signals at other intersections, if required. The signals remain in operation after the operational test.

4-4 PROJECT ACCEPTANCE AND CLOSING REPORTS

    4-4.1 General. When it is desirable or agreeable to the Agency to accept all or a portion of the project prior to formal acceptance, a "Statement of Completion" is processed and issued to the contractor (or permittee). The contractor is then relieved of responsibility for the portion covered by the statement after its issuance.

Such statements are issued following a final inspection and the completion of all corrections reported on the Final Inspection Correction List. Refer to Subsection 4-4.3 for the detailed procedure regarding the issuance of "Statement of Completion."

4-4.2 Policies on Recommending and on Withholding Acceptance. It is the policy of the Agency that a project be "signed off" and recommended for acceptance when all work has been constructed in accordance with the plans and specifications. The Final Inspection Group will be guided by the following additional matters of policy:

(a) Unresolved items which will **not** delay "signing off" a project:

(1) A pending change order or interim change authorization for additional construction which is already constructed.

(2) Dedication or acquisition of a right-of-way.

(3) Damage by Agency departments or bureaus (for example, water and power department breaking a sidewalk during erection of a power pole), except on permit work.

(4) Tree planting by Agency crews after a deposit has been made by the permittee or the contractor.

(5) Street remodeling or other work to be done by Agency forces.

(6) Construction (by property owners or others) of walls, walks, driveways, etc., on public right-of-way without a permit.

(b) Unresolved items which **will** delay "signing off" a project:

(1) A pending change order deleting a portion of the work.

(2) A pending change order involving additional work which has not been started. However, if a promised change order is not forthcoming within 10 days, the Supervisor of Final Inspection will inform the Design Engineer that the job is constructed per plans and specifications.

(3) No clearance or release (when required) from other agencies involved, such as State Division of Highways, County Flood Control District, the Board of Education, etc.

(4) On permit construction, the recommendation for acceptance will be withheld until all utility manholes and vaults in pavement and sidewalk areas have been adjusted to grade, together with necessary resurfacing.

(c) Re-inspection of Assessment District Projects. After final inspection of an assessment act project, but immediately before the confirmation of assessments by the Agency, the Supervisor of Final Inspection will re-inspect the project site to make sure there is no evidence of structural defects in the work.

4-4.3 Statement of Completion. Following corrections (if any) and after the portion in question is found to be complete and acceptable, the Final Inspector will prepare an original and four carbon copies of a "Statement of Completion". The word "PARTIAL" applied on the form with a rubber stamp is used when only a portion of the project is to be accepted. (See Plate 62, Appendix.) After obtaining the signature of the Design Engineer on all five copies they are transmitted to the Supervisor of Final Inspection. A key map is cut from Sheet Number 1 of the project plans, and the portion included in the "partial final" is colored red. Three photocopies of the key map are then prepared. After being signed by the Final Inspection Group Supervisor, the Statement and key map are distributed as follows:

Original of "Statement of Partial Completion":

(a) On subdivision permits: Mail to permittee (no copy of map is required).

(b) On cash contract or assessment projects: Mail to contractor (no copy of map is required).

Carbon copies of "Statement of Partial Completion":

(a) For surface improvements: Transmit copy of Statement with original of map to Agency Street Maintenance Department.

(b) For sewer or storm drain improvements: Transmit copy of Statement with original of map to Agency Sanitation Department.

(c) Transmit copy of statement and copy of map to Engineer.

(d) If it is a partial final, the office file copy of the statement is retained by the Supervisor of Final Inspection, until full final inspection is completed on the project, at which time his copies are placed in the job folder in Main Office files.

(e) If the request for a "partial final" originated with a contractor or sub-contractor on subdivision permit, an additional copy of the "Statement of Partial Completion" will be prepared and mailed to him. This would also apply in the case of a sub-contractor on a cash contract or assessment act project.

4-4.4 Supervisor's Closing Reports. The "Supervisor's Closing Report" has a section reserved for the Supervisor of the Final Inspection Group to rate the contractor's performance on keeping appointments and on his promptness in making corrections or repairs. The amount of corrective work is to be indicated and the number of rechecks is to be recorded.

The date space entitled "Date Acceptable to Final Inspection" is very important and should agree with the date entered on the "Project Record Report" as the date on which acceptance is recommended.

If a completed form entitled "Report of New Paving and Trees Planted" is not in the job envelope, the Final Inspector will request that the District Supervisor have one prepared. If the project is small, the Final Inspector may prepare the form himself. The completed form is transmitted to the Agency street maintenance headquarters by the Supervisor, Final Inspection Group.

The Final Inspector initiates the report entitled "Project Review" (see sample form for surface improvements, Plate 16, Appendix) which is a uniform method of measuring and reporting the standards of quality of construction projects. Such reports are reviewed individually and cumulatively to detect problems of uniformity in the Agency's field operations. Such reviews are helpful in the following areas:

(1) Quality standards

(2) Consistency and uniformity of enforcement

(3) Inspection methods and procedures

(4) Individual and group performance

(5) Contractor performance

Even though the report is initiated by the Final Inspector, it is not intended that his evaluation be the sole criterion or the final determination as to what constitutes the optimum standard of quality. Its purpose is to assist in developing clear, effective standards universally understood and enforced by inspection personnel.

The Final Inspector will complete the report not later than five working days following the issuance of the Final Inspection Correction List and forward the original and one copy to the District Supervisor, plus one carbon copy to the Supervisor of Final Inspection. Normally, it would be expected that such a report be prepared during a subsequent visit to the jobsite. When it is appropriate to do so, the review procedure by the Supervisor should include a visit to the project site with the Inspector assigned during construction.

Work Area Traffic Control Handbook "WATCH"

An important reference addendum to the *Public Works Inspectors' Manual* is the *Work Area Traffic Control Handbook*, more popularly known by the acronym "WATCH." This 52-page, pocket-size booklet sets forth rules for safe and effective warning, control and diversion of vehicular and pedestrian traffic around work areas in public streets and freeways. The WATCH booklet is not only an important book for the public works inspector to use in the discharge of his duties but is also valuable for use by public utilities, police officers, safety engineers and contractors who have a concern with traffic safety. The booklet is well illustrated with multicolored drawings.

Subjects covered include: authority; responsibility; planning; temporary traffic lanes; control, warning and guidance devices; pavement striping and marking; bridging of excavations; pedestrian traffic; flagger control; construction signs; warning signs; regulatory signs; delineators; and barricades.

Control of traffic is well defined and illustrated in the following major work areas: parking lane or shoulders; center of street; right lane; left lane; middle line; half roadways; work within an intersection; and work beyond an intersection.

The WATCH booklet, now in its sixth edition, is approved and endorsed by the American Public Works Association, Southern California Chapter; Institute of Transportation Engineers, So. Calif. Section; and City Traffic Engineers.

The WATCH booklet is another product of the publishers of the *Public Works Inspectors' Manual*, BNI Books, 3055 Overland Avenue, Los Angeles, Calif. 90034, telephone (213) 202-7775. Copies may be purchased ($4 delivered) or further information obtained by contacting the publisher.

TABLE OF PLATES

TABLE OF PLATES (Cont.)

CONSTRUCTION INSPECTOR'S DAILY JOB REPORT

DEPARTMENT OF PUBLIC WORKS
City of Anywhere
Bureau of Contract Administration

CONSTRUCTION INSPECTOR'S DAILY JOB REPORT

JOB TITLE	JOB NO.

Hours	Description of Work Done, Contractor, Units, Quantities, Sampling, Instructions to Contractor, Records & Reports

Type of Work	Inspector
Work Location	Date

PLATE 1
See page 35 (1-3.2)

FINAL INSPECTION CORRECTION LIST

Department of Public Works	**FINAL INSPECTION CORRECTION LIST**	City of Anywhere Bureau of Contract Administration

Job Title: *Hardy St. and Laurel St.*

Contractor:

Permittee: *Able Const. Co.*

Address:

Job No.: *A'11-79262*

Date: *6-14-87*

Mailed ☐   Presented ☑

Final Inspection:

These corrections are required prior to acceptance. Call the Final Inspector for recheck when all items are completed.

TYPICAL ENTRIES FOR 'UNDERGROUND' FINAL:

1.	Correct loose step in manhole, line 2, 2+85.
2.	Install top step on manhole, line 4, 5+64.
*3.	Remove and replace left side stud in manhole to correct line and grades line 5, 4+50.

TYPICAL ENTRIES FOR 'SURFACE' FINAL:

*1.	Complete street light and traffic signal systems.
*2.	Remove and replace 25 sq. ft. of damaged walk in front of 1021 Laurel St.
3.	Remove excess asphalt along gutter edge west side Hardy St. north of Laurel St.

TYPICAL ENTRIES FOR STREET LIGHTING AND TRAFFIC SIGNAL FINAL:

1.	Band conduit in pull box at 1234 Laurel St.
2.	Back fill low parkway and reseed grass at 3216 Hardy St.

SPECIAL NOTES FOR CONTRACTOR

*1. Asterisk (*) preceding a correction item denotes that such correction must be made under inspection.

2. Liquidated damages are chargeable in the amount of $100.00 for each calendar day the contract time is in arrears. The record of contract time on this project as of this date is
☑ Days Remaining
☐ Days in Arrears   *6*

3. If corrections are not made within 30 days, this list is void and a new final inspection must be scheduled.

4. The additional items checked below need to be completed or cleared.
☑ Approval of street lighting system required.
☑ Approval of traffic signal system required.
☐ Test results pending. (Test failure may require remedial work.)
☐ Clearance required from other agency ....
(Agency)

TYPE OF FINAL INSPECTION

☐ Sewer underground only
☐ Storm drain underground only
☐ Street Lighting
☐ Traffic signal
☑ Full final
☐ Other _____

D-21426   P-23606
Plan Numbers
W. Jones
(Engineers) present at final inspection
3 - Thompson
Construction District — Supervisor

PLATE 1A
See page 510 (4-3.8.1)

DAILY INSPECTION REPORTS — CLASS 'A' PERMITS

DEPARTMENT OF PUBLIC WORKS
City of Anywhere
BUREAU OF CONTRACT ADMINISTRATION

JOB MEMORANDUM   N°.

Job Title Class 'A' Permit Report _____ Permit No. _____

(Enter Job Address)

WORK PERFORMED BY (Permittee) _____

(Name, Address & Telephone of Other Person or Contractor)

INSTRUCTIONS

Use this form to report items constructed when white copy of Class 'A' permit is not available. Also, use this form to report **partial progress** of construction when white copy of permit must be left on job for additional entries at a later date. Use the printed spaces and include the information as noted.

PERMIT NOT AVAILABLE: Telephone appropriate District Office and obtain permit number, work items, and permit requirements from office file copy. Fill out this form as required and transmit to appropriate District Office.

PARTIAL PROGRESS: Make appropriate entries both on this form **and** on white copy of permit, if available. Transmit this form to appropriate District Office. Return white copy of permit to contractor or permittee for use by the next inspector to be assigned to the job at a later date.

WORK COMPLETED

(Curb) _____ (Lin. Ft.)

(Gutter) _____ (Sq. Ft.)

(Driveway) _____ (Sq. Ft.)

(Sidewalk) _____ (Sq. Ft.)

(Other Work Such As Roof Drain) _____

(Concrete Source, Class & Ticket #) _____

(Enter Any Appropriate Remarks) _____

This copy can be wasted.

Bureau of Contract Administration

WHITE: Addressee
GREEN: Main Office
PINK: Job Envelope
CANARY: Inspector

Issued on _____ at _____ Not Used _____ By _____
   (Date Work Performed)   (Time)   (Inspector)

(Date)

PLATE 2
See page 313 (3-4.6.5[d])

INSPECTOR'S REPORT
MANUFACTURE OF PIPE

Dept. of Public Works

CITY OF ANYWHERE

INSPECTOR'S REPORT

Bureau of
Contract Administration

MANUFACTURE OF PIPE

Job Title _Hollywood - Wilshire Interceptor_
Sewer Unit II-A   Job or Per. No. _W.O. 31210_

Manufacturer _National Concrete Pipe_   Spec. No. _170_

Period of Report: From _3-1-87_ To _3-5-87_

Reported By _D.L. Black_   (See Over for Individual Record)   Total Hours Worked _40_

DESCRIPTION	Dia. Inches	Length of Pipes	No. of Pipes	D-Load	Batch Number	Class	Kind of Pipe
STRAIGHT	72"	16'	4	1950	587	3000 T-Lock	Cast
BEVELS	72"	16'	9	1750	582	3000 T-Lock	Cast
STUBS	72"	4'	2	1950	553	3000 T-Lock	Cast

(OVER)

PLATE 3
See page 175 (2-7.4.13)

CONCRETE PLANT INSPECTOR'S DAILY REPORT

CITY OF ANYWHERE		
Department of **Public Works**	**Bureau of** **Contract Administration**	Job No. A'11-31210
CONCRETE PLANT INSPECTOR'S DAILY REPORT		Date 11-17-87

Job Title	SYLVAN ST. & TYRONE AVE

Supplier & Plant Location CON ROCK SUN VALLEY	Concrete Contractor A B C CO.

Material Source:	Cement RIVERSIDE II	Sand CON ROCK S.V.	Rock CON ROCK S.V.

Mix Data	Specs. 1976 STD	Concrete Class 560-B-3250	Total Cu. Yds. Produced: 100

Admixture:
Brand & Quantity

Aggregate per Cu. Yds.	No. 2	N. 3	No. 4	Sand	Total Mix	WATER (Gals.)	
% of mix	17	45		38	100%	Max. Allowable	38.4
Dry Weight Lbs.	544	1439		1216	3199	In Aggregate	8.8
% Moisture	0	0		6		Max. Added	29.6
Moisture Lbs.	0	0		73		Cement	560
Batch Weight Lbs.	544	1439		1289	3272		

SCREEN ANALYSIS (% Passing)					Date Last Analysis:		
						Specs.	100%
2 Inch	100	100	100	100		100	Min. 95 100 Max.
1½ Inch	99	100	100	100	100		
1 Inch	18	98	100	100	85	80	96
¾ Inch	3	74	100	100	72	64	80
⅜ Inch	2	9		100	42	40	52
No. 4		2		97	38	35	40
No. 8				81	31	28	38
No. 16				61	23	21	31
No. 30				40	16	10	20
No. 50				16	6	3	9
No. 100				4	1.5	0	3
No. 200				1	0.4	0	2

Cement Sample	TAKEN	Field Inspector A. KLEIN
Notes:		Plant Inspector F. COWAN Hours 4

Notes Over ( )

PLATE 4
See page 122 (2-4.5.10) and page 126 (2-4.5.11[i])

CONCRETE BUNKER CHECK LIST

DATE_____BUNKER_____CLASS_____INSPECTOR_____

ITEM	YES	NO	SEE REMARKS
1. Are materials from approved sources?			
2. Are materials being handled in an approved manner?			
3. Are stockpile separators adequate?			
4. Are segregation precautions taken?			
5. Are bin separators in satisfactory condition?			
6. Does the distributor head function satisfactorily?			
7. Is the cement from an approved source?			
8. Have cement certificates been checked?			
9. Have cement samples been taken?			
10. Does bunker keep a supply of pea gravel?			
11. Have scales been checked within specified time limits?			
12. Is the operation and condition of the scales satisfactory?			
13. Is operation of admixture equipment OK?			
14. Is the condition of the truck mixers, including mixing blades, good?			
15. Are water-metering devices on truck OK?			
16. Are rated capacity plates kept legible?			
17. Are trucks being loaded within rated capacity limits?			
18. Is uniform amount of wash water used?			
19. Are tentative batch weights being kept?			
20. Are weights based on latest sieve analyses?			
21. Are cement and bin weights being recorded on load tickets?			
22. Is all water data being recorded on load tickets?			
23. Has corrective action been taken on previous deficiencies?			
24. Are plant personnel cooperative?			

REMARKS: This section should contain data as to correction required, company personnel notified, action from previous notices, etc.

PLATE 5
See page 113 (2-4.5.5)

JOB SAFETY RECORD ACCIDENT REPORT

City of Anywhere
Department of Public Works
Bureau of Contract Admin.

JOB SAFETY RECORD ACCIDENT REPORT

Job Title: ATWATER AVE & SILVERLAKE BLVD. RLD

Job No.: AC-49153

USE

Use this form to report job related accidents involving either the public or contractor's personnel including vehicular and equipment accidents and property damage. Report any property damage estimated to be in excess of $100 and injuries where lost time in excess of one day is anticipated.

- ☑ Injury
- ☐ Ambulance Required
- ☐ Police Investigation
- ☑ Public Involved
- ☐ Contractor Personnel
- ☐ Property Damage
- ☐ Vehicular
- ☐ Contractor's Equipment

ACCIDENT DESCRIPTION

Time, Location and Nature of Accident: (List names of injured, witnesses, their affiliation and property damaged)

9:30 P.M. Sunday March 27, 1987, Mr. Howard Jones of 2722 Silverlake Blvd, said he fell in excavation for proposed electrolier footing (Base) @ s/w return of Silverlake Blvd. & Sunset Blvd. (Pole #145)

(Attach Police Report, if available)

JOB SAFETY CONDITIONS

Describe associated existing job conditions at time of accident (Barricades, lights, warning signs, trench shoring).

Excavation dug approx. 3-14-87. Barricades set same day. Barricades checked during day and at end of work day. Checked early A.M. Monday March 28, 1987, barricades were in place, no other visible obstructions present. (Dirt, Rocks, etc.)

Original-Main Office
cc: Job Envelope

Inspector's Signature: John Johnson

Date: 3-28-87

Reviewed by: William S. Samson

PLATE 6
See page 54 (1-4.3.2)

RECAPITULATION OF CONTRACT TIME

BEGINNING DATE: 6-15-87
SERIAL NO.: 18

RECAPITULATION OF CONTRACT TIME

JOB TITLE & NO. Broadway And Main

Street Lighting Improvement District

CALENDAR DAYS [ ]   WORKING DAYS [X]

CONTRACTOR:

Reliable Construction Co.
Anywhere, CA

	TOTALS, PRIOR REPORT	CHANGES THIS REPORT	NEW TOTALS
ALLOWABLE CONTRACT TIME	120	10	
DAYS USED	90	10	100
BALANCE	30	0	20
PROGRESS	86%	14%	100%

LEGEND:

NTP—Notice To Proceed
M —Mobilization

Days Charged

X —Worked
O —No Work
C —Final Corrections
LD —Liquidated Damages

Days Not Charged

H —Holiday
UH —Union Holiday
MD —Material Delay
CR —Contract Requirement
AD —Administrative Delay
R —Rain
W —Weather
S —Strike
U —Utility
AW —Awaiting Final
F —To Final
   FF —Field Final
FA —Final Acceptance

AD —Awaiting Change Order

MON.	TUE.	WED.	THUR.	FRI.	SAT.	SUN.	DAYS LEFT	S	DAYS +/=
15	16	17	18	19	20	21			
X	X	R	W	W			28		
22	23	24	25	26	27	28			
X	X	MD	X	X			24		
29	30	1	2	3	4	5			
X	H	X	U	U			22		
6	7	8	9	10	11	12			
X	AD	X	AW	AW			20		
13	14								
F	F						20		20

NOTE: The contractor is allowed 15 days in which to report in writing any disagreement with the content of this report. Otherwise it shall be deemed to have been accepted by the contractor.

JOHN DOE
Director of Bureau Construction

John Doe
(District Supervisor)

13-13-87
(Date)

PLATE 7
See page 509 (4-3.5)

INSTRUCTION FOR THE PREPARATION OF FORM 'MONTHLY PROGRESS ESTIMATE' ➤

Cash Contracts: A progress estimate shall be prepared by the Project Inspector and submitted to the Main Office on the fifteenth of each month, except that none is required if no progress is made and the Project Administrative Control Section in the Main Office is so notified.

A'11 Contracts: On Assessment Act contracts, where the City contributes a portion of the contract amount, a monthly progress estimate shall be prepared and submitted as in the case of a cash contract. If there is no City contribution on an Assessment Act contract, no progress estimates are required.

S'41 Contracts: A final estimate only is to be submitted at the completion of all work.

General: Normally, the reporting period will end on the 15th of month. However, the contractor may request that he be paid for work completed up to seven days before the end of the period or to include or include the first seven days following the end of the period. In either case he must submit a letter to the Project Inspector, stating that a variance from the standard procedure is desired and whether his request is made only for that particular period or is intended to apply to all subsequent periods. The letter is to be forwarded to the Main Office by the Project Inspector with the estimate.

The actual work-period dates must be noted on the estimate in the upper right-hand corner where the period is recorded. For example: "April 16 to May 15" or "April 16 to May 22, incl." Any monthly estimate not accompanied by a letter will be considered to cover the period of work up to the 15th of the month.

The Estimate Form: On contracts, requiring monthly estimates, the Project Administrative Control Section in the Main Office will furnish a supply of forms with the bid items, quantities and unit prices filled in.

Bid Items: In the case of lump sum items, show the percentage of work completed. For items that have a unit price, show the number of units completed. Quantities reported for the first time are shown in the middle column under Quantities headed "This Month" and the last column "Total." Do not report items on which no work has been done. However, once an item has been reported, it must then be shown on each succeeding estimate in the "Previously Reported" column. For second and succeeding estimates, obtain the "Quantities — Previously Reported" from a copy of the estimate for the previous month.

Change Orders: Below the bid items, leave one or two blank lines. Then list change orders by order number and serial number. In general, change orders should not be reported until 100 percent complete. Change orders should be reported as if on a lump sum basis, and this sum entered in the "Unit Price" column. Do **not** enter separate items making up the change order. To report part of a change order for payment, report it as a percentage of the total. Do not enter orders which involve no change of cost.

Money Entries: Dollars and cents amounts will be calculated and filled in by Main Office personnel. The Project Inspector need not make these calculations.

PLATE 8 (Page 1)
See page 42 (1-3.8.1)

MONTHLY PROGRESS ESTIMATE

DEPARTMENT OF PUBLIC WORKS
City of Anywhere
Bureau of Contract Administration

Job Number: AC-91401

Job Title

Estimate Number 2

Inspector: J.K. Smith

Period: From: 6-6-87 To: 7-15-87

Sunset Ave & Parthenia ST ID

Item No.	Item Per Schedule In Bid Proposal	Quantity and Unit	Previously Reported	This Month	Total	Unit Price	Total Value
			QUANTITIES				
1	Removals	Lump. sum	100%		100%	$ 800.00	$
2	Excav	301 cy	180	100	280	3.20	
3	AC pavement	275 tons				12.40	
12	Tree	16 units				8.00	
13	Tree well	10 units				44.00	
14	Street lighting system	Lump. sum	5%	5%	5%	1,550.00	

Amount of Contract: $ 12,696.79

Contractor: Newman and Sons, Inc.

	1. BID ITEM	2. C.O.	3. TOTAL
TOTAL TO DATE	$	$	$
PREVIOUS TOTAL (deduct from amount above)	$	FOR OFFICE USE ONLY $	$
THIS MONTH	$	$	$

PLATE 8 (Page 2) *See page 42 (1-3.8.1)*

INSTRUCTIONS FOR COMPLETING 'RECORD OF SEWER CONSTRUCTION' FORM ('Y' SHEET)

Sewer reports become the permanent record of sewer construction. Such records are used to locate chimneys, tees, wyes, house connection ends, etc., often many years after they are constructed. Accurate measurement to the nearest foot of the actual location of manholes, wyes, tees and upper ends of house connections is of paramount importance.

The following areas of the "Y" Sheet should be carefully checked during preparation and again prior to submittal to the Main Office:

1. Show all pipe batch numbers, segregated by pipe size, on the lower portion of the sheet below the last line entry.

2. Show all pipe stubs constructed at M.H.'s, including their size and direction.

3. Show the length of all house connections — particularly in cul-de-sacs and on curved main lines.

4. Be **sure** all wye and property line stations and depths have been shown **correctly.**

5. Be **sure** to show all manhole, terminal cleanouts or lamphole types as constructed.

6. Be **sure** that all changes, I.C.A. or C.O. have been included in the "Remarks" column — preferably by "number", if known at the time of preparation of the wye sheet.

7. Be **sure** all entries are clear, legible and in ink. The Inspector's original handwritten record is forwarded to District Engineering Offices.

DETAILED INSTRUCTIONS

(a) All sewer construction, relocation, abandonment or reconstruction must be recorded as work progresses. A separate "Y" sheet is required for each line.

(b) Refer to plan for sewer line numbers and sewer line titles. Line titles on all reports should read the same as shown on the plan, except where necessary to reverse the limits to show the lower end as "from" and the upper end as "to". Do not describe a portion of a line.

(c) To determine right and left, face upstream at lower end of line.

PLATE 9 (Page 1)
See page 41 (1-3.5) and page 345 (3-5.13)

INSTRUCTIONS FOR COMPLETING
'Y' SHEET FORM (Continued)

(d) Enter on "Y" sheets the stations of wyes, tees or manholes as main line construction progresses. As house connections are laid, enter the station of the upper end of each house connection, depth, lot number, block number and tract number. Insert house numbers (when available) including those for sewers constructed in alleys or rights-of-way. If lot is vacant, leave the space blank.

(e) Leave all unused spaces on the "Y" sheet blank. Do not make a dash or write "none".

DEPARTMENT OF PUBLIC WORKS City of Anywhere Bureau of Contract Administration			**JOB INSPECTOR'S RECORD OF SEWER CONSTRUCTION ("Y" SHEET)**							Transmit to Main Office AT ONCE as soon as all pipe on this line has been laid. (Both main line and house conn.)	
LINE NO. 2			STREET OR ALLEY, OR R/W HILL STREET							PLAN NO. D-11247	
MAIN LINE PIPE SIZE 10-8 INCHES			FROM (LOWER END) SUNSET BLVD.				TO (UPPER END) ALPINE STREET				
RIGHT SIDE EAST SIDE			PERMITTEE							REPORTED BY F. SMITH	
LEFT SIDE WEST SIDE			CONTRACTOR R&K CONSTRUCTION CO.							MAILING DATE 6-8-87	
JOB OR PERMIT NO. A11-41123			JOB OR PERMIT TITLE SUNSET BLVD. & MAIN STREET S.D.								
			RECORD OF INSPECTORS							**MAIN OFFICE CHECK**	
INSPECTORS ON MAIN LINE F. SMITH				INSPECTORS ON HOUSE CONNECTIONS F. SMITH						CHECKED TO PLAN BY	
										DATE	
STATION OF Y OR Y OR MANHOLE	RIGHT OR LEFT	DEPTH OF Y OR Y	STATION OR HOUSE CONN.	DEPTH OF H. C. AT CURB	AT P. L.	LOT NO.	BLOCK NO.	TRACK NO.	WAIVER NO.	HOUSE NO.	GENERAL INFORMATION
0+00			JCF								8" STUB E'
1+49	R	8/18	1+46		5	1		4372			10' CH
1+49	C	8/18									"
1+49	L	8/18	1+62		5	22		4372			"
1+98	R	18				2					TEE (VERT.)
1+98	L	18				21					" "

(f) Lay blind wye (or tee) to the joint nearest to the station where indicated on the plan. Do not cut a pipe. A signed form entitled "Request for Change of House Connection Sewer" (commonly called a House Connection Waiver) is required to move a blind wye or tee a greater distance. Never omit a blind wye or tee. Do not write "Blind" on the "Y" sheet.

(g) To avoid damaging the main line during future excavation, use only full feet to record depth of all wyes, blind wyes and tees (Example: record 5'9" as 5 feet). Measure on the pro-

PLATE 9 (Page 2)

INSTRUCTIONS FOR COMPLETING 'Y' SHEET FORM (Continued)

file from existing or proposed curb grade to flow line. Use curb profile nearest the main line or when main line is in the center of the street and the curbs for both sides of the street are indicated on the profile, use the average of both curb profiles.

(h) If house connection lengths on the same side of the main line vary (main line laid on a diagonal, curve or not parallel to curb), give lengths of each house connection in "General Information" column.

(i) Inclined tees and wyes are normally installed at an angle of 45 degrees. If the plan calls for a tee or wye to be laid flat, make note of it in the "General Information" column. Tees and wyes lacking special notes are assumed to have been positioned in the main line at a 45-degree angle.

(j) Use two lines to report vertical tees and state in "Lot No." column the lot numbers on both right and left. Vertical tees can be used for two or more lots.

(k) In reporting blind wyes or tees, leave blank the column headed "Station of House Connection" and "Depth of House Connection."

2+47	R	9/18	2+24	5	3		4372		622	10' CH
2+47	R	8/18	2+62	5	4		"			"
2+47	L	8/18	2+62	5	19		"		629	"
2+75		MHB								
2+92	R	8	2+94	5	7		4372			
2+95	L	8	2+96	5	17		"			
3+77	L	8	3+79	5	15		"		651	EXTRA HC. PER CO#2
5+25		MHB		8" LINE NORTH						
5+82	L	7	5+82	5	12		4372		705	MOVED 2' SOUTH
5+92	R	7	5+95	6	4		11267		708	FLAT "Y" 48'H.C.

(l) In the example shown above, the diameter of the sewer main changes from 10 inches to 8 inches at Station 5 + 25.

(m) The "Y" sheet will show the types of manholes, lampholes and terminal cleanout structures in accordance with the project plans and standard designations for such structures.

Take note of all stubs installed in manholes by the appropriate entry in the remarks column. Showing size of

PLATE 9 (Page 3)

INSTRUCTIONS FOR COMPLETING 'Y' SHEET FORM (Continued)

stub and direction (refer to the JCF Manhole at Station $0+00$ in the "Y" sheet illustration on page 2 of this plate).

(n) Use profile to determine house connection depth unless depth of each house connection is shown in a circle on the plan. Check for a special note on the plan regarding depths. Record depth of the house connection where it terminates; at the curb or at the property line — not both.

(o) Upper ends of house connection shall be laid to the exact elevation indicated on the plan and grade sheet, but are recorded only to the nearest whole foot of depth below curb grade as shown on the profile. Write numbers to show the depth of all house connection ends. Do not use dittos.

(p) The inspector is authorized to move house connection ends up to five feet to avoid trees, utility poles, hydrants, gas or water pipes and meters or other obstructions. Required moves should be anticipated during main-line pipe-laying, as relocation of the wye or tee upstream or downstream may be advisable.

(q) A signed "Request for Change of House Connection Sewer" form must be obtained to move a house connection end more than five feet or to change the depth of the upper end of a house connection from the depth indicated on the profile.

(r) Extra house connections not shown on the plan can be added only by Change Order. The property owner affected is required to sign "Request for Change of House Connection Sewer" form in triplicate and advance approval of the added house connection and its location must be obtained by telephone from the Design Engineer by the Inspector prior to permitting any work on the house connection. The name of the Engineer authorizing the additional house connection is to be entered on the form and the copies distributed to the appropriate offices. The property owner **MAY NOT** pay the contractor privately for an added house connection. The Inspector is to enter a remark in the "General Information" column: "Extra HC per C. O. #   ." (Number to be filled in by the office if not available in the field.)

(s) If requested to omit a house connection shown on the plan, have the property owner sign a "Request for Change of

PLATE 9 (Page 4)

INSTRUCTIONS FOR COMPLETING
'Y' SHEET FORM (Continued)

House Connection Sewer" form in triplicate and telephone the Design Engineer to secure a verbal O.K. Note the engineer's name authorizing the omission on the form and distribute the copies of the form to the appropriate offices. Insert in "General Information" column the following: "HC deleted by C.O. # ." (Number to be filled in by the office if not available in the field.) House connections can be omitted only by Change Order.

DEPARTMENT OF PUBLIC WORKS City of Anywhere Bureau of Contract Administration		**JOB INSPECTOR'S RECORD OF SEWER CONSTRUCTION ("Y" SHEET)**							Transmit to Main Office AT ONCE as soon as all pipe on this line has been laid. (Both main line and house conn.)	
LINE NO. 3		STREET OR ALLEY, OR R/W ELKWOOD STREET (H.C.'S ONLY)							PLAN NO. D-13652	
MAIN LINE PIPE SIZE EXIST. 8 INCHES		FROM (LOWER END) FARRALONE AVENUE			TO (UPPER END) GLADE AVENUE					
RIGHT SIDE NORTH SIDE		PERMITTEE CINDERELLA PARK							REPORTED BY L. FARLEY	
LEFT SIDE SOUTH SIDE		CONTRACTOR I. & H. CONSTRUCTION CO.							MAILING DATE 3-25-87	
JOB OR PERMIT NO. B-9971		JOB OR PERMIT TITLE ELKWOOD STREET & CANYON AVENUE I.D.								
RECORD OF INSPECTORS									**MAIN OFFICE CHECK**	
INSPECTORS ON MAIN LINE			INSPECTORS ON HOUSE CONNECTIONS L. FARLEY					CHECKED TO PLAN BY		
								DATE		
STATION OF Y OR Y OR MANHOLE	RIGHT OR LEFT	DEPTH OF Y OR Y	STATION OR HOUSE CONN.	DEPTH OF H. C. AT CURB	DEPTH OF H.C. AT P. L.	LOT NO.	BLOCK NO.	TRACK NO.	WAIVER NO.	HOUSE NO.	GENERAL INFORMATION
0+88		M	HB (EXIST.)								
1+17	R	9	1+24	5		17		23467		1706	
2+03	R	9	2+05	5		20		"		1748	SADDLE INSTALLED
2+63			TCSY (EXIST.)								

(t) Where a plan calls for adding house connections to an existing sewer main, write "HC's only" in the heading of the "Y" sheet and show the main line and manholes existing prior to the work under construction as "existing" (see above). No wye existed at Station 2+03. This necessitated installation of a saddle by the contractor, which was witnessed by the Inspector. Where a new manhole is constructed on an existing sewer, the "Y" sheet should indicate the station of the next adjacent manhole below the new manhole, as well as the station of the next adjacent manhole above, if any. Report the manholes below and above as "existing."

(u) If a sewer line has no wyes or house connections, report the line on a "Y" sheet showing the manhole stations just as though there were house connections on the line.

PLATE 9 (Page 5)

INSTRUCTIONS FOR COMPLETING
'Y' SHEET FORM (Continued)

DEPARTMENT OF PUBLIC WORKS City of Anywhere Bureau of Contract Administration	**JOB INSPECTOR'S RECORD OF SEWER CONSTRUCTION ("Y" SHEET)**	Transmit to Main Office AT ONCE as soon as all pipe on this line has been laid. (Both main line and house conn.)

LINE NO. 5	STREET OR ALLEY, OR R/W R/W S/O CORAL DR.	PLAN NO. D-13430
MAIN LINE PIPE SIZE 8 INCHES	FROM (LOWER END) PARK PLACE	TO (UPPER END) WESTERN AVE.
RIGHT SIDE NORTH SIDE	PERMITTEE MAR-VAL CORP	REPORTED BY F. SMITH
LEFT SIDE SOUTH SIDE	CONTRACTOR VAN HORN BROS.	MAILING DATE 1-8-87
JOB OR PERMIT NO. B-3801	JOB OR PERMIT TITLE CORAL DR. & PARK PL. I.D.	

RECORD OF INSPECTORS		MAIN OFFICE CHECK	
INSPECTORS ON MAIN LINE F. SMITH	INSPECTORS ON HOUSE CONNECTIONS F. SMITH	CHECKED TO PLAN BY	
		DATE	

STATION OF Y OR T OR MANHOLE	RIGHT OR LEFT	DEPTH OF Y OR T	STATION OR HOUSE CONN.	DEPTH OF H. C. AT CURB	DEPTH OF H. C. AT P. L.	LOT NO.	BLOCK NO.	TRACK NO.	WAIVER NO.	HOUSE NO.	GENERAL INFORMATION
2+11	M	HB	— MOVED MH 3' EAST — CO. SER. # 2								
2+24	R	8/14				23	2	3324		8624	6' CH (TYPE "A")
2+24	C	8/14				21	3	"		8627	" "
3+27	R	9/17	3+28		5	35		24467			8' CH (TYPE "C")
3+27	L	9/17	3+12		5	18		"	W-23	8644	" "
3+27	L	8/17	3+46		5	19		"		"	" "

(v) Refer to 2 + 11 M.H. above. Due to some interference encountered during excavation (perhaps a pipe or structure), the manhole was moved three feet east of the original plan location at 2 + 08. A change order was issued authorizing this move. Do not move manholes without prior approval of the Design Engineer.

(w) Where chimneys are built, show the depth of the wye on the chimney and flow line of the tee as a fraction. Example: 8/14 (depth to top of chimney over flow line depth).

A Type "A" chimney has two openings at the top: a wye and the center bell. "Y" branches on Type "A" chimneys not joined to house connection sewers are to be faced to the right looking upstream unless otherwise specified on the sewer plans. This condition is illustrated at Station 2 + 24 above.

A Type "C" chimney has three openings at the top: a double wye with two openings and the center bell. "Y" branches for Type "B," "C" and "D" chimneys face perpendicular to the center line of the sewer main unless otherwise specified on the

PLATE 9 (Page 6)

INSTRUCTIONS FOR COMPLETING
'Y' SHEET FORM (Continued)

sewer plans. Typical entries for a Type "C" chimney are shown above. The center bell opening has been used for the second connection to the left. Use three lines on "Y" sheet for reporting Types "B," "C" and "D" chimneys.

STATION OF Y OR Y OR MANHOLE	RIGHT OR LEFT	DEPTH OF Y OR Y	STATION OR HOUSE CONN.	DEPTH OF H.C. AT CURB	AT P.L.	LOT NO.	BLOCK NO.	TRACK NO.	WAIVER NO.	HOUSE NO.	GENERAL INFORMATION
4+83	L	7	5+03		5	32		23364			MEAS. 12' PAST MH AND 29' L/O MAIN LINE PROD. 39' H.C.
4+86	R	7	4+88		5	20		"		4941	
4+91			MHQ								
4+91	R	7	4+94		5	19		23364			MEAS. 3' PAST MH AND 25' R/O MAINLINE PROD. 25' H.C. GOSE INTO MH
4+93	C	7	5+13		5	18		23364			MEAS. 22' PAST MH ON C/L MAIN LINE PROD. 22' H.C. GOSE INTO MH

| | | | 8" | BATCH | # 453 | | | | | | |
| | | | 6" | " | # 441 | | | | | | |

(x) On dead-end streets and cul-de-sacs, the house connections often extend past the end of the sewer main. (Note the first entry above.) The stations of the wyes are listed consecutively, not the stations of the upper ends of house connections. Where the upper end of a house connection projects beyond the station of the upper manhole, show the distance past the manhole and the number of feet right or left of the centerline of the sewer main produced. In the last two entries above, the connection on the right is stubbed into the side of the manhole and the other connection continues along the line of the sewer main to the property line.

(y) For each line (or portion of a line) that is shown on the plan to be abandoned, make out a "Y" sheet on the date that it is taken out of service.

(z) Transmit "Y" sheet and forms entitled "Request for Change of House Connection Sewer" to the Main Office as soon as all pipe (mainline and all house connection laterals) is laid on each line. Do not wait for completion of manholes and flooding.

PLATE 9 (Page 7)

INSTRUCTIONS FOR FILLING IN POST TENSIONING RECORD FORM

GENERAL

Prestressing System — The prestressing system shall be the same as specified on the shop drawings.

Expected Anchor Set — Shown on shop drawings.

Jack No. and Gauge No. — The jack number and gauge number shall agree with the calibration chart.

Date Calibrated — The jack and gauge shall have been calibrated within 30 days of stressing tendons.

When jacking from one end, one column on the Post Tensioning Record form shall be completed for each tendon jacked. When jacking from both ends, two columns will be required per tendon. Also Items 7, 13 and 14 may be deleted.

Deviations in jacking force, elongation, anchor set, prestressing sequence or procedure should be approved in advance by the Engineer.

ITEM NUMBERS

1. Indicate *girder identification* as shown on the shop drawings. The end jacked shall be specified by abutment or pier number shown on the plans or cardinal points (N, S, E, W).

2. Indicate *tendon identification* as shown on the shop drawings. The No. of Stands shall be verified in the field and must agree with the shop drawings.

3. *Initial jacking pressure* = 10% of Final Jacking Pressure which shall be taken from the calibration chart. Plot 10% of the final jacking force shown on the shop drawings and read the initial jacking pressure.

4. *Final jacking pressure* shall be taken from the calibration chart. Plot the final jacking force shown on the shop drawings and read the final jacking pressure. Do not exceed the final jacking pressure unless approved in advance by the Engineer. Where anticipated gauge pressures are shown on the shop drawings they are theoretical values and should only be used as a guide.

5. *Expected elongation at final jacking pressure* (before seating anchorage) is shown on the shop drawings.

6 and 7. *Length of cable to reference mark* (jacked and unjacked ends). Mark strands and measure cable lengths while holding initial jacking pressure. Cable lengths should be measured from a stable point (such as face of bearing plate) to the reference mark painted on all strands.

8. Measure *cable length* at jacked ends before seating anchorage while holding final jacking pressure.

9. Measured *elongation* before anchor set must agree with expected elongation (Item 5) within 3% unless approved by the Engineer.

10. Measure *cable length* after seating anchorage.

11 and 12. Measured *Anchor Set* at Jacked End must agree with expected anchor set within ⅛″ unless approved by the Engineer.

13. Measure *cable length* after seating anchorage.

14. *Slippage* at unjacked end shall not exceed ⅛″ unless approved by the Engineer.

PLATE 10 (Page 1)
See page 485 (3-13.5.4)

POST TENSIONING RECORD FORM
(SEE PRECEDING PAGE FOR INSTRUCTIONS)

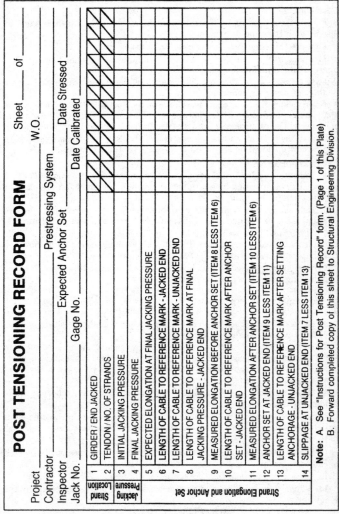

Project _____
Contractor _____
Inspector _____
Jack No. _____

Prestressing System _____
Expected Anchor Set _____
Gage No. _____

Sheet ____ of ____
W.O. _____
Date Stressed _____
Date Calibrated _____

		Strand Location	Jacking Pressure	
1	GIRDER / END JACKED			
2	TENDON / NO. OF STRANDS			
3	INITIAL JACKING PRESSURE			
4	FINAL JACKING PRESSURE			
5	EXPECTED ELONGATION AT FINAL JACKING PRESSURE			
6	LENGTH OF CABLE TO REFERENCE MARK - JACKED END			
7	LENGTH OF CABLE TO REFERENCE MARK - UNJACKED END			
8	LENGTH OF CABLE TO REFERENCE MARK AT FINAL JACKING PRESSURE - JACKED END			
9	MEASURED ELONGATION BEFORE ANCHOR SET (ITEM 8 LESS ITEM 6)			
10	LENGTH OF CABLE TO REFERENCE MARK AFTER ANCHOR SET - JACKED END			
11	MEASURED ELONGATION AFTER ANCHOR SET (ITEM 10 LESS ITEM 6)			
12	ANCHOR SET AT JACKED END (ITEM 9 LESS ITEM 11)			
13	LENGTH OF CABLE TO REFERENCE MARK AFTER SETTING ANCHORAGE - UNJACKED END			
14	SLIPPAGE AT UNJACKED END (ITEM 7 LESS ITEM 13)			

(rows 1–4 grouped under "Jacking Pressure", rows 5–14 grouped under "Strand Elongation and Anchor Set")

Note: A. See "Instructions for Post Tensioning Record" form. (Page 1 of this Plate)
B. Forward completed copy of this sheet to Structural Engineering Division.

PLATE 10 (Page 2)

BATCH WEIGHTS FOR ASPHALTIC CONCRETE MIXTURES

Bureau of Contract Administration

Department of Public Works
City of Anywhere

BATCH WEIGHTS FOR ASPHALTIC CONCRETE MIXTURES
FROM (Plant Supt.) BILL BIRCH
FROM (Inspector) JOHN SMITH

Serial No. 3
Date Issued 8-16-87

The batch weights of material supplied to City of Anywhere projects shall be as follows. Deviations shall be permitted only upon specific authority of the plant inspector. All prior communications regarding batch weights are cancelled.

Plant Name PAVING MATERIALS CO. Address 2633 INDUSTRIAL AVE. Phone No. 131-7833

Batchman A. JASON Fireman Ø Dispatcher (PLANT)

MIX	BIN NO.	4	3	2	1	FILLER	TOTAL	OIL %	TOTAL
B	% of Mix	16%	29%	20%	33%	2%	100%	4.75%	
	Batch Weights	1524	2763	1905	3143	190	9525	475	10,000
	Notes:								
C2	% of Mix		32%	28%	38%	2%	100%	5.6%	
	Batch Weights		3020	2597	3630	188	9435	565	10,000
	Notes:								
D2	% of Mix		25%	30%	43%	2%	100%	6.25%	
	Batch Weights		2340	2818	4030	187	9375	625	10,000
	Notes:								
E	% of Mix			45%	53%	2%	100%	6.75%	
	Batch Weights			4200	4938	187	9325	675	10,000
	Notes:								

REMARKS: The batch weights shall be within the specification range and approach the ideal as closely as possible.

Slight adjustments within the specification limits will be permitted when requested by <u>Bureau of Contract Administration personnel</u> only. The nature of the request (i.e. more soup, less soup, finer texture, etc.), reason for the request and the name of the field inspector and/or other Bureau of Contract Administration personnel requesting the adjustment shall be noted in the plant inspector's report.

Form sent to the field shall include the question "Is the mix OK?" The returned form shall be kept in the locker at the plant.

The plant inspector shall receive information concerning the type, use and quantity of material from the dispatcher at time of assignment.

A new form shall be prepared with new batch weights at any time the results of the screen analysis or experience warrants a change.

PLATE 11
See page 139 (2-5.6) and page 150 (2-6.3.13)

JOINT LOCATIONS CURB, GUTTER, WALK AND DRIVEWAY

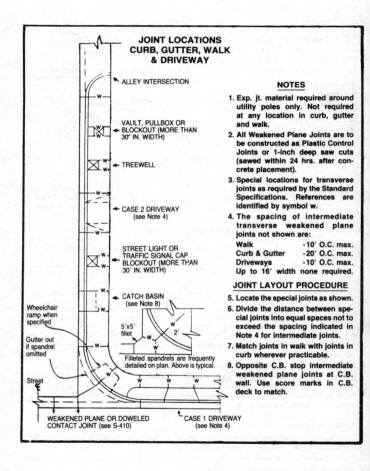

JOINT LOCATIONS CURB, GUTTER, WALK & DRIVEWAY

ALLEY INTERSECTION

VAULT, PULLBOX OR BLOCKOUT (MORE THAN 30" IN. WIDTH)

TREEWELL

CASE 2 DRIVEWAY (see Note 4)

STREET LIGHT OR TRAFFIC SIGNAL CAP BLOCKOUT (MORE THAN 30' IN. WIDTH)

CATCH BASIN (see Note 8)

Wheelchair ramp when specified

Gutter out if spandrel omitted

Street

5'x5' fillet

2'

Filleted spandrels are frequently detailed on plan. Above is typical.

WEAKENED PLANE OR DOWELED CONTACT JOINT (see S-410)

CASE 1 DRIVEWAY (see Note 4)

NOTES

1. Exp. jt. material required around utility poles only. Not required at any location in curb, gutter and walk.
2. All Weakened Plane Joints are to be constructed as Plastic Control Joints or 1-inch deep saw cuts (sawed within 24 hrs. after concrete placement).
3. Special locations for transverse joints as required by the Standard Specifications. References are identified by symbol w.
4. The spacing of intermediate transverse weakened plane joints not shown are:
   Walk — 10' O.C. max.
   Curb & Gutter — 20' O.C. max.
   Driveways — 10' O.C. max.
   Up to 16' width none required.

JOINT LAYOUT PROCEDURE

5. Locate the special joints as shown.
6. Divide the distance between special joints into equal spaces not to exceed the spacing indicated in Note 4 for intermediate joints.
7. Match joints in walk with joints in curb wherever practicable.
8. Opposite C.B. stop intermediate weakened plane joints at C.B. wall. Use score marks in C.B. deck to match.

PLATE 12
See page 303 (3-4.5.6)

INTERFERENCE REPORT

CITY OF ANYWHERE DEPT. OF PUBLIC WORKS		**INTERFERENCE REPORT**		BUREAU OF CONTRACT ADMINISTRATION	

Job Title 9TH ST. STORM DRAIN   **Job No.** W.O. 45782

INTERFERENCE DESCRIPTION

For utility interference, indicate ownership & whether shown on plan or marked on ground. Indicate location or station. If sketch will clarify, show on reverse side.   **Date & Time of Discovery:**

(1) TRAFFIC SIGNAL CONDUIT AT STORM DRAIN LATERAL 3-D NOT SHOWN ON PLAN - NOT MARKED, BROKEN DURING EXCAVATION.

(2) EXISTING STREET LIGHT BASE NOT SHOWN ON PLAN. INTERFERS WITH LATERAL 3-D PLAN LOCATION.

(3) ABANDONED BASEMENT WALL AT PLANNED LOCATION OF 3-D CATCH BASIN.

REPRESENTATIVES AND NOTIFICATIONS

Record of Personnel involved in the Investigation and Solution:

ORGANIZATION	NAME	DATE Notified	DATE On-Site	TIME Notified	TIME On-Site
Design Engineer (4858873)	JOE CABRILLO	5-13-87	5-13-87	0830	1045
Utility Coord. Engineer (485-3891	—				
Change Order Engineer (485-5126)	ROGER CARSON		5-14-87		1300
Utility Co. or Owner's Representative	TRAFFIC SIGNAL REPAIR	5-13-87	5-13-87	0845	1015
Contractor's Representative	JIM BLACK	ONSITE	DURING	OCCURENCE	

EFFECT ON CONSTRUCTION

Indicate time delay, curtailment of operations or extra work required prior to receipt of instructions:

ONE HOUR DELAY — / LABORER + OPERATOR & BACKHOE MOVED TO LATERAL 4-B & RESUMED PRODUCTIVE OPERATIONS.

RESOLUTION

Indicate instructions received and the issuing agency or representative: Date: 5-13-87

CITY TRAFFIC SIGNAL REPAIR CREW RESTORED TRAFFIC SIGNAL SERVICE. CITY STREET LIGHTING CREW REMOVED INTERFERING BASE.
DESIGN ENGINEER AUTHORIZED REMOVAL OF INTERFERING ABANDONED BASEMENT WALL. CHANGE ORDER TO FOLLOW.

Inspector's Name (PRINT) BILL BERK   Inspector's Signature Bill Berk

PLATE 13
See page 71 (1-6.4) and page 327 (3-5.7.5)

STREET LIGHTING EQUIPMENT LIST

City of Anywhere
Dept. of Public Works
Bur. of Contract Admin.

Return for approval to:

BUREAU OF
CONTRACT ADMINISTRATION
CITY HALL, ANYWHERE

STREET LIGHTING EQUIPMENT LIST

Job Title OVERLAND AVENUE – NATIONAL, VENICE	Job. No. W. O. 72680
Contractor POWER ELECTRICAL CONTRACTORS, INC.	Date August 12, 1987

List all electrolier types required by the plans. Show supplier and catalog number for each type listed.

ELECTROLIERS

TYPE	SOURCE	CATALOG NUMBER
CD 953C	Pacific Union Metal Co.	5425C
CD 954	Pacific Union Metal Co.	TC 10203

List the type and light distribution for each luminaire required by the plans. For each type listed, show manufacturer and the catalog number representing the type, size and light distribution specified.

LUMINAIRES

TYPE AND SIZE	LIGHT DISTRIBUTION	MANUFACTURER	CATALOG NUMBER
Multiple 400W	Type II	General Electric	C798G200
Multiple 175W	Type II	General Electric	C760G165
M-40 (3-77)			

PLATE 14
See page 387 (3-9.1)

STANDARD SIZES OF STEEL REINFORCEMENT BARS

STANDARD REINFORCEMENT BARS

Bar Designation Number*	Nominal Weight, lb. per ft.	Nominal Dimensions		
		Diameter, in.	Cross Sectional Area, sq. in.	Perimeter, in.
3	0.376	0.375	0.11	1.178
4	0.668	0.500	0.20	1.571
5	1.043	0.625	0.31	1.963
6	1.502	0.750	0.44	2.356
7	2.044	0.875	0.60	2.749
8	2.670	1.000	0.79	3.142
9	3.400	1.128	1.00	3.544
10	4.303	1.270	1.27	3.990
11	5.313	1.410	1.56	4.430
14	7.65	1.693	2.25	5.32
18	13.60	2.257	4.00	7.09

*The bar numbers are based on the number of $\frac{1}{8}$ inches included in the nominal diameter of the bar.

Type of Steel and ASTM Specification No.	Size Nos. Inclusive	Grade	Tensile Strength Min., psi	Yield (a) Min., psi
Billet Steel A 615	3-11	40	70,000	40,000
	3-11 14, 18	60	90,000	60,000
	11, 14, 18	75	100,000	75,000

PLATE 15 (Page 1)
See page 128 (2-4.8.1)

COMMON TYPES OF STEEL REINFORCEMENT BARS

ASTM specifications for billet steel reinforcing bars (A 615) require identification marks to be rolled into the surface of one side of the bar to denote the producer's mill designation, bar size and type of steel. For Grade 60 and Grade 75 bars, grade marks indicating yield strength must be show. Grade 40 bars show only three marks (no grade mark) in the following order:

1st — Producing Mill (usually an initial)
2nd — Bar Size Number (#3 through #18)
3rd — Type (N for New Billet)

NUMBER SYSTEM — GRADE MARKS

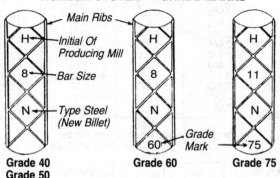

Grade 40
Grade 50   Grade 60   Grade 75

LINE SYSTEM — GRADE MARKS

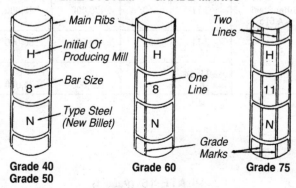

Grade 40
Grade 50   Grade 60   Grade 75

PLATE 15 (Page 2)

WELDED WIRE FABRIC – COMMON STOCK STYLES OF WELDED WIRE FABRIC

Style Designation	Steel Area sq. in. per ft.		Weight Approx. lbs. per 100 sq. ft.
	Longit.	Transv.	
Rolls			
6x6—W1.4xW1.4	.03	.03	21
6x6—W2xW2	.04	.04	29
6x6—W2.9xW2.9	.06	.06	42
6x6—W4xW4	.08	.08	58
4x4—W1.4xW1.4	.04	.04	31
4x4—W2xW2	.06	.06	43
4x4—W2.9xW2.9	.09	.09	62
4x4—W4xW4	.12	.12	86
Sheets			
6x6—W2.9xW2.9	.06	.06	42
6x6—W4xW4	.08	.08	58
6x6—W5.5xW5.5	.11	.11	80
4x4—W4xW4	.12	.12	86

Certain styles of welded wire fabrics as shown in the Table have been recommended by the Wire Reinforcement Institute as common stock styles. Use of these styles is normally based on empirical practice and quick availability rather than on specific steel area designs. Styles of fabric produced to meet other specific steel area requirements are ordered for designated projects, or, in some localities, may be available from inventory.

ASTM SPECIFICATIONS

Welded wire fabric used for concrete reinforcement consists of cold-drawn wire in orthogonal patterns, square or rectangular, resistance welded at all intersections. Welded wire fabric (WWF) is commonly but erroneously called "mesh" which is a much broader term not limited to concrete reinforcement. Welded wire fabric must conform to ASTM A 185 if made of smooth wire or A 497 if made of deformed wire. These Specifications require shear tests on the welds essential to proper anchorage for bond in concrete. ASTM yield strength is 65,000 psi for smooth fabric (A 185) and is 70,000 psi for deformed fabric (A 497).

Unless otherwise specified, welded wire fabric conforming to ASTM A 185 will be furnished.

An example style designation is: WWF 6x12-W16xW8. This designation identifies a style of fabric in which:

Spacing of longitudinal wires	=	6"
Spacing of transverse wires	=	12"
Longitudinal wire size	=	W16
Transverse wire size	=	W8

A deformed fabric style would be designated in the same manner with the appropriate D-number wire sizes.

It is very important to note that the terms "longitudinal" and "transverse" are related to the method of fabric manufacture and have no reference to the position of the wires in a completed concrete structure.

PLATE 15 (page 3)
See page 129 (2-4.8.2)

PROJECT REVIEW — SURFACE IMPROVEMENTS

Bureau of Contract Administration		ROUTING (ORIGINAL COPY) District Supervisor
PROJECT REVIEW — SURFACE IMPROVEMENTS		Chief Const. Division Asst. Director

		Job Title								Job #	

OVERALL PROJECT QUALITY	A. Above Standard	COMPONENT	Curb				Supervisor	
			Gutter					
			Sidewalk				Contractor	
			Driveway					
	B. Standard Acceptability		AC Paving				Sub-Contractors	
			PCC Paving					
			Grading					
	C. Marginal Acceptability		Landscape					
							Final Inspector	
	D. Below Standard		Above Standard ☐ ☐ ☐ Improvement Needed					
			Standard					

	A. CURB			B. GUTTER			C. WALK			D. DRIVEWAY		
1.	Finish		1.	Finish		1.	Finish		1.	Finish		
2.	Align.		2.	Hike-Up		2.	Exp. Jt.		2.	'X'		
3.	Top		3.	Exp. Jts.		3.	Wk. Pl. Jt.		3.	'Y'		
4.	Batter		4.	Wk. Pl. Jt.		4.	Scoring		4.	Joints		
5.	Exp. Jts.		5.	Width		5.	Width		5.	Scoring		
6.	Scoring		6.	Edge		6.	Edges		6.	Width		
7.	Dwy. X		7.	Flow Line		7.			7.			
8.	Returns		8.			**G. OTHER**						
9.	Case IV		**F. AC PAVING**			1.						
10.	Roof Drain		1.	Crown		2.						
11.			2.	"Tee"		3.						
E. GRADING			3.	Texture		4.						
1.	Grade		4.	Transv. Jt.		5.						
2.	Surface		5.	Longtdl. Jt.		6.						
3.			6.	Rolling		7.						
4.			7.	Ride		8.						
5.			8.	Gutter		9.						
6.			9.			10.						

REMARKS:

cc: District Supervisor
Final Inspection Supervisor   Use other side for additional remarks

PLATE 16
See page 528 (4-4.4)

BOLTS IN COMMON USAGE

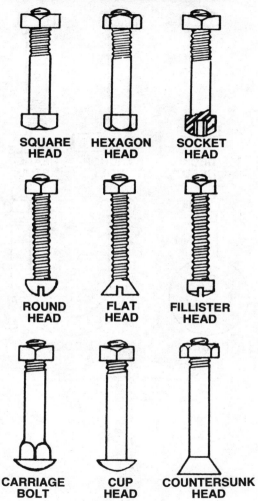

SQUARE HEAD	HEXAGON HEAD	SOCKET HEAD
ROUND HEAD	FLAT HEAD	FILLISTER HEAD
CARRIAGE BOLT	CUP HEAD	COUNTERSUNK HEAD

PLATE 17 (Page 1)
See page 185 (2-8.8) See Plate 54

BOLTS IN COMMON USAGE (Cont.)

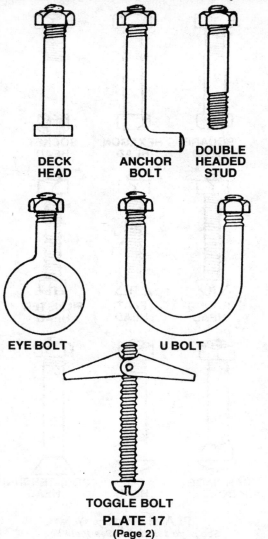

DECK
HEAD

ANCHOR
BOLT

DOUBLE
HEADED
STUD

EYE BOLT

U BOLT

TOGGLE BOLT

PLATE 17
(Page 2)

WIRE AND SHEET METAL GAGES
(In Decimals of an Inch)

Name of Gage	American Wire Gage (A.W.G.) (Corresponds to Brown & Sharpe Gage)	Birmingham Iron Wire Gage (B.W.G.)	United States Standard Gage (U.S.S.G.)	
Principal Use	Electrical Wire & Non-Ferrous Sheet Metal	Iron or Steel Wire	Ferrous Sheet Metal	
Gage No.				Gage No.
00 00000				00 00000
0 00000	.5800			0 00000
00000	.5165	.500		00000
0000	.4600	.454		0000
000	.4096	.425		000
00	.3648	.380		00
0	.3249	.340		0
1	.2893	.300		1
2	.2576	.284		2
3	.2294	.259	23.91	3
4	.2043	.238	.2242	4
5	.1819	.220	.2092	5
6	.1620	.203	.1943	6
7	.1443	.180	.1793	7
8	.1285	.165	.1644	8
9	.1144	.148	.1495	9
10	.1019	.134	.1345	10
11	.0907	.120	.1196	11
12	.0808	.109	.1046	12
13	.0720	.095	.0897	13
14	.0641	.083	.0747	14
15	.0571	.072	.0673	15
16	.0508	.065	.0598	16
17	.0453	.058	.0538	17
18	.0403	.049	.0478	18
19	.0359	.042	.0418	19
20	.0320	.035	.0359	20
21	.0285	.032	.0329	21
22	.0253	.028	.0299	22
23	.0226	.025	.0269	23
24	.0201	.022	.0239	24
25	.0179	.020	.0209	25
26	.0159	.018	.0179	26
27	.0142	.016	.0164	27
28	.0126	.014	.0149	28
29	.0113	.013	.0135	29
30	.0100	.012	.0120	30
31	.0089	.010	.0105	31
32	.0080	.009	.0097	32
33	.0071	.008	.0090	33
34	.0063	.007	.0082	34
35	.0056	.005	.0075	35
36	.0050	.004	.0067	36
37	.0045		.0064	37
38	.0040		.0060	38
39	.0035			39
40	.0031			40

PLATE 18
See page 181 (2-8.9.1)

CONCRETE MIXTURES

ADMIXTURE	PURPOSE	EFFECTS ON CONCRETE	ADVAN-TAGES	DIS-ADVANTAGES
Accelerator	Hasten setting.	Improves cement dispersion and increases early strength.	Permits earlier finishing, form removal, and use of the structure.	Increases shrinkage, decreases sulfate resistance, tends to clog mixing and handling equipment.
Air-Entraining Agent	Increase workability and reduce mixing water.	Reduces segregation, bleeding and increases freeze-thaw resistance. Increases strength.	Increases workability and reduces finishing time.	Excess will reduce strength and increase slump. Bulks concrete volume.
Bonding Agent	Increase bond to old concrete.	Produces a non-dusting, slip resistant finish.	Permits a thin topping without roughening old concrete, self-curing, ready in one day.	Quick setting and susceptible to damage from fats, oils, and solvents.
Densifier	To obtain dense concrete.	Increased workability and strength.	Increases workability and increases waterproofing characteristics, more impermeable.	Care must be used to reduce mixing water in proportion to amount used.
Foaming Agent	Reduce weight.	Increases insulating properties.	Produces a more plastic mix, reduces dead weight loads.	Its use must be very carefully regulated—following instructions explicitly.
Retarder	Retard setting.	Increases control of setting.	Provides more time to work and finish concrete.	Performance varies with cement used—adds to slump. Requires stronger forms.
Water Reducer and Retarder	Increase compressive and flexural strength.	Reduces segregation, bleeding, absorption, shrinkage, and increases cement dispersion.	Easier to place and work, provides better control.	Performance varies with cement. Of no use in cold weather.
Water Reducer, Retarder and Air-Entraining Agent	Increases workability.	Improves cohesiveness. Reduces bleeding and segregation.	Easier to place and work.	Care must be taken to avoid excessive air entrainment.

PLATE 19
See page 103 (2-4.3)

GRADE STAMP GUIDE

INTERPRETING GRADE MARKS

Most grade stamps, except those for rough lumber or heavy timbers, contain five basic elements:

(a) Certification mark of certifying association of lumber manufacturers.

(b) Mill identification. Firm name, brand or assigned mill number.

(c) Grade designation. Grade name, number or abbreviation.

(d) Species identification. Indicates species by individual species or species combination.

(e) Condition of seasoning. Indicates condition of seasoning at time of surfacing:

S-DRY — 19% maximum moisture content
MC-15 — 15% maximum moisture content
S-GRN — Over 19% moisture content (unseasoned)

INSPECTION CERTIFICATE

When an inspection certificate issued by a certifying association is required on a shipment of lumber and specific grade marks are not used, the stock is identified by an imprint of the association mark and the number of the shipping mill or inspector.

CERTIFIED AGENCIES AND TYPICAL GRADE STAMPS

California Lumber Inspection Service
1790 Lincoln Avenue
San Jose, California 95125
(408) 297-8071

MILL 467
CL STAND
IS S-GRN WCLB
® DOUG. FIR

S-GRN
CONST
EASTERN
HEM-TAM

NELMA

Northeastern Lumber Manufacturers Association, Inc.
4 Fundy Road
Falmouth, Maine 04105
(207) 781-2252

PLATE 20 (Page 1)
See page 103 (2-4.3) (Cont. on next page)

CERTIFIED AGENCIES AND TYPICAL GRADE STAMPS
(Continued)

**Northern Hardwood and
Pine Manufacturers
Association, Inc.**
Suite 501, Northern Building
Green Bay, Wisconsin 54301
(414) 432-9161

110 **STUD**
NH&PMA
S-DRY
**BALSAM
FIR**

P.L.I.B.
W-10
CONST
S-GRN
HEM-FIR   WCLB RULES

**Pacific Lumber Inspection
Bureau, Inc.**
1411 Fourth Avenue Building
(Suite 1130)
Seattle, Washington 98101
(206) 622-7327

**Redwood Inspection
Service**
591 Redwood Highway,
Suite 3100
Mill Valley, California 94941
(415) 381-1304

(50)   **F D T N**
S-GRN
REDWOOD   R.I.S.

SPIB®   No. 1
KD 15   (7)

**Southern Pine Inspection
Bureau**
4709 Scenic Highway
Pensacola, Florida 32504
(904) 434-2611

**Timber Products
Inspection**
P.O. Box 919
Conyers, Georgia 30207
(404)922-8000

TP® NO.1 KD-15
000   SYP

MILL 10
WCLB®   **NO. 2**
DOUG FIR   S-DRY

**West Coast Lumber
Inspection Bureau**
Box 23145
Portland, Oregon 97223
(503) 639-0651

**Western Wood Products
Association**
1500 Yeon Building
Portland, Oregon 97204
(503) 224-3930

12
WWP®   **2**   S-DRY

PLATE 20
(Page 2)

CANADIAN GRADE STAMPS

A.F.P.A.® 00

S—P—F

S-DRY STAND

Alberta Forest Products Association
11710 Kingsway Avenue, #204
Edmonton, Alberta T5G OX5, (403) 452-2841

0 · CONST
0 · S GRN
D FIR

Mac Donald Inspection
211 SchoolHouse Street
Coquitlan, B.C. V3K 4X9, (604) 520-3321

C L®A

S-P-F

100

No. 1

S-GRN.

Canadian Lumberman's Association
27 Goulburn Avenue,
Ottawa, Ontario K1N 8C7, (613) 233-6205

Maritime Lumber Bureau
P.O. Box 459, Amherst,
Nova Scotia B4H 4A1, (902) 667-3880

LMA 1 S-GRN 1
1 D FIR (N)

Cariboo Lumber Manufacturers Association
301 Centennial Building
197 Second Avenue North, Williams Lake,
B.C. V2G 1 Z5, (604) 392-7778

O.L.M.A.® O1-1

CONST. S-DRY

SPRUCE - PINE - FIR

Ontario Lumber Manufacture Association
159 Bay Street, Suite 414
Toronto, Ontario M5J 1J7, (416) 367-9717

(FPA® 38

S-P-F S-GRN

CONST

Central Forest Products Association
P.O. Box 1169, Hudson Bay, Saskatcewan
SOE OYO, (306) 865-2595

PIB. NLGA RULE
No 1
00 S-GRN
HEM-FIR-N

Pacific Lumber Inspection Bureau
Suite 1130, 1411 Fourth Avenue Building
Seattle, Washington 98101
B.C. Division: 1460-1055 West Hastings St.
Vancouver, B.C. V6E 2E9, (604) 689-1561

COFI. S-P-F
S-GRN
100 No 1

**Council of Forest Industries
of British Columbia**
1500-1055 West Hastings Street,
Vancouver, B.C. V6E 2H1, (604) 684-0211

ILMA S-DRY 1
00 S-P-F

Interior Lumber Manufacturers Association
203-2350 Hunter Road
Kelowna, B.C. V1 X 6C1, (604) 860-9663

Quebec Lumber Manufactures Association
3555 Boul, Hamel-ouest, Suite 200
Quebec, Canada G2E 2G6, (418) 872-5610

PLATE 20
(Page 3)

GRADE MARKS FOR
PRESSURE TREATED LUMBER

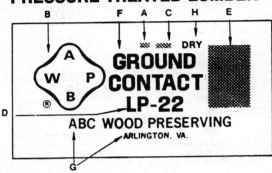

- **A**   Year of treatment
- **B**   American Wood Preservers Bureau trademark or trademark of the AWPB certified agency
- **C**   The preservative used for treatment
- **D**   The applicable American Wood Perservers Bureau quality standard
- **E**   Trademark of the AWPB certified agency
- **F**   Proper exposure conditions
- **G**   Treating company and plant location
- **H**   Dry or KDAT if applicable

Jason Associates, Inc.
Fort Collins, CO 80522

Timber Products
Inspection and
Testing Services
Conyers, GA 30207
Timber Products
Inspection and
Testing Services
Portland, OR 97220

Southwestern Laboratories
Houston, TX 77249

Southern Wood Products
Inspection Company
Pensacola, FL 32504

McCutchan
Inspections, Inc.
Portland, OR 97203

California Lumber
Inspection Services
San Jose, CA 95150

C. M. Rou Service, Inc.
Mobile, AL 36606

Bode Inspection, Inc.
Pake Oswego, OR 97034

PFS Corporation
Madison, WI 53704

Florida Lumber
Inspection Service
Perry, FL 32347

Thurlow Inspection
Sandpoint, ID 83864

PLATE 20
(Page 3)

REDWOOD GRADE MARKS
CALIFORNIA REDWOOD ASSOCIATION

ALL HEARTWOOD	CONSTRUCTION GRADES	MAY CONTAIN SAPWOOD
SELECT HEART — Tight-knotted, heartwood grade with face free of splits or shake. **Sample uses:** decks, posts, garden structures, industrial tanks where decay hazards exist. MILL ONE SEL HT RIS® REDWOOD	**SELECT** — Same general characteristics as Select Heart, but contains sapwood and some imperfections not allowed in Select Heart. **Sample uses:** decking, fence boards and other above ground uses. MILL ONE SEL RIS® REDWOOD	
FOUNDATION GRADE — High quality heartwood grade, specially selected from Construction Heart for durability and resistance to insects. Always grade stamped **Sample uses:** sill plates, crib walls. MILL ONE FDTN RIS® REDWOOD		
CONSTRUCTION HEART — All purpose heartwood grade, contains knots of varying sizes and other slight imperfections. **Sample uses:** decks, posts, retaining walls or other uses on or near soil. MILL ONE CONST HT RIS® REDWOOD	**CONSTRUCTION COMMON** — Versatile grade with same general characteristics as Construction Heart, but contains sapwood. **Sample uses:** decking, railings, and other above ground uses. MILL ONE CONST COM RIS® REDWOOD	
MERCHANTABLE HEART — Economical grade, allows some holes, splits and slightly larger knots than Construction Heart. **Sample uses:** fences, retaining walls, farm uses, structures where decay hazard exists. MILL ONE MERCH HT RIS® REDWOOD	**MERCHANTABLE** — Same general characteristics as Merchantable Heart, but contains sapwood. **Sample uses:** fence boards, railings temporary construction and other above ground uses. MILL ONE MERCH RIS® REDWOOD	

PLATE 21 (Page 1)
See page 199 (2-10.6)

REDWOOD GRADE MARKS
CALIFORNIA REDWOOD ASSOCIATION

ALL HEARTWOOD	FINISH GRADES	MAY CONTAIN SAPWOOD

CLEAR ALL HEART VERTICAL GRAIN — Finest architectural grade, specially selected for grain. Free of defects one face. **Sample uses:** siding, paneling, mill work, processing tanks.

MILL ONE
CLR HT VG RIS®
REDWOOD

CLEAR ALL HEART — Same quality as Clear All Heart Vertical Grain, except contains flat grain pieces. **Sample uses:** siding, trim, fine garden structures, industrial storage.

MILL ONE
CLR HT RIS®
REDWOOD

CLEAR VERTICAL GRAIN — Same general quality as Clear All Heart Vertical Grain, except contains sapwood. **Sample uses:** siding, cabinetry, garden shelters and other above ground uses.

MILL ONE
CLEAR VG RIS®
REDWOOD

CLEAR — Same general quality as Clear All Heart, except contains sapwood. Accepts some imperfections not permitted in Clear All Heart. **Sample uses:** paneling, soffits and other above ground uses.

MILL ONE
CLR RIS®
REDWOOD

B-GRADE — Quality grade, contains sapwood, limited knots and other characteristics not permitted in Clear. **Sample uses:** siding, molding, fascia and other above ground uses.

MILL ONE
B RIS®
REDWOOD

CRA CERTIFIED KILN DRIED CLR RWD RIS®

CRA S-GRN RWD CONST HT RIS®

Redwood Grademarks

Redwood grades are established by the Redwood Inspection Service in the *Standard Specifications for Grades of California Redwood Lumber.* Properly grade-marked lumber will bear the RIS mark or that of another accredited inspection bureau. Grademarks may be on seasoned or unseasoned lumber on face, edge or end of piece. "Certified Kiln Dried" marks lumber kiln dried to accepted standards. CRA trademark is on products of member mills of the California Redwood Association only and is an additional assurance of quality.

PLATE 21
(Page 2)

PLYWOOD – BASIC GRADE MARKS
AMERICAN PLYWOOD ASSOCIATION (APA)

The American Plywood Association's trademarks appear only on products manufactured by APA member mills. The marks signify that the product is manufactured in conformance with APA performance standards and/or U.S. Product Standard PS 1-83 for Construction and Industrial Plywood.

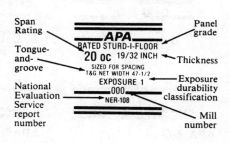

Span Rating

Tongue-and-groove

National Evaluation Service report number

Panel grade

APA
RATED STURD-I-FLOOR
20 OC 19/32 INCH
SIZED FOR SPACING
T&G NET WIDTH 47-1/2
EXPOSURE 1
000
NER-108

Thickness

Exposure durability classification

Mill number

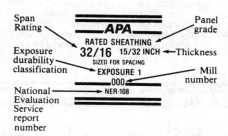

Span Rating

Exposure durability classification

National Evaluation Service report number

Panel grade

APA
RATED SHEATHING
32/16 15/32 INCH
SIZED FOR SPACING
EXPOSURE 1
000
NER-108

Thickness

Mill number

Unsanded and touch-sanded panels, and panels with "B" or better veneer on one side only, usually carry the APA trademark on the panel back. Panels with both sides of "B" or better veneer, or with special overlaid surfaces (such as Medium Density Overlay), carry the APA trademark on the panel edge, like this:

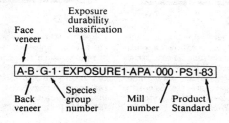

Face veneer

Exposure durability classification

A-B·G-1·EXPOSURE1·APA·000·PS1-83

Back veneer

Species group number

Mill number

Product Standard

PLATE 22 (Page 1)
See page 202 (2-10.9)

PLYWOOD – BASIC GRADE MARKS (Cont.)

APA

B-C   GROUP 1

EXTERIOR

000
PS 1-83

APA

B-D   GROUP 2

INTERIOR

000
PS 1-83

APA B-C

Utility panel for farm service and work buildings, boxcar and truck linings, containers, tanks, agricultural equipment, as a base for exterior coatings and other exterior uses. *Exposure Durability Classification:* Exterior. *Common Thicknesses:* 1/4, 11/32, 3/8, 15/32, 1/2, 19/32, 5/8, 23/32, 3/4.

APA B-D

Utility panel for backing, sides or builtins, industry shelving, slip sheets, separator boards, bins and other interior or protected applications. *Exposure Durability Classifications:* Interior, Exposure 1. *Common Thicknesses:* 1/4, 11/32, 3/8, 15/32, 1/2, 19/32, 5/8, 23/32, 3/4.

APA

A-C   GROUP 1

EXTERIOR

000
PS 1-83

APA

A-D   GROUP 1

EXPOSURE 1

000
PS 1-83

APA A-C

For use where appearance of one side is important in exterior applications such as soffits, fences, structural uses, boxcar and truck linings, farm buildings, tanks, trays, commercial refrigerators, etc. *Exposure Durability Classification:* Exterior. *Common Thicknesses:* 1/4, 11/32, 3/8, 15/32, 1/2, 19/32, 5/8, 23/32, 3/4.

APA A-D

For use where appearance of only one side is important in interior applications, such as paneling, builtins, shelving, partitions, flow racks, etc. *Exposure Durability Classifications:* Interior, Exposure 1. *Common Thicknesses:* 1/4, 11/32, 3/8, 15/32, 1/2, 19/32, 5/8, 23/32, 3/4.

PLATE 22
(Page 2)

PLYWOOD – BASIC GRADE MARKS (Cont.)
SPECIALTY PANELS

HDO · A-A · G-1 · EXT-APA · 000 · PS1-83

Plywood panel manufactured with a hard, semi-opaque resin-fiber overlay on both sides. Extremely abrasion resistant and ideally suited to scores of punishing construction and industrial applications, such as concrete forms, industrial tanks, work surfaces, signs, agricultural bins, exhaust ducts, etc. Also available with skid-resistant screen-grid surface and in Structural I. *Exposure Durability Classification:* Exterior. *Common Thicknesses:* ⅜, ½, ⅝, ¾.

MARINE · A-A · EXT-APA · 000 · PS1-83

Specialty designed plywood panel made only with Douglas fir or western larch, solid jointed cores, and highly restrictive limitations on core gaps and face repairs. Ideal for both hulls and other marine applications. Also available with HDO or MDO faces. *Exposure Durability Classification:* Exterior. *Common Thicknesses:* ¼, ⅜, ½, ⅝, ¾.

```
____APA____
PLYFORM
B-B  CLASS I
EXTERIOR
____000____
PS 1-83
```

APA proprietary concrete form panels designed for high reuse. Sanded both sides and mill-oiled unless otherwise specified. Class I, the strongest, stiffest and more commonly available, is limited to Group 1 faces, Group 1 or 2 crossbands, and Group 1, 2, 3 or 4 inner plies. Class II is limited to Group 1 or 2 faces (Group 3 under certain conditions) and Group 1, 2, 3 or 4 inner plies. Also available in HDO for very smooth concrete finish, in Structural I, and with special overlays. *Exposure Durability Classification:* Exterior. *Common Thicknesses:* 19/32, ⅝, 23/32, ¾.

```
____APA____
M. D. OVERLAY
GROUP 1
EXTERIOR
____000____
PS 1-83
```

Plywood panel manufactured with smooth, opaque, resin-treated fiber overlay providing ideal base for paint on one or both sides. Excellent material choice for shelving, factory work surfaces, paneling, built-ins, signs and numerous other construction and industrial applications. Also available as a 303 Siding with texture-embossed or smooth surface on one side only and Structural I. *Exposure Durability Classification:* Exterior. *Common Thicknesses:* 11/32, ⅜, 15/32, ½, 19/32, ⅝, 23/32, ¾.

PLATE 22
(Page 3)

METHOD FOR LAYING OUT AND SAWING TIMBER

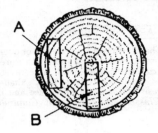

Plank "A" will be flat grained which will wear quickly, sliver easily, have greater shrinkage, and tend to cup or warp.

Plank "B" will be vertically grained which will wear evenly, seldom sliver, and have less shrinkage and tendency to warp.

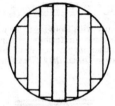

BASTARD SAWING produces variable width planks ranging from vertical to flat grain.

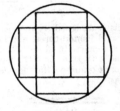

Uniform width and thickness planks are cut by this method, with most having flat grain.

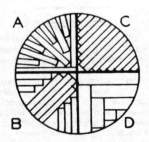

Method "A" produces best quality planks at highest cost and greatest waste.

Method "B" produces high quality planks at lower cost and less waste.

Method "C" costs less with least waste but produces only 1/5 high grade planks.

Method "D" is used to secure large planks and timbers of high quality.

QUARTER SAWING, showing variations. Used to obtain high quality planks.

PLATE 23
See page 201 (2-10.7)

GENERAL INFORMATION ON WELDING

WELDING POSITIONS

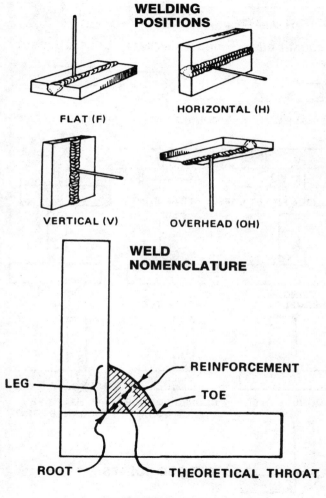

FLAT (F)

HORIZONTAL (H)

VERTICAL (V)

OVERHEAD (OH)

WELD NOMENCLATURE

LEG

REINFORCEMENT

TOE

ROOT

THEORETICAL THROAT

PLATE 24 (Page 1)
See page 193 (2-9.2)

GENERAL INFORMATION ON WELDING

SQUARE BUTT

SINGLE VEE BUTT

DOUBLE VEE BUTT

SINGLE U BUTT

DOUBLE U BUTT

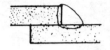

SINGLE FILLET LAP

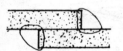

DOUBLE FILLET LAP

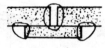

STRAP JOINT

SQUARE TEE

SINGLE BEVEL TEE

DOUBLE BEVEL TEE

SINGLE J TEE

DOUBLE J TEE

CLOSED CORNER (FLUSH) JOINT

HALF OPEN CORNER JOINT

WELDED JOINTS

FULL OPEN CORNER JOINT

PLATE 24
(Page 2)

WELD CHARACTERISTICS

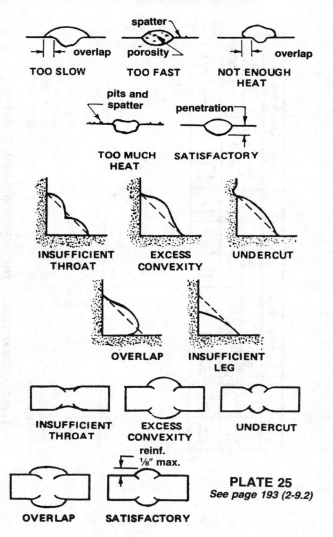

PLATE 25
See page 193 (2-9.2)

WELDING SYMBOLS

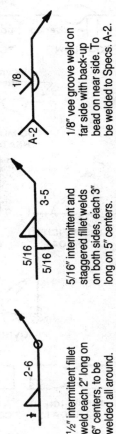

		TYPE OF WELD							SUPPLEMENTARY SYMBOLS				
					GROOVE							CONTOUR	
BEAD	FILLET	PLUG OR SLOT	SQUARE	V	BEVEL	U	J	WELD ALL AROUND	FIELD WELD	FLUSH	CONVEX		

1/2" intermittent fillet weld each 2" long on 6" centers, to be welded all around.

5/16" intermittent and staggered fillet welds on both sides, each 3" long on 5" centers.

1/8" vee groove weld on far side with back-up bead on near side. To be welded to Specs. A-2.

TYPICAL EXAMPLES OF THE USE OF WELDING SYMBOLS

PLATE 26 (Page 1)
See page 194 (2-9.2.5)

WELDING SYMBOLS (Cont.)

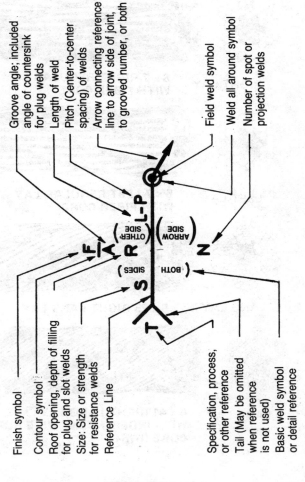

Groove angle; included angle of countersink for plug welds

Length of weld

Pitch (Center-to-center spacing) of welds

Arrow connecting reference line to arrow side of joint, to grooved number, or both

Field weld symbol

Weld all around symbol

Number of spot or projection welds

Finish symbol

Contour symbol

Roof opening, depth of filling for plug and slot welds

Size: Size or strength for resistance welds

Reference Line

Specification, process, or other reference

Tail (May be omitted when reference is not used)

Basic weld symbol or detail reference

PLATE 26
(Page 2)

WIRE ROPE

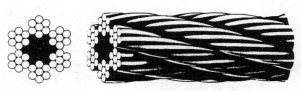

RIGHT LAY   **6 x 7 RIGHT REGULAR LAY
WITH FIBER CORE**

LEFT LAY   **6 x 7 LEFT REGULAR LAY
WITH FIBER CORE**

LANG LAY   **6 x 25 RIGHT LANG LAY**

LANG LAY   **6 x 41 RIGHT LANG LAY
WITH INDEPENDENT WIRE ROPE
CORE (IWRC)**

PLATE 27 (Page 1)
See page 188 (2-8.10)

WIRE ROPE (Cont.)

MEASURING ROPE DIAMETER

RIGHT

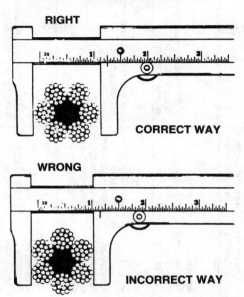

CORRECT WAY

WRONG

INCORRECT WAY

PROPER METHOD FOR ATTACHING WIRE ROPE CLIPS

DEAD END

LIVE END

PLATE 27
Page 2)

SAMPLING SCHEDULE — PLATE 28 (Page 1)
(SEE SUBSECTION 2-1.3 FOR GENERAL SAMPLING AND TESTING INSTRUCTIONS) — SEE PAGE 90

Material	Where Sampled	Sampled By	Frequency of Sampling	Number of Specimens and Size of Sample	REMARKS
ADMIXTURES (CONCRETE)					
Air Entraining Agents	Plant	Lab. or Insp.	As necessary	1 qt. liquid	Dispatchers have available test results for approved lots. Test required before use.
Calcium Chloride	Plant	Lab. or Insp.	Each batch or lot	1 qt. liquid	
Dispersing Agents	Plant	Lab. or Insp.	Each batch or lot	1 qt. liquid	
AGGREGATES					
For Asphalt Paving Mixtures	Plant	Inspector	Daily	Determined by Inspector	Used for determining screen analysis for proportioning.
Lightweight	Job. or Plant	Lab. or Insp.	As necessary	Determined by Lab.	
Rock	Source	Lab.	As necessary	Determined by Lab.	
Sand	Source	Lab.	As necessary	Determined by Lab.	
	Plant	Inspector	As necessary for moisture analysis	Determined by Insp.	
ASPHALT					
Cement	Plant	Inspector	Each material daily	1 pt.	Allow time for adjustments at plant. Avoid sampling first several loads.
Coating (Metal Pipe)	Plant	Lab. or Insp.	As necessary		
Concrete	Plant	Inspector	Composite sample daily	5 lbs. in sack for each mix.	
Emulsified	Plant	Lab. or Insp.	When used for soil stabilization, two to three weeks in advance of use.	1 gallon liquid	
Plastic Cement	Jobsite	Inspector	As necessary	1 qt. liquid	

ASPHALT MIXTURES				
Filler	Plant	Inspector	Once each week	3 lbs. in sack	Take truck sample from top of pile and from opposite sides. Do not sample first several loads to allow time to adjust weights at plant.
Mixes	Plant	Inspector	Daily for each mix laid	5 lbs. in sack for each type mix.	
Stabilized Base Aggregates	Jobsite or source	Lab.	As necessary	Determined by Lab.	Contractor to notify Project Inspector of intention to import materials for use as aggregates.
Mixtures	Jobsite		Each 10,000 sq. ft.	Representative 5 lbs. in sack	
BASE, Untreated for Roadway					See untreated roadway base.
BLOCKS Mortar	Jobsite	Inspector	As necessary	10 blocks	
BOLTS (See Misc. Metal)					
BRICKS	Jobsite	Inspector	As necessary	5 bricks	
CASTINGS Bronze	Source	Inspector	Each melt	4 test coupons to be cast attached to castings	Inspector to be present at time of melt to detach and identify coupons.
Gray Iron	Source	Inspector	Each melt	4 test coupons to be cast separately of castings	Inspector to be present at time of melt to identify coupons.
Steel	Source	Inspector	Each melt	4 test coupons to be cast attached to castings where practicable	Inspector to be present at time of melt to detach and identify coupons, which are to remain attached until annealing or heat treatment.

(Continued on next page)

SAMPLING SCHEDULE — PLATE 28 (Cont., Page 2)

(SEE SUBSECTION 2-1.3 FOR GENERAL SAMPLING AND TESTING INSTRUCTIONS) — SEE PAGE 90

Material	Where Sampled	Sampled By	Frequency of Sampling	Number of Specimens and Size of Sample	REMARKS
CAST IRON Sewer and Storm Drain Fittings	Source When Specified	Sampling Not Normally Required			Certified test by private laboratory when specified; or certificate of compliance.
CEMENT Cement, Portland	Plant	Inspector	Daily	Container furnished by Lab.	Sample to be taken from sacks, bin, silo or other other bulk container. (Sample per ASTM C 150. See Subsection 2-4.2.8.)
Plastic	Plant	Inspector	As necessary	Container furnished by Lab.	Sample per ASTM C 150.
Soil Stabilized Base	Jobsite	Inspector	Daily	One 6"x12" cylinder mold	Cover cylinder mold with paper, etc. and tie on securely.
Waterproof	Jobsite	Inspector	As necessary	Container furnished by Lab.	Sample per ASTM C 150.
CHAIN LINK FENCING Fabric Posts	Jobsite Jobsite	Inspector Inspector	Each lot Each lot	3-ft. square section 1-ft. section.	Test for weight of galvanizing.
COAL TAR COATINGS	Plant	Inspector	Each project	1-ft. square specimen.	Specimen to receive same dipping treatment as the article to be coated.

COMPOUND				
Caulking for Corrugated Metal Pipe	Jobsite	Inspector	As necessary	1 pt.	
Concrete Curing	Jobsite	Inspector	As necessary	1 qt.	
	Source	Lab.	Routine	1 qt.	
Joint Sealing (Concrete)	Jobsite	Inspector	As necessary	1 qt.	
CONCRETE					
Block Masonry	Jobsite	Inspector	As necessary	6 blocks of each size	
Gunite	Jobsite	Inspector	Daily when strength is specified	Two 6"x12" cylinders. Cylinders furnished by contractor.	Cylinders to be made by applying gunite pneumatically in 6" diam. cyl. 12" long, made of wire mesh with 1/4" openings.
Slump Test	Jobsite	Inspector	As necessary	One test, consisting of one slump test and two 6"x12" cylinders (from same sampling).	See strength test.
Strength Test	Jobsite	Inspector	Daily for each class of concrete.		See Subsection 2-4.4.3.
Structural Concrete (3250 psi or more at 28 days)			One test for each 50 cu. yds. or less, up to 100 cu. yds. One additional test for each 100 cu. yds. increment (or fraction thereof) in excess of 100 cu. yds.	One test, consisting of one slump test and two 6"x12" cylinders (from same sampling).	See Subsection 2-4.4.3.
All other classes	Jobsite	Inspector	Daily for each 35 cu. yds. or fraction thereof.	One slump test and one 6"x12" cylinder.	See Subsection 2-4.4.3.

(Continued on next page)

SAMPLING SCHEDULE — PLATE 28 (Cont., Page 3)
(SEE SUBSECTION 2-1.3 FOR GENERAL SAMPLING AND TESTING INSTRUCTIONS) — SEE PAGE 90

Material	Where Sampled	Sampled By	Frequency of Sampling	Number of Specimens and Size of Sample	REMARKS
CONDUIT					
Galvanized	Jobsite	Inspector	As necessary	1-ft. length	Cut from random length of conduit.
Sherardized Steel	Jobsite	Inspector	As necessary	1-ft. length	Cut from random length of conduit.
COUPLINGS (Plain and Sewer Pipe)					
Fiber	Source	Lab.	Prior to use	Determined by Lab.	Engineer to approve prior to use.
Rubber	Source	Lab.	Prior to use	Determined by Lab.	Engineer to approve prior to use.
Stainless Steel Bands	Source	Lab.	Prior to use	Determined by Lab.	Engineer to approve prior to use.
EMULSIFIED ASPHALT (See Asphalt)					
EPOXY (See Resins)					
EXPANSION JOINT FILLER Preformed for Concrete	Jobsite	Inspector	Each 1,000 lin. ft.	One 2-ft. length (Bituminous type) One 3-ft. length (Non-extruding type)	
Redwood	Jobsite	Inspector	Each 1,000 lin. ft.	One 3-ft. length.	

FENCE (See Chain Link)					
GALVANIZING	Plant	Inspector	Each dip, lot or class of coating.	2 coupons, each a minimum of 2.25 in. sq. or 2.54 in. in diameter.	Wire test coupons to top of articles to be galvanized before immersion.
GASKETS Metal (for Sewer Pipe Joints)	Source	Lab.	As necessary	Determined by Lab.	
Neoprene (R.C.P. Joints)	Plant	Inspector	Each lot	3-ft. length	
Rubber (Plain End Pipe)	Source	Lab.	As necessary	Determined by Lab.	
LIME Hydrated	Jobsite	Inspector	As necessary	10 lbs.	
Putty	Jobsite	Inspector	As necessary	10 lbs.	
LINER PLATE Clay	Source	Lab.	Prior to use	Determined by Lab.	Engineer to approve prior to use.
Plastic	Source	Inspector	Each lot	1 sq. ft.	
Plastic Adhesives, Solvents and Activators	Source	Lab. or Insp.	Prior to use	1 pt.	Engineer to approve prior to use.

(Continued on next page)

SAMPLING SCHEDULE — PLATE 28 (Cont., Page 4)
(SEE SUBSECTION 2-1.3 FOR GENERAL SAMPLING AND TESTING INSTRUCTIONS) — SEE PAGE 90

Material	Where Sampled	Sampled By	Frequency of Sampling	Number of Specimens and Size of Sample	REMARKS
LUMBER					
Creosoted	Plant	Inspector	As necessary	As necessary	Bore holes to measure penetration of preservative or check cut ends.
Douglas Fir	Jobsite	Inspector	(Required only under special circumstances)	(Required only under special circumstances)	
Plywood	Jobsite	Inspector	(Required only under special circumstances)	(Required only under special circumstances)	
Redwood	Jobsite	Inspector	(Required only under special circumstances)	(Required only under special circumstances)	
Treated (Chemical Preservative)	Jobsite	Inspector	As necessary	As necessary	Measure penetration of preservative at cut ends or in bored holes.
METAL					
Aluminum Alloys	Plant	Inspector	Each lot	6 sq. in. (or equal)	Coupons to be cast attached to casting where practicable.
Cast Iron (Ni-resist.)	Plant	Inspector	Each heat	2 coupons	
Monel-Metal	Plant	Inspector	Each lot	6 sq. in.	
Stainless Steel	Plant	Inspector	Each lot	6 sq. in.	

MISCELLANEOUS METAL					
Bolts	Jobsite	Inspector	As necessary	2 each size	
Galvanizing (See "Galvanizing" above)					
Grating Bar Assembly	Source	Inspector	As necessary	1-ft. length of bar stock	
Hardware					
Bridge	Jobsite	Inspector	As necessary	As necessary	
Catch Basin	Source	Inspector	As necessary	As necessary	
Manhole	Source	Inspector	As necessary	As necessary	
Rivet Steel	Jobsite	Inspector	Each lot	2 each size	
Sheet Metal	Jobsite	Inspector	As necessary	6 sq. in.	
Stairway Treads	Source	Inspector	As necessary	6 sq. in.	
Tie Rods	Jobsite	Inspector	As necessary	1-ft. length	
Washers	Jobsite	Inspector	As necessary	2 each size	
Welding Rods, Gas	Jobsite or Plant	Inspector	Once each week	2 rods each type being used	
Welding Electrodes	Jobsite or Plant	Inspector	Once each week	2 rods each type being used	
PAINT	Jobsite	Inspector	Each lot	1 qt.	Standard brand paints which have been previously tested and approved by the Laboratory may be used without further testing.

(Continued on next page)

SAMPLING SCHEDULE — PLATE 28 (Cont., Page 5)

(SEE SUBSECTION 2-1.3 FOR GENERAL SAMPLING AND TESTING INSTRUCTIONS) — SEE PAGE 90

Material	Where Sampled	Sampled By	Frequency of Sampling	Number of Specimens and Size of Sample	REMARKS
PILING		(Sampling not normally required)	(Sampling not normally required)		Inspection required during treatment or pre-casting.
PIPE					
Asbestos Cement	Source	Lab.	When requested	Determined by Lab.	Engineer to approve prior to use.
Coupling for Cast Iron	Source	Lab.	When requested	Determined by Lab. Not required where total length of any one size or class of pipe is less than 500 ft.	Engineer to approve prior to use.
Clay	Source	Lab.	Routine	Determined by Lab.	
Concrete	Source	Lab.	Routine	Determined by Lab.	
Corrugated Metal	Source	Lab.	As necessary	Determined by Lab.	
Asphalt Coating for (See "Asphalt Coating for Metal Pipe")					
Joints for (See "Compound, Caulking Corrugated Metal Pipe")					

	Source	Lab. or Insp.	Routine	Spec.	Certificate of compliance from supplier.
Plastic Reinforced Concrete Cast and Spun	Source	Lab.	When requested	1 test for each 50 lengths or fraction materials if req. 3-ft. length Determined by Lab.	
Rubber Gaskets for Rubber Stoppers Stainless Steel Compression Bands	Plant Source	Inspector Lab.	Each lot As necessary	Determined by Lab.	
	Source	Lab.	As necessary	Determined by Lab.	
RESINS (EPOXY)	Jobsite or Plant	Lab. or Insp.	Each lot	1 pt. each of resin and catalyst.	
STEEL Anchor Bolts Pins	Jobsite Plant	Inspector Inspector	Each lot Each project	2 bolts One 6-in. long section. Sample component materials if req.	
Railing	Jobsite	Inspector	See Subsection 201-2.5 Standard Specifications	2 pcs. 3-ft. long (each size)	
Reinforcing	Jobsite	Inspector	Each lot	2 each size	
Rivets Structural and Rivet Steel	Source	Inspector	Each 10 tons of identifiable stock.	2 pcs. 2"x6"	Normally cut from neutral axis of shapes or from waste ends.
Welded Wire Fabric	Jobsite	Inspector	Random from each 3,000 sq. ft.	Two 3-ft. square pieces.	

(Continued on next page)

SAMPLING SCHEDULE — PLATE 28 (Cont., Page 6)
(SEE SUBSECTION 2-1.3 FOR GENERAL SAMPLING AND TESTING INSTRUCTIONS) — SEE PAGE 90

Material	Where Sampled	Sampled By	Frequency of Sampling	Number of Specimens and Size of Sample	REMARKS
STREET LIGHTING SYSTEM COMPONENTS					
Conduit Electrolier	Jobsite	Inspector	As required (Sampling not normally required)	1 pc. 3-ft. long (Sampling not normally required)	
Synthetic Insulation Bare Copper Wire	Jobsite Jobsite	Inspctor Inspector	As necessary Each reel or portion thereof.	1 pc. 3-ft. long 1 pc. 3-ft. long	Not required when reel is tagged and certified.
Cable or Conductor	Jobsite	Inspector	Each reel	1 pc. 3-fl. long	
UNTREATED BASE					
Crushed Aggregate (CAB)	Jobsite or Source	Inspector Lab.	As necessary Routine	50-lb. sack Determined by Lab.	
Crushed Slag (CSB)	Jobsite or Source	Inspector Lab.	As necessary Routine	50-lb. sack Determined by Lab.	
Crushed Miscellaneous (CMB)	Jobsite	Lab. or Insp.	As necessary	50-lb. sack	
Processed Miscellaneous (PMB)	Jobsite	Inspector	As necessary	50-lb. sack	

Material	Location	Inspection	Frequency	Sample	Remarks
Selected Subbase (SSB)	Jobsite		As necessary	25-lb. sack	
WATER-PROOFING MEMBRANE					
Asphalt Plastic Cement	Jobsite	Inspector	As necessary	1 qt. liquid	
Fabric	Jobsite	Inspector	As necessary	3 sq. ft.	
WATERSTOPS (RUBBER)					
G. R. S. (Govt. Rubber Styrene)	Jobsite	Lab. or Insp.	Each lot	1 pc. 3-ft. long	
Neoprene	Jobsite	Lab. or Insp.	Each lot	1 pc. 3-ft. long	
Rubber	Jobsite	Lab. or Insp.	Each lot	1 pc. 3-ft. long	
WIRE AND WIRE RODS					
Barbed	Jobsite	Inspector	Each roll or portion thereof.	1 pc. 3-ft. long	Contractor to furnish to Laboratory the same clamps or attachments to grip wire as used in the work.
Electric Wire and Cable	Jobsite	Inspector	Each reel	1 pc. 3-ft. long	
Prestress	Jobsite	Inspector	As necessary	1 pc. 3-ft. long	
Steel and Iron	Jobsite	Inspector	Each 2-ton. lot or less, each size.	2 pcs. 3-ft. long	

TYPES OF NAILS

COMMON WIRE

CONCRETE

PLASTER BOARD

SMOOTH BOX

SCAFFOLD, (DUPLEX HD)

ROOFING

CASING

SHINGLE

FINISHING

SLATING

BLUED LATH

CUT

Cut Nails. Cut nails are angular-sided, wedge-shaped, with a blunt point.

Wire Nails. Wire nails are round shafted, straight, pointed nails and are used more generally than cut nails. They are stronger than cut nails and do not buckle as easily when driven into hard wood, but usually split wood more easily than cut nails. Wire nails are available in a variety of sizes varying from two penny to sixty penny. (See pages 2 and 3 of this plate).

Nail Finishes. Nails are available with special finishes. Some are galvanized or cadmium plated to resist rust. To increase the resistance to withdrawal, nails are coated with resins or asphalt cement (called cement coated). Nails which are small, sharp-pointed and often placed in the craftsman's mouth (such as lath or plaster board nails) are generally blued and sterilized.

PLATE 29
(Page 1)

COMMON WIRE NAILS (ACTUAL SIZE)

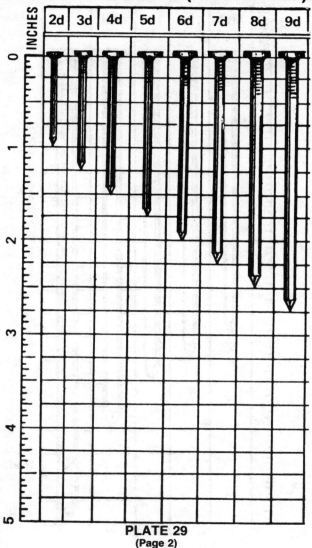

PLATE 29
(Page 2)

COMMON WIRE NAILS (ACTUAL SIZE)

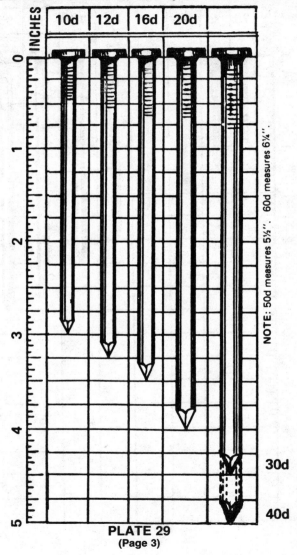

NOTE: 50d measures 5½″. 60d measures 6¼″.

PLATE 29
(Page 3)

SOIL CONSISTENCY TESTS

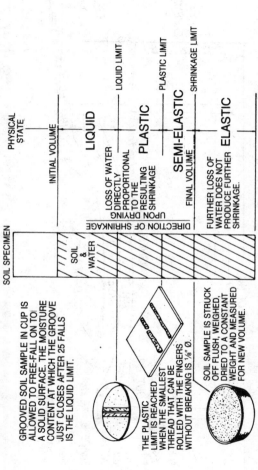

GROOVED SOIL SAMPLE IN CUP IS ALLOWED TO FREE-FALL ON TO A SOLID SURFACE. THE MOISTURE CONTENT AT WHICH THE GROOVE JUST CLOSES AFTER 25 FALLS IS THE LIQUID LIMIT.

THE PLASTIC LIMIT IS REACHED WHEN THE SMALLEST THREAD THAT CAN BE ROLLED WITH THE FINGERS WITHOUT BREAKING IS ⅛" Ø.

SOIL SAMPLE IS STRUCK OFF FLUSH, WEIGHED, DRIED TO A CONSTANT WEIGHT AND MEASURED FOR NEW VOLUME.

PHYSICAL STATE

SOIL SPECIMEN

INITIAL VOLUME

SOIL & WATER

DIRECTION OF SHRINKAGE

LIQUID — LIQUID LIMIT

LOSS OF WATER DIRECTLY PROPORTIONAL TO THE RESULTING SHRINKAGE UPON DRYING

PLASTIC — PLASTIC LIMIT

SEMI-ELASTIC — SHRINKAGE LIMIT

FINAL VOLUME

FURTHER LOSS OF WATER DOES NOT PRODUCE FURTHER SHRINKAGE.

ELASTIC

At some point in the evaporation of a liquid soil-water mix it will no longer flow readily as a liquid. The moisture content at this point is termed — Liquid Limit (LL).

Further evaporation produces a consistency that permits molding. (The plastic stage). It reaches a point upon further drying below which the soil cannot be readily molded. This point is referred to as the Plastic Limit (PL).

As evaporation continues, the mix passes through a semi-elastic stage and reaches a point below which further loss of water does not reduce the soil volume. This point is called the Shrinkage Limit (SL). Below this point the soil is considered to be elastic.

PLATE 30
See page 213 (3-2.1)

STANDARD NOMENCLATURE FOR STREET CONSTRUCTION

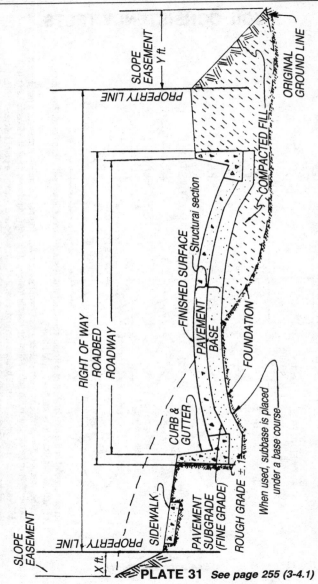

SLOPE EASEMENT — Y ft.

PROPERTY LINE

ORIGINAL GROUND LINE

RIGHT OF WAY

ROADBED

ROADWAY

FINISHED SURFACE

Structural section

PAVEMENT

BASE

FOUNDATION

COMPACTED FILL

CURB & GUTTER

SIDEWALK

SLOPE EASEMENT

PROPERTY LINE

X ft.

PAVEMENT SUBGRADE (FINE GRADE)

ROUGH GRADE ± 1.

When used, subbase is placed under a base course

PLATE 31 *See page 255 (3-4.1)*

CONVERSION FACTORS
ENGLISH TO SI (SYSTEM INTERNATIONAL)

To Convert from	To	Multiply by
LENGTH		
Inches	Millimetres	25.4[a]
Feet	Metres	0.3048[a]
Yards	Metres	0.9144[a]
Miles (statute)	Kilometres	1.609
AREA		
Square inches	Square millimetres	645.2
Square feet	Square metres	0.0929
Square yards	Square metres	0.8361
VOLUME		
Cubic inches	Cubic millimetres	16.387
Cubic feet	Cubic metres	0.02832
Cubic yards	Cubic metres	0.7646
Gallons (U.S. liquid)[b]	Cubic metres[c]	0.003785
Gallons (Canadian liquid)[b]	Cubic metres[c]	0.004546
Ounces (U.S. liquid)[b]	Millilitres[c, d]	29.57
Quarts (U.S. liquid)[b]	Litres[c, d]	0.9464
Gallons (U.S. liquid)[b]	Litres[c]	3.785
FORCE		
Kilograms force	Newtons	9.807
Pounds force	Newtons	4.448
Pounds force	Kilograms force[d]	0.4536
Kips	Newtons	4448
Kips	Kilograms force[d]	453.6
PRESSURE, STRESS, STRENGTH (FORCE PER UNIT AREA)		
Kilograms force per sq. centimetre	Megapascals	0.09807
Pounds force per square inch (psi)	Megapascals	6895
Kips per square inch	Megapascals	6.895
Pounds force per square inch (psi)	Kilograms force per square centimetre[d]	0.07031
Pounds force per square foot	Pascals	47.88
Pounds force per square foot	Kilograms force per square metre[d]	4.882
BENDING MOMENT OR TORQUE		
Inch-pounds force	Metre-kilog. force[d]	0.01152
Inch-pounds force	Newton-metres	0.1130
Foot-pounds force	Metre-kilog. force[d]	0.1383
Foot-pounds force	Newton-metres	1.356
Metre-kilograms force	Newton-metres	9.807
MASS		
Ounce (avoirdupois)	Grams	28.35
Pounds (avoirdupois)	Kilograms	0.4536
Tons (metric)	Kilograms	1000[a]
Tons, short (2000 pounds)	Kilograms	907.2
Tons, short (2000 pounds)	Megagrams[e]	0.9072
MASS PER UNIT VOLUME		
Pounds mass per cubic foot	Kilog. per cubic metre	16.02
Pounds mass per cubic yard	Kilog. per cubic metre	0.5933
Pds. mass per gallon (U.S. liquid)[b]	Kilog. per cubic metre	119.8
Pds. mass p/gal. (Canadian liquid)[b]	Kilog. per cubic metre	99.78
TEMPERATURE		
Degrees Fahrenheit	Degrees Celsius	$tK = (1F - 32)/1.8$
Degrees Fahrenheit	Degrees Kelvin	$tK = (1F + 459.67)/1.8$
Degree Celsius	Degree Kelvin	$tK = 1C + 273.15$

[a] The factor given is exact.
[b] One U.S. gallon equals 0.8327 Canadian gallon.
[c] 1 litre = 1000 millilitres = 10,000 cubic centimetres = 1 cubic decimetre = 0.001 cubic metre.
[d] Metric but not SI unit.
[e] Called "tonne" in England. Called "metric ton" in other metric systems.

PLATE 32 (Page 1)

METRIC CONVERSION TABLE
DECIMAL PART OF A FOOT TO NEAREST .01 FOOT FOR EACH 1/8 INCH

Inch	0	1"	2"	3"	4"	5"	6"	7"	8"	9"	10"	11"
0	0	.08	.17	.25	.33	.42	.50	.58	.67	.75	.83	.92
1/8"	.01	.09	.18	.26	.34	.43	.51	.59	.68	.76	.84	.93
1/4"	.02	.10	.19	.27	.35	.44	.52	.60	.69	.77	.85	.94
3/8"	.03	.11	.20	.28	.36	.45	.53	.61	.70	.78	.86	.95
1/2"	.04	.125	.21	.29	.375	.46	.54	.625	.71	.79	.875	.96
5/8"	.05	.14	.22	.30	.39	.47	.55	.64	.72	.80	.89	.97
3/4"	.06	.15	.23	.31	.40	.48	.56	.65	.73	.81	.90	.98
7/8"	.07	.16	.24	.32	.41	.49	.57	.66	.74	.82	.91	.99

Example: For 6½ inches, refer to 6" column heading. Go down vertically to horizontal line corresponding to ½". Read .54 foot. .54 ft. = 6½".

Since ⅛ of an inch is very close to a hundredth of a foot, mental conversion can be made quickly and easily.

Example: To convert .29 foot to inches: .25 is one-quarter of a foot or 3", .29 is 4 hundredths greater than .25; therefore 3" + 4/8 = 3½ inches or .29 foot = 3½ inches.

PLATE 32
(Page 2)

TYPICAL DESILTING BASIN OUTLET

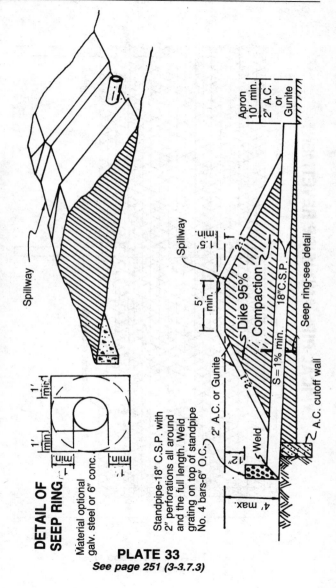

DETAIL OF SEEP RING

Material optional galv. steel or 6" conc.

1' min.

Spillway

Standpipe-18" C.S.P. with 2" perforations all around and the full length. Weld grating on top of standpipe No. 4 bars-6" O.C.

Spillway

Apron 10' min. 2" A.C. or Gunite

Dike 95% Compaction

18" C.S.P.

Seep ring-see detail

A.C. cutoff wall

2" A.C. or Gunite

Weld

S = 1% min.

1.5' min.

5' min.

2:1

2:1

2"

12

4' max.

PLATE 33
See page 251 (3-3.7.3)

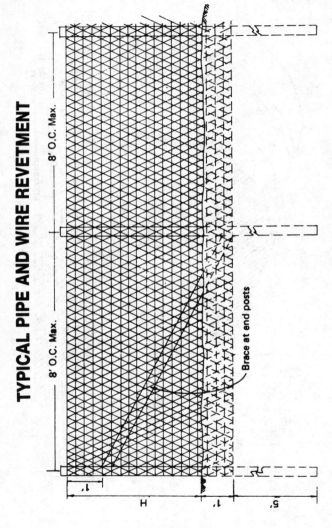

PLATE 34 (Page 1)
See page 251 (3-3.7.3)

TYPICAL PIPE AND WIRE REVETMENT (Cont.)

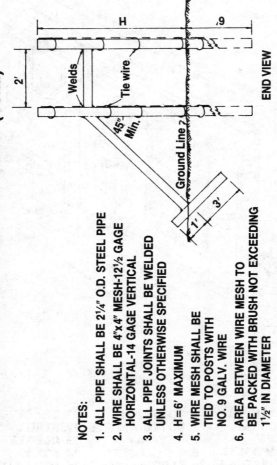

H

.9

2'

Welds

Tie wire

45"
Min.

Ground Line

END VIEW

1'   3'

NOTES:

1. ALL PIPE SHALL BE 2¼" O.D. STEEL PIPE

2. WIRE SHALL BE 4"x4" MESH-12½ GAGE
   HORIZONTAL-14 GAGE VERTICAL

3. ALL PIPE JOINTS SHALL BE WELDED
   UNLESS OTHERWISE SPECIFIED

4. H=6' MAXIMUM

5. WIRE MESH SHALL BE
   TIED TO POSTS WITH
   NO. 9 GALV. WIRE

6. AREA BETWEEN WIRE MESH TO
   BE PACKED WITH BRUSH NOT EXCEEDING
   1½" IN DIAMETER

PLATE 34
(Page 2)

FORM NOMENCLAURE

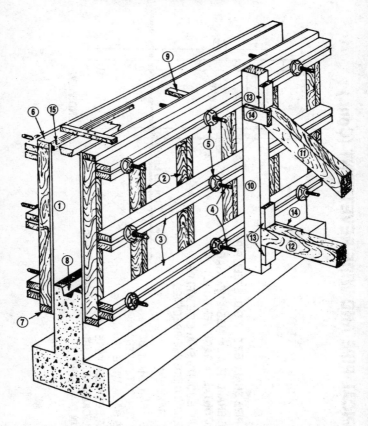

1. SHEATHING	**6. TOP PLATE**	**11. BRACE**
2. STUDS	**7. BOTTOM PLATE**	**12. STRUT**
3. WALES	**8. KEY-WAY**	**13. CLEATS**
4. FORM BOLTS	**9. SPREADER**	**14. SCAB**
5. NUT WASHER	**10. STRONGBACK**	**15. POUR STRIP**

PLATE 35
See page 451 (3-12.4.2) and Plate 56

HAND METHOD FOR SETTING BOTTOM LINE FOR LAYING SMALL DIAMETER PIPE

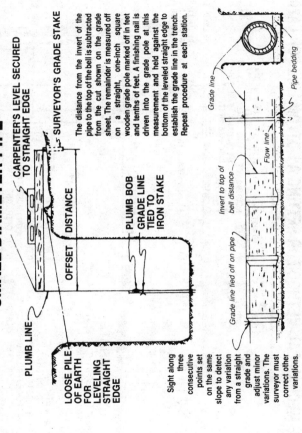

CARPENTER'S LEVEL SECURED TO STRAIGHT EDGE

SURVEYOR'S GRADE STAKE

PLUMB LINE

LOOSE PILE OF EARTH FOR LEVELING STRAIGHT EDGE

OFFSET DISTANCE

PLUMB BOB GRADE LINE TIED TO IRON STAKE

The distance from the invert of the pipe to the top of the bell is subtracted from the cut shown on the grade sheet. The remainder is measured off on a straight, one-inch square wooden grade pole marked off in feet and tenths of feet. A finishing nail is driven into the grade pole at this measurement and held against the bottom of the leveled straight edge to establish the grade line in the trench. Repeat procedure at each station.

Sight along three consecutive points set on the same slope to detect any variation from a straight grade and adjust minor variations. The surveyor must correct other variations.

Grade line tied off on pipe

Invert to top of bell distance

Flow line

Grade line

Pipe bedding

PLATE 36 (Page 1)
See page 328 (3-5.7.6)

ALTERNATE MECHANICAL METHOD FOR SETTING A BOTTOM LINE FOR LAYING PIPE

OFFSET DISTANCE

TAPE READING LINE
LOCK TAPE AT ZERO. ADJUST CHAIN LINKS TO SET PLUMB BOB AT
POINT "A" FOR DIRECT READING OF GRADE SHEET CUTS AT TOP OF BELL
POINT "B" FOR DIRECT READING OF GRADE SHEET CUTS AT FLOW LINE

TAPE LOCKING DEVICE

TELESCOPING TUBE FOR
VARIABLE OFFSETS

CHAIN LINKS, ETC., FOR
ADJUSTING PLUMB BOB
FOR DIFFERENT PIPE
SIZES.

LEVEL LINE

DISTANCE "AB"

POINT "A"

POINT "B"

LEVEL LINE

TOP OF BELL

EQUAL

EQUAL

FLOW LINE

CUT FROM GRADE SHEET

ADJUSTABLE TRIPOD

SPIRIT LEVEL

ANGLE LEG

90°

OFFSET GRADE POINT

TAPE REEL

TO OPERATE

1. ADJUST TELESCOPING TUBE FOR THE PROPER OFFSET DISTANCE.
2. PROJECT TUBE OVER TRENCH.
3. SET ANGLE LEG ON SURVEY POINT AND STABILIZE TRIPOD.
4. LOOSEN TRIPOD SHAFT LOCKING LEVER. ADJUST TUBE FOR LEVEL AND RESET LOCK.
5. LOCK TAPE ON ZERO AT READING LINE.
6. ADJUST PLUMB BOB AS SHOWN ABOVE FOR POINTS "A" OR "B".
7. REEL OUT TAPE TO GRADE SHEET CUT AT READING LINE. LOCK TAPE AT SETTING UNTIL STAKE IS ESTABLISHED IN TRENCH.

IMPORTANT

A NUMBER OF VARIATIONS OF THE BASIC TOOL SHOWN ARE BEING EMPLOYED. THOROUGH UNDERSTANDING OF THE OPERATING CHARACTERISTICS OF THE TOOL ON YOUR PROJECT IS ESSENTIAL FOR THE RECOGNITION OF ERROR AS IT OCCURS.

PLATE 36
(Page 2)

BOTTOM LINE METHOD FOR LAYING LARGE DIAMETER PIPE

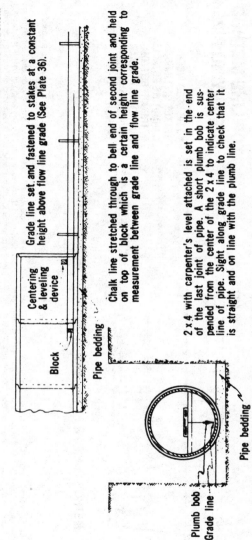

Top of bank

Surveyor's stakes on offset line on bank

NOTE: Use not less than three stakes in trench.

Grade line set and fastened to stakes at a constant height above flow line grade (See Plate 36).

Centering & leveling device

Block

Pipe bedding

Chalk line stretched through to bell end of second joint and held on top of block which is a certain height corresponding to measurement between grade line and flow line grade.

2 x 4 with carpenter's level attached is set in the end of the last joint of pipe. A short plumb bob is suspended from the center of the 2 x 4 to indicate center line of pipe. Sight along grade line to check that it is straight and on line with the plumb line.

Plumb bob
Grade line

Pipe bedding

PLATE 37
See page 328 (3-5.7.6)

TOP LINE METHOD FOR LAYING PIPE

TO BE USED WHEN STAKES OR LINES CANNOT BE ESTABLISHED IN TRENCH BOTTOM, DUE TO WATER, BAD GROUND OR WIDE TRENCH

PLATE 38
See page 328 (3-5.7.6)

METHOD FOR PIPE 24" AND UNDER

A frame, with a horizontal 2 x 8-inch board of sufficient length to span the ditch and extend to offset line, is set perpendicular to the offset line and staked rigidly in place at three or more consecutive stations.

A convenient dimension (shown as A) is established to be used as a constant between top line and flow line grade.

Subtract cuts shown on grade sheet from dimension A and remainder will be distance C to be measured up from bottom of 2 x 8 for setting nail in edge of 1 x 6 upright for top line. This edge of upright must be exactly on center line of pipeline.

Sight along top line for a distance of three or more frames to check for straight grade. Adjust small variations to a straight grade. Surveyor must correct other variations.

FOR 27" AND OVER

Alignment of pipe is set and checked with a plumb bob suspended from the top line and sighting along top of pipe laid.

Grade for pipe sizes 24 inches or less is set and checked with a grade pole. Dimension B (distance from flow line to top of bell) is subtracted from dimension A, and the remainder is measured off on the grade pole. A finishing nail is driven into the grade pole at this measurement and held up against the grade of the tops of the bells of the pipeline. Once set, the grade pole need not be changed unless dimension A or the pipe size is changed.

Grade for pipe sizes 27 inches or larger is established by fastening a shelf bracket to the bottom of the grade pole and measuring from the heel of the bracket the dimension A and driving a finishing nail in the grade pole to set and check flow line grade from the top line as described above.

RECORD OF PILE DRIVING

DEPARTMENT OF PUBLIC WORKS
City of Anywhere

Year _____ 1987 Card No. 2 OF 10
Inspector T.V. Doe

JOB TITLE Vanowen St. (from Coldwater Cyn Ave to Hazeltine Ave) Weight of Hammer 6500 Lbs.

Plan No. D-21821   Type of Pile A-36 H 10 BP 57   Description of Hammer VULCAN #06

Date Driven	Vertical or Batter	Location	Pile No.	Length Below Cut Off	Length Under Ground	Av. Final Drop In Ft. of Hammer	Av. Final Penetration Inches	Safe Bearing Capacity Tons	REMARKS
6-20	V	4-5-5	1	45.5	45.0	3'	.06	114.4	Full Lug 25' fm pile tip
6-20	B	"	2	47.5	47.0	"	.16	70.4	Half " " "
6-23	B	"	3	44.5	44.0	"	.10	91.5	" " " "
6-23	V	"	4	42.0	41.5	"	.10	91.5	Full " 30' " "
6-23	B	"	5	53.0	52.5	"	.12	83.2	Half " " "
6-23	B	"	6	45.5	45.0	"	.15	73.4	" " " "
6-23	V	"	7	46.0	45.5	"	.12	83.2	" " " "
6-23	B	"	8	43.0	42.5	"	.10	91.5	" " 25' "
6-23	B	"	9	43.0	42.5	"	.10	91.5	" " " "

SEE OTHER SIDE FOR SKETCH

PLATE 39 (Page 1)
See page 332 (3-8.8)

RECORD OF PILE DRIVING (Cont.)

To be entered on back of "Record of Pile Driving" form
(see preceding page) as basis for data to be filled in on form.

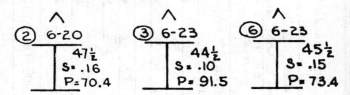

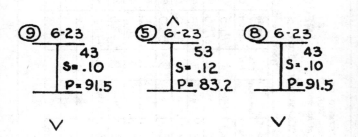

NOTE: CIRCLED NUMBERS SHOW PILE DRIVNG SEQUENCE.

PLATE 39
(Page 2)

RECORD OF PILE DRIVING (Cont.)

DEPARTMENT OF PUBLIC WORKS
City of Anywhere

RECORD OF PILE DRIVING

Year MAY 19 87 Card No. 1
Inspector J.K. Doe
Weight of Hammer 3000 Lbs.
Description of Hammer VULCAN # 02

JOB TITLE Bill Creek Channel at Saticoy St.
Plan No. D-10477 Type of Pile Step Taper (CAST IN PLACE)

Date Driven	Vertical or Batter	Location	Pile No.	Length Below Cut Off	Length Under Ground	Av. Final Drop in Ft. of Hammer	Av. Final Penetration Inches	Safe Bearing Capacity Tons	REMARKS
5/17	V	EAST	E-6	35'	34'	4'	.18	42.5	Piles Listed in
"	"	ABUT.	E-5	34'	33'	4'	.14	50.0	order of driving
"	"		E-4	31'	30'	4'	.18	42.5	
"	"		E-3	31'	30'	4'	.14	50.0	
"	"		E-2	30'	29'	4'	.14	50.0	
"	B		E-7	31'	30'	4'	.18	42.5	
"	"		E-1	30'	29'	4'	.16	46.0	
5/18	V	CENTER PIER	C-12	28'	27'3"	4'	.21	38.5	
"	"		C-13	28'	27'3"	4'	.18	42.5	
"	"		C-14	27'	26'3"	4'	.18	42.5	
"	"		C-15	28'	27'3"	4'	.18	42.5	

SEE OTHER SIDE FOR SKETCH

PLATE 39
(Page 3)

RECORD OF PILE DRIVING (Cont.)

To be entered on back of "Record of Pile Driving" form (see preceding page) as basis for data to be filled in on form.

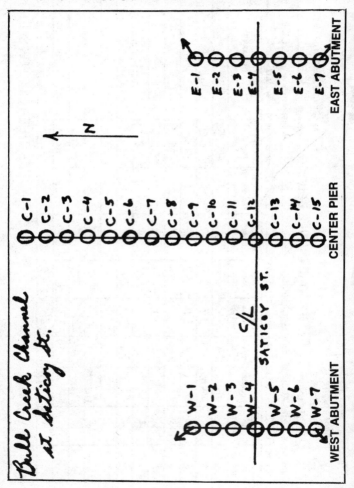

PLATE 39
(Page 4)

PILE CHART

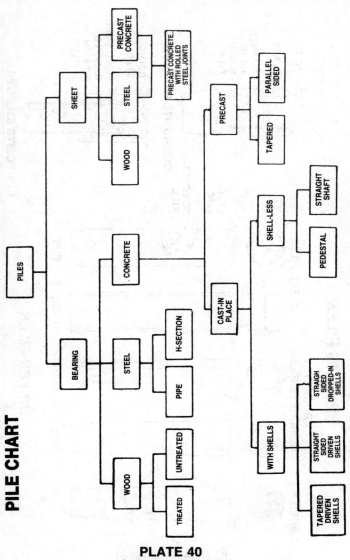

PLATE 40
See page 366 (3-8.1)

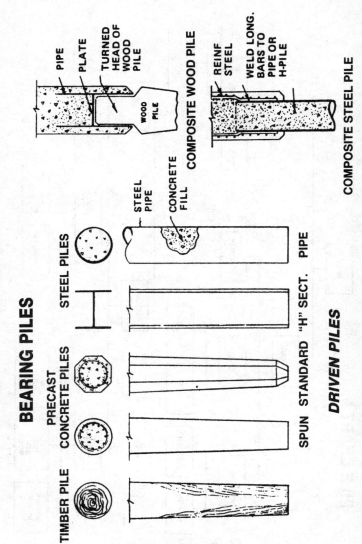

PLATE 41 (Page 1)
See page 366 (3-8.1) and page 370 (3-8.2.5)

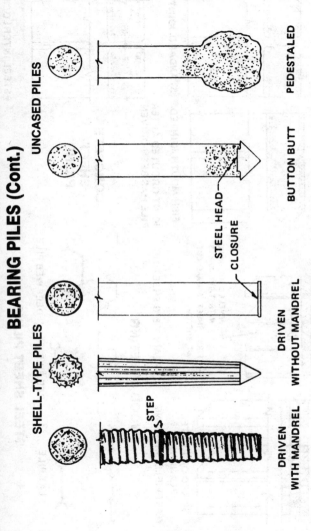

BEARING PILES (Cont.)

UNCASED PILES

PEDESTALED

BUTTON BUTT

STEEL HEAD
CLOSURE

SHELL-TYPE PILES

DRIVEN
WITHOUT MANDREL

STEP

DRIVEN
WITH MANDREL

CAST-IN-PLACE PILES

PLATE 41
(Page 2)

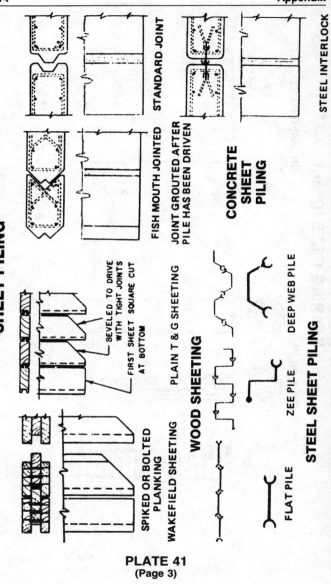

SHEET PILING

STANDARD JOINT

STEEL INTERLOCK

FISH MOUTH JOINTED

JOINT GROUTED AFTER PILE HAS BEEN DRIVEN

CONCRETE SHEET PILING

BEVELED TO DRIVE WITH TIGHT JOINTS

SQUARE CUT

FIRST SHEET CUT AT BOTTOM

PLAIN T & G SHEETING

WOOD SHEETING

SPIKED OR BOLTED PLANKING

WAKEFIELD SHEETING

DEEP WEB PILE

ZEE PILE

FLAT PILE

STEEL SHEET PILING

PLATE 41
(Page 3)

STREET LIGHTING START OF CONSTRUCTION

City of Anywhere Dept. of Public Works Bureau of Contract Administration	STREET LIGHTING CONSTRUCTION START NOTICE	
		Job No. *AC-91848*
Job Title: *Montecito Dr. bet. Griffin Ave.*		Plan No. *P-25058*
& Sinova St.		Tract No. *0*
Street Lighting Contractor: Address: *342 N. Electronics Pl. L.A. 98031*		Telephone: *(213) 406-3872*
Construction of the street lighting portion of the above-mentioned project began on the date shown		Starting Date: *5-4-87*
District Office: *L.A. City Hall*		Telephone: *(213) 485-3002*
Dispatcher: *B. Clark*		

Instructions for Use:

Upon receipt of the first call for inspection of the street lighting portion of the above-mentioned project, the Dispatcher shall complete the information indicated and distribute as follows:

Original: Main Office
    cc: Bureau of Street Lighting
        Electric Utility Street Lighting Engineer
        Job Envelope (via Supervisor)

PLATE 42A
See page 389 (3-9.1)

STANDARD SYMBOLS FOR MARKING CURBS FOR STREET LIGHTING INSTALLATIONS

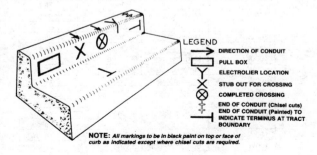

LEGEND

→ DIRECTION OF CONDUIT
▭ PULL BOX
Y ELECTROLIER LOCATION
X STUB OUT FOR CROSSING
⊗ COMPLETED CROSSING
END OF CONDUIT (Chisel cuts)
END OF CONDUIT (Painted) TO INDICATE TERMINUS AT TRACT BOUNDARY

NOTE: *All markings to be in black paint on top or face of curb as indicated except where chisel cuts are required.*

PLATE 42B
See page 389 (3-9.3.1) and page 394 (3-9.6.1)

LAMP SIZE TARGETING COLOR GUIDE

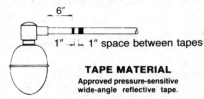

6"

1" →‖← 1" space between tapes

TAPE MATERIAL
Approved pressure-sensitive
wide-angle reflective tape.

LAMP SIZE	LAMP TYPE	TAPE TARGETS		
		NUMBER	WIDTH	COLOR
1000L-6.6A	Incandescent	None		
2500L-6.6A	Incandescent	One	1"	Green
4000L-6.6A	Incandescent	One	1"	Red
4000L15A	Incandescent	Two	1"	Red
6000L6.6A	Incandescent	One	1"	White
6000L-20A	Incandescent	Two	1"	White
10000L-6.6A	Incandescent	One	1"	Blue
		One	1"	White
10000L-20A	Incandescent	One	1"	Blue
15000L-20A	Incandescent	One	1"	Yellow
100W-120V	Incandescent	Two	1"	Green
200W-120V	Incandescent	One	1"	Green
		One	1"	Red
300W-120V	Incandescent	One	1"	Red
		One	1"	White
500W-120V	Incandescent	One	1"	Blue
		One	1"	Yellow
100W	Mercury Vapor	One	½"	Blue
175W	Mercury Vapor	Two	½"	Blue
250W	Mercury Vapor	One	½"	Blue
		One	1"	Blue
400W	Mercury Vapor	Two	1"	Blue
		One	1"	Blue
700W	Mercury Vapor	One	½"	Blue
		One	1"	Blue
1000W	Mercury Vapor	Three	1"	Blue
400W	Metal Halide	Two	1"	White
400W	Sodium Vapor	Two	1"	Yellow
360W	Sodium Vapor	One	1"	Yellow
		One	1"	White
250W	Sodium Vapor	One	½"	Yellow
		One	1"	Yellow
150W	Sodium Vapor	Two	½"	Yellow
100W	Sodium Vapor	One	½"	Yellow

PLATE 43
See page 402 (3-9.7.6)

STEEL REINFORCEMENT FOR REINFORCED CONCRETE PIPE

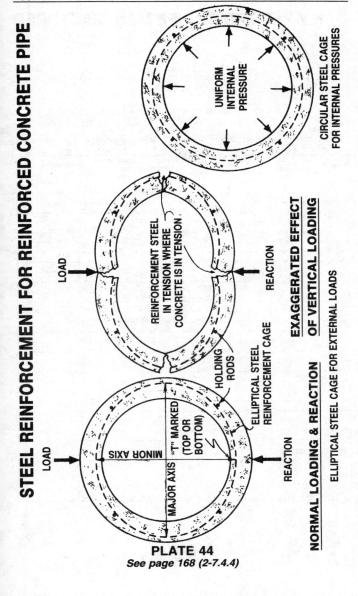

CIRCULAR STEEL CAGE
FOR INTERNAL PRESSURES

UNIFORM INTERNAL PRESSURE

LOAD

REACTION

REINFORCEMENT STEEL IN TENSION WHERE CONCRETE IS IN TENSION.

ELLIPTICAL STEEL REINFORCEMENT CAGE

HOLDING RODS

EXAGGERATED EFFECT OF VERTICAL LOADING
OF EXTERNAL LOADS

LOAD

REACTION

MINOR AXIS

MAJOR AXIS

"T" MARKED (TOP OR BOTTOM)

NORMAL LOADING & REACTION
ELLIPTICAL STEEL CAGE FOR EXTERNAL LOADS

PLATE 44
See page 168 (2-7.4.4)

DAILY RECORD OF PIPE MANUFACTURED

City of Anywhere
Dept. of Public Works
Bureau of Contract Administration

DAILY RECORD OF PIPE MANUFACTURED

JOB NO. AC-51531				JOB TITLE Sycamore Rd. N/o West Channel Rd. Storm Drain			
KIND OF PIPE	**CLASS**	**BATCH NO.**	**D-LOAD**	**SIZE**	**CONTRACTOR**	**PIPE MFG. CO.**
CSRCP	Std.	22B	2000	2T	Lerson	Am. Pipe

DATE	NO. JTS. STRAIGHT	NO. JTS. BEVEL	DESCRIPT. OF BEVEL	PIPE LENGTH	INSPECT. INITIALS	REMARKS	
1-10	3			8'	C.L.J.	1-27-87	
	2			4'	C.L.J.		
		1	HBA	8'	C.L.J.	4	
		1	HBA	8'	C.L.J.	7	
1-11	3			8'	C.L.J.	1-28-87	
		2	HBSA	4'	C.L.J.	1-REJECT 3.5 (EXPOSED STEEL)	
		1	VBA	4'	C.L.J.	1-28-87	1
1-12	1			8'	C.L.J.		
	1			4'	C.L.J.		
		1	VSA	8'	C.L.J.	2	
		1	HBA	4'	C.L.J.	6	
		1	HBSA	4'	C.L.J.	REMAKE	3
			BATCH READY FOR TEST: 1-19-87				
			BATCH TESTED: 1-20-87				
			LAST PIPE STAMPED: 2-14-87				

BEVEL LEGEND:
H – HORIZONTAL
V – VERTICAL
B – BELL
S – SPIGOT
A – ANGLE

PLATE 45
See page 175 (2-7.4.13)

PIPE MANUFACTURING LOG

DATES _12-11-87_ TO*_____   American Pipe
                                   PIPE YARD

F. O.	JOB	LETTER CODE	JOB TITLE	CONTR.	STARTG. DATE	COMPL. DATE
7692	B-2019	RBJZAI	Devonshire St. & Lindley Ave. I.D.	L&M CONST.	12-11-87	12-20-87
7697	81692	HAFFIB	Cabrillo Ave. (Near Miraflores Ave)	TRI-STATE	12-12-87	12-31-87
7739	B-9121	KIAWBA	Quakertown Ave & Redwing St. I.D.	Able Bros.	12-19-87	
7782	22252	BBBCEB	Taxiway K. — L.A. Internat'l Airport	Smith	12-23-87	1-7-88
7821	B-2651	KBFOEA	El Canon Ave & Bessement St. I.D.	Jones & Jackson	1-7-88	

*Date sheet is filled

PLATE 46
See page 175 (2-7.4.13)

GALVANIZING PROCEDURES
— WET GALVANIZING —

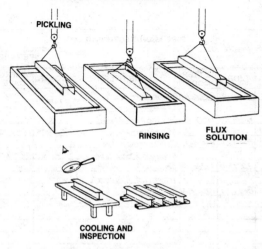

PICKLING

RINSING

FLUX SOLUTION

COOLING AND INSPECTION

— DRY GALVANIZING —

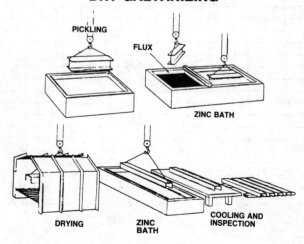

PICKLING

FLUX

ZINC BATH

DRYING

ZINC BATH

COOLING AND INSPECTION

PLATE 47
See page 189 (2-9.1.2)

CONCRETE PROPORTIONING PLANT

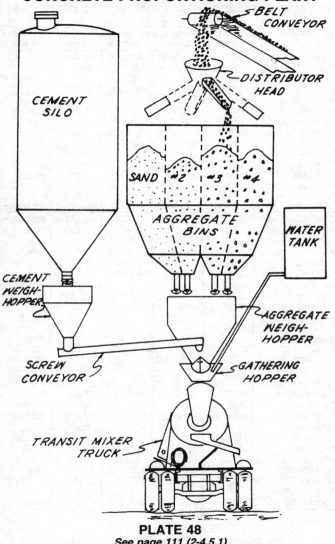

PLATE 48
See page 111 (2-4.5.1)

CONCRETE MIX BATCH WEIGHTS
(REFERENCE NOTES ARE ON PAGE 2 OF PLATE)

Specification Uses	Slurry Backfill	Pipe Bedding, Encasement & Wall Support; Anchors, Thrust Blocks		Tunnel Backfill	Sidehill Drainage Facilities
Specification Class	100-E-100	420-B-2000	420-C-200	480-C-2000	500-C-2500
Supplier ID (Note 2)	100 E	420 B	420 C	480 C	500 C
Cement	100	420	420	480	500
Sand	2334(70)	1261(38)	1377(42)	1348(42)	1348(42)
No. 4 Rock	1000(30)	—	—	—	—
No. 3 Rock	—	1493(45)	1901(58)	1855(58)	1861(58)
No. 2 Rock	—	564(17)	—	—	—
Water, lbs. (gals.)	395(47.4)	305(36.6)	320(38.4)	330(39.6)	310(37.2)
Total Mixture	3829	4043	4018	4009	4029
W/C Ratio	3.95	0.73	0.76	0.69	0.62
Slump, Maximum	5″	4″	4″	5″	3″
Special Notes	—	(Note 3)	(Note 3)	(Note 9)	(Note 9)

Specification Uses	Concrete Pavement	Curb, Integral Pavement, Gutter, Walk; DW & Alley Aprons			
		Standard	Pump Mix	Extruded Curb	Extruded Curb
Specification Class	520-A-2500	520-C-2500	520-C-2500	520-C-2500	520-D-2500
Supplier ID (Note 2)	520 A	520 C	520 PCA	520 CXA	520 DXA
Cement	520	520	520	520	520
Sand	1221(37)	1405(44)	1467(45)	1469(44)	1956(60)
No. 4 Rock	—	—	489(45)	—	1305(40)
No. 3 Rock	1056(32)	1788(56)	1304(40)	1870(56)	—
No. 2 Rock	1023(31)	—	—	—	—
Water (maximum)	290(34.8)	320(38.4)	295(35.4)	265(31.8)	295(35.4)
Total Mixture	4100	4033	4075	4124	4076
W/C Ratio	0.56	0.62	0.62	0.56	0.62
Slump, Maximum	3″	4″	4″	1½″	1½″
Special Notes	—	(Note 5)	(Note 4)	(Note 6)	(Note 6)

Specification Uses	Structural Concrete			Air Place Method 'B'	Pipe Bedding 16 hr. Backfill
	Standard	Standard	Pump Mix		
Specification Class	560-B-3250	560-C-3250	560-C-3250	600-E-3250	660-C-3750
Supplier ID (Note 2)	560 B	560 C	560 PCA	600 E	660 C
Cement	560	560	560	600	660
Sand	1216(38)	1326(42)	1452(45)	2075(70)	1292(42)
No. 4 Rock	—	—	484(15)	889(30)	—
No. 3 Rock	1439(45)	1832(58)	1291(40)	—	1784(58)
No. 2 Rock	544(17)	—	—	—	—
Water lbs. (gals.)	305(36.6)	320(38.4)	295(35.4)	380(45.6)	320(38.4)
Total Mixture	4064	4038	4082	3944	4056
W/C Ratio	0.54	0.57	0.57	0.63	0.48
Slump, Maximum	4″	4″	4″	4″	4″
Special Notes	(Note 7)	(Note 8)	(Note 4)	—	(Note 3)

PLATE 49 (Page 1)
See page 118 (2-4.5.8) and page 122 (2-4.5.11)

CONCRETE MIX BATCH WEIGHTS
SPECIAL NOTES

1. Batch weights are in pounds for one cubic yard, adjusted when necessary to reflect the current screen analysis (% total aggregate and water in gallons are shown in parenthesis). Specification class number represents cement (lbs.) — combined aggregate gradation — 28-day compressive strength (psi).

2. The mix number is the concrete supplier's specific mix design identification for the standard specification class and uses. Some specification classes may have more than one mix design to take care of different placing and handling conditions.

3. For pipe bedding use three pints (1.41 litres) calcium chloride for each 100 pounds (45.5 kilograms) of cement in 420-B or C-2000 for 24-hour backfill and in 660-C-3750 for 16-hour backfill.

*4. Use 3 fl. oz. (89 millilitres) of pozzolith, 300 for each 100# (45.4 kilograms) of cement unless other admixture is approved.

*5. Equivalent special design pump mix or extruded curb mix may be used.

6. Add 3.12 fl. oz. (92 millilitres) of MBVR per C.Y. (0.765 cubic metres) unless other equivalent air entraining agent is approved.

*7. Equivalent special design pump mix may be used when approved by the Engineer. Use 560-C-3250 in thin members 8″ or less in thickness and other locations where reinforcing steel is congested.

8. Equivalent special design pump mix may be used when approved by the Engineer. use 560-B-3250 when placing conditions permit.

9. Use 520 PCA for pump placement.

   *Late model pumps from several manufacturers can pump standard mixes without modification. No special approval is needed in such cases if mix is pumped without exceeding water or slump and there is no change in the aggregate grading. The Inspector should check the pump manufacturer's printed literature for the uses and limitations of particular pumps.

PLATE 49
(Page 2)

METHOD FOR DETERMINING DEPTH FOR HOUSE CONNECTION SEWER TRENCH
(To Avoid Over-Excavation With Backhoe)

1. Employ adequate safety measures.
2. Stretch string line as shown, or by fastening. Dimension "B" must equal Dimension "C."
3. At convenient intervals (10 to 12 feet), measure from string line to surface. Depth of existing wye or tee at main line, less distance from string line to surface, will be depth of trench excavation required at each interval.

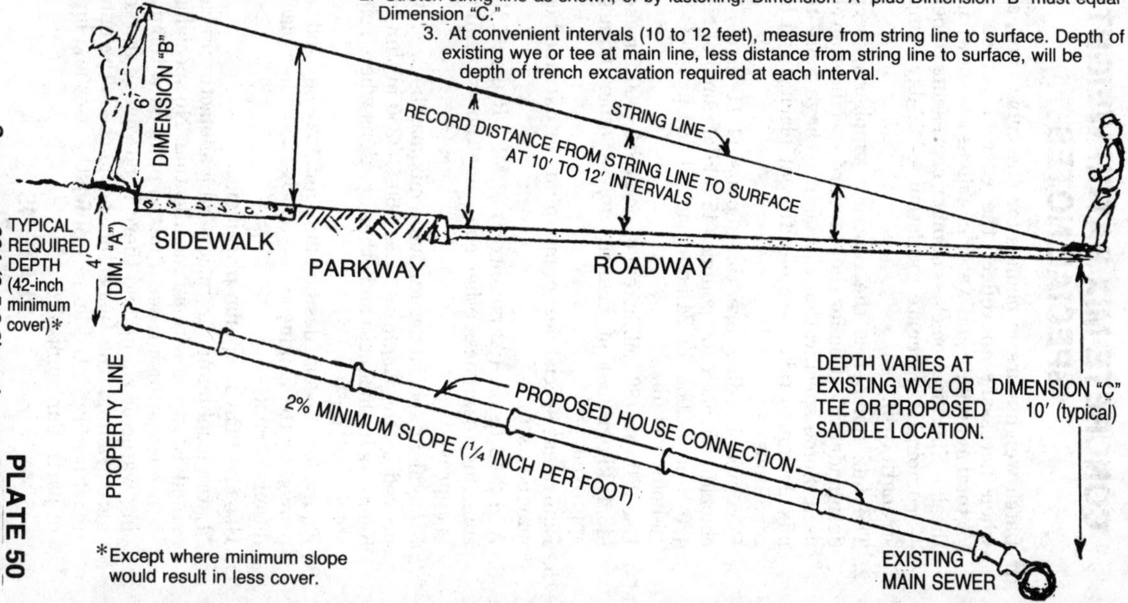

STRING LINE

RECORD DISTANCE FROM STRING LINE TO SURFACE AT 10' TO 12' INTERVALS

ROADWAY

PARKWAY

SIDEWALK

DIMENSION "B" 6'

TYPICAL REQUIRED DEPTH (DIM. "A") 4' (42-inch minimum cover)*

DIMENSION "C" 10' (typical)

DEPTH VARIES AT EXISTING WYE OR TEE OR PROPOSED SADDLE LOCATION.

EXISTING MAIN SEWER

PROPOSED HOUSE CONNECTION

2% MINIMUM SLOPE (1/4 INCH PER FOOT)

PROPERTY LINE

*Except where minimum slope would result in less cover.

PLATE 50
See page 334 (3-5.8.2) and page 358 (3-7.2.2)

LAYING SEWER HOUSE CONNECTIONS

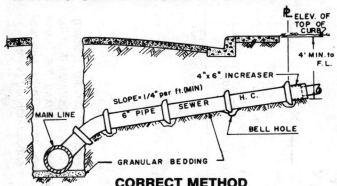

CORRECT METHOD

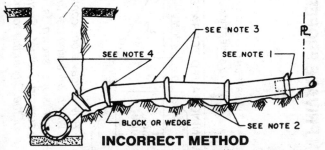

INCORRECT METHOD

INCORRECT METHODS OF LAYING SEWER CONNECTIONS

Note 1. It is not permissible to make a property line connection by telescoping the 4-inch house sewer into the 6-inch sewer lateral. This connection must be made by one of the following methods:

(1) A 4-inch by 6-inch increaser fitting.

(2) A 6-inch wye with 4-inch spur. (6-inch inlet capped).

The bell at the upper end of the sewer lateral shall be no more than 12 inches from the property line.

Note 2. Pipe must not rest upon the bells alone or upon small areas of earth or rock. Supporting pipe with wedges of wood, brick, concrete, etc., is prohibited. The entire length of the barrel of each pipe between bell holes must rest on granular bedding material (natural or imported) shaped to conform to the lower segment of the pipe. Care should be taken to avoid over-excavation during trenching operations. Bell holes should be no larger than necessary.

Note 3. The slope of the pipe line must not change from one pipe to another. All pipe lengths shall be laid to a taut string line on a straight and uniform grade, sloping toward the main line at a minimum grade of ¼-inch per foot.

Note 4. Changes in direction of the pipe must not be accomplished by chipping the spigot end to a bevel or by "pulling" the joints. Spigots shall be centered and firmly seated within each socket.

PLATE 51
See page 333 (3-5.8.2) and page 358 (3-7.2.2)

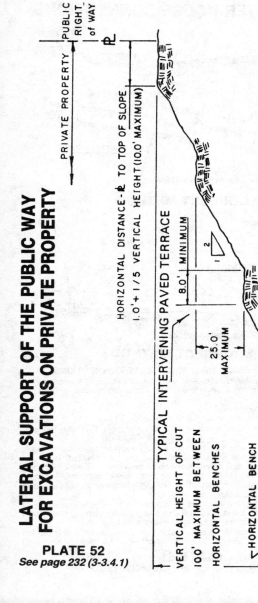

LATERAL SUPPORT OF THE PUBLIC WAY FOR EXCAVATIONS ON PRIVATE PROPERTY

PRIVATE PROPERTY | PUBLIC RIGHT of WAY

HORIZONTAL DISTANCE - ℄ TO TOP OF SLOPE
1.0' + 1/5 VERTICAL HEIGHT (10.0' MAXIMUM)

TYPICAL INTERVENING PAVED TERRACE

8.0' MINIMUM

25.0' MAXIMUM

2 / 1

VERTICAL HEIGHT OF CUT
100' MAXIMUM BETWEEN
HORIZONTAL BENCHES

HORIZONTAL BENCH

30.0' MINIMUM

Any excavation contemplated on private property which will be nearer to the public right-of-way than the cut slope shown is deemed to imperil the lateral support thereof. Such cases require prior approval of the City in the form of a special deposit permit.

PLATE 52
See page 232 (3-3.4.1)

TRAFFIC SIGNAL COMPLETION NOTICE

| City of Anywhere | Bureau of Contract Administration | Dept. of Public Works |

TRAFFIC SIGNAL COMPLETION NOTICE

To: DEPARTMENT OF TRAFFIC (Attention: Anywhere Traffic Signal Superintendent)
City Hall, City of Anywhere

Project Title or Location	Project No.
	Plan No.

Construction of the traffic signal portion of this project has been completed by:

Name of contractor doing work	Phone No.
Address	

Description of traffic signal work done on Class "A" or Excavation Permit and repair of damage on contract construction:

□ Work consists of new construction or relocation.

□ Work authorized by permit for repair only (involves **no** change in location of conduit or signals).

□ Work consists of repair to damage on contract construction as authorized by Traffic Engineer.

□ Work consists of a load change on a non-metered service.
Date & time   (AM)
of change: _____ (PM)

BUREAU OF CONTRACT ADMINISTRATON

□ Work consists of changing from a metered to a non-metered service.
Date & time   (AM)
of change: _____ (PM)

By _____

Date Tested	Date Completed	"As-Built" Plan Required by Contract	[ ] Yes [ ] No

NOTICE OF RECEIPT OF "AS-BUILT" PLAN OF TRAFFIC SIGNAL CONSTRUCTION

To: BUREAU OF CONTRACT ADMINISTRATION
City Hall, City of Anywhere
Attn.: Final Inspection Group   Date _____

An "As-Built" plan for the traffic signal portion of this project.

CITY TRAFFIC ENGINEER

□ has been received.
□ is not required.   By _____

Distribution: Original and first carbon copy to Main Office.
Second carbon copy — insert in job envelope or attach to permit.

PLATE 53
See page 392 (3-9.5.2)

HIGH STRENGTH BOLTS
TIGHTENING PROCEDURES

EQUIPMENT AND POWER

Installation equipment in good working order is vital to proper tightening of high-strength bolts in structural connections. The type of wrench to be used is not designated in the *Specifications for Structural Joints Using ASTM A 325 or A 490 Bolts* as published by the Research Council. However, three methods of tightening are recommended by the Council Specification:

1. *Calibrated Wrench Tightening* requiring the use of a torque-controlled wrench that cuts off when a pre-set torque is reached.

2. *Turn-of-Nut Tightening* which can be accomplished with either a hand wrench or a standard impact wrench.

3. *Tightening by use of a Direct Tension Indicator* which requires use of any device allowing accurate direct measurement of bolts tension, such as the load indicator washer.

Bolts installed with a load indicator washer are tightened with a standard impact wrench.

The usual source of power is compressed air. There must be an adequate pressure at the tool — an absolute minimum of 100 psi for bolts ⅞″ diameter and smaller. For larger bolts, pressure must be higher. Hose lines should be adequate for the number and size of wrenches used.

CALIBRATION

Whether bolts are installed by the calibrated wrench method or by the turn-of-nut method, the use of a calibrating device to check out tools and equipment and to provide a means of reliable inspection is essential.

FIG. 1 — The bolt-tension calibrator is a hydraulic load cell which measures bolt tension created by tightening. As the bolt or nut is turned, the internal bolt tension or clamping force is transmitted through the hydraulic fluid to a pressure gauge which indicates bolt tension directly in pounds. The dial of the gauge may be marked to show the required minimum tension for each bolt diameter. (See Bolt Tension Table as published in the current Research Council Specifications.)

PLATE 54 (Page 1)
See page 185 (2-8.8)

HIGH STRENGTH BOLTS (Cont.)

When torque-control wrenches are used, they must be calibrated at least once each working day by tightening not less than three bolts of each diameter from the bolts to be installed. The average torque determined by this calibration procedure may then be used to pre-set the cut-off device built into torque-control wrench. The torque-control device must be set to provide a bolt tension 5 to 10 percent in excess of the minimum bolt tension. The bolt-tension calibrator is also necessary to calibrate the hand-indicator torque wrenches used by inspectors for checking torque as a measure of tension after tightening by either the calibrated wrench method or the turn-of-nut method.

PROPER TIGHTENING PROCEDURE

Regardless of the method used to tighten high-strength structural bolts, the sequence of operations is basically similar. Accordingly, we show below the step-by-step procedure for tightening a simulated beam-to-girder connection by the turn-of-nut method, using 1-in. diameter A325 bolts. For clarity, the beam is omitted and only the clip angles which had been previously bolted to the girder web are shown.

FIG. 2—First, holes are "faired up" with enough drift pins to maintain dimensions and plumbness. Next, sufficient high-strength bolts of the proper grade and size are installed to hold the connection in place. Only hand tightening is required at this point. Since these bolts will remain in place as permanent fasteners, washers, if required, should be installed with the bolts during fitting-up.

FIG. 3—The balance of the holes are now filled with bolts and assembled with nuts and washers. Note the gap between the angles which will be drawn together during the "snugging" operation. In a true connection, this gap would be filled by the beam web. However, it may be considered representative of "difficult" fitting-up conditions.

PLATE 54
(Page 2)

HIGH STRENGTH BOLTS (Cont.)

FIG. 4 — The bolting crew starts to "snug" the bolts and nuts. ("Snug" is defined as the point at which the wrench begins to impact solidly.) Note that the "snug" condition creates sufficient tension to draw the top half of the angles tightly together while the bottom half still remains open because those bolts are only "hand tight."

FIG. 5 — The crew completes "snugging" the entire connection. As a result, the gap between the angles has entirely disappeared.

FIG. 6 — Now the drift pins are knocked out and the remaining holes filled with bolts and torqued up to "snug." The connection is now ready for final tightening.

FIG. 7 — In this view, the bolts have been numbered to show the suggested tightening sequence. Bolts and nuts should always be tightened progressively *away from the fixed or rigid points to the free edges*.

PLATE 54
(Page 3)

HIGH STRENGTH BOLTS (Cont.)

FIG. 8 — Here, the wrench operator is just starting final tightening of Bolt No. 2 to the required half-turn beyond "snug" condition. (See Nut Rotation Council Specifications.) In final tightening, a hand wrench is used to hold the end *not* being torqued to insure that the true required turn measurement is not lost.

FIG. 9 — Here, the operator has completed the half-turn on Bolt No. 12, as shown by the twin *double* lines on the wrench socket located 90 degrees apart. Notice in Fig. 8 (showing the beginning of a required half-turn) that there are twin *single* lines 90 degrees apart. These socket markings enable the operator to easily measure nut rotation.

FIG. 10 — This is a close-up of a nut after final tightening. Close examination will disclose slight burrs or peening marks near the edge of each nut "flat." These marks are caused by the "hammering" action of the wrench as it impacts. If A 325 nuts show no such markings, a thorough inspection should be made to insure that the bolts were properly tightened. Nuts furnished with A 490 bolts may not show any distortion because of their greater hardness. However, a slight burnishing of the edges should be evident.

LOAD INDICATOR WASHER

The Bethlehem LOAD INDICATOR WASHER (LIW) is a hardened flat circular washer with protrusions on one face. In use, the LIW is placed on the bolt with the protrusions bearing against a hardened surface of the bolt-nut assembly, usually the underside of the bolt head (Figure 1). As the bolt is tightened the protrusions are flattened and the gap reduced (Figure 2).

PLATE 54
(Page 4)

HIGH STRENGTH BOLTS (Cont.)

While tightening, be
sure the bolt head
does not spin on the
load indicator pro-
trusions. At a speci-
fied average gap,
measured by feeler
gauge as in Figure 3,
the induced bolt ten-

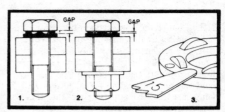

sion will not be less than the minimum required by various standards. If connection details require placing the LIW at the nut
end, or if the fastener must be tightened from the end where the
LIW is located, a supplemental hardened flat washer must be
used against the protrusions. The maximum gaps between load
indicator washer and bolt head (or hardened flat washer) after
tightening are shown in Table 1. Table 2 shows the induced bolt
tensions which correspond to these gaps. The LIW is available
for both A 325 and A 490 bolts, in two distinct configurations.

INSPECTION AND VERIFICATION

Inspection is accomplished by checking the *average* gap of
the LIW bolt assembly with a metal feeler gauge (Figure 3.
Two important rules for inspection should be emphasized:

1. Inspection should be based upon the *average* gap because the bolt will never be perfectly centered in the LIW,
therefore, the protrusions will not collapse uniformally.

2. The feeler gauge is used as a "no go" inspection tool;
that is, if the gauge does not enter the gap (but a gap is evident)
the installation is considered satisfactory.

TABLE 1—Load Indicator Gaps to Give Required Minimum Bolt Tension		
Load Indicator Fitting		
	A 325	A 490
Under Bolt Head		
Black Finish Bolts	0.015 in.	0.015 in.
Under Nut with Hardened Flat Washer		
Black Finish	0.010 in.	0.010 in.
With the gaps shown above, required minimum bolt tensions will be induced as given in Table 2.		

TABLE 2 Minimum Bolt Tensions		
In thousands of pounds (Kips)		
Bolt Dia. (in.)	A 325	A 490
$\frac{1}{2}$	12	—
$\frac{5}{8}$	19	—
$\frac{3}{4}$	28	35
$\frac{7}{8}$	39	49
1	51	64
$1\frac{1}{8}$	56	80
$1\frac{1}{4}$	71	102

PLATE 54
(Page 5)

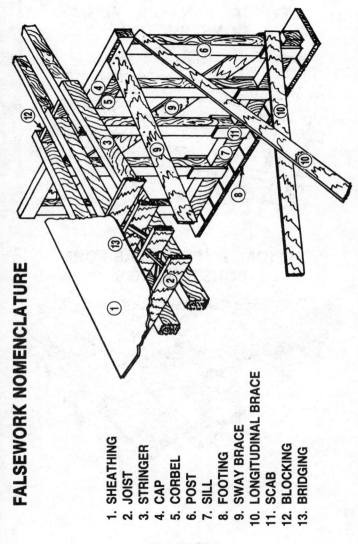

FALSEWORK NOMENCLATURE

1. SHEATHING
2. JOIST
3. STRINGER
4. CAP
5. CORBEL
6. POST
7. SILL
8. FOOTING
9. SWAY BRACE
10. LONGITUDINAL BRACE
11. SCAB
12. BLOCKING
13. BRIDGING

PLATE 56
See page 449 (3-12.4.1)

TYPICAL PAN-JOIST FORM CONSTRUCTION

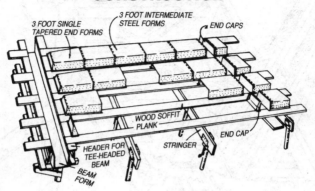

3 FOOT SINGLE TAPERED END FORMS
3 FOOT INTERMEDIATE STEEL FORMS
END CAPS
WOOD SOFFIT PLANK
END CAP
STRINGER
HEADER FOR TEE-HEADED BEAM
BEAM FORM

TYPICAL WAFFLE SLAB FORM CONSTRUCTION

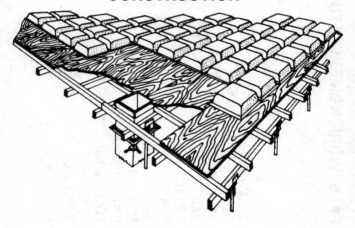

PLATE 57 (Page 1)
See page 449 (3-12.4)

TYPICAL FORM DETAILS

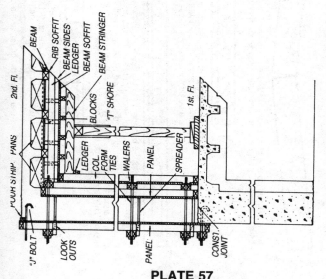

TYPICAL BEAM AND RIB CONSTRUCTION DETAIL

SECTION THROUGH AN EXTERIOR WALL

PLATE 57
(Page 2)

PRINCIPLES OF REINFORCED CONCRETE BEAMS

In the above figure, a plain beam has broken as a result of a load applied at the center. The break first occurs at the bottom, concrete being weak in tension.

The addition of rebar, strong in tension, resists such a break. When such a simply reinforced concrete beam is loaded until it begins to break, cracks appear due to a combination of tension and vertical shear. This stress is known as diagonal tension.

Cracking is best resisted by rebars at right angles to the cracks. This is impractical since it would require very complicated placing of rebar. The compromise then is to let some of the longitudinal bars be straight and these will be at right angles to the cracks near the center. Other bars are bent (called double bent or truss bars) to resist cracks towards the ends and approximate a right angle to the direction of cracks.

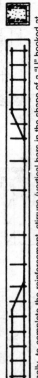

Finally, to complete the reinforcement, stirrups (vertical bars in the shape of a "U" hooked at their upper ends) are added to resist diagonal tension and to firmly anchor the longitudinal steel to the compressed part of the beam. These stirrups are called web reinforcement. In most cases it is not necessary to use web reinforcement for the entire length of the beam, shear being maximum at the supports and decreasing toward the center.

PLATE 58
See page 458 (3-12.5)

CONCRETE REINFORCING STEEL BASIC DETAILS

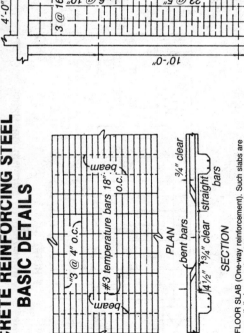

FLOOR SLAB (One-way reinforcement). Such slabs are essentially beams, the width of which is very large. Note the bent bars to provide for the reversal of tension from the lower to the upper portion of the slab over the supporting beams.

FLOOR SLAB (Two-way reinforcement). When floor panels are square or nearly so, two-way reinforcement is often used. Such slabs derive their support from the four edges. Another type of construction known as "flat slab" (not shown here) omits beams and girders and the slab derives its support from the columns only.

PLATE 59 (Page 1)
See page 458 (3-12.5)

CONCRETE REINFORCING STEEL BASIC DETAILS (Cont.)

TYPICAL REINFORCING STEEL DETAILS FOR A CONTINUOUS BEAM

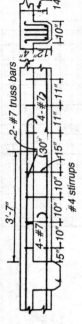

PLATE 59
(Page 2)

For openings of substantial size, details of the rebar placement will normally be shown on the drawings. This is not ordinarily done for openings of moderate size. Rebar should not be interrupted where it is practical to place the rebar as shown for opening "A." Where it is not practical, equivalent rebar for length of the span is added on either side of the opening as shown at "B." Some additional transverse rebar is used to transfer the load to adjacent spanning rebar.

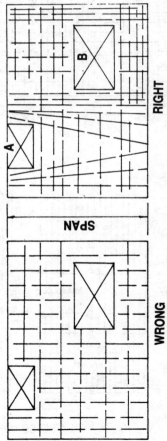

WRONG

RIGHT

REINFORCING AROUND OPENINGS IN SLABS

APPLICATIONS FOR CONDUCTORS USED FOR GENERAL WIRING

	AMBIENT TEMPERATURE						Dry	Dry or Wet	FEATURES
	60°C 140°F	75°C 167°F	85°C 185°F	90°C 194°F	110°C 230°F	200°C 392°F			
R	X						X		Code Rubber
RH		X					X		Heat Resistant
RHH			X				X		More Heat Resistant
RW	X							X	Moisture Resistant
RH-RW	X							X	Moisture and Heat Resistant
		X					X		Moisture and Heat Resistant
RHW		X						X	Moisture and Heat Resistant
RU	X						X		Latex Rubber
RUH		X					X		Heat Resistant
RUW	X							X	Moisture Resistant
T	X						X		Thermoplastic
TW	X							X	Moisture Resistant
THHN				X			X		Heat Resistant
THW		X						X	Moisture and Heat Resistant
THWN		X						X	Moisture and Heat Resistant
MI			X					X	Mineral Insulated Metal Sheathed
V		X					X		Varnished Cambric
AVA					X		X		With Asbestos
AVB			X				X		With Asbestos
AVL					X			X	With Asbestos

This table does not include special condition conductors, thickness of conductor insulation, or reference to all outer protective coverings.

GENERAL CLASSIFICATION OF INSULATIONS:

A .... Asbestos

H .... Heat Resistant

MI .... Mineral Insulation

R .... Rubber

RU ....Latex Rubber

V ....Varnished Cambric

T ....Thermoplastic

W ....(Water) Moisture Resistant

PLATE 60
See page 185 (2-8.9.1)

ASPHALT PLANT INSPECTOR'S DAILY REPORT

CITY OF ANYWHERE

Department of Public Works   **ASPHALT PLANT INSPECTOR'S DAILY REPORT**   **Bureau of Contract Administration**

Job Title **BALBOA BL. & STAGG ST.**

Job No. **AC-71422**

Date **9-9-87**   Sand — Material Source **CON ROCK**   Plant Name **INDUSTRIAL**

Spec. No. **1986**   Rock — **" "**   Plant Location **SUN VALLEY**

Type of Material **I-C AR 8000**   Filler **BAGHOUSE**   Contractor **PDQ PAVERS**

Total Tons **754.00**   L.A. **GULF**   Field Insp. **J. J. JOHNSON**

Plant Insp. **R. W. BELL**   Hrs. **8**   Scale Insp.   Hrs.

SCREEN ANALYSIS

	No. 4 Bin	No. 3 Bin	No. 2 Bin	No. 1 Bin	Filler	Total Agg.	A.C.
% of Mix		28	31	39	2	100%	5 2 %
Wt. in Lbs.		2650	2930	3700	200	9480	520
% Passing						Mix %	Ideal 100%
1½ Inch	100	100	100	100	100		
1"		100	100	100	100		
¾"		100	100	100	100		
½"		96	100	100	100	99	95-100
⅜"		52	100	100	100	87	72-88
No. 4		1	54	100	100	58	46-60
No. 8			2	92	100	39	28-42
No. 30				43	100	19	15-27
No. 50				23	100	11	10-20
No. 200		1.75 x 5 =		8.75	80	5	4-7

ASPHALT		Notes:
	Plant Sample Tank No.	
	Certificate or B.L. No.	
	Certified Viscosity	
	Truck Mix Sample Load No.	

PLATE 61
See page 161 (2-6.6)

STATEMENT OF (PARTIAL) COMPLETION

CITY OF ANYWHERE
U.S.A.
DEPARTMENT OF PUBLIC WORKS

(Rubber stamp reading "PARTIAL" is applied as needed.)

STATEMENT OF (PARTIAL) COMPLETION

Date: 1-20-87

Project Title and No.
Orange Drive and Rose Avenue Improvement District
B-1240

That portion of the above entitled improvement described below has been completed:

Main line sewer and laterals from Sta. 0+00 to 9+50
per Plan D-14226, except for resetting manholes to
grade following street paving.

Acceptance of the improvement by the City will follow upon completion of any remaining work and necessary administrative processing.

City Engineer

Inspector in Charge

By: *M.W. Baker*

By: *L.D. Fisher*

DISTRIBUTION:

PLATE 62
See page 527 (4-4.3)

STREET LIGHTING CONSTRUCTION
RECORD OF REQUEST

STREET LIGHTING CONSTRUCTION RECORD OF REQUEST		
Job Title: Montecito Dr bet. Griffin Ave & Sinova St.		Job No. AC-91848
City of Anywhere		Plan No. P-25058
Bureau of Contract Administration		Supervisor: L.R. Brown

CONTRACTOR REQUEST — INSPECTOR APPROVAL

This is a request for (designate and refer to note)
- ☐ Electrical Utility (See note #1)
- ☐ Electrical Service
- ☒ Burn Test (See note #2) ☐ Maintenance Consent Agreement (reverse side)
- ☐ Tie-in or extension to existing circuit (See note #3)

Anticipated date of Readiness (Burn Test, ~~Tie-in, Extension~~ Scheduled) 10-6-87	Change Orders (Related to Services) #4

Circuit or Locations

Circuits 1, 2, & 3

Contractor: Spark Installers, Inc.	Telephone: 406-3872
Mailing Address: 342 N. Electronics Pl. L.A. 98031	

Requested by *Jack Jones*   Approved by *John Smith*

Street Lighting Contractor
Authorized Representative

Project Street
Lighting Inspector

NOTES

1. The contractor's service equipment must be installed complete in accordance with the project plans and related change orders including pullbox and specified disconnect device (fuses not installed): conduit installed to the service point (either conduit run up the pole for overhead service or conduit run to service location for underground service. Show locations or circuits and related change orders.

2. The Electric Utility's electrical service to supply energy must be completed prior to requesting burn date. On the anticipated date of readiness, all wiring and related circuit work must be complete, ready to be energized. The City will schedule the burn test on the day indicated or as soon thereafter as is practical. Show locations or circuits and anticipated date of readiness. Maintenance agreement requirements on reverse side.

3. On the anticipated date of readiness all wiring and related work must be complete, ready to be energized. Show locations or circuits and anticipated date of readiness.

DISPATCHER RECORD OF SCHEDULING & NOTIFICATION

DISPATCHERS LOG		NOTIFICATIONS & SCHEDULING
Date: 9-24-87	Remarks: Hess notified	☐ EU Notified for Service
9-30-87	Gonzalez (D.W. & P) Scheduled Burn Date	☒ Burn Test Scheduled
10-1-87	Supervisor, Contractor & Inspector notified	☐ Tie-in, Extension Scheduled
Dispatcher: *S. Clark* Telephone: 485-3002		Scheduled Date & Time 10-15-87 10:00 A.M.

Distribution from field:	Distribution from Dispatcher:
First three copies - Dispatcher	1st copy - Dispatchers file
Fourth copy - Job Envelope	2nd copy - Electric Utility
	3rd copy - Contractor

PLATE 65 (Page 1)
See page 405 (3-9.9.1

STREET LIGHTING CONSTRUCTION
RECORD OF REQUEST

STREET LIGHTING SYSTEM MAINTENANCE CONSENT AGREEMENT

Consent is hereby given to operate and maintain the portion of the street lighting system improvement described by the circuits or locations entered on the reverse side of this form, prior to the confirmation of assessments or acceptance of the project.

The City agrees to assume operation, maintenance and protection of the system, as described.

1. The electrolier standards and all electrical components in the circuit have been installed complete with the standards plumb, concrete caps installed, and luminaires oriented and set with the required light distribution.

2. The burn test has been completed satisfactorily (high potential test on series circuits and three night operational test on all circuits).

It is expressly understood that this agreement is for the purpose of protecting the contractor from damage by third parties and does not constitute acceptance of the work which is contingent on the completion of any remaining work and the correction of any deficiencies discovered at final inspection including any corrections or deficiencies associated with requirements (1) and (2) above.

```
_____                    _____
  Street Lighting Contractor                          Date
  Authorized Representative


*By: _____                    _____
  Bureau of Contract Administration                   Date
```

*Dispatcher sign, date and forward to Bureau of Street Lighting on date acceptable for maintenance in accordance with Items 1 and 2.

PLATE 65
(Page 2)

DAILY REPORT FOR
COST PLUS CHANGES

DEPT. OF PUBLIC WORKS
City of Anywhere
Bureau of Engineering

DAILY REPORT
FOR
COST PLUS CHANGES

IDENTIFY FINAL REPORT COMPLETING WORK / FINAL / SERIAL # ≠ 1

Sheet ___ of 2 Sheets

Date 3-22-87

APPROVALS

Jack Smith
Superviso

W. R. Moore
Bureau of Contract Administration

W. R. Moore
Bureau of Engineering

Job Title WALTON & JORDAN I.D.

Job No. W.O. 30677

Change Order Serial No. 3

This invoice is an itemized statement of all claims made upon the City of Anywhere by the Contractor for materials, equipment and services furnished under authority of the above designed Change Order.

REVISE CONST CO.
Contractor

By *John Recon*

INSTRUCTIONS FOR PREPARATION AND PROCESSING OF INVOICE:

The allowable copies are set forth in the applicable sections of the specifications to which the Contractor is referred. Costs must be shown and subtotaled separately for the several classifications involved, such as "Labor," "Materials" and "Equipment". These classifications must be ITEMIZED. Labor costs are to be shown for each day that work is done, with names, labor classifications, wage rates and hours of the person involved. Equipment costs are to be likewise itemized, showing each piece, hours worked, rates and total cost for each day. Materials costs need not be shown on a daily basis but quantities, until prices, where applicable, and total costs of all items must be given. Vendors' bills to the contractor or other substantiating date for equipment and materials costs may be required and will expedite checking and approval of Contractor's invoice. The Bureau of Contract Administration will be responsible for maintaining accurate records of checking and verifying the Contractor's invoices with respect to hours of labor and equipment, quantities of materials and all other facts determinable in the field and affecting the actual cost of work performed.

The Contractor shall submit two signed copies of the invoice to the Project Engineer, who will indicate his approval thereon. The Bureau of Contract Administration will then transmit both approved copies of the Bureau of Engineering for Final approval and issuance of reconciling change orders. The Bureau of Engineering, after approval, will return one copy of the invoice to the Bureau of Contract Administration.

DATE	ITEM OR LABOR BREAKDOWN	QUANTITY OF TIME	UNIT COST	AMOUNT
3-22-87	LABORERS			
	J.H. KING (GUINEA CHASER)	8 HRS		
	GEO BROWN (GEN. CONST.)	8 HRS		
	OPERATORS		(GRADER	
	H.D. NELSON	5 HRS	OPERATOR	
	FOREMAN			
	GEO LAKE	4 HRS		
	EQUIPMENT		(BARE,	
	1 - GRADER - CAT 112	5 HRS	ON-SITE EQUIP.)	
	MATERIAL			
	CRUSHED AGGREG BASE	160 Tons		

PLATE 66 (Page 1)
See page 43 (1-3.8.2)

DAILY REPORT FOR
COST PLUS CHANGES (Cont.)

DEPT. OF PUBLIC WORKS City of Anywhere Bureau of Engineering	**DAILY REPORT** **FOR** **COST PLUS CHANGES**	

Sheet 2 of 2 Sheets

Date 3-22-87

Job Title WALTON & JORDAN I.D.

APPROVALS _Jack Smith_ 19_____
Project Manager
W. R. Moore
Bureau of Contract Administration

Supervisor

Bureau of Engineering

Job No. W. O. 30677

Change Order Serial No. 3

This invoice is an itemized statement of all claims made upon the City of Anywhere by the Contractor for materials, equipment and services furnished under authority of the above designed Change Order.

REVISE CONST CO.
Contractor

By _John Recon_

INSTRUCTIONS FOR PREPARATION AND PROCESSING OF INVOICE:

The allowable copies are set forth in the applicable sections of the specifications to which the Contractor is referred. Costs must be shown and subtotaled separately for the several classifications involved, such as "Labor," "Materials" and "Equipment". These classifications must be ITEMIZED. Labor costs are to be shown for each day that work is done, with names, labor classifications, wage rates and hours of the person involved. Equipment costs are to be likewise itemized, showing each piece, hours worked, rates and total cost for each day. Materials costs need not be shown on a daily basis but quantities, until prices, where applicable, and total costs of all items must be given. Vendors' bills to the contractor or other substantiating date for equipment and materials costs may be required and will expedite checking and approval of Contractor's invoice. The Bureau of Contract Administration will be responsible for maintaining accurate records of checking and verifying the Contractor's invoices with respect to hours of labor and equipment, quantities of materials and all other facts determinable in the field and affecting the actual cost of work performed.

The Contractor shall submit two signed copies of the invoice to the Project Engineer, who will indicate his approval thereon. The Bureau of Contract Administration will then transmit both approved copies of the Bureau of Engineering for Final approval and issuance of reconciling change orders. The Bureau of Engineering, after approval, will return one copy of the invoice to the Bureau of Contract Administration.

DATE	ITEM OR LABOR BREAKDOWN	QUANTITY OF TIME	UNIT COST	AMOUNT
	SUB CONTRACTOR — SPARK ELECTRIC			
	ELECTRICIANS			
	CARL HOTLINE	8 HRS		
	JACK PIFER	8 HRS		
	EQUIPMENT			
	1- PICK UP TRUCK	8 HRS		
	MATERIAL			
	CONDUIT - 1½" ⌀ GALV STEEL	40 L.F.		
	WIRE - #6 THW	250 L.F.		
	PULL BOX - CONC TYPE 2	ONE		

PLATE 66
(Page 2)

INVOICE FOR
COST PLUS CHANGES

DEPT. OF PUBLIC WORKS City of Anywhere Bureau of Engineering	**I N V O I C E** **FOR** **COST PLUS CHANGES**	Sheet __1__ of __5__ Sheets

APPROVALS

Date __August 31, 1987__

_____ 19____
Project Inspector

_____ 19____
Bureau of Contract Administration

_____ 19____
Bureau of Engineering

Job Title __Arthur Street and 2nd Avenue__
__Improvement District__

Job No. __WO-56099__

Change Order Serial No. __7__

This invoice is an itemized statement of all claims made upon the City
of Anywhere by the Contractor for materials, equipment and services
furnished under authority of the above designed Change Order.

_____
Contractor

By _____

INSTRUCTIONS FOR PREPARATION AND PROCESSING OF INVOICE:

The allowable copies are set forth in the applicable sections of the specifications to which the Contractor is referred. Costs must be shown and subtotaled separately for the several classifications involved, such as "Labor," "Materials" and "Equipment". These classifications must be ITEMIZED. Labor costs are to be shown for each day that work is done, with names, labor classifications, wage rates and hours of the person involved. Equipment costs are to be likewise itemized, showing each piece, hours worked, rates and total cost for each day. Materials costs need not be shown on a daily basis but quantities, until prices, where applicable, and total costs of all items must be given. Vendors' bills to the contractor or other substantiating date for equipment and materials costs may be required and will expedite checking and approval of Contractor's invoice. The Bureau of Contract Administration will be responsible for maintaining accurate records of checking and verifying the Contractor's invoices with respect to hours of labor and equipment, quantities of materials and all other facts determinable in the field and affecting the actual cost of work performed.

The Contractor shall submit two signed copies of the invoice to the Project Engineer, who will indicate his approval thereon. The Bureau of Contract Administration will then transmit both approved copies of the Bureau of Engineering for Final approval and issuance of reconciling change orders. The Bureau of Engineering, after approval, will return one copy of the invoice to the Bureau of Contract Administration.

DATE	ITEM OR LABOR BREAKDOWN	QUANTITY OF TIME	UNIT COST	AMOUNT
8–23	Laborers:			
	John Jones (guinea chaser)	8	$5.93	$47.44
	Mill Brown (fine grader)	8	5.95	47.60
	J. H. King (pipe layer)	8	6.16	49.28
	Pat Murphy	8	5.84	46.72
	Pedro Montoya	4	5.84	23.36
	S. A. Goldberg	4	5.84	23.36
	S. O. Hess (foreman)	8	6.50	52.00
	Carpenters:			
	F. G. Smith	8	7.60	60.80
	Homer Bean	4	7.60	30.40
	F. N. Harper (foreman)	8	8.00	64.00
	Reinf. Steel Workers:			
	H. O. Nelson	8	9.36	74.88
8/24	Cement Finishers:			
	Carl Sunburg (power float)	8	7.70	61.60
		Total	Labor	$581.44

PLATE 67 (Page 1)
See page 43 (1-3.8.2)

INVOICE FOR
COST PLUS CHANGES (Cont.)

DEPT. OF PUBLIC WORKS
City of Anywhere
Bureau of Engineering

INVOICE
FOR
COST PLUS CHANGES

Sheet __2__ of __5__ Sheets

Date __August 31, 1987__

Job Title __Arthur Street and 2nd Avenue__
__Improvement District__

Job No. __WO-56099__

Change Order Serial No. __7__

APPROVALS

_____ 19___
Project Inspector

_____ 19___
Bureau of Contract Administration

_____ 19___
Bureau of Engineering

This invoice is an itemized statement of all claims made upon the City of Anywhere by the Contractor for materials, equipment and services furnished under authority of the above designed Change Order.

By _____

Contractor

INSTRUCTIONS FOR PREPARATION AND PROCESSING OF INVOICE:

The allowable copies are set forth in the applicable sections of the specifications to which the Contractor is referred. Costs must be shown and subtotaled separately for the several classifications involved, such as "Labor," "Materials" and "Equipment". These classifications must be ITEMIZED. Labor costs are to be shown for each day that work is done, with names, labor classifications, wage rates and hours of the person involved. Equipment costs are to be likewise itemized, showing each piece, hours worked, rates and total cost for each day. Materials costs need not be shown on a daily basis but quantities, until prices, where applicable, and total costs of all items must be given. Vendors' bills to the contractor or other substantiating date for equipment and materials costs may be required and will expedite checking and approval of Contractor's invoice. The Bureau of Contract Administration will be responsible for maintaining accurate records of checking and verifying the Contractor's invoices with respect to hours of labor and equipment, quantities of materials and all other facts determinable in the field and affecting the actual cost of work performed.

The Contractor shall submit two signed copies of the invoice to the Project Engineer, who will indicate his approval thereon. The Bureau of Contract Administration will then transmit both approved copies of the Bureau of Engineering for Final approval and issuance of reconciling change orders. The Bureau of Engineering, after approval, will return one copy of the invoice to the Bureau of Contract Administration.

DATE	ITEM OR LABOR BREAKDOWN	QUANTITY OF TIME	UNIT COST	AMOUNT
8-23	Material:			
	2" x 6" Construction Grade Lumber	2M	160.00	320.00
	1" x 8" " " "	3.56 M	160.00	569.60
	2" x 4" " " "	0.80 M	160.00	128.00
	#5 reinf. steel (stock) grade 60	600 lbs.	0.10	60.00
	#8 " " (fabricated) grade 60	400 "	0.15	60.00
	Nails	30 "	.25	7.50
	6" C.I. sewer pipe (rubber gasket, Class 150)	60 ft.	3.50	210.00
	8" V. C. Pipe	240 "	1.50	360.00
8-24	Concrete (5.5-C-2500)	18 c.y.	13.00	234.00
		Total		1,949.10
	Less Lumber Salvage (Est.)			150.00
		Total Material		1,799.10

PLATE 67
(Page 2)

INVOICE FOR
COST PLUS CHANGES (Cont.)

DEPT. OF PUBLIC WORKS
City of Anywhere
Bureau of Engineering

INVOICE
FOR
COST PLUS CHANGES

Sheet ___3___ of ___5___ Sheets

Date __August 31, 1987__

Job Title __Arthur Street and 2nd Avenue__
__Improvement District__

Job No. __WO-56099__

Change Order Serial No. ___7___

APPROVALS

_____ 19____
Project Inspector

_____ 19____
Bureau of Contract Administration

_____ 19____
Bureau of Engineering

This invoice is an itemized statement of all claims made upon the City of Anywhere by the Contractor for materials, equipment and services furnished under authority of the above designed Change Order.

By _____
Contractor

INSTRUCTIONS FOR PREPARATION AND PROCESSING OF INVOICE:

The allowable copies are set forth in the applicable sections of the specifications to which the Contractor is referred. Costs must be shown and subtotaled separately for the several classifications involved, such as "Labor," "Materials" and "Equipment". These classifications must be ITEMIZED. Labor costs are to be shown for each day that work is done, with names, labor classifications, wage rates and hours of the person involved. Equipment costs are to be likewise itemized, showing each piece, hours worked, rates and total cost for each day. Materials costs need not be shown on a daily basis but quantities, until prices, where applicable, and total costs of all items must be given. Vendors' bills to the contractor or other substantiating date for equipment and materials costs may be required and will expedite checking and approval of Contractor's invoice. The Bureau of Contract Administration will be responsible for maintaining accurate records of checking and verifying the Contractor's invoices with respect to hours of labor and equipment, quantities of materials and all other facts determinable in the field and affecting the actual cost of work performed.

The Contractor shall submit two signed copies of the invoice to the Project Engineer, who will indicate his approval thereon. The Bureau of Contract Administration will then transmit both approved copies of the Bureau of Engineering for Final approval and issuance of reconciling change orders. The Bureau of Engineering, after approval, will return one copy of the invoice to the Bureau of Contract Administration.

DATE	ITEM OR LABOR BREAKDOWN	QUANTITY OF TIME	UNIT COST	AMOUNT
8-23	Equipment:			
	1 - 210 C.F.M. Air compressor	4 hrs.	$4.50	18.00
	2 - Pavement breakers (50#)	8 "	.80	6.40
	2 - Dump trucks 3 axle	14 "	12.50	175.00
	1 - Loader, crawler, case 750,1.25 cy	3 "	15.00	45.00
	1 - 210 C.F.M. Air compressor	5 "	4.50	22.50
	2 - Dump trucks 3 axle	14 "	13.00	182.00
	Pickup truck	3 "	5.00	15.00
	1 - Northwest 6 crawler w/dragline	8 "	30.00	240.00
8-24	2 - Pavement breakers (50#)	10 "	0.80	8.00
	1 - Loader, crawler case 750,1.25 cy	8 "	15.00	120.00
	Transportation of dragline			75.00
	Transportation of compressor			25.00
	Total Equipment			$931.90

PLATE 67
(Page 3)

INVOICE FOR
COST PLUS CHANGES (Cont.)

| DEPT. OF PUBLIC WORKS
City of Anywhere
Bureau of Engineering | **I N V O I C E**
FOR
COST PLUS CHANGES | Sheet __4__ of __5__ Sheets |

Date __August 31, 1987__

APPROVALS

_____ 19___

_____ 19___
Project Inspector

_____ 19___
Bureau of Contract Administration

Bureau of Engineering

Job Title __Arthur Street and 2nd Avenue__
__Improvement District__

Job No. __WO-56099__

Change Order Serial No. __7__

This invoice is an itemized statement of all claims made upon the City of Anywhere by the Contractor for materials, equipment and services furnished under authority of the above designed Change Order.

Contractor

By _____

INSTRUCTIONS FOR PREPARATION AND PROCESSING OF INVOICE:

The allowable copies are set forth in the applicable sections of the specifications to which the Contractor is referred. Costs must be shown and subtotaled separately for the several classifications involved, such as "Labor," "Materials" and "Equipment". These classifications must be ITEMIZED. Labor costs are to be shown for each day that work is done, with names, labor classifications, wage rates and hours of the person involved. Equipment costs are to be likewise itemized, showing each piece, hours worked, rates and total cost for each day. Materials costs need not be shown on a daily basis but quantities, until prices, where applicable, and total costs of all items must be given. Vendors' bills to the contractor or other substantiating date for equipment and materials costs may be required and will expedite checking and approval of Contractor's invoice. The Bureau of Contract Administration will be responsible for maintaining accurate records of checking and verifying the Contractor's invoices with respect to hours of labor and equipment, quantities of materials and all other facts determinable in the field and affecting the actual cost of work performed.

The Contractor shall submit two signed copies of the invoice to the Project Engineer, who will indicate his approval thereon. The Bureau of Contract Administration will then transmit both approved copies of the Bureau of Engineering for Final approval and issuance of reconciling change orders. The Bureau of Engineering, after approval, will return one copy of the invoice to the Bureau of Contract Administration.

DATE	ITEM OR LABOR BREAKDOWN	QUANTITY OF TIME	UNIT COST	AMOUNT
	SUBCONTRACTOR'S WORK			
8-23	Labor:			
	Howard Jones (Electrical)	2	8.20	16.40
	Hal Newman (Electrician)	2	8.20	16.40
				$ 32.80
	Markup		20%	6.56
	Total Labor			39.36
	Material:			
	Conduit (galv.) 1½"	80 1.ft	2.50	200.00
	Wire #6 THW	320 1.ft	.15	48.00
	Misc. hardware			10.00
				258.00
	Markup		15%	38.70
	Total Material			296.70

PLATE 67
(Page 4)

INVOICE FOR
COST PLUS CHANGES (Cont.)

DEPT. OF PUBLIC WORKS City of Anywhere Bureau of Engineering	**INVOICE FOR COST PLUS CHANGES**	Sheet 5 of 5 Sheets

APPROVALS	
19____	Project Inspector
19____	Bureau of Contract Administration
19____	Bureau of Engineering

Date __August 31, 1987__
Job Title __Arthur Street and 2nd Avenue__
__Improvement District__
Job No. __WO-56099__
Change Order Serial No. ___7___

This invoice is an itemized statement of all claims made upon the City of Anywhere by the Contractor for materials, equipment and services furnished under authority of the above designed Change Order.

Contractor
By _____

INSTRUCTIONS FOR PREPARATION AND PROCESSING OF INVOICE:

The allowable copies are set forth in the applicable sections of the specifications to which the Contractor is referred. Costs must be shown and subtotaled separately for the several classifications involved, such as "Labor," "Materials" and "Equipment". These classifications must be ITEMIZED. Labor costs are to be shown for each day that work is done, with names, labor classifications, wage rates and hours of the person involved. Equipment costs are to be likewise itemized, showing each piece, hours worked, rates and total cost for each day. Materials costs need not be shown on a daily basis but quantities, until prices, where applicable, and total costs of all items must be given. Vendors' bills to the contractor or other substantiating date for equipment and materials costs may be required and will expedite checking and approval of Contractor's invoice. The Bureau of Contract Administration will be responsible for maintaining accurate records of checking and verifying the Contractor's invoices with respect to hours of labor and equipment, quantities of materials and all other facts determinable in the field and affecting the actual cost of work performed.

The Contractor shall submit two signed copies of the invoice to the Project Engineer, who will indicate his approval thereon. The Bureau of Contract Administration will then transmit both approved copies of the Bureau of Engineering for Final approval and issuance of reconciling change orders. The Bureau of Engineering, after approval, will return one copy of the invoice to the Bureau of Contract Administration.

DATE	ITEM OR LABOR BREAKDOWN	QUANTITY OF TIME	UNIT COST	AMOUNT
	RECAPITULATION			
	Sheet 1 – Labor			$872.48
	OASI, Workmen's Comp. Taxes, Union Dues, etc.			
	(Itemize if possible)		39%	340.27
				1,212.75
	Markup, (Sec. 3-32.3)		20%	242.55
	Labor Subtotal			1,455.30
	Sheet 2 – Material			1,799.10
	Markup		15%	269.87
	Material Subtotal			2,068.97
	Sheet 3 – Equipment			931.90
	Markup		15%	139.79
	Equipment Subtotal			1,071.69
	Subcontractor's Work (Sheet 4)			372.99
	Markup		5%	18.65
	Subcontractor Subtotal			391.64
	GRAND TOTAL			4,987.60

PLATE 67
(Page 5)

CONCRETE SLUMP TEST
(Reproduced through courtesy of Master Builders, Inc.)

PURPOSE OF TEST: To determine the consistency of fresh concrete and to check its uniformity from batch to batch. This test is based on ASTM C 143: Standard Method of Test for Slump of Portland Cement Concrete.

Take two or more representative samples — at regularly spaced intervals — from the middle of the mixer discharge; do not take samples from beginning or end of discharge. Obtain samples within 15 minutes or less. **Important:** Slump test must be made within 5 minutes after taking samples.

Combine samples in a wheelbarrow or appropriate container and remix before making test.

Dampen slump cone with water and place it on a flat, level, smooth, moist, non-absorbent, firm surface.

1. Stand on two foot pieces of cone to hold it firmly in place during Steps 1 through 4. Fill cone mold ⅓ full by volume [2½″ (63.5mm) high] with the concrete sample and rod it with 25 strokes using a round, bullet-nosed steel rod of ⅝″ (16mm) diameter x 24″ (61mm) long. Distribute rodding strokes evenly over entire cross section of the concrete by using approximately half the strokes near the perimeter (outer edge) and then progressing spirally toward the center.

2. Fill cone ⅔ full by volume [6″ (23mm) or half the height] and again rod 25 times with rod just penetrating into, but not through, the first layer. Distribute strokes evenly as described in Step 1.

PLATE 68 (Page 1)
See page 109 (2-4.4.3b)

CONCRETE SLUMP TEST (Cont.)

3. Fill cone to overflowing and again rod 25 times with rod just penetrating into but not through the second layer. Again distribute strokes evenly.

4. Strike off excess concrete from top of cone with the steel rod, so that the cone is exactly level full. Clean the overflow away from the base of the cone mold.

5. Immediately after completion of Step 4, the operation of raising the mold shall be performed in 5 to 10 seconds by a steady upward lift with no lateral or torsional notion being imparted to the concrete. The entire operation from the start of the filling through removal of the mold shall be carried out without interruption and shall be completed within an elapsed time of 2½ minutes.

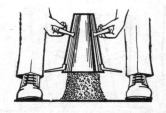

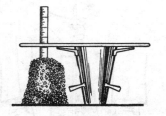

6. Place the steel rod horizontally across the inverted mold, so the rod extends over the slumped concrete. Immediately measure the distance from bottom of the steel rod to the original center of the top of the specimen. This distance, to the nearest ¼ inch (6mm), is the slump of the concrete.

PLATE 68
(Page 2)

CYLINDER CASTING
(Reproduced through courtesy of Master Builders, Inc.)

NOTE: For complete and related procedures see ASTM Designations: C 470 Single-Use Molds for Forming 6 by 12-in. Concrete Compression Test Cylinders; C 31 Standard Method of Making and Curing Concrete Compressive and Flexural Strength Test Specimens in the Field; C 94 Standard Specifications for Ready Mixed Concrete; and C 172 Standard Method of Sampling Fresh Concrete.

USE ONLY NON-ABSORBENT WATERPROOF MOLDS

For casting concrete cylinders in the field, use only approved non-absorbent waterproof molds, 6″ (15 cm) in diameter by 12″ (30 cm) high, with base plates or bottoms. They should be placed on a smooth, firm, level surface for filling and cast in the area where they are to be stored during the first 24 hours and where they will be protected from vibration, jarring, striking, etc.

TAKE 3-PART SAMPLE; COMBINE AND REMIX

Three samples of the concrete should be obtained, at regularly spaced intervals, directly from the mixer discharge. Combine the samples in a wheelbarrow, buggy or metal pan and remix with a shovel to ensure uniformity of the 3-part sample.

FILL MOLDS IN THREE EQUAL LAYERS AND ROD EACH LAYER 25 TIMES

Fill molds in three equal layers and uniformly rod each layer 25 times with a ⅝″ bullet-nosed rod. When rodding the second and third layers, the rod should just break through into the layer beneath. Fill all molds uniformly — that is, place and rod the bottom layer in all cylinders, then place and rod the second layer, etc. The third layer should contain an excess amount of concrete which is struck off smooth and level after rodding.

PLATE 69
(Page 1)

CYLINDER CASTING (Cont.)

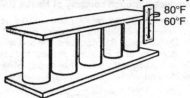

PROTECT CYLINDERS FROM MOISTURE LOSS, MOVEMENT AND TEMPERATURE EXTREMES

Cover the tops of the cylinders to prevent loss of moisture by evaporation. Do not disturb or move cylinders for 24 hours after casting. Protect them against temperatures that fall below 60°F (16C) or exceed 80° (27C). Cylinders left on the job for several days and exposed to high or low temperatures will give substandard results. Additional cylinders used for determining when forms may be stripped or when concrete may be put into service should be removed from the molds after 24 hours and then job-cured adjacent to and under the same conditions as the concrete they represent.

CURE AND HANDLE CYLINDERS WITH CARE

After 24 hours, cylinders for acceptance tests should be placed in moist curing at 73.4°F ± 3°F (23 ± 1.7C) or sent to a laboratory for similar standard curing. Careful handling during moving is necessary since cylinders which are allowed to rattle around in a box, at the back of a car, or pick-up truck, can suffer considerable damage.

IMPORTANT

ALWAY USE ACCEPTED STANDARDS — Standard test procedures were developed to establish lines of uniformity and reproducibility. Only specimens tested according to accepted, reliable standards, such as those established by the American Society for Testing and Materials, give valuable indications of the uniformity and potential quality of the concrete in a structure.

PLATE 69
(Page 2)

SLUMP TABLE

SLUMP

Aggr. Size	2"	2½"	3"	4"	5"	6"
¾"	301/36.1	306/36.7	310/37.2	319/38.3	327/39.2	333/40.0
⅞"	296/35.5	301/36.1	305/36.6	314/37.7	322/38.6	330/39.6
1"	291/34.9	296/35.5	300/36.0	309/37.1	317/38.0	327/39.2
1¼"	281/33.7		290/34.8	299/35.9	307/36.8	316/37.9
1½"	271/32.5		280/33.6	289/34.7	297/35.6	305/36.6

Water requirement in pounds/gals per cubic yard.
Rule of thumb: one gallon will change slump approximately one inch.

TIME TABLE OF CEMENT STRENGTHS (PERCENT*)

Cem. Type	3 Days	7 Days	14 Days	28 Days	60 Days
I	40	60	80	100	
II	33	55	65	80	100
III	60	80	100	120	
IV	20	40	55	75	
V	20	40	60	80	

*Compressive strength rated on percentage of Type I 28-day strength
(All types increased in one year 133%)

EFFECT OF WATER CONTENT ON COMPRESSIVE STRENGTH OF CONCRETE
(Non Air Entrained Concrete)

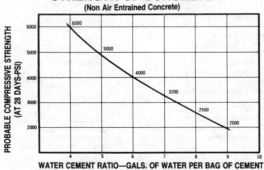

WATER CEMENT RATIO—GALS. OF WATER PER BAG OF CEMENT
From ACI 613: ACI Recommended Practice for Selecting Proportions for Concrete

PLATE 69
(Page 3)

INDEX